Why Do You Need This New Edition?

If you're wondering why you should buy this new edition of *The Penguin Handbook*, here are eight great reasons!

1. Would you like to have a clear and simple overview of the key steps that you should follow when doing research assignments? See the **new research and documentation process maps** at the beginning of Parts 5 and 6, and at the opening of the MLA and APA chapters.

2. Would you find it helpful to see examples of other students working on a research project? **New student "Writer at Work" sections** in Parts 5 and 6 highlight the work of one student as she selects a topic, finds sources, drafts and revises her paper.

3. Would it be helpful to see a quick snapshot of each chapter? New **"Quick Take" boxes** at the beginning of each chapter give you a brief overview of the key points covered in the chapter.

4. Do you learn from looking at assignments created by other students? This edition has **more student writing samples** than ever, including a new sample informative paper, proposal argument paper, a paper based on field research, a film analysis, an extra MLA-style paper and more examples of business and public writing.

5. Does your course emphasize persuasive writing? This handbook now includes two complete chapters on composing position and proposal arguments.

6. Are you being asked to develop visual and multimedia texts in your course? Part 4, on designing and presenting your work, has been completely revised and includes **new help with multimedia assignments** and advice for how to best communicate with words, images and graphics.

7. Are you taking your course online? A new chapter 14 helps you **develop skills for learning in an online course,** to understand how to use courseware as well as how to participate in online discussions and keep track of your online coursework.

8. Do you know how to write in online media? A new chapter, Composing in Online Genres (chapter 17), shows you how to do **assignments requiring the use of online media and software**, such as blogs, wikis, web pages, social media sites, podcasts and videos.

The *Penguin Handbook* gets even better when used with **Pearson's unique MyCompLab site**—the gateway to a world of online resources **and an eText** developed specifically for you!

PEARSON

THE PENGUIN
HANDBOOK

THE PENGUIN HANDBOOK

FOURTH EDITION

LESTER FAIGLEY
University of Texas at Austin

Longman

Boston • Columbus • Indianapolis • New York • San Francisco
Upper Saddle River • Amsterdam • Cape Town • Dubai • London • Madrid • Milan
Munich • Paris • Montreal • Toronto • Delhi • Mexico City • São Paulo • Sydney
Hong Kong • Seoul • Singapore • Taipei • Tokyo

Executive Editor: Lynn M. Huddon
Director of Development: Mary Ellen Curley
Senior Supplements Editor: Donna Campion
Senior Media Producer: Stefanie Liebman
Senior Marketing Manager: Susan E. Grant
Production Manager: Bob Ginsberg
Project Coordination, Text Design, and Electronic Page Makeup: PreMediaGlobal
Senior Cover Design Manager: Nancy Danahy
Cover images *(From left to right)*: ©Glow Images/Alamy; ©Tetra Images/Alamy;
    ©DCPhoto/Alamy; ©Corbis Super RF/Alamy
Cover Designer: Nancy Sacks
Visual Researcher: Rona Tuccillo
Senior Manufacturing Buyer: Dennis J. Para
Printer and Binder: Quad Graphics
Cover Printer: Lehigh Phoenix

For permission to use copyrighted material, grateful acknowledgment is made to the
copyright holders on p. 783, which are hereby made part of this copyright page.

Library of Congress Cataloging-in-Publication Data

Control number is on record at the Library of Congress.

1 2 3 4 5 6 7 8 9 10—QGT—13 12 11 10

Longman
is an imprint of

ISBN-13: 978-0-205-02870-2
ISBN-10:   0-205-02870-5

www.pearsonhighered.com

Contents

PART 3

Writing in the Disciplines   123

PART 4   Designing and Presenting   189

PART 5

Planning Research and Finding Sources   231

PART 6

Incorporating and Documenting Sources   301

PART 9

Understanding Punctuation and Mechanics 599

PART 10

If English Is Not Your First Language   685

Preface

The fourth edition of *The Penguin Handbook* grows out of my experiences as a writing teacher at a time when the tools for writing, the uses of writing, and the nature of writing itself are undergoing astounding and rapid transformation in an era of multimedia. Yet the traditional qualities of good writing—clarity, brevity, readability, consistency, effective design, accurate documentation, freedom from errors, and a human voice—are prized more than ever.

The longer I've taught, the more convinced I've become that a good handbook is invaluable for college writers. A handbook can be a guide for students throughout the composing process, helping them build on what they already know about writing and demonstrate these qualities of good writing in their work. I hope you experience the success teaching with *The Penguin Handbook* that I have enjoyed.

What's new in this edition?

The Penguin Handbook has been revised extensively in order to give students the best, most up-to-date writing instruction available, and to make it easier for them to navigate their handbook.

Process-oriented instruction on documentation styles

- The MLA and APA chapters (Chs. 26 and 27) have been reorganized to emphasize the process for how to create the correct citation for any source. These chapters now open with new documentation process maps that remind students of the key steps when citing sources and also help students find their way into these chapters. New "Writer at Work" student examples show a student figuring out how to cite a source. And newly designed source samples are grouped together in one place in the chapter are easier for students to find and use.

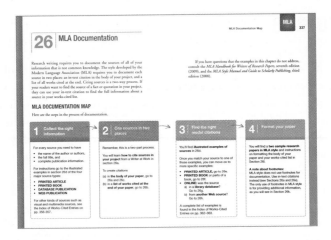

More student models

- New "Writer at Work" sections in the writing, research, and documentation chapters (Parts 5 and 6) highlight the work of one student as she moves through the research process—selecting a topic for a research project, finding and evaluating sources, and drafting a researched argument paper.

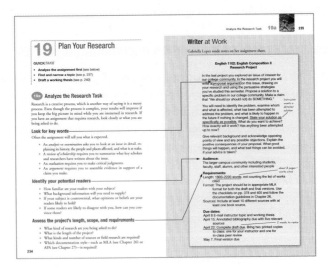

- A new informative paper, a new proposal argument paper, and two MLA model research papers are included in this edition, as well as added models for business writing.

New navigation tools for students

- New step-by-step process maps open Parts 5 and 6 and the MLA and APA documentation chapters, showing students how to use these chapters effectively.
- New "Quick Take" sections now open each chapter in the book. In Parts 1-6, these Quick Takes function as chapter previews of the major points covered in the chapter. In Parts 7-10 (style, grammar, ESL), these feature the questions that students are most likely to ask with quick examples in response to these questions.

More on research, incorporating sources, and avoiding plagiarism

- Coverage of plagiarism has been thoroughly updated and expanded, including new discussion of "patch plagiarism."
- MLA, APA and CMS chapters have been updated to comply with the latest style guidelines.
- The research coverage has been reorganized so that the coverage of finding sources and evaluating sources is now in separate chapters.
- The chapters on incorporating sources and avoiding plagiarism are now in Part 6, emphasizing to students that using sources responsibly and documenting them properly is all part of what responsible researchers do.

More instruction on composing arguments, on designing and presenting information, and composing online

- In Part 2, the argument coverage is expanded to two chapters (one on Position Arguments and one on Proposal Arguments), with sample student papers included in each chapter.
- In Part 4, "Designing and Presenting," chapters have been completely revised and updated to include new discussion of multimedia projects.
- A new chapter 17, "Compose in Online Genres" offers tips and advice on composing in a blog or wiki, or creating podcasts, videos, or social media sites.

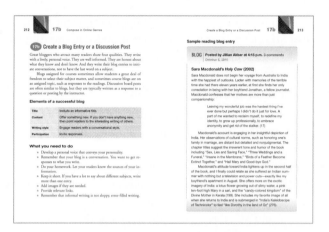

More instruction on writing in other disciplines and genres

- Coverage of writing in Literature and the Humanities, as well as in the Sciences and Social Sciences, has been expanded.
- A new section on creating portfolios has been added.
- An all-new chapter on writing for an online course (chapter 14) is included in Part 3, with tips on using courseware and participating in online discussions.

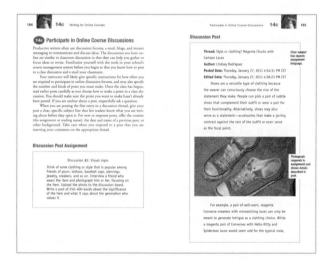

New exercises and examples

- Parts 7-10 (style, grammar, punctuation, and ESL) feature numerous new examples.
- Exercises throughout the book have been updated and revised.

Resources for teachers and students

An array of supplements for both instructors and students accompanies *The Penguin Handbook.*

An interactive Pearson eText in MyCompLab

A dynamic, online version of *The Penguin Handbook* is available in MyCompLab to create an active learning experience for students. MyCompLab, an eminently flexible application, empowers student writers and teachers by integrating a composing space and assessment tools with multimedia tutorials, including online tutoring and exercises for writing, grammar, and research. Teachers can recommend MyCompLab to students for self-study, set up courses to track student progress, and leverage the power of administrative features to be more effective and save time. Learn more at **www.mycomplab.com.**

In the eText students will also find unique, interactive book-specific resources that support and supplement the chapters of *The Penguin Handbook,* such as:

- **Student Writing Samples with Audio Commentary,** offering complete papers in a number of disciplines with additional audio commentaries by the author.
- **Writing and Research Worksheets,** which help students focus on particular stages of the writing, design, and research process.
- **Common Errors Workbook,** providing additional exercises and activities directly related to students' most frequent problem areas encountered by student writers.
- **Common ESL Errors Workbook,** providing additional practice and exercises to help nonnative speakers and writers recognize common grammar and style problems.
- **Punctuation Personality Quiz,** offering students a fun way to discover how punctuation adds personality to their writing.

 References to this eText can be seen throughout the handbook where this icon is displayed.

A CourseSmart eTextbook

The Penguin Handbook is also available as a CourseSmart eTextbook (www.coursesmart.com). Students can subscribe to and search the text, make notes online, print out reading assignments that incorporate lecture notes, and bookmark important passages.

VangoNotes

vango Hear it Students can study on the go with VangoNotes. They down-load chapter reviews of *The Penguin Handbook* and listen to them on any mp3 player. Find out more at www.VangoNotes.com.

Instructor's Resource Manual and Answer Key

An *Instructor's Resource Manual*, revised by Krista Hiser of Kapi'olani Community College, offers guidance to new and experienced teachers for using the handbook and its ancillary package to the best advantage. A separate *Answer Key* to accompany this handbook is also available to instructors.

Social media resources

Join Lester Faigley to create an online community around your course. For additional teaching tips about this book and other resources and an-nouncements, follow him on Pearson's Facebook fan page (http://www.facebook.com/FaigleySeries).

GrammarPrep applications

GrammarPrep are the first grammar apps built specifically for college students and professionals. With multimedia tutorials, quizzes and mastery tests, an-swer feedback, and progress tracking, they are the only grammar apps that offer proven, educational-quality content. Go to www.pearsonhighered.com/grammarprep/ to find apps for ten of the most common grammar errors that your students can download to improve their skills.

To see a complete listing of the supplements available upon adoption of *The Penguin Handbook*, please visit the book's online catalog page, which can be accessed at www.pearsonhighered.com.

Acknowledgments

The scope and complexity of a handbook require a talented, experienced team, and I have been blessed to have the same team as the previous edition. Executive Editor Lynn Huddon and I have worked together on over twenty books and editions—none of which would have achieved success without Lynn's creative mind and hard work. Likewise, I am grateful to have the wise advice of Mary Ellen Curley, director of development, who has brought a wealth of knowledge, thoroughness, and the attention to detail that a handbook demands. She has been a superb editor throughout the long process. Kristen Bowen and Erin Reilly gave valuable advice, and Shannon Kobran worked hard to assemble the manuscript and followed through on the many details of production.

Others at Longman who have contributed their wisdom and experience are Susan Grant, senior marketing manager; Stephanie Liebman, senior media producer; Donna Campion, senior supplements editor; Nancy Danahy, senior cover design manager; Nancy Sacks, cover designer; and Jackie Martin and Bob Ginsberg, production managers. Melena Fenn at PreMediaGlobal has skillfully guided the production. My copy editor, Elsa van Bergen, has worked in some capacity on all four editions, and she has taught me a great deal along the way in addition to being a joy to work with. Victoria Davis created new exercises for the fourth edition and contributed many good ideas. Susan "George" Schorn contributed to the chapters on writing in the disciplines and writing in specific genres. Vernon Nahrgang was a meticulous proofreader of the documentation chapters.

As with previous editions, I've benefitted from the practical knowledge and advice of the English sales specialists at Longman. This talented team includes Aimee Berger, Mike Coons, Gina Gimelli, Kelly Kunert, Kurt Massey, John Meyers, Michael Schmitz and Tanius Stamper.

I am fortunate to have an expert group of reviewers, who were not only perceptive in their suggestions but could imagine a handbook that breaks new ground. They are Ellen Olmstead, Montgomery College; Michael Hricik, Westmoreland County Community College; Teresa Aggen, Pikes Peak Community College; David Sharpe, Ohio University; Jeffrey Janssens, North Central State College; Martha J. Payne, Ball State University; Helen Raica-Klotz, Saginaw Valley State University; Katherine D. Harris, San Jose State University; Leah Zuidema, Dordt College; Krista Hiser, Kapiolani Community College; Ginny Skinner-Linnenberg, Nazareth College; Grace M. Urbanski, Marquette University; Jon Brammer, Three Rivers Community College; Candace Boeck, San Diego State University; Marshall W. Kitchens, Oakland University; Shelley Palmer,

Rowan-Cabarrus Community College; Maria Cahill, Edison College–Fort Myers; Douglas Atkins, University of Kansas. Shanti Bruce of Nova Southeastern University, and Kate Berger of St. Louis Community College offered invaluable advice for students writing in English as a second language.

As always, my greatest debt of gratitude is to my wife, Linda, who makes it all possible.

LESTER FAIGLEY

THE PENGUIN
HANDBOOK

PART 1

Planning, Drafting, and Revising

You **can learn more and do more** with MyCompLab and with the eText version of *The Penguin Handbook*. To find resources in MyCompLab that will help you successfully plan and complete your assignment, go to

Resources

Writing

The Writing Process
Planning | Drafting | Revising | Finishing and Editing

Review the tutorials (Read, Watch, Listen) within each topic, then complete the Exercises and click on the Gradebook to measure your progress.

In the **eText version** of *The Penguin Handbook*, you will also find extra exercises on the rhetorical situation, freewriting and brainstorming, writing effective paragraphs, drafting, revising and proofreading your work.

1 | Think as a Writer

QUICK_TAKE_

- Understand the demands of writing in college (see below)
- Understand the basic process of communicating with readers (see p. 5)
- Know how to get readers to take you seriously (see p. 10)

Think About What College Readers Expect

Writing in college varies considerably from course to course. A lab report for a biology course looks quite different from a paper in your English class, just as a classroom observation in an education course differs from a case study report in an accounting class.

Some common expectations about arguments in college writing extend across disciplines. For example, you could be assigned to write a proposal for a downtown light-rail system in a number of different classes—civil engineering, urban planning, government, or management. The emphasis of such a proposal would change depending on the course. In all cases, however, the proposal would require a complex argument in which you describe the problem that the light-rail system would improve, make a specific proposal that addresses the problem, explain the benefits of the system, esti-mate the cost, identify funding sources, assess alternatives to your plan, and anticipate possible opposition.

Setting out a specific proposal or claim supported by reasons and evi-dence is at the heart of most college writing, no matter what the course. Some expectations of arguments (such as including a thesis statement) may be familiar to you, but others (such as the emphasis on finding alternative ways of thinking about a subject and finding facts that might run counter to your conclusions) may be unfamiliar.

Expectations of college writers

WRITING IN COLLEGE . . .	WRITERS ARE EXPECTED TO . . .
States explicit claims	Know that the main claim is often called a **thesis.** (see pages 22–25)
Supports claims with reasons	Express reasons after making a claim (We should do something *because* _____). (see page 114)
Bases reasons on evidence	Provide evidence for reasons in the form of facts, statistics, testimony from reliable sources, and direct observations. (see pages 89–90)
Considers opposing positions	Help readers understand why there are disagreements about issues by accurately representing differing views. (see pages 101–103)
Analyzes with insight	Provide in-depth analysis. (see pages 68–71)
Investigates complexity	Explore the complexity of a subject by asking "Have you thought about this?" or "What if you discard the usual way of thinking about a subject and take the opposite point of view?" (see pages 105–106)
Organizes information clearly	Make the main ideas evident to readers and to indicate which parts are subordinate to others. (see pages 26–27)
Signals relationships of parts	Indicate logical relationships clearly so that readers can follow an argument without getting lost. (see pages 35–36)
Documents sources carefully	Provide the sources of information so that readers can consult the same sources the writer used. (see pages 338–341)

1b Think About How to Persuade Others

The process of communication involves the interaction of three essential elements: the writer or speaker, the audience, and the subject. These three elements interact with one another. Speakers make adjustments to their presentations of a subject depending on the audience (think of how you talk to small children). Just as speakers adjust to audiences, audiences continually adjust to speakers (think of how your attitude toward speakers changes when they are able to laugh at themselves).

The ancient Greeks represented the dynamic nature of communication with the **rhetorical triangle**. The most important teacher of rhetoric in ancient Greece, Aristotle (384–323 BCE), defined rhetoric as the art of finding the best available means of persuasion in any situation. He set out three primary tactics of persuasion: appeals based on the trustworthiness of the speaker (*ethos*); appeals to the emotions and deepest-held values of the audience (*pathos*); and appeals to logic, reasoning, and evidence (*logos*).

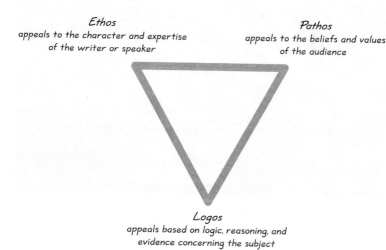

Ethos
appeals to the character and expertise
of the writer or speaker

Pathos
appeals to the beliefs and values
of the audience

Logos
appeals based on logic, reasoning, and
evidence concerning the subject

Figure 1.1   The rhetorical triangle

Figure 1.2 *Ethos.* "Got Milk? Serena Williams"

Figure 1.3 *Logos.* "Spot the five reasons to use an energy 'smart' power strip"

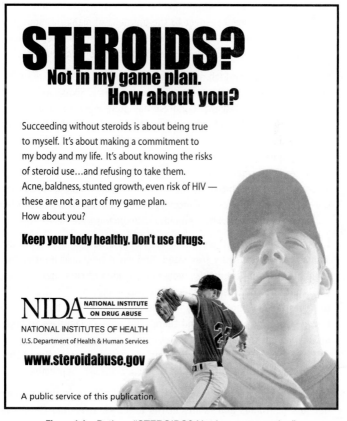

Figure 1.4 *Pathos.* "STEROIDS? Not in my game plan"

Exercise 1.1   Read the following passages and decide which appeal (to logic, to credibility and trustworthiness, to emotions and values) is being addressed.

1. Today I am an inquisitor. And hyperbole would not be fictional and would not overstate the solemnness that I feel right now. My faith in the Constitution is whole; it is complete; it is total. And I am not going to sit here and be an idle spectator to the diminution, the subversion, the destruction, of the Constitution.
   —Barbara Jordan, Speech before the U.S. House Judiciary Committee Impeachment Hearings, 1974

2. When in the course of human events, it becomes necessary for one people to dissolve the political bands which have connected them with one another, and to assume among the powers of the earth, the separate and equal station which the Laws of Nature and of Nature's God entitle them, a decent respect to the opinions of mankind requires that they should declare the causes which impel them to the separation.
   —Thomas Jefferson, *Declaration of Independence,* 1776

3. Since the September 11th attacks, we've seen a shameful increase in the number of hate crimes committed against Muslims, Sikhs, and Americans of Middle Eastern descent. Congress has done much to respond to the vicious attacks of September 11th. We're doing all that we can to strengthen our defenses against hate that comes from abroad. We've spent billions of dollars in the War on Terrorism to ensure that international terrorist organizations such as al' Qaeda are not able to carry out attacks within the United States. There is no reason why Congress should not act to strengthen our defenses against hate that occurs here at home.
   —Senator Edward Kennedy, Introducing Hate Crimes Bill, 2007

4. I got to tell you . . . there are a lot of people here who are very upset, and very angry, and very frustrated. And when they hear politicians . . . thanking one another, it just, you know, it kind of cuts them the wrong way right now. Because literally there was a body on the streets of this town yesterday being eaten by rats, because this woman had been laying in the street for 48 hours. And there's not enough facilities to take her up. Do you get the anger that is out here?
   —Anderson Cooper, Interview with Louisiana Senator Mary Landrieu about Hurricane Katrina, *Anderson Cooper 360°*, September 1, 2005

5. And I am a big supporter of this movement. I believe in this movement. Got lots of friends and family in the lower 48 attending these events across the country, and just knowing that this is the movement, and America is ready for another revolution, and you are a part of this.
   —Sarah Palin, Keynote Address at National Tea Party Convention, February 6, 2010

1c Think About Your Audience

Readers of college writing expect more than what they can find out on Wikipedia or from a Google search. Facts are easy to obtain on the Web. Readers want to know how these facts are connected. Good college writing also involves an element of surprise. If readers can predict exactly where a writer is going, even if they fully agree, they will either skim to the end or stop reading. Readers expect you to tell them something that they don't know already.

WRITING SMART

Understand your audience

- Who is most likely to read what you write?
- How much does your audience know about your subject? Are there any key terms or concepts that you will need to explain?
- How interested is your audience likely to be? If they lack interest in your subject, how can you engage them?
- What is their attitude likely to be toward your subject? If they hold attitudes different from yours, how can you get them to consider your views?
- What would motivate your audience to want to read what you write?

Exercise 1.2 Suppose you are a freelance writer who has lined up several assignments for a variety of publications. Your topics and the publications are listed below. Analyze your intended audience. How much information will they most likely have about your subject (much, none, some); what is their attitude likely to be (positive, negative, neutral); what is their interest level most likely to be (low, moderate, high). In a few cases, you might need to do some research into the readership for the publication.

1. A chapter about the Persian Gulf War in a high school textbook
2. An article about the health benefits of lycopene in *Men's Health*
3. An opinion piece about health care for *The Economist*
4. A feature on "honor killings" in the United States for *Marie Claire*
5. An article comparing hybrid cars in *Car and Driver*

1d Think About Your Credibility

Some writers begin with a strong ethos because of who they are; they have immediate credibility. Most writers, however, have to convince their readers to keep reading by demonstrating knowledge of their subject and concern with their readers' needs. Furthermore, no matter how much you know about a subject or how good your ideas are, your credibility is destroyed if readers in college, in the workplace, or in public life find your writing poor in quality, especially if it is full of errors and sloppy sentences.

WRITING SMART

Build your credibility

- How can you convince your audience that you are knowledgeable about your subject? Do you need to do research?
- How can you convince your audience that you have their interests in mind?
- What strategies can you use that will enhance your credibility? Should you cite experts on your subject? Can you acknowledge opposing positions, indicating that you've taken a balanced view on your subject?
- Does the appearance, accuracy, and clarity of your writing give you credibility?

Exercise 1.3   Evaluate the following passages, as well as the example(s) of appeals to ethos you found in Exercise 1.1, for their appeals to credibility. What sort of ethos does the author represent? How might this affect his or her presentation of the topic?

1. Topic: Gay Marriage
It took years for me to realize that I was gay, years more to tell others and more time yet to form any kind of stable emotional bond with another man. Because my sexuality had emerged in solitude—and without any link to the idea of an actual relationship—it was hard later to reconnect sex to love and self-esteem. It still is. But I persevered, each relationship slowly growing longer than the last, learning in my 20s and 30s what my straight friends had found out in their teens. But even then my parents and friends never asked the question they would have asked automatically if I were straight: So, when are you going to get married? When will we be able to celebrate it and affirm it and support it? In fact, no one—no one—has yet asked me that question.
   —Andrew Sullivan, "Why the M Word Matters to Me," Time, February 8, 2004

2. Topic: Health Care Reform

When I spoke here last winter, this nation was facing the worst economic crisis since the Great Depression. We were losing an average of 700,000 jobs per month. Credit was frozen. And our financial system was on the verge of collapse.

As any American who is still looking for work or a way to pay their bills will tell you, we are by no means out of the woods. A full and vibrant recovery is many months away. And I will not let up until those Americans who seek jobs can find them; until those businesses that seek capital and credit can thrive; until all responsible homeowners can stay in their homes. That is our ultimate goal. But thanks to the bold and decisive action we have taken since January, I can stand here with confidence and say that we have pulled this economy back from the brink.

—President Barack Obama's Health Care Speech to Congress,
September 9, 2009

3. Topic: Spirituality

When I get lonely these days, I think: So BE lonely, Liz. Learn your way around loneliness. Make a map of it. Sit with it, for once in your life. Welcome to the human experience. But never again use another person's body or emotions as a scratching post for your own unfulfilled yearnings.

—Elizabeth Gilbert, Eat, Pray, Love, 2006

 ## Think About Your Purpose

The starting point for effective writing is determining in advance what you want to accomplish. Knowing your purpose shapes everything else you do as a writer—your choice of the kind of writing, your subject matter, your organization, and your style.

WRITING SMART

Identify your purposes for writing

- Are you analyzing a verbal or visual text to understand how it persuades readers, how it makes us think and feel in certain ways? (See Chapter 6.)
- Are you describing and reflecting on people, places, experiences, and ideas? Are you writing a personal essay, blog, or travel narrative? (See Chapter 7.)

(Continued on next page)

- Are you writing to report information, to explain a process, to explore questions and problems, or to analyze patterns, connections, and causes? (See Chapter 8.)
- Are you arguing for a position on a controversial issue? (See Chapter 9.)
- Are you arguing to convince people to take a particular course of action? (See Chapter 10.)

1f Think About the Complex Demands of Writing Today

The nature of work and life in general is changing rapidly because of changing technologies and globalization. So too are the demands placed on writers.

- **Writers today use a variety of writing technologies.** People do not throw away their pencils and ballpoint pens when they buy a laptop. Each writing tool is well suited to particular uses; it's hard to top a pencil for jotting down a grocery list, although some people may be equally comfortable using PDAs for such daily writing tasks.
- **Writers today do many different kinds of writing:** letters, reports, memos, newsletters, evaluations, articles, charts, Web sites, computer-assisted presentations, press releases, brochures, proposals, résumés, agendas, users' manuals, analyses, summaries, Facebook, Twitter, and e-mail. Each kind of writing has its own special set of demands.
- **Writers today have multiple purposes.** An e-mail may convey both business strategies and personal news. A proposal may have as its unacknowledged purpose the request for a new job or wider responsibilities. Even a simple memo often conveys many unstated messages, such as the attitude of the writer toward her coworkers.
- **Writers today have multiple audiences.** Often documents are read by readers who have different interests. The speed of digital media allows many points of view to be expressed simultaneously. Skilled writers in the digital era know they must negotiate among these many points of view.

- **Writers today know how to find and present information relevant to their purposes.** They are efficient researchers who can locate, evaluate, and present information clearly and ethically to their readers. Most readers prefer well-selected information to a barrage of unfiltered data.
- **Writers today often work in teams.** They communicate with colleagues to achieve a common goal, so the ability to collaborate effectively may be an unanticipated need in writing effectively.
- **Writers today know that it is critical to emphasize what is important.** They understand that readers face an overdose of information, have little patience, and want to know quickly what is at stake.
- **Writers today recognize that an active and personal style free from errors is often most effective.** Readers in general prefer a personal and accessible style.
- **Writers today communicate visually as well as verbally.** Computers and digital media give writers the ability to use pictures and graphics in addition to text. Knowing how to communicate visually is important to your success in the digital era.

Exercise 1.4 Write a paragraph describing all of the different types of writing you do in a week. What kinds of tools do you use? How does the audience for the different kinds of writing affect your choice of style? What kind of research do you have to do for this writing? Is there a visual element to any of this writing? If so, what?

2 | Plan and Draft

QUICK*TAKE*

- Establish your goals (see below)
- Explore your topic (see p. 17)
- Write a working thesis (see p. 22)
- Plan a strategy (see p. 26)

Establish Your Goals

Your instructor will give you specific suggestions about how to think about your audience and topic. There are two ways to make your task simpler.

- Be sure you are responding to the assignment appropriately.
- Select a topic that both fits the assignment and appeals to you strongly enough to make you want to write about it.

Look carefully at your assignment

When your instructor gives you a writing assignment, look closely at what you are asked to do. Often the assignment will contain key words such as *analyze, compare and contrast, define, describe, evaluate,* or *propose* that will assist you in determining what direction to take.

- **Analyze:** Find connections among a set of facts, events, or readings, and make them meaningful.
- **Compare and contrast:** Examine how two or more things are alike and how they differ.
- **Define:** Make a claim about how something should be defined, according to features that you set out.
- **Describe:** Observe carefully and select details that create a dominant impression.
- **Evaluate:** Argue that something is good, bad, best, or worst in its class, according to criteria that you set out.
- **Propose:** Identify a particular problem and explain why your solution is the best one.

If you are unclear about what the assignment calls for, talk with your instructor.

Find a topic you care about

If you do not have an assigned topic, a good way to find one is to look first at the materials for your course. You may find something that interests you in the readings for the course or in a topic that came up in class discussion.

If your assignment gives you a wide range of options, you might write more than one list, starting with your personal interests. Think also about campus topics, community topics, and national topics that intrigue you. Your lists might resemble these:

Personal
1. Benefits of weight training
2. Wordplay in Marx brothers movies
3. History of hairstyles

Campus
1. Pros and cons of charging computer fees
2. Should my university have a foreign language requirement?
3. Affirmative action admissions policies

Community
1. Helmet laws for people who ride bicycles and motorcycles
2. Bilingual education programs
3. More bike lanes to encourage more people to ride bicycles
4. Better public transportation

Nation/World
1. Advertising aimed at preschool children
2. Censorship of the Internet
3. Effects of climate change
4. Setting aside the laws that govern police searches, in the effort to stop terrorism

Often you will find that, before you can begin writing, you need to analyze exactly what you mean by a phrase like "censorship of the Internet." For example, do you mean censorship of Web sites, or of everything that goes over the Internet, including private e-mail?

After you make a list or lists, you should review it.

- Put a checkmark beside the topics that look most interesting or the ones that mean the most to you.
- Put a question mark beside the topics that you don't know very much about. If you choose one of these issues, you will have to do research.
- Select the two or three topics that look the most promising.

Exercise 2.1   A student generated the following list to help her finalize a topic for a research paper. She wants to focus on the popularity of specific monsters in mainstream culture. Choose a topic for the paper guided by the list. Then organize items from the list into categories that the student could address effectively in a paper. Eliminate any items that are not useful to the topic.

Nosferatu (1922)
Bela Lugosi in *Dracula* (1931)
zombie, werewolf, and vampire avatars in Second Life
Christopher Lee as Dracula in the 1960s
monster movies in general
Lon Chaney in *The Wolf Man* (1941)
George Romero zombie movies
werewolves
repressed desire
Benicio Del Toro in *The Wolfman* (2010)
Let the Right One In (2008)
28 Days Later (2002)
Teen Wolf (1985)
irony and camp
Vampire Diaries TV series
zombies
Shaun of the Dead (2004)
teen subcultures
Howl TV series
zombie flash mobs
An American Werewolf in London (1981)
romance novels
Bram Stoker's novel Dracula (1897)
Buffy the Vampire Slayer movie and TV show
True Blood TV show
Twilight series of books and movies
vampire proms
teenage angst
online games featuring vampires vs. werewolves

2b Explore Your Topic

Once you have identified a potential topic, the next step is to determine what you already know about that topic and what you need to find out. Experienced writers use many strategies for exploring their knowledge of a topic and how interesting it really is to them. Here are a few.

Ask questions

These classic reporter's questions will assist you in thinking through a topic.

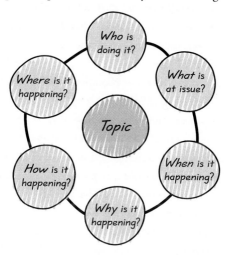

Freewrite

Another way to find out how much you know about a topic is to **freewrite**: write as quickly as you can without stopping for a set time, usually five or ten minutes. The goal of freewriting is to get as much down as possible. Don't stop to correct mistakes. The constant flow of words should generate ideas—some useful, some not.

If you get stuck, write the same sentence over again, or write about how hungry you are, or how difficult freewriting is, until thoughts on your selected topic reappear. After you've finished, read what you have written and single out any key ideas. The following freewrite was composed by Mariela Martinez on a student free speech case that wound up before the United States Supreme Court in March 2007. In 2002 in Juneau, Alaska, high school senior Joseph Frederick was suspended for ten days by principal Deborah Morse after he displayed a banner off of school property during the Winter Olympics Torch Relay. You can read Martinez's essay in Section 9d.

Freewrite on Morse v. Frederick

I did dumb stuff when I was a senior in high school. I can imagine Joe Frederick sitting around with his friends after they found out that the Winter Olympics Torch Relay would pass by his school. I can imagine what happened. Someone said it would be really cool if we held up a banner that said Bong Hits 4 Jesus in front of the cameras. Everyone else said awesome! The principal will totally freak! But what happens next? That's what Joe and his friends didn't think through. And when it happened, the principal didn't think it through either, but give her credit, she had to react on the spot. She did what she thought was right at the time, but she fell right into the trap. The bottom line is when do stupid statements become illegal? A lot of adults and high school students make stupid statements, but unless they are racist, profane, or libelous, they don't get punished. Joe did get punished. In a school he would have been disruptive, but he wasn't in school. He didn't go to class that day. He was outside on a public sidewalk. And school was called off that afternoon because of the parade. So he was just a high school student doing something dumb, not something illegal. Joe made the principal look bad, but he embarrassed his school and his parents, and my guess is that if he had it to do over again, he wouldn't have done it. Still, he shouldn't have been punished. He didn't make a serious argument in favor of doing drugs. Or ridicule Christians. The real argument is about the limits of free speech.

Ideas to Use

1. Joe's banner was in poor taste, but poor taste doesn't meet legal requirement for censorship.
2. The principal was embarrassed and made a knee-jerk reaction without thinking.
3. The real issue is what free speech rights do young people have.

You may want to use a key word or idea as a starting point for a second freewrite. After two or three rounds you will discover how much you already know about your topic and possible directions for developing it.

Brainstorm

An alternative method of discovery is to **brainstorm**. The end result of brainstorming is usually a list—sometimes of questions, sometimes of statements. You might come up with a list of observations and questions, such as these for the free speech case.

- *The student wasn't in the school at the time of the incident.*
- *The principal overreacted.*
- *Drugs are an excuse to give authorities more control.*
- *What is the recent history of free speech cases involving high school students?*
- *Student's citing of Jefferson resulted in more punishment—WHY???*
- *Isn't there protection for satire?*

Make an idea map

Still another strategy for exploring how much you know about a potential topic is to make an **idea map**. Idea maps are useful because they let you see everything at once, and you can begin to make connections among the different aspects of an issue—definitions, causes, effects, proposed solutions, and your personal experience. A good way to get started is to write down ideas on sticky notes. Then you can move the sticky notes around until you figure out which ideas fit together. Figure 2.1 shows what an idea map on the freedom of speech case involving Joseph Frederick might look like.

Respond to something you've read

Most of the writing you do in college will be linked to texts you are reading. Find time to read about your topic before writing about it. Select a book or an article that you find to be a powerful statement about your topic. You don't have to agree with the author completely; in fact, it's more productive if you can "talk back" to the author.

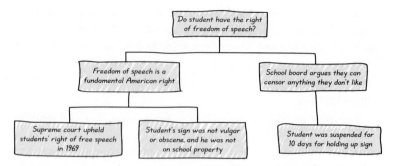

Figure 2.1 Idea map on the Juneau, Alaska, freedom of speech case

Imagine you are sitting down face-to-face with the author. Find places where you can write things like the following:

- *"I agree with your general point, but did you think of this other example? What would you do with it?"*
- *"Here you seem to be arguing for one side, but later you seem to contradict yourself and give credit to the other side."*
- *"Your point about one group might be applied to a different group."*
- *"I don't agree with this claim because your evidence doesn't support your assertion."*

Talking back to a text can help you find your own position: "While X sees it this way, I look at it a different way."

Talk and listen

Writing requires concentration, which for many people depends on quiet and solitude. Nevertheless, many ideas come from conversation, and all ideas are born from other ideas. When we talk and listen, we discover. Productive writers are engaged in a community where ideas are discussed. Your writing class is a writing community. To make the community as useful as possible, it is important to ask your peers for specific and genuine feedback on your drafts and to pay close attention to your classmates' writing as well.

If any of your class communication is done through e-mail or online discussion, you will already have a head start on your assigned writing. E-mails and online discussions can be used the way journals and freewrites are—as material for essays. When you are planning your essay, you may find that you already have a wealth of written material to draw from.

■ You can get one-on-one help in developing your ideas, focusing your topic, and revising your paper at your writing center.

Exercise 2.2 Read the following passage and freewrite for ten minutes. When you are done, look over what you wrote and pick out two or three topics that would be worth pursuing in a paper.

> In the years since Darwin published *The Origin of Species*, the crisp conceptual line that divided artificial from natural selection has blurred. Whereas once humankind exerted its will in the relatively small arena of artificial selection (the arena I think of, metaphorically, as a garden) and nature held sway everywhere else, today the force of our presence is felt everywhere. It has become much harder, in the past century, to tell where the garden leaves off and pure nature begins. We are shaping the evolutionary weather in ways Darwin could never have foreseen; indeed, even the weather itself is in some sense an artifact now, its temperatures and storms the reflection of our actions. For a great many species today, "fitness" means the ability to get along in a world in which humankind has become the most powerful evolutionary force. Artificial selection has become a much more important chapter in natural history as it has moved into the space once ruled exclusively by natural selection.
>
> —Michael Pollan, from *The Botany of Desire*, 2001

2c Write a Working Thesis

The initial stage of the planning process involves finding ideas, expanding and broadening your thoughts, and recording ideas from written sources and conversations. The next stage of thinking, after you have decided on a general topic, is *narrowing* your focus to a specific topic. Having a specific focus is the key to writing a strong essay.

Use questions to focus a broad topic

Childhood obesity is certainly a current and interesting research topic, but it is too broad. Ask questions that will break the big topic into smaller ones.

- Why are children becoming obese?
- Why are children today more obese than children of past generations?
- How has the American food industry contributed to childhood obesity?
- What changes in American culture have contributed to childhood obesity?
- What are the adverse health effects of childhood obesity?
- What strategies are effective for preventing childhood obesity?

Consider other angles to expand a narrow topic

Too-narrow topics are rarer than topics that are too broad. Although candy consumption is certainly one factor contributing to obesity in children, this narrow focus overlooks many other factors that together lead to childhood obesity. For instance:

- Why do some children eat large amounts of candy yet maintain a healthy weight?
- Children have always eaten candy. Why are children today more obese than children of past generations?
- Even when parents keep kids away from candy, some still gain weight. Why?

If you cannot seem to find enough information on your topic to construct an argument, your topic might be too narrow.

Turn your topic into a thesis statement

Your **thesis** states your main idea. Much of the writing that you will do in college and later in your career will have an explicit thesis, usually stated near the beginning. The thesis announces your topic and indicates what points you want to make about that topic.

Your thesis should be closely tied to your purpose—to reflect on your own experience, to explain some aspect of your topic, or to argue for a position or course of action.

Reflective thesis	My experience in a government seminar where other students frequently and sometimes vehemently expressed conflicting views taught me that creating an atmosphere of tolerance can be just as important as passing laws to protect free speech.
Informative thesis	Courts in the United States have consistently upheld the right of free speech on public property if it is not obscene, threatening violence, or inciting violence.
Persuasive thesis	1. A public college or university should have the right to limit free speech in cases of overtly racist or anti-gay language because failing to address such abuses condones intolerance and threatens students' ability to learn.
	2. A public college or university should not have the right to limit free speech, even when it is hateful, because speech that is not obscene or threatening violence is protected on public property.

STAYING ON TRACK

Evaluate your working thesis

Ask yourself these questions about your working thesis.

1. Is it specific?
2. Is it manageable in the length and time I have?
3. Is it interesting to my intended readers?

(continued on next page)

STAYING ON TRACK *(continued)*

Consider the following examples:

Example 1

Eating disorders remain a serious problem on college campuses.

Specific? The thesis is too broad. Exactly who suffers from eating disorders? Is the problem the same for men and women?

Manageable? Because the thesis is not limited to a particular aspect of eating disorders, it cannot be researched adequately.

Interesting? The topic is potentially interesting, but most people know that many college students suffer from eating disorders. If you chose this topic, what could you tell your readers that they don't know already?

Revised thesis

Glamorous images of ultrathin people in the fashion industry, the movie industry, and other media are a contributing cause of eating disorders on college campuses because they influence young people to believe they are fat when in fact their weight is normal.

Example 2

The United States entered World War II when the Japanese bombed Pearl Harbor on December 7, 1941.

Specific? The thesis is too narrow. It states a commonly acknowledged fact.

Manageable? A known fact is stated in the thesis, so there is nothing to research. The general topic of the attack on Pearl Harbor is too large for essay-length treatment.

Interesting? The attack on Pearl Harbor remains interesting to Americans (witness a recent Hollywood film that deals with the subject), but there is no topic to work from.

Revised thesis

Although combat between the United States and Japan began at Pearl Harbor, the unofficial war began when President Roosevelt froze Japanese assets in the United States in July 1940 and later declared a commercial embargo.

These examples suggest that the key to writing an effective thesis is finding a topic that is neither too vast nor too narrow—and not obvious. You may have to adjust your working thesis more than once as you plan and begin drafting.

What makes an effective thesis statement

A thesis should not be a question. The thesis is your answer to your research question.

Not a thesis: *Why did England lose against Germany in the 2010 World Cup?* Along with being specific, manageable, and interesting, your thesis should also tell *what* you plan to argue and an indication of *how* you plan to argue without simply offering a list. Announce how you will be weighing and arranging the points in your argument.

Uninteresting: *The German team's youth, teamwork, and superior coaching led to their victory over England in the 2010 World Cup.* [the typical boring five-paragraph organization: youth, yada yada; teamwork, yada yada; *coaching*, yada yada]

Better: *Although the youth of the German players was certainly a factor in their victory over England in the 2010 World Cup, teamwork and superior coaching had a much greater role.* [arguing that one or two elements are more important breaks out of the five-paragraph formula]

Another way to narrow a potential thesis is to think about possible counterarguments. And then make sure you address these in your argument.

> *Many commentators and fans say that England would have beat Germany in the 2010 World Cup if the contested goal had been good; however, Germany's superior coaching and teamwork would have still made an English victory very difficult, if not impossible.*

A thesis should never be combative or confrontational.

> *Combative: England lost to Germany in the 2010 World Cup because the English team is made up of thugs and millionaires.*

Exercise 2.3 Look at the following theses. What kind (reflective, informative, persuasive) is each?

1. Reading the novel *Push* by Sapphire made me aware of the violence present in some parent-child relationships.
2. Urban policymakers should read novels like *Push* to gain empathy for the population they are affecting when they cut services.
3. Author Sapphire was inspired to create the character Precious by girls she encountered while teaching in Harlem.
4. The change in the voice of *Push's* narrator, Precious, reflects her growing literacy and self-awareness.
5. Having grown up with goats on my grandparent's farm, I know that they are the most fuel-efficient lawnmowers in the world.
6. The city of Los Angeles is using goats instead of lawnmowers to maintain public grounds.

7. More cities should use goats to maintain public parks.
8. The National Center for Science Education promotes the teaching of evolution in schools.
9. My high school biology teacher, one of the best teachers I ever had, firmly believed that science and religion should not be enemies.
10. Schools must teach evolution as a scientific fact or we risk creating a dangerously uninformed generation.

Exercise 2.4 Here are several assignments and the thesis statement that a student has decided to use for each assignment. Evaluate these thesis statements according to their levels of specificity, manageability, and interest. Then, rewrite each one to make it meet all three of the requirements.

1. Design a three-panel brochure intended to educate teenage boys about the responsibilities of fatherhood.
   Thesis: Think before having a baby. They are really expensive.
2. Write a three- to five-page paper for a child development class. The papers from this class will be published on a child advocacy Web site.
   Thesis: Many formerly accepted methods of discipline are now considered child abuse.
3. Write a 10- to 15-page research paper on a revolutionary breakthrough in urban transportation to enter in a contest. Your paper will be evaluated by a panel of graduate students majoring in city planning.
   Thesis: Washington DC has a great subway system called the Metro.
4. Write a 200- to 300- word article for a magazine geared toward 8-12-year-olds.
   Thesis: It's never too early to start thinking about a career.
5. Write a one-page paper for your ethics class. You will use this paper to start class discussion.
   Thesis: Reading employees' e-mail is a violation of privacy.

2d Plan a Strategy

People who write frequently on the job or who make their living by writing have many different ways of producing a successful piece of writing. Some may plan extensively in advance, either individually or as a team, specifying exactly what will go in each section. Other writers find that putting ideas into words often changes the ideas and generates new ones. These writers know that writing drafts is a way of discovering their subject, and they count on one or two or more rewrites to get their document into shape.

Consider making an outline

At some point in school you may have been required to produce a formal outline to submit along with a paper. A **formal outline** typically begins with the thesis statement, which anchors the entire outline. Each numbered or lettered item clearly supports the thesis, and the relationship among the items is clear from the outline hierarchy.

> Thesis statement: The United States needs to take concrete steps to reduce obesity in children.
>
> I. A disturbing aspect of the trend of fatter Americans is that children are increasingly obese.
>   A. More than one third of children 10–17 are obese.
>   B. Obese children suffer many serious health problems today.
>   C. America has had some success in addressing other teenage health problems including smoking, drug use, and teen pregnancy.
> II. Many causes have been proposed for overweight America.
>   A. One proposed cause is the move to the suburbs, but the population shift to the suburbs occurred before the rapid rise in weight gain.
>   B. The couch potato argument is countered by increases in exercise and participation in athletics.
>   C. The simple answer is that Americans consume about twice as many calories per day as they need.

Consider using a working outline

A working outline is more like an initial sketch of how you will arrange the major sections. Jotting down main points and a few subpoints before you begin can be a great help while you are writing. You can read the complete essay that developed from these outlines in Section 26l.

Addressing Childhood Obesity

Section 1: Begin with a description of the problem including statistics on the rising number of obese children.

Section 2: Discuss the causes that have been proposed for childhood obesity.

Section 3: Discuss how the eating patterns of Americans have changed during the last thirty years and how portions served have increased.

Section 4: Examine how food is being marketed to children.
Section 5: Look at the role of parents and why parents
* often don't control much of the environment where*
* children eat.*
Section 6: Describe solutions: (1) restrict marketing of food
* to children, (2) educate parents and children, (3) promote*
* healthier lifestyles.*
Section 7: Discuss how these solutions can be implemented.

Exercise 2.5 Look again at the list of topics in Exercise 2.1 and the freewrite you did for Exercise 2.2. Choose one of these to pursue, and write a short outline for a paper that includes three to five main topics.

2e Compose a Draft

Skilled writers aim at producing a good draft—not a perfect draft. They know that they can go back and revise later.

Essays typically contain an introduction, body, and conclusion. You do not have to write these parts in that order, though. In your **introduction**, you can offer a short example that illustrates the problem being discussed. You can state a surprising fact. You can begin with a fascinating quotation. Your aim is to interest the reader and to let the reader know the topic of the paper, if not necessarily the thesis.

The **body** of the essay consists of the primary discussion. Remember to guide readers through the discussion by letting them know where you are going. Your readers need road signs to tell them where the discussion is taking them. Road signs are transition words and phrases such as *consequently*, *the third reason is . . .* , and *on the other hand*.

The last section, the **conclusion**, often repeats what has already been said. If the essay has been long and complex, sometimes this repetition is necessary, but usually the repetition is just that—annoying redundancy. The final paragraph does not have to repeat the main point. It can give a compelling last example or propose a course of action. It can ponder the larger significance of the subject under discussion. It can pose an important question for the reader to think about.

Write as a Member of a Team

Almost without exception, people in occupations that require a college education write frequently on the job, and much of that writing is done in collaboration rather than alone. The better you understand how to write effectively with other people, the more enjoyable and more productive the process will be for you.

Determine the goals and identify tasks and roles

- Write down the goals as specifically as you can and discuss them as a team.
- Determine what tasks are required to meet those goals. Write down the tasks and arrange them in the order they need to be completed.
- If the team does not possess the necessary skills and resources, adjust the goals to what you can realistically expect to accomplish.

Make a work plan

- Make a time line that lists the dates when specific tasks need to be completed and distribute it to all team members. Charts are useful tools for keeping track of progress.
- Assign tasks to team members.
- Revisit the team's goals often. To succeed, each team member must keep in mind what the team aims to accomplish.
- Decide on a process for monitoring progress. Set up specific dates for review and assign team members to be responsible for reviewing work that has been done.

Understand the dynamics of a successful team

- Teamwork requires some flexibility. Keep talking to each other along the way.
- It may be desirable to rotate roles during the project.

Deal with problems when they come up

- If a team member is not participating, find out why.
- If team members have different ideas about what needs to be done, find time to meet so that the team can reach an agreement.
- Get the team together if you are not meeting the deadlines you established in the work plan and devise a new plan, if necessary.

WRITING SMART

Overcome writer's block

1. **If you have an outline, put it on the computer screen or place it beside you.** The outline will give you prompts to help get you started.

2. **Begin writing what you know best.** If you don't know exactly where you are headed, the introduction can be the hardest section to write. The introduction can wait until last.

3. **Resist the urge to revise too soon.** It's more important to keep moving forward. If you stop to polish a section, you will lose momentum, and in the end you may discard that section anyway.

4. **If you get stuck, try working on another section.** Look again at your notes or outline.

5. **If you are still stuck, talk to someone about what you are trying to write.** If your campus has a writing center, talk to a consultant. Reading more about your subject can also help you to get moving again.

3 | Compose Paragraphs

QUICK*TAKE*

- Focus your paragraphs (see below)
- Organize your paragraphs (see p. 34)
- Make your paragraphs coherent (see p. 35)
- Write effective beginning and concluding paragraphs (see p. 38)

Focus Your Paragraphs

Readers expect sentences in a paragraph to be closely related to one another. Often writers will begin a paragraph with one idea, but other ideas will occur to them while they are writing. Paragraphs confuse readers when they go in different directions. When you revise your paragraphs, check for focus.

In the following example, notice how much stronger the paragraph becomes when we remove the sentences in red. They distract us from the subject, Royal Chitwan National Park in Nepal and how it is different from Western national parks.

> Like everything else in Nepal, Royal Chitwan National Park is different from Western notions of a park. It is a jungle between two rivers, with grass twenty to twenty-five feet tall growing in the swampy land along the rivers. Several rare or endangered species live in the park, including leopards, crocodiles, royal Bengal tigers, and the greater one-horned Asian rhinoceros. In fact, we saw several rhinos during our weeklong visit to the park. To my relief we saw all but one from the safety of an elephant's back. But the boundaries of the park restrict neither the Nepalis nor the animals. The Nepalis cross the river into the park to gather firewood and the tall grass, which they use to make their houses. Some even live within the park. The rhinos and deer raid the Nepalis' fields at night, and the leopards prey on their dogs and livestock. To keep the truce between these competitors, the army patrols the park, mostly to prevent poachers from killing the tigers and rhino. But confrontations do occur; the animals lose habitat and the Nepalis lose their crops and lives.

When to use explicit topic sentences

You were probably taught to begin a paragraph with a topic sentence. Topic sentences alert readers to the focus of a paragraph and help writers stay on

topic. Topic sentences should explain the focus of the paragraph and situate it in the larger argument. However, topic sentences do not have to
begin paragraphs, and they need not be just one sentence. You will decide
what placement and length will best suit your subject.

Topic sentences at the beginning of a paragraph will quickly orient
readers, preparing them for the sentences to come. Each sentence that
follows elucidates the topic sentence.

Topic sentence at the beginning

We live in a world of risks so much beyond our control that
it is difficult to think of anything that is risk free. Even the most
basic human acts involve risk—having sex in an era of AIDS, eating
in an era of genetically altered food, walking outdoors in an ozone-
depleted atmosphere, drinking water and breathing air laden with
chemicals whose effects we do not understand. Should we eat more
fish in our daily diet? Nutritionists tell us that eating fish reduces
the risk of heart disease. Other scientists, however, tell us that fish
are contaminated with a new generation of synthetic chemicals.

When a paragraph builds to make a particular point, the topic sentence is more effective at the end of the paragraph.

Topic sentence at the end

We are continually being summoned to change ourselves for
the better—through fitness programs, through various kinds of
instruction, through advice columns, through self-help books and
videos—and somehow we never quite measure up. The blame always
comes back on us. If we had eaten better, or exercised more, or paid
more attention to our investments, or learned a new skill, or changed
our oil every 3,000 miles, then things would have turned out better.
Very rarely do we ask how a different social organization might have
made things better. Our society incorporates critical thinking
without being much affected by the consequences of that thinking.

When to use implicit topic sentences

In some cases, particularly in narrative prose, writers omit explicit topic
sentences because they would clash with the tone or style of the paragraph.
Instead, these paragraphs use tightly connected, focused sentences to make
the topic implicitly clear.

Implicit topic sentence

By the mid-1970s in the United States, the temporary advantage
of being the only major power with its industries undamaged following
World War II had evaporated, and rust-belt industries failed one after
the other against competition from a revived Europe and an emergent

Asia. The United States seemed to be going the way of other historical world powers, where efficient trading nations beat out bloated military regimes. Japan appeared to be the model for a fast and light capitalism that the rest of the world would imitate. Just a few years later, however, the American decline reversed. The United States again became the economic leader of the world in the 1990s.

The implicit topic sentence is something like "The United States' economy appeared to be in rapid decline in the 1970s, only to bounce back to world leadership in the 1990s."

Exercise 3.1 Find the topic sentence in each of the following paragraphs. If it is implied, write what you think it is.

1. I hate the way the holiday makes all non-mothers, and the daughters of dead mothers, and the mothers of dead or severely damaged children, feel the deepest kind of grief and failure. The non-mothers must sit in their churches, temples, mosques, recovery rooms and pretend to feel good about the day while they are excluded from a holiday that benefits no one but Hallmark and See's.
   —Anne Lamott, "Why I Hate Mother's Day," Salon, May 8, 2010

2. Why is every child forced to memorize "Excuse me," and "Thank you" but so few adults know phrases like, "Looks like you and your kids are having a rough evening. Can I help with anything?" Or, "Hey, my son used to throw tantrums all the time. Don't worry about it. You're doing great." Or, "I understand if you don't want any help. I just want you to know that you've got a beautiful baby there and I hope your day gets better." Why aren't the people who are so busy teaching and enforcing good manners also teaching healthy, effective ways to interrupt violence before it gains traction?
   —Susan Schorn, "Cross, Training" McSweeney's, June 22, 2010

3. At the present time, public education is in peril. Efforts to improve public education are, ironically, diminishing its quality and endangering its very survival. We must turn our attention to improving the schools, infusing them with the substance of genuine learning and reviving the conditions that make learning possible.
   —Diane Ravitch, The Death and Life of the Great American School System, 2010

4. This is the disease. This is the disease in America. It's not just spending, it's not just taxes, it's not just corruption. It is progressivism. And it is in both parties. It is in the Republicans and the Democrats. I mean it's— it really is. I mean, I'm so sick of hearing people say, oh, well the Republicans are going to solve it all. Really? It's just progressive-lite. . . .
   —Glenn Beck, Keynote address to the Conservative Political Action Conference, February 20, 2010

3b Organize Your Paragraphs

Well-organized paragraphs in essays usually follow a pattern similar to that of a well-organized paper, but in miniature. Chances are you'll use a combination of these strategies in order to get your point across.

- **Description.** Descriptive paragraphs are frequent in informative writing. The key is providing concrete details, including sights, sounds, smells, textures, and tastes.
- **Narration.** Narrative paragraphs are organized by time. They are essential for histories and any how-to writing.
- **Comparison and contrast.** Paragraphs of comparison assess one subject in terms of its relation to others, usually highlighting what they have in common. Contrasting paragraphs analyze differences between things.
- **Definition.** Paragraphs organized by definition usually begin with a term and then go on to list its defining characteristics, sometimes using examples.
- **Examples and illustrations.** Examples and illustrations make key points and ideas vivid and memorable.
- **Cause and effect.** Cause and effect paragraphs are structured in two basic ways: they can begin with causes and then state the effect or they can begin with the effect and then analyze the causes.
- **Classification and division.** Classifying places items into categories according to their similarities. Dividing takes a single item or concept and breaks it down into its component parts.

Exercise 3.2 A student is writing a paper on New Orleans Mardi Gras celebrations in the United States. The student has the following ideas for paragraphs. Which of the seven common organizational strategies would work best for each?

1. crowd behavior during Mardi Gras
2. history of Mardi Gras in New Orleans
3. the ways different ethnic groups and social classes celebrate Mardi Gras
4. what Mardi Gras really is
5. the difference between celebrations in other parts of the United States and Mardi Gras in New Orleans
6. key parades of Mardi Gras
7. how Hurricane Katrina changed Mardi Gras

Find a paper you wrote either for this class or for another class. Chose one paragraph and rewrite it, organizing it according to one of the strategies from this section. Make sure you choose a strategy that is different from the one you used when you first wrote the paragraph!

3c Make Your Paragraphs Coherent

You've no doubt heard that good writing should "flow," but what exactly does flow mean? Writing that flows is coherent, which means readers understand how sentences fit together. Repeating key phrases and signaling relationships with transitional terms help in building coherence.

Reiterate key terms and phrases

In the following paragraph, notice how the writer keeps the focus on *Facebook, privacy,* and *personal information* by repeating key terms.

> The value of Facebook as a corporate entity is based on its potential for advertising revenue. In November 2007, Facebook launched Beacon, an advertising system that sent targeted advertising and tracked activities of Facebook members on partner Web sites, even when the members were not logged in on Facebook. Facebook retreated to an opt-in privacy policy only after large-scale protests brought negative publicity, but activists discovered that Facebook was still collecting personal information from those who had opted out. In August 2008, the activists filed a class-action lawsuit against Facebook and its corporate marketing partners, alleging that Facebook's selling of members' personal information is a violation of federal and state privacy laws. Even though Facebook has shut down Beacon, there are no certain safeguards to protect privacy. The BBC program *Click* demonstrated that anyone with a basic knowledge of Web programming could gain access to restricted personal details on Facebook. Furthermore, the information does not go away. Facebook friends are literally friends forever because social networking sites are archived on servers.

Signal relationships with transitional terms

Transitional terms act like warning signs for readers, preparing them for what is around the bend. Notice how transitional terms signal the relationship of one sentence to the next.

> Critics of Web 2.0, including Tim Berners-Lee, who is credited with inventing the Web, dismiss the term as jargon, pointing out that the Web has always been about connecting people. Indeed, in

the late 1970s and early 1980s, e-mail and hobby bulletin boards were the most popular features of the ARPANET, the predecessor of the Internet. **More accurately,** Web 2.0 marked a revival of the mid-1990s ebullience about the Internet as one of the greatest achievements in human history. **For example,** Kevin Kelly speaks of Web 2.0 in terms of religious transcendence: "The Machine provided a new way of thinking (perfect search, total recall) and a new mind for an old species. It was the Beginning."

STAYING ON TRACK

Use transitional terms

Be sure to use transitional terms accurately in order to signal the relationships between your sentences.

- **To enumerate:** again, also, and, as well, finally, furthermore, first, second, third, in addition, last, moreover, next, too

- **To generalize:** commonly, in general, for the most part, on the whole, usually, typically

- **To offer an example:** for example, for instance, indeed, in fact, of course, specifically, such as, the following

- **To situate in time:** after a month, afterward, as long as, as soon as, at the moment, at present, at that time, before, earlier, followed by, in the meantime, in the past, lately, later, meanwhile, now, preceded by, presently, since then, so far, soon, subsequently, suddenly, then, this year, today, until, when, while

- **To situate in space:** above, below, beyond, close to, elsewhere, far from, following, here, near, next to, there

- **To conclude:** as a result, hence, in conclusion, in short, on the whole, therefore, thus

- **To contrast:** although, but, even though, however, in contrast, conversely, in spite of, instead, nevertheless, nonetheless, on the one hand, on the contrary, on the other hand, still, though, yet

- **To compare:** again, also, in the same way, likewise, similarly

- **To signal cause or effect:** as a result, because, consequently, for this reason, hence, if, so, then, therefore, thus

- **To sum up:** as I said, as we have seen, as mentioned earlier, in conclusion, in other words, in short, in sum, therefore, thus

- **To concede a point:** certainly, even though, granted, in fairness, in truth, naturally, of course, to be fair, while it's true

Exercise 3.4 Rewrite the paragraphs below using the strategies presented in Section 3c to make them cohere. The writer has attempted to use the strategies in some places, but may have done so poorly.

1. What do a nineteenth-century rural family, President Andrew Jackson, and two popular movies have in common? The legend of the Bell Witch revolves around a series of strange events experienced by the Bell family of Adams, Tennessee, between 1817 and 1821. Events were witnessed by hundreds of people, among them future President of the United States Andrew Jackson. It represents one of the most famous and documented instances of paranormal events in history. It was used as the basis for the 2006 film *An American Haunting* and influenced production of the 1999 film, *The Blair Witch Project.*

2. This may not be true, but the first haunting occurred in 1817, when John Bell saw a strange animal in his cornfield. It had the body of a dog and the head of a rabbit and vanished when it was shot at. Next, a series of strange beating and gnawing noises were heard around, and eventually inside, the Bell residence. The Bell children's bedclothes were regularly pulled off and tossed onto the floor by an invisible force. A choking, grunting voice was heard. Betsy Bell, the family's younger daughter, was violently assaulted.

3. This became well known in their community. There were reports of a voice conversing loudly and clearly, singing, quoting from the Bible and accurately describing events taking place miles away. Future U.S. President Andrew Jackson heard about them and decided to observe them in person in 1819. Jackson's wagon was stopped in its tracks. He acknowledged that the witch was responsible and the wagon was freed. A man in Jackson's party said he would kill the witch, and he started choking and wriggling. Jackson and his entourage left the Bell property the next day.

4. John Bell was the main target, suffering facial seizures that left him speechless. John Bell died on December 20, 1820. A small bottle containing an unidentified liquid he had apparently ingested was found near the body. The remaining contents were fed to the family cat. It died. The family heard a voice say "I gave Ol' John a big dose of that last night, and that fixed him." Bell's funeral guests heard a voice laughing and singing.

5. Bell died and it stopped, but Lucy Bell later said a voice told her that it would return in 1828. John Bell, Jr. visited later for three weeks and said that a voice communicated with him. It predicted the Civil War, the Great Depression, and both World Wars. Many people believe that the spirit returned in 1935, took up residence on the former Bell property, and remains there to the present day. People on the property today still hear the faint sounds of people talking and children playing. No good pictures have ever been taken of the place.

Exercise 3.5 Choose a paragraph from a paper you have written for either this class or another class. Underline any transitional words or phrases you used, and mark spaces where you think you need a transitional word or phrase. Write out the relationships expressed by the transitions you underlined. Then, write out the relationship that needs to be expressed in each place that you marked. What transitional word or phrase could you add to make that relationship clear?

3d Consider Paragraph Length

Paragraph breaks can signal various kinds of shifts:

- A new concept
- The next step in an argument
- The end of the introduction
- The beginning of the conclusion
- A new speaker in dialogue
- A shift in time or place
- A logical pause that gives the reader a breather

What is the ideal length for a paragraph? It depends on what sort of paragraphs you are writing. Business letter writers strive for short paragraphs so their readers can see the essential information at a glance. Academic writers need space to make and support arguments in depth. As a general rule, readers' eyes glaze over when they see paragraphs in an essay that stretch beyond one page. Nevertheless, too many short paragraphs are a sign that the piece lacks either weighty ideas or sufficient development.

3e Write Effective Beginning and Ending Paragraphs

Beginning and ending paragraphs of essays should behave like a smart suitor meeting "the parents" for the first time: dress well; start with a firm handshake; show you are thoughtful and personable; close on a strong note. Because readers are more likely to remember beginning and ending paragraphs, they are your best opportunity to make a good impression.

Understand what beginning paragraphs do

Effective beginning paragraphs convince the reader to read on. They capture the reader's interest and set the tone for the piece. In essays they often state the thesis and briefly map out the way the writing will progress from paragraph to paragraph. Sometimes the work of the beginning paragraph might be carried through three or four paragraphs. A writer might start with a memorable example, then use the example to launch the rest of the essay.

Start beginning paragraphs with a bang

Getting the first few sentences of an essay down on paper can be daunting. Begin with one of the following strategies to get your reader's attention:

A question — *least favorite*

How valuable are snow leopards? The director of a zoo in Darjeeling, India, was fired when its snow leopard caught a cold and died.

A hard-hitting fact

Poaching is big business—to be exact, a six-billion-dollar business. The only illegal trade that's larger is drugs.

A pithy quotation — *least favorite*

"That the snow leopard is," writes Peter Matthiessen, "that it is here, that its frosty eyes watch us from the mountains—that is enough." And it has to be enough because, while snow leopards are here now, they may not be here much longer.

Images

Tons of animal pelts and bones sit in storage at Royal Chitwan National Park in Nepal. The mounds of poached animal parts confiscated by forest rangers reach almost to the ceiling. The air is stifling, the stench stomach-churning.

An anecdote

The snow leopard stood so still in the frosty bushes, it wasn't until the goat squealed that we saw it. Its mottled white fur was now spattered with the goat's blood. Steam rose from the animal's wounds. We fumbled for our cameras, hoping to capture this terrible beauty.

A problem

Ecologists worry that the construction of a natural gas pipeline in Russia's Ukok Plateau will destroy the habitat of endangered snow leopards, argali mountain sheep, and steppe eagles.

A concisely stated thesis

If the governments of China and Russia don't soon act decisively, snow leopards will be extinct in a few years.

A contradiction or paradox

Snow leopards are tremendously versatile animals, strong enough to kill a horse and fast enough to chase down a hare. What they can't do is hide from poachers in Nepal and India. And this may be their downfall.

An odd, ridiculous, or unbelievable fact

Caterpillar fungus is a hot commodity. Traditional healers and their clients are willing to pay handsomely for illegally harvested ingredients for their treatments. As a result, demand for the fungus, along with other poached items like rhinoceros horns and snow leopard bones, drives a lucrative and destructive black market in endangered species.

Understand what ending paragraphs do

Ending paragraphs remind readers where they've been and invite them to carry your ideas forward. Use the ending paragraph to touch on your key points, but do not merely summarize. Leave your readers with something that will inspire them to continue to think about what you have written.

Conclude with strength

The challenge in ending paragraphs is to leave the reader with something provocative, something beyond pure summary of the previous paragraphs. The following are strategies for ending an essay:

Issue a call to action

Although ecological problems in Russia seem distant, students like you and me can help protect the snow leopard by joining the World Wildlife Fund campaign.

Discuss the implications of your argument

Even though the extinction of snow leopards would be a sad event, their end is not the fundamental problem. Instead, their precarious position is a symptom of a larger dilemma: Environmental damage throughout developing nations in Asia threatens their biodiversity.

Explain the applications of your argument

This study of snow leopard breeding behavior can inform captive breeding programs in zoos.

Make recommendations

Russia's creditors would be wise to sign on to the World Wildlife Fund's proposal to relieve some of the country's debt in order to protect the snow leopard habitat. After all, if Russia is going to be economically viable, it needs to be ecologically healthy.

Speculate about the future

Unless Nepali and Chinese officials devote more resources to snow leopard preservation, these beautiful animals will be gone in a few years.

Tell an anecdote that illustrates a key point

Poachers are so uncowed by authorities that they even tried to sell a snow leopard skin to a reporter researching a story on endangered species.

Describe a key image

As they watched the pile of confiscated furs and bones burn, Nepali forest rangers flashed proud smiles that seemed to say, "This time we mean business."

Offer a quotation that expresses the essence of your argument

Too often, developed nations impose their high-flown priorities, like protecting snow leopards and tigers, on developing nations. A Russian farmer summed up the disjunction succinctly. Tigers ate two cows in his herd of fifty. When he was compensated for the two he asked, "What's this? Can't the tiger come back and eat the remaining forty-eight?"

Ask a rhetorical question

Generally, the larger and more majestic (or better yet, cute) an endangered animal is, the better its chances of being saved. Bumper stickers don't implore us to save blind cave insects; they ask us to save the whales, elephants, and tigers. But snow leopards aren't cave bugs; they are beautiful, impressive animals that should be the easiest of all to protect. If we can't save them, do any endangered species stand a chance?

Exercise 3.6 Write an introductory and a concluding paragraph for each of the essays described here. Label what each paragraph does, using the types shown in Section 3e, such as asking a question or making a recommendation.

1. An essay explaining how to build a computer out of an old manual typewriter
2. A description of a moment when you decided to change something about your life
3. A proposal to make texting while driving a felony
4. An analysis of your favorite CD from a musical artist
5. A several-paragraph blog post responding to another blog post you felt was misinformed or inappropriate, or that presented a viewpoint that opposes your opinion on a subject

4 | Rewrite, Edit, and Proofread

QUICK*TAKE*

- Switch from writer to reader (see below)
- Learn strategies for rewriting (see p. 45)
- Respond to other writers' drafts (see p. 47)
- Proofread carefully (see p. 55)

4a Switch from Writer to Reader

Even the best writers often have to revise several times to get the result they want. To be able to revise effectively, you have to plan your time. You cannot revise a paper or a Web site effectively if you wait until the last minute to begin working. Allow at least a day to let what you write cool off. With a little time you will gain enough distance to "re-see" it, which, after all, is what *revision* means.

You must also have effective strategies for revising if you're going to be successful. The biggest trap you can fall into is starting off with the little stuff first. *Don't sweat the small stuff at the beginning.* When you see a word that's wrong or a misplaced comma, the great temptation is to fix it. But if you start searching for errors, it's hard to get back to the larger concerns.

Begin your revision by pretending you are someone who is either uninformed about your subject or holds an opposing view. If possible, think of an actual person and pretend to be that person. Read your draft aloud, all the way through. When you read aloud, you will probably hear clunky phrases and outright errors, but do no more at this stage than put checks in the margins so you can find these things later. Once again, you don't want to get bogged down with the little stuff.

Use these questions to evaluate your draft. Note any places where you might make improvements.

Does your paper or project meet the assignment?

- Look again at your assignment, especially at the key words, such as *analyze, define, evaluate,* and *propose.* Does your paper or project do what the assignment asks?
- Look again at the assignment for specific guidelines, including length, format, and amount of research. Does your work meet these guidelines?

Does your writing have a clear focus?

- Does your project have an explicitly stated thesis? If not, is your thesis clearly implied?
- Is each paragraph related to your thesis?
- Do you get off the track at any point by introducing other topics?

Are your main points adequately developed?

- Do you support your main points with reasons and evidence?
- Can you add more examples and details that would help to explain your main points?
- Would additional research fill in gaps or make your case stronger?

Is your organization effective?

- Is the order of your main points clear to your reader? (You may want to make a quick outline of your draft if you have not done so already.)
- Are there any places where you find abrupt shifts or gaps?
- Are there sections or paragraphs that could be rearranged to make your draft more effective?

Do you consider your potential readers' knowledge and points of view?

- Do you give enough background if your readers are unfamiliar with your subject?
- Do you acknowledge opposing views that readers might have?
- Do you appeal to common values that you share with your readers?

Do you represent yourself effectively?

- To the extent you can, forget for a moment that you wrote what you are reading. What impression do you have of you, the writer?
- Does "the writer" create an appropriate tone?
- Has "the writer" done his or her homework?
- Is the writing project visually effective? Does "the writer" use headings and illustrations where they are helpful?

Do you conclude emphatically?

- Conclusions that only summarize tend to bore readers. Does your conclusion offer more than a review of ideas you have already fully discussed?
- Could you use your conclusion to discuss further implications?

- Could you conclude by making recommendations for change or improvement, or by urging readers to take action?
- Have you left your audience with a final provocative idea that might invite further discussion?

When you finish, make a list of your goals for the revision. You may have to write another draft before you move to the next stage.

Learn Strategies for Rewriting

Now it's time to go through your draft in detail. You should work on the goals you identified in your review.

1. Keep your audience in mind.   Step back and assess your paper from a reader's perspective. Paragraphs with strong, engaging openers keep an audience's attention, establish a writer's credibility, and above all intrigue readers so that they want to read on. Reread each of your paragraphs' opening sentences and ask yourself whether the language is strong and engaging enough to keep your reader interested in your argument from paragraph to paragraph.

2. Sharpen your focus wherever possible.   You may have started out with a large topic but find now that most of what you wrote concerns only one aspect of it. For example, you may have started with the large topic of privacy, but your focus now is on the current practice of some states' selling their driver's license databases to companies that build junk-mail lists. Revise your thesis and supporting paragraphs as needed.

3. Check that key terms are adequately defined.   What are your key terms? Are they defined precisely enough to be meaningful? If your argument relies on an abstract term such as *justice*, you are obligated to define it specifically.

4. Develop where necessary.   Key points and claims may need more explanation and supporting evidence. Look for opportunities to replace generalizations with specific details.

General statement	Grizzly bears and black bears look different.
Specific details	Rely on body shape rather than size and color to distinguish grizzly bears from black bears. Grizzlies have a hump above their front shoulders; black bears lack this hump. In profile, grizzlies have a depression between their eyes and nose, while black bears have a "Roman" profile with a straight line between the forehead and nose.

5. Check links between paragraphs. Carefully crafted transitions between paragraphs accomplish two things: They explain to your reader why a paragraph logically follows the previous one, and they express the twists and turns of your thinking.

If you are struggling with your transitions, try this quick diagnostic: Underline the first and last sentences of each paragraph in your paper and then read these underlined sentences aloud to a friend. Do these sentences together make a logical and coherent argument? If not, spend more time figuring out the relationships between your ideas. Often you can express these relationships more clearly by choosing accurate transitional phrases such as *although, for example, on the other hand, in contrast, similarly,* and so on (see Section 3c).

6. Consider your title. An effective title makes the reader want to read what you have written. Be as specific as you can in your title, and if possible, suggest your stance. "Use of Anabolic Steroids" as a title is vague and bland, and it suggests a topic far too large to be handled well in a few pages. A stronger title would be "Is Andro a Food Supplement or a Steroid?"

7. Consider your introduction. In the introduction you want to get off to a fast start and convince your reader to keep reading. If your subject is the use of steroids among high school students, don't start with an empty sentence like "Drugs are a big problem in today's high schools." Cut to the chase with a sentence such as "The National Institute of Drug Abuse reports that the number of high school students who abuse anabolic steroids rose steadily during the 1990s, while the perception of the risks involved declined." Then you might follow with a sentence that indicates how you will approach your topic: "My experiences as a high school athlete gave me insights into why students would risk future liver failure, cancer, strokes, heart attacks, and other serious health problems in order to gain a competitive advantage." In two sentences you have established your topic and your own authority to write about it.

8. Consider your conclusion. Restating your claim usually isn't the best way to finish; conclusions that offer only summary tend to bore readers. The worst endings say something like "in my paper I've said this." In contrast, effective conclusions remind readers where your argument has taken them and then invite further discussion. Try to leave your reader with something interesting and provocative. Think about whether there is an implication you can draw or another example you can include that sums up your position. If you are writing a proposal, your ending might be a call for action.

9. Improve the visual aspects of your text. Does the font you selected look attractive? (See Section 16d.) Do you use the same font throughout?

Are you consistent if you use more than one font? Do you include headings and subheadings to identify key sections of your argument? If you include statistical data, would presenting it in charts be effective? (See Section 16d.) Would illustrations help to establish key points? For example, a map could be very useful if you are arguing about the location of a proposed new highway.

4c Respond to Other Writers' Drafts

Your instructor may ask you to review your classmates' drafts. Writing a response to the work of a fellow student may make you feel uncomfortable. You may think you don't know enough to say anything useful. Remember that you are only charged with letting the writer know how you—one of many potential readers—react.

But you do have to put forth your best effort. Responding to other people's writing requires the same careful attention you give to your own draft. To write a helpful response, you should go through the draft more than once. Before you begin, number the paragraphs if the writer has not already done so.

First reading

Read at your normal rate the first time through without stopping. When you finish you should have a clear sense of what the writer was trying to accomplish.

- **Main idea:** Write a sentence that summarizes what you think is the writer's main idea in the draft.
- **Purpose:** Write a sentence that summarizes what you think the writer was trying to accomplish in the draft.

Second reading

In your second reading, you should be most concerned with the content, organization, and completeness of the draft. Make notes as you read.

- **Introduction:** Does the writer's first paragraph effectively introduce the topic and engage your interest?
- **Thesis:** Where exactly is the writer's thesis? Note in the margin where you think the thesis is located.
- **Focus:** Does the writer maintain a focus on the thesis? Note any places where the writer seems to wander off to another topic.
- **Organization:** Are the sections and paragraphs ordered effectively? Do any paragraphs seem to be out of place? Do you note any abrupt shifts? Can you suggest a better order for the paragraphs?

- **Completeness:** Do any sections and paragraphs lack key information or adequate development? Where do you want to know more?
- **Sources:** If the draft uses outside sources, are they cited accurately? If there are quotations, are they used correctly and worked into the fabric of the draft?

Third reading

In your third reading, turn your attention to matters of audience, style, and tone.

- **Audience:** Who is the writer's intended audience? What does the writer assume the audience knows and believes?
- **Style:** Is the writer's style engaging? How would you describe the writer's voice?
- **Tone:** Is the tone appropriate for the writer's purpose and audience? Is the tone consistent throughout the draft? Are there places where another word or phrase might work better?

When you have finished the third reading, write a short paragraph on each bulleted item, referring to specific paragraphs in the draft by number. Then end by answering these two questions:

1. What does the writer do especially well in the draft?
2. What one or two things would most improve the draft in a revision?

Exercise 4.1   Read the draft below and respond in a paragraph or two answering the following questions:

1. What is the writer's main idea and what is his or her purpose for writing this draft? Are these things clear? How could the writer make them clearer?
2. Does all the information serve the thesis? In other words, is the introduction clear and engaging? Do all of the paragraphs maintain a focus on the thesis? Do the paragraphs need to be reorganized? Is any information missing? Is there information that needs to be cited that isn't? Are sources cited correctly?
3. Who is the writer's intended audience? Are the style and tone appropriate for the subject matter and for the audience? How could the writer make this stronger?
4. What are the writer's strengths? What one or two things would most improve this draft?

Remember to resist the urge to edit sentences and correct mechanical errors—the focus here is on clear and effective presentation of ideas.

We've Come Along Way, Baby

Scientists argue about how long humans has existed on the Earth. Until recently, Lucy, an Australopithecus, discovered by Donald Johnson and M. Taieb, for sure wore the crown for oldest human ancestor. Her remains are 3.4 million years old. In 2009, however, scientists announced the discovery of a 4.4 million-year-old *Ardipithecus ramidus* (Ardi, for short). For a while, Ardi, a small-brained, 110-pound (50-kilogram) female was considered more important than Lucy because, as Alan Walker, a paleontologist from Pennsylvania State University, said: "It shows that the last common ancestor with chimps didn't look like a chimp, or a human, or some funny thing in between." (Shreeve)

Ardi's reign did not last long. In 2010, specialists began to argue that she should not be considered a forerunner of the human line (Perlman). And then, that same year, scientists announced the discovery of Kadanuumuu, also called "Big Guy," a five-foot-tall male Australopithecus 400,000 years older than Lucy (Dalton). "Big Guy"'s scapula, which is the oldest hominid scapula to date, is much like a modern humans. This could mean that "Big Guy" lived on land rather than in the trees (Dalton). With the discovery of "Big Guy," Australopithecus maintains the crown as the most likely oldest human ancestor.

Australopithecus africanus, means "southern ape from Africa." They looked more like primates than modern-day Homo Sapiens. Although they walked upright, they had low, sloping foreheads, protruding jaws, and thick body hair. For some reason, they also didn't seem to show any facial expressions (McKie 50).

Humans have evolved a lot over the past three and a half million years. We are almost 6 feet, have lost most of our body hair, have adapted to walking upright all the time, and we've grown brains that are over three times as large as the first Australopithecine's (Larson 123). Besides, humans (Homo Sapiens) have also developed an advanced material culture. We live in cities now and we can grasp abstract concepts like time and we have art and literature.

But we haven't changed all that much, really. We still are related to primates in many ways. This can be seen in the way our hands and feet are structured. Our faces are even very similar, and we share some behaviors, such as tool building (Lemonick).

There have been four agreed-up species of human throughout time: Homo Habilis, Homo Erectus, Homo sapiens Neanderthalesis, and Homo sapiens Sapiens. The first major step in evolution was becoming bipedal, or walking upright (Larson 20). As I said before, Australopithecine's were possibly the first to do this. They were really clumsy, though; because their skeleton weren't really able to support the weight, they probably spent most of their time on all fours. They were tiny, with a tiny (orange size) brain, prominent cheekbones, and thick molars. Like chimps, they had small, underdeveloped thumbs. But their toes were shorter than other primates (IHO).

Australiopithicene also probably lived socailly like chimps. Judging from the way fossils were at their sites, they probably lived in one place in small groups. We think they lived in groups because usually about 5 individuals are found in the same place. One site even had had 13 in the same place! Scientists think that these groups usually had one male in charge and this was because of their sexual dimorphism. Sexual dimorphism, or the difference in size between the genders, usually means that males are larger. So probably the one guy that was big was in charge.

They also weren't very smart. The only tools they had were sticks and rocks. They were also vegetarians. They may not have known animals could be eaten. If they did know, though, they probably couldn't figure out how to kill one anyway. Homo Habilis, though, figured this out (Larson 145). Homo Habilis is the earliest known member of the Homo genus, and has been found only in Africa. Homo Habilis's brain was about 50% larger than Australopithecine's, he was taller, had flatter nostrils, and their faces were nearly hairless (IHO).

Most importantly, though, Homo Habilis figured out, through scavenging, scientists think, that meat was edible. Their teeth show that they started to add meat to their vegetarian diets. Homo Habilis lived in Africa until about 1.6 million years ago, when Homo Erectus emerged, causing their eventual extinction. Homo Erectus was the next step. He had a much larger brain (1060 cc) than Homo Habilis (Mc Kie 80). "Homo Erectus" means "Man who Walks Upright."

The larger brain is the main physical change from H. Hablis to Homo Erectus. But they did have smaller jaws and teeth. They also had a larger brow. The brow-ridge was also slightly larger than Homo Habilis.

Homo Erectus lived until about 100,000 years ago, when Homo sapiens Neanderthalesis took over. Homo sapiens Neanderthalesis, or the Neanderthals, lived during the most recent Ice Age (Larson 160).

Evolution happens so slowly that it almost can't be seen. The changes occur in tiny mutations; if you possess a mutation that makes you survive better than others, you are more likely to reproduce and spread that mutation into the next generation. If you have a bad mutation, you die and you don't pass that mutation on. There are lots of examples that prove this, from the problems in royal families to skin color differences that are related to climate (Larson 30).

We have to remember, though, that all of these things are just physical. Deep down, all humans are really the same so we should love and respect one another. And, we are still not really sure how long humans have existed.

Works Cited

Dalton, Rex. "Africa's Next Top Hominid." *Nature.com*.
21 June 2010. Web. 7 September 2010.

Institute of Human Origins (IHO). *Becoming Human*.
2008. Web. 5 Sept. 2010.

Larsen, Clark Spencer, and Robert M. Matter. *Human
Origins: The Fossil Record*. Waveland Press,
1998. Print.

Lemonick, Michael D. "What Makes Us Different?" *Time
Magazine.com*. 1 Oct. 2006. Web. 5 Sept. 2010.

McKie, Robin. *The Dawn of Man: The Story of Human
Evolution*. London: DK, 2002. Print.

Perlman, David. "Ardi's Place in Human Ancestry
Challenged." *SFGate*. 28 May 2010. Web.
6 Sept. 2010.

Shreeve, Jaimie. "Move over, Lucy. And Kiss the Missing
Link Goodbye." *National Geographic News*, National
Geographic, 1 Oct. 2009. Web. September 6, 2010.

4d Edit for Particular Goals

In your final pass through the text of your paper, you should concentrate on style and eliminate as many errors as you can.

1. Check the connections between sentences. Notice how your sentences are connected. If you need to signal the relationship from one sentence to the next, use a transitional word or phrase.

2. Check your sentences. If you noticed that a sentence was hard to read or didn't sound right when you read your paper aloud, think about how you might rephrase it. Often you can pick up problems with verbs (see Chapters 37 and 38), pronouns (see Chapter 39), and modifiers (see Chapter 40) by reading aloud. If a sentence seems too long, you might break it into two or more sentences. If you notice a string of short sentences that sound choppy, you might combine them. If you notice run-on sentences or sentence fragments, fix them (see Chapter 36).

3. Eliminate wordiness.   Writers tend to introduce wordiness in drafts. Look for long expressions that can easily be shortened (*at this point in time* to *now*) and unnecessary repetition. Remove unnecessary qualifiers (*rather, very, somewhat, little*). See how many words you can take out without losing the meaning (see Chapter 31).

4. Use active verbs.   Any time you can use a verb other than a form of *be* (*is, are, was, were*) or a verb ending in *-ing*, take advantage of the opportunity to make your style more lively. Sentences that begin with *There is (are)* and *It is* often have better alternatives:

Draft	It is true that exercising a high degree of quality control in the manufacture of our products will be an incentive for increasing our market share.
Revised	If we pay attention to quality when we make our products, more people will buy them.

Notice too that the use of active verbs often cuts down on wordiness (see Chapter 30).

5. Use specific and inclusive language.   As you read, stay alert for any vague words or phrases (see Chapter 33). Check to make sure that you have used inclusive language throughout (see Chapter 34).

Example of sentence-level editing to integrate quotations into your text

In ~~the article,~~ "How to Feed the World," Michael Pollan ~~writes,~~ maintains that "agricultural lands make up a precious and finite resource; we should be using it to grow food for people, not for cars or cattle." ~~I definitely agree with Pollan that u~~ Using ten pounds of grain to make one pound of beef doesn't make sense when over a billion people are at the brink of starvation.

~~As for~~ Nevertheless, James McWilliams~~' article, he writes against~~ disagrees with Pollan~~'s argument.~~ about the need to feed as many people as possible. McWilliams believes that citizens shouldn't "have to give up tropical fruits altogether" just for the sake of saving resources.

For more on integrating quotations using signal phrases, see Section 24d.

 **Proofread Carefully**

To proofread effectively, you have to learn to slow down. Some writers find that moving from word to word with a pencil slows them down enough to allow them to find errors. Others read backward to force themselves to concentrate on each word.

1. Know what your spelling checker can and cannot do.   Spelling checkers are the greatest invention since peanut butter. They turn up many typos and misspellings that are hard to catch. But spelling checkers do not catch wrong words (e.g., *to much* should be *too much*), missing endings (*three dog*), and other, similar errors. You still have to proofread carefully to eliminate misspellings.

2. Check for grammar and mechanics.   Nothing hurts your credibility with readers more than a text with numerous errors. Many job application letters get tossed in the reject pile because an applicant made a single, glaring error. Issues of grammar are treated in Chapters 35 through 40. The conventions for using punctuation, capitalization, italics, abbreviations, acronyms, and numbers can be found in Chapters 41 through 50. Get into the habit of referring to these chapters.

4f **Learn to Edit the Writing of Others**

Editing someone else's writing is easier than editing your own. In your own writing you know most of the time what you meant to say and often you don't notice where a reader might be stopped or jarred. But editing someone else's writing is also harder because you want to give the writer useful feedback without taking over the writer's task.

1. Make comments in the margins.   If you find a sentence hard to read, let the writer know. If you think a sentence is repetitive, let the writer know. If you think a word was left out, say so in the margin. Also let the writer know when a sentence is especially successful.

> *Word missing here?*
> *Same point as sentence 1?*
> *Can you join this sentence with the previous sentence?*
> *Vivid description!*

2. Use symbols to indicate possible problems.   Draw a wavy line under any phrase or sentence where you think there may be a problem. Even if you are not sure what the problem is, you can ask the writer to look carefully at a particular sentence. If you think a word is misspelled, draw a circle around it. If you think words can be deleted, put parentheses around them.

WRITING SMART

Standard proofreading symbols

Advanced editing requires learning standard proofreading symbols. Authors, editors, and printers use proofreader's marks to indicate changes. These marks are used in pairs: one mark goes in the text where the change is to be made and the other goes in the margin, close to the change.

Mark in the margin	Mark in the text
ℓ	Delete: take it out
⌒	Close up: foot ball
∧	Caret: insert here
#	Insert a space: a word
(tr)	Transpose: the in beginning
∧	Add a comma: moreover we
∨	Add an apostrophe: Ellens books
∨/∨	Add double quotation marks: James Joyce's Clay
:	Add a colon: 3 45 p.m.
;	Add a semicolon: concluded however, we
⊙	Add a period: last call Next we
¶	Begin a new paragraph
No ¶	No new paragraph
sp	Spell out: 7 dwarfs=>seven dwarfs
stet	Ignore correction: in the beginning

PART 2

Analyzing, Reflecting, Informing, Arguing

You **can learn more and do more** with MyCompLab and with the eText version of *The Penguin Handbook*. To find resources in MyCompLab that will help you successfully complete your assignment, go to

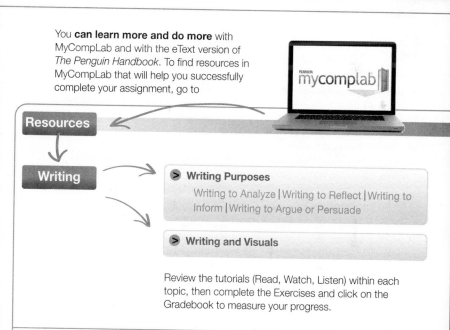

Resources

Writing

> **Writing Purposes**
  Writing to Analyze | Writing to Reflect | Writing to Inform | Writing to Argue or Persuade

> **Writing and Visuals**

  Review the tutorials (Read, Watch, Listen) within each topic, then complete the Exercises and click on the Gradebook to measure your progress.

In the **eText version** of *The Penguin Handbook*, you will also find audio commentary provided by Lester Faigley for the sample student papers in this Part, as well as extra writing assignments.

5 | Read and View with a Critical Eye

- Ask questions while you read (see below)
- Recognize verbal fallacies (see p. 61)
- Recognize visual fallacies (see p. 65)

5a Become a Critical Reader

Critical thinking begins with critical reading. For most of what you read, one time through is enough. When you start asking questions about what you are reading, you are engaging in **critical reading**.

Critical reading is a four-part process. First, begin by asking where a piece of writing came from and why it was written. Second, read the text carefully to find the author's central claim or thesis and the major points. Third, decide if you can trust the author. Fourth, read the text again to understand how it works.

Where did it come from?

- Who wrote this material?
- Where did it first appear? In a book, newspaper, magazine, or online?
- What else has been written about the topic or issue?
- What do you expect after reading the title?

What does it say?

- What is the topic or issue?
- What is the writer's thesis or overall point?
- What reasons or evidence does the writer offer?
- Who are the intended readers? What does the writer assume the readers know and believe?

Can you trust the writer?

- Does the writer have the necessary knowledge and experience to write on this subject?
- Do you detect a bias in the writer's position?
- Can you trust the writer's facts? Where did the facts come from?
- Does the writer acknowledge opposing views and unfavorable evidence? Does the writer deal fairly with opposing views?

How does it work?

- How is the piece of writing organized? How are the major points arranged?
- How does the writer conclude? Does the conclusion follow from the evidence the writer offers? What impression does the reader take away?
- How would you characterize the style? Describe the language that the writer uses.
- How does the writer represent herself or himself?

Exercise 5.1   Find an opinion piece in a newspaper, in a magazine, or online. Analyze the piece by answering the questions in Section 5a.

5b Read Actively

If you own what you are reading, read with a pencil in hand. Pens and highlighters don't erase, and often you won't remember why you highlighted a particular sentence.

Annotate what you read

Using annotating strategies will make your effort more rewarding.

- **Mark major points and key concepts.** Sometimes major points are indicated by headings, but often you will need to locate them.
- **Connect with your experience.** Think about your own experiences and how they match up or don't match up with what you are reading.
- **Connect passages.** Notice how ideas connect to each other. Draw lines and arrows. If an idea connects to something a few pages before, write a note in the margin with the page number.
- **Ask questions.** Note anything that puzzles you, including words to look up.

Critical response

The worldwide crisis over food prices is the direct result of the decision, made by the Bush administration in 2006, to begin feeding large quantities of American corn to American automobiles, in the form of ethanol. This fateful decision led to a run-up in corn prices, which in turn led farmers to plant more corn and less soy and wheat—leading to the surge in the price for all grains. But make no mistake: we've created a situation where American SUVs are competing with African eaters for grain. We can see who is winning.

> *Causes of rise in food prices*
> *corn used to make ethanol =>*
> *corn prices increased =>*
> *farmers planted more corn and less wheat and soy =>*
> *all grain prices went up*

—Michael Pollan, "How to Feed the World"

Map of structure

Causes of rise in food prices

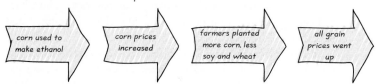

5c Write Summaries

A summary should be concise but thorough.

- Begin your summary with the main point.
- Then report the key ideas. Represent the author's argument in miniature as accurately as you can, quoting exact words for key points (see pages 324–327 for how to quote and integrate an author's words into your summary).
- Your aim is to give your readers an understanding of what the author is arguing for. Withhold judgment even if you think the author is dead wrong. Do not insert your opinions and comments. Stick to what the author is saying and what position the author is advocating.

Usually summaries are no longer than 150 words.

Pollan, Michael. "How to Feed the World." *Newsweek*. Newsweek, 19 May 2008. Web. 17 Sept. 2010.

At a time when world food prices are rising, Michael Pollan maintains that agricultural lands should be used for raising food for people, not for growing corn to make ethanol. When the United States decided in 2006 to subsidize corn to make ethanol, corn prices went up, causing farmers to plant more corn and less wheat and soy, which led to increases in all grain prices. Pollan believes that if the United States reduced ethanol subsidies and dropped import tariffs on ethanol, world food prices would drop. Long-range solutions include decreasing the amount of oil used to produce food and lowering consumption of beef, which requires ten pounds of grain for each pound of meat.

5d Recognize Verbal Fallacies

Reasoning depends less on proving a claim than it does on finding evidence for that claim that readers will accept as valid. The kinds of faulty reasoning called *logical fallacies* reflect a failure to provide sufficient evidence for a claim that is being made.

Fallacies of logic

- **Begging the question.** *People who take 8:00 AM classes are crazy because no sane person would choose to get up that early.* The fallacy of begging the question occurs when the claim is restated and passed off as evidence.

- **Either-or.** *Either fraternities must be forced to cancel all parties, or the university will never be able to control its underage drinking problem.* The either-or fallacy suggests that there are only two choices in a complex situation. Rarely, if ever, is this the case. (In this example, the writer ignores the fact that some students under 21 drink when they are not at a fraternity party.)

- **False analogies.** *Permitting children to play computer games in school is like giving them ice cream for watching television.* Analogies always depend on the degree of resemblance of one situation to another. In this case, the analogy fails to consider the content of the computer games and what children might be learning.

- **Hasty generalization.** *We have been in a drought for three years; that's a sure sign of climate change.* A hasty generalization is a broad claim made on the basis of a few occurrences. Climate cycles occur regularly over spans of a few years; climate trends must be observed over centuries.

- **Non sequitur.** *Janet Jackson's "wardrobe malfunction" during the 2004 Super Bowl shows how far contemporary morals have sunk.* A non sequitur (which is a Latin term meaning "it does not follow") ties together two unrelated ideas. In this case, one person's behavior is not indicative of society's morals.

- **Oversimplification.** *If the federal income tax was doubled for all wage brackets, then we could easily provide comprehensive health care for all citizens.* This claim may be true, but the argument would be unacceptable to most citizens. More complex, if less definitive, solutions are called for.

- ***Post hoc* fallacy.** *The stock market goes down when the AFC wins the Super Bowl in even years.* The *post hoc* fallacy (from the Latin *post hoc ergo propter hoc,* which means "after this, therefore because of this") assumes that things that follow in time have a causal relationship.

- **Rationalization.** *I could have finished my paper on time if my printer was working.* People frequently come up with excuses and weak explanations for their own and others' behavior that avoid actual causes.

- **Slippery slope.** *If the government were to legalize a gateway drug like marijuana, there would be a huge increase in the use of hard drugs like cocaine and heroin.* The slippery slope fallacy maintains that one thing inevitably will cause something else to happen.

Fallacies of emotion and language

- **Bandwagon appeals.** *Since all the power hitters in baseball use steroids, I'll have to use them too if I want to be able to compete.* This argument suggests that everyone is doing it, so why shouldn't you? But on close examination, it may be that everyone really isn't doing it—and in any case, it may not be the right thing to do.
- **Name calling.** Name calling is frequent in politics and among competing groups (*radical, tax-and-spend liberal, racist, fascist, right-wing ideologue*). Unless these terms are carefully defined, they are meaningless.
- **Polarization.** *Feminists are all man haters.* Polarization, like name calling, exaggerates positions and groups by representing them as extreme and divisive.
- **Straw man.** *Liberals want America to lose the war on terror so that our country will have less influence on global affairs.* A straw man argument is a diversionary tactic that sets up another's position in a way that can be easily rejected.

Exercise 5.2   Build a collection of fallacies. See if you can find examples of all thirteen fallacies named in Section 5d. If you can't find them all, make up examples for the ones you are missing. You might start with sources you know to be biased, such as political blogs and the Web sites of political organizations. You should also look at editorials, letters to the editors, and opinion pieces in the newspaper or in newsmagazines. Finally, you might even look at humor publications, such as *The Onion*, and comedy shows that have a news format, such as *The Colbert Reportt and The Daily Show with Jon Stewart*. Make sure you cite the sources for your fallacies.

5e Become a Critical Viewer

Critical viewing is similar to critical reading. An image such as a photograph doesn't float in space but instead has a specific location—in a book with a caption, in a family photo album, in a magazine advertisement, on a Web page—that tells us a great deal about why the photograph was taken and what purpose it is intended to serve. But even without the external context, there are often clues within a photograph that suggest its origins.

We could guess the approximate date of the photograph on page 64 by the content of the billboard. By the end of the 1950s, long-distance travel by passenger train was being replaced by airline travel, so the picture must have been taken before then. The name of the railroad, Southern Pacific, along with the barren landscape, indicates that the photograph was taken in the southwestern United States. In fact, this photograph was taken in 1937 by Dorothea Lange (1895–1955), who gave it the title "Toward Los Angeles, California."

One approach to critical viewing is to examine a photograph in terms of its **composition**. In Lange's photograph the lines of the shoulder of the road, the highway, and the telephone poles slope toward a vanishing point on the horizon, giving the image a sense of great distance. At the same time, the image divides into ground and sky with the horizon line in the center. The two figures in dark clothing walking away contrast to a rectangular billboard with a white background and white frame.

Another approach to critical viewing is to **analyze the content**. In 1937 the United States was in the midst of the Great Depression and a severe drought, which forced many small farmers in middle America to abandon their homes and go to California in search of work. The luxury portrayed on the billboard contrasts with the two walking figures, who presumably do not have bus fare, much less enough money for a luxury train. By placing the figures and the billboard beside each other (a visual relationship called **juxtaposition**), Lange is able to make an ironic commentary on the lives of well-off and poor Americans during the depression.

No one set of questions can cover the great variety of images, but a few general questions can assist you in developing a critical response.

- What kind of an image or visual is it?
- Who created this image (movie, advertisement, television program, and so on)?
- What is it about? What is portrayed in the image?

- Where did it first appear? Where do you usually find images like this one?
- When did it appear?

The following questions are primarily for still images. For animations, movies, and television, you also have to ask questions about how the story is being told.

- What attracts your eye first? If there is an attention-grabbing element, how does it connect with the rest of the image?
- What impression of the subject does the image create?
- How does the image appeal to the values of the audience? (For example, politicians love to be photographed with children.)
- How does the image relate to what surrounds it?
- Was it intended to serve purposes other than art and entertainment?

Exercise 5.3 Find an interesting photo in your textbook, a magazine, or a newspaper, or online. Write a brief (one- or two-page) analysis of the photo following the process outlined in Section 5e. Pay particular attention to the last question. After you have thought about this picture, how has your first impression changed?

5f Recognize Visual Fallacies
Misleading images and videos

■ Can't afford a vacation to Egypt? Photoshop can take you there.

The era of digital imaging has made it possible to create images of lifelike dinosaurs chasing humans, interactions between people now living and those long dead, and human feats that defy human limits and the laws of physics.

Almost from the beginnings of photography, images were staged and negatives were manipulated. In the twentieth century, the technicians in Hitler's and Stalin's darkrooms became experts in removing from photographs people who had fallen out of favor.

The difference in the digital era is that anyone can do it. Perhaps there's nothing wrong with using Photoshop to add absent relatives to family photographs or remove ex-boyfriends and ex-girlfriends. Few people complain when a photographer shaves off a few pounds with the Photoshop liquefy filter. More doubtful is the routine practice of fashion magazines giving already thin models unnatural shapes or adding muscles to male stars, yet we accept that anything goes in advertising.

But where do you draw the line? Not only do many videos on YouTube use outright deception, but newsmagazines and networks have also been found guilty of these practices. Ask questions about what you view.

- Who created the image or video? What bias might the creator have?
- Who published the image or video? What bias might the publisher have?
- Who is the intended audience? For example, political videos often assume that the viewers hold the same political views as the creators.
- What is being shown, and what is not being shown? For example, a video ad promoting tourism for the Gulf of Mexico will look very different from a video showing sources of pollution.
- Who is being represented, and who is not being represented? Who gets left out is as important as who gets included.
- In images, how does the caption influence the interpretation? In videos, how does the voiceover narration shape the meaning?

Misleading charts

A special category of visual fallacies is misleading charts. For example, the fictitious company Glitzycorp might use the chart in Figure 5.1 to attract investors. The chart shows what looks like remarkable growth from 2008 to 2010 and projects additional sales for 2011. But is the picture quite as rosy as it is painted?

Notice that the bars in this bar chart start at 20 rather than at 0. The effect is to make the $22 million sales in 2009 appear to double the $21 million sales of 2008, even though the increase was less than five percent. Three years is also a short span to use to project a company's future profits. Figure 5.2 shows the sales of Glitzycorp over seven years, and it tells quite a different story. The big growth years were in the mid 2000s, followed by a collapse in 2007 and slow growth ever since.

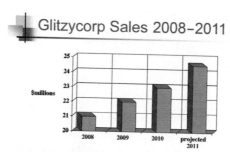

Figure 5.1   Misleading. The starting point on the y-axis is $20 million, not 0.

Figure 5.2   Accurate. The actual increase from 2008 to 2009 was less than 5%.

Glitzycorp's sales charts illustrate how facts can be manipulated in visual presentations.

Exercise 5.4   Altered photos can have a huge impact, especially when they rewrite history or are used to prove a connection between two people who, in reality, have probably never met. But we encounter altered images every day. Find an image that has clearly been altered in an advertisement, on TV, on the Internet, in the newspaper, or even in a textbook (publishers routinely remove logos, tattoos, firearms, and other items from images). Write a few paragraphs about this image. What has been altered? Is the producer of the image up front about the alteration? What, do you think, was the purpose behind the alteration of this photo? What are the possible implications?

6 | Write an Analysis

QUICK_TAKE_

- Analyze the context and the text (see below)
- Organize and write a rhetorical analysis (see p. 72)
- Analyze images and other kinds of visual texts (see p. 80)

6a Understand the Goal of a Rhetorical Analysis

The goal of a **rhetorical analysis** is to understand how a particular act of writing or speaking influenced particular people at a particular time. Rhetorical analysis is not limited to speaking and writing. The tools of rhetorical analysis have been applied to understanding how meaning is made by other human creations, such as art, buildings, photographs, dance, memorials, Web sites, music, advertisements—any kind of symbolic communication.

Writing a rhetorical analysis (also called "critical analysis" or "textual analysis") is frequently an assignment in college. A rhetorical analysis requires you to step back from a text and consider it from multiple perspectives. Writing a rhetorical analysis can give you a heightened awareness of a text and a better appreciation of what the author accomplished.

Understanding how communication works or fails to work is a worthy goal by itself, but rhetorical analysis has other benefits. It enables you to think about a text in more depth, to better understand the arguments it makes, and to appreciate how it is put together. In turn, this knowledge helps you in writing your own text. You will have a much better sense of what has been said and written about your subject and where you have opportunities to contribute your own ideas.

6b Analyze the Context and the Text

A rhetorical analysis begins with a text to analyze. If your instructor does not assign a text, select a text that has significance for you, either because it was important when it was written or it is about a subject that is important to you.

Think of your analysis as running on a continuum between considering the **context**—the relationship between the piece of writing or speaking and the larger society surrounding it—and the **text** itself—what it is about

The Gettysburg Address

Executive Mansion,

Washington,   186

Four score and seven years ago our fathers brought forth, upon this continent, a new nation, conceived in liberty, and dedicated to the proposition that "all men are created equal."

Now we are engaged in a great civil war, testing whether that nation, or any nation so conceived, and so dedicated, can long endure. We are met on a great battle field of that war. We have come to dedicate a portion of it, as a final resting place for those who died here that the nation might live. This we may, in all propriety do. But, in a larger sense, we can not dedicate—we can not consecrate—we can not hallow, this ground—The brave men, living and dead, who struggled here, have hallowed it, far above our poor power to add or detract. The world will little note, nor long remember what we say here, while it can never forget what they did here.

It is rather for us, the living, to stand here,

■ Text

■ Broader context

■ Immediate context

and how it is designed. We can think of the context, which lies at one end of the continuum, in two senses. First, the **immediate context** refers to where the text was written and read or heard. For example, Abraham Lincoln delivered his 10-sentence, 272-word Gettysburg Address on November 19, 1863, at the dedication ceremony of a national cemetery, where he followed a speaker who had talked for two hours. Second, the **broader context** refers to the larger cultural and historical circumstances in which a text is produced and read. The broader context of the Gettysburg Address was, of course, the American Civil War, which had taken thousands of lives and was far from over at the time Lincoln spoke. Lincoln's brief remarks have been immortalized because he could envision an end to the war and a healing process.

At the other end of the continuum lies the text itself. We can consider a text as if it were a piece in a museum, where we closely scrutinize it. For example, if you look carefully at the language of the Gettysburg Address, you'll begin to appreciate Lincoln's tactics and skill. He says of his purpose: "We have come to dedicate a portion of that field, as a final resting place for those who here gave their lives that that nation might live."

But then he immediately turns this purpose on its head: "But in a larger sense, we can not dedicate—we can not consecrate—we can not hallow—this ground. The brave men, living and dead, who struggled here, have consecrated it, far above our poor power to add or detract." Lincoln's words become powerful because they defy expectation: we cannot consecrate the field because the field is already consecrated. Lincoln does not once refer to "the enemy" in the Gettysburg Address. Instead he says, "The brave men, living and dead, who struggled here." Even though the cemetery was a burying ground for Union soldiers, Lincoln's language invokes the heroism and sacrifice of both sides.

Often in the back and forth movement between text and context, you gain surprising insights about how a text achieves certain effects. These questions will help you get started in composing a rhetorical analysis.

Analyze the immediate context
Examine the author

- What is the author's purpose: to change beliefs? to inspire action? to teach about a subject? to praise or blame? to amuse?
- How did the author come to this subject?
- What else did the author write?

Examine the audience

- Who was the intended audience?
- What were their attitudes and beliefs about the subject?
- What were their attitudes and beliefs about the author?
- What does the author assume about the audience?

Analyze the broader context
Examine the larger conversation

- Why did this text appear at this particular time?
- What else has been said or written about this subject?
- What was going on at the time that influenced this text?

Examine the larger society

- What social, political, and economic influences can you find in the text?

Analyze the text
Examine the kind of text

- What kind of text is it: speech? essay? letter? editorial? advertisement?
- What is the medium: print? Web site? voice recording?

Summarize the content

- What is the author's main claim or main idea?
- How is the main claim or main idea supported?
- How is the text organized?

Examine the appeals

- *Ethos:* How does the author represent himself or herself? How does the author build or fail to build trust?
- *Logos:* What kinds of facts and evidence does the author use?
- *Pathos:* How does the author appeal to values shared with the audience?

Examine the language and style

- Is the style formal? informal? academic?
- Does the author use humor or satire?
- What metaphors are used?

Exercise 6.1　Public speeches are usually intended to persuade. You can find many examples of public speeches on the Web on sites such as www. whitehouse.gov, the History Channel at http://www.history.com/speeches, and the University of Houston's Digital History site at http://www.digitalhistory. uh.edu/. Select a speech to analyze and answer the following questions.

1. What is the **rhetorical purpose**? What effect was the speech intended to have?
2. Where was the speech given? How does the speaker connect to the beliefs and attitudes of his or her **audience**?
3. What **appeals** does the speech rely upon: the rational appeal (logos), the emotional appeal (pathos), or the ethical appeal (ethos)?
4. How is the speech **organized**?
5. How formal or informal is the **style**?
6. Does the speaker use any **metaphors**, and for what purpose?

When you have completed your analysis, formulate a thesis about the speech.

 6c **Organize and Write a Rhetorical Analysis**

When you have completed your initial analysis, you are ready to begin writing. Expect to discover additional ideas you can use in the analysis while you are writing and to go back and forth with your analysis.

1 | **Before you write**

Take stock of your initial analysis
- If your selected text isn't working for the assignment, find one that works better.
- Look at your notes on the author, the audience, the circumstances of original publication or delivery, what other texts the author was responding to, and what else was going on at the time.
- Spend some time thinking about how to organize your analysis.

Think about your readers
- How much do readers know about your text? the author? the events surrounding the text? other texts like it?
- What will readers gain from reading your analysis?

2 | Write an introduction

Begin your analysis by giving the necessary background
- Inform your readers about the author and why the author selected this particular topic.
- Tell readers about the original audience and the conversation about the topic that was going on at the time the text was written.

Make a claim
- Make a claim about how the text you are analyzing uses rhetoric for particular purposes.

3 | Organize and write the body of your paper

Support your claim with your detailed analysis of the text and context
- Give examples from the text to show how the author builds credibility with the audience, appeals to their values and beliefs, and convinces them with facts and evidence.
- Analyze the author's style, tone, and language, including metaphors.
- Analyze how the author responded to the immediate context and to the broader context.

4 | Write a conclusion

End with more than a summary
- Draw larger implications from your analysis.
- End with a vivid example from the text.

5 | Revise, revise, revise

Evaluate your draft
- Make sure your analysis meets the requirements of the assignment.
- Consider where you might provide more information about the context.
- Consider where you might provide more evidence supporting your claim about the text.
- When you have finished revising, edit and proofread carefully.

6d Sample Rhetorical Analysis

Samantha Jackson

Professor Janis

English 100

4 May 2009

Rhetorical Strategies in Sojourner Truth's

"Ain't I a Woman?"

Jackson's opening provides background to help readers understand why Truth's personal history is relevant.

Sojourner Truth was born into slavery in 1797 and given the name Isabella Baumfree. Between 1797 and her escape from slavery in 1827, Isabella was "owned" by five different masters. Her last owner, John Dumont, sometimes bragged that she could "do a good family's washing in the night and be ready to go into the field the next morning, where she would do as much raking and binding as his best hands" (Washington 15). However, in 1817, the New York Legislature had passed a law that slavery in New York would end ten years later, on July 4, 1827. With this date fast approaching, Dumont decided to strike a deal with Isabella: he would release her one year early if she worked hard throughout 1826. Isabella agreed, but at the end of the year Dumont refused to release her. Enraged, Isabella escaped. After experiencing mystical visions from God on June 1, 1843, at the age of forty-six, Isabella changed her name to Sojourner Truth and pledged to "'sojourn' the land and speak the 'truth' of God's word" (Washington 15).

Jackson 2

As debates over slavery raged, Sojourner was sometimes harassed. Once she was told that a building she was scheduled to speak in would be burned down if she lectured there. She replied, "Then I will speak to the ashes" (Washington 11). As the Women's Suffrage movement became more popular in the late 1840s, Truth took notice. In 1851 she traveled to Akron, Ohio, to attend a women's rights convention aimed at getting Ohio to add more rights for women in its state constitution. Many Ohioans were against this goal. Many local men, including several ministers, attended the convention just to heckle speakers. Sojourner Truth delivered her famous "Ain't I a Woman?" speech in this intense atmosphere. In her spontaneous lecture, Truth used her own physical and intellectual credibility to make powerful emotional appeals and convincing logical claims. Her arguments redefined the word "womanhood" and made direct connections between women's rights and the abolition of slavery for an all-white audience. Her powerful speech was so successful that her words are the main reason this convention is remembered today.

When Truth began to speak, her words displayed her experience and wisdom. Rather than addressing her audience as "Ladies and gentlemen," or, "Members of the convention," Truth begins this way: "Well children, when there is so much racket there must be something out of kilter" (268). By using the word "children" to address her adult, white audience, Truth draws attention to her age and wisdom, and at the same time proves

This paragraph uses examples to show how slavery and the Women's Suffrage movement shaped the rhetorical situation.

In these two sentences, Jackson makes a claim about the persuasive power of Truth's speech.

Jackson demonstrates how Truth established her relationship to her audience in the opening of her speech.

Jackson 3

that she is equal to, not subservient to, these white adults. She also refers to the heated arguments between the women and men attending the convention as "so much racket," a statement that takes her out of the arguments she is witnessing and therefore makes her seem like a voice of reason in a chaotic environment.

Jackson discusses the humor employed by Truth to defuse tension and put her audience at ease.

Another reason Truth was such an effective speaker at this convention was how she used humor to break down arguments against women's rights. Just after she notes that the convention has become a "racket," she offers a tongue-in-cheek observation: "I think that 'twixt the negroes of the South and the women at the North, all talking about rights, the white men will be in a fix pretty soon" (268). Although Truth is making the serious point that when white women and African Americans get equal rights, white men will be less powerful, she uses humor to break up some of the tension of the moment.

Once Truth has her audience listening through this light tone, she begins to use her status as a former slave woman to bring out feelings of guilt and shame in her audience. She builds her argument slowly.

This paragraph demonstrates how Truth built her argument by drawing on personal experience and by using emotional appeals to her audience's sense of shame.

First, she shows the fallacy in the argument that women do not need rights because male chivalry protects them from harm and guarantees them protection. Truth restates this argument: "That man over there says that women need to be helped into carriages, and lifted over ditches, and to have the best place everywhere." She points out that as a poor, black woman, she is excluded from this definition of womanhood: "Nobody ever helps

Jackson 4

me into carriages, or over mud puddles, or gives me any best place! And ain't I a woman?" (268).

She next shows the connection between women's rights and abolition by referring to the unique horrors of womanhood under slavery: "I could work as much and eat as much as a man—when I could get it—and bear the lash as well! And ain't I a woman? I have borne thirteen children, and seen them most all sold off to slavery, and when I cried out with a mother's grief none but Jesus heard me" (268-69). By using emotional appeals to produce shame in her audience, Truth connects women's rights and abolition. She argues that people who believe women should be protected and treated to "the best" are obliged to treat all women, black and white, with "chivalry."

Although Truth is appealing to her audience's shame here, and asking them to reconsider their positions on women's rights and abolition, her main way of arguing is through logic. Truth tries to expose the flaws in arguments against women's rights, and also in arguments against equal rights for African Americans. First, Truth points out that claiming that chivalry makes rights unnecessary for women is illogical because her audience's definition of "woman" is flawed. Women, she argues, are not only people who need assistance getting into fancy carriages, or those who wear expensive clothes that must be protected from mud puddles. Women are also people like her, who "have ploughed and planted, and gathered into barns" (268).

Jackson analyzes Truth's use of logic to expose fallacies in common arguments against women's rights.

Jackson describes the process Truth used to counter arguments that the Bible authorized male supremacy.

Truth's most powerful logical argument for this audience of mostly religious men is her argument about God, Eve, and women's rights. She first restates their argument: that "women can't have as much rights as men, 'cause Christ wasn't a woman." Then she exposes the flaws in that argument: she asks, "Where did your Christ come from?" and answers, "From God and a woman. Man had nothing to do with Him." Then, turning to her audience's argument that women should not have rights because of Eve's sins, she asks, "If the first woman God ever made was strong enough to turn the world upside down all alone, these women together ought to be able to turn it back, and get it right side up again!" She is arguing here that if these men credit the first woman, Eve, with such a huge amount of power, then they should see that other women are equally powerful and should be given equal rights. If Eve turned the world upside down, these women can turn it right-side up again. Truth argues: "And now they is asking to do it, the men better let them."

Finally, Truth addresses the topic of intelligence: "Then they talk about this thing in the head; what's this they call it?" (269). An audience member reminds her that the word is "intellect," and she replies, "That's it, honey." She then asks, "What's that got to do with women's rights or negro's rights?" (269). This question is deceptive. Although at first it seems like Truth is agreeing with sexist notions when she characterizes women's minds as capable of "hold[ing]

Jackson 6

but a pint" while male minds can "hold a quart," it becomes clear that she is using flattery as a manipulative tool: "if my cup won't hold but a pint, and yours holds a quart, wouldn't you be mean not to let me have my little half measure full?" Clearly, a speaker who can develop such convincing logical arguments is just as intelligent as the audience members whose arguments she exposed as flawed. It is for this reason that Sojourner Truth's "Ain't I a Woman?" speech made such an impression then, and continues to do so today.

Jackson concludes with a powerful example of Truth's wit.

Jackson 7

Works Cited

Truth, Sojourner. "Ain't I a Woman?" *Argument in America: Essential Issues, Essential Texts*. Ed. Jack Selzer. New York: Longman, 2004. 268-69. Print.

Washington, Margaret, ed. *The Narrative of Sojourner Truth*. New York: Random, 1993. Print.

 To hear audio commentary on this piece of writing, visit this page of the eText at **www.mycomplab.com**.

6e Analyze Images and Other Kinds of Visual Texts

The word *text* typically brings to mind words on a printed page. But in the sense that anything that can be "read" can be a text, then nearly everything is a text. We see hundreds of visual texts every day distributed on television, the Web, films, newspapers, advertisements, product labels, clothing, signs, buildings—indeed, on nearly everything. We can analyze how these images create meaning by the same means we use to analyze verbal texts—by examining the relationship between the text and its contexts.

Some culturally significant images, significant at least at the time they were created, are public art and public sculpture. On one of the bridge houses of the Michigan Avenue Bridge crossing the Chicago River in downtown Chicago is a large relief sculpture depicting the massacre of settlers fleeing Fort Dearborn in 1812. The size of the sculpture and its placement on the busiest and most famous street in Chicago attests to its significance at the time it was commissioned.

■ Relief sculpture of the Fort Dearborn Massacre, on the Michigan Avenue Bridge, Chicago

Two central figures—an American soldier and a Potawatomi Indian—battle as an angel hovers above. On the left another Indian is stealthily approaching, crouched with a tomahawk in hand. On the right a man shields a woman and a child from the threat. The sculpture uses a familiar stereotype of American Indians to make a visual argument: The Indians are attacking because they are bloodthirsty and sneaky; the innocent settlers bravely resist. The sculpture does not speak to the circumstances of the massacre: The Potawatomis allied with the British during the War of 1812 to resist settlers who were taking their land, and the settlers waited too long to evacuate Fort Dearborn in the face of growing numbers of Indians surrounding the fort.

It's not surprising that the sculpture represents the settlers as heroic. The bridge and monument were part of a grand plan, begun in 1909, to enhance Chicago's waterfront. Thus, the monument plays its part in obscuring the actual history of the area. Viewers who are unaware of the facts may feel a sense of patriotic pride in the actions of the soldier and the woman. Viewers who are familiar with the whole story may take a different view.

Exercise 6.2 As described in Section 6e, public art and public sculpture are culturally and historically significant. In the same vein, the architecture of public buildings such as government buildings and university buildings convey cultural and historical messages.

Find an example of public art, sculpture, or architecture in your city or town. What messages does this object convey? What do you think the leaders and designers had in mind when they planned for it and created it?

7 | Write a Reflection

QUICK*TAKE*

- Find a topic that has special significance for you (see below)
- Identify a focus for your reflection (see p. 83)
- Write a title, write an introduction, and determine your organization (see p. 84)

7a Find a Reflective Topic

Reflecting on experience

Reflections, whether they appear in print, video, or any other medium, often deal with personal and private experiences, but they do not have to be based on explicitly personal topics. In some cases, being too personal or confessional can limit a writer's ability to connect to his or her audience. The goal of reflection should not be simply to vent pent-up feelings or to expose secrets. Instead, the goal should be to allow the audience to share with the writer his or her discovery of the significance of an experience.

Discovering a reflective topic

Listing is a good way to identify possibilities for reflective essays based on memories.

- List five people who have been significant in your life.
- List five events that have been important in your life. Think about one-time events, such as getting a scholarship, and recurring events, such as a yearly family get-together.
- List five places that have been important in your life.
- Now look through your lists and check the items that are especially vivid.

Another set of possibilities can be drawn from looking at family photographs (see Melissa Dodd's reflection on a family photograph in Section 7d). You can also write about objects that have special significance for your family or just for you, such as a scrapbook that you kept in elementary school.

Not all reflective topics are about the past. You can visit a place or go to an event and focus on your interaction with the place or event instead of on the place or event itself.

Exercise 7.1 Look at your immediate work space. Are you at home, at the library, a coffeehouse, or somewhere else? If the place is familiar, think about people, things, and events that you connect to this place. Can you develop any of these into a brief narrative? Write a one-paragraph narrative inspired by a memory of this place.

If the place is not familiar to you, think about a person, place, thing, or event you are reminded of by this place. Write a one-paragraph narrative inspired by this association.

7b Identify a Focus

Reflections do not often have a formal thesis, but they typically have a **focus** that makes the reflection coherent by communicating a central idea to readers. Why is this experience important? Why is it memorable? In short, why is it worth writing about? Often the focus comes not in the big idea but in the small details that call for reflection.

Exercise 7.2 Find a short, reflective piece of writing in a newspaper, a magazine, or a book, or on the Internet. *The New York Times* magazine, for example, has a regular feature in which people tell brief stories about key moments in their lives. National Public Radio also airs several programs featuring brief personal narratives, such as *This American Life* and *The Moth*. You can find streaming audio or podcasts of these shows online.

Write a paragraph in which you analyze the format of the message. Is the presentation appropriate to what seems to be the intended message? Is the message conveyed to the intended audience? Why or why not?

7c Organize and Write a Reflection

When you have a topic and a focus that communicates the importance of the experience or event to your readers, then it's time to write your reflection. You might not follow this order as writing is often a back-and-forth process.

1 **Before you write**

Think about your readers
- What attitudes are your readers likely to have about your subject?
- How can you make readers care about your subject?
- What will readers gain from reading your reflection?

2 Write an introduction

Engage your readers quickly
- Choose a title that will interest readers.
- Start with the incident, place, or person that is the focus.

3 Organize and write the body of your paper

Should you use a chronological organization?
- Use chronological order to let readers re-live events with you.

Should you use a conceptual organization?
- Use conceptual order to show connections and links between ideas.

Communicate experiences with details
- Give specifics such as dates and names to provide background information.
- Augment visual details with other sensory details (smells, sounds, tastes, tactile feelings).
- Choose specific words to convey details.
- Identify people by more than how they look. Think about typical mannerisms, gestures, and habits.
- If people interact, use dialogue to convey the interaction.

Consider your voice and tone
- Your writing should sound like you. Be yourself.
- If your writing sounds like the voice that makes announcements in the airport, try rewriting as you would talk.
- Let yourself go in the first draft. If you become excessive, you can adjust the language when you revise.

4 Write a conclusion

End by inviting further reflection
- Share any discoveries you made in the process of reflecting.
- Avoid a simple moral lesson, but your conclusion should help your readers to make sense of your reflection.

5 Revise, revise, revise

Evaluate your draft
- Make sure your reflection meets the requirements of the assignment.
- Consider how you might sharpen the focus and significance of your reflection.
- Consider where you might provide more details, dialogue, or background information.
- When you have finished revising, edit and proofread carefully.

7d Sample Reflective Essay

In her film studies class, Melissa Dodd was asked to read excerpts from Michelle Citron's *Home Movies and Other Necessary Fictions*, in which Citron asks why home movies of her childhood do not correspond with her memories of her family. For a course assignment, Melissa Dodd decided to write her own reflection on a family snapshot. The focus of Dodd's reflection is that the objects in a photograph give clues not only to the dynamics of the moment the photo claims to capture, but also to what is missing.

Dodd 1

Melissa Dodd

Professor Mendoza

Introduction to Film

25 April 2009

My Sister and Me on Grandma's Lap

This picture was taken at my paternal grandmother's house in Enid, Oklahoma. I'm on Grandma's lap, and my sister Rhonda is on the floor.

Dodd begins with a descriptive paragraph, bringing the reader into the photo.

Dodd 2

I believe this picture was taken around 1989 or 1990 because I look about two or three years old. It is after supper, and Grandma is reading to me.

The summary of Citron's *Home Movies* is used to pose a question about why Dodd's mother was missing from the photo.

This photograph is interesting to me because it reflects two points that Michelle Citron makes in her book, *Home Movies and Other Necessary Fictions*. First, the person taking the picture is asserting control over the interpretation of the memory. Second, there are clues within the frame that signify what has actually been left out of the frame. The item missing from this picture is my mother.

A detail in the photo, the moccasins, leads to a description of conflict between mother and grandmother.

My father took the picture in order to show me wearing the moccasins my maternal grandfather had just bought for me when we visited him in Holdenville, Oklahoma. My mother had remained there, while we went on to Enid. She rarely came with us to visit Grandma because they did not get along. Like her own mother, my mother could be moody, distant, and bad-tempered. Grandma, on the other hand, was somewhat meddlesome, but affectionate, and over-indulgent with us kids. Consequently, they argued over how we should be treated.

Dodd steps back to reflect on the photograph in the context of what was happening in the family.

Grandma is pointing to the moccasins, which signify my mother's absence. In some ways, the photo is a conciliatory gesture; my father is acknowledging his in-laws' contribution to my happiness and well being. In another, less obvious way, it is an act of spite. Since my mother refused to be there, my father replaced her with his own mother in this happy family scene he has created.

Dodd 3

Her absence is also highlighted by the presence of my sister, Rhonda, who was about nine or ten. When I was a baby, Rhonda and I were always in pictures together. Usually she's playing "mommy" and holding me on her lap. She was very protective of me and would not let me out of her sight. Taking the role of my guardian often got her in trouble, especially when my mother's temper flared. Here, she looks silly and relaxed, more childlike than she does in other family pictures.

Dodd examines how her sister was affected by family conflicts by contrasting her appearance in this photo with her appearance in others.

Citron argues that since they are selective and often taken by men, home movies and family photographs assert a balance of power within the family and strive to promote the "good" memory of family: "parents in control, men in charge, families together" (15). What she does not overtly mention, however, is that these created memories are also punitive. It is the people, things, or events that disrupt the image of the ideal family that are banished from the frame. Importantly, my mother's temper and her refusal to make peace with my grandmother led to her omission from my father's carefully constructed scene of domestic tranquillity.

Dodd moves one step further to explore how good memories are manufactured in family photographs by banishing what is disruptive.

In the end, what is most significant is the fact that this manufactured memory works. Until I began to look at this picture through Citron's eyes, I simply had a memory of my Grandma's house—its warmth, and that it always smelled like bacon and Dr. Pepper. Unfortunately, this is not the whole picture. But this pleasant memory does not have to go away just because I now see things in more detail.

Dodd 4

By recognizing what is missing, I hope I can work to reconcile the fiction to the reality and come to a more complete understanding of my family's dynamics.

Dodd 5

Work Cited

Citron, Michelle. *Home Movies and Other Necessary Fictions*. Minneapolis: U of Minnesota P, 1999 Print.

To hear audio commentary on this piece of writing, visit this page of the eText at **www.mycomplab.com.**

Exercise 7.3   Return to the essay you wrote for Exercise 7.1. Develop this paragraph into a full response using the advice given in Section 7c. Find a focus for your response, and add details to make the reflection come alive for the reader. Remember to give your response an attention-getting introduction and thoughtful conclusion.

8 | Write an Informative Essay

QUICK*TAKE*

- Find a topic that explains or one that explores questions and problems (see below)
- Narrow your topic and write a thesis (see p. 91)
- Identify your main points and decide how to best present them (see p. 92)

8a Find an Informative Topic

Many of the writing tasks assigned in college are informative—from lab reports and essay exams to analyses of literature, research papers, and case studies. Look at your assignment for key words such as *study, analyze, explain,* and *explore,* which indicate what kind of writing you are expected to produce (see Section 2a). Informative writing has four primary functions: to report new or unfamiliar information; to analyze for meaning, patterns, and connections; to explain how to do something or how something works; and to explore questions and problems.

Reporting information

Reporting information takes many forms, ranging from reports of experimental research and reports of library research to simple lists of information. In one sense, writing to reflect (Chapter 7) and writing to persuade (Chapters 9 and 10) also report information. The main difference is that the focus of a report and other informative kinds of writing is on the subject, not on the writer's reflections or on changing readers' minds or on getting them to take action. Writers of reports usually stay in the background and keep their language as neutral as possible.

Analyzing meaning, patterns, and connections

Writers not only report what they read and observe. They often construct meaning through selecting what and what not to include and in organizing that information. Sometimes this construction of meaning is made explicit as **analysis**. The complexity of the world we live in requires making connections. For example, advertisers know that certain kinds of ads (for example, ads that associate drinking beer with social life) sell the product, but often they do not know exactly how these ads work or why some ads are more effective than others.

Explaining how

Often what you know well is difficult to explain to others. You may know how to solve certain kinds of difficult problems, such as how to fix a problem in your car's electrical system, but if you have to tell a friend how to do it over the phone, you may quickly become very frustrated. Often you have to break down a process into steps that you can describe in order to explain it. Explaining a process sometimes requires you to think about something familiar in a new way.

Exploring questions and problems

Not all informative writing is about topics with which you are familiar or ones that you can bring to closure. Often college writing involves issues or problems that perplex us and for which we cannot come to a definitive conclusion. The goal in such writing is not the ending but the journey. Tracing the turns of thought in a difficult intellectual problem can result in writing far beyond the ordinary. Difficult issues often leave us conflicted; readers appreciate it when we deal honestly with those conflicts.

Finding a topic

When your general subject is specified in your assignment, you can make your work more enjoyable by choosing a specific topic that is either more familiar to you or that you find particularly interesting. Your level of engagement in a topic can have a real impact on your readers' level of interest. Here are guidelines you can use when choosing a topic.

- Choose a topic you will enjoy writing about.
- Choose a topic that readers will enjoy reading about.
- Choose a topic for which you can make a contribution of your own, perhaps by viewing something familiar in a new way.
- If you choose an unfamiliar topic, you must be strongly committed to learning more about it.

Exercise 8.1 Informative writing in college often involves explaining a concept. Pick an academic discipline that interests you and that you already know something about (such as psychology, biology, engineering, art, and so on) or another broad subject area (such as social media, vegan cooking, college athletics, and so on). List at least five central concepts for that discipline or area of interest. When you finish, review your list and select one concept as a possible topic.

Take five minutes to write what you know about that concept. Why does it interest you? What else would you like to know about it?

Next, make a quick survey of information about the concept. If your library has online resources such as specialized encyclopedias, look up the concept. You can also do a Web search or go to the library. Do you have enough information to write about this concept?

8b Narrow Your Topic and Write a Thesis

A central difficulty with writing to inform is determining where to stop. For any large subject, even a lifetime may be insufficient. The key to success is to limit the topic. Find a topic you can cover thoroughly in the space you have. Broad, general topics are nearly impossible to cover in an essay of five pages. Look for ways of dividing large topics such as *the use of steroids among college students* into smaller categories and select one that is promising. *Why college athletes ignore the risks of steroids* is a topic that you are more likely to be able to cover in a short paper.

Often your readers will lack initial interest in your topic. If you ignore their lack of interest, they in turn will likely ignore you. Instead, you can take your readers' knowledge and interest into account when you draft your thesis. For example, someone who knows a lot about birds in the parks of your city might write this informative thesis:

> Watching birds in urban areas is interesting because unusual birds often show up in city parks.

It doesn't sound like a topic that most college students would find as interesting as the writer does. But if the writer puts the audience's attitude in the foreground, challenging them to consider a subject they have likely not thought much about, a college audience might read beyond the title:

> Although most college students think of bird watching as an activity for retired people, watching birds gives you a daily experience with nature, even in urban areas.

This thesis also gives the writer a stance from which to approach the topic.

Exercise 8.2 If you completed exercise 8.1, look at the topic you explored. If you did not, look at a paper you have already written for this class or another, or think about a topic you would like to write about for this class or another.

An informative thesis statement should contain the topic and indicate your focus. To sharpen that focus, ask the following questions.

1. Who are your readers? What are they likely to know about your topic?
2. What particular features of this topic have led to your interest in it?
3. What are the main subtopics your topic can be broken down into? Which ones would you focus on?
4. What key terms are important to your topic?

Write a clear, focused thesis statement based on your answers to these questions.

8c Organize and Write an Informative Essay

Successful reporting of information requires a clear understanding of the subject and a clear presentation. How much information you need to include depends on your readers' knowledge of and potential interest in your topic. You might not follow this order as writing is often a back-and-forth process.

1 Before you write

Think about your readers
- What do your readers already know about the subject?
- What questions or concerns might they have about your subject?
- What is their attitude toward the subject? If it is different from yours, how can you address the difference?

Review your thesis and scope
- When you learn more about your topic, you should be able to identify one aspect or concept that you can cover thoroughly.

2 Write an introduction

Engage your readers quickly
- Write a title and an introduction that will make readers take an interest in your topic.

3 Organize and write the body of your paper

Think about your main points
- Use an idea map to organize your main points (see Section 2b).
- Make a working outline to identify your main points and the relationships among them.

Decide how your points are best ordered
- Chronological organization often works best for a topic that occurs over time.
- Conceptual organization focuses on how important concepts are related.
- Compare and contrast organization helps to show how two things are similar or different.

Write a conclusion

End with more than a summary
- Make a point that readers can take away.
- Raise an interesting question.
- End with a vivid example.

 Revise, revise, revise

Evaluate your draft
- Examine the order of your ideas and reorganize if necessary.
- Add detail or further explanation where needed.
- When you have finished revising, edit and proofread carefully.

WRITING SMART

Use visuals to report information

Complex statistical data can often be presented effectively in a table or a chart. Other visuals such as maps and photos can help readers to understand your subject. Be sure to provide the sources of your data and the source of any visual that you do not create.

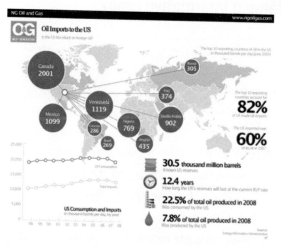

■ *O&G* magazine published this graphic created by BP's Energy Information Administration. Why do you think BP created this graphic? Is the purpose to persuade as well as to inform?

Exercise 8.3 The way you should organize your information in an informative essay depends on the subject you have chosen. If you are writing about a topic that occurs over time, a **chronological organization** works best. If your subject requires you to identify the major aspects of a subject and discuss each in turn, a **conceptual organization** may work best (outlines and idea maps are useful for this). If you are writing about two things that are similar or different, a **compare and contrast organization is appropriate**. In this case, you might describe one thing and then the other, closing with a summary of similarities or differences.

Which of the methods of organization described above would work best for each of the following topics?

1. How to apply for a job
2. A survey of New Year's celebrations around the world
3. An analysis of the speeches of gubernatorial candidates
4. What subcultures are currently popular in American high schools
5. How to bake a cheesecake
6. A comparison of two plans for a promenade along the river
7. A history of the Yellow Fever Epidemic of 1878 in Memphis
8. A description of Hindu wedding traditions
9. The evolution of the character Spike over the course of the television series *Buffy the Vampire Slayer*
10. An analysis of a plan to create a local business district

8d Sample Informative Essay

Haddad 1

Akilah Haddad

Professor Swift

English 1102

5 October 2010

Haddad's title, given as a question, piques reader interest.

Protecting Your Privacy on the Internet:

Is There an App for That?

Early in 2010, Google and Facebook found themselves in trouble for breaching the public's trust with their privacy policies. Google caught the attention of privacy regulators for collecting data as they

Haddad 2

captured images for its Street View project. Facebook enraged its users by not only altering its privacy controls to make more of its users' personal data public by default, but also by creating a complicated interface for changing privacy options (Hartley). In addition, Facebook unveiled a service called "Instant Personalization," which automatically shares information about customers with external sites unless the customer opts out, site by site (Manjoo). The result of these two events is a revival of the fear that, as the *Economist* puts it, "online privacy is being trampled underfoot as Internet behemoths race to grab as much data as possible" ("Dicing"). And the behemoths want these data because of the potential for huge profits, especially for Facebook, which generates most of its revenue from targeted advertisements based on users' demography (Robinson).

Haddad's thesis is given in the last two sentences of the first paragraph.

The debates about Internet privacy are nothing new; they have been raging since Web sites started leaving "cookies" on users' hard drives to trace their Internet behavior. At the center of this debate has been the question of who is responsible for making sure that information collected by Web sites is not misused—the government, the Internet companies, or consumers themselves. Vice President Albert Gore was an early advocate of government intervention, and he announced an "Electronic Bill of Rights" in 1998, defining privacy as a basic human right protected by the Constitution and numerous federal laws (Broder). In light of the recent Google and Facebook scandals,

Haddad 3

other people, such as social-networking expert Danah
Boyd, are again thinking that the Internet should be
regulated by the government, perhaps as a utility.

Advocates of self-regulation believe that since
Internet companies are financially motivated to make
consumers feel secure about their Internet use, they
should be trusted to police themselves. However,
if self-regulation is to work, there have to be
consequences for bad behavior, which leads to the next
question: How can self-regulation be enforced? TRUSTe,
a program operated by a nonprofit that grants certificates
to Web sites posting a privacy statement that meets
TRUSTe's standards and submitting to an audit, was
created as a partial solution to this issue ("Tailed").

In addition, companies have to recognize their
culpability, which they are often reluctant to do. Google,
for example, apologized for its mistake, but the data
collection had been going on for several years. Google
did not admit to violating laws until German officials
asked them to come clean (Heining). The CEO of
Facebook, Mark Zuckerberg, was also reluctant to accept
blame for his company's actions, arguing that Facebook
should be entirely public. He believes that most users are
agreeable to Facebook being open by default because, as
he says, "people have really gotten comfortable not only
sharing information and different kinds, but more openly
and with more people. That social norm is just something
that has evolved over time" (Kirkpatrick).

These controversies have spurred discussion about
whether or not the idea of privacy itself has changed,

**Haddad
provides an
analysis of the
problems of
regulating the
Internet.**

Haddad 4

and consequently, how responsible consumers are for
protecting themselves. Like Zuckerberg, Facebook's
Barry Schnitt believes that the world is becoming
more open, as evidenced by Twitter, My Space, and
reality TV (Kirkpatrick). In his book *Delete*, Viktor
Mayer-Schönberger warns of the costs of what he calls
the "digital panopticon," in which every move and
decision is recorded into digital memory, incapable of
being forgotten. Thus, compromising photos, candid
statements about our jobs, embarrassing searches,
and controversial acts can be used against us in a
variety of contexts (11). Since users voluntarily
disclose information about themselves every day, "in
that strict sense, they bear responsibility for the
consequences of their disclosures" (5). However, there
are also times when users disclose without knowing,
as is the case with the recent Facebook and Google
privacy scandals. Are users then still responsible for
not adequately securing their networks, as in the case
with Google, or not being vigilant enough about their
privacy settings, as in the case with Facebook?

These questions still consider privacy a matter
of culture, however. Issues become more thorny when
privacy enters the legal realm. Helen Nissenbaum
in *Privacy in Context* argues that the changes to the
Internet have happened too fast for us to be able to
accurately assess how harmful the aggregation and
dissemination of information will be. In particular,
increasing sophistication of both software and users
has made what was once rather boring and disconnected

A conceptual organization has been used to explain the threats to privacy and how both Facebook and Google have responded to critics of the policies.

Haddad 5

information gathering dust in databases vulnerable to being "remixed" into full, recognizable profiles of individuals by savvy programmers and hackers (17). In addition, some of Google's new Map features have raised unexpected questions in law enforcement. Specifically, why do you need a warrant to search a property for drugs when Google Earth and Street View can show you what's growing in someone's yard? And is evidence gathered in this way admissible in court (Morozov)?

As the Internet continues to grow and change, these debates over responsibility will continue. Regarding government intervention, experts agree that it is unlikely that the Internet will be regulated as a utility since sites such as Facebook and Google are not essential services, nor do they enjoy a monopoly. In addition, regulating the Internet in this way could restrict further innovation ("Dicing"). What will probably happen in the next two years, however, is some form of FCC regulation ("Price"). As for the companies themselves, it is in their best interest to keep consumers happy, which was certainly the case for Facebook. Even though the activist-initiated "Quit Facebook Day" only saw 31,000 users out of 450 million follow through on their pledge to quit the site on May 31, 2010, it was still enough to convince Zuckerberg to address publicly its new privacy policies and make changes, including creating one single page where users can control who sees their information. In addition, Facebook also enabled users to block outside software developers from accessing users' personal information (Hartley). In fact, according to Tom Spring in *PC World* magazine, on several other occasions from 2007 to the present, public pressure has led Facebook to change policies and page layouts. But the problem still remains that, despite these lessons, Facebook continues to engage in practices that enrage consumers. As Spring points out, Facebook would be "well served to be more pro-active about communicating changes to its terms and services rather than reactive." Until that happens, it remains the user's job to police what is being made of his or her information online.

Haddad concludes with a key point for readers to take away—namely it is up to each of us to safeguard our privacy on the Internet.

Works Cited

Boyd, Danah. "Facebook Is a Utility; Utilities Get Regulated." *apophenia*. N.p., 15 May 2010. Web. 13 Sept. 2010.

Broder, John M. "Gore to Announce 'Electronic Bill of Rights' Aimed at Privacy." *New York Times* 14 May 2010, late ed.: 16. *LexisNexis Academic*. Web. 15 Sept. 2010.

"Dicing with Data: Facebook, Google and Privacy." *Economist* 22 May 2010, US ed.: 16. *LexisNexis Academic*. Web. 15 Sept. 2010.

Haddad 8

Manjoo, Farhad. Interview with Neal Conan. *Talk of the
   Nation*. NPR, 12 May 2010. Radio.

Hartley, Matt. "Facebook Founder Mark Zuckerberg to
   Blame for Privacy Mess." *National Post*. National
   Post, 28 May 2010. Web. 14 Sept. 2010.

Heining, Andrew. "What's So Bad about the Google
   Street View Flap?" *The Christian Science Monitor*.
   csmonitor.com, 15 May 2010. Web. 16 Sept. 2010.

Kirkpatrick, Marshall. "Facebook's Zuckerberg Says that
   the Age of Privacy is Over." *ReadWriteWeb*. N.p.,
   9 Jan. 2010. Web. 14 Sept. 2010.

Mayer-Schönberger, Viktor. *Delete: The Virtue of
   Forgetting in the Digital Age*. Princeton: Princeton
   UP, 2009. Print.

Morozov, Evgeny. "e-outed." Rev. of *Privacy in Context*
   by Helen Nissenbaum. *Times Literary Supplement*
   12 Mar. 2010: 8. Print.

"The Price of Privacy." *On the Media*. Natl. Public Radio.
   WNYC New York, 28 May 2010. Web. 14 Sept. 2010.

Robinson, James. "Facebook Users Revolt Against Mark
   Zuckerman Over Privacy." *Guardian*. Guardian.co.uk,
   23 May 2010. Web. 15 Sept. 2010.

Spring, Tom. "Quit Facebook Day Was a Success Even as
   It Flopped." *PC World*. pcworld.com, 1 June 2010.
   Web. 14 Sept. 2010.

"You Are Being Tailed." *Economist* 27 June 1998, US
   ed.: 62. *LexisNexis Academic*. Web. 15 Sept. 2010.

*To hear audio commentary on this piece of writing, visit this page
of the eText at* **www.mycomplab.com**.

9 | Write a Position Argument

QUICKTAKE

- Find and narrow a topic (see below)
- Make sure your arguments are convincing (see p. 105)
- Acknowledge opposing viewpoints (see p. 106)

 ## Position Arguments and Proposal Arguments

When you imagine an argument, you might think of two people with different views, engaged in a heated debate—maybe even shouting slogans. In college courses, in public life, and in professional careers, written arguments are meant to persuade readers who refuse to accept a **claim** when it is expressed as a slogan. Extended written arguments attempt to change people's minds by convincing them that a new idea or point of view is valid, or that a particular course of action is the best one to take.

Written arguments

- offer evidence and reason,
- examine the assumptions on which the evidence and reason are based,
- explore opposing arguments, and
- anticipate objections.

How you develop a written argument depends on your goals. You may want to convince your readers to change their way of thinking about an issue or perhaps get them to consider the issue from your perspective. Or you may want your readers to take some course of action based on your argument. These two kinds of arguments can be characterized as **position** and **proposal arguments** (see Chapter 10).

 ## Find an Arguable Topic and Make a Claim

In a position argument you make a claim about a controversial issue. You

- define or rebut the issue,
- take a clear position,

- make a convincing argument, and
- acknowledge opposing views.

Position arguments often take two forms—definition arguments and rebuttal arguments.

Definition arguments. People argue about definitions (for example, is graffiti vandalism or is it art?) because of the consequences of something being defined in a certain way. If you can get your audience to accept your definition, then usually your argument will be successful.

Definition arguments take the form shown here.

Something is (or is not) _____ because it has (or does not have) Criteria A, Criteria B, and Criteria C (or more).

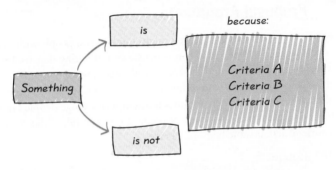

Graffiti is art because it is a means of self-expression, it shows an understanding of design principles, and it simulates both the senses and the mind.

Rebuttal arguments take the opposite position. You can challenge the criteria a writer uses to make a definition or you can challenge the evidence that supports the claim. Often the evidence presented is incomplete or wrong. Sometimes you can find counterevidence. Often when you rebut an argument, you identify one or more fallacies in that argument. (See pages 61–63.)

Rebuttal arguments take this form.

The opposing argument has serious shortcoming that undermine the claim because

            flawed reason 1

            flawed reason 2

because:

Something	is not	flawed reason 1 flawed reason 2

The great white shark gained a false reputation as a "man eater" from the 1975 movie *Jaws,* but in fact *attacks on humans are rare* and *most bites have been "test bites,"* which is a common shark behavior with unfamiliar objects.

Exercise 9.1 Identify which of the following are definition arguments, which are rebuttals, and which are neither.

1. Critics blinded by *Avatar's* strange beauty have missed the cynical use of thinly veiled native stereotypes and post-Vietnam imperialist critiques to sell high-tech gimmickry.
2. The national ban on gay marriage is unconstitutional.
3. Hate speech is not free speech protected by the First Amendment.
4. Although it is a common practice in many states, senators should not be appointed by the governor because it reduces the power of the voters.
5. The television show *Glee* in its extreme artificiality and sentimentality is an example of the cultural concept of "camp."

Finding an arguable topic

Probably you know people who will argue about almost anything. Some topics, however, are much better suited than others for writing an extended argument. One way to get started is to make a list of topics you care about. Below are examples of other starting points.

Think about issues that are debated on your campus

- Should admissions decisions be based solely on academic achievement?
- Should varsity athletes get paid for playing sports that bring in revenue?

Think about issues that are debated in your community

- Should people who ride bicycles and motorcycles be required to wear helmets?
- Should the public schools be privatized?

Think about national and international issues

- Should advertising be banned on television shows aimed at pre-school children?
- Should capital punishment be abolished?

Read about your issue

- What are the major points of view on your issue?
- Who are the experts on this issue? What do they have to say?
- What major claims are being offered?
- What reasons are given to support the claims?
- What kinds of evidence are used to support the reasons?
- How can you add to what has been said about your subject?

Supporting claims with reasons

The difference between a slogan, such as *Oppose candidate X*, and an arguable claim, such as *Oppose candidate X because she will not lower taxes and not improve schools*, is the presence of a reason linked to the claim. A reason is typically offered in a ***because* clause**, a statement that begins with the word *because* and provides a supporting reason for the claim. The word *because* signals a **link** between the reason and the claim.

Claims must be specific and contestable

In addition to being supported by reasons that are appropriately linked to it, your claim must also be *specific*. Broad general claims such as *The United States has become too crowded* are nearly impossible to argue effectively. Often general claims contain more restricted claims that can be argued, such as *The United States should increase its efforts to reduce illegal immigration* or *The amount of land in national parks should be doubled to ensure adequate wild spaces for future generations.*

Your claim must also be contestable. Your claim that you like sour cream on a baked potato is specific, but not contestable. No matter how often you are told that a baked potato is less fattening without sour cream, the fact that you like sour cream won't change. You may stop eating the sour cream, but you won't stop wanting to eat it.

Exercise 9.2 Collect five slogans that state a position from advertisements, posters, the Internet, social media, the news media, and even bumper stickers and evaluate whether or not each presents an arguable claim by answering the following questions.

1. Is there a reason linked to the claim? If not, is it assumed that the audience knows the reason?
2. Is there evidence to stand up to the questions *So what? Why?* and *How?* If so, what is this evidence? If not, what evidence is needed to support the argument against the challenges?
3. Is the claim specific or is it too broad? How could it be made more specific?
4. Is the claim contestable? Why or why not?

9c Organize and Write a Position Argument

Thinking of reasons to support a claim is not hard. What *is* hard is convincing your audience that your reasons are good ones. Imagine you will have critical readers. Whenever you put forward a reason, they will ask *So what?* You will have to have evidence, and you will have to link that evidence to your claim in ways they will accept if they are to agree that your reason is a good reason. Be open to new ideas while you are writing. Often you will go back and forth in developing a position argument.

1 Before you write

Think about your readers
- What do your readers already know about the subject?
- What is their attitude toward the subject? If it is different from your position, how can you address the difference?
- What are the chances of changing the opinions and beliefs of your readers? If your readers are unlikely to be moved, can you get them to acknowledge that your position is reasonable?
- Are there any sensitive issues you should be aware of?

2 Write an introduction

Engage your readers quickly
- Get your readers' attention with an example of what is at stake.
- Define the subject or issue.
- State your thesis to announce your position.

3 Organize and write the body of your paper

Develop reasons
- Can you argue from a definition? Is _____ a _____?

EXAMPLES

Are cheerleaders athletes?

Are zoos guilty of cruelty to animals?

- Can you compare and contrast? Is _____ like or unlike _____?
- Can you argue that something is good (better, bad, worse)?
- Can you argue that something caused (or may cause) something else?
- Can you refute objections to your position?

Support reasons with evidence
- Can you support your reasons by going to a site and making observations?
- Can you find facts, statistics, or statements from authorities to support your reasons?

Consider opposing views
- Acknowledge other stakeholders for the issue, and consider their positions.
- Explain why your position is preferable.
- Make counterarguments if necessary.

4 Write a conclusion

End with more than a summary
- Think of a strong way to end by offering more evidence in support of your thesis, reinforcing what is at stake, or giving an example that gets at the heart of the issue.

5 Revise, revise, revise

Evaluate your draft
- Make sure your position argument meets the assignment requirements.
- Can you sharpen your thesis to make your position clearer?
- Can you add additional reasons to strengthen your argument?
- Can you supply additional evidence?
- Examine your language for bias and emotionally loaded words and reword if needed.
- When you have finished revising, edit and proofread carefully.

9d Sample Position Argument

Martinez 1

Mariela Martinez

Professor Barnes

English 102

13 April 2009

Should Students Have the Right

of Freedom of Speech?

In January 2002, students at Juneau-Douglas
High School in Juneau, Alaska, were dismissed from
classes for a parade sponsored by a local business for the
Winter Olympic Torch Relay, which passed in front of
the school. Across the street and off of school grounds,
high school senior Joseph Frederick, who had not
attended school that day, and his friends waited until
the torch and cameras approached. They then unfurled
a banner that read "Bong Hits 4 Jesus." The outraged
school principal, Deborah Morse, ran across the street
and seized the banner. She then suspended Frederick
for five days and later increased the penalty to ten
days when Frederick quoted Thomas Jefferson on the
right of freedom of speech (Sherman).

> The first and
> second paragraphs
> give the back-
> ground of an issue
> that likely is
> unfamiliar to most
> readers.

Frederick appealed to the Superintendent and the
Juneau School Board, which denied his appeal. He then
filed suit against Morse and the school board, claiming
they had violated his First Amendment right to freedom
of speech. The federal district court ruled in favor of
Morse and the school board. The United States Court of

Martinez 2

Appeals for the Ninth Circuit, however, reversed the
district court in a unanimous decision, ruling that
Frederick's right to freedom of speech had been violated
(Hussain). The Juneau School Board then took the case
to the United States Supreme Court, which heard oral
arguments on March 19, 2007. Kenneth Starr, the
Whitewater prosecutor during the Clinton administration,
presented the case for the school board.

> In the third
> paragraph
> Martinez gives
> her interpretation
> that the event
> was not worthy
> of the attention it
> received. Then
> she states her
> thesis that
> students' rights
> to freedom of
> speech should be
> protected.

At first glance the incident seems blown
enormously out of proportion, certainly unworthy
of consuming many hours of a federal judge's time.
Frederick's banner was a stupid prank done in poor
taste by an adolescent. He is far from the ideal poster
child for free speech. But the underlying issue is huge.
I maintain that there is no reason to restrict
the First Amendment rights of students when they are
not disrupting the school. To give school authorities
the right to control anything a student says anywhere
far exceeds any reasonable interpretation of our
Constitution.

Attorney Kenneth Starr argued before the
Supreme Court that Morse's censorship of Frederick
was justified because of the precedent set in Bethel
School District v. Fraser. In that 1986 case, the
Supreme Court ruled that public schools could limit
student speech at a school assembly. Vulgar or
obscene speech could be censored. The court decided
that "[T]he undoubted freedom to advocate unpopular
and controversial views in schools and classrooms

> Martinez
> examines the
> opposing position.
> She concludes
> that the evidence
> cited by the
> opposition does
> not apply to the
> Juneau case.

Martinez 3

must be balanced against the society's countervailing interest in teaching students the boundaries of socially appropriate behavior." But that case involved a school assembly on school property. Starr argued that Frederick v. Morse is comparable because students had been collectively released from school to watch the Olympic torch pass by and were accompanied by their teachers.

The case Morse v. Frederick is not, as Starr maintained, about protecting young people from "the scourge of drugs." The drug reference is a red herring. Frederick described the words as nonsense meant to get the attention of the television cameras (Biskupic). The banner was not pornographic or obscene. The banner did not incite violence. The only violent act was the principal's seizing the banner. Neither could it be interpreted as attacking Christianity. Organizations that litigate on behalf of the religious right including the Christian Legal Society and the American Center for Law and Justice, founded by the Rev. Pat Robertson, have sided with Frederick (Greenhouse).

Martinez argues that Frederick's banner neither broke any laws nor did it insult Christian organizations because the religious right sided with Frederick.

Instead the case is an effort by school administrators supported by their professional organizations to get the Supreme Court to allow them to censor anything they disagree with. This effort is chilling because they currently have the power to censor obscene, violent, and libelous speech. It is an attempt to use the public's fear about illegal drugs to justify heavy-handed authoritarian control of student

Martinez 4

expression, whether on or off campus. Morse and Starr may not like to admit it, but the First Amendment does apply in our nation's public schools. The U.S. Supreme Court decided in 1969, in the case of Tinker et al. v. Des Moines Independent Community School District, that students do have the right of political expression. The court ruled that as long as the student's expression does not disrupt the educational environment, officials cannot suppress it (Haynes). The Supreme Court has long maintained that speech that is unpleasant or uncomfortable is nonetheless protected.

> Martinez supplies evidence that students do have the right of political expression when they are not disruptive.

Frederick's prank was stupid and boorish, but imagine that Frederick held up a banner protesting racial segregation in the South in 1961. We would now see his act as courageous. Indeed, students were at the forefront of the Civil Rights movement, and many school administrators opposed their actions. Principal Morse was not wrong to disagree with Frederick's message, but she was wrong to censor it. The Supreme Court declared in its Tinker ruling in 1969 that students do not "shed their constitutional rights to freedom of speech or expression at the 'schoolhouse gate.'" The First Amendment is fundamental to our sense of what the United States is about, and we should always be vigilant when those in power seek to limit freedom of speech.

> In her conclusion, Martinez reiterates that she does not think Frederick's prank was a good idea, but the principal was wrong to deny his right to freedom of speech off of school property. She gives additional evidence that the Supreme Court has ruled in the past that students do have freedom of speech.

Martinez 5

Works Cited

Bethel School Dist. v. Fraser. 478 US 675. Supreme
    Court of the US. 1986. *Supreme Court Collection*.
    Legal Information Inst., Cornell U Law School, n.d.
    Web. 3 Apr. 2009.

Biskupic, Joan. "Justices Debate Student's Suspension
    for Banner." *USA Today*. 20 Mar. 2007: 3A. Print.

Greenhouse, Linda. "Free Speech Case Divides Bush and
    Religious Right." *New York Times*. 18 Mar. 2007,
    final ed.: A22. Print.

Haynes, Charles C. "T-shirt Rebellion in the Land of the
    Free." *First Amendment Center*. First Amendment
    Center, Vanderbilt U, 14 Mar. 2004. Web. 4 Apr. 2009.

Hussain, Murad. "The 'Bong' Show: Viewing Frederick's
    Publicity Stunt Through Kulmeier's Lens." *Yale Law
    Journal Pocket Parts*. Yale U Law School, 9 Mar.
    2007. Web. 2 Apr. 2009.

Sherman, Mark. "'Bong Hits 4 Jesus' Banner Case Reaches
    Supreme Court." *Lansing State Journal*. Lansing State
    Journal, 16 Mar. 2007. Web. 2 Apr. 2009.

Tinker et al. v. Des Moines Independent Community
    School Dist. 393 US 503. Supreme Court of the US.
    1969. *Supreme Court Collection*. Legal Information
    Inst., Cornell U Law School, n.d. Web. 3 Apr. 2009.

 *To hear audio commentary on this piece of writing, visit this page
of the eText at* **www.mycomplab.com**.

10 | Write a Proposal Argument

QUICKTAKE

- Find a topic that proposes a solution (see below)
- Make sure your solution is convincing and feasible (see p. 114)
- Be sure to include other possible solutions and argue why your solution is better (see p. 116)

10a Find an Arguable Topic and Make a Proposal

Every day we hear and read arguments that some action should be taken. We even make these arguments ourselves: We should eat better; we should exercise more; we should change our work habits. Convincing others to take action for change is always harder. Other people may not see the problem that you see or they may not think it is important. Nevertheless, most people aren't satisfied with doing nothing about a problem that they think is important. The problem we face in persuading others is not so much that people are resistant to change, but that they need to be convinced that the change we propose is the right one and worthy of their efforts to make it happen.

In a proposal argument you present a course of action in response to a recognizable problem. The proposal says what can be done to improve the situation or change it altogether. You

- define the problem,
- propose a solution or solutions, and
- explain why the solution will work and is feasible.

Proposal arguments take the form shown here.

SOMEONE should (or should not) do SOMETHING because _____

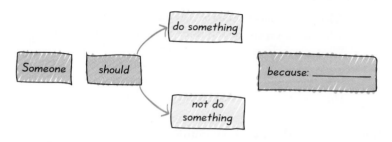

We should convert existing train tracks in the downtown areas to a light-rail system and build a new freight track around the city because we need to relieve traffic and parking congestion downtown.

Finding an arguable topic

Probably you know people who will argue about almost anything. If you think long enough, you too can find ways to argue about almost anything. Some topics, however, are much better suited than others for writing an extended argument. One way to get started is to make a list of topics you care about. Below are examples of other starting points.

Think about issues that are debated on your campus

- Should admissions decisions be based exclusively on academic achievement?
- Should fraternities be banned from campuses if they are caught encouraging alcohol abuse?

Think about issues that are debated in your community

- Should bike lanes be built throughout your community to encourage more people to ride bicycles?
- Should more tax dollars be shifted from building highways to public transportation?

Think about national and international issues

- Should the government be allowed to monitor all phone calls and all e-mail to combat terrorism?

- Should handguns be outlawed?
- Should the United States punish nations with poor human rights records?

Read about your issue

- What are the major points of view on your issue?
- Who are the experts on this issue? What do they have to say?
- What major claims are being offered?
- What reasons are given to support the claims?
- What kinds of evidence are used to support the reasons?
- How can you add to what has been said about your subject?

Supporting claims with reasons

The difference between a slogan, such as *Support light rail now!*, and an arguable claim, such as *Support light rail now because it will reduce traffic and air pollution, and encourage the development of neighborhoods near rail routes* is the presence of a reason linked to the claim. A reason is typically offered in a ***because* clause**, a statement that begins with the word *because* and provides a supporting reason for the claim. The word *because* signals a **link** between the reason and the claim.

Claims must be specific and contestable

In addition to being supported by reasons that are appropriately linked to it, your claim must also be *specific*. Broad general claims such as *The baby food in most supermarkets is overprocessed and unhealthy* are nearly impossible to argue effectively. Often general claims contain more restricted claims that can be argued, such as *The baby food brands sold in Green's supermarket contain high fructose syrup and several preservatives, which are unhealthy for infants and toddlers* or *The collection and use of video surveillance data should be regulated by the government.*

Your claim must also be contestable. Everyone would agree that people should not litter, but not everyone agrees that states or countries should collect deposits for water, juice, and soda bottles and cans.

Exercise 10.1 Collect five statements that propose some kind of change or action from advertisements, posters, the Internet, social media, the news media, and even bumper stickers, and evaluate whether or not each presents an arguable claim by answering the following questions.

1. Is there a reason linked to the claim? If not, is it assumed that the audience knows the reason?

2. Is there evidence to stand up to the questions So what? Why? and How? If so, what is this evidence? If not, what evidence is needed to support the argument against the challenges?
3. Is the claim specific or is it too broad? How could it be made more specific?
4. Is the claim contestable? Why or why not?

10b Organize and Write a Proposal Argument

Writing an effective proposal argument takes time. Often you start out with something that bothers you but no one seems to be doing much about it. Writing about the problem can inspire you to learn more about what causes it and how the solution you are proposing might actually be put into practice.

1 Before you write

Think about your readers
- How much are your readers affected by the problem you are addressing?
- Do your readers agree that the problem you are addressing is important?
- If your readers are unaware of the problem, how can you make them think that solving the problem is important?

2 Write an introduction

Identify the problem
- Do background research on what has been written about the problem and what solutions have been attempted.
- Summarize the problem for your readers and identify whose interests are at stake.
- Describe what is likely to happen if the problem isn't addressed.

3 Organize and write the body of your paper

Describe other solutions that have been attempted or proposed

- Explain why other solutions don't solve the problem or are unrealistic.

Present your solution

- Make clear the goals of your solution. Some solutions do not completely solve the problem.
- Describe the steps of your proposal in detail.
- Describe the positive consequences (or how negative consequences might be avoided) as a result of your proposal.

Argue that your solution can be done

- Your proposal is a good idea only if it can be put into practice, so explain how it is feasible.
- If your proposal requires money, explain where the money will come from.
- If your proposal requires people to change their present behavior, explain how they can be convinced to change.

4 Write a conclusion

End with a call to action

- Think about shared community values—such as fairness, justice, or clean air and water—that you might raise with your readers.
- Put your readers in a position that if they agree with you, they will take action.
- Explain exactly what they need to do.

5 Revise, revise, revise

Evaluate your draft

- Make sure your proposal argument meets the requirements of the assignment.
- Can you better explain the problem or provide more evidence about it?
- Can you add additional evidence that your proposal will solve the problem?
- Can you supply additional evidence that your proposal can be implemented?
- Do you explain why your solution is better than other possible solutions?
- When you have finished revising, edit and proofread carefully.

10c Sample Proposal Argument

Lee 1

Kim Lee

Professor Patel

RHE 306

31 March 2010

Let's Make It a Real Melting Pot with
Presidential Hopes for All

The image the United States likes to advertise is
a country that embraces diversity and creates a land of
equal opportunity for all. As the Statue of Liberty cries
out, "give me your tired, your poor, your huddled masses
yearning to breathe free," American politicians gleefully
evoke such images to frame the United States as a bastion
for all things good, fair, and equal. As a proud American,
however, I must nonetheless highlight one of the cracks
in this façade of equality. Imagine that an infertile couple
decides to adopt an orphaned child from China. They
follow all of the legal processes deemed necessary by both
countries. They fly abroad and bring home their (once
parentless) six-month-old baby boy. They raise and nurture
him, and while teaching him to embrace his ethnicity,
they also teach him to love Captain Crunch, baseball, and
The Three Stooges. He grows and eventually attends an
ethnically diverse American public school. One day his
fifth-grade teacher tells the class that anyone can grow up
to be president. To clarify her point, she turns to the boy,
knowing his background, and states, "No, you could not
be president, Stu, but you could still be a senator.
That's something to aspire to!" How do Stu's parents

Lee 2

Lee sets out the problem with a concrete scenario.

explain this rule to this American-raised child? This scenario will become increasingly common, yet as the Constitution currently reads, only "natural-born" citizens may run for the offices of president and vice president. Neither these children nor the thousands of hardworking Americans who chose to make America their official homeland may aspire to the highest political position in the land. While the huddled masses may enter, it appears they must retain a second-class citizen ranking.

The "natural-born" stipulation regarding the presidency stems from the self-same meeting of minds that brought the American people the Electoral College. During the Constitutional Convention of 1787, the Congress formulated the regulatory measures associated with the office of the president. A letter sent from John Jay to George Washington during this period reads as follows:

> "Permit me to hint," Jay wrote, "whether it would not be wise and seasonable to provide a strong check to the admission of foreigners into the administration of our national government; and to declare expressly that the Commander in Chief of the American army shall not be given to, nor devolve on, any but a natural-born citizen."
> (Mathews A1)

Shortly thereafter, Article II, Section I, Clause V, of the Constitution declared that "No Person except a natural born Citizen, or a Citizen of the United States at the time of the Adoption of this Constitution, shall

Lee 3

be eligible to the Office of President." Jill A. Pryor
states in the *Yale Law Journal* that "some writers have
suggested that Jay was responding to rumors that
foreign princes might be asked to assume the
presidency" (881). Many cite disastrous examples of
foreign rule in the eighteenth century as the impetus
for the "natural-born" clause. For example, in 1772—
only fifteen years prior to the adoption of the
statute—Poland had been divided up by Prussia,
Russia, and Austria (Kasindorf). Perhaps an element of
self-preservation and not ethnocentrism led to the
questionable stipulation. Nonetheless, in the twenty-
first century this clause reeks of xenophobia.

> Lee gives
> the historical
> background
> of the
> "natural-born"
> restriction.

The Fourteenth Amendment clarified the difference
between "natural-born" and "native-born" citizens by
spelling out the citizenship status of children born to
American parents outside of the United States (Ginsberg
929). John McCain claimed that the Fourteenth
Amendment made him eligible to run for president in
2008. Even though McCain was allowed to run against
Barack Obama, legal experts including Professor Gabriel J.
Chin argued that McCain was technically ineligible
because the law clarifying citizenship was passed in
1937, a year after McCain's birth (Liptak).

The issue of McCain's eligibility would never have
come up if the natural-born clause had been struck from
the Constitution. I propose that the United States abolish
the natural-born clause and replace it with a stipulation
that allows naturalized citizens to run for president. This

> Lee states her
> proposal in this
> paragraph.

Lee 4

amendment would state that a candidate must have been naturalized and must have lived in residence in the United States for a period of at least twenty-five years. The present time is ideal for this change. This amendment could simultaneously honor the spirit of the Constitution, protect and ensure the interests of the United States, promote an international image of inclusiveness, and grant heretofore-withheld rights to thousands of legal and loyal United States citizens.

In our push for change, we must make clear the importance of this amendment. It would not provide special rights for would-be terrorists. To the contrary, it would fulfill the longtime promises of the nation. The United States claims to allow all people to blend into the great stew of citizenship. It has already suffered embarrassment and international cries of ethnic bias as a result of political moves such as Japanese American internment and the Guantanamo Bay detention center. This amendment can help mend the national image as every American takes one more step toward equality. Naturalized citizens have been contributing to the United States for centuries. Many nameless Mexican, Irish, and Asian Americans sweated and toiled to build the American railroads. The public has welcomed naturalized Americans such as Bob Hope, Albert Pujols, and Peter Jennings into their hearts and living rooms. Individuals such as German-born Henry Kissinger and Czechoslovakian-born Madeleine Albright have held high posts in the American government and have served as respected aides to its presidents. The amendment must

Lee gives examples of people who are qualified to become president yet are ineligible.

Lee 5

make clear that it is not about one man's celebrity. Approximately seven hundred foreign-born Americans have won the Medal of Honor and over sixty thousand proudly serve in the United States military today (Siskind 5). The "natural-born" clause must be removed to provide each of these people—over half a million naturalized in 2003 alone—with equal footing to those who were born into citizenship rather than working for it (United States).

Since the passing of the Bill of Rights, only seventeen amendments have been ratified. This process takes time and overwhelming congressional and statewide support. To alter the Constitution, a proposed amendment must pass with a two-thirds "super-majority" in both the House of Representatives and the Senate. In addition, the proposal must find favor in two-thirds (38) of state legislatures. In short, this task will not be easy. In order for this change to occur, a grassroots campaign must work to dispel misinformation regarding naturalized citizens and to force the hands of senators and representatives wishing to retain their congressional seats. We must take this proposal to ethnicity-specific political groups from both sides of the aisle, business organizations, and community activist groups. We must convince representatives that this issue matters. Only through raising voices and casting votes can the people enact change. Only then can every American child see the possibility for limitless achievement and equality. Only then can everyone find the same sense of pride in the possibility for true American diversity in the highest office in the land.

Lee explains the process of amending the Constitution and ends with a call for action.

Works Cited

Ginsberg, Gordon. "Citizenship: Expatriation: Distinction between Naturalized and Natural Born Citizens." *Michigan Law Review* 50 (1952): 926-29. *JSTOR*. Web. 6 Mar. 2010.

Kasindorf, Martin. "Should the Constitution Be Amended for Arnold?" *USA Today* 2 Dec. 2004. *LexisNexis Academic*. Web. 8 Mar. 2010.

Liptak, Adam. "A Hint of New Life to the McCain Birth Issue." *New York Times* 11 July 2008: A11. *LexisNexis Academic*. Web. 6 Mar. 2010.

Mathews, Joe. "Maybe Anyone Can Be President." *Los Angeles Times* 2 Feb. 2005: A1. *LexisNexis Academic*. Web. 6 Mar. 2010.

Pryor, Jill A. "The Natural Born Citizen Clause and Presidential Eligibility: An Approach for Resolving Two Hundred Years of Uncertainty." *Yale Law Journal* 97.5 (1988): 881-99. Print.

Siskind, Lawrence J. "Why Shouldn't Arnold Run?" *Recorder* 10 Dec. 2004: 5. *LexisNexis Academic*. Web. 10 Mar. 2010.

United States. Dept. of Commerce. Census Bureau. "The Fourth of July 2005." *Facts for Features*. US Dept. of Commerce, 27 June 2005. Web. 17 Mar. 2010.

To hear audio commentary on this piece of writing, visit this page of the eText at **www.mycomplab.com**.

PART 3

Writing in the Disciplines

You **can learn more and do more** with MyCompLab and with the eText version of *The Penguin Handbook*. To find resources in MyCompLab that will help you successfully complete assignments in other disciplines and in your business writing, go to

Resources

Writing

> **Writing Samples: Technical and Workplace**
>
> Memos | E-mails | Career Correspondence | Proposals | Abstracts | Reports | Letters | Instructions and Procedures | Descriptions and Definitions | Technical Writing

Review within each topic, then complete the Exercises and click on the Gradebook to measure your progress.

In the **eText version** of *The Penguin Handbook*, you will also find audio commentary provided by Lester Faigley for the sample student work in this Part.

11 | Write About Literature and the Humanities

QUICK_TAKE_

- Know the purposes and genres of disciplines in the humanities (see below)
- Know the types of evidence required in humanities disciplines (see p. 126)
- Analyze literature and develop an interpretation (see p. 128)
- Write a literary analysis (see p. 130)
- Write a film analysis (see p. 138)

11a What Are the Humanities?

Researchers and writers in the humanities write to explore, explain, and interpret aspects of the human experience. Most of this chapter deals with writing about literature and film, beginning with Section 11c, but the general approach of analyzing and interpreting texts and works of arts is shared across humanities and fine arts disciplines. The texts you read in the humanities may include novels, poems, plays, philosophical treatises, historical documents, paintings, or films to be analyzed and interpreted as primary sources. Researchers and writers in the humanities also rely on secondary sources, including books and articles that present the interpretations of others.

The groupings can vary from one institution to another, but the chart on page 126 shows the most common fields and majors within the humanities and fine arts. Note, however, that there is significant overlap and sharing of knowledge among various fields. For example, archaeology is often housed in humanities programs, yet the study of ancient civilizations combines many of the scientific methods used in natural sciences like paleontology.

Ask your instructor for advice and for examples of the writing genres common in your field. Some genres, such as case studies, vary considerably from discipline to discipline, so locate an example from your field.

DISCIPLINES, PURPOSES, AND GENRES				
Discipline	Common fields or majors	Purposes	Genres	Preferred documentation style
Fine Arts	Theater, dance, studio art, art history, music	Creation of art-work; history and reception of art	Essay, critique, review, visual analysis, iconography, research paper, grant proposal, creative writing	MLA and CMS (see Ch. 26 and 28)
Humanities	Literature, history, classics, languages, philosophy, education	Interpreting, appreciating, and imagining the human experience	Essay, research paper, abstract, case study, grant proposal, oral history, ethnography	Primarily MLA, but also APA and CMS (see Chs. 26, 27, and 28)

11b What Counts as Evidence in the Humanities?

What counts as acceptable evidence to make a point or build an argument in one field may be less persuasive to experts in a different field. The types of evidence noted below are those that carry the most weight in the humanities.

Look for key words and phrases in the assignment that signal what you should use as evidence (see Section 2a for a list of key words in assignments). For example, if in an American history class you are asked to

FIELDS OF STUDY AND TYPES OF EVIDENCE										
Field	Controlled experimental data	Non-participatory observation	Participatory observation	Material data (fossil record, human artifacts, material properties)	Historical records (letters, maps)	Literary texts	Man-made artifacts: buildings, paintings	Pre-existing, gathered statistics	Interviews, surveys	Articles by other experts
Archaeology				✓	✓	✓	✓			✓
Literature					✓	✓				✓
Classics					✓	✓	✓			✓
History	✓				✓	✓	✓	✓	✓	✓
Fine Arts		✓	✓		✓	✓	✓			✓

describe with examples a trend in the United States from 1850 to 1900, you will need to use the *ProQuest Historical Newspapers*, which includes the *New York Times* from 1851 onward with an index (see Section 20b for more on using databases). If you have any doubts about the kind of evidence to use, you should always check with your instructor.

Experts in the various disciplines look for different kinds of evidence because they are trying to solve different problems. For example, here are questions the experts in five fields might ask in beginning to explore the topic of global climate change.

Field	Possible questions
History	What percentage of recorded famines might be attributable in part to global climate change?
Classics	What ancient texts describe possible effects of global climate change, and what can these texts tell us about humans' response to such change?
Literature	How do literary descriptions of climate-related catastrophes (floods, drought, hurricanes) change over time?
Fine Arts	How might a performance piece utilizing dance and music demonstrate the impact of global climate change on human beings?
Archaeology	What effect did global climate change have on ancient human population and migration patterns?

11c Become a Critical Reader of Literature

Reading literature requires a set of practices different from those you might use while reading the Sunday paper or a magazine article. Think of yourself as an active critical observer. Carry on a dialogue with the text using marginal notes. Keeping a record of your reading will force you to engage with a text; being an active reader is practice toward being a thoughtful reader. And marginal comments will be your best resource to use in generating a paper topic.

As you read make notes, using the following list as a guide.

- Study the plot of the story. Determine how the events in the story relate to each other. What is the conflict and how is it resolved?
- Examine the principal characters in the story. What are their most defining characteristics? Are there minor characters? What purpose do they serve?
- Describe the setting of the story. What role does it play?

- Identify the point of view—the perspective from which the story is told. Does a major character relay the events? Does a minor character? Or a fly on the wall?
- Look for shifts in the tone, style, and language of the story.
- Look for symbols, imagery, and interesting metaphors. Are sounds, images, or motifs repeated? What role do they play?
- Identify the story's central theme or main idea. Consider the title of the story and how the main characters fit the theme.

When reading poetry also pay attention to the following.

- Identify the rhyme scheme. For example, when the first and third lines rhyme and the second and fourth do, the rhyme scheme is *abab*.
- Listen to the meter. The most common meter in English is *iambic*, where an unstressed syllable is followed by a stressed syllable (for example, "To swell the gourd, and plump the hazel shells," from John Keats, "To Autumn").
- Listen for alliteration, the repetition of initial consonant sounds (for example, *M*arch *m*adness, *r*oad *r*age, *W*orld *W*ide *W*eb).
- Note the stanza, the unit of poetry. The shortest stanza is the two-line couplet.

11d Develop an Interpretation

Assignments for English classes tend to be more open-ended than writing assignments in other disciplines so you can focus on an aspect of the text that interests you. Develop an original idea. Ideally your audience will see the text differently after reading your interpretation.

Opinion versus interpretation

Papers about literature are often called *critical analyses*. Don't let the term trip you up. *Critical* in this sense doesn't mean judgmental. The fact is, your understanding of the text is much more interesting to a reader than whether you like it or not. Avoid making an argument about your opinion of a text unless the assignment specifically asks for one. Instead, develop an interpretation that illuminates some aspect of the text.

Exercise 11.1 Decide whether the following statements about works of literature are interpretation or opinion.

1. Remarque's *All Quiet on the Western Front* is critical of the romanticization of war, patriotism, and nationalism.

2. *Jazz*, by Toni Morrison, is hard to understand.
3. The character Victor Frankenstein in Mary Shelley's *Frankenstein* is cowardly.
4. In *Dubliners*, James Joyce brings the reader's attention to everyday events and objects.
5. Jeanette Winterson's novel *Oranges Are Not the Only Fruit* is autobiographical.

Develop your thesis

Ask *what*, *how*, and *why* questions. These questions will lead you from observation, to exploration, to an interpretation.

Observation: What's going on in the text?

What did you observe in the text that was unexpected, odd, powerful, or central? What questions did you ask? Wonderful interpretations frequently evolve from a question or confusion about the text.

> Why does the concluding scene of *Pride and Prejudice* feature the Gardiners, two secondary characters?

Although you won't have an interpretation yet, answering *why* questions will help you narrow your focus to a potentially fruitful topic for interpretation.

Exploration: How does the text do what it's doing?

The answer to this question may consider technical, stylistic, or thematic aspects of the text. At this point you'll begin to develop the first stages of your interpretation.

> How does Austen feature the Gardiners in the last scene of *Pride and Prejudice*? Throughout the novel Austen shows us strained or broken marriages, but the Gardiners are an exception. She presents them as a well-matched, well-adjusted couple.

Analysis and interpretation: Why does the text do what it's doing?

Consider to what end or for what purpose the text functions as it does. What are the ultimate implications of this feature of the text? Frequently answers will fall into one of the following lines of inquiry.

- It advances or complicates a major theme of the text.
- It engages in commentary about larger political, social, philosophical, or literary issues of the author's day.
- It reflects the influence of another writer or text.
- It advances the plot or adds depth to a character.
- It's attempting to be technically innovative. It highlights a capability or limitation in the author's choice of theme, genre, structure, stylistic elements, or narrative technique.

Why does the end of *Pride and Prejudice* feature secondary characters, the Gardiners? The Gardiners exemplify successful marriage. By ending the novel with them, Austen lends a note of hope for Elizabeth and Darcy's union. The novel, then, is not a condemnation of marriage as an institution but of the social forces that promote bad matches. We can analyze Austen's characterization of the Gardiners to better understand the kind of marriage making she wants to advocate.

Exercise 11.2 Think about a work of fiction (novel, short story, graphic novel, poem) you've read recently or a film you've seen recently and write a *what* (observation), *how* (exploration), and *why* (analysis) question for it.

WRITING SMART

Library database resources for writing about literature

Check your library's database page for these valuable resources. Your library should have one or more available.

- **Literature Online** (LION) is a fully searchable library of over 250,000 full-text works of English and American literature.
- **Literature Resource Center** provides access to biographies, bibliographies, and critical analyses of authors from every age and literary discipline, including more than 90,000 novelists, poets, essayists, journalists, and other writers.
- **MLA International Bibliography** indexes critical materials on literature, criticism, drama, languages, linguistics, and folklore.
- **Contemporary Literary Criticism** offers significant published criticism on the works of novelists, poets, playwrights, short story writers, and other creative writers now living or who died after December 31, 1959.
- **Oxford English Dictionary** records the history of a word's meaning, tracking where it first appeared and how its definition has changed through the years.

11e   Write a Literary Analysis

Keep your audience in mind when writing a literary analysis. Those who have already read the work will be bored by plot summary. Quote or paraphrase passages that advance your interpretation. Never use the text as evidence without analyzing it. Your analysis should explain how the text you've chosen illustrates your interpretation.

1 Before you write

Read and analyze closely
- Go through your text line by line, annotating your responses.
- Develop a thesis for your interpretation that might start with a question and turn into a claim.
- When you have a thesis, reread the text to look for evidence.

2 Write an introduction

Engage your reader
- Raise what is at stake in your literary text. Many literary texts speak to large issues, whether about art or about life. What issues does your text raise?

3 Organize and write the body of your paper

Use literary concepts to examine your text
- Take into account literary concepts such as character, setting, theme, motif, symbol, point of view, or imagery, to express your ideas.
- Your analysis will likely answer such questions as who are the characters, what is the setting and what role does it play, what are themes or motifs in the text, from what point of view is the work told, what language choices are made, and what is the significance of the title?

Support your interpretation
- Cite the precise passages in the text that support your interpretation.
- Attribute every direct quotation and explain its significance.
- If your instructor asks you to use secondary sources, either literary criticism or biographical information about the author, decide where these sources are relevant.

4 Write a conclusion

End with something other than a summary
- Draw larger implications from your analysis.
- End with a vivid example from the text.

5 | Revise, revise, revise

Evaluate your draft

- Make sure your analysis meets the requirements of the assignment.
- Make sure your thesis is specific and significant. If you identify a pattern but say nothing about why it is important, your reader will ask "So what?" What does the pattern contribute to an overall interpretation?
- Make sure your evidence and examples are relevant to your thesis. Explain the significance of the evidence for your thesis.
- When you have finished revising, edit and proofread carefully.

Incorporating critical strategies

Your instructor might ask you to use particular critical strategies, such as to consider a literary work from a feminist approach. Ask your instructor to recommend major critical books and articles that deal with your topic. Then consider ways you can advance or revise the conversation about your topic. Does your interpretation of the text advance or complicate an existing critical perspective? Is there a scene or an aspect of the text that the critics don't consider but should? By developing original responses to these questions, you enter the critical conversation.

STAYING ON TRACK

Use the literary present tense

The disciplinary convention in English is to employ the **literary present tense**. The literary present tense requires the use of present tense when analyzing any literary text such as a poem, a play, a work of fiction, an essay, or a sermon. Also use the present tense when discussing literary criticism.

Incorrect	In *Song of Myself* Walt Whitman tempered his exuberant language with undercurrents of doubt about whether language could do all he asked of it.
Correct	In *Song of Myself* Walt Whitman tempers his exuberant language with undercurrents of doubt about whether language can do all he asks of it.

However, you should employ the past tense when discussing literary history. The author's life, the creation of the text, the text's publication,

(*continued on next page*)

STAYING ON TRACK (continued)

and the critical reception of the text all exist outside the work itself and require the past tense. The following passage uses the past tense to discuss the publication history and critical reception of *Leaves of Grass*.

Correct   Beyond doubting whether his audience would understand the spirit of his verse, Whitman worried that *Leaves of Grass* would never reach an audience at all. He was so concerned, in fact, that he published reviews of the book under false names to drum up publicity.

11f Sample Literary Analysis

The following student paper responds to the assignment "Analyze how W. B. Yeats's poem 'A Prayer for My Daughter' uses poetic language to describe a father's ambitions for his child's future. What does the speaker's 'prayer' tell us about his own conceptions of femininity?"

Samuel 1   Include your last name and page number as the header on each page.

Renee Samuel

Professor Reitz

Literature and Culture

4 April 2010

Yeats's Conception of Womanhood   Include name, instructor, course number, and date.

in "A Prayer for My Daughter"

Whether or not they ever speak their hopes out loud, parents dream of brilliant futures for their children: high school valedictorian? law school? the ballet? the White House? Although these dreams are usually well-intentioned, often a parent's definition of   Center the title. Italicize words that would be italicized in the text.

his or her child's "brilliant future" is filtered through that parent's own desires, fears, and prejudices. The speaker in W. B. Yeats's 1919 poem "A Prayer for My Daughter" is a father who at first seems to have his

Samuel 2

daughter's best interests at heart. As his child sleeps
in her cradle, immune to a raging storm outside, the
speaker "walk[s] and pray[s] for this young child"
for hours on end (9). But despite such protective
behavior, the father's prayers contain old-fashioned and
conservative notions about femininity. By describing
the kind of woman he hopes his daughter will one
day become, Yeats's speaker also gives the reader a
definition of his "perfect woman." By analyzing this
definition, we learn more about how this father's past
has influenced his ideas about women than we do
about his concern for his daughter's future.

This father's first prayer for his daughter concerns
ideal beauty. He prays, "May she be granted beauty and
yet not / Beauty to make a stranger's eye distraught, / Or
hers before a looking glass" (17-19). The speaker wants
his daughter to be beautiful, but not *too* beautiful,
because "being . . . beautiful overmuch" might allow
her to slide by on her beauty and "consider beauty a
sufficient end" (20-21). The father fears that this vanity
will lead to other life problems: she will "lose natural
kindness," miss out on "heart-revealing intimacy," and
worst of all, "never find a friend" (12-24).

By "a friend" the speaker means a husband, and
Yeats makes this clear in the next stanza when the
speaker declares that he wants his less-than-beautiful
daughter "chiefly learned" in the art of "courtesy" (33),
because "Hearts are not had as a gift but hearts are
earned / By those that are not entirely beautiful"
(34-35). According to the speaker, men who have been

*Thesis statement
appears at end of
first paragraph.*

*The interpretation
is supported by
quotations from
the poem.*

*Line numbers
are given in
parentheses for
each quotation
from the poem.*

Samuel 3

seduced by and "played the fool" for "beauty's very self"
(37) will eventually prefer a woman with "glad kindness"
instead of "charm" (40). The father also prays that his
daughter will not be too intellectual or opinionated,
because such women are unattractive and "choked with
hate" (52). He states that "Intellectual hatred is the
worst" (57) and prays that his daughter will grow up to
"think opinions are accursed" (58). In this way he will
avoid becoming like a woman her father once knew, who

> Because of her opinionated mind
> Barter[ed] that horn and every good
> By quiet natures understood
> For an old bellows full of an angry wind? (61-64)

If his daughter follows this definition of ideal
womanhood (ideal women are courteous rather than
too beautiful, and avoid the bitterness caused by
intellect and opinion), this father believes she will
marry well, live in "a house / where all's accustomed,
ceremonious" (73-74) and "be happy" (72).

This father's prayer for his daughter is not all bad;
surprisingly, this poem's speaker idolizes non-perfect
women and believes that true love should come from
courtesy and kindness rather than just lust. As Elizabeth
Cullingford argues, "It is refreshing to be offered the
'not-entirely-beautiful' woman as an ideal. . . . Pleasing,
too, is the notion of love as a gradual development rather
than a thunderbolt" (136). However, behind this open-
mindedness is anger over how he was treated by
beautiful, opinionated women in his past, and anxiety

A secondary source is introduced to supply a context for the interpretation.

Samuel 4

over the dying out of old traditions. This anger and anxiety leads to some sexist ideas about femininity.

For most of his early life, Yeats was in love with Maud Gonne, a beautiful, smart, opinionated, and political woman who rejected his affection. However, Yeats felt that she used her beauty to manipulate him into writing beautiful poetry about her. In 1917, Yeats finally married a less beautiful, but also less independent woman: Georglie Hyde-Lees. When the poem's speaker prays that his daughter will be "not entirely beautiful," he is also wishing that she will be more gentle and kind, and less opinionated, than Maud Gonne with her "opinionated mind" and "angry wind" (61, 64). Here we see the father's protective sexism: he would selfishly prefer a submissive daughter over a smart one who would remind him of the "loveliest woman born" (57) for whom he once "played the fool" (36).

Furthermore, this kind of daughter will be less likely to "dance to [the] frenzied drum" (15) of modern womanhood. Instead, she will carry on old traditions, and "live like some green laurel / Rooted in one dear perpetual place" (47-48). Here, the speaker shows his desire to keep his daughter protected against the modern violence of the twentieth century (which Yeats symbolizes through images of "howling," "roof-leveling" storms and "flooded," "murderous" seas) by hiding her away in past traditions. The father prays that his daughter will marry into a family rooted in old aristocratic tradition, and he chooses this "hypothetical son-in-law" not because he is

Samuel 5

a good match for his daughter, but "because of his aristocratic social status and ownership of landed property" (Cullingford 138). The father is so anxious about the future that he prays his daughter will give up her individual identity and free will to become an "innocent," "beautiful" ambassador of tradition (Cullingford 76).

If the author of a secondary source is not mentioned, include the author's last name and page number in the in-text citation.

Even though the speaker in "A Prayer for My Daughter" selfishly projects his own past onto his daughter's future, Yeats does not seem to want us to think we are hearing the prayer of an unreliable narrator. Although Yeats believed in gender equality, this poem "marks a regression in Yeats's acceptance of changing gender roles" (Cullingford 136). Perhaps the point, though, is just this: When it comes to their children's futures, even open-minded parents sometimes become conservative and reactionary.

Samuel 6

Center heading on new page.

Works Cited

Secondary source

Cullingford, Elizabeth. *Gender and Sexuality in Yeats's Love Poetry*. Syracuse: Syracuse UP, 1996. Print.

Poem

Yeats, W. B. "A Prayer for My Daughter." *The Collected Poems of W. B. Yeats*. Ed. Richard J. Finneran. New York: Collier, 1989. Print.

To hear audio commentary on this piece of writing, visit this page of the eText at **www.mycomplab.com**.

11g Write a Film Analysis

When you write an analysis of a film, you view with a critical eye and develop an interpretation just as you would in writing about a print text. The goal is to interpret the film and support that interpretation with evidence. More simply, a film analysis makes a discovery about a film that you share with your readers. The steps you would take to develop your thesis about a film—observation, exploration, and interpretation—are similar to those for a print text (see 11d).

Ask questions and take notes in order to do a close, careful reading of a film. After a first viewing, write down your impressions and questions. Then be ready to review the film while taking notes and jotting down anything that is confusing or interesting. Include details about scenes—describing setting, colors, camera angles, or any other visual or stylistic elements—along with key quotes.

Analyzing Text and Context

An analysis of a film may be concerned with either the text or the context, but it often examines both. Textual analysis focuses on the features of the text—the words and evidence in speech, the images and patterns in the pictures, and so on. For a textual analysis, ask

- What is the medium? film, television, or Web short? What is the genre? a documentary? an independent drama? a science fiction blockbuster?
- What is the subject?
- If you are analyzing a documentary film, what are the main ideas?
- If you are analyzing a fictional film, what is the plot and who are the characters?
- How is the film organized?
- What kind of style does the filmmaker use? Formal or informal, satirical or humorous? Are any metaphors used?

Contextual analysis reconstructs the cultural environment, or context, that existed when a particular film was made, and then depends on that recreation to produce clues about persuasive tactics and appeals. For a contextual analysis, ask

- Who is the filmmaker? What other films has she made? Who does she borrow from or quote? What motivates her to address this issue or subject?
- Who is the audience? Who are the viewers the filmmaker is addressing?

- What is the other films are in this genre? When did the film appear? Why did it appear at that particular moment? Who or what might this film be responding to?

Sample Film Analysis

The following excerpt is from an essay written by a student in a first-year writing course. Her essay responds to an assignment prompt to focus closely on an aspect of a film and reflect on her personal response to that element of the film while offering a close reading. The essay follows the MLA documentation guidelines in Chapter 26.

Koenig 1

Anna Koenig

Professor Callahan

English 1000

13 October 2010

The Triumph of Technology in Avatar

In addition to being a huge commercial success, *Avatar* represents a sophisticated technical achievement in the history of film. The rich detail and newness of the viewing experience excited the first audiences. The dazzling special effects produce a fully realized place with beautiful, luminous creatures and plant life. *Avatar* manages to thrill audiences with powerful visuals, even though the screenplay and plot often feel clunky and familiar. It is on one level a movie about using cutting-edge technology to get back to an unspoiled, more natural environment. But the aspect of the film that is most important and has the most long-term impact is its revolutionary uses of technology.

Annotations:

Include name, instructor, course number, and date.

Center the title. Italicize words that would be italicized in the text.

Introductory paragraph sets out focus of essay on specific aspect of film.

Thesis statement appears at end of first paragraph.

Koenig 2

Use the present tense to analyze the film.

What the filmmakers and their technology achieve in the form of beautiful, complex images is what is most engaging about *Avatar*. The film's use of special effects prompts viewers to think about how technology shapes our view of reality The use of groundbreaking 3-D technology helps viewers admire and feel a part of the Na'vi's world. The effects are not used to propel creatures out of the screen and into viewers' laps. Instead the subtler 3-D experience allows viewers to feel closer to the creatures of Pandora. Viewers are invited to experience wonder.

Quotation from film. Include the quoted performer in the Works Cited entry.

"Try to see the forest through her eyes," Sigourney Weaver's character says. By connecting with *Avatar* in 3-D glasses we are a little like the characters in the film who plug in to machines to gain access to an alien world.

Focus on particular details and images to illustrate main point.

The colorful and alien landscapes of Pandora are filled with carefully constructed plants and animals that add to the movie magic. In interviews director James Cameron explains how he took pains to create a fully realized world and name "every plant, every creature, in Latin and in the Na'vi language" ("James Cameron").

Quotation from source without an author. Title given in parenthetical citation.

He hired scientists and experts including a botanist, ethnomusicologist, and astrophysicist along with other specialists to create a realistic culture and ecosystem for the film.

Koenig 3

Works Cited

Avatar. Dir. James Cameron. Perf. Sigourney Weaver.

20th Century Fox, 2010. DVD

"James Cameron, A King with a Soft Touch?" *National*

Public Radio. Natl. Public Radio, 18 Dec. 2009.

Web. 8 Oct. 2010.

Center heading
on new page.

Film

Article found
on the Web

To hear audio commentary on this piece of writing, visit this page of the eText at **www.mycomplab.com**.

12 | Write in the Sciences and Social Sciences

QUICK*TAKE*

- Know the types of evidence required in science and social science disciplines (see p. 144)
- Learn to write an observation (see p. 146)
- Learn to write a case study (see p. 148)
- Learn to write a lab report in the sciences (see p. 150)

12a What Are the Sciences and Social Sciences?

In the sciences and social sciences—as in any discipline—good writing is likely to exhibit some standard qualities: it will be clear, concise, and logical, supplying appropriate evidence in sufficient amounts to persuade the audience. But because the individual disciplines have different purposes, they use different vocabularies, formats, and evidence to make and support claims. Researchers and writers in the sciences and social sciences write to explain or record their research, documenting the steps, methods, and results for experiments or observations.

Social sciences and *sciences* are broad cover terms for an array of specific fields. Social sciences include fields like psychology, government, sociology, and anthropology, but the many fields in education and communication also are often classified as social sciences. At the core of the sciences are fields like physics, mathematics, biology, astronomy, chemistry, and geology, but engineering, computer science, nursing, medicine, and other health fields are often grouped with the sciences. With so many different fields involved, it's no wonder that a common genre like a lab report is written in many different formats.

	DISCIPLINES, PURPOSES, AND GENRES			
Discipline	Common fields or majors	Purposes	Genres	Preferred documentation style
Education	Curriculum and instruction, education administration	Training teachers and developing effective teaching methods	Lesson plan, literature review, abstract, case study, grant proposal	APA (see Ch. 27)

(*continued on next page*)

		DISCIPLINES, PURPOSES, AND GENRES		
Discipline	**Common fields or majors**	**Purposes**	**Genres**	**Preferred documentation style**
Media/ communications	Journalism, radio/television /film studies, advertising, information management	Informing and entertaining the public, promoting commerce, and effecting the exchange of information	Article, analysis, advertising, scripts, screenplays	APA and CMS (see Chs. 27 and 28)
Social Sciences	Psychology, sociology, anthropology, geography, social work, government, human ecology	Exploring human behavior in individuals and groups—both in the past and the present—with a strong desire to learn to predict human behavior in the future	Literature review, abstract, case study, oral history, grant proposal, poster presentation	Primarily APA (see Ch. 27)
Natural Sciences	Physics, math, astronomy, biology (botany, zoology, marine science), geology, ecology, chemistry	The study of living things, inanimate matter, systems, and processes	Literature review, lab report, abstract, grant proposal, poster presentation	APA and CSE (see Chs. 27 and 29); some sciences, like chemistry and physics, have their own style guides
Engineering	Civil, industrial, chemical, petroleum, aerospace, biomedical, mechanical, electrical	Practical application of science and technology to improve human civilization	Case study, design report, progress report, lab report, proposal	Primarily CSE and APA (see Chs. 29 and 27)
Health Sciences	Nursing, pharmacy, kinesiology, premed, veterinary medicine	Improving health and well-being	Lab report, case study, poster presentation	APA and CSE
Computer Science and Technology	Information management, technical communications, computer engineering	Building, maintaining, and optimizing electronic communications systems and databases	User manuals, support documentation, technical reports, journal articles	CSE and IEEE (Institute of Electrical and Electronics Engineers)

Exercise 12.1 Look at some journals or textbooks that are used frequently in your field of study. Do you notice any common elements of format, style, or language? Do some journals follow a style that differs from others in the field? Why do you think this is? Write out a list of the elements that define writing in your field.

12b What Counts as Evidence in the Sciences and Social Sciences?

Experts in most fields ask particular kinds of questions that require certain types of evidence. Experts in the various disciplines look for different kinds of evidence because they are trying to solve different problems. For example, here are questions the experts in ten fields might ask in beginning to explore the topic of global climate change.

Field	Possible questions
Geography	What constitutes a "normal" range of global climate conditions?
Psychology	How has the "clean energy" movement changed individuals' norms regarding fossil fuels?
Sociology	How does a community's assumptions about socioeconomic values affect its response to the threat of global climate change?
Economics	What burdens do carbon dioxide emissions controls impose on large businesses versus small businesses?
Geology	What do worldwide coal deposits tell us about the global Paleolithic climate?
Astronomy	What can humans' impact on earth's atmosphere and climate teach us about making other planets habitable?
Biology	Is recent deforestation responsible for an increase in CO_2 in the earth's atmosphere?
Chemistry	To what extent has the reduced production of chlorofluorocarbons "solved" the problem of ozone depletion?
Engineering	How can engineers protect coastal urban areas from the stronger hurricanes associated with global warming?
Government	How might rising sea levels affect the stability of governments in coastal third-world nations?

To answer questions like these, the different fields rely on different kinds of evidence, as shown in the chart below.

FIELDS OF STUDY AND TYPES OF EVIDENCE

Field	Controlled experimental data	Non-participatory observation	Participatory observation	Material data (fossil record, human artifacts, material properties)	Historical records (letters, maps)	Man-made artifacts: buildings, paintings	Pre-existing, gathered statistics	Interviews, surveys	Articles by other experts
Government		✓			✓		✓	✓	✓
Psychology	✓	✓	✓	✓	✓		✓	✓	✓
Sociology		✓	✓		✓		✓	✓	✓
Economics		✓			✓		✓	✓	✓
Geography	✓		✓	✓	✓		✓		✓
Astronomy	✓	✓		✓	✓		✓		✓
Chemistry	✓			✓			✓		✓
Biology	✓	✓		✓			✓		✓
Engineering	✓	✓	✓	✓		✓	✓		✓

12c   Write an Observation

Observations are common in the sciences and in the social sciences. Observations begin as notes taken firsthand by the writer as he or she observes an event, phenomenon, or place and should include as many relevant and specific details as possible.

Elements of an observation

Title	Include a precise title. **EXAMPLE** Doppler Profile of the Structure of Tornadoes Near Attica, Kansas, on 12 May 2004
Description and context	Be specific about what or whom you are observing. How did you limit your site or subject? What background information do readers need? How will a deeper understanding of your subject help people? **EXAMPLE** Eleven mixed-breed puppies six weeks old were observed during feeding and play periods over a five-week period. Each puppy's tendency to exhibit alpha- or omega-dog behaviors changed relatively little over this period.
Record of observations	Report what you observed in some logical order: chronologically, from most obvious features to least obvious, or some other pattern. **EXAMPLE** On the second day of observation, between 8:00–11:00 a.m., a significantly higher number of migratory birds were seen in the feeding area.
Conclusion or summary	Give your readers a framework in which to understand your observations. What conclusions can you draw from them? What questions are left unanswered? **EXAMPLE** It appears that the toddlers observed were often aware of social expectations even when they were unable to meet those expectations in their own behavior. This indicates that an awareness of norms probably develops independently from an individual's ability to control impulsive behavior.

What you need to do

- Carry a notebook and make extensive field notes. Provide as much information as possible about the situation in which your observations occurred.
- Record in your notebook exactly when you arrived and left, where you were, and exactly what you saw and heard.
- Analyze your observations before you write about them. Identify patterns, and organize your report according to those patterns.

Sample observation

Animal Activity in Barton Springs Pool

from 15 April to 22 April 2010

Barton Springs Pool is a 225-meter-long, natural spring-fed pool in a limestone creek bed in Austin, Texas. It is both a wildlife habitat and a busy hub of human activity. Because of the constant flow from the springs, the water temperature is constant at 68°F (20°C), allowing swimmers to use the pool year around.

Specific times, weather conditions, numbers of individual species, and behaviors are recorded.

My first observation was on 15 April from 1:45–4:00 p.m. on a warm sunny day with the air temperature at 74°F (23°C). I used a mask and snorkel to observe below the water. It was remarkable how oblivious people and wildlife were of each other. While from forty to fifty-five Austinites splashed on the surface, many fish (mostly smallmouth bass with two large channel catfish on the bottom) swam below them, and large numbers of crayfish crept along the rocky portion of the pool's bottom. Eight small turtles (red-eared sliders) alternately swam at the surface or dove below near the dam at the deep end. Twelve endangered Barton Springs salamanders (Eurycea sosorum), ranging in color from bright orange to paler yellow, were active by the larger spring at the center of the pool.

At the times when humans are not present or nearly absent, animal activity noticeably increases. From the side of the pool on 16 April (clear, 72°) from 7:25 p.m. until closing at 8 p.m., I observed smallmouth bass schooling near the dam and feeding on mosquitoes and mayflies. Nine ducks (seven lesser scaup and two mallards) landed on the pool at 7:40 p.m. and remained when I left. (Lesser scaup migrate to the area in large numbers in the winter; the mallards are likely domesticated ducks.) A pair of wood ducks (male and female) were also on the cliff above the shallow end.

To hear audio commentary on this piece of writing, visit this page of the eText at **www.mycomplab.com.**

12d Write a Case Study

Case studies are used in a wide range of fields such as nursing, psychology, business, and anthropology. Their exact structure can vary from discipline to discipline, so be sure to get instructions from your professor. Case studies are narrow in focus. Rather than giving the "big picture" about phenomena, they provide a rich, detailed portrait of a specific event or subject.

Elements of a case study

Introduction	Explain the purpose of your study and how or why you selected your subject. Use language appropriate to your discipline, and specify the boundaries of your study.
Methodology	Explain the theories or formal process that guided your observations and analysis during the study. **EXAMPLE** A face-to-face survey methodology was used, where interviewers asked respondents a set of prepared questions and noted answers on the survey sheet.
Observations	Describe the "case" of the subject under study by writing a narrative, utilizing interviews, research, and other data to provide as much detail and specificity as possible. **EXAMPLE** The subject reported a lengthy history of heart trouble, beginning at age 37, involving multiple trips to the emergency room.
Discussion	Explain how the variables in your case might interact. Don't generalize from your case to a larger context; stay within the limits of what you have observed.
Conclusion	What does all this information add up to? What is implied, suggested, or proven by your observations? What new questions arise?
References	Using the appropriate format, cite all the outside sources you have used. (See Chapter 27 for APA documentation and Chapter 29 for CSE documentation.)

What you need to do

- Understand the specific elements of your assignment. Ask your instructor if you aren't sure about the focus, context, or structure your case study should have.
- Use careful observation and precise, detailed description to provide a complex picture with a narrow focus.
- Write your observations in the form of a narrative, placing yourself in the background (avoid using *I* or *me*).
- Analyze your findings and interpret their possible meanings, but draw your conclusions from the observed facts.

Sample case study

Underage Drinking Prevention Programs

in the Radisson School District

INTRODUCTION

This study examines the effect of Smith and Bingham's drinking-prevention curriculum on drinking rates in the Radisson School District, 2000-2006. Prior to 2002, the Radisson School District offered no formal drinking-prevention education. In 2000, as part of a state initiative, the district proposed several underage drinking education curricula for possible adoption. After substantial debate and input from parents, Smith and Bingham's curriculum was chosen for implementation in ninth through twelfth grades. This study tracks student drinking rates from 2000 to 2006, and compares the results after introduction of the curriculum to district rates prior to implementation.

DISCUSSION

The data from this study showed no correlation between the curriculum and student drinking rates. Drinking rates remained unchanged before, during, and after the implementation of the curriculum. Additionally, survey data indicate that levels of student drinking remained constant as well. Therefore, in this case, it cannot be said that Smith and Bingham's curriculum had any measurable effect on changing students' drinking behavior.

CONCLUSION

In terms of reducing student drinking, Smith and Bingham's curriculum does not appear to be any more effective than no drinking-prevention education at all. Since no measurable results were obtained, the strong administrative support for the curriculum in the school district cannot be attributed to its success. A possible explanation for that support may be the approval expressed by parents who preferred it to the other curricula proposed. Further studies might usefully expand the scope of this study and compare multiple school districts' use of Smith and Bingham's curriculum to identify variables that might alter its effectiveness.

Some disciplines require title pages. See page 000 for an example of an APA title page.

The introduction identifies both the problem and the particular subject of the case study.

The conclusion sums up what has been observed. Many case studies do not give definitive answers but rather raise further questions to explore.

To hear audio commentary on this piece of writing, visit this page of the eText at **www.mycomplab.com.**

12e Write a Lab Report in the Sciences

Lab reports follow a strict structure, enabling specialists in a given field to assess quickly the experimental methods and findings in any report. Though the basic elements are usually the same, details of formatting can vary among disciplines in the sciences. Check with your instructor for the specific elements needed in your report.

Elements of a lab report

Title	The title of a lab report should state exactly what was tested, using language specific to the field.
Abstract	The abstract briefly states the questions and the findings in the report.
Introduction	The introduction gives the full context of the problem, defining the hypothesis being tested.
Methods	Describe the materials used, as well as the method of investigation. Your methods and procedure sections should be specific enough to allow another researcher to replicate your experiment. EXAMPLE A double-blind structure was used so the investigators did not know which subjects received placebos.
Procedure	Step by step, narrate exactly what you did and what happened. In most fields, you will use the passive voice to avoid distracting the reader with references to yourself. EXAMPLE The salts were dissolved in distilled water to achieve a salinity level of 3%.
Results	State the outcomes you obtained, providing well-labeled charts and graphics as needed. EXAMPLE The tempered glass plates resisted fracture 2.3 times better than the standard glass plates.
Discussion	State why you think you got the results you did, using your results to explain. If there were anomalies in your data, note them as well. EXAMPLE Since all of the plants grew normally, it appears that the high acidity levels in the soil were not harmful to their early development. However, the low fruit yields indicate that high acidity is detrimental to reproduction.

Conclusion	Briefly, what was learned from this experiment? What still needs to be investigated?
References	Using the appropriate format, cite all the outside sources you have used. (See Chapter 27 for pyschology lab reports and Chapter 29 for science lab reports.)

What you need to do

- Understand the question you are researching and the process you will use before you begin. Ask your instructor if you need clarification.
- Take thorough notes at each step of your process. You may be asked to keep a lab notebook with a specific format for recording data. Review your notes before you begin drafting your report.
- Don't get ahead of yourself. Keep methods, procedure, discussion, and conclusion sections separate. Remember that other scientists will look at specific sections of your report expecting to find certain kinds of information. If that information isn't where they expect it to be, your report will not make sense.
- Write your abstract last. Writing all the other sections of the report first will give you a much clearer picture of your findings.

Sample lab report

Wave interference in visible light using

the double-slit method

Abstract

Filtered light was projected through one slit in a piece of cardboard, producing a single bar of light, brightest in the center and shaded darker toward the edges, on the wall behind the cardboard. When a second slit was added to the cardboard, the projected image changed to alternating bands of bright light and darkness. The conclusion reached is that wavelength patterns in the light cancelled or reinforced one another as they reached the wall, increasing or decreasing the observed light. These results are consistent with the wave theory of light.

To hear audio commentary on this piece of writing, visit this page of the eText at **www.mycomplab.com.**

For another example of a lab report, see pages 471–473.

13 | Write Portfolios and Essay Exams

QUICK*TAKE*

- Know the purposes and genres of portfolios (see below)
- Learn to write a portfolio letter (see p. 154)
- Learn to write effective exam essays (see p. 158)

13a Create a Portfolio

A portfolio includes a range of documents, giving readers a broader, more detailed picture of your writing than a single document could. Portfolios have different purposes and different requirements. For some portfolios, you might assemble a collection of printouts of your writing, while for others you might submit documents online into an electronic portfolio system. For any kind of portfolio, your goal is to provide tangible evidence of your learning.

Your instructor should give you instructions about the purpose of your portfolio, what it should contain, and how you should arrange and submit it.

Types of portfolios

What you choose to include will depend on your portfolio guidelines. Here are some common portfolio types, their purposes, and documents they might contain.

A **developmental portfolio** demonstrates a writer's developing skills over a given period of time—perhaps a semester, a year, or several years. Developmental portfolios may focus on skills like critical thinking, research, argument, style, collaboration, and correct grammar and mechanics. A developmental portfolio will usually include examples of revised work, providing evidence to readers that you have learned to evaluate and improve your own work. Often, writing in a developmental portfolio ranges from simple, short pieces to longer, more complex work. Your selections may demonstrate how you built upon or combined earlier ideas to produce a more substantial project.

A **disciplinary portfolio** or professional writing portfolio demonstrates the writer's mastery of important writing forms in a field or discipline. An engineering writing portfolio might include examples of a survey, an accident report, an e-mail to clients, a competitive bid, and similar documents. A business writing portfolio might include examples of a complaint resolution letter, an interoffice memo, a prospectus, an executive summary, and a PowerPoint presentation. A portfolio for a creative writing class might include examples of different genres, such as personal essays, short fiction, poetry, drama, and criticism.

Like a developmental portfolio, a disciplinary portfolio may also reflect how your knowledge of a subject progressed over a period of time. To show how you learned, you might provide examples of informal writing where you wrestle with new concepts; short papers where you research, expand, or connect your growing knowledge; and drafts or sections of longer analytical papers that demonstrate how you have learned to manipulate complex ideas.

Stylistic portfolios are used to give readers a sense of the various styles and genres a writer can employ. Such a portfolio might include humorous writing, formal oratory, descriptive writing, and other types of writing that aim to produce different effects for the reader.

Many schools now use electronic portfolio systems, or **e-portfolios**, for the collection and review of student work. E-portfolios allow you to include many types of media, such as PowerPoint presentations and video, and to link them together or organize them in different ways. You can link early and late drafts of projects to show how they changed and improved over time. Or you might link projects from several classes to show how you transferred skills from one situation to another.

Learning outcomes

Most college-writing portfolios will involve specific learning outcomes that your writing samples and reflections must speak to. These are the skills and abilities that your work should demonstrate—writing a research paper, solving complex problems, writing clearly about data, and so on. If the learning outcomes for your portfolio are not clear, talk to your instructor about them. Also look closely at any grading criteria or rubrics that will apply to your portfolio. Ideally, your instructor will have models of strong portfolios to share with you.

Think of a writing portfolio as a way to begin constructing your professional identity. The items in your portfolio add up to a snapshot of you and your abilities. How will these look to potential employers or clients?

Elements of a portfolio

Conclusion letter or summary statement	Give an overview of your materials and experience. It should help readers track your experience, using the samples as a step-by-step guide to your learning.
Contents	List each item in the portfolio, in the order they will appear.
Documents	What you include depends on the purpose of the portfolio and the instructions from your instructor.

What you need to do

- Understand the specific requirements for your portfolio. Ask your instructor if you aren't sure about the purpose or documents your portfolio should have.
- Assemble and organize the documents for your portfolio, including earlier drafts of your submitted papers and projects to show the revisions you made to them.
- Analyze your documents and perform an honest, impartial examination of your work.
- Write your reflective letter or summary, briefly describing the documents you include, then explaining why you chose the pieces you did and how they add up to a comprehensive picture of your challenges, setbacks, and successes.

13b Sample Portfolio Letter and Contents

Sample portfolio assignment

> **End of Semester Portfolio Requirements**
> **Pharmacy 5230 Practicum**
>
> The writing you do for this class will count toward your final grade in two ways—your regular assignments and your portfolio. Thirty-five % of your final grade will be based on your written work (entries on your Rotation Journal, responses to patient communication scenarios which I will post online weekly, and several longer analytical papers). Additionally, 25% of your grade will be based on a writing portfolio that you will assemble and turn in at the end of the semester. You will choose the documents for your portfolio, and you will write a reflective letter explaining how the documents you chose show your growth and learning during the course.
>
> To write an effective portfolio, you should first take each and every writing assignment seriously. Ask yourself, "How does a pharmacist think? With whom does a pharmacist need to communicate? What does a pharmacist need to say?"

When you make entries in your Rotation Journal, don't just record the events that happened that day. You should also think and write about what these events taught you. What did you learn? What surprised you? What questions have occurred to you as a result?

When you begin assembling materials for your portfolio, don't choose only your best work. Remember that your goal is to show how you have grown and gained knowledge and experience during this course. Ideally, you will include some examples of work from early in the semester, to give me a better sense of the skills and knowledge you brought into the class. Include later projects that show how you have built on your earlier skills.

The reflective letter you write is perhaps the most important part of your portfolio. Briefly summarize the documents you have included and explain what you think they show about your progress during the course. Your portfolio does not need to prove that you have learned all the facts we covered in class; that's what the final exam measures. Instead, your portfolio should give me a sense that this course has helped you clarify your professional goals, understand the responsibilities of a pharmacist, and acquire some tools to communicate appropriately in the field of pharmacy.

You are always welcome to meet with me to discuss your writing assignments and portfolio. I recommend that you take your reflective letter to the writing center for feedback before submitting your final portfolio. Portfolios will be turned in at the beginning of class on December 2.

Sample portfolio reflective letter

December 2, 2010

Dear Professor Nguyen,

The documents I chose for my portfolio demonstrate how I have gained the skills and insight a working pharmacist needs to communicate professionally.

The first three selections are from my Rotation Journal. I chose entries that show how I learned something significant from my experience on rotation. The first entry relates how I learned that the ongoing concerns of the community served by a pharmacist can affect day-to-day operations. The second and third entries address my realization that mistakes do happen in a real-world pharmacy and part of a pharmacist's job is to catch and correct mistakes as quickly and professionally as possible. These entries show me gaining practical, professional knowledge during the class.

The fourth entry is one of my two critical reports on ethics topics. In this report, I examined the Oregon Death with Dignity Act in light of our reading on professional ethics. One reason I included this report is that I found writing it did a great deal to focus me on a career pathway involving older adult care. Reading about the issues that motivated advocates of the Death with Dignity Act really made me understand the lack of options available to people of advanced age. I began to feel that the controversy over assisted suicide focuses more on younger, terminally ill patients, and neglects the challenges facing those who are approaching death "normally." Therefore, I believe this document demonstrates how I have thought critically about my career options in pharmacy, and my goals in that career.

The fifth entry is my evaluation of a health news article in the popular press. This project fit in perfectly with my experience on rotation because of the flu outbreak that happened right after I started observing at the pharmacy. I was shocked at how much bad information there was on flu vaccines in the article I analyzed. I became more aware how much work pharmacists have to do when consulting with patients who may not just be uninformed but misinformed. I have appended to this document a short fact sheet I later wrote up for customers, answering "Questions About the Flu Vaccine." My rotation supervisor actually posted this sheet at the pharmacy counter to help educate customers.

The last five selections in the portfolio are "patient communication scenarios" written in response to the online prompts. I chose some of these from very early in the semester because I grew better at writing them as the semester went on. Also, I have included rough drafts of each scenario to show how I worked on adjusting their tone and language. I learned how to provide detailed information more precisely, without using a lot of wordy phrases. I also found it that it was usually better to start with directive information, such as what the patient should or should not do, and then move on to more general information about a drug or illness. That way I would be more certain that the important actions would be taken. The last scenario, dealing with the breach of confidentiality for a minor patient, was the most interesting to write. While I would definitely not like to be in this situation in real life, it was fascinating to find out what the legal responsibilities were for the pharmacist and the physician's office in that kind of case.

The Pharmacy Practicum has given me a thorough understanding of the nuts-and-bolts issues pharmacists must deal with every day. In writing these documents, I have really enjoyed wrestling with the ethical problems involved in pharmacological care. The work also reassured me that I have chosen the right career path, because I always found the background information and the problems being considered fascinating and important.

Sincerely,
Lindsay Baumgartner

Sample portfolio contents

Portfolio Contents

1. Rotation Journal Entry, 9/4
2. Rotation Journal Entry, 9/27
3. Rotation Journal Entry, 11/15
4. Aging with Dignity: What the Death with Dignity Act Leaves Out
5. Analysis of "Flu Vaccines a Risky Business"
   5a. Questions about the Flu Vaccine—Patient Fact Sheet
6. Scenario 1: Who Do You Ask for Help?
   6a. Rough Draft
7. Scenario 3: Confusing Labels
   7a. Rough Draft
8. Scenario 8: Language Barriers
   8a. Rough Draft
9. Scenario 13: Dr. Who?
   9a. Rough Draft
10. Scenario 15: Confidentiality
    10a. Rough Draft

13c Write an Essay Exam

Instructors use essay exams to test your understanding of course concepts and to assess your ability to analyze ideas independently. To demonstrate these skills, you must write an essay that responds directly and fully to the question being asked.

Elements of an essay exam

Introduction	Briefly acknowledge the question, and give the thesis for the answer you will provide.
	EXAMPLE QUESTION
	Analyze an incident in Pride and Prejudice *that reveals the character of one of Elizabeth Bennet's four sisters: Jane, Mary, Catherine ("Kitty"), or Lydia.*
	EXAMPLE
	The letter Lydia Bennett leaves after eloping highlights several of her most important character traits: her failure to take her own mistakes seriously, her casual attitude toward morality, and her disregard for the pain she causes others.

Body paragraphs	Each paragraph should address a major element of the question. Order them so the reader can tell how you are responding to the question.
	EXAMPLE
	Of the many factors leading to the downfall of Senator Joseph McCarthy, the Army-McCarthy hearings were the most important.
Conclusion	*Briefly* restate your answer to the question, not the question itself.
	EXAMPLE
	Thus, the three things all responsible creditors assess before making a loan are the borrower's capacity, credit history, and collateral.

What you need to do

- Make sure you understand the question. Actively respond with the kinds of information and analysis the question asks you to provide; don't just write generally about the topic.
- Plan your response before you begin writing, with an outline, list, or diagram. Note how much time you have to write your response.
- Respond to each element of the question, providing support and being as specific as possible.
- Save a few minutes to read over your essay, correcting errors and adding information where needed.

13d Sample Essay Exam

Exam assignment

HIS 312: Early American History Describe the economic, cultural, and political variables that led to the establishment of slavery in the American South.

Unsatisfactory essay exam

One student who skipped the planning stage gave a response to the essay question that lacked organization and specifics.

This essay provides few details and relies on vague qualifiers. What kind of "power"? How much is "a lot"? ⟶

There were many variables leading to the establishment of slavery in the American South. One of these variables was the way laws were made. Plantation owners held a lot of power and were able to make slavery the law of the land.

Another variable was the racist ideology that was prevalent in the South. Racism was used to justify the power whites had over blacks.

Passive constructions do not tell the reader very much about why racism was prevalent in the south, or who held racist ideologies. ⟵

Instead of organizing the variables or showing relationships among them, the author presents a "laundry list" and offers only brief and superficial explanation for each claim. ⟶

A third variable was the need for cheap labor to sustain the plantation system. The big plantations needed many workers to sustain them. Plantation owners wanted the cheapest labor possible, to maximize their profits.

Successful essay exam

Amy Zhao began her response to the essay question by jotting down ideas for each of the three categories mentioned. Her outline also served as a map for the structure of her essay.

economic	*cultural*	*political*
plantation economy	racist ideologies	elite leadership of southern colonies
trade with Europe	divide with indentured servants	legislature limited to large landowners
need for cheap labor		

Multiple variables in economics, culture, and politics combined to help institutionalize slavery in the American South. Most important among these variables were the plantation economy, racist ideologies, conflict among the lowest social classes, and the stranglehold of elite landowners on the legislative process. Economic variables arose primarily from the Southern colonies' ◄——— unique geographical situation. Physically isolated from the large markets of Europe but blessed with huge quantities of arable land, the region required cheap labor in order to exploit its full economic potential. Relatively wealthy white colonists secured large tracts of land and strongly resisted any forces that pushed for the breakup of these plantations into smaller, individually owned farm holdings. The concentrated wealth and power of the plantation owners allowed them to arrange conditions to protect their land. Slavery came to be seen as the best way to maintain their power.

Amy uses the key terms from the question to indicate where she is addressing that element of the question.

To hear audio commentary on this piece of writing, visit this page of the eText at **www.mycomplab.com**.

Exercise 13.1   Read the essay questions below. Underline the question words and phrases that indicate what the prompt asks you to do. Pay close attention to the question words (*who, what, why, how*) or verbs (*analyze, define, identify*) for important clues about how to respond.

1. Think about the importance of educational institutions in society. What would happen if there were no educational institutions? Specifically, imagine our present society with no schools. What would it look like?

2. In *Utilitarianism*, by John Stuart Mill, how much or how little does justice protect the individual? Does Mill provide any safeguards? If so, could these safeguards fail? How?

3. Analyze why the Tet Offensive, which technically was an overwhelming American victory, affected not only the course of the war in Vietnam, but also American politics and society.

4. In Stendhal's *The Red and the Black*, does the character Julien Sorel have free will? If yes, how does he use it? If no, what is limiting him?

5. Do you believe animals have rights? If you do, define those rights as specifically as you can. If you don't, should it be legal, for example, to torture dogs and cats? Why or why not?

14 | Writing for Online Courses

QUICKTAKE

- Know how to use online courseware (see below)
- Know how to manage online coursework (see p. 163)
- Know how to participate in online course discussions (see p. 164)
- Know how to manage your online writing projects (see p. 168)

When you enroll in a course with an online component, your participation and engagement are the keys to your success. You will excel in online courses if you communicate well and stay motivated and disciplined. Fully online courses and hybrid courses that have online components allow flexibility, ample writing practice, and opportunity for in-depth and engaging conversations, but if you miss assignments, you can fall behind in a hurry.

14a Use Courseware

Many courses—not just those that meet only online—now offer online tools and content that are located within a course management system (such as Blackboard, Moodle, or Sakai). Instructors use course management systems to deliver assignments and grades along with tools for communication and collaboration. While working in these online spaces you may be required to read and write a wide range of materials, from course content from the instructor, discussion boards, or wikis that represent the collaborative work of students in the class.

Whatever course management system your school uses, take advantage early in the semester of tutorials and help documents that guide you in how to e-mail, post to a discussion, or submit an assignment for your course. After the course begins, you will want to be comfortable with these features. If you are not at ease with technology or sometimes feel uncomfortable with learning new computer tools, it will be especially important to get familiar with the online course tools early. Even if you may not be face-to-face with your instructor, you'll need to know when to ask for help.

14b Keep Track of Online Coursework

Plan your time

Even more than in traditional face-to-face-classes, online courses require self-discipline and strong organization to keep your work on track. At the beginning of the term, use the course syllabus or online course schedule to create your own detailed schedule to be sure you keep up with reading and assignments. Some students choose to use a traditional planner, others do well using an online calendar or other reminders. The important thing is to stay on top of due dates.

Don't forget to include required participation in discussion forums in your planning and schedule. Participating in online discussion can require a big investment of time. Be sure to give yourself ample time to read and write responses to the posts of others in discussion forums. Your instructor will be able to gauge the time you spend in discussion forums and the quality of your contributions and these may both contribute to your grade for the course.

Then stick to the schedule you have outlined. Know the course policy for late assignments, for written work, and other participation. The sooner you start the work for the course the better. As in any other class, keeping up with reading and due dates is essential. Many students who take online courses report that it is especially important not to fall behind. Without the reminders that face-to-face interaction in the classroom can provide, it is up to you to remember what you should be working on and when.

Stay organized

Hard drive failure or Internet service interruptions tend to happen when it is least convenient. As in any course, be sure you back up files as a regular part of your routine. Anticipate other technical problems such as Internet outages. You are expected to have adequate and regular access to the Internet in order to participate in discussion and to submit assignments. Technical problems will not excuse you from online work. Plan to have multiple ways to access the Internet, e-mail, and your course materials if your usual means of access is down.

Staying connected also means keeping up communication with your instructor and participating in required discussion forums. You have the responsibility to communicate with or meet your instructor and fellow students; note your instructor's policies for conferences or other sessions and keep track of these meetings. Regardless of whether your class meets online or both online and face-to-face, success in online courses comes when you participate fully in the community and discussions.

14c Participate in Online Course Discussions

Productive writers often use discussion forums, e-mail, blogs, and instant messaging to communicate and discuss ideas. The discussions you have online are similar to classroom discussion in that they can help you gather or focus ideas or revise. Familiarize yourself with the tools in your school's course management system before you begin so that you know how to post to a class discussion and e-mail your classmates.

Your instructor will likely give specific instructions for how often you are required to participate in online discussion forums, and may also specify the number and kinds of posts you must make. Once the class has begun, read earlier posts carefully as you choose how to make a point in a class discussion. You should make sure the point you want to make hasn't already been posted. If you are unclear about a post, respectfully ask a question.

When you are posting the first entry in a discussion thread, give your post a clear, specific subject line that lets readers know what you are writing about before they open it. For new or response posts, offer the context (the assignment or reading name), the date and name of a previous post, or other background. Take care when you respond to a post that you are inserting your comments on the appropriate thread.

Discussion Post Assignment

Discussion #2: Visual signs

Think of some clothing or style that is popular among friends of yours: tattoos, baseball caps, piercings, jewelry, sneakers, and so on. Interview a friend who wears the item and photograph him or her, focusing on the item. Upload the photo to the discussion board. Write a post of 250–400 words about the significance of the item and what it says about the generation who values it.

Discussion Post

Clear subject line repeats assignment language.

Thread: Style or clothing? Magenta Chucks with Cartoon Laces

Author: Lindsey Rodriguez

Posted Date: Thursday, January 27, 2011 4:54:31 PM CST

Edited Date: Thursday, January 27, 2011 4:58:23 PM CST

Shoes are a versatile type of clothing because the wearer can consciously choose the size of the statement they make. People can pick a pair of subtle shoes that complement their outfit or wear a pair for their functionality. Alternatively, shoes may also serve as a statement—accessories that make a jarring contrast against the rest of the outfit or even serve as the focal point.

Photograph responds to assignment and shows details described in post.

For example, a pair of well-worn, magenta Converse sneakers with mismatching laces can only be meant to generate intrigue as a clothing choice. While a magenta pair of Converses with Hello-Kitty and Spiderman laces would seem odd for the typical male,

Post relates results of interview.

Rick Wang's closet is a sea of black, white, and shades of purple with the occasional ironic or vintage T-shirt lying on the floor. Rick is unlike any person I've ever met. For his senior yearbook portrait, he wore the same rented tux that was required for all guys with one exception: after much convincing of the photographer, on his shoulder sat the turtle beanie-baby he named Cornelius Alfonso Laramy Galileo III Esq. His eighteenth birthday party was held at Chuck E. Cheese's, where he gallivanted around with the cape and Chuck E. Cheese mask given to all birthday children. Like many of his generation, the shoes convey his embrace of the strange, fun, and colorful without any regard to dignity. The cartoon shoelaces are a display of his eccentricity and still lively inner-child.

As the technological revolution gave power and prestige to nerds, Converse's "Chucks" became popular among the generation that values socially awkward yet intelligent and quirky individuals. Crazy colored shoes have also grown in popularity because they express creativity and individualism for a generation that resists becoming boring.

Post length is appropriate to assignment.

Reply to a Discussion Post

Re: Style or clothing? Magenta Chucks with Cartoon Laces

Author: Ahsika Richter

Posted Date: Thursday, January 27, 2011 7:49:28 PM CST

Edited Date: Thursday, January 27, 2011 7:49:28 PM CST

> One of the best things about Converse sneakers is how many varieties you can buy of the same shoe design. Students on our campus sport the classic black model along with red, turquoise, and even patterns such as the Union Jack. With so many choices students can fit into a growing trend while still showing their unique flavor. My friend Risa owns several pairs of these inexpensive shoes. I asked Risa why she chose the purple plaid ones, and she replied "because they seemed funky and awesome, and it was not likely that many people would have that particular style of shoe." Risa and other students attempt to stand out from everyone else not only with "Chucks" but also with many other trends like jewelry and tattoos.

Subject line for response clearly relates to original post

Response post contributes an additional point about significance of these sneakers.

Additional example connects to original post's main point about how sneakers express creativity.

To hear audio commentary on this piece of writing, visit this page of the eText at **www.mycomplab.com.**

In online courses, your discussion posts, wiki entries, and other written work speak for and create an impression of you. Your instructor and classmates will rely on your comments and conversations in writing to relate to you and assess your ideas. Even if the online conversation is casual, use a respectful tone and keep your language clear and to the point. Think about the voice your writing creates and how classmates and your instructor will hear it. Follow commonsense rules of etiquette and avoid posting angry, unfair, or personal attacks, taking special care to use a respectful tone when you disagree. Finally, take time to reread and edit your work before posting.

The community that is created in online courses thrives when participants are fully engaged and contributing responsibly. These interactions can be extremely rewarding. Some students who may feel reluctant to speak up in a face-to-face classroom report that online discussions offer a way to be heard and can be especially gratifying. Participating in online discussion offers opportunities for additional writing practice, which will help you develop ideas and confidence as a writer.

> **Exercise 14.1** On the discussion board for your class, identify the two or three posts that drew the most responses. Why did students respond more to these posts? Can you make any conclusions about what makes an effective discussion board post?

14d Manage Your Writing Projects

For many assignments your instructor will ask you to submit drafts electronically. It is also likely in most online courses that you will be saving and then exchanging drafts with classmates. To avoid problems with lost drafts or confusing file names, develop a system for organizing drafts for each course. Set up a system of folders with one for your drafts, and one for those from classmates; save files in these separate folders.

Give each of your drafts a name that includes specifics of the assignment and, if you plan to share it with others, your name (*Sheri Harrison Reflection Draft 1*). Your instructor may require or suggest a system for you. Including your name in the draft's file name helps your instructor and classmates keep track.

When you are sharing drafts, be sure you know what formats your instructor recommends and your classmates can read and open. If you are not sure what file format is appropriate, use Rich Text Format to save your document before sharing.

You'll find more about writing in online genres in Chapter 17, including blogs (Section 17b), wikis (Section 17c), Web pages (Section 17d), professional social media sites (Section 17e), podcasts (Section 17f), and videos (Section 17g).

15 | Compose for Business and Public Writing

15a What Is Business Writing?

Written communication is central to success in the workplace. Whatever disciplines you study in college or whatever field you enter for work, you will need to write efficiently and effectively for your job. Written communication is part of every work setting, from corporations to at-home businesses to nonprofit groups.

Business writing assignments usually specify an audience and call on you to write clearly and concisely. Business writers, like writers in other disciplines, are expected to observe conventions of format, organization, and tone. As in other kinds of writing, business writers need to carefully consider the needs of their audience.

Readers of business documents are busy and juggling many competing demands. Write with your readers in mind, showing that you respect their time by following some guidelines for business communication.

- Focus your writing; be concise, using short paragraphs.
- Write clearly, using a simple, straightforward style. State your purpose early on.
- Use a professional tone, be courteous, and avoid informal language.
- Choose an accessible, readable format and organization.
- Follow rules of grammar and punctuation and proofread carefully. Accuracy, appearance, and correctness reflect well on you and your organization.
- Include a closing that uses a positive tone to build goodwill.

15b Write a Letter of Application

Successful letters of application place the reader's needs first and show why you are the best candidate. Great jobs attract many applicants. Convince your readers that you are worthy of an interview. A well-written letter of application gets your foot in the door.

Elements of a letter of application

Inside address and salutation	Use the name and title of the person doing the hiring whenever possible. If you don't know them, call the organization for the person's name and official title.
First paragraph	Name the position for which you are applying.
Body	Explain why your education, experience, and skills make you a good candidate for the position.
Conclusion	Mention that you've enclosed your résumé and your contact information.

What you need to do

- Limit yourself to one page.
- Find out as much as you can about the organization or company.
- Don't fall into the trap of emphasizing why the job would be good for you; instead, show why you are well suited for the employer's needs.
- List in your résumé the qualifications and work experience that make you well suited for the position, then describe them in your letter and remember to bring them up if you get an interview.
- If you are applying by e-mail, name the position you are applying for in the subject line (*Application for production assistant position*).

Exercise 15.1 Look on the Internet, the newspaper, or school or local bulletin boards for a job or internship for which you would like to apply. Write a cover letter and update (or create) your résumé tailored for this position.

Sample letter of application

609 McCaslin Lane
Manitou Springs, CO 80829

November 2, 2010

Ann Darwell
100 Pine Street
Colorado Springs, CO 80831

Dear Ms. Darwell:

Please consider my application for Fox 45's *Kids' Hour* production assistant position.

During my senior year at Boston College, I interned for the Emmy-winning children's program *Zoom*. Through the internship I learned not only the technical skills necessary to produce a weekly, hour-long show, but the finesse required to manage an all-child cast.

My experience as the producer of *All the News* also gave me intensive training in the skills of a successful producer. Under my direction, a staff of fifteen crew members and reporters regularly broadcast creative campus news pieces. Because I produced this weekly show for three years, I would need little initial supervision before being able to make significant contributions to *Kids' Hour*.

After one year at *Zoom*, I want to continue production work in a position that offers more responsibility in the field of children's television. My work at *Zoom*, particularly my authoring and producing a series of spots to teach children Spanish, has given me hands-on experience in creating the kind of innovative television for which *Kids' Hour* is known.

Thank you for considering my application. Enclosed is my résumé. I would be happy to send my references if you wish to see them. You can reach me at (719) 555-0405 or c.popolo@hotmail.com. I look forward to speaking with you about the production assistant position.

Sincerely,

Christian Popolo
Christian Popolo

To hear audio commentary on this piece of writing, visit this page of the eText at **www.mycomplab.com**.

15c Write a Résumé

Finding the right job depends on writing a successful résumé, one of the most important pieces of writing that you will ever compose. The secret of a successful résumé is understanding its purpose—to place you in the small group of candidates to be interviewed.

Elements of a résumé

Objective section	Target the objective section to the position you are applying for. Be as specific as possible. **EXAMPLE** Special education teacher in the greater Atlanta area specializing in brain-injured patients and requiring familiarity with coordinating ARDS and completing IED documentation.
Overview section	List your education in reverse chronological order, beginning with certificates or degrees earned. List work experience in reverse chronological order, focusing on your more recent jobs and including details of your duties. **EXAMPLE** Reviewed real estate investments and loan portfolios for documentation, structure, credit analysis, risk identification, and credit scoring.

What you need to do

- Focus on the employer's needs. Imagine you are the person hiring. List the qualifications and work experience an ideal candidate would have.
- Make a list of your qualifications and work experience.
- Compare the two lists. What qualifications and work experience do you have that make you well suited for the position? Put checks beside the items on your list that you find are most important for the position.
- Create two printed résumés—a scannable résumé and a traditional résumé. Many companies now scan résumés and store the information in a database. Make your scannable résumé simple and clean, and avoid any graphics such as bulleted points and lines.

Sample résumé

Christian Popolo
609 McCaslin Lane
Manitou Springs, CO 80829
(719) 555-0405
c.popolo@hotmail.com

OBJECTIVE
Production assistant position for an innovative Colorado television program requiring prior experience in children's television and a strong technical background.

SUMMARY OF SKILLS
On-location production, studio-based production, news production, children's television, management, fund raising, animation, AVID Media Composer, AVID Xpress DV, MS Word, MS Office, fluent Spanish, detail-oriented, articulate, excellent writer

EDUCATION
Bachelor of Arts in Communications, Boston College, May 2010
GPA: 3.65/4.0

WORK EXPERIENCE
Producer, All the News, BCTV Campus Television, Chestnut Hill, MA, August 2007–May 2010. Produced a weekly, half-hour campus news program. Supervised seven studio staffers and eight reporters. Spearheaded successful initiative to increase Student Services funding of the program by fifteen percent.
Intern, Zoom, Boston, MA, May 2009–May 2010. Interned in the production department of award-winning national children's television program. Wrote and produced three 2-minute "Hablamos" segments, designed to teach Spanish phrases.
Technician, Communications Media Lab, Chestnut Hill, MA, August 2007–April 2009. Maintained over $300,000 worth of the latest filming and editing technology.

HONORS
Presidential Scholar, August 2007–May 2010
BCTV Excellence Award, May 2008 and May 2009

REFERENCES
Available upon request from the Career Center, Boston College, Southwell Hall, Chestnut Hill, MA 02467 at (617) 555-3430.

To hear audio commentary on this piece of writing, visit this page of the eText at **www.mycomplab.com**.

Write a Memo

Memoranda, or memos, are a type of internal communication and are one of the most common forms of workplace writing. Memos are circulated internally, meaning within a company or among members of a team working on a particular project. While e-mail is quickly replacing memos for day-to-day communication in many workplaces, the memo remains the preferred method for more formal and more extended communication. In particular, memos are valued for creating a paper trail that can be used later to confirm information and process. The primary purpose of a memo is to distribute information. Typical uses for a memo include summarizing the results of an important meeting, announcing a new policy, or updating team members of progress on a project.

Elements of a Memo

Date	Include date that the memo is distributed.
To	List all recipients.
From	List yourself and any other authors.
Subject	Create a subject line that offers a brief preview of the memo's contents.
Introduction	Provide any necessary background information as briefly as possible. Include only the background information that your readers are likely to *need* in order to understand the memo.
Body	Detail all necessary information as clearly and concisely as possible. Many memos use design elements such as short paragraphs or bulleted lists to make the content easy for a busy reader to absorb at a glance.
Conclusion	If appropriate, use a brief conclusion to suggest any necessary follow-up steps.

What you need to do

- Use your company memo template (if available). If your company does not have a template, basic templates are available within most word processing programs.
- Begin with a header that includes each of the following on a new line: *Date, To, From, Subject.*
- Determine your purpose and stick to it. Focus on a single topic within your memo.
- Be brief and direct. Busy readers need to be able to absorb the information in your memo as quickly as possible.

- Use a professional tone.
- Format your memo for easy skimming. Provide ample white space, and make use of bulleted or numbered lists to make important information stand out.
- Conclude with a call to action, if appropriate to your purpose.

Sample Memo

s@fetyNET

Memo

Date: March 2, 2010
To: Information Design Department
From: Trichelle Mim
Subject: REQUEST FOR WEBSITE DEVELOPMENT

s@fetyNET has had an overwhelming response to our recent sales campaign. We are expecting to add a number of new clients in the next few weeks. Obviously, our clients expect a network security company to have a Website. Therefore, we must work very quickly to develop this online portal to our company.

The Web site should include the following:

- <u>About Us</u> – an explanation of our company's values, a description of our vision, and how we can help meet customer needs.

- <u>Training and Support</u> – bullet points describing types of training and support available to our prospective clients.

- <u>Services Offered</u> – a listing with explanations of the various types of customized services we offer.

- <u>Shopping Cart</u> – a feature of the site including an order form clients can use to augment or order service directly from our site.

I have always been able to depend on your quick response to challenges. We are planning another mailing in four weeks; please provide at least two possible designs by our next weekly meeting. Let's work to stay on schedule so we may include our new Websites in next month's mailing!

To hear audio commentary on this piece of writing, visit this page of the eText at **www.mycomplab.com**.

15e Write a Business E-mail

E-mail is now the preferred form for most day-to-day communication in the business world. An e-mail is faster than a letter and, unlike a phone call, leaves a record of the conversation between sender and recipient. It's important to remember that e-mail is easily shared and forwarded. You should never assume that e-mails you send will remain private.

Elements of a Business E-mail

Addresses **To:** **Cc:** **Bcc:**	Use the address line for the primary recipient or recipients—those you address directly in your salutation. Use the "cc:" field for address of people who also need to know about the issue. "Bcc:" recipients receive a copy but are hidden from the main recipient.
Subject Line	Always provide a subject. Make it informative and specific. Avoid words and phrases that are likely to trigger a recipient's junk mail filter, such as "Opportunity," "Credit," "Loans," or "Please read—URGENT."
Salutation	Always include a formal salutation, especially when e-mailing someone from a different company or organization.
Body	Keep business e-mail as short as possible. Skip a line between paragraphs instead of indenting the first line.
Signature	Many e-mail programs allow you to automate your signature, so your name, title, and contact information appear at the bottom of every e-mail. You should always "sign" your name at the end of an e-mail.

What you need to do

- Keep an e-mail brief, and limit it to one topic. If you need to communicate about more than one issue, send another e-mail.
- The subject line is critical in business e-mail to reference the contents. Business projects often produce hundreds of messages.
- Be specific about what you want the recipient to do, and when. Make deadlines, dates, and desired actions clear and prominent.
- Use a professional, straightforward tone. Proofread messages for grammar and punctuation errors.

Sample business e-mail

To: Shane Brewer, Brewer Showcases Ltd. (shane@showcases.com)
Cc:
Bcc:
Subject: Imperial Electronics Rental Rate Quote

Dear Mr. Brewer,

In response to your request during our phone conversation this morning, I have put together the following rate schedule for the equipment you will need on December 21 and 22, 2010:

–16 channel analog mixing console: $190

–Digital DLP Projector (3 chip): $200

–Truss screen, 6 x 8': $150

–Subwoofer speakers, three pair: $100/pair

–Cabling, setup, and breakdown: $280

–Total (state sales tax not included): $1120

In order to guarantee these rates, we will need your confirmation by 5 p.m. Friday, October 27, and payment of a $300 deposit no later than November 21st. The balance of the rental charges will be invoiced to you after your event.

Please let me know if you have any other questions. Our team looks forward to hearing from you.

Sincerely,
Laurie Hernandez
AV Sales and Customer Care
Imperial Electronics
789-232-6978

To hear audio commentary on this piece of writing, visit this page of the eText at **www.mycomplab.com**.

15f What Is Public Writing?

Like business writing, public writing is designed to inform or persuade. Public writing serves a central purpose of sharing information on causes, informing citizens and groups, and calling people to action. Public writing that addresses a need or proposes a solution to a problem is effective when it is informative, credible, and helps readers find information or accept and implement a course of action. Being able to effectively write in these contexts is an important form of communication that addresses real needs and problems in your community.

Many writing courses now ask students to undertake community-based writing projects. These courses often connect students with work in or for a nonprofit or community organization or other volunteer group. Learning to communicate with community organizations using some of the same genres (letters, memos) as in business writing situations helps you relate as a citizen and informed member of a community. Other forms of public writing include letters and e-mails to elected officials; editorials, or blogs addressing an issue; and newsletters, brochures, or flyers promoting a cause, event, or organization.

As in other kinds of writing, public writing requires you to carefully consider the needs of your audience. Think in concrete terms about your audience—both the primary readers who may be in a position to take action and also any other stakeholders who may be affected by your work. Consider, for example, that a proposal you are making to a nonprofit group might directly complicate the work of people at the group. Writing for a public audience that you do not know personally requires you to pay special attention to create a professional and fair tone and to anticipate and respond to their objections. It is useful as you work on a public writing project to gather information about your audience, including talking with members of the audience to get their reactions and experiences. Knowing whether members of your audience are indifferent or enthusiastic about your information or solutions will help you address what details and other persuasive information you need to include as you write.

Often the public writing you do will be collaborative, requiring you to work with others at various stages. Many large, formal documents are written collaboratively. For example, when working on a report as a volunteer for a community organization, you may be asked to write a draft that is then reviewed for content and tone by one person and for design by another.

As with business documents, readers of public writing are busy and will want to see a clear statement of your purpose for writing and what you are calling on them to do early on. Establish your credibility by showing that you understand your audience's needs and expectations. Keep your writing clear, focused, and concise. Choose a format and organization for your documents that relates to your purpose. Accuracy, appearance, and correctness reflect well on you and any organization you represent. Finally, be sure to follow rules of grammar and punctuation and proofread carefully.

15g Write a Report

Reports are documents that offer information or the results of research, written for a specific purpose. Reports are written for a variety of purposes, for example to inform and share information about a trip, to update on the progress with a project, or to relate investigations and analyze the results of research. The audience for a report can be internal readers in your organization or group, or an outside audience beyond your organization. Many reports will require you to gather data or carry out research, including interviews, observations, or surveys to use as evidence. If your assignment requires you to do research, you will need to document your sources. Effective reports are clearly organized and structured with design elements that help readers find information easily.

Think visually

Readers want to take in information at a glance. You don't need fancy graphics to convey information efficiently. For example, action oriented goals are easier to understand in a table rather than in running text.

Goals for Children and Youth	Goals for Family, School & Community Supports	Frameworks for Decision Making and Communications
Clear, measurable outcome goals established for children and youth that reflect what we know about learning and development, as evidenced by:	Clear, measurable performance goals that address the quantity, quality and consistency of supports, as evidenced by:	Goals for children and youth and for family/school/community supports are memorable and marketable as evidenced by:
• Age range: across age ranges and developmental stages, from birth to young adulthood (at least 21). • Breadth: across developmental areas, balancing academic outcomes with social, physical, emotional, vocational, spiritual. • Reach: applicable to all young people but built to acknowledge key sub-populations (e.g., special needs, SES, geography). • Balance: addressing "problem reduction" and "prevention" needs with "preparation" and "leadership" aspirations.	• Breadth of supports: based on the full range of key setting supports (e.g., safety, structure, positive relationships, high expectations, challenging activities, opportunities for skill building). • Breadth of usage: usage across family, school and community settings, including formal systems and informal connections. • Accountability: supports used to define performance measures by multiple systems.	• Communications power: specific goals developed are linked to core messages for the general public and for specific stakeholder groups. • Planning/decision making power: outcome and performance goals are linked to planning and decision making frameworks and reported on together.

■ Goal statements in a table give the big picture vision.

Elements of a report

Title page	Include for longer, more formal reports. Follow the format given by your instructor or organization.
Abstract or executive summary	Give a concise overview of the key points in the report, including any significant findings and conclusions.
Table of contents	Longer, formal reports require a detailed list of the contents. Long reports may also include lists of figures or tables.
Introduction	State the topic and why it is of interest or important.
Body	Be concise and clear while including appropriate detail. Describe the data or information used in the report and methods for gathering it. Include necessary documentation and clear headings, bulleted lists, or other appropriate design elements.
Conclusion	State the important information or recommendations. Be sure they are supported in the report with evidence.

What you need to do

- Choose an appropriate format for your report. Check with your supervisor or instructor for the specific format you should follow.
- Understand the required organization and parts of the report—depending on your purpose—before you begin (do you need a title page? executive summary? bibliography?).
- Conduct necessary research and keep detailed notes about the information you gather.
- Write clearly and concisely in each part, including necessary details.
- End with a strong conclusion or persuasive recommendation that offers evidence.

Sample report

True/False Film Festival: Greater than Fiction

Prepared by Owen Skoler

Report Distributed October 22, 2010

Title page
includes title,
author, and
date informa-
tion, centered.

Prepared for True/False Film Festival

True/False 2

Executive Summary

The True/False Film Festival is a bold showcase
for nonfiction films that has successfully established
Columbia, Missouri on the cultural map. Filmmakers,
volunteers, and audiences are engaged and inspired
by the festival. To assist this festival's mission,
interested public institutions and private organizations
should take into account and help develop the prestige
and economic and cultural impact the festival has on
our city.

Page num-
bered with
abbreviated
title.

The executive
summary
briefly
summarizes
the report's
research and
recommenda-
tions.

True/False 3

Introduction

Introduction sets out the purpose for the report.

Now in its eighth year, the True/False Film Festival has brought unprecedented acclaim and leading-edge cultural experiences to Columbia. Screenings of excellent documentaries—those also shown at larger, world-renowned festivals like Sundance and Cannes— show that the festival's reputation is solidly established in the film world. Though the success of the festival contributes to the health of the mid-Missouri economy, True/False brings esteem and adds value to Columbia that goes beyond its numbers.

A Film Festival that Works for Columbia

The body begins with heading that suggests the research results.

The festival has been a big success for its organizers, David Wilson and Paul Sturtz. The festival overcame the remote location of Columbia and assembled an impressive and diverse set of screening spaces. They estimate that last year 6,000 people attended the festival. Even more impressively, there were 25,000 viewings of films (this counts viewers who see more than one screening), and the numbers go up every year (Waters, 2008).

Filmmakers love the True/False experience because of the enthusiastic response of audiences and the lack of big-city attitude. Because the size is small and the focus is on the films, the atmosphere is unpretentious and inviting to a wide variety of filmmakers, not only those who have already made it big. Filmmakers appreciate connecting with the audiences and one another at True/False. The festival has established credibility in the industry and its appeal to audiences continues to grow.

True/False 4

The economic impact to the city is not its main benefit, but it is substantial. The costs of this festival, held in theaters, churches, and ballrooms across the city, are relatively small. Organized as a nonprofit venture, the festival is known for its egalitarian treatment of the filmmakers and musicians who present their work.

Lorah Seiner, director of the Columbia Convention and Visitors Bureau, believes the buzz about the film festival is worth more to the community than the revenues it generates. True/False is large enough that it gets national attention. It creates a positive perception about the community, both because of the high quality of the festival programs. But even more impressive to the filmmakers who travel here is the community involvement and enthusiasm. Seiner reports that "time after time, the directors that come in from Europe, Los Angeles, New York, they are astounded by the attendance at the films" (Waters, 2008).

There are other important implications for mid-Missourians who attend the thought-provoking festival. Many films help open conversations on thorny political and cultural issues. These films that provoke conversations and engage citizens are on both global and local topics. Government officials who attend come away with ideas and lots to think about. One such figure, State Representative Chris Kelly, commented that "True/False is a manifestation of the slogan, 'Think globally; act locally'" (Putnam, 2009).

> Format for business report uses bold headings and leaves spaces between paragraphs, rather than using paragraph indents.

> Quotes a respected source.

True/False 5

Statements in the conclusion are supported by statements and research in the body of the report.

Conclusion

The True/False Film Festival puts our community on the world stage, attracting important films and filmmakers from the wider world of documentary cinema. The films allow our community to enter into a conversation about thorny and valuable global and local issues. Even in the face of economic hard times, community support and sponsorship must remain strong and focused on the needs of the festival in order to help it thrive and continue at its level of success.

True/False 6

Center heading *References* and include list of sources following APA style.

Article from online periodical that did not appear in print includes retrieval information.

References

Putnam, S. (2009, March 1). True/False offers intimacy other festivals lack [Electronic version]. *Columbia Missourian.*

Szczepanski, C. (2010, February 24). True/False film festival puts Missouri on the cinematic map. *The Pitch.* Retrieved October 13, 2010, from http:// blogs.pitch.com/plog/2010/02/truefalse_film_ festival_puts_missouri_on_the_cinematic_map.php

Waters, H. J. (2009, March 11). True/False: More than the numbers [Electronic version]. *Columbia Daily Tribune.*

To hear audio commentary on this report, visit this page of the eText at **www.mycomplab.com.**

15h Write a Proposal

Proposals are documents that offer solutions designed to persuade readers to solve a problem or recommend a change. Effective proposals are clearly organized and structured, clearly state the problem, and rely heavily on facts and persuasive details. Your proposal should anticipate and then provide answers to readers' questions and objections. Proposals can be internal, designed to persuade readers within the same organization. Or the audience for a proposal can be outside your organization, such as potential clients.

ELEMENTS OF A PROPOSAL	
Title page	Include only for longer, formal proposals. Follow the format given by your instructor or organization.
Headings	For internal proposals, follow memo format and include heading elements (see p. 174).
Abstract or summary	Give a concise overview of the key points, including any significant findings and conclusions.
Table of contents	Longer, formal proposals require a detailed list of the contents.
Introduction	Identify the existing problem and explain why it needs solving or why it is important.
Body	Be concise and clear while including appropriate detail. Include persuasive details, figures, and other data. Include necessary documentation and clear headings, bulleted lists, or other appropriate design elements.
Conclusion	State the important recommendations and explain the benefits of your proposal. Be sure they are supported in the proposal with evidence.

What you need to do

- Understand the required organization and parts of the proposal before you begin (title page, executive summary, table of contents, bibliography) depending on your purpose.
- Conduct necessary research, keeping detailed notes.
- Write clearly, including details and facts to support your proposal.
- Anticipate readers' objections and questions and include answers.
- Conclude with a proposed solution, summarizing the benefits of the proposal, explaining the advantages of your solution over other possible solutions

Sample proposal

Memorandum

Date: August 19, 2010

Internal proposals follow memo format.

To: Claudia La Fountain, Vice President for Business Affairs

From: Kathy Harris, Health Services Administrative Assistant

Subject: Garage Sale Fund-raising Proposal for Wellness Week 2011

Overview of proposal.

SUMMARY

The upcoming West Virginia University Wellness Week event requires funds and requests support for a garage sale fund-raiser to be held in early October.

Explains the purpose and goals for the proposed event.

NEED

This fall's proposed fund-raising focus will be a garage sale. The garage sale does not require many hours of labor but many students and community organizations are willing to help with the event and donate items for the sale. The sale could involve students in early October and be held outdoors to coincide with other events to increase community participation. The goal is to raise at least $3,000 for promoting and sponsoring Wellness Week. That event's budget for last year was $3,204.

Includes necessary detail.

PLAN

The proposed dates for the sale are Friday, October 8 and Saturday, October 9, 8:30 AM to 3 PM. Set-up day would be Thursday, October 7. The timing of the sale would also be coordinated with the Division of Theatre and Dance's vintage costume sale. That sale traditionally offers a variety of garments including dresses, separates, and coats along with accessories such as hats and gloves. Because of the delicate nature of the items in that sale, I request that we have access to both the lobby of the Rec Center in case of rain, and the visitor parking lot to the north.

Also needed is promotional space in campus newsletters and publications in the three weeks preceding the event. Portions of this work will be coordinated with Anne Gilman through the Office of Marketing and Public Relations. Note that the $150 budget for flyers promoting the garage sale is covered by the Health Services department.

WELLNESS WEEK BUDGET

Funds are needed to promote Wellness Week, scheduled for the week before spring break, March 21–25. Based on budget numbers for the 2010 Wellness Week event these are costs for 2011.

Guest speakers	$1,500
Literature	400
T-shirts	300
Promotional posters, flyers	200
Attendance prizes and giveaways	500
Logo contest award	100

VOLUNTEERS

Volunteer workers will be needed to collect and sort donations, set up, administer, and take down the sale. A minimum of eight student volunteers are needed for each of the three days, but the goal is to recruit twelve to fifteen. Students can be credited volunteer points for work on one or two days. I will be on hand to promote the garage sale event as an option at the Volunteer Fair, September 8 in Union Lobby.

States a benefit of the proposal to students.

CONCLUSION

Although WVU has not held a campus-wide garage sale fund-raiser in recent years, there are similar successful sales held annually for other large community organizations. The sale offers students volunteer credit and can be timed to coincide with an existing, smaller upscale sale on campus of vintage costumes.

To hear audio commentary on this piece of writing, visit this page of the eText at **www.mycomplab.com.**

PART 4

Designing and Presenting

You **can learn more and do more** with MyCompLab and with the eText version of *The Penguin Handbook*. To find resources in MyCompLab that will help you successfully complete your assignment, go to

Resources

Writing

> **Writing Samples: Technical and Workplace**
> Web sites | Presentations | Brochures

> **Writing and Visuals**
> Multimedia: Informational Graphics

Review the Instruction and Multimedia resources within each topic, then complete the Exercises and click on the Gradebook to measure your progress.

In the **eText version** of *The Penguin Handbook*, you will also find extra worksheets, student writing samples, and assignments.

16 | Communicate in Multimedia

QUICK*TAKE*

- Compose in multimedia (see below)
- Think about verbal and visual relationships (see p. 192)
- Choose type (see p. 200)
- Create tables, charts, and graphs (see p. 205)

16a Multimedia Composing

Digital technologies now make it possible to create on your home computer multimedia projects that formerly required entire production staffs. You can publish multimedia projects on the Internet (either as Web sites or as downloadable files), as stand-alone media distributed on CDs and DVDs, or in print with posters, brochures, and essays with images.

Start with the audience

Most college assignments specify the medium, which is typically a printed paper that you submit to the instructor. In the workplace and in life outside college, the choice of medium often isn't immediately evident. For example, if you want to address a neighborhood issue, would a brochure or a Web site be more effective?

College viewers and listeners have the same expectations of multimedia projects that they do of essays and research papers. They expect

- your project to be well organized and free of errors,
- your claims to be supported with evidence,
- your analysis to be insightful,
- your sources to be documented, and
- your work clearly distinguished from the work of others.

Examples of multimedia projects

- Web page (see Section 17d)
- Podcast (see Section 17f)
- Video (see Section 17g)
- Oral presentation with visuals (see Chapter 18)
- Essay with images (see Section 22f)

16b Think About Verbal and Visual Relationships

Knowing when to use audio, video, images, and graphics and when to use words requires you to think about them as **media**—as different means of conveying information and ideas. The word *writing* makes us think of words, yet in our daily experience reading newspapers, magazines, advertisements, posters, and signs, we find words combined with images and graphics. On the flip side, television uses words extensively (think of the words you see on commercials when you have the sound off or the text running across the bottom of the screen on news, sports, and financial programs).

Think about what an image communicates

What are the expectations of your audience?

- Most essays don't use images. Most Web sites, brochures, and instructions do use images.
- Think about the purpose of including an image. Does it communicate a concept? Does it show something hard to explain in words alone?
- Think about the focus of the image. You may need to crop the image.
- Provide an informative caption for the images you include and refer to them in your text.

■ Sometimes images are used in place of words.

■ Sometimes words bring images to mind.

STAYING ON TRACK

Scanning and the law

Images in books and magazines published in the last seventy-five years are almost always owned by someone. If you copy an image for redistribution of any kind, including putting it on a Web site, you must find out who holds the copyright and obtain permission to use the image. Always give credit for any image that you copy, even if it is in the public domain.

Organization in verbal texts

Organization is the path the writer creates for readers to follow. Even in a reference book like this one, in which readers consult particular chapters and sections according to their needs, there is still a path from beginning to end.

Titles, headings, and paragraphs

Titles and headings combine verbal and visual indicators of levels of importance and major divisions in subject matter. Paragraphs give visual cues to the progression of ideas in verbal texts. Other visual indicators such as boldface and italics provide emphasis at the level of words and phrases. Print, after all, is a visual as well as a verbal medium.

Organization in visual texts

Organization is often called *composition* by photographers, artists, and designers. Both of the pictures below are of the same subject.

Static versus dynamic

The image on the left is a typical snapshot. The person is placed at the exact center, and the horizon is about at the midpoint. Putting the subject in the exact center is what happens when people take snapshots without thinking about how they are composed. The effect is static.

The image on the right moves the person away from the center and places him in relation to a large rock illuminated by the setting sun. Instead of focusing on the man, we now see him in relation to objects on the beach and the sea and sky behind.

Point of view in verbal texts

At the most basic level, **point of view** means selecting among first person (*I, we*), second person (*you*), and third person (*he, she, it*) when you write about your subject. Using *I* emphasizes the writer or the teller of the story in fiction. Using *you* puts the relationship between writer and reader in the foreground. Using *he, she,* or *it* keeps the focus more on the subject and diminishes the prominence of the writer.

Point of view is also determined by how you locate yourself in relation to your subject. Whether you write in first or third person, you can write about a subject from close, firsthand experience or you can place yourself at a distance from your subject, giving the sense of being an impartial observer offering an overview.

Point of view in visual texts

Where we choose to stand when we take a photograph makes all the difference in how the audience sees the subject. The photographer gives the audience a vantage point to take in the subject by allowing the audience to see what the photographer sees, creating an effect comparable to the use of *I* in writing.

Photographing people at close range creates a sense of interaction between subject and photographer.

Focus and frame in verbal texts

When you write, maintain focus on one subject at a time. You achieve focus by what you choose to include and what you choose either to leave out or to postpone until later.

When you write about a complex subject, sort the issues and present them one at a time

Our era is not unique as a time of uncertainty. The Four Horsemen of the Apocalypse—war, disease, famine, and death—have been the daily reality for most humans in times before modernity and for many living now. There are two major differences between uncertainty today and in the past.

First is the degree to which risk is produced by humans. Science and technology are both the cause of and the solution to our present risks. Every new technology brings associated risks; trains brought train wrecks, airplanes brought plane crashes, automobiles brought traffic accidents, nuclear power brought radiation leaks, the Internet brought rapidly spreading computer viruses.

Second is the absence of traditions to account for risks. In the past spirits or demons took the blame for catastrophes. Today the blame circles back on us. We chose the wrong lifestyle or the wrong partner or the wrong kind of food or the wrong occupation. When things go wrong, it is the individual's responsibility to seek counseling, to retrain herself, to pull himself up by his bootstraps.

Focus and frame in visual texts

Beginning photographers tend to see only what is at the center of the viewfinder. More experienced photographers pay attention to the edges of the frame because they know the frame is critical to how the viewer sees the subject.

■ Most of the time you should aim for simplicity in images.

Interest in Verbal Texts

Readers will plow through pages of boring writing if they have a strong purpose for reading, such as a financial report for a company they plan to invest in. Most of the time, however, you have to create and hold readers' interest if you expect them to finish what you write. When you create interest, you also build your credibility as a writer.

Details make writing lively

> Lamesa is typical of the hard towns of west Texas, which you quickly associate with the smell of sulfur. Coming into town you pass the lots of oil field suppliers surrounded by chain-link fences with red dirt blown over the lower third. Inside are rusted oil tanks, mutated steel skeletons of derrick parts, and squat buildings with plank porches lined with orange and blue oil drums—model railroad buildings blown up to full scale. On the small lots in between are shabby motels and windowless liquor stores with names like "Pinkies" on art deco signs above.

Interest in visual texts

Interest in visual texts is created by composition and subject matter. Some subjects possess inherent interest, but the photographer or artist must build on that interest.

■ Even potentially interesting subjects can be rendered boring if they are photographed in stereotypical ways.

■ Children often express a spontaneity lacking in adults, which provides visual interest.

Know where visuals work best

"A picture is worth a thousand words" is an old cliché. It's not that images are necessarily more powerful than words but that images and words are different media. Our eyes and brains are able to take in a great deal of visual information and sort that information for relevance.

Visuals are typically used in combination with text. Visuals work well when they

- Deliver spatial information, especially through maps, floor plans, and other graphic representations of space
- Represent statistical relationships
- Produce a strong immediate impact, even shock value
- Emphasize further a main point you've made in words

Know where words work best

Words can do many things that images cannot. Written words work best when they

- Communicate abstract ideas
- Report information
- Persuade using elaborated reasoning
- Communicate online using minimal bandwidth

- Adapt to specific users' needs (Computers can convert words from spoken to written language for those who are hearing impaired, or from written to spoken for those who are visually impaired.)

Exercise 16.1   Find an example of words and visuals used effectively to convey a message. The example can be an advertisement, a poster announcing a public service, a brochure, an article in a periodical, a page in a textbook or other book, a manual, a work of art, a flyer for a concert or show, a Web site, or anything else that appeals to you. Describe the work accomplished by the visuals and by the text, both separately and in combination with one another. Why is the example you've chosen effective?

16c Design Documents

MLA style (the major style in the humanities and fine arts) and APA style (the major style in the social sciences and education) both provide extensive guidelines for formatting papers. See the sample papers for MLA in section 26l and the sample paper for APA in section 27g.

Use color effectively

Color can provide contrast to draw attention to headings and emphasized words. We are surrounded by so much color that sometimes the strongest

■ The red used in the titles and headings both matches and balances the red uniforms in the image.

effects are created by using color in minimal ways. Limited use of warm colors—yellow, orange, and especially red—can make an impact.

Design brochures and other documents

With today's easy-to-use software, you can produce a professional-looking project. Handsome brochures are one example. Templates take care of the basic layout, allowing you to focus on the content and design. If you are creating a brochure, select the size of paper you want, fold the sheet of paper, and number the panels. Make a sketch of what you want to appear on each panel, including headings, text, images, and graphics.

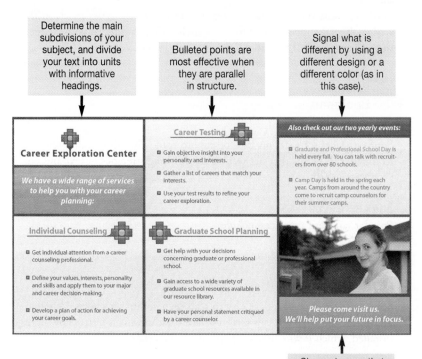

■ The inside panels of a three-panel brochure fold out to show the services offered by the Career Exploration Center.

16d Choose Type

Writing on a computer enables you to use dozens of different typefaces and fonts. (A particular style of type is called a **typeface**, such as Times New Roman or Arial. A specific kind of typeface, such as Verdana bold, is called a **font**.) At first, typefaces may all appear similar, but when you pay attention to various typefaces, you will notice how they differ.

Use typefaces effectively

Serif type

Serif and **sans serif** are major categories of typefaces. Serifs are the little wedge-shaped ends on letter forms, which scribes produced with wedge-tipped pens. Four of the most common serif typefaces are

> Times
> Palatino
> Bookman
> Garamond

Serif typefaces were designed to be easy to read. They don't call attention to themselves. Thus they are well suited for long stretches of text and are used frequently.

Sans serif type

Popular sans serif typefaces include

> Helvetica
> Arial
> Verdana

Some sans serif typefaces are easy to read on a computer screen. Verdana, Helvetica, and Arial are sans serif typefaces that most computers now have installed, which is why they are popular on Web sites.

Script and decorative type

There are many script and decorative typefaces. These typefaces tend to draw attention to themselves. They are harder to read, but sometimes they can be used for good effects.

Popular script typefaces include Nuptial Script and Dorchester Script:

> *When you want only the very best*
>
> *Snead, Potter, and Jones, Attorneys at Law*

Some decorative typefaces, including Lazyvermont and ComicStrip Classic, are informal, almost irreverent:

That's a no brainer.

Totally awesome!

Use a readable type size

It's easy to change the size of type when you compose on a computer. For long stretches of text, use at least 10- or 12-point type. Use larger type for headings and for text that will be read on a screen.

Use other effects as needed

Finally, use font formats such as **boldface**, *italics*, and <u>underlining</u> for emphasis.

16e Compose Images

Think about what an image communicates

- Think about your readers' expectations for the medium you are using. Most essays don't use images. Most Web sites and brochures do use images.
- Think about the purpose for an image. Does it illustrate a concept? highlight an important point? show something that is hard to explain in words alone? If you don't know the purpose, you may not need the image.
- Think about the focus of an image. Will readers see the part that matters? If not, you may need to crop the image.
- Provide informative captions for the images you use and refer to them in your text.

Format images for the medium you are using

Images that you want to print need to be of higher quality than those intended for the Web or the screen. Pay attention to the settings on your camera or scanner.

Digital cameras frequently make images with 72 ppi (pixels per inch), which is the maximum you can display on the screen. Most printers use a resolution from 300 to 600 ppi. Use the high-quality setting on your camera for images you intend to print.

Scanners typically offer a range of resolution from 72 to 1600 ppi. The higher the number, the finer the image, but the file size becomes larger. Images on the Web or a screen display at 72 ppi, so higher resolutions do not improve the quality but do make the image slow to load.

Take pictures that aren't boring

No matter how easy it is now to take photographs, the great majority of pictures look alike. Why? It's because most people hold their cameras at eye level and put the subject in the center.

Learn what your camera can do

Many digital cameras have special features, such as the macro setting that captures much more detail than the standard setting when photographing at close range. Read the manual that came with your camera, and try the different settings.

■ Changing the angle from the usual view often produces interesting photos.

■ Look for details. If your camera has a zoom, use it.

■ The macro setting on your camera (usually a flower symbol) allows you to take finely detailed photos from a few inches away.

■ Usually the closer you can get to your subject, the better.

Fill the frame

Most people include too much in their photographs. Decide what is essential and concentrate on getting those elements in the frame.

16f Edit Images

No matter which image editor you use, there are a few manipulations that you will need to use frequently. It's always a good idea to copy an image first and work on the copy.

■ Cropping often improves the image by emphasizing details. Smaller images use less memory and thus load faster on the screen.

- **Cropping.** Most images can be trimmed to improve visual focus and file size. To crop an image, select the rectangle tool, draw the rectangle over the area you want to keep, and select the **Crop** or **Trim** command. The part of the image outside the rectangle will be discarded. Every pixel you can squeeze out of an image intended for use on the Web makes the image display faster on a user's screen.

WRITING SMART

Save a copy of an image before editing it

Always keep a copy of your original scan or digital photo. Once you change an image and save it, you cannot restore what you changed. Use the **Save As** command to save a copy before you start editing an image.

- **Rotating images.** Often you'll find that you held your camera at a slight angle when taking pictures, especially if your subjects were moving. You can make small adjustments by using the **Rotate Image** command. You can also rotate images 90° to give them a vertical orientation.
- **Sizing images.** All photo editing programs will tell you the height and width of an image. You can resize images to fit in a particular area of a Web page or printed page. You can also change the resolution in the ppi window. Remember that if the image is intended for the Web, 72 ppi is the maximum the screen will display. Higher resolution images look no better and are slower to load.
- **Adjusting colors.** Often the colors in photographs that you scan appear "off" when you view the image on a computer monitor. The image may appear too dark or lack contrast. Sometimes the color balance appears off and you want to correct it. The basic controls for brightness, contrast, and color saturation are similar to those on your color TV. Be aware that colors look different on different monitors and what you print may not show the colors you saw on your screen.

16g Create Tables, Charts, and Graphs

Tables, charts, and graphs are easy to create in editing and presentation software, and they can be imported from one program (e.g., Excel) to another (e.g., Word). While software does much of the formatting of tables, charts, and graphs, you still have to supply the labels for the different parts of the graphic and an accurate title or caption.

STAYING ON TRACK

Use and evaluate tables

When to use tables
- To present a summary of several factors
- To present exact numbers
- To give an orderly arrangement so readers can locate and compare information

Evaluating tables
- Does the table have a clear purpose?
- Does the title indicate the purpose?
- What units do the numbers represent (dollars, people, voters, percentages, and so on)?
- What is the source of the data?
- Is the table clearly organized?
- Is the table clearly labeled?

Sample table format

Name of item	Factor 1	Factor 2	Factor 3
AAA	000	00	0
BBB	00	0	000
CCC	0	000	00

Like any graphic, tables, charts, and graphs can be used to mislead readers. Small differences can be exaggerated, for example, or relevant differences concealed (see Section 5f). You have an ethical responsibility to create accurate tables, charts, and graphs.

Tables

Extensive statistical data can be dull or cumbersome to communicate in sentences and paragraphs. Readers can more quickly and easily grasp data when they are displayed in a table. A table allows readers to view an entire set of data at once or to focus only on relevant aspects (see Table 16.1).

Table 16.1 U.S. Population by Sex and Age, 2000–2008

	2000 (April)	2005	2006	2007	2008
Resident population (1,000)	281,425	295,561	298,363	301,290	304,060
Male (1,000)	138,056	145,465	146,946	148,466	149,925
Female (1,000)	143,368	150,096	151,417	152,824	154,135
Under 5 years old (1,000)	19,176	20,301	20,436	20,730	21,006
5 to 17 years old (1,000)	53,119	53,077	53,158	53,129	52,936
18 to 44 years old (1,000)	112,184	112,665	112,737	112,891	113,190
45 to 64 years old (1,000)	61,954	72,765	74,768	76,598	78,058
65 years old and over (1,000)	34,992	36,752	37,264	37,942	38,870

Source: United States. Census Bureau. *U.S. Statistics in Brief.* 20 Nov. 2009. Web. 23 Sept. 2010.

Bar charts

Bar charts are useful for comparing data.

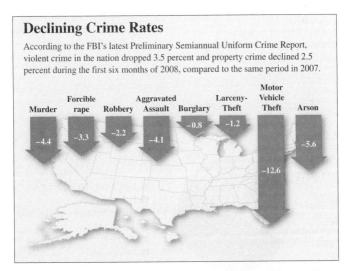

Source: United States. Dept. of Justice. Federal Bureau of Investigtion. *Some Good News: Crime Is Declining.* 12 Jan. 2009. Web. 9 Oct. 2010.

Line graphs

Line graphs are well suited for displaying changes in data across time. Line graphs can have one line, or two or more sets of data can be displayed on different lines, emphasizing the comparative rates of change.

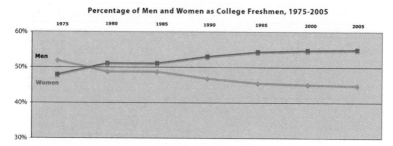

Source: United States. Census Bureau. *Statistical Abstract of the United States: 2007.* Washington: GPO, 2007. 177.

Pie charts and flowcharts

Pie charts are commonly used to represent the relationship of parts to a whole. You must have data in percentages to use a pie chart, and the slices of the pie must add up to 100%. If the slices are too small, a pie chart becomes confusing. Six or seven slices are about the limit for a pie chart that is easy to interpret.

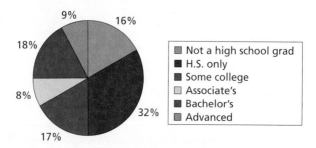

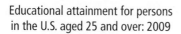 Pie charts display the relationship of parts to a whole.

Stage 1: Planning

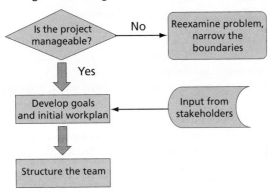

■ Flowcharts are useful for representing steps in a process.

STAYING ON TRACK

Use and evaluate charts

When to use charts
- To direct readers to what is important
- To give evidence for claims
- To show factual information visually
- To show statistical relationships more clearly than either words or numbers alone permit

Selecting the right chart

	Bar charts	Make comparisons in particular categories
	Line graphs	Show proportional trends over time
	Pie charts	Show the proportion of parts in terms of the whole
	Flowcharts	Show the steps in a process

(Continued on next page)

STAYING ON TRACK *(Continued)*

Evaluating charts
- Does the chart have a clear purpose?
- Does the title indicate the purpose?
- What do the units represent (dollars, people, voters, percentages, and so on)?
- What is the source of the data?
- Is the type of chart appropriate for the information presented?
- Is there any distortion of information (see Section 5f)?

17 | Compose in Online Genres

QUICK*TAKE*

- Know readers' expectations for online writing (see below)
- Learn how to create a blog or a discussion post (see p. 212)
- Learn how to create Web pages (see p. 216)
- Learn how to create podcasts and videos (see p. 218 and p. 220)

17a Tips for Online Writing

Meeting the expectations of online readers is critical for gaining and keeping their attention.

- **Use a clear title.** Your topic should be evident from the title.
- **Keep it short and to the point.** Cut to the chase. Online readers are scanners, and they need to find the point quickly.
- **Don't waste readers' time.** Delete unnecessary words and phrases. You don't have to say things like "In my opinion."
- **Attribute sources.** Readers think you are making up facts if you don't list your sources.
- **Link often.** No one has time to read everything. Readers appreciate writers who offer them useful links.
- **Keep blocks of text short.** Long paragraphs are hard to read on the screen. Keep text blocks five lines or shorter.
- **Use formatting.** Insert headings where needed. Create a bulleted list for a series of points.
- **Spell check and proofread carefully.** Errors stand out more in short blocks of text. They destroy your credibility.

17b Create a Blog Entry or a Discussion Post

Great bloggers who attract many readers share four qualities. They write with a lively, personal voice. They are well informed. They are honest about what they know and don't know. And they write their blog entries to initiate conversations, not to have the last word on a subject.

Blogs assigned for courses sometimes allow students a great deal of freedom to select their subject matter, and sometimes course blogs are on an assigned topic, such as responses to the readings. Discussion board posts are often similar to blogs, but they are typically written as a response to a question or posting by the instructor.

Elements of a successful blog

Title	Include an informative title.
Content	Offer something new. If you don't have anything new, then point readers to the interesting writing of others.
Writing style	Engage readers with a conversational style.
Participation	Invite responses.

What you need to do

- Develop a personal voice that conveys your personality.
- Remember that your blog is a conversation. You want to get responses to what you write.
- Do your homework. Let your readers know the sources of your information.
- Keep it short. If you have a lot to say about different subjects, write more than one entry.
- Add images if they are needed.
- Provide relevant links.
- Remember that informal writing is not sloppy, error-filled writing.

Sample reading blog entry

BLOG | **Posted by Jillian Akbar at 4:18 p.m.** 3 comments
October 5, 2010

Sara Macdonald's *Holy Cow* (2002)

Sara Macdonald does not begin her voyage from Australia to India
with the happiest of outlooks. Laden with memories of the terrible
time she had there eleven years earlier, at first she finds her only
consolation in being with her boyfriend Jonathan, a fellow journalist.
Macdonald confesses that her motives are more than just
companionship:

> Leaving my wonderful job was the hardest thing I've
> ever done but perhaps I didn't do it just for love. A
> part of me wanted to reclaim myself, to redefine my
> identity, to grow up professionally, to embrace
> anonymity and get rid of the stalker. (17)

Macdonald's account is engaging in her insightful depiction of
India. Her observations of cultural norms, such as honoring one's
family in marriage, are distant but detailed and nonjudgmental. The
chapter titles suggest the irreverent tone and humor of the book
including "Sex, Lies and Saving Face," "Three Weddings and a
Funeral," "Insane in the Membrane," "Birds of a Feather Become
Extinct Together," and "Hail Mary and Good-bye God."

Macdonald's attitude toward India lightens up in the second half
of the book, and I finally could relate as she suffered an Indian summer with nothing but a television and power cuts—exactly like my
boyfriend's apartment in August. She offers more on the exotic
imagery of India: a lotus flower growing out of slimy water, a pink
ten-foot high Mary in a sari, and the "candy-colored kingdom" of the
Divine Mother in Kerala (199). She includes my favorite image of all
when she returns to India and is submerged in "India's Kaleidoscope
of Technicolor" to feel "like Dorothy in the land of Oz" (276).

17c Compose Wikis

Mention the word "wiki" and most people associate it with Wikipedia, the hugely popular people's encyclopedia. No doubt Wikipedia has had an enormous impact on our culture, but there are many other wikis besides Wikipedia, and many differ significantly from Wikipedia.

The underlying goal of wikis is to create a collective knowledge base. Unlike blogs and discussion posts, wikis are written and edited by a number of people. Individuals not only contribute their own ideas but edit the work of others. A wiki, in theory at least, is never finished.

Elements of a Wiki

Collaboration	Everyone can access the same information and can contribute.
Content	Wikis are "encyclopedic," meaning that they aim at creating comprehensive knowledge.
Revision	Wikis are by definition always works in progress. Everyone can add and revise.
Writing style	Writing in wikis should be factual and neutral.
Community building	No one takes individual ownership of a wiki.

What you need to do

- If you are selecting a subject for a wiki, ask is it worth your and your colleagues' effort? Who will be interested in reading it? Can you find enough information?
- If you are contributing to an article on a wiki, think about what you might add.
- Stay on the topic.
- Do your homework on the subject, and provide references for all facts.
- Avoid taking sides on an issue or interpretation.
- Respect others' views and convictions.
- Write clearly and in a neutral style.

Sample educational Wiki

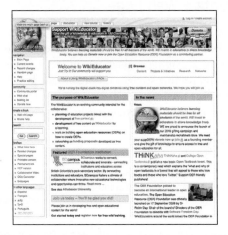

■ The WikiEducator project invites experts from around the world to create free educational materials for both schools and informal learning settings.

WRITING SMART

Know how to edit a wiki

Wikis represent the collective effort of many people. You have a responsibility to respect their effort by being a helpful contributor.

1. **Understand your goal:** Wikis allow you to contribute your knowledge to a larger project. You may change or add to the content that others have contributed or you may post new articles on new subjects.
2. **Learn the tools:** Wikis have a different set of tools than those on a standard word processor. Find the markup tools before you start editing.
3. **Assume a neutral point of view:** Wikis are usually informative rather than persuasive. Attempt to represent all relevant viewpoints. If you include opinions, note them as opinions and attribute them if possible (e.g., Senator X maintains global warming is a hoax.)
4. **Cite sources:** The sources of any information or facts that are not common knowledge should be cited.
5. **Copyright:** Don't cut and paste the work of others into a wiki. Paraphrase in your own words and cite the source.
6. **Courtesy:** Be open about disagreements, but don't resort to name calling.

17d Create a Web Page

Readers approach Web pages differently than they do older media like books and newspapers. Readers of Web pages expect to be able to move through your site according to their own interests, rather than starting on the first page and reading straight through to the last. Thus the information on a Web page needs to be clearly connected to other information on the site, but it must also, to a certain extent, stand on its own.

Elements of a Web page

Title and Subheadings	The title of your Web page should appear in the page itself and at the top of the reader's browser window. Use subheadings to divide your information into readable sections.
Navigation Menu	Navigation elements are the "table of contents" for a Web site. They should be clear and easy to find, but should not distract readers from the main content of the page.
Content	"Content" refers to the text, images, embedded videos, sound files, and all other material on your page.
Affiliation and Credentials	To earn readers' trust, you will need to provide information about you, your organization, and your affiliations. Such information often appears in footers or sidebars to the main content.

What you need to do

- If you do not have Web editing software such as Dreamweaver on your computer, find out where this software is available on your campus.
- Capture your readers' attention, and don't waste their time. Unlike readers of books, readers of Web pages can, with the click of their mouse, leave your page for thousands of other entertaining and informative sites. You must give them a reason to spend time on your site.
- Avoid large blocks of unbroken text. Divide your information into chunks, and if it runs longer than a page, consider dividing it between two or more Web pages.
- Build navigation into your content. Think about where people will need to go next after they read your page. Provide links that direct them to more information, or related topics.
- Provide links to sources. One great strength of Web writing is the way it makes other voices in the conversation instantly available to readers.
- Proofread carefully for mechanics, grammar, and spelling; they can make or break your credibility with readers.

Sample Web page for a student organization

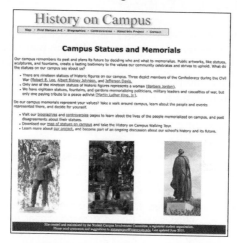

■ Campus organizations, like nearly all organizations, create Web sites to publicize their mission and activities.

WRITING SMART

Evaluate the design of a Web site

You can learn a great deal about effective Web design by keeping these criteria in mind when you visit Web sites.

1. **Audience and purpose:** How does the site identify its intended audience? Why was the site created?
2. **Content:** How informative is the content? Has the site been updated recently? What do you want to know more about?
3. **Readability:** Is there sufficient contrast between the text and the background to make it legible? Are there paragraphs that go on too long and need to be divided? Are headings inserted in the right places, and if headings are used for more than one level, are the levels indicated consistently?
4. **Visual design:** Does the site have a consistent visual theme? Do the images contribute to the visual appeal or do they detract from it?
5. **Navigation:** Does the first page indicate what else is on the site? How easy or difficult is it to move from one page to another on the site? Are there any broken links?

17e Create a Podcast

Podcasts are easy to create using your own audio editor and your Web site or you can create them in a multimedia lab and post them on a third-party site. You'll need a headset with a noise-canceling microphone, a portable voice recorder, and podcasting software. All these may be available from your campus multimedia lab.

The process for creating a podcast

Identify your subject and purpose	What exactly do you want to accomplish?
Plan your content	Do you want to conduct interviews about a subject or an issue? Do a documentary of an event? Give practical advice or instructions? Give a history or an analysis? Make a persuasive argument?
Compose your audio	Arrange and record interviews. Write a script.
Know the law	If you use music created by someone else, you likely will have to pay for the right to broadcast that music. If someone agrees to be your guest, you have the right to broadcast that person's voice.
Record your podcast	Reserve a campus audio production lab or record on your computer. Create an audio file by combining the interviews with your narration.
Edit your podcast	Your multimedia lab may have instructions or consultants for using audio editing software. Allow ample time for editing.
Publish your podcast	Export the audio into a format such as WAV or MP3 that you can put on the Web or share as a downloadable file.

Sample audio editor

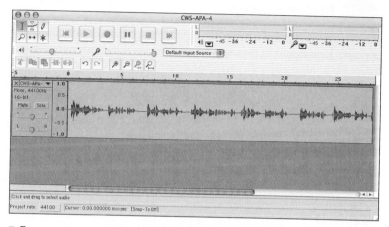

■ Free open-source audio editors are available for Windows, Mac, and Linux.

■ Many organizations, including the U.S. Geological Survey, distribute podcasts.

17f Create a Video

The cost and technical barriers for creating video have been significantly reduced. Phones and PDAs can now record video along with simple-to-use camcorders. Most new computers come with video editors installed including Apple's iMovie or Windows MovieMaker. YouTube and other video-sharing Web site make it easy to publish your video.

Nonetheless, making a high-quality video requires a great deal of effort. In addition to the technical demands, producing quality videos requires the hard work of planning and revising that extended writing tasks demand.

The process for creating a video

Identify your subject and purpose	What exactly do you want to accomplish?
Decide on your approach	Do you want to conduct interviews? Do a documentary of an event? Make an announcement? Re-enact a past event?
Plan your content	Will all the video be original? Will you incorporate other video such as YouTube clips? Will you include still images? Maps or graphs? Music? Voiceover?
Draft a script and a storyboard	A storyboard is a shot-by-shot representation of your project that will help you organize your shooting schedule.
Make a schedule and plan your locations	Quality videos take many hours to shoot and edit. Visit all locations in advance to take into account issues such as lighting and noise.
Arrange for your equipment	At minimum you will need video and sound recording equipment and an editing suite. Find out what is available from your campus multimedia lab.
Compose your video	You can create more dynamic video by using techniques of still photographers. See pages 212–215. You can add movement by using the zoom feature on your camera.
Capture audio	The microphone installed in your camera is usually not the best option. Your multimedia lab may have external microphones that will give you better quality. Microphones record ambient noises—such as the wind noise, traffic, and computer fans—which you need to minimize.
Edit your video	Editing software allows you to combine video clips and edit audio. Your multimedia lab may have instructions or consultants for using video editing software. Allow ample time for editing.
Publish your video	Export the video into a format such as QuickTime that you can put on the Web or share as a downloadable file.

Sample video editor

■ Video editors work with a time line. You can insert video clips and make transitions between clips.

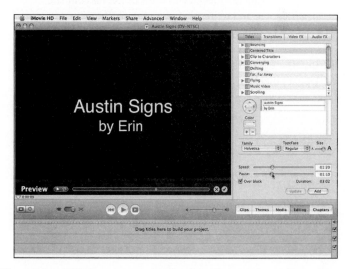

■ You can insert title frames and other frames with text using a video editor.

17g Create a Professional Social Media Site

Few could have imagined that social media would challenge the popularity of television and other traditional media in the first years of the 2000s. The rise of Facebook is a case in point. Facebook began as Facemash at Harvard University in 2003 when Mark Zuckerberg added photographs to the student directory. When Facebook was expanded to other universities and later to everyone over age 13, the number of users grew to over 500 million worldwide. By 2010 Facebook had become the second-most-visited site on the Web, closing in on frontrunner Google.

With so many people on Facebook, the uses of Facebook quickly spread beyond individual profiles. Creating a professional Facebook page or using other social media for professional purposes is more challenging than making an individual page. You must think carefully about how best to create and maintain a professional presence.

Besides reaching a large audience, social media also allow you to promote an ongoing relationship with your audience.

What you need to do

- Select or create the images you want to use on your site.
- Insert images and write headers and descriptions.
- Choose a page layout.
- Change background color and styles.
- Install the page on your Facebook account.
- Update the page regularly.

18 | Design Presentations

QUICK*TAKE*

- **Planning an effective presentation requires putting the audience first** (see below)
- **Keep your slides simple** (see p. 225)
- **Delivering an effective presentation is all about you** (see p. 226)

18a Plan a Presentation

If you are assigned to give a presentation, look carefully at the assignment for guidance on finding a topic. The process for finding a topic is similar to that for a written assignment (see Chapter 2). If your assignment requires research, you will need to document the sources of information just as you do for a research paper (see Chapters 19–25).

Start with your goal in mind

What is the real purpose of your presentation? Are you informing, persuading, or motivating? Take the elevator test. Imagine you are in an elevator with the key people who can approve or reject your ideas. Their schedule is very tight. You have only thirty seconds to convince them. Can you make your case?

This scenario is not far-fetched. One executive demanded that every new idea had to be written in one sentence on the back of a business card. What's your sentence?

It's all about your audience

Who is your audience? In college your audience is often your instructor and fellow students—an audience you know well. Many times you will not have this advantage. Take a few minutes to answer these questions.

My audience
  Will they be interested in the topic?
  Why does it matter to them?
  What are they likely to know and believe about
    the topic?
  What are they likely to not know?

Where are they likely to disagree?
What do I want them to do?
How much time do I have?
If they remember only one thing, what should it be?

Get organized

Start with pen and paper before you begin creating slides. Post-it notes are another useful planning tool.

- **Make a list of key points.** Think about the best order for your major points.
- **Plan your introduction.** Your success depends on your introduction. You must gain the attention of your audience, introduce your topic, indicate why it's important, and give a sense of where you are headed. It's a tall order, but if you don't engage your audience in the first two minutes, you will lose them.
- **Plan your conclusion.** You want to end on a strong note. Stopping abruptly or rambling on only to tail off leaves your audience with a bad impression. Give your audience something to take away, a compelling example or an idea that captures the gist of your presentation.

Build content

Content alone does not make a presentation successful, but you cannot succeed without solid content. Support your major points with relevant evidence. Consider creating a handout so your audience can refer to important facts, statistics, and quotations.

- **Facts.** Speakers who know their facts build credibility.
- **Statistics.** Effective use of statistics can give the audience the impression that you have done your homework. Statistics can also indicate that a particular example is representative.
- **Statements by authorities.** Quotations from credible experts can support key points.
- **Narratives.** Narratives are brief stories that illustrate key points. Narratives can hold the attention of the audience—but keep them short or they will become a distraction.

Exercise 18.1 Think about oral presentations you have recently seen—class lectures, presentations at work, public talks, sermons, televised speeches—and choose one that you felt was very effective and one that you felt was not at all effective. Make two lists—one on what makes a presentation effective and another on what makes a presentation ineffective.

18b Design Visuals for a Presentation

With slides, less is more. One text-filled slide after another is mind-numbingly dull. Presentations using slides can be better than a series of slides with bulleted points, one after the other seemingly forever.

Keep it simple

Compare the following examples.

Food Crisis in the United States

- The U.S. Agriculture Department reported that households struggling to buy enough food in 2008 jumped 31% over the previous year.

- The 2008 survey results suggest that almost 15% of U.S. households had trouble putting enough food on their tables, up from 11% in 2007.

- About 49 million people, including 17 million children, worried about having enough to eat.

■ Which slide makes the point most effectively?

Simple design rules!
   One point per slide
   Very few fonts
   Quality photos, not clip art
   Less text, more images
   Easy on the special effects

But what if you have a lot of data to show? Make a handout that the audience can study later. They can make notes on your handout, which gives them a personal investment. Keep your slides simple and emphasize the main points in the presentation.

Use effective charts

Again simpler is better. Limit your charts to only the detail you need to make the point. If you have a complicated table or chart, distribute it as a handout.

Food Security Status of U.S. Households, 2008

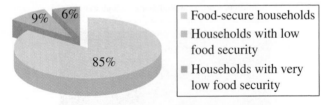

■ Limit the number of slices on a pie chart to four or fewer.

Use audio and video clips strategically

Short audio and video clips can offer concrete examples and add some variety to your presentation. An audience appreciates hearing and even seeing the people you interview. PowerPoint makes it simple to embed the files within a presentation. Be careful, however, in using the built-in sound effects in PowerPoint such as canned applause. Most sound effects are annoying and make you come off as inexperienced.

18c Deliver an Effective Presentation

If you are not passionate about your subject, you will never get your audience committed to your subject, no matter how professional looking your slides are. Believe in what you say; enthusiasm is contagious.

It's all about you

The audience didn't come to see the back of your head in front of slides. Move away from the podium and connect with them. Make strong eye contact with individuals. You will make everyone feel like you are having a conversation instead of giving a speech.

Prepare in advance

Practice your presentation, even if you have to speak to an empty chair. Check out the room and equipment in advance. If you are using your laptop with a projector installed in the room, make sure it connects. If the room has a computer connected to the projector, bring your presentation on a flash drive and download it to the computer. PowerPoint works much the same on a Mac or Windows platform.

Be professional

Pay attention to the little things.

- **Proofread carefully.** A glaring spelling error can destroy your credibility.
- **Be consistent.** If you randomly capitalize words or insert punctuation, your audience will be distracted.
- **Pay attention to the timing of your slides.** Stay in synch with your slides. Don't leave up a slide when you are talking about something else.
- **Use the "B" key.** If you get sidetracked, press the "B" key, which makes the screen go blank so the audience can focus on you. When you are ready to resume, press the "B" key again and the slide reappears.
- **Involve your audience.** Invite response during your presentation where appropriate, and leave time for questions at the end.
- **Add a bit of humor.** Humor can be tricky, especially if you don't know your audience well. But if you can get your audience to laugh, they will be on your side.
- **Slow down.** When you are nervous, you tend to go too fast. Stop and breathe. Let your audience take in what's on your slides.
- **Finish on time or earlier.** Your audience will be grateful.
- **Be courteous and gracious.** Remember to thank anyone who helped you and the audience for their comments. Eventually you will run into someone who challenges you, sometimes politely, sometimes not. If you remain cool and in control, the audience will remember your behavior long after the words are forgotten.

Avoid Death by PowerPoint

PowerPoint and similar slideware programs have become prevalent in businesses, organizations, and colleges alike, yet there are many critics of PowerPoint culture. And it's no mystery why. Think about all the bad presentations you have sat through. Write down what you don't like. Your list may look like the following:

> *What I don't like about PowerPoint presentations*
> > *Data dump presentations—too much information*
> > *Too much text on the slides, making it hard to*
> > > *read it all*
> > *Text too small to read*
> > *One bulleted point after another*
> > *Cutesy clip art and distracting transitions*
> > *Presenter reading word-for-word off the slides*

The basic problem is that presenters don't acknowledge the difference between an oral presentation and a written document. PowerPoint, Apple Keynote, and other slideware were designed to support presentations with graphics, not to be the focus of the presentation. Why should an audience take the time to come to a presentation when they are asked to read the slides? Your audience expects to be informed and motivated by you.

18d Convert a Written Text into a Presentation

The temptation when converting a written text such as a report into a presentation is to dump reams of words onto the slides. Indeed, it's simple enough to cut and paste big chunks of text, but you risk losing your audience.

Too much information on slides overloads your audience. If they try to read slides, they tune you out. If your goal is to have your audience read, then give them a printed text. Remember that they came to hear you.

People learn better when your oral presentation is accompanied by engaging images and graphics. Your voice supplies most of the information; your slides help your audience to remember and organize your presentation. Slides can also add emotional involvement.

Unwanted dogs

Carlos

a playful mixed-breed pup who was recently adopted

■ Arrange your slides so they tell a story. See Section 22f to read the project that originated this presentation.

> *Problem: 64% of animals that enter shelters are killed*

> *Joyce: "pets not neutered and arrive sick at shelters"*

■ The worst mistake you can make in a presentation besides not showing up is to read from note cards. If you must have note cards as a security blanket, put words or phrases on them that will help you remember what you had planned to say. Better yet, use your slides to jog your memory so you can keep eye contact with your audience.

Planning Research and Finding Sources

You **can learn more and do more** with MyCompLab and with the eText version of *The Brief Penguin Handbook*. For help with planning your research project and finding and evaluating your sources successfully, go to MyCompLab and click on "Resources," then select "Research." Review the tutorials (Read, Watch, Listen) within each topic, then complete the Exercises and click on the Gradebook to measure your progress.

In the **eText version** of *The Penguin Handbook*, you will also find extra worksheets and student writing samples.

RESEARCH MAP 1: CONDUCTING RESEARCH

College research writing requires that you

- determine your goals,
- find a topic,
- ask a question about that topic,
- find out what has been written about that topic,
- evaluate what has been written about that topic, and
- make a contribution to the discussion about that topic.

Here are the steps in planning research and finding sources.

1 | Plan the research project

First, analyze what you are being asked to do and set a schedule; go to Sections 19a and 19b.

Ask a question about a topic that interests you and narrow that topic. Go to 19c.

Determine what kinds of research you will need; go to 19d.

Conduct field research if it is appropriate for your project. See strategies for

- **CONDUCTING INTERVIEWS**; go to 22b.
- **ADMINISTERING SURVEYS**; go to 22c.
- **MAKING OBSERVATIONS**; go to 22d.

2 | Draft a working thesis

Draft a working thesis. Go to 19e.

Create a working bibliography. Go to 19f.

If you are assigned to create an annotated bibliography, go to 19g.

You'll see in Parts 5 and 6 the process Gabriella Lopez used to produce her research project. Gabriella's final version of her project is on pages 379–391.

See Research Map 2 (page 302) for guidance on incorporating and documenting sources.

---

3 | **Find and track sources**

Consult with a research librarian if possible, and determine where and how to start looking.

Find sources online and in print:

- for sources in **DATABASES**, go to 20b.
- for sources on the **WEB**, go to 20c.
- for **VISUAL** sources, go to 20d.
- for **PRINT** sources, go to 20e.

Keep track of sources. Go to 20f.

---

4 | **Evaluate sources**

Decide which sources are going to be useful for your project. For each source you'll need to determine the

- **RELEVANCE** to your research question; go to 21a.
- **QUALITY** for your purposes; go to 21b.

Evaluate the different types of sources you are using:

- **DATABASE and PRINT SOURCES**; go to 21c.
- **WEB SOURCES**; go to 21d.

19 | Plan Your Research

QUICK*TAKE*

- **Analyze the assignment first** (see below)
- **Find and narrow a topic** (see p. 237)
- **Draft a working thesis** (see p. 240)

19a Analyze the Research Task

Research is a creative process, which is another way of saying it is a messy process. Even though the process is complex, your results will improve if you keep the big picture in mind while you are immersed in research. If you have an assignment that requires research, look closely at what you are being asked to do.

Look for key words

Often the assignment will tell you what is expected.

- An *analysis* or *examination* asks you to look at an issue in detail, explaining its history, the people and places affected, and what is at stake.
- A *review of scholarship* requires you to summarize what key scholars and researchers have written about the issue.
- An *evaluation* requires you to make critical judgments.
- An *argument* requires you to assemble evidence in support of a claim you make.

Identify your potential readers

- How familiar are your readers with your subject?
- What background information will you need to supply?
- If your subject is controversial, what opinions or beliefs are your readers likely to hold?
- If some readers are likely to disagree with you, how can you convince them?

Assess the project's length, scope, and requirements

- What kind of research are you being asked to do?
- What is the length of the project?
- What kinds and number of sources or field research are required?
- Which documentation style—such as MLA (see Chapter 26) or APA (see Chapter 27)—is required?

Writer at Work

Gabriella Lopez made notes on her assignment sheet.

English 1102: English Composition II
Research Project

In the last project you explored an issue of interest for our college community. In the research project you will write a (proposal argument) on this issue, drawing on your research and using the persuasive strategies you've studied this semester. Propose a solution to a specific problem in our college community. Make a claim that "We should (or should not) do SOMETHING."

Instructor wants a detailed solution

You will need to identify the problem, examine whom and what is affected, what has been attempted to address the problem, and what is likely to happen in the future if nothing is changed. State your solution as specifically as possible. What do you want to achieve? How exactly will it work? Has anything been attempted up to now?

Give relevant background and acknowledge opposing points of view and any possible objections. Explain the positive consequences of your proposal. What good things will happen, and what bad things can be avoided, if your advice is taken?

Audience:
The larger campus community including students, faculty, staff, alumni, and other interested people

about 8 pages + works cited

Requirements:
Length: 1800–2200 words, not counting the list of works cited
Format: The project should be in appropriate MLA format for both the draft and final versions. Use the checklists on pp. 378 and 405 and follow the documentation guidelines in Chapter 26.
Sources: Include at least 10 different sources with at least one book source.

Due dates:
April 8 E-mail instructor topic and working thesis
April 15: Annotated bibliography due with five relevant sources
2 weeks to revise
April 22: Complete draft due. Bring two printed copies to class: one for your instructor and one for in-class peer review
May 6: Final version due

Exercise 19.1 Determine the research strategy required for each of the assignment topics below: analysis/examination, review of scholarship, evaluation, or argument.

1. Should the university reduce the number of foreign language course offerings?
2. Why do some medical professionals believe early cancer screening tests cause more harm than good?
3. What has caused a decline in the bee population in the United States?
4. Do antiwar movies actually glamorize war?
5. Should states be allowed to opt out of national curriculum standards?

 Set a Schedule

Writer at Work

Gabriella used the assignment to create her work schedule.

TASK	DATE
Find topic and decide what research is needed	April 1
Start a working bibliography and draft a working thesis	April 1–8
E-mail instructor topic and working thesis	April 8
Read and evaluate sources and write annotations	April 8–15
Submit annotated bibliography	April 15
Summarize and paraphrase sources; plan an organization; write a draft	April 15–21
Review my draft	April 21
Bring 2 copies of draft to class	April 22
Revise, edit, and check formatting and documentation	April 22–May 5
Submit final version	May 6

19c Find and Narrow a Topic

If you ask meaningful questions, research will be enjoyable. Your courses may give you ideas about questions to ask, or you may simply want to pursue an interest of your own. One good way to begin is by browsing, which may also show you the breadth of possibilities included in a topic and possibly lead you to new topics.

You might begin browsing by doing one or more of the following.

- **Visit "Research by Subject" on your library's Web site.** Clicking on a subject such as "African and African American Studies" will take you to a list of online resources. Often you can find an e-mail link to a reference librarian who can assist you.
- **Look for topics in your courses.** Browse your course notes and readings. Are there any topics you might want to explore in greater depth?
- **Browse a Web subject directory.** Web subject directories, including Yahoo Directory (dir.yahoo.com), are useful when you want to narrow a topic or learn what subcategories a topic might contain. In addition to the Web subject directories, the Library of Congress Virtual Reference Shelf (www.loc.gov/rr/askalib/virtualref.html) may help you identify sites relevant to your topic.
- **Consult a specialized encyclopedia.** Specialized encyclopedias focus on a single area of knowledge, go into more depth about a subject, and often include bibliographies. Check if your library database page has a link to the Gale Virtual Reference Library, which offers entries from many specialized encyclopedias and reference sources.
- **Look for topics as you read.** When you read actively, you ask questions and respond to ideas in the text. Review what you wrote in the margins or the notes you have made about something you read that interested you. You may find a potential topic.

Writer at Work

Gabriella Lopez knew immediately that she wanted to write about the general topic of sustainable food on campus. Gabriella was personally aware of the difficulty of healthy eating on campus, and she had voiced concerns in her dormitory about the few options for eating organic food. But she was also aware that many students, including herself, were struggling to pay for college and didn't want to pay more for campus food. She drew different possibilities she might pursue and what objections might be raised.

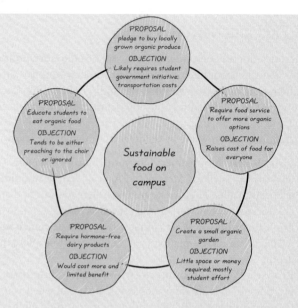

Two possibilities looked promising—creating a student organization to pledge to buy fresh, locally grown produce and creating a small organic garden on campus. She decided to go with the garden because the idea is simpler to implement.

STAYING ON TRACK

Decide if a topic is manageable

It can be tricky to find a balance between what you want to say about a topic and the amount of space you have to say it in. Usually your instructor will suggest a length for your project, which should help you decide how to limit your topic. If you suspect your topic is becoming unmanageable and your project may be too long, look for ways to narrow your focus.

Off track	A 5-page paper on European witch hunts
On track	A 5-page paper tracing two or three major causes of the European witch hunts of the fifteenth and sixteenth centuries
Off track	A 10-page paper on accounting fraud
On track	A 10-page paper examining how a new law would help prevent corporate accounting fraud

Exercise 19.2 Think about a general topic you might write about for one of your courses (immigration laws, the Harlem Renaissance, the Mexican Revolution, green building, H1N1 influenza, or any other). Then, gather lists of subtopics by consulting your class notes and readings, researching by subject on your library's Web site, using a Web subject directory, and consulting a specialized encyclopedia (if applicable). Answer the questions that follow.

1. What subtopics do all of the resources provide for this general topic?
2. Do any of the subtopics lead to other subtopics? Which ones?
3. Which resource produced the most useful list of subtopics for this general topic?
4. Which of the subtopics generated seems the most fruitful to pursue? Why?

19d Determine What Kind of Research You Need

When you begin your research, you will have to make a few educated guesses about where to look. Ask these questions before you start.

- How much information do you need? The assignment may specify the number of sources you should consult.
- Are particular types of sources required? If so, do you understand why those sources are required?
- How current should the information be? Some assignments require you to use the most up-to-date information you can locate.
- Do you need to consider point of view? Argument assignments sometimes require you to consider opposing viewpoints on an issue.

Secondary research

Most people who do research rely partly or exclusively on the work of others as sources of information. Research based on the work of others is called **secondary research**. In the past this information was contained almost exclusively in collections of print materials housed in libraries, but today enormous amounts of information are available on the Internet and in various recorded media. Chapters 20 and 21 explain in detail how to find and evaluate database, Web, and print sources.

Primary research

Much of the research done at a university creates new information through **primary research**: experiments, data-gathering surveys and interviews, detailed observations, and the examination of historical documents. If you are researching a campus issue such as the problem of inadequate parking for students, you may need to conduct interviews, make observations, and take a survey. Or, if you are training in a field where primary research is important, you may be required to conduct research in order to learn research methods. Chapter 22 explains how to plan and conduct three types of field research: interviews (22b), surveys (22c), and observations (22d).

19e Draft a Working Thesis

If you ask a focused and interesting research question, your answer will be your **working thesis**. This working thesis will be the focus of the remainder of your research and ultimately your research project.

Ask questions about your topic

When you have a topic that is interesting to you, manageable in scope, and possible to research using sources or doing field research, then your next task is to ask researchable questions.

Explore a definition

- While many (most) people think X is a Y, can X be better thought of as a Z?

   Most people think of deer as harmless animals that are benign to the environment, but their overpopulation devastates young trees in forests, leading to loss of habitat for birds and other species that depend on those trees.

Evaluate a person, activity, or thing

- Can you argue that a person, activity, or thing is either good, better, or best (or bad, worse, or worst) within its class?

   Fender Stratocasters from the 1950s remain the best electric guitars ever made because of their versatility, sound quality, and player-friendly features.

Examine why something happened

- Can you argue that while there were obvious causes of Y, Y would not have occurred had it not been for X?

  College students are called irresponsible when they run up high credit card debts that they cannot pay off, but these debts would not have occurred if credit card companies did not aggressively market cards and offer high lines of credit to students with no income.

- Can you argue for an alternative cause rather than the one many people assume?

  The defeat of the Confederate Army at the Battle of Gettysburg in July 1863 is often cited as the turning point in the Civil War, but in fact the South was running out of food, equipment, and soldiers, and it lost its only real chance of winning when Great Britain failed to intervene on its side.

Counter objections to a position

- Can the reverse or opposite of an opposing claim be argued?

  New medications that relieve pain are welcomed by runners and other athletes, but these drugs also mask signals that our bodies send us, increasing the risk of serious injury.

Propose a solution to a problem

- Can you propose a solution to a local problem?

  The traffic congestion on our campus could be eased by creating bike lanes on College Drive, which would encourage more students, faculty, and staff to commute by bicycle.

Turn your answers into a working thesis

Topic	Reading disorders
Researchable question	Why do some people learn to read top-to-bottom Chinese characters more easily than left-to-right alphabetic writing?
Working thesis	The direction of text flow may be an important factor in how an individual learns to read.

Writer at Work

Garbriella's working thesis answered her research question.

TOPIC	Sustainable food on our campus
RESEARCHABLE QUESTION	How can our campus increase the amount of locally grown food that students eat without adding to the cost they pay and increase student awareness of environmental stewardship?
WORKING THESIS	Establishing a small organic garden can provide both fresh, healthy food and a low-cost way to support our school's environmental mission.

Exercise 19.3 Choose one of the subtopics you found for Exercise 19.2. Do some preliminary research on this subject and develop a topic, research question, and working thesis, using the advice given in Section 19e.

19f Create a Working Bibliography

When you begin to collect your sources, make sure you get full bibliographic information for everything you might want to use in your project: articles, books, Web sites, and other materials. Decide which documentation style you will use. If your instructor does not tell you which style is appropriate, ask. (The major documentation styles—MLA, APA, CMS, and CSE—are dealt with in detail in Chapters 26-29.)

Find the necessary bibliographic information

Chapter 20 gives instructions on what information you will need to collect for each kind of source. In general, as you research and develop a working bibliography, the rule of thumb is to write down more information rather than less. You can always delete unnecessary information when it comes time to format your citations according to your chosen documentation style (APA, MLA, CMS, or CSE), but it is time-consuming to go back to sources to find missing bibliographic information.

Record bibliographic information

There are many ways to record and organize your sources. You can record each source's bibliographic information on individual note cards; you can print out or photocopy relevant pages from each source; you can e-mail articles to yourself from library databases; and you may be able to use your library's bibliographic software to manage citations (but be aware that the software often does not get everything you need). Whichever way you choose, always check that you have complete and accurate publication information for each source.

Alternatives to copying from a source are cutting and pasting into a file (for online sources) or making photocopies (for a print source). Both methods ensure accuracy in copying sources, but in either case make sure you attach full bibliographic information to the file or photocopy.

If you are not careful about putting quotation marks around material you cut and paste, you can get confused about where the material came from and plagiarize unintentionally (see Chapters 23 and 24 for information on incorporating sources and avoiding plagiarism). In Chapter 26 you'll find detailed instructions on how to find the information you need for MLA documentation. See Chapter 27 for APA, Chapter 28 for CMS, and Chapter 29 for CSE documentation.

Writer at Work

Gabriella was careful to distinguish her notes from material she quoted directly. She identified by page number any quoted material.

Pollan, Michael. The Omnivore's Dilemma: A Natural History
  of Four Meals. New York: Penguin, 2006. Print.

Pollan sums up the big problem I want to write about.
     "Our ingenuity in feeding ourselves is prodigious, but
     at various points our technologies come into conflict
     with nature's way of doing things, as when we seek
     to maximize efficiency by planting crops or raising
     animals in vast monocultures. This is something nature
     never does, always and for good reason practicing
     diversity instead." (9)

19g Create an Annotated Bibliography

A **working bibliography** is an alphabetized list of sources with complete publication information that you collect while researching your topic. An **annotated bibliography** builds on the basic citations of a working bibliography by adding a brief summary or evaluation of each source. Annotated bibliographies must include

- a complete citation in the documentation style you are using (MLA, APA, CMS, CSE).
- a concise summary of the content and scope.

In addition, your instructor may ask you to include one or more of the following:

- a comment on the relevance of the source to your research topic.
- an evaluation of the background and qualifications of the author.
- a comparison to another work on your list.

Writer at Work

Gabriella Lopez

Professor Kimbro

English 1102

15 Apr. 2010

Annotated Bibliography

Bartholemew, Mel. *All New Square Foot Gardening: Grow More in Less Space*. Franklin, TN: Cool Spring P, 2006. Print.

Mel Bartholemew is the expert on square foot gardening. This book explains everything you need to know about constructing and maintaining a square-foot garden. It will help me show not only how to create small campus gardens, but all of the options available and how easy and inexpensive it will be.

Berman, Jillian. "Sustainability Could Secure a Good Future: College Students Flock to "Green" Degrees, Careers." *USA Today* 3 Apr. 2009, final ed.: 7D. *LexisNexis Academic*. Web. 6 Apr. 2010.

This article describes how the growth in "green" jobs is making students seek colleges that provide them with opportunities to learn about sustainability. This trend will be useful in helping me argue that our college needs to offer students opportunities to learn about sustainability in real ways.

Lewington, Jennifer. "Lean Green Campus Machines:

> Students Are at the Forefront of a Grassroots
>
> Environmental Revolution As They Coax—and
>
> Sometimes Embarrass—Administrators into Walking
>
> the Walk with Them." *The Globe and Mail* [Toronto] 23
>
> Oct. 2008: 14. *LexisNexis Academic*. Web. 8 Apr. 2010.

This article talks about how students in Canada are

getting administrators to support sustainability. It shows

how a new kind of collaborative, rather than

confrontational, student activism works.

Rozin, Paul, Rebecca Bauer, and Dana Catanese. "Food

> and Life, Pleasure and Worry, among American
>
> College Students: Gender Differences and Regional
>
> Similarities." *Journal of Personality and Social*
>
> *Psychology* 85.1 (2003): 132–141. *PsycARTICLES*.
>
> Web. 10 Apr. 2010.

This scientific article describes a study of how students think

about food. It not only complements Michael Pollan's

argument that we have developed an unhealthy relationship

with food, but it also shows how important the college years

are for establishing that relationship.

"Starting a College Farm: Stories from the Yale Sustainable

> Food Project." *Yale Sustainable Food Project*. Yale
>
> Sustainable Food Project, n.d. Web. 9 Apr. 2010.

This document is invaluable in showing how Yale

students gained and maintain support for the

Sustainable Food Project. It is written by students who

work in that program.

20 | Find Sources

Develop Strategies for Finding Sources

Libraries still contain many resources not available on the Web. Even more important, libraries have professional research librarians who can help you locate sources quickly.

Determine where to start looking

Searches using *Google* or *Yahoo!* turn up thousands of items, many of which are often not useful for research. Considering where to start is the first step.

Scholarly books and articles in scholarly journals often are the highest quality sources, but the lag in publication time makes them less useful for very current topics. Newspapers cover current issues, but often not in the depth of books and scholarly journals. Government Web sites and publications are often the best for finding statistics and are also valuable for researching science and medicine.

Learn the art of effective key word searches

Key word searches take you to the sources you need. Start with your working thesis and generate a list of possible key words for researching your thesis.

First, think of key words that make your search **more specific**. For example, a search for sources related to youth voter participation might focus more specifically on young adults *and*

> voter registration
> historical participation rates
> voter turnout

WRITING SMART

Find the right kinds of sources

Type of Source	Type of Information	How to Find Them
Scholarly books	Extensive and in-depth coverage of nearly any subject	Library catalog
Scholarly journals	Reports of new knowledge and research findings by experts	Online library databases
Trade journals	Reports of information pertaining to specific industries, professions, and products	Online library databases
Popular magazines	Reports or summaries of current news, sports, fashion, entertainment subjects	Online library databases
Newspapers	Recent and current information; foreign newspapers are useful for international perspectives	Online library databases
Government publications	Government-collected statistics, studies, and reports; especially good for science and medicine	Library catalog and city, state, and federal government Web sites
Videos, audios, documentaries, maps	Information varies widely	Library catalog, Web, and online library databases

Also think about **more general** ways to describe what you are doing—what synonyms can you think of for your existing terms? Instead of relying on "young adult," try key words like

under 30
Generation Y
college students

You can even search using terms that refer to related people, events, or movements that you are familiar with

> Rock the Vote
> MTV voter registration drive

Many databases have a thesaurus that can help you find more key words.

WRITING SMART

Adjust searches to improve results

If your search turns up hundreds or thousands of hits, consider the following options:

- Try more specific search terms.
- Use a phrase within quotation marks or specify "the exact phrase."
- Specify NOT for terms you are not interested in finding.
- Limit your search by a date range.
- Limit the search by domain name (site:.edu, site:.gov).

If your search turns up fewer than ten hits, you could use these options.

- Check your spelling.
- Try broader search terms.
- Try another index or search engine.

Writer at Work

Gabriella Lopez wanted the most recent information she could locate about student-run farms, so she searched the *LexisNexis Academic* database, which is an excellent tool for searching newspapers. She first used "campus farms" as her key words, but this search produced over 2,000 sources, most off her topic. She next tried "college organic farm" and limited the search to the last five years, which produced a more manageable sixteen sources.

LexisNexis *Academic*		Home
General Searching	**Power Search**	Help Clear
» Easy Search™	Use of this service is subject to Terms and Conditions	
» Power Search ▶		
» **Tip:** Click the headings below to view links to specialized search forms and other useful features.	Search Type: ● Terms & Connectors ○ Natural Language	
	Search Terms: college organic farm	Search
	Specify Date: Previous 5 years	

Exercise 20.1   What kind of source (scholarly book, scholarly journal, trade journals, popular magazines, newspapers, government publications, or multimedia) would provide the most useful information about the following?

1. nutritional guidelines for school lunches
2. public opinion on a local ordinance
3. what cars will be on the market next year
4. the history of "doping" in the Olympics
5. the efficacy of light therapy in treating depression
6. a day in the life of a soldier deployed in Afghanistan

20b Find Sources in Databases

Sources found through library databases have already been filtered for you by professional librarians. They will include some common sources like popular magazines and newspapers, but the greatest value of database sources are the many journals, abstracts, studies, e-books, and other writing produced by specialists whose work has been scrutinized and commented upon by other experts. When you read a source from a library database, chances are you are hearing an informed voice in an important debate.

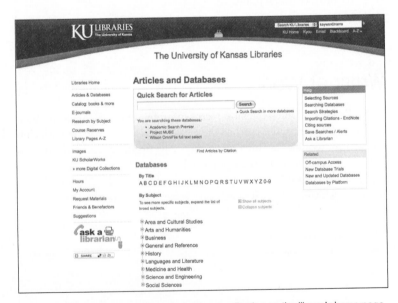

■ You can find a link to your library's database collection on the library's home page.
Reprinted by permission of The University of Kansas Libraries.

WRITING SMART

Know the advantages of database versus Web sources

	Library database sources	**Web sources**
Speed	✓ Users can find information quickly	✓ Users can find information quickly
Accessibility	✓ Available 24/7	✓ Available 24/7
Organization	✓ Materials are organized for efficient search and retrieval	User must look in many different places for related information
Consistency and quality	✓ Librarians review and select resources	Anyone can claim to be an "expert," regardless of qualifications
Comprehensiveness	✓ Collected sources represent a wide and representative body of knowledge	No guarantee that the full breadth of an issue will be represented
Permanence	✓ Materials remain available for many years	Materials can disappear or change in an instant
Free of overt bias	✓ Even sources with a definite agenda are required to meet certain standards of documentation and intellectual rigor	Sources are often a "soapbox" for organizations or individuals with particular agendas and little knowledge or experience
Free of commercial slant	✓ Because libraries pay for their collections, sources are largely commercial-free	Sources are often motivated primarily by the desire to sell you something

Locate databases

You can find databases on your library's Web site. Sometimes you will find a list of databases. Sometimes you select a subject, and then you are directed to databases. Sometimes you select the name of a database vendor such as EBSCO or ProQuest. The vendor is the company that provides databases to the library.

Use databases

Your library has a list of databases and indexes by subject. If you can't find this list on your library's Web site, ask a reference librarian for help. Follow these steps to find articles.

1. Select a database appropriate to your subject. (For example, if you are researching multiple sclerosis, you might start with *Health Reference Center, MEDLINE, PsycINFO,* or *PubMed.*)
2. Search the database using your list of key words. (You could start with *multiple sclerosis* and then combine *MS* with other terms to narrow your search.)
3. Once you have chosen an article, print or e-mail to yourself the complete citation to the article. Look for the e-mail link after you click on the item you want.
4. Print or e-mail to yourself the full text if it is available. The full text is better than cutting and pasting because you might lose track of which words are yours, leading to unintended plagiarism.
5. If the full text is not available, check the online library catalog to see if your library has the journal.

Your library will probably have printed handouts or information on the Web that tells you which database to use for a particular subject. Ask a librarian who works at the reference or information desk to help you.

If you wish to get only full-text articles, you can check that option. Full-text documents give you the same text you would find in print. Sometimes the images are not reproduced in the HTML versions, but the PDF versions show the actual printed copy.

Results of articles in the PDF format are scans of the printed text with page numbers. Get the PDF version if it is available. Articles in HTML format usually do not contain the page numbers.

Writer at Work

Gabriella did a full-text search for "sustainable farm" on *Academic Search Complete*.

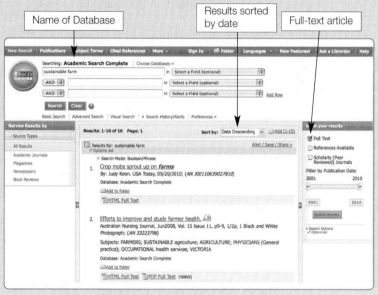

Image courtesy of EBSCO PUBLISHING

Common Databases

Academic OneFile	Indexes periodicals from the arts, humanities, sciences, social sciences, and general news, with full-text articles and images. (*Formerly Expanded Academic ASAP*)
Academic Search Premier and Complete	Provides full-text articles for thousands of scholarly publications, including social sciences, humanities, education, computer sciences, engineering, language and linguistics, literature, medical sciences, and ethnic-studies journals.
ArticleFirst	Indexes journals in business, the humanities, medicine, science, and social sciences.
Business Search Premier	Provides full-text articles in all business disciplines.

EBSCOhost Research Databases	Gateway to a large collection of EBSCO databases, including *Academic Search Premier* and *Complete*, *Business Source Premier* and *Complete*, *ERIC*, and *Medline*.
Factiva	Provides full-text articles on business topics, including articles from *The Wall Street Journal*.
Google Books	Allows you to search within books and gives you snippets surrounding search terms for copyrighted books. Many books out of copyright have the full text. Available for everyone.
Google Scholar	Searches scholarly literature according to criteria of relevance. Available for everyone.
General OneFile	Contains millions of full-text articles about a wide range of academic and general-interest topics.
JSTOR	Provides scanned copies of scholarly journals.
LexisNexis Academic	Provides full text of a wide range of newspapers, magazines, government and legal documents, and company profiles from around the world.
ProQuest Databases	Like EBSCOhost, ProQuest is a gateway to a large collection of databases with over 100 billion pages, including the best archives of doctoral dissertations and historical newspapers.

WRITING SMART

Why Database Searches Are Often Better Than the First 10 Hits on Google

If you did a Google search for *oil spill* in summer 2010, the first link you saw on the list was www.BP.com/OilSpillNews, a site that issued BP press releases giving their spin on the oil spill. BP paid Google a large sum to have their site show up first. Similarly, a search for *oil spill lawsuits* produced three law firms looking for business at the top of the list for the same reason—the law firms paid to be first.

There's nothing wrong with Google making money through advertising, but the first hits on Google searches are often of limited value for research. Library databases are supported by subscriptions from libraries, not through advertising, and you don't have to wade through the commercial clutter.

Exercise 20.2 Explore the following databases listed in the table on p. 263 through the Web or your library. In which of these would you be able to find the following

1. full-text scholarly articles about feminism and the *Twilight* series of books?
2. articles about the increase of gluten allergies in the United States
3. full text articles about job growth
4. full-text general interest articles about tourism in Vietnam
5. full issues of the journal *Asian Music*

20c Find Sources on the Web

Because anyone can publish on the Web, there is no overall quality control and there is no system of organization—two strengths we take for granted in libraries. Nevertheless, the Web offers you some resources for current topics that would be difficult or impossible to find in a library. The key to success is knowing where you are most likely to find current and accurate information about the particular question you are researching, and knowing how to access that information.

Use search engines wisely

Search engines designed for the Web work in ways similar to library databases and your library's online catalog but with one major difference. Databases typically do some screening of the items they list, but search engines potentially take you to everything on the Web—millions of pages in all. Consequently, you have to work harder to limit searches on the Web or you can be deluged with tens of thousands of items.

Kinds of search engines
A search engine is a set of programs that sort through millions of items at incredible speed. There are four basic kinds of search engines.

1. **Key word search engines** (e.g., *Bing, Google, Yahoo!*). Key word search engines give different results because they assign different weights to the information they find.
2. **Meta-search engines** (e.g., *Dogpile, MetaCrawler, Surfwax*). Meta-search engines allow you to use several search engines simultaneously. While the concept is sound, meta-search agents are limited because many do not access Google or Yahoo!
3. **Web directories** (e.g., *Britannica.com, Yahoo! Directory*). Web directories classify Web sites into categories and are the closest equivalent to the cataloging system used by libraries. On most directories professional editors decide how to index a particular Web site. Web directories also allow key word searches.

4. **Specialized search engines** are designed for specific purposes:
   - regional search engines (e.g., *Baidu* for China)
   - medical search engines (e.g., *WebMD*)
   - legal search engines (e.g., *Lexis*)
   - job search engines (e.g., *Monster.com*)
   - property search engines (e.g., *Zillow*)
   - comparison-shopping search engines (e.g., *Froogle*)

Advanced searches

Search engines often produce too many hits and are therefore not always useful. If you look only at the first few items, you may miss what is most valuable. The alternative is to refine your search. Most search engines offer you the option of an advanced search, which gives you the opportunity to limit numbers.

The advanced searches on *Google* and *Yahoo!* give you the options of using a string of words to search for sites that contain (1) all the words, (2) the exact phrase, (3) any of the words, or (4) that do not contain certain words. They also allow you to specify the site, the date range, the file format, and the domain. For example, if you want to limit a search for *multiple sclerosis* to government Web sites such as the National Institutes of Health, you can specify the domain as **.gov**.

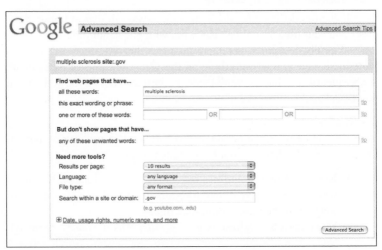

■ Limiting the domain to .gov eliminates commercial sites from the search.

The **OR** operator is useful if you don't know exactly which term will get the results you want, especially if you are searching within a specific site. For example, you could try this search: "face-to-face OR f2f site: webworkerdaily.com."

WRITING SMART

Keep track of Web research

One of the easiest ways to return to Web sites you find useful for your research is to use the **Add to Favorites** or **Add Bookmark** command on your browser. You can arrange the sites you mark in folders and even download them onto a keychain drive or other storage device so you can retrieve the Web sites on other computers.

You can also use the **History** menu on your browser to obtain a list of sites you have visited. Most allow you to go back a few days, so if you remember a site you visited but didn't add to your favorites list, you can probably find it again.

You can also exclude terms with the – operator. If you want to search for social network privacy, but not Facebook, try "social network privacy – Facebook."

Find online government sources

The federal government has made many of its publications available on the Web. Also, many state governments now publish important documents on the Web. Often the most current and most reliable statistics are government statistics. Among the more important government resources are the following:

- **Bureau of Labor Statistics** (www.bls.gov/). Source for official U.S. government statistics on employment, wages, and consumer prices
- **Census Bureau** (www.census.gov/). Contains a wealth of links to sites for population, social, economic, and political statistics, including the *Statistical Abstract of the United States* (www.census.gov/compendia/statab/)
- **Centers for Disease Control** (www.cdc.gov/). Authoritative and trustworthy source for health statistics
- **CIA World Factbook** (www.cia.gov/library/publications/the-world-factbook/). Resource for geographic, economic, demographic, and political information on the nations of the world
- **Library of Congress** (www.loc.gov/). Many of the resources of the largest library in the world are available on the Web.
- **National Institutes of Health** (www.nih.gov/). Extensive health information including MedlinePlus searches
- **NASA** (www.nasa.gov/). A rich site with much information and images concerning space exploration and scientific discovery

- **Thomas** (thomas.loc.gov/). The major source of legislative information, including bills, committee reports, and voting records of individual members of Congress
- **USA.gov** (www.usa.gov/). The place to start when you are not sure where to look for government information

Find online reference sources

Your library's Web site has a link to **reference site**s, either on the main page or under another heading like **research tools**.

Reference sites are usually organized by subject, and you can find resources under the subject heading.

- **Business information** (links to business databases and sites like *Hoover's* that profile companies)
- **Dictionaries** (including the *Oxford English Dictionary* and various subject dictionaries and language dictionaries)
- **Education** (including *The College Blue Book* and others)
- **Encyclopedias** (including *Britannica Online* and others)
- **Government information** (links to federal, state, and local Web sites)
- **Reference books** (commonly used books like atlases, almanacs, biographies, handbooks, and histories)
- **Statistics and demographics** (links to federal, state, and local government sites; *FedStats* [www.fedstats.gov/] is a good place to start)

Find and explore archives

An archive is traditionally a physical place where historical documents, such as manuscripts and letters, are stored. Recently the term has come to mean any collection of documents, typically preserved for educational purposes, and many are now available online.

For example, if you want to do a research project on how people living at the time of the American Civil War understood the war, you will need to look at documents written at the time—letters, diaries, newspapers, speeches, and sermons. *The Valley of the Shadow* project has made available on the Web thousands of documents written at the time of the Civil War from Augusta County, Virginia, and Franklin County, Pennsylvania (valley.vcdh.virginia.edu/).

Other extensive archive sites include the following:

- **American Memory** (memory.loc.gov/ammem/) Library of Congress site offering over 11 million digital items from more than a hundred historical collections
- **A Chronology of U.S. Historical Documents** (www.law.ou.edu/hist/) Sponsored by the University of Oklahoma College of Law,

this site contains chronologically ordered primary sources ranging from the Federalist Papers to recent presidential addresses.

- **JSTOR: The Scholarly Journal Archive** (www.jstor.org) Electronic archive of the back issues of over a hundred scholarly journals, mainly in the humanities and social sciences fields
- **University of Michigan Documents Center** (www.lib.umich.edu/government-documents-center/) Huge repository of local, state, federal, foreign, and international government information; Includes an extensive subject directory

Search interactive media

The Internet allows you to access other people's opinions on thousands of topics. Millions of people post messages on discussion lists and groups, Facebook groups, blogs, RSS feeds, Twitter, and so on. Much of what you read on interactive media sites is undocumented and highly opinionated, but you can still gather important information about people's attitudes and get tips about other sources, which you can verify later.

Several search engines have been developed for interactive media. Facebook and Twitter also have search engines for their sites.

Discussion list search engines

- **Big Boards** (www.big-boards.com). Tracks over 2,000 of the most active discussion forums
- **Google Groups** (groups.google.com). Archives discussion forums dating back to 1981
- **Yahoo Groups** (groups.yahoo.com). A directory of groups by subject

---

WRITING SMART

Know the limitations of Wikipedia

Wikipedia is a valuable resource for current information and for popular culture topics that are not covered in traditional encyclopedias. You can find out, for example, that SpongeBob SquarePants's original name was "SpongeBoy," but it had already been copyrighted.

Nevertheless, many instructors and the scholarly community in general do not consider Wikipedia a reliable source of information for a research project. The fundamental problem with Wikipedia is stability, not whether the information is correct or incorrect. Wikipedia and other wikis constantly change. The underlying idea of documenting sources is that readers can consult the same sources that you consulted. To be on the safe side, treat Wikipedia as you would a blog. Consult other sources to confirm what you find on Wikipedia and cite those sources.

Blog search engines

- **Google Blog Search** (blogsearch.google.com). Searches blogs in several languages besides English
- **IceRocket** (blogs.icerocket.com). Searches blogs, MySpace, and Twitter
- **Technorati** (www.technorati.com). Searches blogs and other user-generated content

20d Find Multimedia Sources

Massive collections of images; audio files including music, speeches, and podcasts; videos, maps; charts; graphs; and other resources are now available on the Web. For example, the Hubble Space Telescope discovered a planet being devoured by a star in 2010. A search for "hubble star eats planet" turns up the image below on NASA's Web site.

Find images

The major search engines for images include the following:

- **Bing Images** (www.bing.com/images/)
- **Google Image Search** (images.google.com/)

■ The Hubble Space Telescope finds a star eating a planet (www.nasa.gov/mission_pages/hubble/science/planet-eater.html).

- **Picsearch** (www.picsearch.com/)
- **Yahoo! Image Search** (images.search.yahoo.com)

Libraries and museums also offer large collections. For example, the American Memory collection in the Library of Congress offers an important visual record of the history of the United States (memory.loc.gov/ammem/).

Find videos

- **Bing Videos** (www.bing.com/videos/)
- **blinkx** (www.blinkx.com/)
- **Google Videos** (video.google.com/)
- **Yahoo! Video Search** (video.search.yahoo.com)
- **YouTube** (www.youtube.com)

Find podcasts

- **iTunes Podcast Resources** (www.apple.com/itunes/podcasts/)
- **PodcastDirectory.com** (http://www.podcastdirectory.com/)

Find charts, graphs, and maps

You can find statistical data represented in charts and graphs on many government Web sites.

- **Statistical Abstract of the United States** (www.census.gov/compendia/statab/)
- **Google Earth** (earth.google.com/)
- **National Geographic Map Machine** (mapmachine.nationalgeographic.com/)
- **Perry Casteñada Map Collection, University of Texas** (www.lib.utexas.edu/maps/map_sites/map_sites.html)

Respect copyright

Just because images, videos, and other multimedia files are easy to download from the Web does not mean that everything is available for you to use. Look for the creator's copyright notice and suggested credit line. This notice will tell you if you can reproduce the multimedia file.

For example, the Cascades Volcano Observatory makes their images available to all: "The maps, graphics, images, and text found on our website, unless stated otherwise, are within the Public Domain. You may download and use them. Credit back to the USGS/Cascades Volcano Observatory is appreciated." Most images on government Web sites can be reproduced, but check the copyright restrictions. You should acknowledge the source of any image you use.

In many cases you will find a copyright notice that reads, "Any use or retransmission of text or images in this website without written consent of the copyright owner constitutes copyright infringement and is prohibited." You must write to the creator to ask permission to use an image from a site that is not in the public domain, even if you cannot find a copyright notice.

> **Exercise 20.3**   Use the image search engines and video search engines mentioned in this chapter to research images and video for three or more keywords related to a current event (the Gulf oil disaster, for example), or a person or thing in the news (Kim Jong Il or the iPad, for example). Compare the first few results. What differences do you see? What similarities? What might this tell you about the sources for the images and videos? Why do you think the images and videos are presented in this order on each site? How are the sources for the images presented on each site? Can you think of instances when you might choose one image or video search site over another?

20e Find Print Sources

Print sources may seem "old fashioned" if you grew up with the Internet. You might even feel a little bit intimidated by them. But they are the starting point for much of the research done by experts. In college and beyond, they are indispensable. No matter how current the topic you are researching, you will likely find information in print sources that is simply not available online.

Print sources have other advantages as well.

- Books are shelved according to subject, allowing easy browsing.
- Books often have bibliographies, directing you to other research on the subject.
- You can search for books in multiple ways: author, title, subject, or call letter.
- The majority of print sources have been evaluated by scholars, editors, and publishers, who decided whether they merited publication.

Find books

Nearly all libraries now shelve books according to the Library of Congress Classification System, which uses a combination of letters and numbers to give you the book's unique location in the library. The Library of Congress call number begins with a letter or letters that represent the broad subject area into which the book is classified.

Writer at Work

Gabriella found this book by doing a subject search for "farming" AND "sustainability."

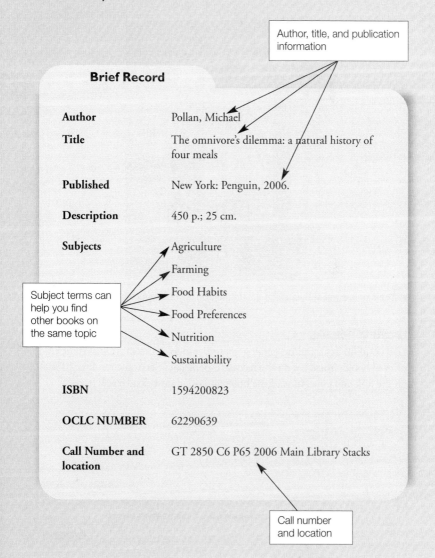

Author, title, and publication information

Brief Record

Author	Pollan, Michael
Title	The omnivore's dilemma: a natural history of four meals
Published	New York: Penguin, 2006.
Description	450 p.; 25 cm.
Subjects	Agriculture
	Farming
	Food Habits
	Food Preferences
	Nutrition
	Sustainability
ISBN	1594200823
OCLC NUMBER	62290639
Call Number and location	GT 2850 C6 P65 2006 Main Library Stacks

Subject terms can help you find other books on the same topic

Call number and location

Locating books in your library

The floors of your library where books are shelved are referred to as the stacks. The call number will enable you to find the item in the stacks. You will need to consult the locations guide for your library, which gives the level and section where an item is shelved.

■ The signs in the stacks guide you to the books you are looking for.

Locating e-books

Use your library's online catalog to find e-books the same way you find printed books. You'll see on the record "e-book" or "electronic resource." Click on the link and you can read the book and often download a few pages.

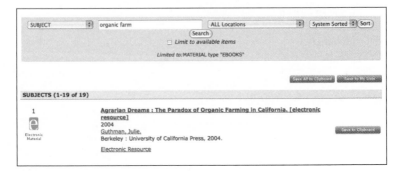

■ Books are increasingly becoming available in electronic form through your library's online catalog.

Locating book reviews

Book Review Digest is available in the print version in your library's reference room or else your library's Web site has a link to the online version, *Book Review Digest Plus.* Library databases also contain reviews.

- **Academic OneFile** (Search for the title or author and add the word "review." [for example, *The Omnivore's Dilemma* and review].)
- **Academic Search Complete** (Enter the title of the book and limit the *Document Type* to "Book Review.")

Find journal articles

Like books, scholarly journals provide in-depth examinations of subjects. The articles in scholarly journals are written by experts, and they usually contain lists of references that can guide you to other research on a subject.

Popular magazines are useful for gaining general information. Articles in popular magazines are usually short with few, if any, source references and are typically written by journalists. Some instructors frown on using popular magazines, but these journals can be valuable for researching current opinion on a particular topic. (See Section 21b for more on scholarly journals and popular magazines.)

Many scholarly journals and popular magazines are available on your library's Web site. Find them the same way you look for books, using your library's online catalog. Databases increasingly contain the full text of articles, allowing you to read and copy the contents onto your computer. If the article you are looking for isn't available online, the paper copy will be shelved with the books in your library.

20f Keep Track of Sources

As you begin to collect your sources, make sure you get full bibliographic information for everything you might want to use in your project. Decide which documentation style you will use. (The major documentation styles—MLA, APA, Chicago, and CSE—are dealt with in detail in Chapters 26–29.)

MLA style no longer requires URLs unless your readers cannot locate the source without it. Nevertheless, your instructor may require you to list the URL, and it's a good idea to copy and paste the URL or add a bookmark on your browser for your own reference. Pages on the Web are often difficult to relocate.

Locate elements of a citation in database sources

For any sources you find on databases, MLA style requires you to provide the full print information, the name of the database in italics,
the medium of publication (*Web*), and the date you accessed the database.
If page numbers are not included, use *n. pag.* Do *not* include the URL
of the database.

Author's name	Shefner, Ruth
Title of article	"Politics Deserve Teens' Attention"
Publication information	
Name of periodical	*Post-Standard* [Syracuse]
Date of publication (and edition for newspapers)	28 Nov. 2006, final ed.
Section and page number	B3
Database information	
Name of database	*LexisNexis Academic*
Date you accessed the site	28 Apr. 2010

The citation would appear as follows in an MLA-style works-cited list
(see Section 26g).

> Shefner, Ruth. "Politics Deserve Teens' Attention." *Post-Standard*
> [Syracuse] 28 Nov. 2006, final ed.: B3. *LexisNexis Academic*.
> Web. 28 Apr. 2010.

APA style no longer requires listing the names of common databases
or listing the date of access, unless the content is likely to change (see Section 27e). If you name the database, do not list the URL.

> Shefner, R. (2006, November 28). Politics deserve teens' attention.
> *The Post-Standard*, p. B3. Retrieved from LexisNexis Academic
> database.

*For a tutorial on finding and citing information using databases,
visit this page of the Pearson eText at* **www.mycomplab.com.**

Locate elements of a citation in Web sources

As you conduct your online research, make sure you collect the necessary
bibliographic information for everything you might want to use as a
source. Because of the potential volatility of Web sources (they can and do

disappear overnight), their citations require extra information. Depending on the citation format you use, you'll arrange this information in different ways.

Collect the following information about a Web site:

Author's name, if available (if not, use the associated institution or organization)	Samadzadeh, Nozlee
Title of article	"Farm Update: The Third Annual Jack Hitt Annual Last Day of Classes Pig Roast"
Publication information	
Name of site or online journal	*Yale Sustainable Food Project Student Blog*
Publisher or Sponsor of the site (for MLA style)	Yale Sustainable Food Project
Date of publication (for an article) or of site's last update	3 May 2010
Date you accessed the site	10 May 2010
URL (for some APA formats including blogs)	http://yalesustainablefood project.wordpress.com/ 2010/05/03/farm-update- the-third-annual-jack-hitt- annual-last-day-of-classes- pig-roast/

An MLA works-cited entry for this article would look like this:

Samadzadeh, Nozlee. "Farm Update: The Third Annual Jack Hitt Annual Last Day of Classes Pig Roast." *Yale Sustainable Food Project Student Blog*. Yale Sustainable Food Project, 3 May 2010. Web. 10 May 2010.

In an APA references list, the citation would look like this:

Samadzadeh, N. (2010, May 3). Farm update: The Third Annual Jack Hitt Annual Last Day of Classes Pig Roast. Message posted to http://yalesustainablefoodproject.wordpress.com/2010/05/03/ farm-update-the-third-annual-jack-hitt-annual-last-day-of- classes-pig-roast/

You can find more examples of how to cite Web sources in MLA style (Section 26h) and APA style (Section 27e).

Locate elements of a citation in print sources

For books you will need, at minimum, the following information, which can typically be found on the front and back of the title page.

Author's name	Ojito, Mirta
Title of the book	*Finding Mañana: A Memoir of a Cuban Exile*
Publication information	
Place of publication	New York
Name of publisher	Penguin
Date of publication	2005
Medium of publication	Print

Here's how the book would be cited in an MLA-style works-cited list.

Ojito, Mirta. *Finding Mañana: A Memoir of a Cuban Exile*. New York:
Penguin, 2005. Print.

Here's the APA citation for the same book.

Ojito, M. (2005). *Finding mañana: A memoir of a Cuban exile*. New
York, NY: Penguin.

You will also need the page numbers if you are quoting directly or referring to a specific passage, and the title and author of the individual chapter if your source is an edited book with contributions by several people.

For journals you will need the following:

Author's name	Romano, Susan
Title of article	"'Grand Convergence' in the Mexican Colonial Mundane: The Matter of Introductories"
Publication information	
Name of journal	*Rhetoric Society Quarterly*
Volume number and issue number	40.1
Date of publication (and edition for newspapers)	2010
Page numbers of the article	71–93
Medium of publication	Print
Document Object Identifier (DOI) if available for APA	10.1080/02773940903413407

An entry in an MLA-style works-cited list would look like this:

> Romano, Susan. "'Grand Convergence' in the Mexican Colonial
>   Mundane: The Matter of Introductories." *Rhetoric Society
>   Quarterly* 40.1 (2010): 71-93. Print.

And in APA style, like this:

> Romano, S. (2010). "Grand convergence" in the Mexican colonial
>   mundane: The matter of introductories. *Rhetoric Society
>   Quarterly, 40,* 71–93. doi: 10.1080/02773940903413407

21 | Evaluate Sources

QUICK*TAKE*

- **Determine the relevance of sources** (see below)
- **Determine the quality of sources** (see p. 271)
- **Evaluate database and print sources** (see p. 274)
- **Evaluate Web sources** (see p. 276)

21a Determine the Relevance of Sources

Whether you use print or online sources, a successful search will turn up many more items than you can expect to use in your final product. You have to make a series of decisions as you evaluate your material. Use your research question and working thesis to create guidelines for yourself about importance and relevance.

For example, if your research question asks why the Roman Empire declined rapidly at the end of the fourth and beginning of the fifth centuries CE, you may find older sources as valuable as new ones. Edward Gibbon's three-volume history, *The Decline and Fall of the Roman Empire*, remains an important source even though it was published in 1776 and 1781.

But if you ask a research question about contemporary events—for example, why Chinese businesses are thriving in African nations at a time when the Western presence is dwindling—you will need to find current information. Statistics such as the growth of Chinese trade with Africa to $106 billion in 2008 or the fact that over a million Chinese live and work in Africa describe the trend, but statistics alone do not explain why. An article on the new popularity of Chinese food in some African cities might be interesting, but it is not relevant. Relevant articles will discuss China's willingness to invest in factories and businesses in Africa while Western investment in the continent has decreased.

Use these guidelines to determine the importance and relevance of your sources to your research question.

- Does your research question require you to consult primary or secondary sources?
- Does a source you have found address your question?
- Does a source support or disagree with your working thesis? (You should not throw out work that challenges your views. Representing opposing views accurately enhances your credibility.)

- Does a source add significant information?
- Is the source current? (For most topics try to find the most up-to-date information.)
- What indications of possible bias do you note in the source?

Determine the Quality of Sources

In the Internet era, we don't lack for information, but we do lack filters for finding quality information. Two criteria will help you to make a beginning assessment of quality: individual vs. edited sources and popular vs. scholarly sources.

Distinguish individual and anonymous sources from edited sources

Anyone with a computer and access to the Internet can put up a Web site. Furthermore, they can put up sites anonymously or under an assumed name. It's no wonder that there are so many sites that contain misinformation or are intentionally deceptive on the Web.

In general, sources that have been edited and published in scholarly journals, scholarly books, major newspapers, major online and print magazines, and government Web sites are considered of higher quality than what an individual might put on a personal Web site, a Facebook page, a user review, or in a blog. Nevertheless, people tend to believe reports from individuals. Corporations are well aware that blogs and user reviews on sites like Amazon are now more trusted than newspaper and magazine articles, and they regularly send bloggers information about new products and pay them for favorable mentions. Some corporations have gone even further, hiring public relations firms to write favorable reviews and favorable blogs.

Edited sources can have biases, and indeed some are quite open about their perspectives. *National Review* offers a conservative perspective, the *Wall Street Journal* is pro-business, and *The Nation* is a liberal voice. The difference from individual and anonymous sites is that we know the editorial perspectives of these journals, and we expect the editors to check the facts. On self-published Web sites and in self-published books, anything goes.

Distinguish popular sources from scholarly sources

Scholarly books and **scholarly journals** are published by and for experts. Scholarly books and articles published in scholarly journals undergo a **peer review** process in which a group of experts in a field reviews them for their scholarly soundness and academic value. Scholarly books and articles in scholarly journals include

- author's name and academic credentials and
- a list of works cited.

Newspapers, popular books, and **popular magazines** vary widely in quality. Newspapers and popular magazines range from highly respected publications such as the *Los Angeles Times, Scientific American* and *The Atlantic Monthly* to the sensational tabloids at grocery-store checkouts. Popular sources are not peer reviewed and require more work on your part to determine their quality.

POPULAR VS. SCHOLARLY SOURCES			
	Popular books and magazines	**Newspapers**	**Scholarly books and journals**
Author	staff writers, journalists	journalists	scholars, researchers
Audience	general public	general public	scholars, college students
Reviewed by	professional editor	professional editor	other scholars and researchers
Purpose	entertain, express an opinion	entertain, express an opinion, inform	share information with the scholarly community
Documentation	usually none	usually none	extensive, with lists of works cited or footnotes
Advertisements	frequent in magazines	frequent	a few ads for scholarly products
Evidence of bias	usually some bias	usually some bias	little bias
Examples	[magazines] *Cosmopolitan, GQ, Rolling Stone, Sports Illustrated, Time* [book] Elizabeth Gilbert, *Eat, Pray, Love*	*New York Times, Toronto Globe and Mail, The Independent* (London), *Washington Times*	[journals] *College English, JAMA: Journal of the American Medical Association*; [book] Robert Putnam, *Bowling Alone: The Collapse and Revival of American Community*

Exercise 21.1 Decide what kind of periodical (popular or scholarly) you would turn to for information on each of the following topics.

1. an essay arguing for legislation banning texting while driving
2. an article describing how multitasking affects human learning
3. an article on how to use your Web-enabled cell phone to help you multitask
4. an article on the shift in the organization of tasks within corporations from a Tayloristic (specialization) model to a holistic model
5. review of a book called *The Myth of Multitasking: How "Doing It All" Gets Nothing Done*

Distinguish primary sources from secondary sources

Another key distinction for researchers is primary versus secondary sources. In the humanities and fine arts, **primary sources** are original, creative works and original accounts of events written close to the time they occurred. **Secondary sources** interpret creative works and primary sources of events.

In the sciences, **primary sources** are the factual results of experiments, observations, clinical trials, and other factual data. **Secondary sources** analyze and interpret those results.

PRIMARY VS. SECONDARY SOURCES		
Examples	**Humanities and fine arts**	**Sciences**
Primary sources	• Novels, short stories, poems, plays, music • Paintings, sculpture, photographs, maps • Speeches • Diaries, letters, journals • Interviews with witnesses and participants • Government records	• Published results • Collections of data • Collections of observations
Secondary sources	• Histories • Biographies • Literary criticism • Reviews	• Publications interpreting the results of experiments and clinical trials • Reviews of several studies or experiments

Read sources critically

Evaluating sources requires you to read critically, which includes the following:

- Identifying the source, which is not always easy on the Web
- Identifying the author and assessing the author's credentials
- Understanding the content—what the text says
- Recognizing the author's purpose—whether the author is attempting to reflect, inform, or persuade
- Recognizing how the purpose influences the choices of words, examples, and structure
- Recognizing biases in the choices of words, examples, and structure
- Recognizing what the author does not include or address
- Developing an overall evaluation that takes into account all of the above

(For more on critical reading, see Chapter 5.)

Evaluate the quality of visual sources

Evaluating the quality of visual sources involves skills similar to critical reading. Similar to critical reading, you should

- identify and assess the source,
- identify the creator,
- identify the date of creation,
- describe the content,
- assess the purpose, and
- recognize how the purpose influences the composition of the image or graphic.

For graphics including charts and graphs, pay attention to the source of any data presented and that the data are presented fairly, (For more on the evaluation of visual sources, see Sections 5e and 5f.)

21c Evaluate Database and Print Sources

Books are expensive to print and distribute, so book publishers generally protect their investment by providing some level of editorial oversight. Printed and online materials in your library undergo another review by professional librarians who select them to include in their collections. Library database collections, which your library pays to access, also are screened, which eliminates many poor-quality sources.

This initial screening doesn't free you, however, from the responsibility of evaluating the quality of the sources. Many printed and database sources contain their share of inaccurate, misleading, and biased information. Also, all sources carry the risk of becoming outdated if you are looking for current information.

WRITING SMART

Checklist for evaluating database and print sources

Over the years librarians have developed a set of criteria for evaluating sources, and you should apply them in your research.

1. **Source.** Who published the book or article? Enter the publisher's name on Google or another search engine to learn about the publisher. Scholarly books and articles in scholarly journals are generally more reliable than popular magazines and books, which tend to emphasize what is sensational or entertaining at the expense of accuracy and comprehensiveness.

2. **Author.** Who wrote the book or article? What are the author's qualifications? Enter the author's name on Google or another search engine to learn more about him or her. Does the author represent an organization?

3. **Timeliness.** How current is the source? If you are researching a fast-developing subject such as treating ADHD, then currency is very important, but even historical topics are subject to controversy or revision.

4. **Evidence.** Where does the evidence come from—facts, interviews, observations, surveys, or experiments? Is the evidence adequate to support the author's claims?

5. **Biases.** Can you detect particular biases of the author? How do the author's biases affect the interpretation offered?

6. **Advertising.** For print sources, is advertising a prominent part of the journal or newspaper? How might the ads affect the credibility or the biases of the information that gets printed?

Exercise 21.2 Here is a working bibliography on hate crimes. Evaluate these sources as if you would be using them for a research paper dealing with hate crime legislation in Texas. Answer these two questions for each:

How relevant is this source (very, somewhat, slightly, not at all)? Why?
How reliable is this source (very, somewhat, slightly, not at all)?

1. "Governor of Texas Signs New Hate Crime Bill." *Jet*. Print. 28 May 2001: 16.

    Short article (262 words) about Governor Perry signing the James Byrd Jr. Hate Crime Act.

2. King, Joyce. *Hate Crime: The Story of a Dragging in Jasper, Texas*. New York: Pantheon, 2002. Print.

    King writes about the trial following the dragging death of James Byrd, Jr. in Jasper, Texas, in 1998.

3. Jonsson, Patrick. "Fewer Hate Crimes in 2008, Obama's Election Year, Data Show." *Christian Science Monitor* 20 Nov. 2009: 2. *LexisNexis Academic*. Web. 15 September 2010.

    This article describes how the slight increase in hate mongering followed by the decline in hate crimes after the election of Obama may or may not be the result of the election.

4. Spong, John. "The Hate Debate." *Texas Monthly* April 2001: 64. *LexisNexis Academic*. Web. 15 September 2010.

    Article dealing specifically with the controversy over hate crime legislation in Texas.

5. Texas Civil Rights Project. *Hate Crime in Texas: Where We've Come, Where We're Going*. Austin, TX: The Project, 1995. Print.

    This very short book (88 pages) is a history of hate crime legislation in Texas, published by a community grassroots foundation that provides legal assistance and education to low-income and minority persons and individuals victimized by discrimination.

21d Evaluate Web Sources

Researching on the Web has been compared to drinking from a fire hose. The key to success is not only getting the torrent down to the size of a glass, but also making sure the water in the glass is pure enough to drink.

Pay attention to domain names

Domain names can give you clues about the quality of a Web site.

- **.com** Commercial site. The information on a .com site is generally about a product or company. While the information may be accurate, keep in mind that the purpose of the site is to sell a product or service.
- **.edu** Educational institution. The suffix tells you the site is on a school server, ranging from kindergarten to higher education. If the information is from a department or research center, it is generally credible, but if the site is an individual's, treat it as you would other kinds of self-published information.
- **.gov** Government. If you see this suffix, you're viewing a government site. Most government sites are considered credible sources.
- **.org** Nonprofit organization. Initially, nonpartisan organizations like the Red Cross used this domain, but increasingly partisan political groups and commercial interests have taken the .org suffix. Treat this domain with scrutiny.
- **.mil** Military. This domain suffix is owned by the various branches of the armed forces.
- **.net** Network. Anyone can use this domain.

Be alert for biased Web sites

Nearly every large company and political and advocacy organization has a Web site. We expect these sites to represent the company or the point of view of the organization. Many sites on the Web, however, are not so clearly labeled.

For example, if you do a search for "Sudden Infant Death Syndrome (SIDS)" and "vaccines," you'll find near the top of the list an article titled "Vaccines and Sudden Infant Death Syndrome (SIDS): A Link?" (www.thinktwice.com/sids.htm). The article concludes that vaccines cause SIDS. If you look at the home page—www.thinktwice.com—you'll find that the site's sponsor, Global Vaccine Institute, opposes all vaccinations of children.

Always look for other objective sources for verification of your information. The U.S. Centers for Disease Control publishes fact sheets with the latest information about diseases and their prevention. The fact sheet on SIDS and vaccines reports that people associate sudden infant death syndrome with vaccinations because babies begin vaccinations between two and four months, the same age babies die of SIDS. There is no scientific evidence that vaccines cause SIDS.

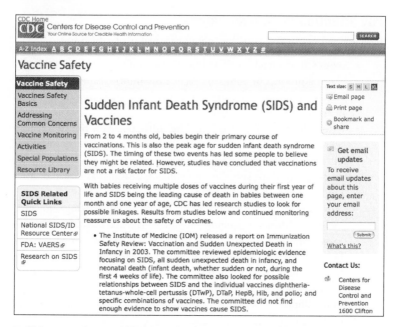

- FAQ on vaccines and SIDS from the Centers of Disease Control (www.cdc. gov/vaccinesafety/Concerns/sids_faq.html)

WRITING SMART

Checklist for evaluating Web sources

Web sources present special challenges for evaluation. When you find a Web page by using a search engine, you will often go deep into a complex site without having any sense of the context for that page. To evaluate the credibility of the site, you would need to examine the home page, not just the specific page you get to first.

Use these criteria for evaluating Web sites.

1. **Source.** What organization sponsors the Web site? Look for the site's owner at the top or bottom of the home page or in the

(Continued on next page)

WRITING SMART *(Continued)*

Web address. Enter the owner's name on Google or another search engine to learn about the organization. If a Web site doesn't indicate ownership, then you have to make judgments about who put it up and why.

2. **Author.** Is the author identified? Look for an "About Us" link if you see no author listed. Enter the author's name on Google or another search engine to learn more about the author. Often Web sites give no information about their authors other than an e-mail address, if that. In such cases it is difficult or impossible to determine the author's qualifications. Be cautious about information on an anonymous site.

3. **Purpose.** Is the Web site trying to sell you something? Many Web sites are infomercials that might contain useful information, but they are no more trustworthy than other forms of advertising. Is the purpose to entertain? To inform? To persuade?

4. **Timeliness.** When was the Web site last updated? Look for a date on the home page. Many Web pages do not list when they were last updated; thus you cannot determine their currency.

5. **Evidence.** Are sources of information listed? Any factual information should be supported by indicating where the information came from. Reliable Web sites that offer information will list their sources.

6. **Biases.** Does the Web site offer a balanced point of view? Many Web sites conceal their attitude with a reasonable tone and seemingly factual evidence such as statistics. Citations and bibliographies do not ensure that a site is reliable. Look carefully at the links and sources cited, and peruse the "About Us" link if one is available.

Writer at Work

Gabriella Lopez's topic, college gardens, focuses on a quite recent development and has been treated in few scholarly books and scholarly articles. She had to expand her searches to include popular books, newspapers, and Web sources. One of the books she found was Mel Bartholomew's *All New Square-Foot Gardening*. Here is her evaluation.

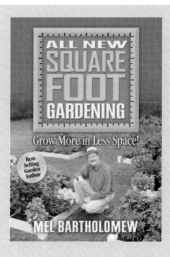

Source:	*popular book; Cool Springs Press, according to its Web site, is the largest publisher of gardening books*
Author:	*Mel Bartholomew has published on this topic for 30 years and has a Web site*
Purpose:	*persuade people to move to square-foot gardening and to inform how to do it*
Timeliness:	*published in 2006*
Evidence:	*almost all the author's experience*
Biases:	*author strongly committed to his method but isn't trying to sell anything*
Conclusion:	*book is repetitive but author is convincing about the subject; published reviews and user reviews on Amazon are strongly favorable*

Exercise 21.3 A recent search on Google with the phrase *hate crimes* resulted in a list of the following URLs. Answer the questions below. Look for clues provided by the URLs before visiting the sites.

(A) http://www.humanrightsfirst.org/discrimination/index.aspx

(B) http://en.wikipedia.org/wiki/Hate_crime

(C) http://www.fbi.gov/hq/cid/civilrights/hate.htm

(D) http://psychology.ucdavis.edu/rainbow/html/hate_crimes.html

(E) http://www.infoplease.com/spot/hatecrimes.html

(F) http://www.asianam.org/hate.htm

1. On which of the sites are you most likely to find advertisements?
2. Which sites are most likely to feature the opinions of an individual?
3. Which sites have unknown authors?
4. Which sites probably contain out-of-date information?
5. Which sites are probably funded by grants from the government or public donations?
6. Which site provides information from the federal government?

22 | Plan Field Research

QUICKTAKE

- **Conduct informative interviews** (see p. 283)
- **Design and administer focused surveys** (see p. 284)
- **Make detailed observations** (see p. 287)
- **Gather data from other original sources** (see p. 288)

22a Know What You Can Obtain from Field Research

Even though much of the research you do for college courses will be secondary research conducted at a computer or in the library, some topics do call for primary research, requiring you to gather information on your own. Field research of this kind can be especially important for exploring local issues. It is also used extensively in professions that you may be joining after college, like sociology, anthropology, and marketing.

To conduct field research effectively, you should start with a well-formed research question. You will also want to prepare by learning about your area of research online or at the library.

Remember, you're not a huge polling organization with thousands of employees and unlimited resources. The data you collect will necessarily be limited in scope. You won't be able to sample a wide range of people in a survey, and you can't spend years observing wildlife in a distant location. But you can use field research to provide concrete evidence about attitudes, environments, and opinions in your immediate location. If you are making an argument about a local issue, local opinions or conditions are an important part of that argument. Field research that directly measures those opinions or conditions will give your argument much more credibility.

Be aware that the ethics of conducting field research require you to inform people about what you are doing and why you are gathering information. If you are uncertain about the ethics of doing field research, talk to your instructor.

However, you shouldn't overstate the weight of your findings. While field research can give very accurate, detailed information, it isn't always representative. You may find that 90% of the students responding to your survey are concerned about crime on campus, but that doesn't mean that 90% of *all* students share this concern. Similarly, one interview subject may have very strong feelings on a subject, but there may be many other people who feel differently. Or, you may observe a lot of activity at a local café while you are observing there, but it's possible you just happened to arrive on a particularly busy day.

Three types of field research that can usually be conducted in college are **interviews, surveys,** and **observations.** You can also **find data** that has been gathered for some other purpose, and interpret it in light of your own research question.

- **Interviews.** College campuses are a rich source of experts in many areas, including those on the faculty and in the surrounding community. Interviewing experts on your research topic can help build your knowledge base. You can use interviews to discover what the people most affected by a particular issue are thinking and feeling.
- **Surveys.** Extensive surveys that can be projected to large populations, like the ones used in political polls, require the effort of many people. Small surveys, however, often can provide insight on local issues.
- **Observation.** Local observation can be a valuable source of data. For example, if you are researching why a particular office on your campus does not operate efficiently, observe what happens when students enter and how they are handled by the staff.
- **Gathering data.** You don't always have to conduct a controlled experiment to get relevant data about a question or issue. Many types of data can be gathered quite easily if you simply go and look for them. To determine whether low-income families have more trouble accessing financial services, for example, you could count the number of banks, pawn shops, and check-cashing services in various neighborhoods, look them up in the phone book, or map them online.

22b Conduct Interviews

Before you contact anyone to ask for an interview, think carefully about your goals; knowing what you want to find out through your interviews will help you determine whom you need to interview and what questions you need to ask.

- Decide what you want or need to know and who best can provide that for you.
- Schedule each interview in advance, and let the person know why you are conducting the interview.
- Plan your questions in advance. Write down a few questions and have a few more in mind. Listen carefully so you can follow up on key points.
- Come prepared with a notebook and pencil or laptop for taking notes and jotting down short quotations. Record the date, time,

place, and subject of the interview. A tape recorder sometimes can intimidate the person you are interviewing. If you want to use a tape recorder, ask for permission in advance.

- Someone who can't meet face-to-face or find the time for a phone interview may be able to answer a series of questions sent by e-mail. When you set up an e-mail interview, be sure to state that you will want to ask a few follow-up questions after you receive the initial reply. This will let you clear up any confusing points in your subject's answers.

- When you are finished, thank your subject and ask his or her permission to get in touch again if you have additional questions.

- Immediately after the interview, make notes about your impressions and ideas that occurred to you during the interview. Do this while the interview is fresh in your mind.

- When you are ready to incorporate the interview into a paper or project, think about what you want to highlight from the interview and which direct quotations to include.

Exercise 22.1 Think of a specific person who fits one of the categories below. Then think of a specific purpose and write 5–10 interview questions to solicit the information you need. For example, you might write questions to ask your U.S. Senator about immigration policy.

1. a politically active celebrity
2. a potential employer or employee
3. the author of a book you read recently
4. the CEO of a controversial company
5. someone in the service or maintenance industry that you see every day but rarely interact with
6. a scientist in a field you know little about

22c Administer Surveys

Use surveys to find out what large groups of people think about a topic (or what they are willing to admit they think). Surveys need to be carefully designed. There are two important components: the survey instrument itself—which is the list of questions you will ask—and the place, time, and way in which the survey will be administered.

- Write a few specific questions. Make sure that they are unambiguous. People will fill out your survey quickly, and if the questions are confusing, the results will be meaningless. To make sure your questions are clear, test them on a few people before you conduct the survey.

- Include one or two open-ended questions, such as "What do you like about X?" "What don't you like about X?" Open-ended questions can be difficult to interpret, but sometimes they turn up information you had not anticipated.
- Decide whom you need to survey and how many people to include. If you want to claim that the results of your survey represent the views of residents of your dormitory, your method of selecting respondents should give all residents an equal chance to be selected. Don't select only your friends.
- Decide how you will contact participants in your survey. If you are going to mail or e-mail your survey, include a statement about what the survey is for and a deadline for returning it. You may need to get permission to conduct a survey in a public place.
- Think about how you will interpret your survey. Multiple-choice formats make data easy to tabulate, but often they miss key information. Open-ended questions will require you to figure out a way to analyze responses.
- Using online survey systems, you can now collect data from many people much more quickly than if you had to contact them all face-to-face. Services like Survey Monkey, Zoomerang, and Survey Gizmo offer more basic versions of the service for free, or allow students to set up a free account. Your school may also subscribe to an online survey system like Survey Station. Ask your instructor or librarian about survey software that is available to you. Most of these systems have tutorials to help you set up your survey, administer it, and interpret the data. If you use an online survey instrument, be sure to download a copy of your data and store it on your won computer.
- When writing about the results, be sure to include information about who participated in the survey, how the participants were selected, and when and how the survey was administered.

STAYING ON TRACK

Keep survey language impartial

Writers of effective surveys must take into account people's subconscious biases; reading, writing, and listening patterns; and other subtle factors. For a small survey, you probably won't be able to control many of the variables important in large polls. Still, you want your survey results to be as accurate and credible as possible. That means you have to let people make up their own minds. So take care that the questions you ask don't actively encourage people to give the answers you may hope to hear.

(Continued on next page)

STAYING ON TRACK *(Continued)*

Off track	Would you like the library to stop closing at the ridiculous hour of 9 p.m.?
On track	Would you like the library to stay open later at night?
Off track	Do you want the Student Council spending your student fees on things like chips and soda?
On track	Do you think the Student Council should have discretion to use student fees for entertainment costs?

An example of a survey on study habits that a student could administer in the student union or library appears below.

Study Habits Survey

Your answers to these questions will help me determine if the library's schedule ought to be altered.

1. How often do you use the library?	<ul><li>Daily</li><li>Three or more times a week</li><li>Once a week</li><li>Once a month</li><li>Once a semester</li><li>Never</li></ul>
2. At what time do you most often use the library?	<ul><li>8 a.m.–noon</li><li>noon–4:00 p.m.</li><li>4 p.m.–8 p.m.</li><li>After 8 p.m.</li></ul>
3. Have you ever had to leave the library because it was closing?	<ul><li>Yes</li><li>No</li></ul>
4. Have you ever had to wait to use the library because it wasn't yet open?	<ul><li>Yes</li><li>No</li></ul>
5. In general, how well do the library's current hours meet your study needs?	<ul><li>Not at all well</li><li>Somewhat well</li><li>Quite well</li><li>Extremely well</li></ul>
6. What for you would be the ideal hours for the library to be open?	

Exercise 22.2 Find a survey consisting of at least 5 questions in print or online. Think of yourself as a consultant for the person, group, or company administering the survey and analyze it according to the pointers on pages 294–295. Give clear feedback to your "client" about how the survey could be improved to gather the information desired. Make sure to note who is administering the survey, what information the survey is supposed to gather, and to whom the survey is targeted.

22d Make Observations

Simply observing what goes on in a place can be an effective research tool. Your observations can inform a controversy or topic by providing a vivid picture of real-world activity. For example, you might observe a local swimming pool to see what age groups use it the most and at what times of day. Or you might observe a drainage pond to see what forms of wildlife it attracts. Here are some tips on making observations.

- Choose a place where you can observe with the least intrusion. The less people wonder about what you are doing, the better. Get permission, if necessary, and be ready to identify yourself and explain your project if anyone asks.
- Carry a notebook and write extensive field notes. Get down as much information as you can, and worry about analyzing it later. If you take photos or video, be respectful. While it is not usually illegal to photograph people in a public place, you do not necessarily have the right to photograph strangers in a private space like an amusement park.
- Record the date, exactly where you were, exactly when you arrived and left, and important details like the number of people present. Plan on visiting the location more than once, so you know what constitutes "normal" activity.
- Write on one side of your notebook so you can use the facing page to note key observations and analyze your data later.

A sample page of observations of a preschool classroom might look like this.

Observations	Analysis
8 a.m.	
Dimonte and Lilly dropped off. Lilly cries when her mother leaves.	Lilly's teacher says she always cries when her mother drops her off, but not when her father does. Some of the other children also exhibit this pattern.

8:15	
Carissa tries to take the scissors outside onto the playground and is stopped by a increased.	

8:30	
All the children are playing outside; the noise level has gradually increased.	It's interesting that the morning starts off fairly quietly, then gets louder and louder until snack time. Are the kids getting reacquainted, with each other every morning, or just waking up?

8:40	
Carissa has managed to sneak the scissors outside again. The teacher takes them away.	Carissa does this over and over again during the day; does anyone know what she wants to do with the scissors outside?

8:45	
Snack time. Carissa shares her goldfish crackers with Lilly.	The girls are sharing more often now, although they also use "not sharing" as a way to punish others or show their displeasure.

Once you begin taking extensive notes about what you observe, you will collect a great deal of data. At some point you have to interpret the data. When you analyze your observations, think about what constitutes normal and unusual activities for this place. What can you determine about the purposes of these activities?

22e Gather Data from Other Sources

In disciplines like science, medicine, and engineering, controlled laboratory experiments are commonly used to collect evidence. In a biology class, you may learn how to set up and conduct a lab experiment, and how to report and interpret your data. But there are many ways to gather information firsthand that don't involve setting up an experiment. Data is constantly being collected in many places, if you know how to look for it. In fact, looking at this kind of data can generate questions that lead you to a researchable hypothesis.

- Computer and Internet technologies continually collect user data for commercial purposes, and if you can access it and make sense of it, you can learn a lot. For example, Google Trends allows you to see how Internet searches for certain terms have varied over time. Log file data, collected on every Web site, lets site designers see how users enter and move around within a site.
- Online message forums and comment threads are obvious sources for direct quotes from individuals interested in a topic, but they can also be used as a kind of informal survey or group interview. You could look through the comments on a Web page to see how often people mention a certain politician, use a particular phrase, or express agreement or disagreement on an issue.
- Social networking sites like Facebook and Twitter provide a great deal of information about links between people and groups, the popularity of ideas and celebrities, and the paths by which information spreads.
- In the nonelectronic world, accumulated evidence of human behavior can also provide clues about trends and events. The due dates stamped in an old library book can provide information about how popular the book was in the 1980s, for example. The depth and width of footpaths worn into the grass outside a dorm may tell you how often students head to the library compared to how often they turn toward the gym. The number of empty pizza boxes outside your next-door neighbor's apartment can help you estimate how many classmates he had studying with him the night before.
- Natural phenomena frequently leave evidence behind. You might notice debris at different levels of foliage by a river, indicating how high various flood levels have reached. Trees and shrubs all growing in one direction can indicate where prevailing winds come from. And you can trace the prior path of a river by locating old ox-bow lakes on a map. Many disciplines have specific methods like these for collecting existing data—especially disciplines like astronomy, geology, and ecology, where testing theories in a laboratory is difficult or impossible.

Exercise 22.3 The top blue line of this Google Trends chart shows the number of Internet searches performed from the United States using the search phrase "how to study."

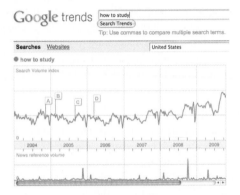

1. What might explain the drop in the number of searches at the end of each calendar year?
2. Do you notice any other regular fluctuations in the data that you can explain?
3. What might be some possible causes of the overall rise in searches beginning in 2008?

22f Sample Project Using Field Research

Janet Duong received the following assignment in her Writing and Photography course. The assignment required her to select a nonprofit organization as a focus for the project, interview people at the site, take photographs, and report on the work of the organization. Here is her assignment.

Documentary Project

Class draft due: November 3, 2010
Final version due: November 17, 2010

Thousands of people in central Texas are volunteering to improve the lives of other people, the lives of wild animals and our pets, and the environment we live in. Your documentary project will focus on socially involved people (or a person) in central Texas. Important social issues are not always in the headlines daily. For example, Austin, like other cities, has a significant problem with pet overpopulation. The Town Lake

Animal Center, which relies on volunteers, shelters over 23,000 animals each year. Bike lanes and hiking trails are also important social issues.

You can find a list of community volunteer organizations on the Get Involved page of the KUT Web site. KUT has another list of volunteer organizations. The UT Dean of Students Office also has a list of volunteer links. Another place to look is Giving City Austin.

Volunteering is not the purpose of this project, and you are not required to volunteer. You are required to engage with and observe people in our community who are working to improve it.

Your documentary project should be intriguing, original, well researched, and socially meaningful. Like most documentaries, you will focus on a few people, or even one person, who represents a larger issue. You can draw your own conclusions about the issue, or you can let the people you observe tell their story.

The project should include:

- at least 1500 words of text
- at least 5 original photographs

Grading criteria

- The documentary project should be exceptionally well written and free from grammatical errors.
- The fieldwork should be extensive and detailed, providing in-depth observation, detailed accounts, and especially vivid portraits of a particular person or people. The project should center on thick, carefully crafted and selected description. Concrete details and direct quotations make places and people come alive.
- The project should explore a socially meaningful question about contemporary Texas.
- The narrative should demonstrate a deep interest in and concern for the people being studied; you need to show enthusiasm for your topic.
- You need to show originality and give academic as well as social insight into your topic.

When you visit your site

- Don't take your photographs at the outset. Plan to hang out to get a sense of what goes on.
- See your *Penguin Handbook* for more on how to make observations.

Conduct interviews

- See your *Penguin Handbook* for advice on conducting interviews.

Janet chose to write about Austin Dog Rescue, a no-kill animal shelter.

Duong 1

Janet Duong

Professor Faigley

RHE 330C

17 November 2009

Austin Dog Rescue

Overview

Austin Dog Rescue is a non-profit organization composed of volunteers that give shelter, food, training, and love to Austin-area stray and street dogs. It was founded in 2007 by seven people who were passionate about dogs and experienced in a wide variety of areas in rescuing animals (Joyce). The volunteers rescue dogs from area shelters and through anonymous calls from people who provide information about abandoned or stray dogs. Austin Dog Rescue goes to great lengths to bring rescued dogs back to good health, even from the worst of medical conditions. The organization also makes strong efforts to match the dogs with adoption families. It serves not only serves Austin shelters but also reaches out to nearby communities and cities.

Fig. 1. Future pet owners visit a dog at Town Lake Animal Shelter.

Duong 2

Problem

Town Lake Animal Shelter reports that they take in around 23,000 animals each year. Due to limited space and housing, many animals are euthanized, which is a national trend. According to the American Humane Society, approximately 64% of the animals that enter animal shelters are killed. Austin Dog Rescue fights to rescue as many dogs as they can to save them from being put to sleep. Too often people obtain dogs from local pet shops. Typically, pets from the shops come from puppy mills, where the animals are bred for profit and genetic quality. The living conditions are often disease-ridden, and the pups often suffer from hereditary defects.

The new dog owners frequently take a dog that hasn't met expectations to shelters to get rid of the problem. The overcrowded shelters have little choice but to euthanize most these unwanted dogs. That's where Austin Dog Rescue steps in. Austin Dog Rescue helps the dogs regain health and then cares for and trains the dogs with the goal of eventually matching the dogs with responsible families and pet owners. Austin Dog Rescue believes that every animal that can be saved deserves a good home.

The Volunteers

Joyce, Executive Director. Joyce was one of the original seven who began Austin Dog Rescue. Her responsibility includes visiting the shelters, assessing the dogs' behaviors before choosing them to be rescued, and

Duong 3

running Austin Dog Rescue in an organized and professional manner. Prior to starting Austin Dog Rescue, Joyce worked with several area non-profits and was known as the "church-girl" for her devotion to these organizations and their work. She strives to give dogs a better lifestyle that is full of nurture and healthy support.

In an interview Joyce discussed two important problems regarding dogs in the Austin community. Pet owners should neuter their dogs and treat and prevent their dogs from heartworm disease. Many of the dogs are sick when they arrive at a shelter and end up getting worse to the point where they have to be euthanized. Joyce believes educating new pet owners about these basic caring-and-keeping steps for their dogs will allow the pup to live a longer and happier life.

Joyce is currently caring for a Labrador pup named Butter. Butter did not interact with humans much when she first arrived at the shelter. Joyce has slowly eased the awkwardness and sometimes fearful interaction that Butter has with people. Once comfortable, Butter has become a sweet and gentle dog.

Ryan, Director of Fosters. Ryan currently works from home. He found that his time at his house could be put to good use. When he learned about Austin Dog Rescue, Ryan decided to jump on board. The most challenging part of his responsibility is potty training the dogs that come into his foster home. Ryan says that "finding a home for the dogs" and "receiving positive reinforcement from his work" keeps him going in caring for the dogs.

Duong 4

Ryan kept a mixed breed pup named Carlos, otherwise known as "Carlito Puppito," who lived at Ryan's foster home for three months (see fig. 2). Carlos is a very playful puppy and loves to get attention from people. Carlos was recently adopted and is featured on the "Happy Endings Success Stories" on the Austin Dog Rescue Web site.

Fig. 2. Carlos, a recently adopted dog.

Kelly, Director of Special Events and Fundraiser. Kelly and her husband have been volunteering and rescuing dogs for seven years and have provided a foster home for 61 dogs. Kelly is concerned with keeping the public informed about ways these dogs could receive help. Kelly and her husband organize several events throughout the year to get the people of Austin involved, and they campaign to raise funds each season. She finds that the most difficult aspect of her role at Austin Dog Rescue is balancing her own dogs' needs with those that she adopts. She also realizes

Duong 5

that the volunteer needs are high because there is always a need for more foster parents and more space to take in more dogs.

Kelly kept a black Labrador named Garbo, who was recently adopted. I accompanied Kelly to a meeting of Garbo and her potential adoptee family (see fig. 3). The family's two young children immediately bonded with the puppy, and they all enjoyed playing together at the park.

Fig. 3. Potential pet owner meeting Garbo.

Amanda, Foster Parent. Amanda is a foster parent for dogs that need housing and training in the program. Austin Dog Rescue is Amanda's first experience working with a non-profit organization. She works at a law firm and has a flexible schedule that allows her to care for each of the dogs at her foster house. Amanda decided to work with Austin Dog Rescue after she had found a feral litter of puppies that needed to be rescued. She had contacted all the area shelters and rescue organizations in the area, but none would take the puppies except Austin Dog Rescue.

Duong 6

Fig. 4. Amanda petting her dog, Maybelline.

Amanda recently adopted Maybelline, who was a very ill dog when initially rescued (see fig. 4). The dog was scared of people and was surely to be euthanized at Town Lake Animal Shelter. Within her first week of being rescued, Maybelline had a fever of 104 degrees. The veterinarian found that she had two tick diseases: Bartonella and Hypaticinosis. Amanda told me that Austin Dog Rescue reaches out to unwanted, stray, and street dogs. Many of those dogs are from shelters in the area. Every day, Austin Dog Rescue receives a list of all the dogs that are to be euthanized at these shelters. Depending on the amount of room that is available, the list is narrowed down to match the conditions and breeds with the foster households. The dogs are then assessed for condition and personality. When dogs are selected, they are treated for any medical conditions encountered, neutered or spayed, vaccinated, and a micro-chip is inserted in each dog. They are then put in a suitable foster home with parents who train

Duong 7

and acquaint the dogs with human as well as other dog interactions. At Austin Dog Rescue, each household is allowed one to two rescued dogs at once. By setting this limit, the foster parent can adequately care for each dog and the pups can keep each other company.

Fig. 5. Trainer at Town Lake Animal Shelter assessing Sam, one of the dogs taken in.

At the right time, the dogs are made available for adoption. The dogs are photographed and featured on Austin Dog Rescue's Web site. The foster parents usually include a short description of the dog's personality, daily routine, level of care, and needs. Potential dog owners may fill out an adoption form on the Web site. This step allows them to declare their interest in a particular dog and have the opportunity to meet up with the dog. The foster parent will choose a day and location for the dog to meet its potential owner. In efforts to make sure that the dogs will receive good care, Austin Dog Rescue volunteers ask for a detailed profile of the potential owner, especially to check for history

Duong 8

of animal abuse. Sometimes Austin Dog Rescue may ask
to visit the household to examine its conditions. When
the right match is found, the paperwork is completed
and the dog is adopted.

Fig. 6. Children meet Garbo at a dog park.

To ensure that adoptions are not impulsive, there
is a 48-hour return policy with no questions asked that
allows the adoptee to give the dog back to Austin Dog
Rescue for any reason. Returns or abandonments often
happen when the family or pet owner cannot take care
of the dog or if other dogs in the household cannot get
along with the newly adopted pup. Occasionally, these
adopted dogs will be returned to the shelter or streets.
Since each dog that is received by Austin Dog Rescue is
micro-chipped, the shelters will notify the organization
when one of their dogs has been taken in. At that
point, the dogs will be placed in available foster homes
and the caring-to-adoption process repeats.

Duong 9

Works Cited

Amanda. Personal interview. 4 Nov. 2010.

"Animal Shelter Euthanasia." *American Humane Association*. American Humane Association, 2010. Web. 3 Nov. 2010

Austin Dog Rescue. Austin Dog Rescue, 2010. Web. 31 Oct. 2010.

Joyce. Personal interview. 29 Oct. 2010.

Kelly. Personal interview. 5 Nov. 2010.

"Puppy Mills." *ASPCA: We Are Their Voice*. American Society for the Prevention of Cruelty to Animals, 2010. Web. 1 Nov. 2010.

Ryan. Personal interview. 4 Nov. 2010.

You **can learn more and do more** with MyCompLab and with the eText version of *The Penguin Handbook*. For help with documenting your sources successfully, go to MyCompLab and click on "Resources," then select "Research." Review the tutorials (Read, Watch, Listen) within each topic, then complete the Exercises and click on the Gradebook to measure your progress.

In the **eText version** of *The Penguin Handbook with Exercises*, find extra worksheets, tutorials, and student writing samples.

RESEARCH MAP 2: WORKING WITH SOURCES

Using sources effectively requires that you

- avoid plagiarism in taking notes, summarizing, and paraphrasing,
- employ sources to provide evidence and points of departure,
- integrate quotations, summaries, paraphrases, and visuals,
- write and revise your research project, and
- document all sources using the format of a major documentation style.

Here are the steps in incorporating and documenting sources.

1 | Understand plagiarism

First, understand exactly how plagiarism is defined; go to Section 23b.

Avoid patch plagiarism when taking notes by distinguishing source words from your own words; go to 23c.

Avoid patch plagiarism when quoting sources by putting words from the source within quotation marks; go to 23d.

Avoid patch plagiarism when summarizing and paraphrasing by putting ideas from the source into your own words; go to 23e.

2 | Integrate sources

Use sources to provide evidence; go to 24a.

Use sources as points of departure; go to 24b.

Integrate quotations, summaries and paraphrases into your research project; go to 24d and 24e.

Integrate visuals into your research project; go to 24f.

You'll see in Parts 5 and 6 the process Gabriella Lopez used to produce her research project. Gabriella's final version of her project is on pages 379–391.

See Research Map 1 (on page 232) for guidance on planning research and finding sources.

3 | Write and revise

Take stock of your research to determine which sources are critical to your project and what further research you may need to do; go to 25a.

Plan your organization by creating a working outline; go to 25b.

Begin your draft by writing a specific title, an introduction, and a conclusion; go to 25c.

Review your project and revise, beginning with high-level issues of content and organization; go to 25d.

4 | Document sources

Decide which documentation style you will use:

- **MODERN LANGUAGE ASSOCIATION (MLA):** go to Chapter 26.
- **AMERICAN PSYCHOLOGICAL ASSOCIATION (APA):** go to Chapter 27.
- **CHICAGO MANUAL OF STYLE (CMS):** go to Chapter 28.
- **COUNCIL OF SCIENCE EDITORS (CSE):** go to Chapter 29.

23 | Understand and Avoid Plagiarism

QUICK*TAKE*

- **What is plagiarism?** (see p. 305)
- **Avoid plagiarism when taking notes** (see p. 308)
- **Avoid plagiarism when quoting sources** (see p. 310)
- **Avoid plagiarism when summarizing and paraphrasing** (see p. 313)

23a Understand the Purposes of Sources

From a student's point of view, documenting sources can seem like learning Latin—something obscure and complicated that has little use in daily life. You don't see footnotes or lists of works cited in magazines and newspapers, so you may wonder why they are so important in college writing. Careful documentation of sources, however, is essential to developing knowledge and allows scholars and researchers to build on the work of other scholars and researchers.

Sources build knowledge

Knowledge is built through ongoing conversations that take place in writing as well as talking. The practice of citing sources provides a disciplinary map, indicating the conversation in which the writer is participating and how that writer responds to what has been said before. Often knowledge building does not move in a straight line but reflects wrong turns and backtracking. Tracing these movements would be extremely difficult if writers did not acknowledge their sources.

Sources must be accurate

Accurate referencing of sources allows you or any reader the opportunity to consult those sources. For example, historians who write about the distant past must rely on different kinds of evidence, including letters, records, public documents, newspaper articles, legal manuscripts, and other material from that time; they also take into account the work of contemporary scholars. Other historians working in the same area must be able to find and read these primary sources to assess the accuracy of the interpretation. Research using sources requires that summaries and paraphrases be accurate, that words taken from the original be set off in quotation marks, and that full information be provided to locate the source.

Sources and fairness

Another basic issue is fairness. When historians draw on the interpretations of other historians, they should give those historians credit. In this respect citing sources builds community with writers of both the present and the past. When you begin to read the published research in an academic discipline, your awareness of that community takes shape. But the issue of fairness also is part of the much larger issues of intellectual property and scholastic honesty—issues that need to be considered carefully when you use sources.

23b What Is Plagiarism?

Plagiarism means claiming credit for someone else's intellectual work no matter whether it's to make money or get a better grade. Intentional or not, plagiarism has dire consequences. Reputable authors have gotten into trouble through carelessness by copying passages from published sources without acknowledging those sources. A number of famous people have had their reputations tarnished by accusations of plagiarism, and several prominent journalists have lost their jobs and careers for copying the work of other writers and passing it off as their own.

Deliberate plagiarism

If you buy a paper on the Web, copy someone else's paper word for word, or take an article off the Web and turn it in as yours, it's plain stealing, and people who take that risk should know that the punishment can be severe—usually failure for the course and sometimes expulsion. Deliberate plagiarism is easy for your instructors to spot because they recognize shifts in style, and it is easy for them to use search engines to find the sources of work stolen from the Web.

Patch plagiarism

The use of the Web has increased instances of plagiarism in college. Some students view the Internet as a big free buffet where they can grab anything, paste it in a file, and submit it as their own work. Other students intend to submit work that is their own, but they commit patch plagiarism because they aren't careful in taking notes to distinguish the words of others from their own words (see Section 23c).

What you are not required to acknowledge

Fortunately, common sense governs issues of academic plagiarism. The standards of documentation are not so strict that the source of every fact you cite must be acknowledged. You do not have to document the following.

- **Facts available from many sources.** For example, many reference sources report that the death toll of the sinking of the *Titanic* on April 15, 1912, was around 1,500.
- **Results of your own field research.** If you take a survey and report the results, you don't have to cite yourself. You do need to cite individual interviews.

What you are required to acknowledge

The following sources should be acknowledged with an in-text citation and an entry in the list of works cited (MLA style) or the list of references (APA style).

- **Quotations.** Short quotations should be enclosed within quotation marks, and long quotations should be indented as a block. See Section 24d for how to integrate quotations with signal phrases.
- **Summaries and paraphrases.** Summaries represent the author's argument in miniature as accurately as possible (see Section 5c). Paraphrases restate the author's argument in your own words.
- **Facts that are not common knowledge.** For facts that are not easily found in general reference works, cite the source.
- **Ideas that are not common knowledge.** The sources of theories, analyses, statements of opinion, and arguable claims should be cited.
- **Statistics, research findings, examples, graphs, charts, and illustrations.** As a reader you should be skeptical about statistics and research findings when the source is not mentioned. When a writer does not cite the sources of statistics and research findings, there is no way of knowing how reliable the sources are or whether the writer is making them up.

STAYING ON TRACK

Plagiarism in college writing

If you find any of the following problems in your academic writing, you may be guilty of plagiarizing someone else's work. Because plagiarism is usually inadvertent, it is especially important that you understand what constitutes using sources responsibly. Avoid these pitfalls.

- **Missing attribution.** Make sure the author of a quotation has been identified. Include a lead-in or signal phrase that provides attribution to the source, and identify the author in the citation.

- **Missing quotation marks.** You must put quotation marks around material quoted directly from a source.

- **Inadequate citation.** Give a page number to show where in the source the quotation appears or where a paraphrase or summary is drawn from.

- **Paraphrase relies too heavily on the source.** Be careful that the wording or sentence structure of a paraphrase does not follow the source too closely.

- **Distortion of meaning.** Don't allow your paraphrase or summary to distort the meaning of the source, and don't take a quotation out of context, resulting in a change of meaning.

- **Missing works-cited entry.** The Works Cited page must include all the works cited in the project.

- **Inadequate citation of images.** A figure or photo must appear with a caption and a citation to indicate the source of the image. If material includes a summary of data from a visual source, an attribution or citation must be given for the graphic being summarized.

Exercise 23.1 Decide which of the following are instances of plagiarism or scholastic dishonesty and which are not

1. You cut and paste information from a well-known political blog into your notes for a government paper. Unfortunately, you lose track of what information you were quoting directly and what information you were paraphrasing. You try to sort out which ideas were yours and which came from the blog, but you don't have time to check everything before the paper is due.

2. You are swamped with work for other courses so you ask your friend to read over your paper. She rewrites a few awkward sentences and corrects some of your facts. You type in her changes and turn in your paper.

3. You have two papers due on the same day. You write the one for the course in your major, but since the other one is for a required course that

doesn't really interest you, you find an old paper on a similar topic, update about 20% of the information, and turn it in.

4. A passage in your English paper on the book *1919* by John Dos Passos is a paraphrase of a lecture your history professor gave about World War I. Much of the lecture was factual, but some was analysis. You don't document the lecture because your English professor did not require outside sources or a works-cited sheet for the paper.

5. You need a picture of virus for a biology paper, so you find one using Google Images. Since you see that multiple sites use the same image, you decide it must be in the public domain and you put it in your paper without documenting the source.

Exercise 23.2 Which of the following pieces of information require a citation and which do not?

1. Spike Lee was born March 20, 1957, in Atlanta, Georgia.
2. Lee's movies often explore urban life, race relations, the role of media in society, and politics.
3. His first feature film, 1986's *She's Gotta Have It,* featured a Michael Jordan–loving character played by Lee himself.
4. After being blamed for a rash of inner-city violence involving Air Jordan basketball shoes, Lee said that social conditions were really at fault.
5. Many Hollywood insiders believed that Lee's 1989 film, *Do the Right Thing,* deserved a nomination for Best Picture.
6. *Driving Miss Daisy* won the Academy Award for Best Picture in 1989.
7. According to an interview in *New York* magazine, Lee felt that *Driving Miss Daisy's* win hurt him more than not being nominated.
8. In 2006, Lee directed *When the Levees Broke: A Requiem in Four Acts,* a documentary about the devastation wrought on New Orleans when the levees failed after Hurricane Katrina.
9. Lee told ABC News that the devastation to New Orleans was not solely the work of nature; people were also not doing their jobs.
10. Lee interviewed nearly 100 people of diverse backgrounds for the film and he plans to follow up with them at least once more.

23c Avoid Plagiarism When Taking Notes

The best way to avoid unintentional plagiarism is to take care to distinguish source words from your own words. Don't mix words from the source with your own words. Create a folder for your sources on your computer and clearly label the files.

- **Create a working bibliography and make separate files for content notes.** Create a file for each source. If you work on paper, use a separate page for each source. Also write down all the information you need for a list of works cited or a list of references in your working bibliography (see Section 20f).

- **If you copy anything from a source when taking notes, place those words in quotation marks and note the page number(s) where those words appear.** If you copy words from an online source, take special care to note the source. You could easily copy online material and later not be able to find where it came from.
- **Print out the entire source so you can refer to it later.** Having photocopies or complete printed files allows you to double-check later that you haven't used words from the source by mistake and that any words you quote are accurate.

Writer at Work

Gabriella Lopez made a photocopy of "An Eater's Manifesto," the Introduction to Michael Pollan's *In Defense of Food*. She made notes in the margins of the photocopy.

Pollan, Michael. In Defense of Food: An Eater's Manifesto. New York: Penguin, 2008. 8-9. Print.

We forget that, historically, people have eaten for a great many reasons other than biological necessity. Food is also about pleasure, about community, about family and spirituality, about our relationship to the natural world, and about expressing our identity. As long as humans have been taking meals together, eating has been as much about culture as it has been about biology.

Important point: food is about more than nutrition.

That eating should be foremost about bodily health is a relatively new and, I think, destructive idea—destructive not just of the pleasure of eating, which would be bad enough, but paradoxically of our health as well. Indeed, no people on earth worry more about the health consequences of their food choices than we Americans do—and no people suffer from [p. 9] as many diet-related health problems. We are becoming a nation of orthorexics: people with an unhealthy obsession with healthy eating.

Pollan notes the paradox that Americans worry more about food than anyone else yet suffer from the most health problems from diet.

"orthorexics" means "right diet"

23d Avoid Plagiarism When Quoting Sources

Most people who get into plagiarism trouble lift words from a source and use them without quotation marks. Where the line is drawn is easiest to illustrate with an example. In the following passage, Nell Irvin Painter discusses the African Diaspora, the dispersion of African people from their native lands in Africa. She describes the cultural differences that distinguish contemporary African Americans from their ancestors. Note the words in green.

■ Nell Irvin Painter

The three centuries separating African Americans from their immigrant ancestors profoundly influenced their identity. A strong case can be made for seeing **African Americans as a new, Creole people, that is, as a people born and forged in the Western Hemisphere.** Language provides the most obvious indicator: **people of African descent in the Diaspora do not speak languages of Africa as their mother tongue. For the most part, they speak Portuguese, Spanish, English, and French as a mother tongue, although millions speak Creole languages (such as Haitian Creole and South Carolinian Gullah) that combine African grammars and English vocabulary.**

As the potent engine of culture, language influences thought, psychology, and education. Language boundaries now divide descendants whose African ancestors may have been family and close neighbors speaking the same language. One descendant in Nashville, Tennessee, may not understand the Portuguese of her distant cousin now living in Bahia, Brazil. Today, with immigrants from Africa forming an increasing proportion of people calling themselves African American, the woman in Nashville might herself be an African immigrant and speak an African language that neither her black neighbors in Tennessee nor her distant cousin in Brazil can understand. Religion, another crucial aspect of culture, distinguishes the different peoples of the African Diaspora. Millions of Africans are Muslims, for instance, while most African Americans see themselves as Christian. They would hardly agree to place themselves under the Sharia, the legal system inspired by the Koran, which prevails in Northern Nigeria.

—Nell Irvin Painter, *Creating Black Americans:*
African-American History and Its Meanings,
1619 to the Present (New York: Oxford
University Press, 2006), 5.

If you were writing a paper or creating a Web site that concerned African American cultural heritage, you might want to refer to Painter's arguments about cultural differences resulting from different languages. Your options are to paraphrase the source or to quote it directly.

If you quote directly, you must place quotation marks around all words you take from the original:

> One scholar notes the numerous linguistic differences among Americans of African descent: "[P]eople of African descent in the Diaspora do not speak languages of Africa as their mother tongue. For the most part, they speak Portuguese, Spanish, English, and French as a mother tongue" (Painter 5).

Notice that the quotation is introduced and not just dropped in. This example follows MLA style, where the citation goes outside the quotation marks but before the final period. In MLA style, source references are made according to the author's last name, which refers you to the full citation in the works-cited list at the end. Following the author's name is the page number where the quotation can be located.

If the author's name appears in the sentence, cite only the page number, in parentheses:

> According to Nell Irvin Painter, "people of African descent in the Diaspora do not speak languages of Africa as their mother tongue" (5).

If you want to quote material that is already quoted in your source, use single quotes for that material:

> Nell Irvin Painter traces a long history of African American interest in Egyptian culture: "Hoping that past greatness portended future glory, black Americans often recited a verse from the Bible that inspired this hope: 'Princes shall come out of Egypt; Ethiopia shall soon stretch forth her hands unto God' (Psalms 63:31)" (7).

Exercise 23.3 Using the following excerpts about Elizabeth Gilbert's book *Eat, Pray, Love* copied directly from sources, rewrite the numbered items that incorporate quotations to correct punctuation and citation errors.

Source 1: Egan. Jennifer. "The Road to Bali." *New York Times.com*. The New York Times, 26 February 2006. Web. 1 October 2010.

"Eat, Pray, Love" is built on the notion of a woman trying to heal herself from a severe emotional and spiritual crisis. . . .

Lacking a ballast of gravitas or grit, the book lists into the realm of magical thinking: nothing Gilbert touches seems to turn out wrong; not a single wish goes unfulfilled. What's missing are the textures and confusion and unfinished business of real life, as if Gilbert were pushing these out of sight so as not to come off as dull or equivocal or downbeat.

Source 2: Calahan, Maureen. "Eat, Pray, Loathe." *New York Post.com*. The New York Post, 23 December 2007. Web. 1 October 2010.

. . . it is the worst in Western fetishization of Eastern thought and culture, assured in its answers to existential dilemmas that have confounded intellects greater than hers. You may be a well-off white woman, but if you are depressed, the answer can be found in the East, where the poor brown people are sages. . . .

But the anecdotal evidence suggests that its readers are using "Eat, Pray, Love" as a shortcut to finding a spiritual "truth" (one that is not even theirs, but Gilbert's), as an excuse to have that extra glass of wine, and as a license to abandon all critical thinking.

Source 3: Roiphe, Katie. "Should you read the best-selling memoir *Eat, Pray, Love?*" *Slate.com*. 3 July 2007. Web. 1 October 2010.

How does one get better? If one has the stamina to narrate the process, to write frank and chatty postcards from this immensely difficult transition, then one is in fact putting rare and valuable information out into the world. And so I would say for summer, *Eat, Pray, Love* is a transcendently great beach book.

Source 4: Gilbert, Elizabeth. *Eat, Pray, Love*. New York: Penguin, 2006.

. . . I am a professional American woman in my mid thirties, who has just come though a failed marriage and a devastating, interminable divorce followed immediately by a passionate love affair that ended in sickening heartbreak (7).

. . .

My God, but I wanted a spiritual teacher (25).

. . .

And I can actually *afford* to do this [live in Italy] because of a staggering personal miracle: in advance, my publisher has purchased the book I shall write about my travels (35)

1. *Eat, Pray,* Love is built on the notion of a woman trying to heal herself from a severe emotional and spiritual crisis. The author describes herself as a professional American woman in my mid thirties, who has just come though a failed marriage and a devastating, interminable divorce followed immediately by a passionate love affair that ended in sickening heartbreak (Gilbert 7).

2. The book was wildly popular; Gilbert's story of personal redemption resonated with millions of women. For these readers, Gilbert not only

answers the question how does one get better?, but she does so with humor and grace: If one has the stamina to narrate the process, to write frank and chatty postcards from this immensely difficult transition, then one is in fact putting rare and valuable information out into the world.

3. Other critics see Gilbert's message as evidence of something more troubling. For example, . . . it is the worst in Western fetishization of Eastern thought and culture, assured in its answers to existential dilemmas that have confounded intellects greater than hers. You may be a well-off white woman, but if you are depressed, the answer can be found in the East, where the poor brown people are sages.

4. Critics who adhere to this view cite Gilbert's own privileged position. After all, she can afford to live in Italy because of a staggering personal miracle; her publisher has given her an advance on a book she will write about this journey of spiritual growth. And, as someone who has just been paid to seek enlightenment, she goes shopping: My God, but I wanted a spiritual teacher (25).

5. Reviewers and readers more ambivalent than hostile about Gilbert's message read her constant luck as magical thinking: nothing Gilbert touches seems to turn out wrong; not a single wish goes unfulfilled. The only danger here is that Gilbert leaves out the textures and confusion and unfinished business of real life. Critics less kindly inclined see her message as very dangerous indeed, inspiring readers to find a shortcut to finding a spiritual "truth" and as an excuse to have that extra glass of wine, and to abandon all critical thinking.

 ## Avoid Plagiarism When Summarizing and Paraphrasing

Summarize

When you summarize, you cite your source but, instead of quoting it directly, you state the major ideas of the entire source, or part of a source, in a paragraph or perhaps even a sentence. The key is to put the summary in your own words.

Plagiarized

Nell Irvin Painter argues in *Creating Black Americans* that we should consider African Americans as a new Creole people, born and forged in the Western Hemisphere.

Most of the words of this example of patch plagiarism are lifted directly from the original.

Acceptable summary

Nell Irvin Painter argues in *Creating Black Americans* that African Americans' experiences in the Western Hemisphere made them so culturally different from their ancestors that we can think of them as a separate people.

Paraphrase

When you paraphrase, you represent the idea of the source in your own words at about the same length as the original. You still need to include the reference to the source of the idea. The following paraphrase is an example of patch plagiarism.

Plagiarized

Nell Irvin Painter contends that cultural factors like language and religion divide African Americans from their ancestors. People of African descent no longer speak the languages of Africa as their first language. Since language is a potent engine of culture, the thought, psychology, and education of contemporary African Americans is radically different from that of their ancestors. Religion, another crucial aspect of culture, also divides African Americans from Africans. Sharia, the legal system inspired by the Koran, may prevail in Northern Nigeria, but it is foreign to Christian African Americans (5).

Even though the source is listed, this paraphrase is unacceptable. Too many of the words in the original are used directly here, including much or all of entire phrases. When a string of words is lifted from a source and inserted without quotation marks, the passage is plagiarized. Changing a few words in a sentence is not a paraphrase. Compare these two sentences.

Source

People of African descent in the Diaspora do not speak languages of Africa as their mother tongue.

Unacceptable paraphrase

People of African descent no longer speak the languages of Africa as their first language.

The paraphrase keeps the structure of the original sentence and substitutes a few words. It is much too similar to the original.

A true paraphrase represents an entire rewriting of the idea from the source.

Acceptable paraphrase

Nell Irvin Painter contends that cultural factors like language and religion divide African Americans from their ancestors. Black Americans speak a wide variety of languages, but usually these are not African. Painter notes how important language is in shaping our cultural identity; it dictates in large part how we think and feel. Linguistic differences create significant boundaries between peoples. Religion, like language, is a fundamental part of how many people identify themselves. Many African Americans identify as Christians, and they would probably see sharp contrasts between their faith and the Muslim faith common in much of Africa (5).

Even though there are a few words from the original in this paraphrase, such as *identity* and *language,* these sentences are original in structure and wording while accurately conveying the meaning of the source.

 For guidelines on avoiding plagiarism and exercises in responsible documentation, visit this page of the eText at **www.mycomplab.com**.

Exercise 23.4 Two sources dealing with Abraham Lincoln and his association in American pop culture with the log cabin are excerpted here. Decide whether the numbered paraphrases and summaries of the two sources are correct. If not, rewrite to eliminate problems.

Source 1: Tarbell, Ida Minerva. *The Early Life of Abraham Lincoln.* New York: S. S. McClure, 1896. Print.

[Thomas Lincoln's] home was a log cabin, but at that date few people in the state had anything else (40).

. . .

Mr. Lincoln said in his short autobiography of 1860, which he wrote in the third person: "Here they built a log cabin, into which they removed, and made sufficient of rails to fence ten acres of ground, fenced and broke the ground, and raised a crop of sown corn upon it the same year. There are, or are supposed to be, the rails about so much is being said just now, though these are far from being the first or only rails ever made by Abraham" (101).

Source 2: Loewen, James W. *Lies My Teacher Told Me: Everything Your American History Textbook Got Wrong.* **New York: Touchstone, 2007. Print.**

The strange career of the log cabin in which Abraham Lincoln was born symbolizes in a way what textbooks have done to Lincoln. The actual cabin fell into disrepair probably before Lincoln became president. According to research by D. T. Pitcaithley, the new cabin, a hoax built in 1894, was leased to two amusement park owners, went to Coney Island, where it got commingled with the birthplace cabin of Jefferson Davis (another hoax), and was finally shrunk to fit inside a marble pantheon in Kentucky, where, reassembled, it still stands. The cabin also became a children's toy: Lincoln Logs, invented by Frank Lloyd Wright's son John in 1920, came with instructions on how to build both Lincoln's log cabin and Uncle Tom's cabin! The cabin still makes its archetypal appearance in our textbooks, signifying the rags-to-riches legend of Abraham Lincoln's upward mobility. No wonder one college student could only say of him, in a much-repeated blooper, "He was born in a log cabin which he built with his own hands."

1. The description that Tarbell gives of Lincoln hand hewing logs to build a log cabin is the story we are taught as schoolchildren.

2. James Loewen, in his book *Lies My Teacher Told Me,* focuses instead on the career of the log cabin of Lincoln's childhood. He argues that the cabin's story symbolizes in some way what the textbooks student read have done to Lincoln (187).

3. It is interesting to note how Tarbell's account strives to be meticulous in its reportage, from her assurance that living in a log cabin was not an indicator of low class—at that date few people in the state had anything else—to her clarification that Lincoln uses the third person voice in his short autobiography of 1896.

4. According to Loewen, however, Lincoln's cabin has led a comparatively unhealthy life. In his research he found that a new "Lincoln" cabin, a hoax built in 1894, was leased to two amusement park owners and went to Coney Island, where it got commingled with the birthplace cabin of Jefferson Davis. The cabin, shrunk down to fit inside a marble pantheon, now stands in Kentucky (187). Has the legend of Lincoln suffered the same fate?

24 | Use Sources Effectively

QUICK_TAKE_

- **Use sources to provide evidence** (see below)
- **Use sources as points of departure** (see p. 318)
- **Integrate quotations into your project** (see p. 324)
- **Integrate summaries and paraphrases into your project** (see p. 326)
- **Integrate visuals into your project** (see p. 328)

24a Use Sources to Provide Evidence

A common saying is that 88% of all statistics (or whatever percentage) are made up on the spot, which of course is an example of the error it describes. Readers expect to see evidence to support claims, and they want to know where the evidence came from. For example, polls and studies are often funded by those who have an interest in the outcome.

Your obligation is to find the most reliable evidence and to document the sources of that evidence. Let's consider an example of a student, George Abukar, writing on the topic of identity theft. Abukar had a friend whose driver's license was stolen. The thief then applied for a credit card in George's friend's name and made thousands of dollars of fraudulent purchases. None of the people who could have stopped the thief did so: The credit card company did not bother to verify the friend's identity, and the three major credit card reporting agencies did not remove the information about unpaid bills from her file, leaving her with a bad credit rating. Abukar's thesis proposes that the United States Congress pass federal legislation making credit-reporting agencies liable for damages when their actions or negligence leads to loss from identity theft.

Sources can help you build a case for why your claim matters. To argue for his thesis, Abukar had to establish first that the problem affected many more people besides his friend. He found statistics on the Federal Trade Commission's _Consumer Sentinel Data Book, January-December 2009_ and included them in his paper.

Readers expect evidence to support claims and reasons.

The Federal Trade Commission (FTC) reports that of 1.3 million complaints received in 2009, the number one complaint category was identity theft with 21% of the total (3). The number of identity theft complaints rose from 31,140 in 2000 to 278,078 in 2009 (5).

24b Use Sources as Points of Departure

All good research writing responds to sources. Every significant issue has an extensive history of discussion with various points of view.

Keep your voice when using sources

Your task as a researcher is to enter ongoing discussions by "talking" to your sources. Just as you would in a conversation with several people who hold different views, you may disagree with some people, agree with some, and agree with others only up to a point and then disagree.

Think about assuming roles in relation to your sources:

- The **skeptic**, who disagrees with a source,
- The **contributor**, who agrees with a source and has another point to add,
- The **analyst**, who agrees with a source up to a point but has reservations.

George Abukar uses all three strategies to position his sources in relation to his argument.

Take the role of the skeptic

You can use this template.

A common way of thinking about this issue is _____, but this view is mistaken because _____.

George Abukar argues that there are inadequate safeguards against identity theft because credit card companies and reporting agencies have no financial interest in preventing identity theft and in some ways even profit from it. He needed to establish that a common view is that individuals are responsible for identity theft. He found a Federal Trade Commission Web site that puts forth this view and included a quotation from the site in his paper.

Abukar quotes common sense advice from the FTC Web site.

> Mostly, consumers are being told to protect themselves. The Federal Trade Commission has an entire Web site devoted to telling consumers how to minimize their risk of identity theft. Some of their advice is obvious, like "Keep your purse or wallet in a safe place at work." Some tips are more obscure: "Treat your mail and trash carefully." Some assume that people have a lot more time, patience, and knowledge than they really do:
>
> > Ask about information security procedures in your workplace or at businesses, doctor's offices, or other

institutions that collect your personally identifying information. Find out who has access to your personal information and verify that it is handled securely. Ask about the disposal procedures for those records as well. Find out if your information will be shared with anyone else. If so, ask how your information can be kept confidential. ("Deter")

Abukar points out how impractical the FTC advice is.

However, not many people are prepared to spend twenty minutes grilling the checkout person at Old Navy when she asks for their phone number.

Take the role of the contributor

You can use this template.

I agree with _____ because my experience confirms that _____.

Sources should not make your argument for you. Indicate exactly how they support your position by making an additional point.

The credit reporting agencies are not content with letting consumers and banks foot the bill for their sloppy handling of our digital identities. They want to make more money off the insecurity they have created. Kevin Drum reports in *Washington Monthly*:

The source describes how credit card reporting agencies make money off the fear of identity theft, supporting Abukar's claim.

For their part, the major credit-reporting bureaus—Experian, Equifax, and TransUnion—don't seem to care much about the accuracy of their credit reports. In fact, they actually have a positive incentive to let ID theft flourish. Like mobsters offering "protection" to frightened store owners, credit-reporting agencies have recently begun taking advantage of the identity-theft boom to offer information age protection to frightened consumers. For $9.95 a month, Equifax offers "Credit Watch Gold," a service that alerts you whenever changes are made to your credit report. Experian and TransUnion offer similar services. In effect, customers are being asked to pay credit agencies to protect them from the negligence of those same agencies.

Abukar makes an additional point that builds on his source.

Unlike consumers, who usually at least try to act responsibly to protect their credit rating, credit-reporting agencies avoid responsibility for, and profit from, identity theft. Therefore, the most important step to take in reducing identity theft is

to implement legislation that holds credit reporting agencies responsible for the damage their actions or inactions cause consumers.

Take the role of the analyst

You can use this template.

I agree with _____ up to a point, but I disagree with the conclusion _____ because _____ .

Incorporating sources is not a matter of simply agreeing or disagreeing with sources. Often you will agree with a source up to a point, but you will object to the conclusions. Or you may agree with the conclusions but not with the reasoning. In other words, you may find someone's views are correct but not for the reasons put forth.

Abukar used a source with which he was in basic agreement, but he found one part of the argument in the source much stronger than the other part.

Abukar summarizes the position of his source.

In his book *The Digital Person: Technology and Privacy in the Information Age*, Daniel J. Solove proposes that the way to reduce identity theft is to change the structure, or "architecture," of the systems we use to collect and store personal information. He recommends giving individuals more control over their personal information, and requiring the companies that use that information to inform people whenever something unusual happens to their files.

Abukar goes on to argue that the source misses how the solution proposed might be implemented.

While Solove's plan sounds good, he neglects the key for implementing the solution. Solove says that any new system should be "premised on the notion that the collection and use of personal information is an activity that carries duties and responsibilities" (121). This statement is an indirect way of saying, "Companies that handle personal information ought to be held liable for damages caused by identity theft." I would argue that if you make companies responsible to consumers by making them liable (the second half of Solove's plan), then they will automatically give consumers more control over their own information (the first half).

WRITING SMART

Determine the relationship of each source to your thesis

Gather the list of sources you have found in your research. You may have assembled these sources in a working bibliography or an annotated bibliography. Examine each source in relation to your working thesis. Note beside each source how it relates to your argument, using the "skeptic," "contributor," and "analyst" strategy.

- Does the source provide evidence for your claim or your reasons?
- Do you disagree with the source and can you use it as a jumping-off point for your argument?
- Do you agree with the source and find you can expand on it?
- Do you agree with the source up to a point and can you use it to show how your argument is different and perhaps better?

Exercise 24.1   Find an argumentative essay or essays in which the author is using the roles discussed in this section: skeptic, contributor, analyst. Highlight examples of these roles being used in the text.

24c Decide When to Quote and When to Paraphrase

Use sources to support what you say; don't expect them to say it for you. Next to plagiarism, the worst mistake you can make with sources is to string together a series of long quotations. This strategy leaves your readers wondering whether you have anything to say. Relying too much on quotations from others also makes for a bumpy read. Think about how each source relates to your thesis (see Section 24b).

When to quote and when to paraphrase

The general rule in deciding when to include direct quotations and when to paraphrase lies in the importance of the original wording.

- If you want to refer to an idea or fact and the original wording is not important, make the point in your own words.
- Save direct quotations for language that is memorable or conveys the character of the source.

Writer at Work

For background for her proposal to create a campus garden, Gabriella Lopez wanted to cite two ideas from Michael Pollan's *In Defense of Food*—that food has meanings beyond nutrition and that the industrialization of food production has led to less variety in the American diet with negative consequences for health.

Pollan, Michael. In Defense of Food: An Eater's Manifesto. New York: Penguin, 2008. 8-10. Print.

We forget that, historically, people have eaten for a great many reasons other than biological necessity. Food is also about pleasure, about community, about family and spirituality, about our relationship to the natural world, and about expressing our identity. As long as humans have been taking meals together, eating has been as much about culture as it has been about biology.

QUOTE SENTENCE "Food is also about pleasure, about community, about family and spirituality, about our relationship to the natural world, and about expressing our identity" (8).

That eating should be foremost about bodily health is a relatively new and, I think, destructive idea—destructive not just of the pleasure of eating, which would be bad enough, but paradoxically of our health as well. Indeed, no people on earth worry more about the health consequences of their food choices than we Americans do—and no people suffer from as many diet-related health problems. We are becoming a nation of orthorexics: people with an unhealthy obsession with healthy eating.

. . .

All of our uncertainties about nutrition should not obscure the plain fact that the chronic diseases that now kill most of us can be traced directly to the industrialization of our food: the rise of highly processed foods and refined grains; the use of chemicals to raise plants and animals in huge monocultures; the superabundance of cheap calories of sugar and fat produced by modern agriculture; and the narrowing of the biological diversity of the human diet to a tiny handful of staple crops, notably wheat, corn, and soy. These changes have given us the Western diet that we take for granted: lots of processed foods and meat, lots of added fat and sugar, lots of *everything*—except vegetables, fruits, and whole grains.

PARAPHRASE This promotion of discrete nutrients over whole food has lead to industrialization of food production—more processed foods, more artificial grains, more chemicals to raise animals and vegetables in vast "monocultures," more sugars and fats, and less variety in our diet that has been reduced to a glut of wheat, corn, and soy (Pollan 10).

Exercise 24.2 For each of the rhetorical situations described below, decide whether you would quote, paraphrase, or summarize the sources mentioned. Keep in mind that for some, you might want to do a combination of quoting, paraphrasing, or summarizing.

1. You are writing an article arguing that a local judge is a racist. You have collected several inappropriate remarks made by this judge as she conducted the business of the court.
2. You are writing an e-mail to your friend comparing two movies you may go to see based on online reviews.
3. You are tasked with submitting a proposal for purchasing new multimedia software for the computer lab. You will be using technical manuals and reviews to argue which software should be purchased.
4. You are writing a paper on the *Twilight Saga* series of books and the controversy over the message the books send to young female readers.
5. You are writing a response to a letter in the newspaper. You want to emphasize the other author's factual errors.

WRITING SMART

Use quotations effectively

Quotations are a frequent problem area in research projects. Review every quotation to ensure that each is used effectively and correctly.

- **Limit the use of long quotations.** If you have more than one block quotation on a page, look closely to see if one or more can be paraphrased or summarized. Use direct quotations only if the original wording is important.
- **Check that each quotation is supporting your major points rather than making major points for you.** If the ideas rather than the original wording are what's important, paraphrase the quotation and cite the source.
- **Check that each quotation is introduced with a signal phrase and attributed.** Each quotation should be introduced and the author or title named. Check for verbs that signal a quotation: Smith *claims*, Jones *argues*, Brown *states*.
- **Check that each quotation is properly formatted and punctuated.** Prose quotations longer than four lines (MLA) or forty words (APA) should be indented ten spaces in MLA style or five spaces in APA style. Shorter quotations should be enclosed within quotation marks.

(Continued on next page)

> ## WRITING SMART   *(Continued)*
>
> - **Check that you cite the source for each quotation.** You are required to cite the sources of all direct quotations, paraphrases, and summaries.
> - **Check the accuracy of each quotation.** It's easy to leave out words or mistype a quotation. Compare what is in your project to the original source. If you need to add words to make the quotation grammatical, make sure the added words are in brackets. Use ellipses to indicate omitted words.
> - **Read your project aloud to a classmate or a friend.** Each quotation should flow smoothly when you read your project aloud. Put a check beside rough spots as you read aloud so you can revise later.

24d   Integrate Quotations

All sources should be well integrated into the fabric of your project. Introduce quotations by attributing them in your text:

> Even those who fought for the United States in the U.S.-Mexican War of 1846 were skeptical of American motives: "We were sent to provoke a fight, but it was essential that Mexico should commence it" (Grant 68).

The preceding quotation is used correctly, but it loses the impact of the source. Compare it with the following:

> Many soldiers who fought for the United States in the U.S.-Mexican War of 1846 were skeptical of American motives, including Civil War hero and future president Ulysses S. Grant, who wrote: "We were sent to provoke a fight, but it was essential that Mexico should commence it" (68).

Use signal phrases

Signal verbs often indicate your stance toward a quotation. Introducing a quotation with "X says" or "X believes" tells your readers nothing. Find a livelier verb that suggests how you are using the source. For example, if you write "X contends," your reader is alerted that you likely will disagree with the source. Be as precise as possible.

Signal phrases that report information or a claim

X argues that . . .

X asserts that . . .

X claims that . . .

X observes that . . .

As X puts it, . . .

X reports that . . .

As X sums it up, . . .

Signal phrases when you agree with the source

X affirms that . . .

X has the insight that . . .

X points out insightfully that . . .

X theorizes that . . .

X verifies that . . .

Signal phrases when you disagree with the source

X complains that . . .

X contends that . . .

X denies that . . .

X disputes that . . .

X overlooks that . . .

X rejects that . . .

X repudiates that . . .

Signal phrases in the sciences

Signal phrases in the sciences often use the past tense, especially for interpretations and commentary.

X described . . .

X found . . .

X has suggested . . .

Introduce block quotations

Long direct quotations, called **block quotations**, are indented from the margin instead of being placed in quotation marks. In MLA style, a quotation longer than four lines should be indented one inch. A quotation of forty words or longer is indented one-half inch in APA style. In both MLA and APA styles, long quotations are double-spaced. You still need to integrate a block quotation into the text of your project by mentioning who wrote or said it.

- No quotation marks appear around the block quotation.
- Words quoted in the original retain the double quotation marks.

- The page number appears after the period at the end of the block quotation.

It is a good idea to include at least one or two sentences following the quotation to describe its significance to your thesis.

Double-check quotations

Whether they are long or short, you should double-check all quotations you use to be sure they are accurate and that all words belonging to the original are set off with quotation marks or placed in a block quotation. If you wish to leave out words from a quotation, indicate the omitted words with ellipses (. . .), but make sure you do not alter the meaning of the original quote (see Section 47e). If you need to add words of your own to a quotation to make the meaning clear, place your words in square brackets (see Section 47d).

 Integrate Summaries and Paraphrases

Summaries and paraphrases likewise need introductions. The following paragraph is the summary of a book. The source is noted at the end, but the reader cannot tell exactly which ideas come from the source.

> In 2001 it became as fashionable to say the Internet changes nothing as it had been to claim the Internet changes everything just two years before. While the profit-making potential of the Internet was overrated, the social effects were not. The Internet is demolishing old castles of expertise along with many traditional relationships based on that expertise (Lewis).

In the following summary, signal phrases make it clear which ideas come from the source. The summary also indicates the stance of Lewis and includes a short quotation that gives the flavor of the source.

> In 2001 it became as fashionable to say the Internet changes nothing as it had been to claim the Internet changes everything just two years before. In the midst of the Internet gloom, one prominent contrarian has emerged to defend the Internet. Michael Lewis observes in *Next: The Future Just Happened* that it's as if "some crusty old baron who had been blasted out of his castle and was finally having a look at his first cannon had said, 'All it does is speed up balls'"(14). Lewis claims that while the profit-making potential of the Internet was overrated, the social effects were not. He sees the Internet demolishing old castles of expertise along with many traditional relationships based on that expertise.

STAYING ON TRACK

Weave sources into your paper

Sources should be well integrated into your project. A common mistake is to drop in quotations without introducing them or indicating their significance. We don't know how the following long quotation fits into the writer's argument.

Off track
Cell phones and the Internet have not made the world a more harmonious place just because people have the increased potential to talk with each other.

> I see a world where people can't talk to each other in any meaningful way. Global networking will be a tool of business communication, consumerism, propaganda, banal conversations, and mindless entertainment. We will have forgotten how to tell stories or how to hear them. The majority of the world's population will be very young people without extended families or intact cultures, with fanatical allegiances to dead religions or live dictatorships. We have what Jonas Salk called a "wisdom deficit." (Laurel 102–03)

Introduce each quotation and make clear its significance to your text. Compare the following paragraph with the paragraph above.

On track
Cell phones and the Internet have not made the world a more harmonious place just because people have the increased potential to talk with each other. The tone of public discourse–be it in political campaigns, opinion in print and in pixels, talk radio, and discussion boards–has taken a turn toward the ugly. More information seems to have led to less understanding. Brenda Laurel, one of the more insightful commentators on the effects of digital media, fears we are moving toward "a world where people can't talk to each other in any meaningful way," a world where "we will have forgotten how to tell stories or how to hear them" (102). Laurel uses Jonas Salk's description of our culture as suffering from a "wisdom deficit" to sum up her point (103).

The second example introduces Brenda Laurel in relation to the writer's claim that more information has led to less understanding. The writer weaves Brenda Laurel's words into his own but preserves Laurel's distinctive voice.

Remember: Quotations don't speak for themselves.

Exercise 24.3 Rewrite the following to better integrate the quotes and paraphrases. Note that paraphrased text is underlined.

1. The novel *Infinite Jest* by David Foster Wallace is about sadness: "The sadness that the book is about, and that I was going through, was a real American type of sadness" (Wallace 2).

2. Wallace says this sadness "is something that doesn't have very much to do with physical circumstances, or the economy, or any of the stuff that gets talked about in the news. It's more like a stomach-level sadness. I see it in myself and my friends in different ways. It manifests itself as a kind of lostness. Whether it's unique to our generation I really don't know" (1).

3. Frank Bruni wrote a profile of Wallace in 1996 for *The New York Times Magazine*. He said that Wallace's place in literature could be compared to Jim Carrey's or Robin Williams's place in comedy. Wallace is "a creator so maniacally energetic and amused with himself that he often follows his riffs out into the stratosphere, where he orbits all alone."

4. Wallace was known for his heavy and creative use of footnotes. Footnotes are used to disrupt the narrative to represent his perception of reality. He said that he could have jumbled up the sentences instead. He also said "but then no one would read it." He said all of this in a 1997 interview with Charlie Rose.

24f Integrate Visuals

Like quotations, visuals should not be dropped in without introductions.

- Place all visuals as close as possible to the related text.
- Introduce each visual in your text.
- In MLA style, give each visual a figure number (abbreviated *Fig.*) and a caption.
- Give complete information about the source in the caption.
- If the source is not mentioned in the text, you do not need to include it in the list of works cited.

In April 1947, Jackie Robinson became the first African American to play baseball in the major leagues in the twentieth century, ending the segregation practice that restricted black players to the Negro leagues. Robinson's superior athletic ability quickly became evident, and he won the Most Valuable Player award in the National League in 1949. His success made him a popular culture icon, with a hit song written about him, a Hollywood movie about his life, and even a comic book (see fig. 3).

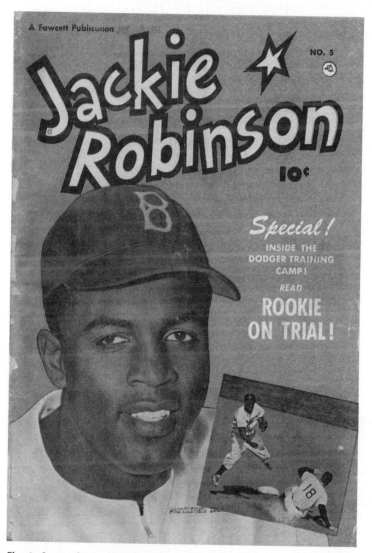

Fig. 3. Cover of a Jackie Robinson comic book (1951); rpt. "Baseball and Jackie Robinson." *American Memory*. Lib. of Cong., n.d. Web. 26 Oct. 2010.

25 | Write and Revise the Research Project

QUICKTAKE

- **Revisit your research** (see below)
- **Plan your organization** (see p. 331)
- **Review and revise** (see p. 333)

25a Revisit Your Research

Before you begin writing your project, review the assignment and your goals (see Chapter 19). Your review of the assignment will remind you of your purpose (analysis, review, survey, evaluation, argument), your potential readers, your stance on your subject, and the length and scope you should aim for.

Take stock of your research

Gather the source material and any field research you have generated (see Chapters 20, 21, and 22). Often additional questions come up in the course of your research. Group your notes by subject. Ask yourself

- Which sources provide evidence that supports your thesis or main points?
- Which sources turned out not to be relevant?
- Which ideas or points lack adequate sources? You may need to do additional research before starting to write your project.

Revise your working thesis

Often you will find that one aspect of your topic turned out to be more interesting and produced more information. If you have ample material, narrowing your subject is a benefit. At this stage in the writing process, your working thesis may be rough and may change as you write your draft, but having a working thesis will help keep your project focused (see Section 2d).

Revise or write out your working thesis.

I plan to (analyze, review, survey, evaluate, argue) that _____ .
This subject matters to my readers because _____ .

> **Exercise 25.1** Go back to the working thesis you developed in Exercise 19.3. After doing research on this topic, you likely changed your thesis, and perhaps even your topic and research questions. Revise your topic, research questions, and thesis to reflect these changes.

25b Plan Your Organization

After you have drafted a thesis, look back over your notes and determine how to group the ideas you researched. Decide what your major points will be, and how those points support your thesis. Group your research findings so that they match up with your major points.

Now it is time to create a working outline. Always include your thesis at the top of your outline as a guiding light. Some writers create formal outlines with roman numerals and the like; others compose the headings for the paragraphs of their project and use them to guide their draft; still others may start writing and then determine how they will organize their draft when they have a few paragraphs written (see Section 2d).

Writer at Work

Gabriella Lopez made a working outline for her project.

Establishing a Campus Garden	
Section 1	Give background on why students are increasingly interested in sustainability and where campus farms have been established
Section 2	Propose establishing a campus garden as the least expensive way our campus can "go green"
Section 3	Argue that gardening can promote a healthy relationship with food at a time many students suffer from eating disorders
Section 4	Argue for the social, environmental, and educational benefits
Section 5	Explain the specifics for making the garden
Section 6	Explain how support for the garden can be generated and maintained
Section 7	Conclude by returning to the importance of sustainability for the future

**Exercise 25.2** Using the advice given in Section 2d develop an outline for your research paper (Exercise 25.1). Remember that your outline does not have to be formal; use a system that works best for you.

25c Write a Draft

Some writers begin by writing the title, first paragraph, and concluding paragraph.

Write a specific title

A bland, generic title says to readers that you are likely to be boring.

> Generic   Good and Bad Fats

Specific titles are like tasty appetizers; if you like the appetizer, you'll probably like the main course.

> Specific   The Secret Killer: Hydrogenated Fats

Write an engaging introduction

Get off to a fast start. If, for example, you want to alert readers to the dangers of partially hydrogenated oils in the food we eat, you could begin by explaining the difference in molecular structure between natural unsaturated fatty acids and trans fatty acids. And you would probably lose your readers by the end of the first paragraph.

Instead, let readers know what is at stake along with giving some background and context (see Section 3e). State your thesis early on. Then go into the details in the body of your project.

> Americans today are more heath conscious than ever before, yet most are unaware that they may be ingesting high levels of dangerous fat in the form of partially hydrogenated oils. Hydrogenation is the process of passing hydrogen bubbles through heated oil, which makes the oil taste like butter. Nearly all processed food contains some level of hydrogenated oils. The food tastes good, but the oil it contains will make you fat and can eventually kill you.

Write a strong conclusion

The challenge in writing ending paragraphs is to leave the reader with something provocative, something beyond pure summary of the previous paragraphs. Connect back to your thesis, and use a strong concluding image, example, question, or call to action to leave your readers with something to remember and think about (see Section 3e).

25d Review and Revise

After you've finished your first draft, you'll want to get comments from other writers. A good source of help is fellow students. Your instructor may include a peer review session as part of the assignment.

Reading another student's project

It is usually best to read through a project twice, looking at different levels (see Chapter 4). The first time you read through a project, concentrate on comprehension and overall impressions. See if you can summarize the project after reading it once.

Once you've read through the project a second time, write concluding suggestions and comments about how the writer could improve the project. Be specific. Saying "I liked your project" or "It's a good first draft" does not help the writer. Comments like "You need to cite more sources" or "You might consider switching paragraphs 2 and 4" give the writer specific areas to concentrate on in the revision. Remember it's important to be supportive in the peer editing process, so try to offer comments that are positive and encouraging.

Reading your own project

Reading your project aloud to yourself will help you find rough places. Parts that are difficult for you to speak aloud are going to be hard for your readers to get through. Try to imagine yourself as a reader who does not know much about your subject or who holds a viewpoint different from yours. What could you add that would benefit that reader?

Revise, Revise, Revise

After you've gone through the peer editing process or assessed your own draft, sit down with your project and consider the changes you need to make. Start from the highest level, reorganizing paragraphs and possibly even cutting large parts of your project and adding new sections. If you make significant revisions, likely you will want to repeat the overall evaluation of your revised draft when you finish.

When you feel your draft is complete, begin the editing phase. Use the guidelines in Section 4d to revise style and grammatical errors. Finally, proofread your project, word by word, checking for mistakes (see Section 4e). After you print out the final project, check each page for formatting errors (see Section 26l for MLA-style formatting and Section 27g for APA-style formatting).

STAYING ON TRACK

Check for missing documentation

When you reach the proofreading stage, make one pass though your draft to check for missing documentation. Print your draft and your works-cited list, then place them beside each other.

1. Check that every parenthetical citation and every mention of an author's name in your text has an entry in your works-cited list. Put a check beside each when you find they match and note what is missing.
2. Read your text carefully for missing citations. For example, if you find a sentence similar to the following, you'll need to insert a parenthetical citation.

Off track   One critic of the exuberance over Web 2.0 writes, "today's amateur monkeys can use their networked computers to publish everything from uninformed political commentary, to unseemly home videos, to embarrassingly amateurish music, to unreadable poems, reviews, essays and novels."

On track   One critic of the exuberance over Web 2.0 writes, "today's amateur monkeys can use their networked computers to publish everything from uninformed political commentary, to unseemly home videos, to embarrassingly amateurish music, to unreadable poems, reviews, essays and novels" (Keen 3).

3. Check for missing page numbers for sources that have pagination.

Off track   Andrew Keen describes Wikipedia as "an online encyclopedia where anyone with opposable thumbs and a fifth-grade education can publish anything on any topic from AC/DC to Zoroastrianism."

On track   Andrew Keen describes Wikipedia as "an online encyclopedia where anyone with opposable thumbs and a fifth-grade education can publish anything on any topic from AC/DC to Zoroastrianism" (3).

Remember: Faulty documentation hurts your credibility as a researcher and can be a cause of plagiarism.

MLA, APA, CMS, and CSE

You **can learn more and do more** with MyCompLab and with the eText version of *The Penguin Handbook*. For help with documenting your sources successfully, go to MyCompLab and click on "Resources," then select "Research." Review the tutorials (Read, Watch, Listen) within each topic, then complete the Exercises and click on the Gradebook to measure your progress.

In the **eText version** of *The Penguin Handbook with Exercises*, find extra worksheets, tutorials, and student writing samples.

26 | MLA Documentation

Research writing requires you to document the sources of all of your information that is not common knowledge. The style developed by the Modern Language Association (MLA) requires you to document each source in two places: an in-text citation in the body of your project, and a list of all works cited at the end. Citing sources is a two-way process. If your readers want to find the source of a fact or quotation in your project, they can use your in-text citation to find the full information about a source in your works-cited list.

MLA DOCUMENTATION MAP

Here are the steps in the process of documentation.

1 | Collect the right information

For every source you need to have

- the name of the author or authors,
- the full title, and
- complete publication information.

For instructions go to the illustrated examples in section 26d of the four major source types:

- **PRINTED ARTICLE**
- **PRINTED BOOK**
- **DATABASE PUBLICATION**
- **WEB PUBLICATION**

For other kinds of sources such as visual and multimedia sources, see the Index of Works-Cited Entries on pp. 366-367.

2 | Cite sources in two places

Remember, this is a two-part process.

You will learn **how to cite sources in your project** from a Writer at Work in section 26a.

To create citations

(a) in **the body of your paper**, go to 26a and 26c.
(b) in a **list of works cited at the end of your paper**, go to 26b.

If you have questions that the examples in this chapter do not address, consult the *MLA Handbook for Writers of Research Papers*, seventh edition (2009), and the *MLA Style Manual and Guide to Scholarly Publishing*, third edition (2008).

3 | Find the right model citations

You'll find **illustrated examples of sources** in 26d.

Once you match your source to one of those examples, you can move on to more specific examples:

- **PRINTED ARTICLE,** go to 26e.
- **PRINTED BOOK** or parts of a book, go to 26f.
- **ONLINE:** was the source
  a) in a **library database**? Go to 26g.
  b) from **another Web source**? Go to 26h.

A complete list of examples is found in the Index of Works-Cited Entries on pp. 356–357.

4 | Format your paper

You will find a **two sample research papers in MLA style** and instructions on formatting the body of your paper and your works-cited list in Section 26l.

A note about footnotes:
MLA style does not use footnotes for documentation. Use in-text citations instead (see Sections 26a and 26e). The only use of footnotes in MLA style is for providing additional information, as you will see in Section 26k.

26a Citing Sources in an MLA-Style Project

Writer at Work

Gabriella Lopez chose to make a proposal argument for a campus garden as her research project. She wanted to argue that the garden was important for her school for reasons beyond providing a few fresh vegetables and that the garden could be created without massive effort or expense. You can see the complete paper in Section 26l at the end of this chapter.

How to quote and cite a source in the text of an MLA-style paper

Gabriella searched for an article on the *LexisNexis Academic* database using the search terms "green" and "college." She found the article below, and she printed a copy.

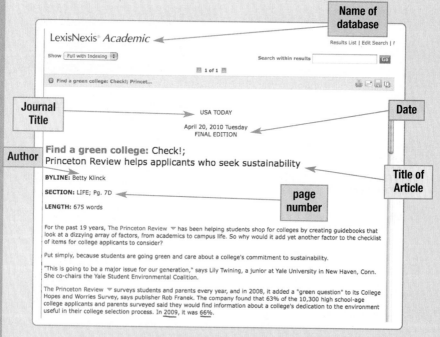

To support her argument that many students consider a college's commitment to sustainability when selecting a college, she wanted to quote the statistic that 66% of students and parents surveyed would find it useful to have information about a college's dedication to the environment.

Gabriella can either (a) mention Betty Klinck in the text of her paper with a signal phrase (see page 324) or (b) place the author's name inside parentheses following the quotation. Either with or without the signal phrase, in most cases she must include the page number where she found the quotation inside parentheses. Gabriella could omit the page number for this source because MLA does not require including the page number for one-page sources.

Author's name in signal phrase

Betty Klinck reports that in 2009, the *Princeton Review* found that 66% of high school-age college applicants and parents surveyed "would find information about a college's dedication to the environment useful in their college selection process" (7D).

OR

Author's name in parenthetical citation

In 2009, the *Princeton Review* found that 66% of high school-age college applicants and parents surveyed "would find information about a college's dedication to the environment useful in their college selection process" (Klinck 7D).

If Gabriella includes a quotation that is four lines or longer, she must doublespace and indent the quotation in her paper 1 inch (see example on page 379).

Include in-text citations for summaries and paraphrases

To argue for the feasibility of the garden proposal, Gabriella supplied specific details of how square-foot gardens work. She used information from a book by Mel Bartholomew, who is an expert on square-food gardening. The wording was not especially important, so Gabriella summarized Bartholomew's recommendations and gave the page numbers from her source.

The size of each square in the grid depends on what plants are planted there; certain plants require larger and deeper grids (Bartholomew 15-16). The main benefit of square-foot gardening is that one can grow the same amount of produce in a 140-square-foot grid that is typically grown in the average 700 square foot, single-row garden (Bartholemew 42).

26b Creating the List of Works Cited

Writer at Work

Gabriella is ready to create an entry for the list of works cited at the end of her paper. Gabriella kept a copy of this screenshot from her library database and made notes about the proper information to create the works-cited entry.

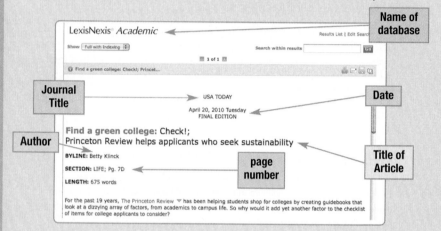

Gabriella asked herself a series of questions to create an entry for this source in her list of Works Cited.

1. What information do I need to pull from this screenshot?

For a source like this article from an online database, she needs to know five things: (1) what type of source it is; (2) the author; (3) the title; (4) the publication information; and (5) information about the online database.

2. I know this is from my library's online database, but that could be one of several different types of sources. What kind of source is this?

The kinds of sources you'll find in a database are an article from a periodical (newspaper or a scholarly journal), a business or financial report, a legal case, or an abstract. Gabriella selected newspapers for the source type in her *LexisNexis Academic* search; thus she knew that her source type would be an article.

3. Now how do I find the author's name?

Look for a bold heading that says something like "AUTHOR" or "BYLINE." If more than one author is listed, take note of all names listed.

4. What is the title of my source?

If the title is not immediately evident, look for a heading that says "TITLE" or "HEADLINE."

5. Where do I find the publication information?

The name and date of the periodical are usually listed at the top of the page but sometimes are found at the bottom. In this case the page number is listed beside "SECTION."

6. Where do I find the name of the database?

For databases distributed by EBSCO, you have to look for the name of the database. EBSCO is the vendor who sells access to many databases such as *Academic Search Complete*. LexisNexis is the vendor that distributes access to *LexisNexis Academic* and other LexisNexis databases.

Gabriella listed the information.

AUTHOR	Klinck, Betty
TITLE OF ARTICLE	"Find a Green College: Check! Princeton Review Helps Applicants Who Seek Sustainability"
PUBLICATION INFORMATION	
Name of periodical	USA Today
Date of publication	20 Apr. 2010, final ed.
Section and page number	7D
DATABASE INFORMATION	
Name of database	LexisNexis Academic
Date the site was accessed	20 Apr. 2010

Then she used the instruction on page 353 to format her citation. You can see Gabriella's complete list of works cited on pages 389–391 at the end of this chapter.

Lopez 10

Works Cited

Klinck, Betty. "Find a Green College: Check! Princeton Review Helps Applicants Who Seek Sustainability." *USA Today* 20 Apr. 2010, final ed.: 7D. *LexisNexis Academic*. Web. 20 Apr. 2010.

26c In-text Citations in MLA Style

Paraphrase, summary, or short quotation

A short quotation takes four lines or fewer in your paper.

> The computing power of networked technology is growing at an accelerating rate, prompting some visionaries to argue that the Internet "may actually become self-aware sometime in the next century" (Johnson 114).

Here, the author's name is provided in the parenthetical reference.

> Science writer and cultural critic Steven Johnson poses the question this way: "Is the Web itself becoming a giant brain?" (114).

Note that the period goes *after* the parentheses.

The author of the quotation is named in this sentence, so only a page number is needed in the parenthetical reference.

Quotations longer than four lines

The sentence introducing the quotation names the author, so only the page number needs to appear in the parenthetical reference.

> Technology writer and cultural commentator Steven Johnson relates how he often responded to questions about whether or not networked computers would ever be able to think or develop awareness:
>
>> For there to be a single, global consciousness, the Web itself would have to be getting smarter, and the Web wasn't a single, unified thing—it was just a vast sum of interlinked data. You could debate whether the Web was making us smarter, but that the Web itself might be slouching toward consciousness seemed ludicrous. (114)
>
> Despite his initial scepticism, however, Johnson slowly began to change his mind about the idea of artificial consciousness or intelligence.

Note that the period appears *before* the parentheses in an indented block quote.

WHEN DO YOU PROVIDE A PAGE NUMBER?

- If the source is longer than one page, provide the page number for each quotation, paraphrase, and summary.
- If an online source includes paragraph numbers rather than page numbers, use *par.* with the number.

(Cello, par. 4)

- If the source does not include page numbers, consider citing the work and the author in the text rather than in parentheses.

In a hypertext version of James Joyce's *Ulysses*, . . .

Index of in-text citations

Include in-text citations as you are writing your project rather than waiting until you finish. Use this index to determine the right format.

Sample in-text citations for sources in general

1. Author named in a signal phrase

Put the author's name in a signal phrase in your sentence.

> Sociologist Daniel Bell called this emerging U.S. economy the "postindustrial society" (3).

2. Author not named in your text

> In 1997, the Gallup poll reported that 55% of adults in the United States think secondhand smoke is "very harmful," compared to only 36% in 1994 (Saad 4).

3. Work by one author

The author's last name comes first, followed by the page number. There is no comma.

> (Bell 3)

4. Work by two or three authors

The authors' last names follow the order of the title page. If there are two authors, join the names with *and*. If there are three, use a comma between the first two names and a comma with *and* before the last name.

> (Francisco, Vaughn, and Lynn 7)

5. Work by four or more authors

You may use the phrase *et al.* (meaning "and others") for all names but the first, or you may write out all the names. Make sure you use the same method for both the in-text citations and the works-cited list.

> (Abrams et al. 1653)

6. Author unknown

Use a shortened version of the title that includes at least the first important word. Your reader will use the shortened title to find the full title in the works-cited list.

> A review in the *New Yorker* of Ryan Adams's new album focuses on the artist's age ("Pure" 25).

Notice that "Pure" is in quotation marks because it is the shortened title of an article. If it were a book, the short title would be in italics.

7. Work by a group or organization

Treat the group or organization as the author. Try to identify the group author in the text and place only the page number in parentheses.

> According to the *Irish Free State Handbook*, published by the Ministry for Industry and Finance, the population of Ireland in 1929 was approximately 4,192,000 (23).

8. Quotations longer than four lines

NOTE: When using indented ("block") quotations that are longer than four lines, the period appears *before* the parentheses enclosing the page number.

> In her article "Art for Everybody," Susan Orlean attempts to explain the popularity of painter Thomas Kinkade:
>> People like to own things they think are valuable. . . . The high price of limited editions is part of their appeal: it implies that they are choice and exclusive, and that only a certain class of people will be able to afford them. (128)
> This same statement could also explain the popularity of phenomena like PBS's *Antiques Road Show*.

If the source is longer than one page, provide the page number for each quotation, paraphrase, and summary.

9. Two or more works by the same author

Use the author's last name and then a shortened version of the title of each source.

> The majority of books written about coauthorship focus on partners of the same sex (Laird, *Women* 351).

Note that *Women* is italicized because it is the title of a book.

10. Different authors with the same last name

If your list of works cited contains items by two or more different authors with the same last name, include the initial of the first name in the parenthetical reference. Note that a period follows the initial.

> Web surfing requires more mental involvement than channel surfing (S. Johnson 107).

11. **Two or more sources within the same sentence**

Place each citation directly after the statement it supports.

> Many sweeping pronouncements were made in the 1990s that the Internet is the best opportunity to improve education since the printing press (Ellsworth xxii) or even in the history of the world (Dyrli and Kinnaman 79).

12. **Two or more sources within the same citation**

If two sources support a single point, separate them with a semicolon.

> (McKibbin 39; Gore 92)

13. **Work quoted in another source**

When you do not have access to the original source of the material you wish to use and only an indirect source is available, put the abbreviation *qtd. in* ("quoted in") before the information about the indirect source.

> National governments have become increasingly what Ulrich Beck, in a 1999 interview, calls "zombie institutions"—institutions which are "dead and still alive" (qtd. in Bauman 6).

Sample in-text citations for particular kinds of sources

14. **One-page source**

A page reference is unnecessary if you are citing a one-page work.

> Economists agree that automating routine work is the broad goal of globalization (Lohr).

15. **Web sources including Web pages, blogs, podcasts, wikis, videos, and other multimedia sources**

MLA prefers that you mention the author in your text instead of putting the author's name in parentheses.

> Andrew Keen ironically used his own blog to claim that "blogs are boring to write (yawn), boring to read (yawn) and boring to discuss (yawn)."

If you cannot identify the author, mention the title in your text.

> The podcast "Catalina's Cubs" describes the excitement on Catalina Island when the Chicago Cubs came for spring training in the 1940s.

16. Work in an edited anthology

Cite the name of the author of the work within an anthology, not the name of the editor of the collection. For example, Melissa Jane Hardie published the chapter "Beard" in *Rhetorical Bodies*, a book edited by Jack Selzer and Sharon Crowley. Note that Hardie, not Selzer and Crowley, is named in a parenthetical citation.

(Hardie 278-79)

17. Work in more than one volume

Give the volume number in the parenthetical reference before the page number, with a colon and a space separating the two.

(Walther and Metzger 2: 647).

18. Poems, plays, and classic works

Poems

If you quote all or part of two or three lines of poetry that do not require special emphasis, put the lines in quotation marks and separate the lines using a slash (/) with a space on each side.

John Donne's "The Legacy" associates the separation of lovers with death: "When I died last, and, Dear, I die / As often as from thee I go" (1-2).

Plays

Give the act, scene, and line numbers when the work has them, the page numbers when it does not. Abbreviate titles of famous works (like *Hamlet*).

(*Ham.* 3.2.120-23).

Classic Works

To supply a reference to classic works, you sometimes need more than a page number from a specific edition. Readers should be able to locate a quotation in any edition of the book. Give the page number from the edition that you are using, then a semicolon and other identifying information.

"Marriage is a house" is one of the most memorable lines in *Don Quixote* (546; pt. 2, bk. 3, ch. 19).

19. Sacred texts

Cite a sacred text such as the Bible or the Qur'an the first time with the name of the edition you use along with the book, chapter, and verse. In subsequent citations you need to give only the book, chapter, and verse. Abbreviate the names of books with five or more letters (*Prov.* for *Proverbs*).

The memorable phrase from the Vietnam War, "hearts and minds," actually comes from the New Testament (*New Oxford Annotated Bible*, Phil. 4.7).

26d Illustrated Samples and Index of Works Cited in MLA Style

Printed Article

You can find recent issues of printed scholarly journals and popular magazines in your library's periodicals room. Older issues are shelved on the stacks with books. Use your library's online catalog to find the location.

Scholarly journals usually list the publication information at the top or bottom of the first page. Popular magazines often do not list volume and issue numbers. You can find the date of publication on the cover.

> **Name of journal, volume number, issue number, date of publication, page numbers**

> *Ecological Applications*, 17(6), 2007, pp. 1742–1751
> © 2007 by the Ecological Society of America

Title of Article

A CROSS-REGIONAL ASSESSMENT OF THE FACTORS AFFECTING ECOLITERACY: IMPLICATIONS FOR POLICY AND PRACTICE

SARAH PILGRIM, DAVID SMITH, AND JULES PRETTY[1]

Authors

Centre for Environment and Society, Department of Biological Sciences, University of Essex, Wivenhoe Park, Colchester CO4 3SQ United Kingdom

Abstract. The value of accumulated ecological knowledge, termed ecoliteracy, is vital to both human and ecosystem health. Maintenance of this knowledge is essential for continued support of local conservation efforts and the capacity of communities to self- or co-manage their local resources sustainably. Most previous studies have been qualitative and small scale, documenting ecoliteracy in geographically isolated locations. In this study, we take a different approach, focusing on (1) the primary factors affecting individual levels of ecoliteracy, (2) whether these factors shift with economic development, and (3) if different knowledge protection strategies are required for the future. We compared non-resource-dependent communities in the United Kingdom with resource-dependent communities in India and Indonesia ($n = 1250$ interviews). We found that UK residents with the highest levels of ecoliteracy visited the countryside frequently, lived and grew up in rural areas, and acquired their knowledge from informal word-of-mouth sources, such as parents and friends, rather than television and schooling. The ecoliteracy of resource-dependent community members, however, varied with wealth status and gender. The least wealthy families depended most on local resources for their livelihoods and had the highest levels of ecoliteracy. Gender roles affected both the level and content of an individual's ecoliteracy. The importance of reciprocal oral transfer of this knowledge in addition to direct experience to the maintenance of ecoliteracy was apparent at all sites. Lessons learned may contribute to new local resource management strategies for combined ecoliteracy conservation. Without novel policies, local community management capacity is likely to be depleted in the future.

Key words: ecoliteracy; India; Indonesia; knowledge; natural resource; oral traditions; resource management; sustainable management; United Kingdom.

Citation in the List of Works Cited

Pilgrim, Sarah, David Smith, and Jules Pretty. "A Cross-Regional Assessment of the Factors Affecting Ecoliteracy: Implications for Policy and Practice." *Ecological Applications* 17.6 (2007): 1742-51. Print.

Elements of the citation

Author's Name

The author's last name comes first, followed by a comma and the first name.

For two or more works by the same author, see page 405.

Title of Article

Use the exact title and put it inside quotation marks. If a book title is part of the article's title, italicize the book title.

Publication Information

Name of journal or newspaper
Italicize the title of the journal or newspaper.

Abbreviate the title if it commonly appears that way.

Volume, issue, and page numbers
For scholarly journals give the volume number and issue number. Place a period between the volume and issue numbers: "55.3" indicates volume 55, issue 3.

Some scholarly journals use issue numbers only.

Give the page numbers for the entire article, not just the part you used.

Medium of publication
Print.

Find the right example as your model (you may need to refer to more than one model)

What type of article do you have?

A scholarly journal article?

- For a scholarly journal, go to page 359, #28–#29.

A review, editorial, or letter to the editor NOT in a newspaper?

- For a review, go to page 360, #30.
- For an editorial, go to page 360, #32.
- For a letter to the editor, go to page 360, #31.

A newspaper article, review, editorial, or letter to the editor?

- For a newspaper article, go to pages 360–361, #34–#39.
- For a review, go to page 361, #40.
- For an editorial, go to pages 361–362, #42–#43.
- For a letter to the editor, go to page 362, #41.

A government document?
Go to page 362, #44–#45.

How many authors are listed?

- One, two, or more authors: go to page 358, #20–#22.
- Unknown author: go to page 358, #23.

What kind of pagination is used?

- For a scholarly journal, go to page 359, #28.
- For a journal that starts every issue with page 1, go to page 359, #29.

Printed Book

Use your library's online catalog to locate printed books on your library's shelves. Find the copyright date on the copyright page, which is on the back of the title page. Use the copyright date for the date of publication, not the date of printing.

Citation in the List of Works Cited

Pollan, Michael. *In Defense of Food: An Eater's Manifesto*. New York: Penguin, 2008. Print.

Elements of the citation

Author's or Editor's Name

The author's last name comes first, followed by a comma and the first name.

For edited books, put the abbreviation *ed.* after the name, preceded by a comma:
Kavanagh, Peter, ed.

Book Title

Use the exact title, as it appears on the title page (not the cover).

Italicize the title.

Publication Information

Place of publication

If more than one city is given, use the first.

For cities outside the U.S., add an abbreviation of the country or province if the city is not well known.

Publisher

Omit words such as *Publisher* and *Inc*.

For university presses, use *UP*: New York UP

Shorten the name. For example, shorten *W. W. Norton & Co.* to *Norton*.

Date of publication

Give the year as it appears on the copyright page.

If no year of publication is given, but can be approximated, put a *c.* ("circa") and the approximate date in brackets: [c. 1999].

Otherwise, put n.d. ("no date"): Boston: Harvard UP, n.d.

Medium of publication

Print.

Find the right example as your model (you may need to refer to more than one model)

How many authors are listed?

- One, two, or more authors: go to page 364, #53–56.
- Unknown author: go to page 364, #57.
- Group or organization as the author: go to page 365, #59.

Do you have a book with an editor, translator, or illustrator?

- For a focus on the editor, go to page 367, #72.
- For a focus on the author of an edited book, go to page 367, #73.
- For a book with a translator, go to page 367, #74.
- For an illustrated book, go to page 367, #76.

Do you have only a part of a book?

- For an introduction, foreword, preface, or afterword, go to page 366, #66.
- For a chapter in an anthology or edited collection, go to page 366, #68.
- For more than one selection in an anthology or edited collection, go to page 366, #69.

Do you have two or more books by the same author?

- Go to page 364, #54.

Library Database Publication

You will find library databases linked off your library's Web site (see page 250). A few databases including Google Scholar are available to everyone, but most library databases are password protected if you access them off campus.

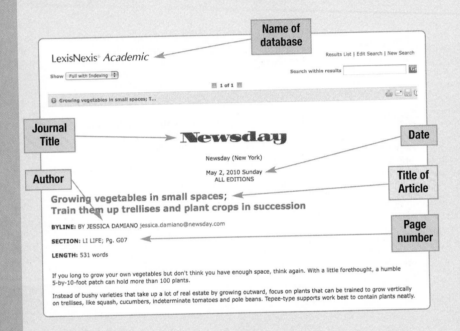

Citation in the List of Works Cited

> Damiano, Jessica. "Growing Vegetables in Small Spaces: Train Them
>
> up Trellises and Plant Crops in Succession." *Newsday* 2 May
>
> 2010: G107. *LexisNexis Academic.* Web. 8 Apr. 2010.

Take Note

Don't confuse the name of the vendor—the company that sells access to the database—with the name of the database. For example, EBSCO or EBSCO Host is not the name of a database but the name of the vendor that sells access to databases such as *Academic Search Complete.*

Elements of the citation

Start with the citation with the exact format of a print citation. Replace the word *Print* at the end with the name of the database, the medium (*Web*), and the date you accessed the source.

Author's Name

The author's last name comes first, followed by a comma and the first name. For two or more works by the same author, see page 405.

Title of Source

Use the exact title and put it inside quotation marks. If a book title is part of the article's title, italicize the book title.

Publication Information for an Article

Name of journal or newspaper
Italicize the title of the journal or newspaper. Abbreviate the title if it commonly appears that way.

Volume, issue, date, and page numbers
List the same information you would for a print item. If there are no page numbers, put *n. pag.* where the page numbers would ordinarily go.

Database Information

Name of the database
Italicize the name of the database, followed by a period.

Medium of publication
For all database sources, the medium of publication is *Web*.

Date of access
List the date you accessed the source (day, month, year).

Find the right example as your model (you may need to refer to more than one model)

Most databases allow you to search by document type, such as scholarly journal, newspaper article, financial report, legal case, or abstract. Use these categories to identify the type of publication.

> **What kind of publication do you have?**
>
> - For an article in a scholarly journal, go to page 368, #79
> - For a magazine article, go to page 368, #80
> - For a newspaper article, go to page 368, #83
> - For a legal case, go to page 368, #84
> - For a company report, go to page 369, #85

> **Do you have a publication with an unknown author?**
>
> Go to page 368, #81.

Web Publication

Date, volume, and issue

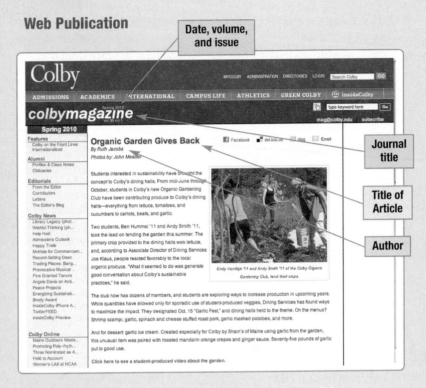

Journal title

Title of Article

Author

Citation in the List of Works Cited

Jacobs, Ruth. "Organic Garden Gives Back." *Colby Magazine* 99.1 (2010): n. pag. Web. 2 Apr. 2010.

When Do You List a URL?

MLA style no longer requires including URLs of Web sources. URLs are of limited value because they change frequently and they can be specific to an individual search. Include the URL as supplementary information only when your readers probably cannot locate the source without the URL.

Elements of the citation

Author's Name

Authorship is sometimes hard to discern for online sources. If you know the author or creator, follow the rules for books and journals.

If the only authority you find is a group or organization, list its name after the date of publication or last revision.

Title of Source

Place the title of the work inside quotation marks if it is part of a larger Web site.

Untitled works may be identified by a label (e.g., *Home page, Introduction*). List the label in the title slot without quotation marks or italics.

Italicize the name of the overall site if it is different from the work. The name of the overall Web site will usually be found on its index or home page.

Some Web sites are updated, so list the version if you find it (e.g., *Vers. 1.2*).

Publication Information for Web Sources

List the publisher's or sponsor's name followed by a comma. If it isn't available, use *N.p.*

List the date of publication by day, month, and year if available. If you cannot find a date, use *n.d.*

Give the medium of publication (*Web*).

List the date you accessed the site by day, month, and year.

Find the right example as your model (you may need to refer to more than one model)

Do you have a Web page or an entire Web site?

- For an entire Web site, go to page 369, #87
- For a page on a Web site, go to page 369, #86

What kind of publication do you have, and who is the author?

- For a known author, go to page 369, #88
- For a group or organization as the author, go to page 369, #89
- For a publication with print publication data, go to page 369, #90
- For a PDF or digital file, go to page 370, #91
- For an article in a scholarly journal, newspaper, or magazine, go to page 370, #92–94
- For a government publication, go to page 371, #100

Do you have a source that is posted by an individual?

- For e-mail or text messaging, go to page 372, #102
- For a post to a discussion list, go to page 372, #103
- For a personal home page, go to page 372, #105
- For a blog, go to page 372, #106–107

Index of Works Cited Entries

26e Journals, Magazines, Newspapers, and Other Print Sources

JOURNAL AND MAGAZINE ARTICLES

20. **Article by one author**

> Bhabha, Jacqueline. "The Child—What Sort of Human?"
> *PMLA* 121.5 (2006): 1526-35. Print.

21. **Article by two or three authors**

The second and subsequent authors' names are printed first name first.

> Kirsch, Gesa E., and Jacqueline J. Royster. "Feminist Rhetorical
> Practices: In Search of Excellence." *CCC* 61.4 (2010): 640-72.
> Print.

Notice that a comma separates the authors' names.

22. **Article by four or more authors**

You may use the phrase *et al.* (meaning "and others") for all authors but the first, or you may write out all the names.

> Breece, Katherine E., et al. "Patterns of mtDNA Diversity in
> Northwestern North America." *Human Biology* 76.5 (2004):
> 33-54. Print.

23. **Article by an unknown author**

Begin the entry with the title.

> "The Fire Next Time." *Newsweek* 5 July 2010: 83. Print.

24. **Article with a title within a title**

If the title of the article contains the title of another short work, include it in single quotation marks. Italicize the title or a word that would normally be italicized.

> Happel, Alison, and Jennifer Esposito. "Vampires, Vixens, and
> Feminists: An Analysis of *Twilight*." *Educational Studies*
> 46.5 (2010): 524-31. Print.

25. Abstract of a journal article

Add the word *Abstract* after the title.

Salsberry, Pamela J., and Patricia B. Reagan. "Dynamics of Early
Childhood Overweight." Abstract. *Pediatrics* 116.6 (2005):
1329. Print.

MONTHLY, WEEKLY, AND BIWEEKLY MAGAZINES

26. Monthly or seasonal magazines or journals

For magazines and journals identified by the month or season of publication, use the month (or season) and year in place of the volume. Abbreviate the names of all months except May, June, and July.

Huang, Yasheng. "China's Other Path." *Wilson Quarterly* Spring
2010: 58-64. Print.

27. Weekly or biweekly magazines

For weekly or biweekly magazines, give both the day and month of publication, as listed on the issue.

Toobin, Jeffrey. "Crackdown." *New Yorker* 5 Nov. 2001: 56-61. Print.

DIFFERENT TYPES OF PAGINATION

28. Article in a scholarly journal

After the title of the article, give the journal name in italics, the volume and issue numbers, the year of publication in parentheses, a colon, the inclusive page numbers, and the medium of publication.

Duncan, Mike. "Whatever Happened to the Paragraph?" *College
English* 69.5 (2007): 470-95. Print.

29. Article in a scholarly journal that uses only issue numbers

If a journal begins each issue on page 1, list the issue number after the name of the journal.

McCall, Sophie. "Double Vision Reading." *Canadian Literature* 194
(2007): 95-97. Print.

REVIEWS, EDITORIALS, LETTERS TO THE EDITOR

30. Review

Provide the title, if given, and name the work reviewed. If there is no title, just name the work reviewed. For film reviews, name the director.

Mendelsohn, Daniel. "The Two Oscar Wildes." Rev. of *The Importance of Being Earnest*, dir. Oliver Parker. *New York Review of Books* 10 Oct. 2002: 23-24. Print.

31. Letter to the editor

Add the word *Letter* after the name of the author.

Patai, Daphne. Letter. *Harper's Magazine* Dec. 2001: 4. Print.

32. Editorial

If the editorial is unsigned, put the title first. Add the word *Editorial* after the title.

"Stop Stonewalling on Reform." Editorial. *Business Week* 17 June 2002: 108. Print.

33. Published interview

Phipps, Simon. Interview. *Linux Journal* 1 June 2007: 33-34. Print.

NEWSPAPER ARTICLES

34. Article by one author

Rojas, Rick. "For Young Sikhs, a Tie That Binds Them to Their Faith." *Washington Post* 20 June 2010, final ed.: C03. Print.

35. Article by two or three authors

The second and subsequent authors' names are printed in regular order, first name first:

Chazen, Guy, and Dana Cimilluca. "BP Amasses Cash for Oil-Spill Costs." *Wall Street Journal* 26 June 2010: A1. Print.

Notice that a comma separates the authors' names.

36. Article by four or more authors

You may use the phrase *et al.* (meaning "and others") for all authors but the first, or you may write out all the names. Use the same method in the in-text citation as you do in the works-cited list.

Watson, Anne, et al. "Childhood Obesity on the Rise." *Daily Missoulian* 7 July 2003: B1. Print.

37. **Article by an unknown author**

Begin the entry with the title.

> "Democratic Candidates Debate Iraq War." *Austin American-Statesman* 19 Jan. 2004: A6. Print.

38. **Article with a title in a foreign language**

If the title is in a foreign language, copy it exactly as it appears on the title page, paying special attention to accent marks and capitalization.

> "Iraq, Liberati gli Ostaggi Sudcoreani." *Corriere Della Sera* 8 Apr. 2004: A1. Print.

39. **Article that continues to a nonconsecutive page**

Add a plus sign after the number of the first page.

> Kaplow, Larry, and Tasgola Karla Bruner. "U.S.: Don't Let Taliban Forces Flee." *Austin American-Statesman* 20 Nov. 2001, final ed.: A11+. Print.

NEWSPAPER REVIEWS, EDITORIALS, LETTERS TO THE EDITOR

40. **Review**

List the reviewer's name and the title of the review. Then write *Rev. of* followed by the title of the work, the word *by*, and the author's name.

> Garner, Dwight. "Violence Expert Visits Her Dark Past?" Rev. of *Denial: A Memoir of Terror*, by Jessica Stern. *New York Times* 25 June 2010: 28. Print.

41. **Letter to the editor**

> Leach, Richard E. Letter. *Boston Globe* 2 Apr. 2007, first ed.: A10. Print.

42. **Editorial**

Add the word *Editorial* after the title.

> Pachon, Harry P. "Pricing Out New Citizens." Editorial. *Los Angeles Times* 2 Apr. 2007, home ed.: A13. Print.

43. Unsigned editorial

If the editorial is unsigned, put the title first.

"High Court Ruling Doesn't Mean Vouchers Will Work." Editorial. *Atlanta Journal and Constitution* 28 June 2002, home ed.: A19. Print.

GOVERNMENT DOCUMENTS

44. Government documents other than the *Congressional Record*

If you are citing a congressional document other than the *Congressional Record*, be sure to identify the congress and, when necessary, the session after the title of the document.

Malveaux, Julianne. "Changes in the Labor Market Status of Black Women." *A Report of the Study Group on Affirmative Action to the Committee on Education and Labor.* 100th Cong., 1st sess. H. Rept. 100-L. Washington: GPO, 1987. 231-55. Print.

To cite an act, include the name, Public Law (*Pub. L.*) number, Statutes at Large volume number followed by the abbreviation *Stat.* and pages, the date enacted, and medium.

American Recovery and Reinvestment Act of 2009. Pub. L. 111-5. 50 Stat. 664. 17 Feb. 2009. Print.

45. *Congressional Record*

Cong. Rec. 8 Feb. 2000: 1222-46. Print.

BULLETINS, PAMPHLETS, AND LETTERS

46. Bulletin or pamphlet

Watkins Health Center. *The Common Cold.* Lawrence: U of Kansas, 2010. Print.

47. Published letter

Wilde, Oscar. "To Lord Alfred Douglas." 17 Feb. 1895. In *The Complete Letters of Oscar Wilde.* Ed. Merlin Holland and Rupert Hart-Davis. New York: Holt, 2000. 632-33. Print.

48. Unpublished letter

Welty, Eudora. Letter to Elizabeth Bowen. 1 May 1951. MS. Harry
Ransom Humanities Research Center, Austin.

DISSERTATIONS

49. Published dissertation or thesis

Mason, Jennifer. *Civilized Creatures: Animality, Cultural Power, and
American Literature, 1850-1901*. Diss. U of Texas at Austin,
2000. Ann Arbor: UMI, 2000. Print.

50. Unpublished dissertation or thesis

Schorn, Susan. "The Merciful Construction of Good Women:
Actresses in the Marriage-Plot Novel." Diss. U of Texas at
Austin, 2000. Print.

51. Abstract of a dissertation

Give the author, title, and dissertation information following the
abbreviation *Diss.* Then include the publication information for *DAI* (*Dissertation Abstracts International*) or *DA* (*Dissertation Abstracts*), with page
number and medium. If you access the abstract via a database, add the item
number, database, medium, and date of access.

LaVally, Rebecca Jean. "Political Contradictions: Discussions of
Virtue in American Life." Diss. U of Texas at Austin, 2010.
*DAI*71.9 (2011): AAT3417468. *ProQuest Dissertations and
Theses*. Web. 15 Feb. 2011.

CONFERENCE PROCEEDINGS

52. Published proceedings of a conference

Abadie, Ann, and Robert Hamblin, eds. *Faulkner in the Twenty-first
Century: Proceedings of the 27th Faulkner and Yoknapatawpha
Conference, Aug. 10-16, 2000*. Jackson: U of Mississippi P,
2003. Print.

26f Books

ONE AUTHOR

53. Book by one author

> Mayer-Schönberger, Viktor. *Delete: The Virtue of Forgetting in the Digital Age*. Princeton: Princeton UP, 2009. Print.

54. Two or more books by the same author

In the entry for the first book, include the author's name. In the second entry, substitute three hyphens and a period for the author's name. List the titles of books by the same author in alphabetical order.

> Krakauer, Jon. *Into the Wild*. New York: Villard, 1996. Print.

> ---. *Where Men Win Glory: The Odyssey of Pat Tillman*. New York: Doubleday, 2009. Print.

MULTIPLE AUTHORS

55. Book by two or three authors

The second and subsequent authors' names appear first name first.

> Burger, Edward B., and Michael Starbird. *Coincidences, Chaos, and All That Math Jazz*. New York: Norton, 2006. Print.

56. Book by four or more authors

You may use the phrase *et al.* (meaning "and others") for all authors but the first, or you may write out all the names. Use the same method in the in-text citation as you do in the works-cited list.

> North, Stephen M., et al. *Refiguring the Ph.D. in English Studies*. Urbana: NCTE, 2000. Print.

ANONYMOUS AND GROUP AUTHORS

57. Book by an unknown author

Begin the entry with the title.

> *Encyclopedia of Americana*. New York: Somerset, 2001. Print.

58. Book revised by a second author

Place the editor's name after the book title.

> Strunk, William. *Elements of Style*. Ed. E. B. White. 4th ed. Boston: Allyn, 2000. Print.

59. Book by a group or organization

Treat the group as the author of the work.

> United Nations. *The Charter of the United Nations: A Commentary.*
> New York: Oxford UP, 2000. Print.

TITLES WITHIN TITLES AND FOREIGN TITLES

60. Title within a title

If the title contains the title of another book or a word normally italicized, do not italicize that title or word.

> Higgins, Brian, and Hershel Parker. *Critical Essays on Herman*
> *Melville's* Moby-Dick. New York: Hall, 1992. Print.

61. Title in a foreign language

If the title is in a foreign language, copy it exactly as it appears on the title page.

> Fontaine, Jean. *Etudes de Littérature Tunisienne.* Tunis: Dar
> Annawras, 1989. Print.

IMPRINTS, REPRINTS, AND UNDATED BOOKS

62. Book published before 1900

You may omit the publisher for books published prior to 1900.

> Rodd, Renell. *Rose Leaf and Apple Leaf.* Philadelphia, 1882. Print.

63. Book from a publisher's imprint

In the example below, Flamingo is a special imprint of Harper.

> O'Brien, Flann. *The Poor Mouth.* London: Flamingo-Harper, 1993.
> Print.

64. Book with no publication date

If no year of publication is given, but it can be approximated, put a *c.* ("circa") and the approximate date in brackets: [c. 1999]. Otherwise, put *n.d.* ("no date").

> O'Sullivan, Colin. *Traditions and Novelties of the Irish Country Folk.*
> Dublin, [c. 1793]. Print.

> James, Franklin. *In the Valley of the King.* Cambridge: Harvard UP,
> n.d. Print.

65. Reprinted works

For works of fiction that have been printed in many different editions or reprints, give the original publication date after the title.

> Wilde, Oscar. *The Picture of Dorian Gray*. 1890. New York: Norton, 2001. Print.

PARTS OF BOOKS

66. Introduction, foreword, preface, or afterword

> Benstock, Sheri. Introduction. *The House of Mirth*. By Edith Wharton. Boston: Bedford-St. Martin's, 2002. 3-24. Print.

67. Single chapter by the same author as the book

> Ardis, Ann. "Mapping the Middlebrow in Edwardian England." *Modernism and Cultural Conflict: 1880-1922*. Cambridge: Cambridge UP, 2002. 114-42. Print.

68. Chapter in an anthology or edited collection

> Sedaris, David. "Full House." *The Best American Nonrequired Reading 2004*. Ed. Dave Eggers. Boston: Houghton, 2004. 350-58. Print.

69. More than one selection from an anthology or edited collection

Multiple selections from a single anthology can be handled by creating a complete entry for the anthology and shortened cross-references for individual works in that anthology.

> Adichie, Chimamanda Ngozi. "Half of a Yellow Sun." Eggers 1-17.
> Eggers, Dave, ed. *The Best American Nonrequired Reading 2004*. Boston: Houghton, 2004. Print.
> Sedaris, David. "Full House." Eggers 350-58.

70. Article in a reference work

> "Utilitarianism." *The Columbia Encyclopedia*. 6th ed. 2001. Print.

THE BIBLE AND OTHER SACRED TEXTS

71. Sacred texts

> *The New Oxford Annotated Bible*. Ed. Bruce M. Metzger and Roland E. Murphy. New York: Oxford UP, 1991. Print.

Use a period to separate the chapter and verse in the in-text note: (John 3.16)

EDITIONS, TRANSLATIONS, AND ILLUSTRATED BOOKS

72. Book with an editor—focus on the editor

Lewis, Gifford, ed. *The Big House of Inver*. By Edith Somerville and
Martin Ross. Dublin: Farmar, 2000. Print.

73. Book with an editor—focus on the author

Somerville, Edith, and Martin Ross. *The Big House of Inver*. Ed.
Gifford Lewis. Dublin: Farmar, 2000. Print.

74. Book with a translator

Mallarmé, Stéphane. *Divagations*. Trans. Barbara Johnson.
Cambridge: Harvard UP, 2007. Print.

75. Second or subsequent edition of a book

Hawthorn, Jeremy, ed. *A Concise Glossary of Contemporary Literary
Theory*. 3rd ed. London: Arnold, 2001. Print.

76. Illustrated book or graphic narrative

After the title of the book, give the illustrator's name, preceded by the
abbreviation *Illus.* If the emphasis is on the illustrator's work, place the illustrator's name first, followed by the abbreviation *illus.*, and list the author
after the title, preceded by the word *By.*

Strunk, William, Jr., and E. B. White. *The Elements of Style
Illustrated*. Illus. Maira Kalman. New York: Penguin, 2005. Print.

MULTIVOLUME WORKS

77. One volume of a multivolume work

Samuel, Raphael. *Theatres of Memory*. Vol. 1. London: Verso, 1999. Print.

78. Book in a series

Give the series name after the publishing information.

Watson, James. *William Faulkner: Self-Presentation and Performance*.
Austin: U of Texas P, 2000. Print. Literary Modernism Ser.

26g Library Database Sources

Give the print citation followed by the name of the database in italics, the medium (Web), and the date you accessed the database. You do not need to list the URL of common library databases.

79. Scholarly journal article from a library database

> Klesges, Robert C., Mary L. Shelton, and Lisa M. Klesges. "Effects of Television on Metabolic Rate: Potential Implications for Childhood Obesity." *Pediatrics* 91 (1993): 281-86. *Academic Search Complete*. Web. 14 Nov. 2010.

80. Magazine article from a library database

> "The Trouble with Immortality: If We Could Live Forever, Would We Really Want To?" *Newsweek* 5 July 2010, US ed.: 78. *Academic Search Complete*. Web. 9 Dec. 2010.

81. Article with unknown author from a library database

> "Dicing with Data: Facebook, Google and Privacy."*Economist* 22 May 2010, US ed.: 16. *LexisNexis Academic*. Web. 15 Sept. 2010.

82. Abstract of a journal article from a library database

Cite the abstract including print information, adding the word *Abstract* after the publication information and before the name of the database.

> Li, Ji, and Neal H. Hooker. "Childhood Obesity and Schools: Evidence from the National Survey of Children's Health." *Journal of School Health* 80.2 (2010): 96. Abstract. *Academic Search Premier*. Web. 15 Oct. 2010.

83. Newspaper article from a library database

> Franciane, Valerie. "Quarter Is Ready to Rock." *Times-Picayune* [New Orleans] 3 Apr. 2007: 1. *LexisNexis Academic*. Web. 23 Jan. 2010.

84. Legal case from a library database

> Bilski v. Kappos. US 08-964. Supreme Court of the US 28 June 2010. *LexisNexis Academic*. Web. 28 June 2010.

85. Company report from a library database

> "Nike, Inc." 3 Aug. 2010. *Factiva*. Web. 3 Aug. 2010.

26h Web Sources and Other Online Sources

WEB SITES

86. Page on a Web site

The basic format for citing a Web page includes the author or editor, the title of the page, the title of the site (in italics), the sponsor or publisher of the site, the date of publication, the medium (*Web*), and the date you accessed the site.

> Boerner, Steve. "Leopold Mozart." *The Mozart Project: Biography*. Mozart Project, 21 Mar. 1998. Web. 30 Oct. 2010.

87. Entire Web site

> Boerner, Steve. *The Mozart Project*. Mozart Project, 20 July 2007. Web. 30 Oct. 2010.

PUBLICATIONS ON THE WEB

88. Publication by a known author

> Samadzadeh, Nozlee. "Farm Update: The Third Annual Jack Hitt Annual Last Day of Classes Pig Roast." *Yale Sustainable Food Project Student Blog*. Yale Sustainable Food Project, 3 May 2010. Web. 10 May 2010.

89. Publication by a group or organization

If a work has no author's or editor's name listed, begin the entry with the title.

> "State of the Birds." *Audubon. National Audubon Society*, 2010. Web. 19 Aug. 2010.

90. Publication on the Web with print publication data

Include the print publication information. Then give the name of the Web site or database in italics, the medium of publication (*Web*), and the date of access (day, month, and year).

> Kirsch, Irwin S., et al. *Adult Literacy in America*. Darby: Diane, 1993. *Google Scholar*. Web. 30 Oct. 2010.

91. PDFs and digital files

PDFs and other digital files can often be downloaded through links. Determine the kind of work you are citing (e.g., article, paper, photograph, song), include the appropriate information for the particular kind of work, and list the type of file.

> Glaser, Edward L., and Albert Saiz. "The Rise of the Skilled City."
> Discussion Paper No. 2025. Harvard Institute of Economic
> Research. Cambridge: Harvard U, 2003. PDF file.

PERIODICALS ON THE WEB

92. Article in a scholarly journal on the Web

Some scholarly journals are published on the Web only. List articles by author, title, name of journal in italics, volume and issue number, and year of publication. If the journal does not have page numbers, use *n. pag.* in place of page numbers. Then list the medium of publication (*Web*) and the date of access (day, month, and year).

> Fleckenstein, Kristie. "Who's Writing? Aristotelian Ethos and the
> Author Position in Digital Poetics." *Kairos* 11.3 (2007): n.
> pag. Web. 6 Apr. 2010.

93. Article in a newspaper on the Web

List the name of the newspaper in italics, followed by a period and the publisher's name. Follow the publisher's name with a comma. The first date is the date of publication; the second is the date of access.

> Brown, Patricia Leigh. "Australia in Sonoma." *New York Times*. New
> York Times, 5 July 2008. Web. 3 Aug. 2010.

94. Article in a popular magazine on the Web

> Brown, Patricia Leigh. "The Wild Horse Is Us." *Newsweek*.
> Newsweek, 1 July 2008. Web. 12 Dec. 2010.

95. Review on the Web

> Ebert, Roger. Rev. of *Gran Torino*, dir. Clint Eastwood.
> *rogerebert.com*. Chicago Sun-Times, 17 Dec. 2008. Web.
> 28 Jan. 2010.

BOOKS, ARCHIVES, AND SCHOLARLY PROJECTS ON THE WEB

96. Book on the Web

If the book was printed and then scanned, give the print publication information. Then give the name of the database or Web site in italics, the medium of publication (*Web*), and the date of access (day, month, and year).

> Prebish, Charles S., and Kenneth K. Tanaka. *The Faces of Buddhism in America*. Berkeley: U of California P, 2003. *eScholarship Editions*. Web. 2 May 2010.

97. Scholarly project or archive on the Web

Give the name of the editor if available, the name of the scholarly project or archive in italics, and the publisher or sponsor followed by a comma. Then give the date (if unavailable, use *n.d.*), the medium of publication (*Web*), and the date of access (day, month, and year).

> McGann, Jerome J., ed. *The Rossetti Archive*. U of Virginia, n.d. Web. 30 Mar. 2010.

98. Document within a scholarly project or archive

Give the print information, then the title of the scholarly project or archive in italics, the medium of publication (*Web*), and the date of access (day, month, and year).

> "New York Quiet." *Franklin Repository* 5 Aug. 1863, 1. *Valley of the Shadow*. Web. 23 Feb. 2010.

99. Film or recording in an archive

If you download a film or recording from an archive, treat the works-cited entry as a digital file (see sample entry 91).

> Dickson, William Kennedy-Laurie, prod. *Buffalo Dance*. 1894. Lib. of Cong., Washington. MPEG file.

GOVERNMENT PUBLICATIONS ON THE WEB

100. Government publication

Government publications are issued in many formats. If you cannot locate the author of the document, give the name of the government and the agency that published it.

> United States. Dept. of Health and Human Services. *Salmonellosis Outbreak in Certain Types of Tomatoes*. US Dept. of Health and Human Services, 5 July 2008. Web. 30 Nov. 2010.

UNEDITED ONLINE SOURCES

101. Wiki entry

Wiki content is written collaboratively, thus no author is listed. Because the content on a wiki changes frequently, wikis are not considered reliable scholarly sources.

> "Snowboard." *Wikipedia*. Wikimedia Foundation, 2010. Web.
> 30 Jan. 2010.

102. E-mail and text messaging

Give the name of the writer, the subject line, a description of the message, the date, and the medium of delivery (*E-mail, Text message*).

> Ballmer, Steve. "A New Era of Business Productivity and Innovation."
> Message to Microsoft Executive E-mail. 30 Nov. 2006. E-mail.

103. Posting to a discussion list

Give the name of the writer, the subject line, the name of the list in italics, the publisher, the date of the posting, the medium (*Web*), and the date of access.

> Dobrin, Sid. "Re: ecocomposition?" *Writing Program Administration*.
> Arizona State U, 19 Dec. 2008. Web. 5 Jan. 2009.

104. Course home page

> Sparks, Julie. "English Composition 1B." Course home page. San
> Jose State U, Fall 2008. Web. 17 Sept. 2008.

105. Personal home page

List *Home page* without quotation marks in place of the title. If no date is listed. use *n.d.*

> Graff, Harvey J. Home page. Dept. of English, Ohio State U, n.d.
> Web. 15 Nov. 2008.

106. Blog entry

If there is no sponsor or publisher for the blog, use *N.p.*

> Arrington, Michael. "Think Before You Voicemail." *TechCrunch*.
> N.p., 5 July 2008. Web. 10 Sept. 2010.

107. Blog

Cite a blog as you would a Web site, including the sponsor, if available.

> Silver, Nate. *FiveThirtyEight*. New York Times, 18 Oct. 2010. Web.
> 18 Oct. 2010.

26i Visual Sources

108. Cartoon or comic strip

Give the author's name, the title of the cartoon or comic strip in quotation marks, and the description *Cartoon* or *Comic strip*.

> Trudeau, G. B. "Doonesbury." Comic strip. *Washington Post* 21 Apr. 2008. C15. Print.

109. Advertisement

Begin with the name of the advertiser or product, then the word *Advertisement*.

> Nike. Advertisement. ABC. 8 Oct. 2010. Television.

110. Map, graph, or chart

Specify *Map, Graph,* or *Chart* after the title.

> *Greenland.* Map. Vancouver: International Travel Maps, 2004. Print.

111. Table reproduced in your text

This is how a table might appear in your text:

> In *The Republic*, Plato explains how the three parts of the individual soul should be repeated in the structure of the ideal city-state (see Table 1).
>
> Table 1
> Plato's Politics
>
> | Soul | Reason | Courage | Appetites |
> |------|--------|---------|-----------|
> | State | Elite guardians | Soldiers | Masses |
>
> Source: Richard Osborne, *Philosophy for Beginners* (New York: Writers and Readers, 1992; print; 15).

This is how a table appears in your list of works cited:

> *Plato's Politics.* Table. New York: Writers and Readers, 1992. 15. Print.

112. Painting, sculpture, or photograph

Give the artist's name if available, the title of the work in italics, its date of creation, the medium of composition, the name of the institution that houses the work and the city, or the name of the collection. In the text, mentioning the work and the artist is preferable to a parenthetical citation.

> Manet, Edouard. *Olympia*. 1863. Oil on canvas. Musée d'Orsay,
> Paris.

VISUAL SOURCES ON THE WEB

113. Video on the Web

Video on the Web often lacks a creator and a date. Begin the entry with a title if you cannot find a creator. Use *n.d.* if you cannot find a date.

> Wesch, Michael. *A Vision of Students Today*. *YouTube*. YouTube,
> 2007. Web. 28 May 2010.

114. Work of art on the Web

Include the artist, title of the work in italics, and the date. For works found on the Web, omit the medium but include the location or museum, then add the name of the Web site, the medium (*Web*), and the date of access.

> Mapplethorpe, Robert. *Self Portrait*. 1972. Palm Springs Art
> Museum. *Robert Mapplethorpe Foundation*. n.d. Web.
> 3 Nov. 2010.

115. Photograph on the Web

Include the photographer, title of the image, and the date. Include the location of the photograph, if available, then the name of the Web site, the medium (*Web*), and the date of access.

> Swansburg, John. *The Illinois Monument at the Vicksburg National
> Military Park*. 2010. *Slate.com*. Web. 18 Oct. 2010.

116. Map on the Web

> "Lansing, Michigan." Map. *Google Maps*. Google, 2008. Web.
> 19 Nov. 2010.

117. Cartoon or comic strip on the Web

> Tomorrow, Tom. "Modern World." Comic strip. *Huffington Post*.
> HuffingtonPost.com, 2 Jan. 2009. Web. 20 Jan. 2009.

26j Multimedia Sources

118. Work in more than one medium

Follow the format of the medium you primarily used and specify all the media you consulted.

> Shakespeare, William. *Hamlet*. Ed. Terri Bourus. New York:
> Longman, 2007. CD-ROM, print.

119. CD-ROM by a known author

When page numbers are not available, use the author's name in the text to avoid an awkward parenthetical citation.

> Hagen, Edward, and Phillip Walker. *Human Evolution: A Multimedia*
> *Guide to the Fossil Record*. New York: Norton, 2002. CD-ROM.

120. Multidisc CD-ROM

Follow the publication medium with either the total number of discs or the number of the specific disc you are using.

> Rey, H. A., and Margaret Rey. *The Complete Adventures of Curious*
> *George*. New York: Houghton, 2006. CD-ROM. 5 discs.

121. Musical composition

For a published musical score, follow the format for a book. If the publication is part of a series, list the series.

> Gershwin, George. *An American in Paris*. Secaucus: Warner Bros.,
> 1987. Print. Gershwin 50th anniversary ed.

122. Sound recording

List the composer, performer, or group first, depending on which you wish to emphasize. Place a comma between the publisher and the date. Indicate the medium after the date.

> McCoury, Del, perf. "1952 Vincent Black Lightning." By Richard
> Thompson. *Del and the Boys*. Ceili, 2001. CD.

123. Podcast

Provide all relevant information, including the name of the host, the name of the program, the number of the episode if available, the name and publisher of the podcast if available, and original broadcast information if the podcast is a rebroadcast.

> Sussingham, Robin. "All Things Autumn." No. 2. *HighLifeUtah*.
> N.p., 20 Nov. 2006. Web. 28 Feb. 2010.

124. Film

Begin with the title in italics. List the director, the distributor, the date, and the medium. Other data, such as the names of the screenwriters and performers, is optional.

> *Wanted.* Dir. Timur Bekmambetov. Perf. James McAvoy, Angelina
> Jolie, and Morgan Freeman. Universal, 2008. Film.

125. DVD

Follow the format for films.

> *No Country for Old Men.* Dir. Joel Coen and Ethan Coen. Perf.
> Tommy Lee Jones, Javier Bardem, and Josh Brolin. Paramount,
> 2007. DVD.

126. Television or radio program

Provide the title of the episode or segment, followed by the title of the program and series (if any). After the titles, list any performers, narrators, directors, or others who might be pertinent. Then give the name of the network, call numbers and city for any local station, the broadcast date, and the medium of reception (*television* or *radio*).

> "Kaisha."*The Sopranos.* Perf. James Gandolfini, Lorraine Bracco,
> and Edie Falco. HBO. 4 June 2006. Television.

127. Broadcast interview

> Cage, Nicolas. Interview by Terry Gross. *Fresh Air.* WHYY-FM,
> Philadelphia. 13 June 2002. Radio.

128. Musical, dramatic, dance, or artistic performance

> *Lipstick Traces.* By Griel Marcus. Adapted by Kirk Lynn. Dir. Shawn
> Sides. Perf. Lana Lesley and Jason Liebrecht. Off Center,
> Austin. 31 Aug. 2000. Performance.

129. Speech, debate, mediated discussion, or public talk

> Clinton, Hillary Rodham. "Remarks on Internet Freedom."
> Newseum. Washington. 21 Jan. 2010. Address.

TELEPHONE AND PERSONAL INTERVIEWS

130. Telephone interview

> Minnelli, Liza. Telephone interview. 5 Mar. 2008.

131. Personal interview

> Zuckerberg, Mark. Personal interview. 8 Jan. 2011.

26k Informational Notes

The MLA style is designed to avoid the need for either footnotes or endnotes. Documentation should be handled using in-text citations and a list of works cited. However, two kinds of notes sometimes appear in MLA style. Notes may be placed at the bottom of the page or at the end of the paper.

Content notes supply additional information that would interrupt the flow of the text, yet may be important to provide the context of a source.

Much speculation has blamed electronic media, especially television, for an alleged decline in literacy, following Newton N. Minow's famous 1961 description of television as a "vast wasteland."[1]

The note explains who Minow was and why the remark was newsworthy.

1. Minow, the newly appointed chairman of the Federal Communications Commission, told the assembled executives of the National Association of Broadcasters in May 1961 that "[w]hen television is bad, nothing is worse" (Adams). Minow's efforts to upgrade programming were met with cries of censorship from the television industry, and Minow resigned two years later.

You need to include any sources you use in notes in the list of works cited.

Work Cited

Adams, Val. "F.C.C. Head Bids TV Men, Reform 'Vast Wasteland.'" *New York Times* 10 May 1961, late ed.: 11. Print.

Bibliographic notes give either evaluative comments about sources or additional references.

"Fordism" is a summary term for the system of mass production consolidated by Henry Ford in the early decades of this century.[1]

The note gives the origin of the term "Fordism."

1. The term Fordism was first used by Italian political theorist Antonio Gramsci in his prison notebooks, written while he was jailed under Mussolini's fascist dictatorship.

Work Cited

Gramsci, Antonio. *Selections from the Prison Notebooks of Antonio Gramsci.* Ed. and trans. Quintin Hoare and Geoffrey Nowell Smith. New York: International, 1971. Print.

26l Two Sample Research Papers with MLA Documentation

Chapters 19 through 25 discuss how to plan and write a research paper. The two sample research papers that follow are annotated to show specific features of MLA style and to show how the works-cited page is organized.

FORMATTING A RESEARCH PAPER IN MLA STYLE

MLA offers these general guidelines for formatting a research paper.

- **Use white, 8½-by-11-inch paper.** Don't use colored or lined paper.
- **Double-space everything—the title, headings, body of the paper, quotations, and works-cited list.** Set the line spacing on your word processor for double spacing and leave it there.

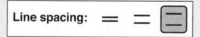

- **Put your last name and the page number at the top of every page, aligned with the right margin, ½ inch from the top of the page.** Your word processor has a header command that will automatically put a header with the page number on every page.
- **Specify 1-inch margins.** One-inch margins are the default setting for most word processors.
- **Do not justify (make even) the right margin.** Justifying the right margin throws off the spacing between words and makes your paper harder to read. Use the left-align setting instead.

- **Indent the first line of each paragraph ½ inch (5 spaces).** Set the paragraph indent command or the tab on the ruler of your word processor at ½ inch.
- **Use the same readable typeface throughout your paper.** Use a standard typeface such as Times New Roman, 12 point.
- **Use block format for quotations longer than four lines.** See page 382.

- **MLA does not require a title page.** Unless your instructor asks for a separate title page, put 1 inch from the top of the page your name, your instructor's name, the course, and the date on separate lines. Center your title on the next line. Do not underline your title or put it inside quotation marks.

MLA style does not require a title page. Check with your instructor to find out whether you need one.

1"

1/2"

Lopez 1

Include your last name and page number as page header, beginning with the first page, 1/2" from the top.

Gabriella Lopez

Professor Kimbro

English 1102

6 May 2010

1/2"

Establishing a Campus Garden

Center the title. Do not underline the title, put it inside quotation marks, or type it in all capital letters.

1"

When high school seniors begin to look at colleges and universities, they consider many factors: location, academics, and the quality of campus life, including food service. Now prospective students are also considering sustainability. Sustainability has become a buzzword in many fields, including architecture, energy, urban planning, and nutrition. And it seems to have a particular popularity on college campuses (Egan). According to a 2006 article in *USA Today*, students are increasingly interested in schools with "green" practices, which offer local, sustainable, and organic options in their food service (Horovitz). In 2009, the *Princeton Review* found that 66% of high school-age college applicants and parents surveyed "would find information about a college's dedication to the environment useful in their college selection process" (Klinck).

Do not include a page number for items without pagination, such as Web sites.

1"

1"

Lopez 2

Higher education is responding. Colleges and universities lead other institutions and industries with 3,850 LEED (Leadership in Energy and Environmental Design) certified buildings (Klinck), and show commitment to recycling and waste-reduction programs. Furthermore, schools are increasingly devoting at least a portion of food budgets to buying from local farms and producers (Pino). And this trend should only grow: the 2009–2014 Strategic Plan of the National Association of College and University Food Service (NACUFS) calls for the organization to become an integral player in sustainability policy-making and programming for higher education by advocating for and providing education on sustainable food service policies and practices. Some schools, most notably Yale University, have even established farms and gardens on or near campus that serve as living classrooms for environmental studies and provide food for students as well as the community (Samadzadeh).

"Going green" is not easy, nor is it inexpensive. For those reasons, many schools, including our own, are finding it difficult to move beyond campus-wide recycling programs to other initiatives such as increasing the amount of local organic foods in the dining halls. The fact that many colleges contract with outside food service vendors makes this goal even more difficult. An alternative approach, however, can provide both fresh, healthy food and hands-on experience in environmental stewardship. Establishing a small

Lopez 3

organic campus garden is a low-cost, high-yield way to support our school's mission, our students, the local community, and the global environment.

Lopez's thesis appears here, at the end of her third paragraph.

Our school in particular has a stated commitment to creating a campus in which students feel safe and sustained in an environment that is, according to the Web page, "contingent on the every-day learning process." One of the immediate benefits to establishing a campus organic garden is promoting a healthy relationship to food. According to a survey of 2,200 American college students, a significant number of women and a smaller group of men have "major concerns about eating and food with respect to both weight and health" (Rozin, Bauer, and Catanese 132). The negative feelings about food that result from these concerns can lead to eating disorders, primarily in young women (Rozin, Bauer, and Catanese 140). In short, Americans have become neurotic about eating. Michael Pollan attributes this anxiety to "nutritionism": the belief, fueled by food scientists and the food industry, that nutrients and the energy (or calorie) count is more important than actual food, and since nutrients exist at the molecular level, we believe we need to eat "scientifically," under the direction of the experts (8). This promotion of discrete nutrients over whole food has led to the industrialization of food production—more processed foods, more artificial grains, more chemicals to raise animals and vegetables in vast "monocultures," more sugars and fats, and less

Give page numbers for paraphrases as well as direct quotations.

Lopez 4

variety in our diet that has been reduced to a glut of

Use a signal
phrase to
include the
author's name
before a quota-
tion from a
source.

wheat, corn, and soy (Pollan 10). Thus, not only is our

industrialized diet making us physically sick; in fact, it

is also making us emotionally unhealthy. Pollan

observes that food concerns much more than nutrition:

"Food is all about pleasure, about community, about

family and spirituality, about our relationship to the

natural world, and about expressing our identity"(8).

Colleges are becoming increasingly aware of the

relationships among individual, social, and environmental

health, and that projects like campus farms and gardens

Lopez introduces
the block quota-
tion, naming the
source in the
text.

serve not only students, but also the local population,

and even the planet (Pino). The Dartmouth Organic Farm

Web site points to these connections:

> The very nature of an agricultural
>
> enterprise lies in the intersection of culture
>
> and the environment, to identify and respond

Quotations of
more than four
lines should be
indented 1" or
ten spaces. Do
not use quota-
tion marks.

> to the needs of a society while recognizing
>
> the limits and demands of the immediate,
>
> local ecosystem. A farm is one of the last
>
> institutionalized vestiges of our direct
>
> connection to the natural world that
>
> surrounds and supports us.

There is evidence to support these claims. A study in

the United Kingdom found that people with the highest

levels of "ecoliteracy" (accumulated ecological

knowledge) acquired that knowledge through direct

experience and talking with others rather than from

schooling and television (Pilgrim, Smith, and Pretty).

Lopez 5

One of the missions of our school, as stated on our Web site, is "the development of men and women dedicated to the service of others." Establishing a campus organic farm that could immediately serve as a model of sound nutritional and environmental practices, and perhaps one day provide food for local relief organizations, certainly supports this mission.

Another benefit to establishing a campus organic garden is that it would provide educational opportunities to students who are interested in the growing field of sustainability. As concern about the environment grows, colleges and universities are beginning to incorporate sustainability into their programs. Environmental studies classes and majors are growing and diversifying. Students can now get MBAs in sustainable-business practices and train to build and operate wind turbines, among other things (Berman). In the area of public policy, a major in this field is also becoming more valuable. The *New York Times Magazine* notes this cultural trend: "Time was, environmental-studies majors ran campus recycling programs. Now they run national campaigns" ("Learn").

Sources not identified with an author are referenced by a shortened title.

Because our school is much smaller and has fewer resources than Yale or most of the other schools with well-known and successful sustainable food projects including Dartmouth, Rutgers, Dickinson, Boston College, Colby, Columbia, Wisconsin-Madison, Iowa State, UCSD (University of California, San Diego), UCLA,

Lopez 6

and the University of Nebraska, establishing a farm or a
large garden seems improbable. I propose that we
establish a campus garden following the very simple
principles of organic "square foot" gardening. Square
foot gardening is raised bed gardening that takes place
in 6- to 12-inch-deep frames that have been segmented
into a grid (see Fig. 1). The size of each square in the
grid depends on what plants are planted there; certain
plants require larger and deeper grids (Bartholomew
15-16). The main benefit of square-foot gardening is
that one can grow the same amount of produce
in a 140-square-foot grid that is typically grown
in the average 700 square foot, single-row garden
(Bartholomew 42). Thus, a garden—or multiple gardens,
placed strategically according to the sunlight needs of the
plants—can be fitted into small spaces around campus.
We don't need to find one large, dedicated space. Another
benefit is that since the beds are filled with a high-
nutrient mix of compost, peat moss, and vermiculite, the
quality of soil the beds are built on top of does not
matter (Bartholomew 30-31). Thus, no money needs to
be spent on testing the soil, as Yale and other schools
had to do when they chose the land for their farms. In
fact, the beds can be placed on pavement, a patio, or
even a roof (Bartholomew 51). Dickinson College offers a
model for establishing a rooftop garden ("History"). The
main considerations are sunlight and water drainage. The
frames can even be built to be portable; again, requiring
no dedication of a large space for the garden.

Margin note: Position figures close to the text where they are mentioned. Include a figure number followed by a caption.

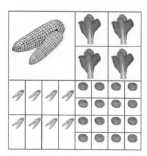

Fig. 1. The grid in a square foot gardening plot is divided according to the mature size of each plant.

Because Lopez illustrates the point with a figure she created, no source information is needed.

Another great benefit to the square-foot garden is that the smaller beds are easily adapted to grow seasonal crops, making it easier to recognize and explore the foods within our foodshed, or regional food chain, as the locavore movement encourages ("Why"). The smaller size of the beds also means that crops and harvests can be staggered. Regular row planting replicates the same kinds of yields as industrial farming, meaning that an entire row of the same item is harvested all at once, which can lead to waste. Staggering crops ensures that only what is needed is grown and harvested (Bartholomew 18), and staggering maximizes use of the space. For example, planting fast-growing plants that mature quickly between rows of slower growing plants means that early crops can be harvested and plants removed before the slower growers need the space (Damiano). Finally, the smaller beds and loose soil reduce the amount of labor needed. There is no need for tilling, and weeding

Lopez 8

is much easier. Also, the high-quality soil mixture
requires no fertilizer, and planting pest-resistant
plants, such as marigolds, alongside the produce and
herbs eliminates the need for pesticides. In short,
square-foot gardening is ideal for a small group of
beginning gardeners (Bartholomew 13). In addition, it
is easy to modify as need and skill level dictates, as
amateur gardeners show in their YouTube videos (see,
for example, mokahdeelyte).

Gardening is still a fickle enterprise, and beginners
(as most student volunteers will be) will have difficulty
assessing the right amount to plant and anticipate
harvesting. In *All New Square Foot Gardening: Grow
More in Less Space*, Mel Bartholomew says that it is
best to start small in the spring season, with a garden
about one-third of the ideal size. For phase two, the
summer season, more beds can be added as needed or
beds can be relocated or reconfigured. For phase three,
the fall season, beds can again be added, relocated, or
reconfigured as needed (Bartholomew 44).

Even though our campus organic garden will not
be built on the same scale as at the larger schools, much
can still be learned from them, especially regarding
how they gain support and how they maintain interest
in their project. The key to both Yale's Sustainable
Food Project and Dartmouth's Organic Farm is activist
students. Unlike student activists of the past, however,
today's students are working with school administrators
to make change possible. And school administrators

Lopez mentions a YouTube video and parenthetical reference leads to entry in Works Cited list.

Cite publications within the text by the name of the author (or authors).

are seeing the surge in green activism on campus as something that could appeal to prospective freshmen and alumni alike (Lewington). Establishing a core group of students responsible for shepherding the project is essential; these students can then start finding allies on campus. Other successful activist student groups are a good possibility, as are like-minded faculty, and food service administration and staff.

Once support is gained from students, faculty, staff, and administration, the logistics of building the gardens can get underway. Little space and few resources and tools are necessary for square foot gardening but supplies such as building materials, ingredients for the soil mixture, and seeds will still have to be gathered. Frames for the beds can be made from discarded building materials as long as wood is not painted or treated (Bartholomew 57). Compost for the soil mixture can be made from existing kitchen waste. Seeds, peat moss, vermiculite, and small tools are not expensive and can be bought with donated funds. Partnering with a community organic gardening organization or individuals in the community may not only yield donated or discounted supplies, but also training for student volunteers and a tie to the local community, which can help maintain support for the project in the long term.

Maintaining interest is important to keeping support, getting volunteer labor, and allowing for

Lopez 10

future growth. Holding events is one way to keep the excitement going. Yale's Sustainable Food Project offers cooking classes, uses a pizza oven installed on the farm to bake pizzas every Friday to thank volunteers, and even hosts an annual pig roast to celebrate the end of classes (Samadzadeh). Events of this scale are probably not an option for a smaller garden, but working with food service to create theme menus, such as Colby's "Garlic Fest" can attract attention (Jacobs). In addition, highlighting the farm or garden during student orientation and during parent weekends not only helps garner financial support, but also attracts new volunteers. Finally, inviting members of the community to visit and donating produce to local organizations will publicize the garden and gain further support.

> Lopez uses sources to show how proposal has worked for other campuses.

As sustainability becomes increasingly important in society, colleges and universities have increased responsibility not only to be models of sustainable practices, but also to train students for jobs in an economy and environment informed by sustainability. The Sustainable Endowments Institute urges, "Colleges and universities, as leaders of innovation in our society, have the potential to demonstrate sustainable principles in their campus operations and endowment policies. Their examples can provide a road map for others to follow" ("Frequently"). For our college to remain competitive with other schools, we need to increase our commitment to these important ideas. Establishing a campus garden should be the first step.

> The conclusion uses a quotation that appeals to readers' values and repeats call to action.

Lopez 11 Center "Works Cited" on a new page.

Works Cited

"About the Student Sustainable Farm at Rutgers."

Student Sustainable Farm at Rutgers. Rutgers U,

n.d. Web. 2 Apr. 2010.

Bartholomew, Mel. *All New Square Foot Gardening: Grow*

More in Less Space. Franklin: Cool Spring P, 2006.

Print.

Berman, Jillian. "Sustainability Could Secure a Good

Future: College Students Flock to 'Green' Degrees,

Careers." *USA Today* 3 Apr. 2009, final ed.: 7D.

LexisNexis Academic. Web. 6 Apr. 2010.

Damiano, Jessica. "Growing Vegetables in Small Spaces:

Train Them up Trellises and Plant Crops in

Succession." *Newsday* 2 May 2010: G107.

LexisNexis Academic. Web. 8 Apr. 2010.

"Dartmouth Organic Farm." *Dartmouth Outdoor Club*.

Dartmouth Coll., n.d. Web. 5 Apr. 2010.

Egan, Timothy. "The Greening of America's Campuses."

New York Times 8 Jan. 2008, final ed.: 4A.

LexisNexis Academic. Web. 5 Apr. 2010.

"Frequently Asked Questions." *The College Sustainability*

Report Card. Sustainable Endowments Institute,

n.d. Web. 2 Apr. 2010.

"The History of the Dickinson Garden." *Dickinson*

College Farm. Dickinson Coll., n.d. Web. 2 Apr.

2010.

Horovitz, Bruce. "More University Students Call for

Organic, 'Sustainable' Food." *USA Today*. USA

Today, 26 Sept. 2006. Web. 2 Apr. 2010.

Double-space all entries. Indent all but the first line in each entry 1/2 inch.

If the date of publication is not available, use the abbreviation *n.d.*

Alphabetize entries by the last names of the authors or by the first important word in the title if no author is listed.

Lopez 12

Jacobs, Ruth. "Organic Garden Gives Back." *Colby*
      Magazine 99.1 (2010): n. pag. Web. 2 Apr. 2010.

Klinck, Betty. "Find a Green College: Check! Princeton
      Review Helps Applicants Who Seek Sustainability."
      USA Today 20 Apr. 2010, final ed.: 7D. *LexisNexis*
      Academic. Web. 20 Apr. 2010.

"Learn," *New York Times Magazine* 20 Apr. 2008: 61.
      LexisNexis Academic. Web. 2 Apr. 2010.

Lewington, Jennifer. "Lean Green Campus Machines:
      Students Are at the Forefront of a Grassroots
      Environmental Revolution As They Coax—and
      Sometimes Embarrass—Administrators into
      Walking the Walk with Them." *Globe and Mail*
      [Toronto] 23 Oct. 2008: 14. *LexisNexis Academic*.
      Web. 8 Apr. 2010.

mokahdeelyte. *Square Foot Gardening Modified Tutorial*.
      YouTube. YouTube, 17 May 2008. Web. 3 Apr. 2010.

NACUFS. "Strategic Plan, 2009-2014." *NACUFS*. Natl.
      Assn. of Coll. and Univ. Food Services, n.d. Web.
      5 Apr. 2010.

Pilgrim, Sarah, David Smith, and Jules Pretty. "A Cross-
      Regional Assessment of the Factors Affecting
      Ecoliteracy: Implications for Policy and Practice."
      Ecological Applications 17.6 (2007): 1742-51.
      Print.

Pino, Carl. "Sustainability on the Menu: College
      Cafeterias Are Buying Local and Going Organic."
      E-Magazine.com. E-The Environmental Magazine,
      Mar./Apr. 2008. Web. 3 Apr. 2010.

When the city of publication is not included in the name of a newspaper, add the city name in brackets after the name of the newspaper.

List the title of videos or films in italics if the work is independent. Include in quotation marks if it is part of a larger work.

Journal article

Lopez 13

Pollan, Michael. *In Defense of Food: An Eater's*   Book

Manifesto. New York: Penguin, 2008. Print.

Rozin, Paul, Rebecca Bauer, and Dana Catanese. "Food

and Life, Pleasure and Worry, among American   Journal article

College Students: Gender Differences and Regional   from a database

Similarities." *Journal of Personality and Social*

Psychology 85.1 (2003): 132-41. *PsycARTICLES*.

Web. 6 Apr. 2010.

Samadzadeh, Nozlee. "Farm Update: The Third Annual

Jack Hitt Annual Last Day of Classes Pig Roast."   Blog entry

Yale Sustainable Food Project Student Blog. Yale

Sustainable Food Project, 3 May 2010. Web. 5 Apr.   Go through your
text and make

2010.   sure all the
sources you have

"Why Eat Locally?" *Locavore*. Locavores, n.d. Web.   used are in the
list of works

6 Apr. 2010.   cited.

 *To hear audio commentary on this piece of writing, visit this page
of the eText at* **www.mycomplab.com**.

MLA

MLA style does not require a title page. Check with your instructor to find out whether you need one.

Ashley Walker

Professor Avalos

English 102

30 April 2010

Include your last name and page number as page header, beginning with the first page, 1/2" from the top.

Preventing Obesity in Children

1/2"

Americans are among the fattest people on the planet and continue to expand. According to results from the 2005-2006 National Health and Nutrition Examination Survey (NHANES), of adults over the age of 20, 32.7% are overweight, 34.3% are obese, and 5.9% are extremely obese (United States). Excess weight is not just a matter of looks. Obesity magnifies the risk of heart disease, diabetes, high blood pressure, and other ailments—already overtaking tobacco as the leading cause of chronic illness (Brownell and Horgen 4). An especially disturbing aspect of this trend is that children are increasingly obese. The Center for Disease Control and Prevention reports that the rates of obesity in children have more than tripled since the 1980s (see Fig. 1). After years of steady increase, these numbers may have peaked, as the 2008 NHANES shows (Ogden, Carroll, and Flegel 2401). Nonetheless, the number of children with unhealthy BMIs remain far too high, as shown by data from the 2007 National Survey of Children's Health (NSCH). More than one third of children ages 10-17 are obese (Levi et al. 7; Ogden, Carroll, and Flegel 2402-03). Obese children have a 70% chance of becoming obese adults with a much

Center the title. Do not underline the title, put it inside quotation marks, or type it in all capital letters.

Specify 1" margins all around. Double-space everything.

Number figures and include a reference to each in the body of the text.

Cite a work with four or more authors using the first author's name and the phrase *et al.*

Walker 2

higher risk of serious illness than those of normal
weight (Brownell and Horgen 46). Furthermore, obese
children suffer many serious health problems today.
Pediatricians now routinely treat atherosclerosis and
type 2 diabetes, diseases that used to be frequent only
among older people (Tyre 38). Today's children are
among the first generation in American history who
may die at earlier ages than their parents.

*Walker identifies
the problem her
proposal will
address*

*Position figures
close to the text
where they are
mentioned.
Include a figure
number followed
by a caption
and source
information.*

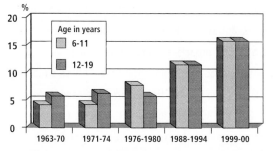

NOTES: Excludes pregnant women starting with 1971-74. Pregnancy status not available for
1963-65 and 1966-70. Data for 1963-65 are for children 6-11 years of age, data for 1966-70 are
for adolescents 12-17 years of age, not 12-19 years.
SOURCE CDC/NCHS, NHES and NHANES.

Fig 1. Prevalence of overweight among children and
adolescents ages 6-19 years, 1988-2006.
Source: United States, Dept. of Health and Human Services,
Centers for Disease Control and Prevention; *Prevalence of
Overweight among Children and Adolescents: United States,
1988-2006;* US Dept. of Health and Human Services. Web.
4 Apr. 2010.

Walker 3

For most people in the United States, obesity is a matter of individual choice and old-fashioned willpower (Lee and Oliver). The usual advice for overweight people is to eat less and exercise more, but how applicable is this advice for children unless they have strong guidance from adults? How can children make intelligent choices about eating in an environment where overeating is normal and where few adults know what's in the food they eat? The United States has been successful in addressing teenage health problems: drug use has dropped, teenage pregnancy has been reduced, and teen smoking has declined. We need to take a similar proactive response by taking concrete steps to reverse the trend toward more obese children.

Many have blamed the rise in obesity on a more sedentary life style, including the move to the suburbs, where people drive instead of walk, and increased viewing of television. One study of children watching television found a significant drop in the average metabolic rate during viewing (Klesges, Shelton, and Klesges). Another study reports that reducing children's television viewing also affects their eating behavior (Robinson and Killen). No doubt that children who exercise less tend to weigh more, but the couch potato argument does not explain why the enormous weight gains have occurred over the past 25 years. The move to the suburbs and the widespread viewing of television began in the 1950s. Furthermore, the couch potato argument neglects the extraordinary rise of

Walker's thesis appears here, at the end of her second paragraph. The preceding questions establish a context for her thesis.

Indent each paragraph five spaces (1/2" on the ruler in your word processor).

Cite publications within the text by the name of the author (or authors).

Walker 4

female participation in athletics. Today, 1 in 3 high
school girls play sports compared with 1 in 27 in 1971
(Parker-Pope). Yet girls, like boys, have gained weight.

 The simple answer to why Americans of all ages
have steadily gained weight over the past three
decades is that we're consuming more food high in
calories and high in fat than ever before—about 350
more per child per day and about 500 more per adult
per day than in the 1970s. Counteracting this increase
with exercise is also not realistic as a child would have
to walk 150 more minutes per day and adult would
have to walk 110 more minutes per day (Shute).

 Patterns of eating in America have changed over
the past three decades. With more people working
longer hours and fewer staying at home, annual
spending in adjusted dollars at restaurants increased
nearly by a factor of 10 between 1970 and 2003, from
$42.8 billion to $426.1 billion ("Industry"). The growth
was most rapid among fast-food chains, which by 1999
were opening a new restaurant every two hours
(Schlosser, "Bitter"). According to Eric Schlosser,

> in 1970, Americans spent about $6 billion on
> fast food; in 2001, they spent more than $110
> billion. Americans now spend more money on
> fast food than on higher education, personal
> computers, computer software, or new cars.
> They spend more money on fast food than on
> movies, books, magazines, newspapers, videos,
> and recorded music—combined. (*Fast* 3)

Walker identifies causes of the problem.

Do not include a page number for items without pagination, such as Web sites.

If more than one publication is by the same author, include an abbreviated title in the reference.

Quotations of more than four lines should be indented 1" or ten spaces. Do not use quotation marks.

Include the parenthetical reference at end of block quote after the period.

Walker 5

As the restaurant business became more competitive, fast-food chains realized that the cost of the food they served was small in comparison to the costs of buildings, labor, packaging, and advertising, so they began increasing the size of portions. Amanda Spake and Mary Brophy Marcus note: "When McDonald's opened, its original burger, fries, and 12-ounce Coke provided 590 calories. Today, a supersize Extra Value Meal with a Quarter Pounder With Cheese, supersize fries, and a supersize drink is 1,550 calories" (44). Large portions may represent good value for the dollar, but they are not good value for overall health.

Another significant change in the American diet beginning in the 1970s has been the introduction of high-fructose corn syrup into many foods. Listed at the top of food labels today are fructose, dextrose, maltrose, or a similar name—all corn syrup products— in foods like peanut butter, crackers, and ketchup, not associated with high levels of sugar. Food producers found that sweetness is an important component of taste, and they have been dumping in sweet corn syrup ever since. High-fructose corn syrup is cheap to produce and enjoys government subsidies, enabling soft drink manufacturers to increase size without increasing cost. The 8-ounce soft drink bottle of the 1950s has been replaced with the 12-ounce can, 20-ounce bottle, and 32-ounce fountain drink. Harvard researcher David Ludwig has found that food high in sugar makes people hungrier in a short time because it

Walker offers background for the problem.

Clear topic sentence alerts readers to the focus of the paragraph.

Walker 6

creates a spike in blood sugar followed by a crash, triggering overeating (Uhlenhuth). In other words, one cookie does lead to another.

Also contributing to the rise of obesity is the widespread availability of food. Stores that formerly did not sell food, such as drug stores, now have aisles of food. Gas stations have been replaced by mini-marts. Vending machines are found nearly everywhere, particularly in cash-strapped schools where students can be tempted with high-fat snacks and candy. And food companies have produced an endless line of good-tasting snack foods for consumption at home and at work. When we eat food high in sugar and feel hungry two hours later, usually food is close by.

These factors have contributed to a general rise in obesity, but they do not explain why the rate of obesity among children has skyrocketed. One prominent cause is the huge increase in marketing food to children, which has not only doubled since 1992 but also become increasingly sophisticated. An average child in the United States who watches television now sees a food ad on Saturday morning every 5 minutes and a total of over 10,000 a year, overwhelmingly ads for high-sugar and high-fat food (Brownell and Horgen 101-02). Restaurant and food companies spend 15 billion dollars in marketing to children each year with sophisticated advertising campaigns that include product tie-ins (Barboza C1). Even children of parents who limit or ban television watching are exposed to a

Give page numbers for paraphrases as well as direct quotations.

Walker 7

Cite a quote included in another source using the abbreviation *qtd. in* before the information about the indirect source.

massive amount of food advertising in movies and video games, on the Internet, and even in schools. Walter Willett, a Harvard professor of nutrition, observes, "The vast majority of what [food companies] sell is junk. . . . How often do you see fruits and vegetables marketed?" (qtd. in Barboza C1).

Obesity in children is a health crisis comparable to the illnesses caused by smoking. Defenders of the food industry argue that smoking is voluntary, but everyone has to eat. The crisis for children is more analogous to secondhand smoke, which has been proven to be harmful to children. To blame children for choosing to be fat is like blaming a baby for being born to parents who smoke. Most children lack the knowledge to make intelligent food choices, and they often have no access to healthy food. Parents of course can make a difference, but parents do

Walker describes solutions that have not successfully addressed the problem.

not control much of the environment where children eat, including school lunch programs and vending machines in schools. Furthermore, the majority of adults have inadequate skills for controlling their weight.

Some changes have begun to occur. Several states have passed laws banning junk food in vending machines in schools. McDonald's and other fast-food companies have begun to offer healthier alternatives to their fat-laden foods. Kraft Foods, the largest food company in the United States, has begun an antiobesity initiative by reducing portions of popular snacks and providing more nutritional information (Walker). Also, the Health Care Bill requires chain

Walker 8

restaurants to display nutrition information on menus, menu boards, and drive-throughs (Goldstein). But these are small steps in addressing the biggest health crisis of the twenty-first century.

The first major step in reducing obesity in children is to restrict marketing of junk food to children. When the American public realized how effective Joe Camel ads were in reaching children, their outrage led to a ban on many forms of cigarette advertising. The food industry has no such restrictions and uses popular cartoon characters and actors to pitch their products. According to advertising professor Vijay Netaji, children under age 8 cannot distinguish programs from advertising, particularly when the same characters are participating in both. Other countries including Belgium, Greece, Norway, and Sweden now limit advertising directed toward children (Brownell and Horgen 123). The United States should join these nations.

Walker presents steps to solve the problem.

The second major step is to develop a campaign to educate children and parents about healthy and unhealthy food. Children and their parents need to know more about the health risks of obesity and how to follow healthier eating habits. Parents play an important role in selecting what children eat, but children also need to be able to make good choices about eating on their own.

The third major step is to promote a healthy lifestyle through more exercise. Exercise, like eating, is not simply a matter of personal choice. Many schools

Walker 9

cannot afford to provide physical education programs and activities that encourage exercise, and many communities lack public space and facilities where people can exercise. More exercise for children needs to be made a priority in schools and communities.

Step one can be accomplished either by voluntary restriction of marketing to children or by legislation, and steps two and three have already received some attention. In February 2010, First Lady Michelle Obama launched the Let's Move initiative to combat childhood obesity by promoting more nutrition information, physical activity, access to healthier foods, and personal responsibility (Givhan). This initiative has faced controversy, however. Some, such as Margo Wootan of the consumer advocacy group Center for Science in the Public Interest, feel that Obama needs to use her power to eliminate junk food from schools and junk food advertising from children's television programming. Others say that childhood obesity should not be a priority in tough economic times when school budgets are already stretched thin (Travis). Others have proposed so-called "fat taxes" on fattening foods and beverages. These food tax proposals have been extremely controversial. The Center for Consumer Freedom, a group supported by the restaurant and food industry, has launched ads against "fat taxes" and legal actions against junk food, arguing that healthy food is a choice ("CCF"). The choice argument, however, is more difficult to make for children.

Cite a work without an author using a shortened form of the title

Walker 10

If food taxes are the best way to promote healthier eating and more exercise among children, would Americans support such a tax? A 2003 opinion poll sponsored by the Harvard Forums on Health found that Americans are overwhelmingly in favor of measures to fight obesity in children, including banning vending machines that sell unhealthy foods in schools and providing healthier school lunches (Robinson and Killen 266). Over three quarters of the people sampled in the poll support a government-sponsored advertising campaign for healthier eating and the creation of more public spaces for exercise. The poll indicates that Americans are willing to pay higher taxes for these programs, although the majority opposed specific taxes on junk food. Just as Americans eventually woke up to the risks of smoking among young people and took decisive action, they are gradually becoming aware of the threat of obesity to their children's future and, more important, starting to do something about it.

Concluding paragraph explains how Walker's solution is feasible

Walker 11

Works Cited

Barboza, David. "If You Pitch It, They Will Eat." *New
York Times* 3 Aug. 2003, late ed.: C11. *LexisNexis
Academic*. Web. 4 Apr. 2010.

Brownell, Kelly D., and Katherine Battle Horgen. *Food
Fight: The Inside Story of the Food Industry, America's
Obesity Crisis, and What We Can Do about It*. Chicago:
Contemporary, 2004. Print.

"CCF Ad Campaigns." *ConsumerFreedom.com*. Center for
Consumer Freedom, 2010. Web. 5 Apr. 2010.

Givhan, Robin. "First Lady Michelle Obama: 'Let's Move'
and Work on Childhood Obesity Problem."
Washington Post. Washington Post, 10 Feb. 2010.
Web. 3 Apr. 2010.

Goldstein, Katherine. "Calorie Count Disclosure and the
Health care Bill. Will This Lead to a Food
Revolution?" *Huffington Post*, 23 Mar. 2010.
Web. 4 Apr. 2010.

"Industry at a Glance." *Restaurant.org*. National
Restaurant Association, 2007. Web. 3 Apr. 2010.

Klesges, Robert C., Mary L. Shelton, and Lisa M. Klesges.
"Effects of Television on Metabolic Rate: Potential
Implications for Childhood Obesity." *Pediatrics* 91
(1993): 281-86. *Academic OneFile*. Web. 3 Apr. 2010.

Lee, Taeku, and J. Eric Oliver. "Public Opinion and the
Politics of America's Obesity Epidemic." Faculty
Research Working Paper Series, RWP02-017. John
F. Kennedy School of Government, Harvard U, May
2002. Web. 2 Apr. 2010.

Center "Works Cited" on a new page.

Double-space all entries. Indent all but the first line in each entry five spaces.

Alphabetize entries by the last names of the authors or by the first important word in the title if no author is listed.

Walker 12

Levi, Jeffrey F., et al. *F as in Fat: How Obesity Policies Are Failing Health in America, 2009.* Trust for America's Health, July 2009. Web. 4 Apr. 2010.

Netaji, Vijay. Telephone interview. 20 Mar. 2010.

Ogden, Cynthia L., M. D. Carroll, and K. M. Flegel. "High Body Mass Index for Age Among U.S. Children and Adolescents, 2003-2006" *JAMA* 299.20 (2008): 2401-05. Print.

Parker-Pope, Tara. "As Girls Become Women, Sports Pay Dividends." *Well.* New York Times, 15 Feb. 2010. Web. 3 Apr. 2010.

Robinson, Thomas N., and Joel D. Killen. "Obesity Prevention for Children and Adolescents." *Body Image, Eating Disorders, and Obesity in Youth: Assessment, Prevention, and Treatment.* Ed. J. Kevin Thompson and Linda Smolak. Washington: APA, 2001.261-92. Print.

Schlosser, Eric. "The Bitter Truth about Fast Food." *Guardian* 7 Apr. 2001, weekend sec. 13. Print.

---. *Fast Food Nation: The Dark Side of the All-American Meal.* New York: Perennial, 2002. Print.

Shute, Nancy. "Today's Kids Are Fat. Why? They Eat More." *U.S. News & World Report.* U.S. News & World Report, 11 May 2009. Web. 3 Apr. 2010.

Spake, Amanda, and Mary Brophy Marcus. "A Fat Nation." *U.S. News & World Report* 19 Aug. 2002: 40-47. *Academic Search Premier.* Web. 2 Apr. 2010.

List a work with four or more authors using the first author's name and the phrase *et al.*

Italicize the titles of books and periodicals.

If an author has more than one entry, list the entries in alphabetical order by title. Use three hyphens in place of the author's name for the second and subsequent entries.

Walker 13

Travis, Karen. "First Lady Michelle Obama Says 'Let's
Move' to Fight Childhood Obesity, Encourage
Healthy Eating." *ABC News.com*. ABC News,
9 Feb. 2010. Web. 2 Apr. 2010.

Tyre, Peg. "Fighting 'Big Fat.'" *Newsweek* 5 Aug. 2002:
38-40. Print.

Uhlenhuth, Karen. "Spoonful of Sugar Makes Appetites
Go Up." *Advertiser* 19 Jan. 2003: 39. *LexisNexis
Academic*. Web. 2 Apr. 2010.

United States. Dept. of Health and Human Services.
Centers for Disease Control and Prevention.
*Prevalence of Overweight, Obesity, and Extreme
Obesity among Adults: United States, Trends
1976-1980 through 2005-2006*. NCHS E-Stats,
December 2008. Web. 3 Apr. 2010.

Walker, Andrea K. "Chipping Away at Fat." *Baltimore
Sun* 26 Sept. 2003, final ed.: C1. *LexisNexis
Academic*. Web. 1 Apr. 2010.

Go through your text and make sure all the sources you have used are in the list of works cited

*To hear audio commentary on this piece of writing, visit this
page of the eText at* **www.mycomplab.com**.

FORMATTING THE WORKS CITED IN MLA STYLE

- **Begin the works-cited list on a new page.** Insert a page break with your word processor before you start the works-cited page.
- **Center "Works Cited" on the first line at the top of the page.**
- **Double-space all entries.**
- **Alphabetize each entry by the last name of the author or, if no author is listed, by the first content word in the title (ignore *a, an, the*).**
- **Indent all but the first line in each entry ¹/₂ inch.**
- **Italicize the titles of books and periodicals.**
- **If an author has more than one entry, list the entries in alphabetical order by title. Use three hyphens in place of the author's name for the second and subsequent entries.**

  Murphy, Dervla. *Cameroon with Egbert*. Woodstock, NY: Overlook, 1990.
  Print.

  ---. *Full Tilt: Ireland to India with a Bicycle*. London: Murray, 1965.
  Print.

- **Go through your paper to check that each source you have used is in the works-cited list.**

27 | APA Documentation

Social sciences disciplines—including government, linguistics, psychology, sociology, and education—frequently use the American Psychological Association (APA) documentation style. The APA style is similar to the MLA style in many ways. Both styles use parenthetical citations in the body of the text, with complete bibliographical citations in the list of references at the end. Both styles avoid using footnotes for references.

APA DOCUMENTATION MAP

Here are the steps in the process of documentation.

1 | Collect the right information

For every source you need to have

- the name of the author or authors,
- the full title, and
- complete publication information.

For instructions go to the illustrated examples in section 27b of the three major source types:

- **PERIODICAL SOURCES**
- **BOOKS AND NONPERIODICAL SOURCES**
- **ONLINE SOURCES**

For other kinds of sources such as visual and multimedia sources, see the Index of References on pp. 418–419.

2 | Cite sources in two places

Remember, this is a two-part process.

To create citations

(a) in **the body of your paper**, go to 27a.
(b) in a **list of references at the end of your paper**, go to 27b.

If you have questions that the examples in this chapter do not address, consult the *Publication Manual of the American Psychological Association*, sixth edition (2010).

3 | Find the right model citations

You'll find **illustrated examples of sources** in Section 27b.

Once you match your source to one of those examples, you can move on to more specific examples:

- **PERIODICAL SOURCES,** go to 27c.
- **BOOKS AND NONPERIODICAL SOURCES,** go to 27d.
- **ONLINE SOURCES,** go to 27e.

A complete list of examples is found in the Index of References on pp. 418–419.

4 | Format your paper

You will find a **sample research paper in APA style** and instructions on formatting the body of your paper and your References list in Section 27g.

A note about footnotes:
APA style does not use footnotes for documentation. Use in-text citations instead (see Section 27a).

27a In-text Citations in APA Style

APA style emphasizes the date of publication. When you cite an author's name in the body of your paper, always follow it with the date of publication. Notice too that APA style includes the abbreviation for page (p.) in front of the page number. A comma separates each element of the citation.

> Zukin (2004) observes that teens today begin to shop for themselves at age 13 or 14, "the same age when lower-class children, in the past, became apprentices or went to work in factories" (p. 50).

If the author's name is not mentioned in the sentence, the reference looks like this:

> One sociologist notes that teens today begin to shop for themselves at age 13 or 14, "the same age when lower-class children, in the past, became apprentices or went to work in factories" (Zukin, 2004, p. 50).

The corresponding entry in the references list would be

> Zukin, S. (2004). *Point of purchase: How shopping changed American culture.* New York, NY: Routledge.

Paraphrase, summary, or short quotation

In APA style a short quotation has fewer than 40 words.

> "The appeal of a shopping spree," one sociologist comments, "is not that you'll buy a lot of stuff; the appeal is that, among all the stuff you buy, you'll find what you truly desire" (Zukin, 2004, p. 112).

↑

The author's name is provided in the parenthetical reference.

In this example, the author's name is provided inside the parentheses at the end of the sentence. Put the author's name in a signal phrase in your sentence when you want to give an affiliation or title to indicate the authority of your source.

"The appeal of a shopping spree," noted sociologist Sharon Zukin ◄───
(2004) comments, "is not that you'll buy a lot of stuff; the appeal
is that, among all the stuff you buy, you'll find what you truly
desire" (p. 112).

Put the page number in
parentheses after the quotation.
Note that the period comes
after the parentheses.

When the author of the
quotation is clearly named in
the sentence, add the date in
parentheses after the author's
name.

Quotations 40 words or longer

Orlean (2001) has attempted to explain the popularity of the painter
Thomas Kinkade:
> People like to own things they think are valuable. . . . The high
> price of limited editions is part of their appeal; it implies that
> they are choice and exclusive, and that only a certain class of
> people will be able to afford them. (p. 128)

The sentence introducing the
quotation names the author.

Note that the period appears
before the parentheses in an indented "block" quote.

The date appears in parentheses immediately following the
author's name.

Index of in-text citations

Sample in-text citations

1. **Author named in your text**

The influential sociologist Daniel Bell (1973) noted a shift in the United States to the "postindustrial society" (p. 3).

2. **Author not named in your text**

In 1997, the Gallup poll reported that 55% of adults in the United States think secondhand smoke is "very harmful," compared to only 36% in 1994 (Saad, 1997, p. 4).

3. **Work by a single author**

(Bell, 1973, p. 3)

4. **Work by two authors**

List both authors' last names, joined with an ampersand.

(Suzuki & Irabu, 2002, p. 404)

When you cite the authors' names in a sentence, use *and* in place of the ampersand.

Suzuki and Irabu (2002) report . . .

5. **Work by three to five authors**

The authors' last names follow the order of the title page.

(Francisco, Vaughn, & Romano, 2006, p. 7)

Subsequent references can use the first name and *et al.*

(Francisco et al., 2006, p. 17)

6. **Work by six or more authors**

Use the first author's last name and *et al.* for all in-text references.

(Swallit et al., 2007, p. 49)

7. **Work by a group or organization**

Identify the group in the text and place the page number in parentheses.

The National Organization for Women (2001) observed that this "generational shift in attitudes towards marriage and childrearing" will have profound consequences (p. 325).

If you use the name of the group in an in-text citation, the first time you cite the source put its acronym (if there is one) in brackets.

(National Organization for Women [NOW], 2001)

Use the acronym in subsequent in-text citations.

(NOW, 2001)

8. Work by an unknown author

Use a shortened version of the title (or the full title if it is short) in place of the author's name. Capitalize all key words in the title. If it is an article title, place it inside quotation marks.

("Derailing the Peace Process," 2003, p. 44)

9. Two works by one author published in the same year

Assign the dates letters (*a*, *b*, etc.) according to their alphabetical arrangement in the references list.

The majority of books written about coauthorship focus on partners of the same sex (Laird, 2007a, p. 351).

10. Parts of an electronic source

If an online or other electronic source does not provide page numbers, use the paragraph number preceded by the abbreviation *para.*

(Robinson, 2007, para. 7)

11. Two or more sources within the same sentence

Place each citation directly after the statement it supports.

Some surveys report an increase in homelessness rates (Alford, 2004) while others chart a slight decrease (Rice, 2006a) . . .

If you need to cite two or more works within the same parentheses, list them in the order in which they appear in the references list.

(Alford, 2004; Rice, 2006a)

12. Work cited in another source

Saunders and Kellman's study (as cited in Rice, 2006a)

27b Illustrated Samples and Index of References in APA Style

Periodical Sources

Title of article ——▶

Practicing Engineers Talk about the Importance of Talk: A Report on the Role of Oral Communication in the Workplace

Authors' names ——▶ Ann L. Darling and Deanna P. Dannels

In the last decade engineering education and industry have requested assistance from communication educators. Responding to increased attention on the changing expectations for practicing engineers and an attendant need for better communication skills, these teams of engineering and communication educators have been working to incorporate speaking and writing in engineering education. Despite a great deal of anecdotal evidence that communication is important to working engineers, relatively little data based information is available to help us understand better the specifics of how and why communication is important for these particular professionals. This paper reports the results of practicing engineers' descriptions of the importance of oral communication. These data suggest that engineering practice takes place in an intensely oral culture and while formal presentations are important to practicing engineers, daily work is characterized more by interpersonal and small group experiences. Communication skills such as translation, clarity, negotiation, and listening are vital. **Keywords:** communication in the professions, workplace teams, engineering education, oral presentations

Abstract ——▶ Increasingly, oral communication is recognized as an essential element of the curriculum in technical disciplines (Beaufait, 1991; Bjorklund & Colbeck, 2001; Denton, 1998; Yu & Liaw, 1998). Disciplines such as biology, chemistry, engineering, and mathematics, with a long curricular tradition focused on technical knowledge, have begun to explore the role of oral performance as both a learning tool (e.g., use of cooperative learning groups) and outcome (i.e., students in these disciplines are expected to be proficient both technically and communicatively).

Engineering is one such discipline experiencing a shift toward incorporating oral communication instruction within a highly technical curriculum (Beaufait, 1991). The 1995 report from the National Board of Engineering Education includes recommendations for a redesign of the engineering curriculum toward a more professional focus with specific attention on instruction in communication. Additionally, the Accreditation Board for Engineering and Technology (ABET) has developed new standards for accreditation to evaluate departments and colleges of engineering around the country. Specifically, ABET assessment procedures are driven by 11 student outcome measures, one of which states that students should

Ann L. Darling (PhD, University of Washington) is Associate Professor and Chair of the Department of Communication at the University of Utah. *Deanna P. Dannels* (PhD, University of Utah) is Assistant Professor of Communication and Assistant Director of the Campus Writing and Speaking Program at North Carolina State University. The authors wish to thank the gracious and abundant contributions of the College of Engineering at the University of Utah, especially on the part of Professor Robert Roemer.

Communication Education, Vol. 52, No. 1, January 2003, pp. 1–16
Copyright 2003, National Communication Association

Publication information

Darling, A. L., & Dannels, D. P. (2003). Practicing engineers talk about the importance of talk: A report on the role of oral communication in the workplace. *Communication Education*, *52*, 1–16.

Elements of the citation

Author's Name

The author's last name comes first, followed by the author's initials.

Join two authors' names with a comma and an ampersand.

Date of Publication

Give the year the work was published in parentheses.

Newspapers and popular magazines are referenced by the day, month, and year of publication.

Title of Article

- Do not use quotation marks. If there is a book title in the article title, italicize it.

- Titles of articles in APA style follow standard sentence capitalization.

Publication Information

Name of journal

- Italicize the journal name.

- Put a comma after the journal name.

Volume, issue, and page numbers

- Italicize the volume number.

- If each issue of the journal begins on page 1, give the issue number in parentheses, followed by a comma.

- If the article has been assigned a DOI (Digital Object Identifier), list it after the page numbers but without a period at the end.

Find the right example as your model (you may need to refer to more than one model)

What type of article do you have?

A scholarly journal article or abstract?

- For an article in a journal with continuous pagination, go to page 420, #20.
- For an article in a journal paginated by issue, go to page 420, #21.
- For a weekly, biweekly, or monthly publication, go to page 420, #22–#23.
- For an abstract, go to page 421, #24–#25.

A newspaper article, review, or letter to the editor

- For a newspaper article, go to page 421, #26.
- For a review, go to page 421, #27.
- For a letter to the editor, go to page 421, #28.

A government document?
Go to page 425, #53–#54.

How many authors are listed?

- One, two, or more authors: go to page 419, #13–#15.
- Unknown author: go to page 420, #17.

Books and Nonperiodical Sources

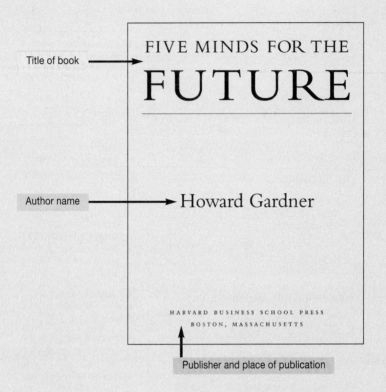

Title of book →

FIVE MINDS FOR THE
FUTURE

Author name → Howard Gardner

HARVARD BUSINESS SCHOOL PRESS
BOSTON, MASSACHUSETTS

Publisher and place of publication

Gardner, H. (2007). *Five minds for the future.* Boston, MA: Harvard
Business School Press.

Elements of the citation

Author's or Editor's Name

The author's last name comes first, followed by a comma and the author's initials.

If an editor, put the abbreviation *Ed.* in parentheses after the name.
Kavanagh, P. (Ed.).

Year of Publication

- Give the year the work was copyrighted in parentheses.

- If no year of publication is given, write *n.d.* ("no date") in parentheses.

Book Title

- Italicize the title.

- Titles of books in APA style follow standard sentence capitalization. Capitalize only the first word, proper nouns, and the first word after a colon.

Publication Information

Place of publication

- For all books, list the city with a two-letter state abbreviation (or full country name) after the city name.

- If more than one city is given on the title page, list only the first.

Publisher's name

Do not shorten or abbreviate words like *University* or *Press*. Omit words such as *Co.*, *Inc.*, and *Publishers*.

Find the right example as your model (you may need to refer to more than one model)

How many authors are listed?

- One, two, or more authors: go to pages 422, #30–33.
- Unknown author: go to page 423, #38.
- Group or organization as the author: go to page 423, #39.

Do you have only a part of a book?

- For a chapter written by the same author as the book, go to page 424, #43.
- For a chapter in an edited collection, go to page 424, #44.
- For an article in a reference work, go to page 424, #46.

Do you have a printed document other than a book or article?

- For a technical report, go to page 424, #48.
- For published conference proceedings, go to page 425, #49.
- For a dissertation or thesis, go to page 425, #52.
- For a government document, go to page 425, #53.

Online Sources

Journal Title

Title of article

Author

Date

Volume, page, and DOI

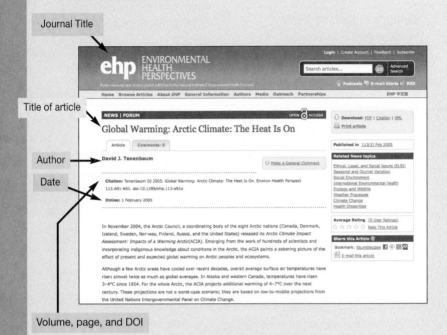

Tennenbaum, D. J. (2005). Global warming: Arctic climate: The heat
is on. *Environmental Health Perspectives, 113,* A91.
doi:10.1289/ehp.113–a91a

TITLES AND URLS IN APA-STYLE REFERENCES

If you are citing a page or an article that has a title, treat the title like an
article in a periodical.

Heiney, A. (2004). A gathering of space heroes. Retrieved from
the National Aeronautics and Space Administration Web
site: http://www.nasa.gov/missions/

Otherwise, treat the name of the Web site itself as you would a book. No
retrieval date is necessary if the content is not likely to be changed or updated. If no DOI is assigned, provide the home or entry page for the
journal or report publisher.

Elements of the citation

Author's Name or Organization

- Authorship is sometimes hard to discern for online sources. if you do have an author or creator to cite, follow the rules for periodicals and books.

- If the only authority you find is a group or organization, list its name as the author.

Dates

Give the date the site was produced or last revised (sometimes the copyright date) after the author.

Title of Page or Article

- Web sites are often made up of many separate pages or articles. Each page or article on a Web site may or may not have a title.

URL

- Copy the address exactly as it appears in your browser window. You can even copy and paste the address into your text for greater accuracy.

- Break a URL at the end of a line *before* a mark of punctuation. Do not insert a hyphen.

- If the article has a DOI (Digital Object Identifier), give the DOI after the title. Do not list the URL.

Find the right example as your model (you may need to refer to more than one model)

What kind of publication do you have?

- For a publication in a database, go to page 426, #57
- For an article with a DOI assigned, go to page 427, #66
- For an article with no DOI assigned, go to page 428, #67
- For an article in a newspaper or magazine, go to page 428, #68–69
- For a government publication, go to page 427, #65

Who is the author?

- For a known author, go to page 426, #60
- For a group or organization as the author, go to page 427, #61

Do you have a source that is posted by an individual?

- For a blog, go to page 428, #70
- For a post to a discussion list, go to page 428, #71
- For e-mail or text messaging, go to page 428, #73

Index of References Entries

27c Periodical Sources in the APA-style References List

JOURNAL AND MAGAZINE ARTICLES

13. Article by one author

> Kellogg, R. T. (2001). Competition for working memory among writing processes. *American Journal of Psychology, 114,* 175–192.

14. Article by two authors

> McClelland, D., & Eismann, K. (1998).

15. Article by three or more authors

List last names and initials for up to seven authors, with an ampersand between the last two names. For works with eight or more authors, list the first six names, then an ellipsis, then the last author's name.

> Andis, S., Franks, D., Gee, G., Ng, K., Orr, V., Ray, B., . . . Tate, L.

16. Authors listed with the word *with*

> Bettinger, M. (with Winthorp, E.).

17. Article by an unknown author

The green gene revolution [Editorial]. (2004, February). *Scientific American*, *291*, 8.

18. Article by a group or organization

Smithsonian Institution. (2003). The player. *Diamonds are forever: Artists and writers on baseball*. San Francisco, CA: Chronicle Books.

19. Two or more works by the same author in the same year

Arrange in alphabetical order according to the titles of the articles. Add lowercase letters to the year of publication.

Butler, D. (2010a). Food: The growing problem. *Nature, 466*, 546–547.

Butler, D. (2010b). What will it take to feed the world. *Nature, 464*, 969.

20. Article in a journal with continuous pagination

Include only the volume number and the year, not the issue number.

Engen, R., & Steen, S. (2000). The power to punish: Discretion and sentencing reform in the war on drugs. *American Journal of Sociology, 105*, 1357–1395.

21. Article in a journal paginated by issue

If each issue of the journal begins on page 1, give the issue number in parentheses (not italicized) after the volume number.

Bunyan, T. (2010). Just over the horizon—the surveillance society and the state in the EU. *Race and Class, 51*(3), 1–12.

MONTHLY, WEEKLY, AND BIWEEKLY PERIODICALS

APA DOES NOT ABBREVIATE ANY MONTH.

22. Weekly or biweekly periodicals

Hurtley, Stella. (2004, July 16). Limits from leaf litter. *Science, 305*, 311–313.

23. Monthly publications

Barth, A. (2010, March). Brain science gets squishy. *Discover*, 11–12.

ABSTRACTS

24. Abstract from an original source

de Watteville, C. (1904). On flame spectra [Abstract]. *Proceedings of the Royal Society of London, 74*, 84.

25. Abstract from a printed secondary source

Van Schaik, P. (1999). Involving users in the specification of functionality using scenarios and model-based evaluation. *Behaviour and Information Technology, 18*, 455–466. Abstract obtained from *Communication Abstracts*, 2000, *24*, 416.

NEWSPAPERS

26. Newspaper article

Olsen, E. (2010, June 22). A campaign for M&Ms with a salty center? Sweet. *The New York Times*, p. B6.

If an article has no author, list and alphabetize by the first significant word in the title of the article.

Incorrect cancer tests can be costly. (2004, December 16). *USA Today*, p. 8D.

REVIEWS, INTERVIEWS, AND LETTERS TO THE EDITOR

27. Review

Henig, R. N. (2010, June 27). The psychology of bliss [Review of the book *How Pleasure Works* by Paul Bloom]. *The New York Times*, p. BR6.

28. Letter to the editor or editorial

Wilkenson, S. E. (2001, December 21). When teaching doesn't count [Letter to the editor]. *The Chronicle of Higher Education*, p. B21.

29. Published interview

Bush, L. (2001, April). [Interview with P. Burka]. *Texas Monthly*, pp. 80–85, 122–124.

27d Books and Nonperiodical Sources in the APA-style References List

BOOKS

30. Book by one author

The author's last name comes first, followed by a comma and the first initial of the author's first name and middle initial, if any.

> Ball, E. (2000). *Slaves in the family*. New York, NY: Ballantine Books.

If an editor, put the abbreviation *Ed.* in parentheses after the name.

> Rasgon, N. L. (Ed.). (2006). *The effects of estrogen on brain function*. Baltimore, MD: Johns Hopkins University Press.

31. Two or more books by the same author

Arrange according to the date, with the earliest publication first, or alphabetically according to the names of additional authors.

> Jules, R. (2003). *Internal memos and other classified documents*. London, England: Hutchinson.

> Jules, R. (2004). *Derelict cabinet*. London, England: Corgi-Transworld.

32. Book by two authors

> Hardt, M., & Negri, A. (2000). *Empire*. Cambridge, MA: Harvard University Press.

33. Book by three or more authors

List last names and initials for up to seven authors, with an ampersand between the last two names. For works with eight or more authors, list the first six names, then an ellipsis, then the last author's name.

> Anders, K., Child, H., Davis, K., Logan, O., Orr, J., Ray, B., . . . Wood, G.

34. Book with an editor

> Miller, N. K. & Tougaw, J. (Eds.). (2002). *Extremities: Trauma, testimony, and community*. Champaign, IL: University of Illinois Press.

35. **Book with a title within a title**

> Grilli, G. (2007). *Myth, symbol, and meaning in* Mary Poppins: *The governess as provocateur.* New York: Routledge.

36. **Republished book**

> Brand, M. (2010). *The outward room.* New York, NY: New York Review Books. (Original work published 1937)

37. **Authors listed with the word *with***

> Bettinger, M. (with Winthorp, E.).

38. **Book by an unknown author**

> *Survey of developing nations.* (2003). New York, NY: Justice for All Press.

39. **Book by a group or organization**

> Centers for Disease Control and Prevention. (2003). *Men and heart disease: An atlas of racial and ethnic disparities in mortality.* Atlanta, GA: Author.

40. **Translated book**

> Freud, S. (2010). *Three contributions to the theory of sex* (A. A. Brill, Trans.). Las Vegas, NV: IAP Publishing. (Original work published 1909)

41. **Revised or later edition of a book**

> Weintraub, A. (2004). *Yoga for depression: A compassionate guide to relieve suffering through Yoga* (2nd ed.). New York, NY: Broadway Books.

42. **Multivolume book**

> Schwarzer, M., & Frensch, P. A. (2010). *Personality, human development and culture: International perspectives on psychological science* (Vol. 2). London, UK: Psychology Press.

43. Chapter written by the same author as the book

Add the word *In* after the chapter title and before the book title. Include inclusive page numbers for the chapter inside parentheses.

> Savage, T. (2004). Challenging mirror modeling in group therapy. In *Collaborative practice in psychology and therapy* (pp. 130–157). New York, NY: Haworth Clinical Practice Press.

44. Chapter in an edited collection

> Boyaton, D. (2010). Behaviorism and its effect upon learning in schools. In G. Goodman (Ed.), *The educational psychology reader: The art and science of how people learn* (pp. 49–66). New York, NY: Peter Lang.

45. Chapter in a volume in a series

> Jackson, E. (1998). Politics and gender. In F. Garrity (Series Ed.) & M. Halls (Vol. Ed.), *Political library: Vol. 4. Race, gender, and class* (2nd ed., pp. 101–151). New York, NY: Muse.

46. Article in a reference work

> Viscosity. (2001). In *The Columbia encyclopedia* (6th ed.). New York, NY: Columbia University Press.

47. Selection reprinted from another source

> Thompson, H. S. (1997). The scum also rises. In K. Kerrane & B. Yagoda (Eds.), *The art of fact* (pp. 302–315). New York, NY: Touchstone. (Reprinted from *The great shark hunt*, pp. 299–399, by H. S. Thompson, 1979, New York, NY: Simon & Schuster)

RESEARCH REPORTS, CONFERENCE PROCEEDINGS, AND DISSERTATIONS

48. Technical and research reports

> Austin, A., & Baldwin, R. (1991). *Faculty collaboration: Enhancing the quality of scholarship and teaching* (ASCHE-ERIC Higher Education Report 7). Washington, DC: George Washington University.

49. Published conference proceedings

Abarkan, A. (1999). Educative physical planning: Housing and the emergence of suburbia in Sweden. In T. Mann (Ed.), *Power of imagination. Proceedings of the 30th annual conference of the Environmental Design Research Association* (pp. 24–32). Edmond, OK: Environmental Design Research Association.

50. Unpublished paper presented at a symposium or meeting

Kelly, M. (2004, November). *Communication in virtual terms.* Paper presented at the annual meeting of the National Communication Association, Chicago, IL.

51. Poster session

Wilson, W. (2005, September). *Voting patterns among college students, 1992–2004.* Poster session presented at the annual meeting of the American Political Science Association, Washington, DC.

52. Dissertation or thesis

Tzilos, G. K. (2010). *A brief computer-based intervention for alcohol use during pregnancy* (Doctoral dissertation). Available from ProQuest Dissertations and Theses database. (UMI No. 3373111)

GOVERNMENT AND LEGAL DOCUMENTS

53. Government document

When the author and publisher are identical, use the word *Author* as the name of the publisher.

U.S. Environmental Protection Agency. (2002). *Respiratory health effects of passive smoking: Lung cancer and other disorders* (EPA Publication No. 600/6–90/006 F). Washington, DC: Author.

In-text

(U.S. Environmental Protection Agency [EPA], 2002)

54. *Congressional Record* (Senate resolution)

S. Res. 103, 107th Cong., 147 Cong. Rec. 5844 (2001) (enacted).

In-text

(S. Res. 103, 2001)

55. Religious or classical texts

Reference entries are not required for major classical works or the Bible, but in the first in-text citation, identify the edition used.

> John 3.16 (Modern Phrased Version)

56. Bulletins or pamphlets

> University Health Center. (2001). *The common cold* [Brochure].
> Austin, TX: Author.

Online Sources in the APA-style References List

57. Document from a database

APA no longer requires listing the names of well-known databases. Include the name of the database only for hard-to-find books and other items.

> Holloway, J. D. (2004). Protecting practitioners' autonomy.
> *Monitor on Psychology, 35*(1), 30.

58. Electronic copy of an abstract retrieved from a database

> Putsis, W. P., & Bayus, B. L. (2001). An empirical analysis of firms'
> product line decisions. *Journal of Marketing Research, 37*(8),
> 110–118. Abstract retrieved from PsychINFO database.

59. Online encyclopedia

> Swing. (2002). In *Britannica Online*. Retrieved April 29, 2010,
> from http://www.britannica.com/

60. Online publication by a known author

> Carr, A. (2003, May 22). *AAUW applauds Senate support of title IX
> resolution*. Retrieved from http://www.aauw.org/about
> /newsroom/press_releases/030522.cfm

61. Online publication by a group or organization

Girls Incorporated. (2003). *Girls' bill of rights*. Retrieved from
http://www.girlsinc.org/gc/page.php?id=9

62. Informally published or self-archived work

Bjork, O. (2004, May 5). *MOO bots*. Retrieved from http://www
.cwrl.utexas.edu/professional/whitepapers/2004/040512-1.pdf

63. Online publication with no known author or group affiliation

Begin the reference with the title of the document.

Halloween costumes from my warped mind. (n.d.). Retrieved from
http://home.att.net/~jgola/hallow01.htm

64. Online publication with no copyright or revision date

If no copyright or revision date is given, use *(n.d.)*, as shown in entry 63.

65. Online government publication

U.S. Public Health Service. Office of the Surgeon General. (2001,
March 11). *Women and smoking*. Retrieved from http://www
.surgeongeneral.gov/library/womenandtobacco/

In-text

(U.S. Public Health Service [USPHS], 2001)

ONLINE PERIODICALS

Because URLs frequently change, many scholarly publishers have begun
to use a Digital Object Identifier (DOI), a unique alphanumeric string that
is permanent. If a DOI is available, use the DOI instead of the URL.

66. Article with DOI assigned

You may need to click on a button such as "Article" or "PubMed" to
find the DOI. There is no need to list the database, the retrieval date, or
the URL if the DOI is listed.

Erdfelder, E. (2008). Experimental psychology: Good news.
Experimental Psychology, 55(1), 1–2. doi:0.1027
/1618-3169.55.1.1

67. Article with no DOI assigned

> Brown, B. (2004). The order of service: the practical management of
> customer interaction. *Sociological Research Online, 9*(4).
> Retrieved from http://www.socresonline.org.uk/9/4/brown.html

68. Article in an online newspaper

> Erard, M. (2001, November 16). A colossal wreck. *Austin Chronicle.*
> Retrieved from http://www.austinchronicle.com/

69. Article in an online magazine

> Resinkoff, N. (2010, June 22). Media ignores Gulf tragedy:
> Focuses on campaign narrative. *Salon*. Retrieved from
> http://www.salon.com/

UNEDITED ONLINE SOURCES

70. Blog entry

> Spinuzzi, C. (2010, January 7). In the pipeline [Web log post].
> Retrieved from http://spinuzzi.blogspot.com/search?updated
> -max=2010-01-25T12%3A35%3A00-06%3A00

71. Online posting

> Tjelmeland, A. (2010, January 26). Zacate Creek [Electronic
> mailing list message]. Retrieved from http://server1
> .birdingonthe.net/mailinglists/TEXS.html#1264558433

72. Wiki entry

> Mount Everest [Wikipedia entry]. (n.d.). Retrieved November 12,
> 2010, from http://en.wikipedia.org/wiki/Mt._Everest

73. E-mail

E-mail sent from one individual to another should be cited as a personal communication. Personal communication is cited in text but not included in the reference list.

> (D. Jenkins, personal communication, July 28, 2010)

27f Visual and Multimedia Sources in the APA-style References List

MULTIMEDIA

74. Television program

Ball, A. (Writer), & Winant, S. (Director). (2008). The first taste [Television series episode]. In A. Ball (Producer), *True Blood*. New York, NY: HBO.

75. Film, Video, or DVD

Stroller, N. (Writer and Director). (2010). *Get him to the greek* [Motion picture]. United States: Universal Studios.

76. Musical recording

Waits, T. (1980). Ruby's arms. On *Heartattack and vine* [CD]. New York, NY: Elektra Entertainment.

77. Graphic, audio, or video files

Aretha Franklin: A life of soul. (2004, January 24). *NPR Online*. Retrieved from http://www.npr.org/features /feature.php?wfId=1472614

78. Software or computer program

Second Life [Computer software]. (2010). San Francisco, CA: Linden Research.

VISUAL SOURCES

79. Photograph or work of art

American Heart Association. (2009). Hands-only CPR graphic [Photograph]. Retrieved from http://handsonlycpr.org/assets /files/Hands-only%20me.pdf

80. Map, chart, or graph

Information Architects. (2010). Web Trend Map 4 [Map]. Retrieved from http://www.informationarchitects.jp/en/wtm4/

27g Sample Research Paper with APA Documentation

Major kinds of papers written in APA style include the following.

Reports of research

Reports of experimental research follow a specific organization in APA style:

- **The abstract** gives a brief summary of the report.
- **The introduction** identifies the problem, reviews previous research, and states the hypothesis that was tested. Because the introduction is identified by its initial position in the report, it does not have to be labeled "introduction."
- **The method section** describes how the experiment was conducted and how the participants were selected.
- **The results section** reports the findings of the study. This section often includes tables and figures that provide statistical results and tests of statistical significance. Tests of statistical significance are critical for experimental research because they give the probability that the results could have occurred by chance.
- **The discussion section** interprets the findings and often refers to previous research.

Case studies

Case studies report material about an individual or a group that illustrates some problem or issue of interest to the field. See pages 148–149.

Reviews of literature

Reviews of literature summarize what has been published on a particular subject and often evaluates that material to suggest directions for future research.

Thesis-driven arguments

Thesis-driven arguments are similar to reviews of research, but they take a particular position on a theoretical or a real-life issue. The APA paper that follows by John M. Jones is a thesis-driven proposal argument that advocates a particular course of action.

FORMATTING A RESEARCH PAPER IN APA STYLE

APA offers these general guidelines for formatting a research paper.

- **Use white, $8^1/_2$-by-11-inch paper.** Don't use colored or lined paper.
- **Double-space everything—the title page, abstract, body of the paper, quotations, and list of references.** Set the line spacing on your word processor for double spacing and leave it there.
- **Include a running head aligned with the left margin on every page.** The running head is an abbreviated title set in all caps with a maximum of 50 characters. Include a page number for every page aligned with the right margin.
- **Specify 1-inch margins.** One-inch margins are the default setting for most computers.
- **Do not justify (make even) the right margin.** Justifying the right margin throws off the spacing between words and makes your paper harder to read. Use the left-align setting instead.
- **Indent the first line of each paragraph $^1/_2$ inch.** Set the paragraph indent command or the tab on the ruler at $^1/_2$ inch.
- **Use block format for quotations longer than 40 words.** See page 449.
- **Create an abstract.** The abstract appears on a separate page after the title page. Insert and center "Abstract" at the top. Do not indent the first line of the abstract. The abstract should be a brief (120 words or under) summary of the paper.
- **Create a title page.** Follow the format below for your title page. It should have

  1. a running head beginning with the words "Running head:" followed by a short title in ALL CAPS at the top left and a page number at the top right,
  2. a descriptive title that is centered in the top half of the page with all words capitalized except *a, an, the*, prepositions, and conjunctions under four letters,
  3. your name centered on a separate line,
  4. your school centered on a separate line.

Include a running head, consisting of a short version of your title in ALL CAPS and the page number. This header should be about ¹/₂" from the top of the page. Set the margins of your paper to 1".

SURVEILLANOMICS   1

Surveillanomics: The Need for Governmental Regulation

of Video Surveillance

John M. Jones

The University of Texas at Austin

Center your title in the top half of the page. The title should clearly describe the content of the paper and should be no longer than 12 words. If the title runs to 2 lines, double-space it.

On the line below the title, include your name, also centered. On the next line below, include the name of your school. Double-space between these lines.

SURVEILLANOMICS   2 Continue the
                                                     running head.

Abstract

Because recent technological advances have made it
possible to use surveillance video to gather information
about private citizens, and because unregulated data-
mining has made this information economically
valuable, the collection and use of video surveillance
data should be regulated by the government. This
regulation, based on the model introduced by Taylor
(2002), should mandate that all video surveillance
must be in accordance with the law, have a legitimate
objective, and be necessary for the maintenance of a
free society. These guidelines would ensure that
surveillance data could not be used for purposes other
than those for which they were collected, and would
make the primary concerns in debates over the use
of surveillance democratic, not economic as they
are now.

The abstract
appears on a
separate page
with the title
Abstract
centered at
the top.

Do not indent
the first line of
the abstract.

The abstract
should be a brief
(120 words or
fewer) summary
of your paper's
argument.

Surveillanomics: The Need for Governmental
Regulation of Video Surveillance

On September 5, 2005, the operators of the social
networking site Facebook gave the service a facelift. One
of the innovations they introduced was the "news feed"
feature, which "automatically alerted users when their
friends made changes to their online profiles," like
changing personal details or adding new "friends"
(Meredith, 2006). This service, which was automatically
installed for all accounts, outraged users, 700,000 of
whom formed the group "Students Against Facebook
News Feeds." Before Facebook altered its implementation
of this feature, the members of this group were preparing
to protest the changes at the company's headquarters.

At first, this negative reaction by users took the
company completely by surprise. As Schneier (2006) puts
it, in their eyes, all they had done "was take available
data and aggregate it in a novel way for what [they]
perceived was [their] customers' benefit"; however, users
realized that this change "made an enormous difference"
in the way that their information could be aggregated,
accessed, and distributed. In other words, although
Facebook news feeds did nothing more than take
information that was already publicly available and
repackage it in a new form, this new information source
was seen by users as a massive invasion of their privacy.

In light of this reaction, it is interesting to note
that right now companies referred to as "data brokers"
are creating their own "news feeds" of private citizens'

Center your title
at the beginning
of the body of
your paper. If it
runs to 2 lines,
double-space it.

SURVEILLANOMICS 4

lives, collating individuals' public information, such as
credit reports and vehicle registration histories, and
then selling that information to practically anyone who
can pay for it. Whereas Facebook was semiprivate—in
September 2005 its membership was restricted to those
with .edu email addresses and news feeds were
distributed only to a member's online friends—data
brokers like USAData, Acxiom, and ChoicePoint collect
information about anyone, then package and sell that
information to third parties in what has become "a
multibillion-dollar, unregulated business that's growing
larger by the day" (Whiting, 2006). This "unregulated"
activity, known as data-mining, has recently come
under increased scrutiny, the need for which was
highlighted when ChoicePoint sold sensitive
information to thieves who posed as the
representatives of legitimate businesses.

All quotations should be cited by author, date, and page number. A page number does not appear in this example because the source is a Web page without paragraph numbers.

The rapid growth of data-mining has provoked
worries that continually improving technology has made
it possible to mine other kinds of data as well. Like the
consumer information already gathered by data brokers,
the video collected by surveillance cameras and webcams
is quickly becoming an economically valuable data
source. Department stores can now analyze movement in
video data to prevent shoplifting or to increase sales, and
face recognition software can be used to find particular
individuals on security tapes (O'Harrow, 2005, p. 296).
Similarly, Sweeney and Gross (2005) have developed
software that can monitor public webcams for suspicious

SURVEILLANOMICS 5

If you include the author's name in the text, include the publication year in parentheses immediately after it. If necessary, include the page number in parentheses with the abbreviation *p.* following the citation.

activity. Currently, video data is largely in the hands of private companies, for, as Koskela (2003) has noted, "cameras run by private market forces outnumber those used by the authorities" such that governments "have very little control on how and where surveillance is used" (p. 302). In short, surveillance has become an economic activity managed by "private market forces" and data miners, and this surveillanomics represents a significant new challenge to personal privacy.

In light of these facts, it is clear that we are in dire need of governmental regulation of video surveillance. Following the model for surveillance regulation in the European Convention on Human Rights as outlined by Taylor (2002), I agree that the government should mandate that all video surveillance must be in accordance with the law, have a legitimate objective, and be necessary for the maintenance of a free society (pp. 67–69). Further, any organization, public or private, that uses video surveillance should be required to register with the government in order to ensure that the use of surveillance data does not violate these three guidelines (p. 78). While the first guideline, that video surveillance practices be in accordance with the law, would reinforce the applicability of current statutes to surveillance activity—for example, the documented tendency of surveillance camera operators to voyeuristically stalk women in public spaces (Koskela, 2000, pp. 255–256; O'Harrow, 2005, p. 179)—for the purposes of this

If you cite the works of multiple authors in a sentence, format as normal, but separate the individual sources with a semicolon.

SURVEILLANOMICS   6

paper I will focus more on the necessity of the latter
two guidelines and their beneficial effects.

In the first place, demanding that video surveillance
operations have a legitimate objective would place
surveillance video out of the reach of data miners. Under
these guidelines, in order to obtain permission to install
surveillance equipment, it would be necessary for
potential operators to establish a clear objective for their
surveillance. The resulting data could then be used only
for purposes relevant to that objective. A similar
restriction has been successfully implemented in a
program to limit weigh-station stops by trucks. While
truckers were initially skeptical of the program because
they feared that the system of transponders used to track
weight information "would be used to catch them for
speeding or check their routines" (O'Harrow, 2005,
p. 217), the data collected was used only for a single,
clear purpose—automating the weighing process. After
that task was accomplished, the data was destroyed,
making it impossible for it to be used for other
purposes, such as tracking speeders, as some tollbooth
cameras are used now (Nieto, Johnston-Dodds, &
Simmons, 2002, p. 24). Following this example, if the
government were to use video surveillance in airports
to look for terrorist activity, that video would not be
allowed to be used for other applications, such as
using facial recognition to find private citizens with
outstanding arrest warrants. Having clear objectives for
the collection of video surveillance, and regulating the

In a parenthetical citation, use & instead of *and* when listing more than one author.

SURVEILLANOMICS   7

use of the data collected through surveillance operations so as to prevent it from being used for other purposes, would eliminate surveillance video as a source for data-mining, thus protecting individual privacy.

Second, since video surveillance would be subject to government regulation, defining what "needs" necessitate the use of video surveillance would be the subject of open debate. The last guideline, that video surveillance be conducted only for the purpose of maintaining a free society, would help define the terms of that debate in such a way as to make the needs of private citizens of primary concern. Currently, the use of video surveillance and the storage of surveillance data is primarily motivated by economic concerns. In the past ten years, video surveillance has become a billion-dollar industry (see Table 1). As pointed out earlier, most video surveillance is conducted by private

Title tables by number (Table 1, Table 2, . . .).

Provide your table with a descriptive title that is italicized and flush with the left margin.

Table 1

Sales Revenues Generated by CCTV Surveillance Cameras

Year	Sales (in billions)
1996	0.29
1997	0.31
1998	0.49
1999	0.7
2000	1
2001	1.6

Note. From the Security Industry Association, 2001, qtd. in Nieto et al. (2002).

SURVEILLANOMICS 8

companies (Koskela, 2003). Although arguments for surveillance systems are generally described in terms of public safety, when used in public places like shopping malls, video surveillance has become a key element of what Koskela (2000) calls "policing for profit," identifying "groups that are marginal in relation to the mall's purpose": consumption (p. 246). In malls

> the guards' routine work is to use surveillance cameras to look for 'undesirables' (Sibley, 1995: xi). The reason for excluding someone is that person's appearance. A person's appearance is considered as reflecting that person's ability to consume (Crawford, 1992: 27): one must always look as if one has bought something or is about to buy (Shields, 1989: 160) [. . .] Thus, ostensibly public spaces are not public for everyone—public space can be seen as if it 'refers to places under public scrutiny' (Domosh, 1998: 209). (p. 246)

The transformation of public spaces into "places under public scrutiny" is contrary to the democratic principle of freedom of movement. Unfortunately, the shopping mall, where any activity that is considered "undesirable"—defined by a person's "ability to consume"—is excluded, has become the template for public space (Koskela, 2000, p. 246).

Although some might argue that giving market forces a free hand would be the best solution to the surveillance problem, this is not necessarily true, for

Quotations of more than 40 words should be indented 1/2" from the margin. Include citations from the original text, but do not list those works in your references unless you cite them again elsewhere in the paper.

For block quotations, parenthetical citations go outside closing punctuation.

SURVEILLANOMICS   9

economists have shown that market solutions are not
always the best ones (Waldrop, 1992, pp. 40–41). In
either case, as a society do we really want economic
concerns to determine how video surveillance is used?
Based on current trends, if surveillance standards
are left entirely in private hands, or if individual
government agencies are allowed to determine
standards for surveillance use independently, this will
certainly be the result. However, if the government
were to regulate surveillance and to base its regulation
on the principle of a free and open society, this
economic motive could be subverted through the use of
openly debatable standards based on individual rights,
rights that are unlikely to be protected in a situation
dominated by economic concerns.

    I believe that this solution—government
regulation of video surveillance—is the best one
because it responds to both of the problems I have
outlined: the ability of private companies to mine
video sources for information about private citizens,
and the use of economic concerns to define
surveillance standards. Before this solution is likely to
be accepted, however, it will be necessary to deal with
a possible objection to government regulation: the
fear that giving the government control of video
surveillance would turn it into a de facto Big Brother.
As Mieszkowski (2003) reports, some argue that the
fact that the government conducts video surveillance is
already a sign that we are entering an Orwellian future.

SURVEILLANOMICS   10

If the government were to regulate video surveillance, the argument might go, this situation would only get worse, for it would have access to all public and private surveillance data, thereby realizing Orwell's dark vision of the future. However, Lee (2005) points out that in current practice the government *already* has access to this data, for private surveillance video is regularly provided to government agencies when they request it. What, then, would be the danger in allowing the government to regulate information it already has access to? The government already regulates many important aspects of our personal lives without widespread panic over the potential for abuse: the FDA regulates our food and medicine, the SEC regulates our finances, and the FCC regulates telecommunications. While no one would argue that the government is perfect, it does occasionally get things right. At the very least, if it gets policies wrong, it can be held accountable for its mistakes and faulty policies can be changed. If the guidelines I have presented here were to be adopted, neither the government nor any other entity would be allowed to access video data for purposes other than those for which that data was collected, a fact which would reduce the chances of Big-Brother-type outcomes. Further, there would be the added benefits of open, debatable standards for government surveillance and a marked increase in accountability for private sector surveillance activities.

SURVEILLANOMICS 11

Allowing the government to regulate video surveillance would eliminate the access of data-miners and government agencies to surveillance data. More important, in the face of the rampant use of surveillance technology, decisions over how that technology is implemented, how the data it produces is stored, and who gets to have access to it should be decided in an open, democratic manner, not a private, economic one. Governmental regulation is our best chance for achieving this end.

SURVEILLANOMICS 12

Center *References* at the top.

References

Koskela, H. (2000). "The gaze without eyes": Video-surveillance and the changing nature of urban space. *Progress in Human Geography, 24*, 243–265.

Koskela, H. (2003). "Cam era"—the contemporary urban panopticon. *Surveillance & Society, 1*, 292–313. Retrieved from http://www.surveillance-and-society.org

Lee, J. (2005, May 22). Caught on tape, then just caught; private cameras transform police work. *The New York Times*. Retrieved from http://www.nytimes.com

Meredith, P. (2006, September 22). Facebook and the politics of privacy. *Mother Jones*. Retrieved from http://www.motherjones.com/

Alphabetize entries by last name of the first author.

Indent all but the first line of each entry.

Double-space all entries.

SURVEILLANOMICS   13

Mieszkowski, K. (2003, September 25). We are all
    paparazzi now. *Salon*. Retrieved from http://
    archive.salon.com/

Nieto, M., Johnston-Dodds, K., & Simmons, C. W.
    (2002). *Public and private applications of video
    surveillance and biometric technologies.*
    Sacramento, CA: California Research Bureau,
    California State Library. Retrieved from http://
    www.library.ca.gov/CRB/02/06/02-006.pdf

O'Harrow, R. (2005). *No place to hide*. New York, NY:
    Free Press.

Schneier, B. (2006, September 21). Lessons from the
    Facebook riots. *Wired News*. Retrieved from http://
    www.wired.com

Sweeney, L., & Gross, R. (2005). *Mining images in
    publicly-available cameras for homeland security.*
    Paper presented at the AAAI Spring Symposium on
    AI Technologies for Homeland Security, Palo Alto,
    CA. Retrieved from http://privacy.cs.cmu.edu
    /dataprivacy/projects/videocount/index.html

Taylor, N. (2002). State surveillance and the right to
    privacy. *Surveillance & Society, 1*, 66–85. Retrieved
    from http://www.surveillance-and-society.org

Waldrop, M. M. (1992). *Complexity: The emerging
    science at the edge of order and chaos*. New York,
    NY: Simon & Schuster.

Go through your text and make sure that everything you have cited, except for personal communication, is in the list of references.

SURVEILLANOMICS   14

Whiting, R. (2006, July 10). Data brokers draw

    increased scrutiny. *InformationWeek*. Retrieved

    from http://www.informationweek.com

To hear audio commentary on this piece of writing, visit this page of the eText at **www.mycomplab.com**.

FORMATTING THE REFERENCES IN APA STYLE

- **Begin the references on a new page.** Insert a page break with your word processor before you start the references page.
- **Center "References" on the first line at the top of the page.**
- **Double-space all entries.**
- **Alphabetize each entry by the last name of the author or, if no author is listed, by the first content word in the title (ignore *a, an, the*).**
- **Indent all but the first line in each entry $^1/_2$ inch.**
- **Italicize the titles of books and periodicals.**
- **Go through your paper to check that each source you have used (except personal communication) is in the list of references.**

28 CMS Documentation

QUICK*TAKE*

- **Use in-text citations in CMS style** (see below)
- **Create citations for books and nonperiodical sources** (see p. 448)
- **Create citations for periodical sources** (see p. 454)
- **Create citations for online, electronic, and multimedia sources** (see p. 458)
- **Format a paper in CMS style** (see p. 462)

Writers who publish in business, social sciences, fine arts, and humanities outside the discipline of English often use *The Chicago Manual of Style* (CMS) method of documentation. CMS guidelines allow writers a clear way of using footnotes and endnotes (rather than MLA and APA in-text citations) for citing the sources of quotations, summaries, and paraphrases. If you have questions after consulting this chapter, you can consult *The Chicago Manual of Style*, sixteenth edition (Chicago: University of Chicago Press, 2010), or visit the Web site (www.chicagomanualofstyle.org).

28a In-text Citations in CMS Style

In-text citations

CMS describes two systems of documentation, one similar to APA and the other a style that uses footnotes or endnotes, which is the focus of this chapter. In the footnote style CMS uses a superscript number directly after any quotation, paraphrase, or summary. Notes are numbered consecutively throughout the essay, article, or chapter. This superscript number corresponds to either a footnote, which appears at the bottom of the page, or an endnote, which appears at the end of the text.

> In *Southern Honor: Ethics and Behavior in the Old South*, Wyatt-Brown argues that "paradox, irony, and guilt have been three current words used by historians to describe white Southern life before the Civil War."[1]

Note

> 1. Bertram Wyatt-Brown, *Southern Honor: Ethics and Behavior in the Old South* (Oxford: Oxford University Press, 1983), 3.

Bibliography

Wyatt-Brown, Bertram. *Southern Honor: Ethics and Behavior in the Old South.* Oxford: Oxford University Press, 1983.

Footnote and endnote placement

Footnotes appear at the bottom of the page on which each citation appears. Begin your footnote four lines from the last line of text on the page. Double-space footnotes and endnotes.

Endnotes are compiled at the end of the text on a separate page titled *Notes.* Center the title at the top of the page and list your endnotes in the order they appear within the text. The entire endnote section should be double-spaced—both within and between each entry. Even with endnotes it's still possible to include explanatory footnotes, which are indicated by asterisks or other punctuation marks.

CMS Bibliography

Because footnotes and endnotes in CMS format contain complete citation information, a separate list of references is often optional. This list of references can be called the *Bibliography,* or if it has only works referenced in your text, *Works Cited, Literature Cited,* or *References.*

THE CHICAGO MANUAL OF STYLE AND PUBLISHING

The *Chicago Manual of Style* is the favorite of the publishing industry because it is far more comprehensive than either the *MLA Handbook* or the *Publication Manual of the American Psychological Association.* The sixteenth edition has been updated to include instruction on how to create and edit electronic publications, including Web sites and e-books. Because many business and organizations now produce electronic publications, a basic knowledge of the electronic publishing process could be a valuable item on your résumé.

The *Chicago Manual* also gives advice on copyright law, such as how a work is granted copyright, what may constitute copyright violation, and what is fair use.

In addition, writers and publishers turn to the *Chicago Manual* for the fine points of writing. For example, there are two kinds of dashes: a longer dash called an *em dash* (discussed in Chapter 41) and a shorter dash called an *en dash.* If you want to know when to use an en dash, the *Chicago Manual* is the place to look.

Index of CMS Documentation

28b   Books and Nonperiodical Sources in CMS Style

Note

1. Nell Irvin Painter, *Creating Black Americans: African-American History and Its Meanings, 1619 to the Present* (New York: Oxford University Press, 2006), 5.

Bibliography

Painter, Nell Irvin. *Creating Black Americans: African-American History and Its Meanings, 1619 to the Present.* New York: Oxford University Press, 2006.

Author's or Editor's Name

In a note, the author's name is given in normal order.

In the bibliography, give the author's last name first. If an editor, put ed. after the name.

Book Title

Use the exact title, as it appears on the title page (not the cover).

Italicize the title.

Capitalize all nouns, verbs, adjectives, adverbs, and pronouns, and the first word of the title and subtitle.

Publication Information

In a note, the place of publication, publisher, and year of publication are in parentheses.

Place of publication

- Add the state's postal abbreviation or country when the city is not well known (Foster City, CA) or ambiguous (Cambridge, MA, or Cambridge, UK).

- If more than one city is given on the title page, use the first.

Publisher's name

- You may use acceptable abbreviations (e.g., Co. for Company).

- For works published prior to 1900, the place and date are sufficient.

Year of publication

- If no year of publication is given, write *n.d.* ("no date") in place of the date.

- If it is a multivolume edited work published over a period of more than one year, put the span of time as the year.

Sample citations for books and nonperiodical sources

BOOKS

1. Book by one author

In a note the author's name is given in normal order.

> 1. Thomas Friedman, *The World Is Flat: A Brief History of the Twenty-first Century* (New York: Farrar, Straus, and Giroux, 2005), 9.

In subsequent references, cite the author's last name only:

> 2. Friedman, 10.

If the reference is to the same work as the preceding note, you can use the abbreviation *Ibid.*:

> 3. Ibid., 10.

In the bibliography, give the author's name in reverse order.

> Friedman, Thomas. *The World Is Flat: A Brief History of the Twenty-first Century*. New York: Farrar, Straus, and Giroux, 2005.

For edited books, put *ed.* after the name.

> Chen, Kuan-Hsing, ed. *Trajectories: Inter-Asia Cultural Studies*. London: Routledge, 1998.

2. Book by multiple authors

For books with two or three authors, in a note, put all authors' names in normal order. For subsequent references, give only the authors' last names:

> 4. Taylor Hauser and June Kashpaw, *January Blues* (Foster City, CA: IDG Books, 2003), 32.

In the bibliography, give second and third names in normal order.

> Hauser, Taylor, and June Kashpaw. *January Blues*. Foster City, CA: IDG Books, 2003.

When there are more than three authors, in a note, give the name of the first author listed, followed by *et al.* List all of the authors in the bibliography.

3. Book by an unknown author

Begin both the note and the bibliography entries with the title.

Note

> 6. *Remarks upon the Religion, Trade, Government, Police, Customs, Manners, and Maladys of the City of Corke* (Cork, 1737), 4.

Bibliography

> *Remarks upon the Religion, Trade, Government, Police, Customs, Manners, and Maladys of the City of Corke*. Cork, 1737.

4. **Book by a group or organization**

Treat the group or organization as the author of the work.

Note

7. World Health Organization, *Advancing Safe Motherhood through Human Rights* (Geneva, Switzerland: World Health Organization, 2001), 18.

Bibliography

World Health Organization. *Advancing Safe Motherhood through Human Rights*. Geneva, Switzerland: World Health Organization, 2001.

PARTS OF BOOKS

5. **A single chapter by the same author as the book**

Note

1. Ann Ardis, "*The Lost Girl, Tarr*, and the Moment of Modernism," in *Modernism and Cultural Conflict, 1880–1922* (New York: Cambridge University Press, 2002), 78–113.

Bibliography

Ardis, Ann. "*The Lost Girl, Tarr,* and the Moment of Modernism." In *Modernism and Cultural Conflict, 1880–1922*. New York: Cambridge University Press, 2002.

6. **A selection in an anthology or a chapter in an edited collection**

Note

2. Renato Constantino, "Globalization and the South," in *Trajectories: Inter-Asia Cultural Studies*, ed. Kuan-Hsing Chen (London: Routledge, 1998), 57–64.

Bibliography

Constantino, Renato. "Globalization and the South." In *Trajectories: Inter-Asia Cultural Studies*, edited by Kuan-Hsing Chen, 57–64. London: Routledge, 1998.

7. **Article in a reference work**

Publication information is usually omitted from citations of well-known reference volumes. The edition is listed instead. The abbreviation *s.v.* (*sub verbo* or "under the word") replaces an entry's page number.

Note

4. *Encyclopaedia Britannica*, 2009 ed., s.v. "mercantilism."

8. Introduction, foreword, preface, or afterword

When citing an introduction, foreword, preface, or afterword written by someone other than the book's main author, the other writer's name comes first, and the main author's name follows the title of the book.

Note

> 5. Edward Larkin, introduction to *Common Sense*, by Thomas Paine (New York: Broadview, 2004).

Bibliography

> Larkin, Edward. Introduction to *Common Sense*, by Thomas Paine, 1–16. New York: Broadview, 2004.

REVISED EDITIONS, VOLUMES, AND SERIES

9. A revised or later edition of a book

Note

> 1. Fred S. Kleiner, *Gardner's Art through the Ages: A Global History*, 13th ed. (Boston: Wadsworth, 2010), 85.

Bibliography

> Kleiner, Fred S. *Gardner's Art through the Ages: A Global History*. 13th ed. Boston: Wadsworth, 2010.

10. Work in more than one volume

Note

> 1. Oscar Wilde, *The Complete Works of Oscar Wilde*, vol. 3 (New York: Dragon Press, 1998), 1024.

Bibliography

> Wilde, Oscar. *The Complete Works of Oscar Wilde*. Vol. 3. New York: Dragon Press, 1998.

EDITIONS AND TRANSLATIONS

11. Book with an editor

Note

> 1. Thomas Hardy, *Jude the Obscure*, ed. Norman Page (New York: Norton, 1999), 35.

Bibliography

> Hardy, Thomas. *Jude the Obscure*. Edited by Norman Page. New York: Norton, 1999.

12. Book with a translator

Follow the style shown in entry 11, but substitute "trans." for "ed." in the note and "Translated" for "Edited" in the bibliographic entry.

GOVERNMENT DOCUMENTS

13. Government document

Note

> 5. US House Committee on Armed Services, *Comptroller General's Assessment of the Iraqi Government's Record of Performance* (Washington, DC: Government Printing Office, 2008), 40.

Bibliography

> US Congress House Committee on Armed Services. *Comptroller General's Assessment of the Iraqi Government's Record of Performance*. Washington, DC: Government Printing Office, 2008.

14. *Congressional Record*

For legal documents including the *Congressional Record*, CMS now follows the recommendations in *The Bluebook: A Uniform System of Citations* issued by the Harvard Law Review. The *Congressional Record* is issued in biweekly and permanent volumes. If possible, cite the permanent volumes.

Note

> 6. 156 Cong. Rec. 11,265 (2010).

RELIGIOUS TEXTS

15. Religious texts

Citations from religious texts appear in the notes but not in the bibliography. Give the version in parentheses in the first citation only.

Note

> 4. John 3:16 (King James Version).

LETTERS

16. Published letter

Note

> 5. Oscar Wilde to Robert Ross, 25 November 1897, in *The Complete Letters of Oscar Wilde*, ed. Merlin Holland and Rupert Hart-Davis (New York: Holt, 2000), 992.

Bibliography

Wilde, Oscar. *The Complete Letters of Oscar Wilde*. Edited by Merlin Holland and Rupert Hart-Davis. New York: Holt, 2000.

17. **Personal letter to author**

Personal communications are not usually listed in the bibliography because they are not accessible to the public.

Note

7. Ann Williams, letter to author, May 8, 2007.

DISSERTATIONS AND CONFERENCE PROCEEDINGS

18. **Unpublished dissertation**

Note

7. James Elsworth Kidd, "The Vision of Uncertainty: Elizabethan Windows and the Problem of Sight" (PhD diss., Southern Illinois University, 1998), 236.

Bibliography

Kidd, James Elsworth. "The Vision of Uncertainty: Elizabethan Windows and the Problem of Sight." PhD diss., Southern Illinois University, 1998.

19. **Published proceedings of a conference**

Note

8. Joyce Marie Jackson, "Barrelhouse Singers and Sanctified Preachers," in *Saints and Sinners: Religion, Blues, and (D)evil in African-American Music and Literature: Proceedings of the Conference held at the Université de Liège*, (Liège: Société Liègeoise de Musicologie, 1996), 14–28.

Bibliography

Jackson, Joyce Marie. "Barrelhouse Singers and Sanctified Preachers." In *Saints and Sinners: Religion, Blues, and (D)evil in African-American Music and Literature: Proceedings of the Conference held at the Université de Liège*, 14–28. Liège: Société Liègeoise de Musicologie, 1996.

28c Periodical Sources in CMS Style

Note

> 1. Michael Hutt, "A Nepalese Triangle: Monarchists, Maoists, and Political Parties," *Asian Affairs* 38 (2007): 11–22.

Bibliography

Hutt, Michael. "A Nepalese Triangle: Monarchists, Maoists, and Political Parties." *Asian Affairs* 38 (2007): 11–22.

Author's or Editor's Name

In a note, the author's name is given in normal order.

In a bibliography, give the author's last name first.

Title of Article

- Put the title in quotation marks. If there is a title of a book within the title, italicize it.
- Capitalize nouns, verbs, adjectives, adverbs, and pronouns, and the first word of the title and subtitle.

Publication Information

Name of journal

- Italicize the name of the journal.
- Journal titles are normally not abbreviated in the arts and humanities unless the title of the journal is an abbreviation (*PMLA, ELH*).

Volume, issue, and page numbers

- Place the volume number after the journal title without intervening punctuation.
- For journals that are paginated from issue to issue within a volume, do not list the issue number.
- When citing an entire article, with no page numbers, place the abbreviation *vol.* before the volume number.

Date

- The date or year of publication is given in parentheses after the volume number, or issue number, if provided.

Sample citations for periodical sources

JOURNAL ARTICLES

20. Article by one author
Note

> 1. Sumit Guha, "Speaking Historically: The Changing Voices of Historical Narration in Western India, 1400–1900," *American Historical Review* 109 (2004): 1084–98.

In subsequent references, cite the author's last name only:

> 2. Guha, 1085.

If the reference is to the same work as the reference before it, you can use the abbreviation *Ibid.*:

> 3. Ibid., 1087.

Bibliography

> Guha, Sumit. "Speaking Historically: The Changing Voices of Historical Narration in Western India, 1400-1900," *American Historical Review* 109 (2004): 1084–98.

21. Article by two or three authors
Note

> 3. Pamela R. Matthews and Mary Ann O'Farrell, "Introduction: Whose Body?" *South Central Review* 18, no. 3–4 (Fall/Winter 2001): 1–5.

All authors' names are printed in normal order. For subsequent references, give both authors' last names.

> 4. Matthews and O'Farrell, 4.

Bibliography

> Matthews, Pamela R., and Mary Ann O'Farrell. "Introduction: Whose Body?" *South Central Review* 18, no. 3–4 (Fall–Winter 2001): 1–5.

22. Article by more than three authors
Note
Give the name of the first listed author, followed by *et al.*

> 5. Michael J. Thompson et al., "The Internal Rotation of the Sun," *Annual Review of Astronomy and Astrophysics* 41 (2003): 602.

Bibliography

List all the authors (inverting only the first author's name).

Thompson, Michael J., Jorgen Christensen-Dalsgaard, Mark S.
Miesch, and Juri Toomre. "The Internal Rotation of the Sun."
Annual Review of Astronomy and Astrophysics 41 (2003):
599–643.

23. **Article by an unknown author**

Note

6. "Japan's Global Claim to Asia," *American Historical Review*
109 (2004): 1196–98.

Bibliography

"Japan's Global Claim to Asia." *American Historical Review* 109
(2004): 1196–98.

DIFFERENT TYPES OF PAGINATION

24. **Journals paginated by volume**

Note

4. Susan Welsh, "Resistance Theory and Illegitimate
Reproduction," *College Composition and Communication* 52
(2001): 553–73.

Bibliography

Welsh, Susan. "Resistance Theory and Illegitimate Reproduction."
College Composition and Communication 52 (2001): 553–73.

25. **Journals paginated by issue**

For journals paginated separately by issue, list the issue number after
the volume number.

Note

5. Tzvetan Todorov, "The New World Disorder," *South Central
Review* 19, no. 2 (2002): 28–32.

Bibliography

Todorov, Tzvetan. "The New World Disorder." *South Central Review*
19, no. 2 (2002): 28–32.

POPULAR MAGAZINES

26. Weekly and biweekly magazines

For a weekly or biweekly popular magazine, give both the day and month of publication as listed on the issue.

Note

> 5. Malcolm Gladwell, "Pandora's Briefcase," *New Yorker*, May 10, 2010, 72–78.

Bibliography

> Gladwell, Malcolm. "Pandora's Briefcase." *New Yorker*, May 10, 2010, 72–78.

27. Regular features and departments

Do not put titles of regular features or departments of a magazine in quotation marks.

Note

> 3. Conventional Wisdom, *Newsweek*, May 14, 2007, 8.

Bibliography

> Newsweek. Conventional Wisdom. May 14, 2007, 8.

REVIEWS AND EDITORIALS

28. A review

Provide the title, if given, and name the work reviewed. If there is no title, just name the work reviewed.

Note

> 1. Jeff Severs, review of *Vanishing Point,* by David Markson, *Texas Observer*, February 2, 2004.

Bibliography

> Severs, Jeff. Review of *Vanishing Point,* by David Markson. *Texas Observer*, February 2, 2004.

29. A letter to the editor or an editorial

Add *letter* or *editorial* after the name of the author (if there is one). If there is no author, start with the descriptor.

Note

> 2. Mary Castillo, letter to the editor, *New York Magazine*, May 14, 2007, 34.

Bibliography

> Castillo, Mary. Letter to the editor. *New York Magazine*, May 14,
>   2007, 34.

NEWSPAPERS

30. **Newspaper article**

Note

> 1. Melena Ryzik, "Off the Beaten Beat," *New York Times*,
> May 11, 2007, late edition, sec. E.

- The month, day, and year are essential in citations of materials from daily newspapers. Cite them in this order: Month–Day–Year (November 3, 2007).
- For an item in a large city newspaper that has several editions a day, give the edition after the date.
- If the newspaper is published in sections, include the name, number, or letter of the section after the date or the edition (sec. C).
- Page numbers are usually omitted. If you put them in, use *p.* and *col.* (column) to avoid ambiguity.

 Online Sources in CMS Style

ONLINE PUBLICATIONS

31. **Document or page from a Web site**

To cite original content from within a Web site, include as many descriptive elements as you can: author of the page, title of the page, title and owner of the Web site, and the URL. Include the date accessed only if the site is time-sensitive or is frequently updated. If you cannot locate an individual author, the owner of the site can stand in for the author.

Note

> 11. National Organization for Women, "NOW History," accessed
> October 8, 2010, http://www.now.org/history/history.html.

Bibliography

> National Organization for Women. "NOW History." Accessed
>   October 8, 2010. http://www.now.org.history/history.html.

32. Online book

Note

12. Angelina Grimké, *Appeal to the Christian Women of the South* (New York: New York Anti-Slavery Society, 1836), accessed November 2, 2010, http://history.furman.edu/~benson/docs/grimke2.htm.

Bibliography

Grimké, Angelina. *Appeal to the Christian Women of the South*. New York: New York Anti-Slavery Society, 1836. Accessed November 2, 2010. http://history.furman.edu/~benson/docs/grimke2.htm.

33. Article in a scholarly online journal (using 007)

Note

13. Margaret Cohen, "Literary Studies on the Terraqueous Globe." *PMLA* 125, no. 3 (2010): 657-62, doi:10.1632/pmla.2010.125.3.657.

Bibliography

Cohen, Margaret. "Literary Studies on the Terraqueous Globe." *PMLA* 125, no. 3 (2010): 657-62. doi:10.1632/pmla.2010.125.3.657.

34. Article in an online database (using URL)

Note

18. George R. Boyer and Timothy P. Schmidle, "Poverty among the Elderly in Late Victorian England," *The Economic History Review* 62, no. 2 (2009): 249-278, http://www.jstor.org/stable/20542911.

Bibliography

Boyer, George R. and Timothy P. Schmidle. "Poverty among the Elderly in Late Victorian England." *The Economic History Review* 62, no. 2 (2009): 249-278. http://www.jstor.org /stable/20542911.

35. Article in an online newspaper

Note

28. Liz Alderman, "Dubai Struggles with Environmental Problems after Growth," *New York* Times, October 28, 2010, http://www.nytimes.com/2010/10/28/business /energy-environment/28dubai.html?ref=todayspaper.

Bibliography

> Alderman, Liz. "Dubai Struggles with Environmental Problems after
> Growth." *New York Times*, October 28, 2010. http://
> www.nytimes.com/2010/10/28/business
> /energy-environment/28dubai.html.

CITING ONLINE SOURCES IN CMS STYLE

CMS advocates a style for citing online and electronic sources that is adapted from its style for citing print sources. Titles of complete works are italicized. Quotation marks and other punctuation in citations for online sources should be used in the same manner as for print sources.

Access dates: List the date of access before the URL or DOI.

Revision dates: Due to the inconsistency in the practice of Internet sites stating the date of last revision, CMS recommends against using revision dates in citations.

DOIs and URLs: If the book or article has a Document Object Identifier (DOI) assigned, list it and not the URL. Otherwise, list the URL. If a URL has to be broken at the end of a line, the line break should be made before a slash (/) or punctuation mark (other than a colon or double slash). CMS does not advocate the use of angle brackets (<>) to enclose URLs.

For details not covered in this section, consult *The Chicago Manual of Style*, sixteenth edition, sections 14.4–14.13.

OTHER ELECTRONIC SOURCES

36. Podcast

Note

> 4. Joseph Ellis, interview by Neal Conan, "Dear John, Dear
> Abigail: A Love Story Through Letters," *Talk of the Nation*, NPR,
> podcast audio, October 27, 2010, http://www.npr.org/templates
> /story/story.php?storyId=130862704.

Bibliography

> Ellis, Joseph. Interview by Neal Conan. "Dear John, Dear Abigail:
> A Love Story Through Letters." *Talk of the Nation*. NPR.
> Podcast audio. October 27,2010. http://www.npr.org
> /templates/story/story.php?storyId=130862704.

37. Posting to a discussion list or group

To cite material from archived Internet forums, discussion groups or blogs, include the name of the post author, the name of the list or site, the date of the posting, and the URL. Limit your citation to notes or in-text citations.

Note

> 16. Jason Marcel, post to U.S. Politics Online Today in Politics Forum, April 4, 2004, http://www.uspoliticsonline.com/forums /forumdisplay.php?f=24.

38. E-mail

Because personal e-mails are not available to the public, they are not usually listed in the bibliography.

Note

> 11. Erik Lynn Williams, "Social Anxiety Disorder," e-mail to author, August 12, 2007.

28e Multimedia Sources in CMS Style

39. Musical recording

Note

> 8. Judy Garland, "Come Rain or Come Shine," *Judy at Carnegie Hall: Fortieth Anniversary Edition*, Capitol B000059QY9, compact disc.

Bibliography

> Garland, Judy. "Come Rain or Come Shine." *Judy at Carnegie Hall: Fortieth Anniversary Edition*. Capitol B000059QY9, compact disc.

40. Film or video

Note

> 9. *Invictus*, directed by Clint Eastwood (2009; Hollywood, CA: Warner Home Video, 2009), DVD.

Bibliography

> *Invictus*. Directed by Clint Eastwood. Hollywood, CA: Warner Home Video, 2009. DVD.

41. Speech, debate, mediated discussion, or public talk

Note

> 16. Ellen Arthur, "The Octoroon, or Irish Life in Louisiana" (paper presented at the 2001 Annual Convention of the American Conference for Irish Studies, New York, June 2001).

Bibliography

Arthur, Ellen. "The Octoroon, or Irish Life in Louisiana." Paper presented at the 2001 Annual Convention of the American Conference for Irish Studies, New York, June 2001.

42. **Interview**

Note

15. Gordon Wood, interview by Linda Wertheimer, *Weekend Edition,* National Public Radio, May 14, 2005.

Bibliography

Wood, Gordon. Interview by Linda Wertheimer. *Weekend Edition.* National Public Radio, May 14, 2005.

43. **Illustrations, figures, and tables**

When citing figures from sources, use the abbreviation *fig.* However, spell out the word when citing tables, graphs, maps, or plates. The page number on which the figure appears precedes any figure number.

Note

16. Christian Unger, *America's Inner-City Crisis* (New York: Childress, 2003), 134, fig. 3.4.

28f Sample Pages with CMS Documentation

Laker 1

Jason Laker

American History 102

January 28, 2011

The Electoral College: Does It Have a Future?

Until the presidential election of 2000, few Americans thought much about the Electoral College. It was something they had learned about in civics class and had then forgotten about as other, more pressing bits of information required their attention. In November 2000, however, the Electoral College took center stage and sparked an argument that

Laker 2

continues today: Should the Electoral College be abolished?

The founding fathers established the Electoral College as a compromise between elections by Congress and those by popular vote.[1] The College consists of a group of electors who meet to vote for the president and vice president of the United States. The electors are nominated by political parties within each state and the number each state gets relates to the state's congressional delegation. The process and the ideas behind it sound simple, but the actual workings of the Electoral College remain a mystery to many Americans.

The complicated nature of the Electoral College is one of the reasons why some people want to see it abolished. One voter writes in a letter to the editor of the *New York Times* that the elimination of the Electoral College is necessary "to demystify our voting system in the eyes of foreigners and our own citizenry."[2] Other detractors claim that it just does not work, and they cite the presidential elections of 1824, 1876, 1888, and, of course, 2000 as representative of the failures of the College. Those who defend the Electoral College, however, claim that the failures of these elections had little to do with the Electoral College itself.[3]

According to Gary Gregg, director of the McConnell Center for Political Leadership, a new study shows that much of what Americans think we know about the Electoral College is wrong. Consequently, we should actively question the wisdom of those who want to see it abolished.[4]

Notes

1. Lawrence D. Longley and Neal R. Peirce, *The Electoral College Primer 2000* (New Haven: Yale University Press, 1999).

2. William C. McIntyre, "Revisiting the Electoral College," *New York Times*, November 17, 2001, late edition, sec. A.

3. Avagara, *EC: The Electoral College Webzine*, accessed January 21, 2011, http://www.avagara.com/e_c/.

4. Gary Gregg, "Keep the College," *National Review Online*, November 7, 2001, accessed January 19, 2011, http://www.lexisnexis.com/universe/.

Bibliography

Avagara. *EC: The Electoral College Webzine*. Accessed January 21, 2011. http://www.avagara.com/e_c/.

Gregg, Gary. "Keep the College." *National Review Online*, November 7, 2001. Accessed January 19, 2011. http://www.lexisnexis.com/ universe/.

Longley, Lawrence D., and Neal R. Peirce. *The Electoral College Primer 2000*. New Haven: Yale University Press, 1999.

McIntyre, William C. "Revisiting the Electoral College." *New York Times*. November 17, 2001. Late edition, sec. A.

29 | CSE Documentation

QUICK*TAKE*

- Use in-text references in CSE style (see p. 466)
- Create references for books and nonperiodical sources (see p. 467)
- Create references for periodical sources (see p. 469)
- Create references for online sources (see p. 470)
- Format a paper in CSE style (see p. 471)

Within the disciplines of the natural and applied sciences, citation styles are highly specialized. Many disciplines follow the guidelines of particular journals or style manuals within their individual fields. Widely followed by writers in the sciences is the comprehensive guide published by the Council of Science Editors: *Scientific Style and Format: The CSE Manual for Authors, Editors, and Publishers*, seventh edition (2006).

The preferred documentation system in CSE places references in the body of the text marked by a superscript number preceded by a space and placed inside punctuation. For example:

> Cold fingers and toes are common circulatory problems found in most heavy cigarette smokers [1].

This number corresponds to a numbered entry on the CSE source list, titled *References*.

The CSE References page lists all sources cited in the paper. To create a CSE References page, follow these guidelines:

1. Title your page "References," and center this title at the top of the page.
2. Double-space the entire References page, both within and between citations.
3. List citations in the order they appear in the body of the paper. Begin each citation with its citation number, followed by a period, flush left.
4. Authors are listed by last name, followed by initials. Capitalize only first words and proper nouns in cited titles. Book titles are not underlined and article titles are not placed between quotation marks. Names of journals should be abbreviated where possible.
5. Cite publication year, and volume or page numbers if applicable.

In-text References in CSE Style

CSE documentation of sources does not require the names of authors in the text but only a number that refers to the References list at the end.

> In 1997, the Gallup poll reported that 55% of adults in the United States think secondhand smoke is "very harmful," compared to only 36% in 1994 [1].

The superscript [1] refers to the first entry on the References list, where readers will find a complete citation for this source.

What if you need more than one citation in a passage?

If the numbers are consecutive, separate with a hyphen. If nonconsecutive, use a comma.

> The previous work [1, 3, 5–8, 11]

Index of CSE Documentation

Books and Nonperiodical Sources in CSE-Style References

1. Nance JJ. What goes up: the global assault on our atmosphere. New York: W Morrow; 1991.

Author's or Editor's Name

The author's last name comes first, followed by the initials of the author's first name and middle name (if provided). If an editor, put the word *editor* after the name.

Book Title

- Do not italicize or underline titles.
- Capitalize only the first word and proper nouns.

Publication Information

Year of publication

- The year comes after the other publication information. It follows a semicolon.

- If it is a multivolume edited work published over a period of more than one year, give the span of years.

Page numbers

- When citing part of a book, give the page range for the selection: *p. 60–90.*

Sample references

BOOKS

1. Book by a single author/editor

> 2. Minger TJ, editor. Greenhouse glasnost: the crisis of global warming. New York (NY): Ecco; 1990.

2. Book by two or more authors/editors

> 3. O'Day DH, Horgen PA, editors. Sexual interactions in eukaryotic microbes. New York (NY): Academic Press; 1981.

3. Book by a group or organization

> 4. IAEA. Manual on radiation haematology. Vienna (Austria): IAEA; 1971.

4. **Two or more books by the same author**

Number the references according to the order in which they appear in the text.

5. Gould SJ. The structure of evolutionary theory. Cambridge (MA): Harvard University Press; 2002.

8. Gould SJ. Wonderful life: the Burgess Shale and the nature of history. New York (NY): Norton; 1989.

PARTS OF BOOKS

5. **A single chapter written by the same author as the book**

6. Ogle M. All the modern conveniences: American household plumbing, 1840–1890. Baltimore (MD): Johns Hopkins University Press; 2000. Convenience embodied; p. 60–92.

6. **A selection in an anthology or a chapter in an edited collection**

7. Kraft K, Baines DM. Computer classrooms and third grade development. In: Green MD, editor. Computers and early development. New York (NY): Academic; 1997. p. 168–79.

REPORTS

7. **Technical and research reports**

9. Austin A, Baldwin R, editors. Faculty collaboration: enhancing the quality of scholarship and teaching. ASCHE-ERIC Higher Education Report 7. Washington (DC): George Washington University; 1991.

Periodical Sources in CSE-Style References

> 1. Bohannon J. Climate change: IPCC report lays out options for taming greenhouse gases. Science. 2007;316(5826):812–814.

Author's Name

The author's last name comes first, followed by the initials of the author's first name and middle name (if provided).

Publication Information

Name of journal

- Do not abbreviate single-word titles. Abbreviate multiple-word titles according to the National Information Standards Organization (NISO) list of serials.

- Capitalize each word of the journal title, even if abbreviated.

Title of Article

- Do not place titles inside quotation marks.

- Capitalize only the first word and proper nouns.

Date of publication, volume, and issue numbers

- Include the issue number inside parentheses if it is present in the document. Leave no spaces between these items.

JOURNAL ARTICLES

8. **Article by one author**

> 1. Board J. Reduced lodging for soybeans in low plant population is related to light quality. Crop Science. 2001;41:379–387.

9. **Article by two or more authors/editors**

> 2. Simms K, Denison D. Observed interactions between wild and domesticated mixed-breed canines. J Mamm. 1997; 70:341–342.

10. **Article by a group or organization**

> 4. Center for Science in the Public Interest. Meat labeling: help! Nutrition Action Health Letter: 2. 2001 Apr 1.

11. **Article with no identifiable author**

If you cannot find an indentifiable author or organization, begin the entry with the article title.

12. Journals paginated by issue

Use the month or season of publication (and day, if given) for journals paginated by issue. Include the issue number in parentheses after the volume number.

> 8. Barlow JP. Africa rising: everything you know about Africa is wrong. Wired. 1998 Jan:142–158.

13. Article in newspaper

> 32. Meier B, Krauss C. Inquiry puts Halliburton in familiar hot seat. New York Times (New York Ed.). 2010 Oct 29;Sect. A20.

29d Online Sources and Multimedia Sources in CSE-Style References

14. Online journal articles

> 2. Schunck CH, Shin Y, Schirotzek A, Zwierlein MW, Ketterle A. Pairing without superfluidity: the ground state of an imbalanced fermi mixture. Science [Internet]. 2007 [cited 2007 June 15]; 316(5826):867–870. Available from: http://www.sciencemag. org/cgi/content/full/3165826/867/DC1

15. Article from a database

> 18. Williams SE, Slice DE. Regional shape change in adult facial bone curvature with age. Am J Phys Anthropol. 2010; 143(3):437–47. PubMed [database on the Internet]. Bethesda (MD): National Library of Medicine; [cited 2010 Oct 28]. Available from: http://www.ncbi.nlm.nih.gov/pubmed/20949614

16. Web site

> 28. Centers for Disease Control and Prevention. [Internet]. Atlanta (GA): Centers for Disease Control and Prevention; 2010 [cited 2010 Dec 12]. Available from: http://www.cdc.gov

17. **Message posted to a discussion list**

> 25. Wilson CB. What works; what works best. On the road with
> Dr. Wilson [discussion list on the Internet]. Chicago (IL):
> American Medical Association; 2010 Oct 28 [cited 2010
> Oct 29]. Available from: http://www.ama-assn.org/ama
> /pub/ama-president-blog

18. **Scientific databases on the Internet**

> 3. Comprehensive Large Array-data Stewardship System [Internet].
> 2007. Release 4.2. Silver Spring (MD): National Environmental
> Satellite, Data, and Information Service (US). [updated 2007
> May 2; cited 2007 May 14]. Available from: http://
> www.class.noaa.gov/saa/products/welcome

19. **Audio or video recording**

> 48. Planet Earth [DVD-ROM]. London (UK): BBC; 2006.

 Sample Pages with CSE Documentation

Do 1

Thuydung Do

BIO 206L Fall 2010

November 13, 2010

The Preference of Home Soil over Foreign Soil in

Pogonomyrmex barbatus

Abstract

Tests were conducted to see whether or not
harvester ants of the species *Pogonomyrmex barbatus*
can actually distinguish home soil from foreign soil.

Do 2

These ants were exposed to different types of soils and the time they spent on each soil was recorded. The Wilcoxan Signed Rank test was performed to analyze the collected data. It was observed that *Pogonomyrmex barbatus* does show preference for home soil over foreign soil.

Introduction

Pieces of food are sometimes seen surrounded by hundreds of ants a while after they were dropped on the table or on the ground. There are also trails of ants that line up in an orderly fashion leading from the food to the nests. How do these ants know to follow each other in a line instead of scattering all over? The main method is through releasing pheromones [1]. The pheromones allow the ants to trail after one another, but where will they go? What makes these different ant mounds unique from one another? Based on research done by Wagner and her group, soil biota and soil chemistry of each nest can set themselves apart [2]. Can the harvester ants detect these differences in the soils at all or are all soils the same to them? In this experiment, the null hypothesis that harvester ants *Pogonomyrmex barbatus* cannot distinguish home soil from foreign soil and neutral soil was tested in attempt to find the answer to this question.

Do 3

References

1. Holldobler B, Morgan ED, Oldham NJ, Liebig J. Recruitment pheromone in the harvester ant genus *Pogonomyrmex*. J Insect Phys. 2001;47:369–374.

2. Wagner D, Brown M, Gordon D. Harvester ant nests, soil biota and chemistry. Oceologia. 1997;112:232–236.

PART 7

Effective Style and Language

You **can learn more and do more** with MyCompLab and with the eText version of *The Penguin Handbook*. To find resources in MyCompLab that will help you successfully complete your assignment, go to

Resources

Grammar

> **Usage and Style**

  Bias in Language and Sexist Language | Faulty Comparison | Inference from Speech | Parallel Structure | Shifts in Point of View | Redundancy and Wordiness | Stringy Sentences

Review the Instruction and Multimedia resources within each topic, then complete the Exercises and click on the Gradebook to measure your progress.

In the **eText version** of *The Penguin Handbook*, you will also find extra instruction, examples and practice exercises.

30 | Write with Power

QUICK*TAKE*

- **How do you make your writing active?** (see p. 479)
  Passive: The snowboard was invented by Sherman Poppen.
  Active: Sherman Poppen invented the snowboard.
- **What are agents, and how do you use them in your writing?**
  (see p. 481)
  No agent: It was made as a plaything for his daughter.
  With agent: Poppen made the first snowboard as a plaything for his
  daughter.
- **How do you vary your sentences?** (see p. 483)
  Choppy and repetitive: It was called the Snurfer. The name was a combina-
  tion of snow and surfer. It was a skateboard without wheels. It was manufac-
  tured as a toy the next year.
  Variety: Poppen named his snowboard the Snurfer, which was a combination
  of snow and surfer. Essentially a skateboard without wheels, the Surfer was
  manufactured as a toy the next year.

Keeping a few principles in mind can make your writing a pleasure to read
instead of a boring slog.

In visuals
You imagine actions when subjects are captured in
motion.

In writing
Your readers expect actions to be expressed in
verbs: *gallop, canter, trot, run, sprint, dash, bound,
thunder, tear away.*

In visuals
Viewers interpret the most prominent person or
thing as the subject—what the visual is about.

In writing
Readers interpret the first person or thing they
meet in a sentence as what the sentence is about
(the jockey, the horse). They expect that person or
thing to perform the action expressed in the verb.

30a Pay Attention to Verbs

A teacher may once have told you that verbs are "action words." Where are the action words in the following paragraph?

> Red hair flying, professional snowboarder and skateboarder Shaun White became a two-time Olympic gold medalist with a record score of 48.4 at the 2010 Winter Olympics. White was a skier before he was five, but became a snowboarder at age six, and by age seven he had become a professional, receiving corporate sponsorships. At age nine, White became friends with professional skateboarder Tony Hawk, who became White's mentor in becoming a professional skateboarder. White is known for accomplishing several "firsts" in snowboarding, including being the first to land back-to-back double corks and to master a trick called a Cab 7 Melon Grab. He is also the holder of record for the highest score in the men's halfpipe at the winter Olympics.

No action words here! The paragraph describes a series of actions, yet most of the verbs are *is, was,* and *became.* These sentences typify writing that uses *be* verbs (*is, are, was, were*) when better alternatives are available. Think about what the actions are and choose powerful verbs that express those actions.

> Red hair flying, professional snowboarder and skateboarder Shaun White scored a 48.4 during the 2010 Winter Olympics and won his second gold medal. White skied before he was five,

---

STAYING ON TRACK

Express actions as verbs

Many sentences contain words that express action, but those words are nouns instead of verbs. Often the nouns can be changed into verbs. For example:

> The arson unit ~~conducted an investigation of~~ investigated the mysterious fire.

> The committee ~~had a debate over~~ debated how best to spend the surplus funds.

Notice that changing nouns into verbs also eliminates unnecessary words.

but switched to snowboarding at age six, and by age seven received corporate sponsorships. At age nine, White befriended professional skateboarder Tony Hawk, who mentored White and helped him become a professional skateboarder. White has accomplished several "firsts" in snowboarding, including landing back-to-back double corks and mastering a trick called a Cab 7 Melon Grab. He also holds the record for the highest score in the men's halfpipe at the Winter Olympics.

30b Stay Active

When you were a very young child, you learned an important lesson about language. Perhaps you can remember the day you broke the cookie jar. Did you tell Mom, "I knocked over the jar"? Probably not. Instead, you might have said, "The jar got broken." This short sentence accomplishes an amazing sleight of hand. Who broke the jar and how the jar was broken remain mysterious. Apparently, it just broke.

"Got" is often used for "was" in informal speech. In written language, the sentence would read, "The jar was broken," which is an example of the passive voice. Passives can be as useful for adults as for children to conceal who is responsible for an action:

> The laptop containing our customers' personal information was misplaced.

Who misplaced the laptop? Who knows?

Active vs. passive voice

Sentences with transitive verbs (labeled "TV" below; verbs that need an object; see Section 38c) can be written in the active or passive voice. In the active voice the subject of the sentence is the actor. In the passive voice the subject is being acted upon.

	┌───── SUBJ ─────┐ ┌──TV──┐
Active	**Leonardo da Vinci** painted *Mona Lisa* between 1503 and 1506.

	┌── SUBJ ──┐ ┌──TV──┐
Passive	*Mona Lisa* was painted by Leonardo da Vinci between 1503 and 1506.

The passive is created with a form of *be* and the past participle of the main verb. In a passive voice sentence, you can either name the actor in a *by* phrase following the verb or omit the actor altogether.

| Passive | *Mona Lisa* was painted between 1503 and 1506. |

Shifts in voice

Watch for unintended shifts from active (*I ate the cookies*) to passive voice (*the cookies were eaten*).

| Incorrect | The sudden storm **toppled** several trees and numerous windows **were shattered**. |
| Correct | The sudden storm **toppled** several trees and **shattered** numerous windows. |

STAYING ON TRACK

Prefer the active voice

To write with power, consider different ways of saying the same thing. The extra effort will bring noticeable results.

| Passive | A request on your part for special consideration based on your experience working in the profession **will be reviewed** by the admissions committee. |
| Active | If you ask for special consideration because you have worked in the profession, the graduate admissions committee **will review** your request. |

Exercise 30.1 Underline the active or passive verbs in the following paragraph. If a sentence contains a passive, rewrite the sentence to make it active.

| Example | Many kinds of human behavior <u>are</u> now <u>being understood</u> as the products of brain structures by researchers in neuroscience. |
| Rewrite | Researchers in neuroscience now understand many kinds of human behavior as the products of brain structures. |

It has been reported by researchers in neuroscience that food advertising often succeeds because of the structure of our brains. Some people are surprised by this finding. That people buy things they don't need because of advertising has long been rejected by economists. Studies using brain imaging have proven otherwise. When people see and smell their favorite food, a brain structure called the dorsal striatum is stimulated. This brain structure was found to be different from the neural circuits that are stimulated when we are truly hungry. When the dorsal striatum is activated, food is desired to be consumed, even if we are not hungry. Probably the dorsal striatum was important for human survival in past times when food wasn't plentiful. Food needed to be eaten and stored in our bodies for times when food wouldn't be available. But today with food everywhere, an epidemic of obesity is caused by the drive to eat when we aren't hungry.

30c Find Agents

The **agent** is the person or thing that does the action. The most powerful writing usually highlights the agent in a sentence.

Focus on people

Read the following sentence aloud.

> Mayoral approval of the recommended zoning change for a strip mall on Walnut Street will negatively impact the traffic and noise levels of the Walnut Street residential environment.

It sounds dead, doesn't it? Think about the meaning of the sentence for a minute. It involves people—the mayor and the people who live on Walnut Street. Putting those people in the sentence makes it come alive.

With people

> If the mayor approves the recommended zoning change to allow a strip mall on Walnut Street, people who live on the street will have to endure much more noise and traffic.

Identify characters

If people are not your subject, then keep the focus on other types of characters.

Without characters

> The celebration of Martin Luther King Day had to be postponed because of inclement weather.

With characters

> A severe ice storm forced the city to postpone the Martin Luther King Day celebration.

STAYING ON TRACK

Include people

Including people makes your writing more emphatic. Most readers relate better to people than to abstractions. Putting people in your writing also introduces active verbs because people do things.

Without people

> Remembering that the ghosts in the arcade game Pac Man move directly in response to the player's movements can aid greatly in winning the game.

STAYING ON TRACK (*Continued*)

With people

If you remember that the ghosts in the arcade game Pac Man move directly in response to the player's movements, you increase your chances of winning the game.

Exercise 30.2 The following paragraph includes nouns used to express action. Underline all nouns that show action and the *be* verbs they follow. Then rewrite the entire paragraph, changing the underlined nouns to verbs and deleting *be* verbs. More than one set of correct answers is possible.

Example An amputee is likely to have the experience of "phantom limb sensations," as the brain can misinterpret activity from the nervous system.

Rewrite An amputee may feel "phantom limb sensations," as the brain can misinterpret activity from the nervous system.

Though few people celebrate the experience of pain, the human body is dependent on unpleasant impulses for survival. Without pain, an individual is at a disadvantage in terms of self-preservation. When a diseased brain is a failure at communication, the entire body is in jeopardy. Pain is a signal to the body of injured or strained joints, bones, or muscles and is integral in forcing an individual to alter his or her behavior to aid the healing process. Those who are without the ability to sense pain often die by early adulthood, as unchecked infections and injuries overwhelm the body.

Exercise 30.3 In the following paragraph, underline the subject of each sentence. Then rewrite the entire paragraph so that living agents are performing the actions expressed by the verbs.

Example Halloween customs and traditions have been traced back in time to the ancient Druids.

Rewrite Historians have traced Halloween customs back to the times of the ancient Druids.

The observation of these old customs in parts of Europe where the inhabitants are Celtic proves their Druid origin. To mark the beginning of winter, the burning of fires on November 1 was customary. These Halloween fires are lit even today in Scotland and Wales. Also, it was the belief of Druid custom that on the night of November 1, the earth was roamed by such groups as witches, demons, and evil spirits. To greet the beginning of "their season," Halloween was the night when these demons celebrated the long nights and early sunsets of the coming winter. It was important to have fun at the expense of mortals on this night, and to offer treats as appeasement was the only way mortals could stop the evil, demonic tricks. To give these treats became a tradition, which has continued in to modern Halloween celebrations.

Vary Your Sentences

Read the following passage.

> On the first day Garth, Jim, and I paddled fourteen miles down Johnstone Strait. The morning was moist and deceptively calm. We stopped to watch a few commercial fishing boats net salmon on the way. Then we set up camp on a rocky beach. We headed down the strait about five more miles to Robson Bight. It is a famous scratching place for orcas. The Bight is a small bay. We paddled out into the strait so we could see the entire Bight. There were no orcas inside. By this time we were getting tired. We were hungry. The clouds assumed a wintry dark thickness. The wind was kicking up against us. Our heads were down going into the cold spray.

The subject matter is interesting, but the writing isn't. The paragraph is a series of short sentences, one after the other, that have a thumpety-thump, thumpety-thump rhythm. When you have too many short sentences one after the other, try combining a few of them. The result of combining some (but not all) short sentences is a paragraph whose sentences match the interest of the subject.

Revised

> On the first day Garth, Jim, and I paddled fourteen miles down Johnstone Strait on a moist and deceptively calm morning. We stopped to watch a few commercial fishing boats net salmon before we set up camp on a rocky beach and headed down the strait about five more miles to Robson Bight, a small bay known as a famous scratching place for orcas. We paddled out into the strait so we could see the entire Bight, but there were no orcas inside. By this time we were tired and hungry, the clouds had assumed a wintry dark thickness, and the wind was kicking up against us—our heads dropped going into the cold spray.

Ahead of us we heard what sounded like a series of distant shotgun blasts, and when it happened again, we could see the fins of a pod of orcas. We stopped paddling. **The orcas were feeding on the salmon, surfacing at six- to eight-second intervals, coming straight at us, swimming in twos and threes, at least twelve of them, a mix of the long fins of the bulls and the shorter, more rounded fins of the cows, the noise of their exhaling becoming louder and louder.**

30e Give Your Writing Personality

Nobody likes listening to the voice of a robot. Good writing—no matter what the genre—has two unfailing qualities: a human personality that bursts through the page or screen and a warmth that suggests the writer genuinely wishes to engage the readers.

> From age eleven to age sixteen I lived a spartan life without the usual adolescent uncertainty. I wanted to be the best swimmer in the world, and there was nothing else.
>
> —Diana Nyad

> You don't choose your family. They are God's gift to you, as you are to them.
>
> —Desmond Tutu

Sentences like these convince your readers that you are genuinely interested in reaching out to them.

31 | Write Concisely

QUICK*TAKE*

- **How do you eliminate unnecessary words?** (see p. 486)
  Wordy: I was fourteen years of age when my friends and I happened upon the totally abandoned house in the exact middle of the woods.
  Less wordy: I was fourteen when my friends and I happened upon the abandoned house in the middle of the woods.

- **How do you reduce wordy phrases?** (see p. 488)
  Wordy: At that point in time I was of the opinion that I alone amongst all the people in my family of origin recognized the hypocrisy of a bourgeois, middle-class existence.
  Less wordy: At that time, I believed that in my family I alone recognized the hypocrisy of middle-class life.

- **How do you simplify tangled sentences?** (see p. 490)
  Wordy: There were no words exchanged by us as we surveyed the unsettling array of stuff left behind by the house's former occupants.
  Less wordy: Nobody said a word as we surveyed the unsettling array of stuff that the house's former occupants had left behind.

Clutter creeps into our lives every day.

Clutter also creeps into our writing in the form of unnecessary words, inflated constructions, and excessive jargon.

> In regards to the Web site, the content is pretty successful in consideration of the topic. The site is fairly good writing-wise and is very unique in telling you how to adjust the rear derailleur one step at a time.

485

The words in red are clutter. Get rid of the clutter. You can say the same thing with half the words and gain more impact as a result.

> The well-written Web site on bicycle repair provides step-by-step instructions on adjusting your rear derailleur.

31a Eliminate Unnecessary Words

Empty words resemble the foods that add calories without nutrition. Put your writing on a diet.

Redundancy

Some words act as modifiers, but when you look closely at them, they repeat the meaning of the word they pretend to modify. Have you heard expressions such as *red in color, small in size, round in shape, several in number, past history, attractive in appearance, visible to the eye,* or *honest truth?* Imagine *red* not referring to color or *round* not referring to shape.

Legalese

Legal language often attempts to remove ambiguity through repetition and redundancy. For example, think about what a flight attendant says when your plane arrives.

> Please remain seated, with your seatbelt fastened, until the airplane has come to a full and complete stop; when you deplane from the airplane, be sure to take with you all your personal belongings.

Is there a difference between a *full* stop and a *complete* stop? Can you *deplane* from anything but an airplane? Would you have any *nonpersonal* belongings?

Some speech situations like the flight attendant's instructions may require redundancy to ensure that listeners understand, but in writing, say it once.

COMMON ERRORS

Empty intensifiers

Intensifiers modify verbs, adjectives, and other adverbs, and they often are overused. One of the most overused intensifiers is *very*.

The new copper roof was very bright on a sunny day.

A new copper roof reflects almost all light. *Very bright* isn't an accurate description. Another adjective would be more accurate:

The new copper roof was blinding on a sunny day.

Very and *totally* are but two of a list of empty intensifiers that usually can be eliminated with no loss of meaning. Other empty intensifiers include *absolutely, awfully, definitely, incredibly, particularly,* and *really*.

Remember: When you use *very*, *totally*, or another intensifier before an adjective or adverb, always ask yourself whether there is a more accurate adjective or adverb you could use instead to better express the same thought.

For step-by-step discussion, examples, and practice exercises, visit this page of the eText at **www.mycomplab.com**.

Exercise 31.1 The following paragraph is littered with redundant words and phrases. Rewrite wordy sentences to make them concise.

Example ~~Threatening in concept, a~~ black hole is often incorrectly
thought of as an ^threatening^ astronomical force that possesses a pull
so strong ~~in force~~ it can engulf anything in its path.

    Because we cannot visibly see a black hole up close distance-wise, we must use our own imaginations to consider its characteristic properties. For example, imagine taking a jumping leap feet first into a black hole. As you fall, you would descend downward at a slow speed; however, from your personal perception you would seem to be falling faster in speed as time elapsed. In fact, a personal friend observing your downward descent would see that you were in fact moving more and more slowly. In addition, that self-same friend would see that your body was being elongated lengthwise as the center of the black hole pulled more strongly in force on the part of your body which was closest in distance to its center. Simultaneously, your body would begin to start collapsing toward its center, as the forceful force pulled both sides of your body toward the middle of the black hole's center. Unlike in science fiction make-believe, black holes do not serve as either a menacing threat to human life or as a possible means of space or time travel.

Exercise 31.2 In the following paragraph, underline empty intensifiers and the modifiers they intensify. Replace them with more specific and effective modifiers.

Example   The American CIA conducted a <u>very long</u> search for a drug that could serve as a truth serum.

Rewrite   The American CIA conducted an extensive search for a drug that could serve as a truth serum.

In 1942, the American Office of Strategic Services (OSS) Chief William Donovan gathered six incredibly respected scientists to develop a truth serum. The American Psychiatric Association and the Federal Bureau of Narcotics, both very respectable organizations, also participated in this rather secretive search for the truth drug. After definitely varying results and very interesting visions occurred with drugs such as peyote and scopolamine, the group turned to marijuana as a really serious possibility. Creating very different forms of the drug, both strong and diluted, the group tested knowing and unknowing subjects. They tried incredibly unique methods of administering the drug, such as placing a laced gel in foods or injecting a serum into cigars or cigarettes, but they found it very hard to settle on an exact dosage or suitable method. Also, they discovered that individuals did not react very regularly, and the drug could cause a subject to become either absolutely too talkative or particularly quiet. Despite the initial setbacks with marijuana, the American government would really pursue its quest to find a really good substance to serve as a truth serum.

31b Reduce Wordy Phrases

We acquire bad writing and speaking habits because we read and hear so much wordy language. Many inexperienced writers use phrases like "It is my opinion that" or "I think that" to begin sentences. These phrases are deadly to read. If you find them in your prose, cut them. Unless a writer is citing a source, we assume that the ideas are the writer's. (See "When to use *I*" on p. 504.)

Coaches are among the worst in using many words for what could be said in a few:

> After much deliberation about Brown's future in football with regard to possible permanent injuries, I came to the conclusion

that it would be in his best interest not to continue his pursuit of playing football again.

The coach might have said simply:

Because Brown risks permanent injury if he plays football again, I decided to release him from the team.

Perhaps the coach wanted to sound impressive, authoritative, or thoughtful. But the result is the opposite. Speakers and writers who impress us are those who use words efficiently.

STAYING ON TRACK

Replace wordy phrases

Certain stock phrases plague writing in the workplace, in the media, and in academia. Many wordy phrases can be replaced by one or two words with no loss in meaning.

Wordy Within the time period of no more than the past decade, e-mail has replaced handwritten and printed personal letters.

Concise In the past decade e-mail has replaced handwritten and printed personal letters.

Wordy	Concise
at this point in time	now
at that point in time	then
due to the fact that	because
for the purpose of	for
have the ability to	can
in spite of the fact that	although
in the event that	if
in the modern world of today	today
in the neighborhood of	about
it is possible that there might be	possibly
make an attempt	try
met with her approval	she approved
The great writer by the name of Henry David Thoreau	Henry David Thoreau

Exercise 31.3 The following paragraph includes many wordy phrases. Rewrite each sentence to eliminate wordiness. Make sure you retain the original meaning of each sentence.

> Example The parasite ~~that goes by the name of~~ *Cymothoa exigua* is also called the tongue-eating louse.

> *C. exigua* is in the ballpark of 3 to 4 centimeters, or if one prefers 1.2 to 1.6 inches in length. This totally unique parasite makes its way into the body of a fish, specifically the spotted rose snapper, through the gills and works to attach itself at the very base of the aforementioned fish's tongue. The parasite proceeds to extract blood through the claw-like appendages on its front, at this point in time causing the tongue to atrophy. In a very real sense the parasite then replaces the fish's tongue by the action of attaching its own body to the stub of tongue muscle that happens to be left in the fish's mouth. For all intents and purposes, the fish proceeds to use the parasite like a normal tongue. In spite of the fact that the parasite has effectively destroyed the fish's tongue, it does not seem to cause any other damage. Day in and day out, the fish continues to eat normally, and the parasite feeds on the fish's blood. This case of a parasite functionally replacing an organ in its host is the only one known to man.

31c Simplify Tangled Sentences

Long sentences can be graceful and forceful. Such sentences, however, often require several revisions before they achieve elegance. Too often long sentences reflect wandering thoughts that the writer did not bother to go back and sort out. Two of the most important strategies for untangling long sentences are described in Chapter 30: using active verbs (Section 30a) and naming your agents (Section 30c). Here are some other strategies.

Revise expletives

Expletives are empty words that can occupy the subject position in a sentence. The most frequently used expletives are *there is*, *there are*, and *it is*.

> Wordy There is another banking option that gives you free checking.

To simplify the sentence, find the agent and make it the subject.

> Revised Another banking option gives you free checking.

> Wordy There were several important differences between their respective positions raised by the candidates in the debate.

Revised   The candidates raised several important differences
between their respective positions in the debate.

A few kinds of sentences—for example, *It is raining*—do require you
to use an expletive. In most cases, however, expletives add unnecessary
words, and sentences usually read better without them.

Use positive constructions

Sentences become wordy and hard to read when they include two or more
negatives such as the words *no*, *not*, and *nor* and the prefixes *un-* and *mis-*.
For example:

Difficult   A not uncommon complaint among employers of new
                college graduates is that they cannot communicate
                effectively in writing.

Revised   Employers frequently complain that new college
                graduates cannot write effectively.

Even simpler   Employers value the rare college graduate who can
                write well.

Phrasing sentences positively usually makes them more economical.
Moreover, it makes your style more forceful and direct.

Simplify sentence structure

Long sentences can be hard to read, not because they are long but because
they are convoluted and hide the relationships among ideas. Consider the
following sentence.

> Some historians are arguing that World War II actually ended
> with German reunification in 1990 instead of when the Japanese
> surrendered in 1945, after which time the Cold War got in the way
> of formal legal settlements amongst the involved nations and
> Germany was divided between the Western powers and the Soviet
> Union meaning that no comprehensive peace treaty was signed.

This sentence is hard to read. To rewrite sentences like this one, find the
main ideas, then determine the relationships among them.

After examining the sentence, you decide there are two key ideas:

1. Some historians argue that World War II actually ended in 1990
   with German reunification, not when the Japanese surrendered
   in 1945.

2. The Cold War and the division of Germany between the Western powers and the Soviet Union hindered formal legal settlements amongst the involved nations.

Next ask what the relationship is between the two ideas. When you identify the key ideas, the relationship is often obvious; in this case (2) is the cause of (1). Thus the word you want to connect the two ideas is *because.*

> **Because** the Cold War and the division of Germany between the Western powers and the Soviet Union hindered formal legal settlements amongst the involved nations, some historians argue that World War II actually ended in 1990 with German reunification rather than with the Japanese surrender in 1945.

The revised sentence is both clearer and more concise, reducing the number of words from sixty-one to forty-seven.

Exercise 31.4 The following paragraph includes negative constructions and expletives (there is, it is). Rewrite the sentences for clarity and concision. Some expletives may remain.

Example ~~Not unlike~~ *Similar to* anthropology and sociology, paleontology *the discipline of*
~~is an attempt~~ *attempts* to uncover information ~~that is yet unknown~~ about both living things and civilizations.

There are a number of ways fossils can help paleontologists gain additional information about ancient eras. Though not without problems and informational gaps, fossils aid in locating data that are missing regarding location, time, and traits of both past and future organisms. For example, data have been determined by the not uncontested notion of "uniformitarianism," a theory that assumes certain interactions of matter have not been inconsistent throughout time. Because there is this assumption regarding the constancy of certain processes, it is not illogical to believe there is a way by which fossil age and other characteristics may be determined by considering the effects of constant processes on the aged relic. There is controversy in the scientific community, however, regarding the constancy of such scientific processes and interactions.

32 | Write with Emphasis

QUICKTAKE

- **How do you manage emphasis in your sentences?** (see below)
  Main idea unclear: Pluto was once classified as a planet. Now it is classified as a dwarf planet. It does not meet the IAU's official definition of a planet.
  Main idea made clear: Pluto's classification changed from planet to dwarf planet because it does not meet the IAU's official definition of a planet.
- **What is parallelism, and how do you use it correctly?** (see p. 498)
  Not parallel: To be a planet, a celestial body must be in orbit around the Sun, mass must be sufficient to assume a nearly round shape, and enough gravitational force to have no other comparably sized objects in its orbit must be shown.
  Parallel: To be a planet, a celestial body must orbit around the Sun, have sufficient mass to assume a nearly round shape, and show enough gravitational force to have no other comparably sized objects in its orbit.

32a Manage Emphasis in Sentences

Put your main ideas in main clauses

Emphasize your most important information by placing it in main clauses and your less important information in subordinate clauses (for a description of main and subordinate clauses, see Section 35c).

In the following paragraph all the sentences are main clauses.

> Lotteries were common in the United States before and after the American Revolution. They eventually ran into trouble. They were run by private companies. Sometimes the companies took off with the money. They didn't pay the winners.

This paragraph is grammatically correct, but it does not help the reader understand which pieces of information the author wants to emphasize. Combining the simple sentences into main and subordinate clauses and phrases can significantly improve the paragraph.

First, identify the main ideas.

> Lotteries were common in the United States before and after the American Revolution. They eventually ran into trouble.

These ideas can be combined into one sentence.

> Lotteries were common in the United States before and after the American Revolution, but they eventually ran into trouble.

Now think about the relationship of the three remaining sentences to the main ideas. Those sentences explain why lotteries ran into trouble; thus the relationship is *because*.

> Lotteries were common in the United States before and after the American Revolution, but they eventually ran into trouble **because** they were run by private companies that sometimes took off with the money instead of paying the winners.

Put key ideas at the beginning and end of sentences

Read these sentences aloud.

1   The Cottingley Fairies, a series of five photographs taken in 1917 by Elsie Wright and Frances Griffiths, depict the girls interacting with what seem to be fairies.

2   A series of photographs showing two girls interacting with what seem to be fairies known as the Cottingley Fairies, was taken by Elsie Wright and Frances Griffiths in 1917.

3   The series of photos Elsie Wright and Frances Griffiths took in 1917 showing them interacting with what seem to be fairies is called the Cottingley Fairies.

Most readers put the primary emphasis on words at the beginning and end of sentences, usually at the front of a sentence is what is known: the topic. At the end is the new information about the topic. Subordinate information is in the middle. If a paragraph is about the Cottingley Fairies, we would not expect the writer to choose sentence 2 over 1 or 3. In sentence 2, the reference to the Cottingley Fairies is buried in the middle.

Photographs and writing gain energy when they emphasize key ideas.

In visuals

Photographers create emphasis by composing the image to direct the attention of the viewer. Putting people and objects in the foreground and making them stand out against the background gives them emphasis.

In writing

You have many tools for creating emphasis. Writers can design a page to gain emphasis by using headings, white space, type size, color, and boldfacing. Just as important, learning the craft of structuring sentences will empower you to give your writing emphasis.

Exercise 32.1   The following paragraph includes many short sentences. Locate the main and subordinate ideas, and combine groups of sentences into longer, more concise, and clearer sentences. In the revised sentences, underline the main information twice and the subordinate information once.

Example   Muscular Christianity was popular in the late nineteenth
and early twentieth centuries. It focused on regaining
the church for men. It sought to change the image of
Jesus Christ.

(handwritten edits: "P" above "popular"; ", Muscular Christianity sought to regain" inserted; "by changing" inserted)

Rewrite   Popular in the late nineteenth and early twentieth
centuries, Muscular Christianity sought to regain
the church for men by changing the image of Jesus Christ.

American religion was thought of as very feminine in the nineteenth century. It catered to moralism. Some thought it deterred market capitalism. There were more women than men in congregations. Pictures of Jesus Christ portrayed a sickly, effeminate man. Men wanted to reclaim religion. They did not want to aspire to an effeminate God. They wanted to change the image of Jesus. They refocused on Jesus' carpentry. Carpentry was associated with America's self-made man. Billy Sunday was a major spokesman for Muscular Christianity. He was an exprofessional baseball player. He had left baseball. He disapproved of the fact that one did not need morality for success in baseball. He demanded men be manly like Jesus. He was popular. *American Magazine* voted him the eighth greatest man in the United States. This vote was in 1914. This helped to rejuvenate religion. Menwere allowed to be religious. They were also allowed to be strong.

32b Forge Links Across Sentences

When your writing maintains a focus of attention across sentences, the reader can distinguish the important ideas and how they relate to each other. To achieve this coherence, control which ideas occupy the positions of greatest emphasis. The words and ideas you repeat from sentence to sentence act as links.

Link sentences from front to front

In front-to-front linkage, the subject of the sentence remains the focus from one sentence to the next. In the following sequence, sentences 1 through 5 are all about Arthur Wright. The subject in each of sentences 2–5 refers to the first sentence by using the pronouns *he* and *his*.

1   Arthur Wright was one of the first electrical engineers in England.

2   He loaned his camera to his daughter Elsie, who took the fairy pictures in the yard behind their house.

3   His opinion was that the pictures were fake.

4   However, his wife Polly was convinced that they were real.

5   Nevertheless, he banned Elsie from ever using his camera again.

Each sentence adds more information about the repeated topic, Arthur Wright.

Link sentences from back to front

In back-to-front linkage, the new information at the end of the sentence is used as the topic of the next sentence. Back-to-front linkage allows new material to be introduced and commented on.

1   By summer of 1919, the girls and their photographs had become so well known that author Sir Arthur Conan Doyle even wrote an article for a leading magazine claiming that the photos and the fairies were real.

2   Not everyone believed that the Cottingley Fairies were authentic, however, and other public figures wrote the papers calling the photographs a hoax.

3   The hoax continued until the 1980s when both Elsie and Frances finally admitted that all but one of the pictures were fake.

Back-to-front linkage is useful when ideas need to be advanced quickly, as when you are telling stories. Rarely, however, will you use either front-to-front linkage or back-to-front linkage for long. You will mix them, using front-to-front linkage to add more information and back-to-front linkage to move the topic along.

STAYING ON TRACK

Check links across sentences

Where in the following paragraph is your attention disrupted?

In February 1888, Vincent van Gogh left cloudy Paris for Arles in the sunny south of France. Later that year he persuaded fellow painter Paul Gauguin to join him. Gauguin, who had traveled in the tropics, did not find Arles colorful and exotic. Critics hail this period as the most productive in van Gogh's brilliant but short career.

(Continued on next page)

> ## STAYING ON TRACK *(Continued)*
>
> The last sentence connects distantly with what has come before by mentioning art and van Gogh, but it jars you when you read it because new information, "critics," comes where we expect to find known information. Adding a clause provides a bridge between the old and new information.
>
> > In February 1888, Vincent van Gogh left cloudy Paris for Arles in the sunny south of France. Later that year he persuaded fellow painter Paul Gauguin to join him. Gauguin, who had traveled in the tropics, did not find Arles colorful and exotic. **Although van Gogh and Gauguin argued and soon parted company,** critics hail this period as the most productive in van Gogh's brilliant but short career.

32c Use Parallel Structure with Parallel Ideas

What if Patrick Henry had written "Give me liberty or I prefer not to live"? Would we remember those words today? We do remember the words he did write: "Give me liberty or give me death." Writers who use parallel structure often create memorable sentences.

Use parallelism with *and, or, nor, but*

When you join elements at the same level with coordinating conjunctions, including *and, or, nor, yet, so, but,* and *for,* use parallel grammatical structure.

Awkward

> In today's global economy, the method of production and where factories are located has become relatively unimportant in comparison with the creation of new concepts and marketing those concepts.

Parallel

> In today's global economy, how goods are made and where they are produced has become relatively unimportant in comparison with creating new concepts and marketing those concepts.

COMMON ERRORS

e <u>E</u>dit He<u>l</u>p

Faulty parallel structure

When writers neglect to use parallel structure, the result can be jarring. Reading your writing aloud will help you catch problems in parallelism. Read this sentence aloud.

> At our club meeting we identified problems in finding new members, publicizing our activities, and maintenance of our Web site.

The end of the sentence does not sound right because the parallel structure is broken. We expect to find another verb + *ing* following *finding* and *publicizing*. Instead, we run into *maintenance*, a noun. The problem is easy to fix: Change the noun to the *-ing* verb form.

> At our club meeting we identified problems in finding new members, publicizing our activities, and maintaining our Web site.

Remember: Use parallel structure for parallel ideas.

For step-by-step discussion, examples, and practice exercises, visit this page of the eText at **www.mycomplab.com.**

Use parallelism with *either/or, not only/but*

Make identical in structure the parts of sentences linked by correlative conjunctions: *either . . . or, neither . . . nor, not only . . . but also, whether . . . or.*

Awkward

> Purchasing the undeveloped land **not only** gives us a new park **but also** is something that our children will benefit from in the future.

Parallel

> Purchasing the undeveloped land **not only** will give our city a new park **but also** will leave our children a lasting inheritance.

The more structural elements you match, the stronger the effect.

Correct

> Either we find a way to recruit new members or we settle for the current number of sailboats.

Improved

Either we find a way to recruit new members or we drop the plan to increase our fleet.

The first sentence is correct but still clunky. The parallelism is limited to *we find/we settle*. The second sentence delivers more punch by extending the parallelism: *we find a way to recruit new members/we drop the plan to increase our fleet.* Matching structural elements exactly—verb for verb, article for article, adjective for adjective, object for object—provides the strongest parallelism.

Exercise 32.2 The following paragraph contains many examples of non-parallel sentence structure. Find the faulty constructions and either delete them or replace them with parallel constructions, as necessary.

Example A "dark ride" is an indoor amusement ride where visitors ride through specially lit scenes featuring sound, animation, music, and ~~sometimes~~ special effects ~~are used~~.

The first dark rides were built in the late 19th century and using small boats to carry riders through water-filled canals. These rides were called "scenic railways" or they were described as pleasure railways. A dark ride does not have to be dark, but ride mechanisms are hidden by dark, and the drama of the ride is enhanced by the dark. Most do use special lighting to create effects but there are wide variations in how they use it. Smaller-scale rides often use the same simple animation and sounds used since the early days, while more complex multimedia effects and unconventional vehicles are used by others. The tunnels of dark rides either curve and bend frequently to surprise the rider or they may excite the rider with sudden ascents or descents. Both Disneyland's Haunted Mansion and another ride known as It's a Small World are well known dark rides.

32d Use Parallel Structure with Lists

Lists are frequently used in visual aids for oral presentations and in announcements, brochures, instructions, and other kinds of writing. The effectiveness of a bulleted list is lost, however, when the items are not in parallel form. In a list of action items, such as a list of goals, beginning each item with a verb emphasizes the action. See the example below.

Sailing Club goals

- Increase the membership by 50% this year
- Compete in all local regattas
- Offer beginning and advanced classes
- Purchase eight new Flying Juniors
- Organize a spring banquet
- Publicize all major events

Exercise 32.3 You're invited to Howard's party on Saturday. The following directions to Howard's house contain several examples of faulty parallelism. Revise the directions, making the structure of each parallel to the first entry.

Directions to Howard's

1. Turn left onto Route 22 N at the end of Maple Street.
2. You'll come to the Dewdrop Inn after following Route 22 N 3 miles.
3. There's a sharp right turn onto Geoffrey Drive at the fourth traffic signal after the Dewdrop.
4. The red mailbox you're looking for is halfway down the block.
5. Directly across from the mailbox there's a driveway—turn in there.
6. You can reverse the directions and follow them to come home.

32e Use Parallel Structure in Paragraphs

Use parallelism to create rhythm

Parallel structure does not have to be used in rigid, mechanical ways. Repeating elements of structure can build a rhythm that gives your prose a distinctive voice.

> If you don't like my book, write your own. If you don't think you can write a novel, that ought to tell you something. If you think you can, do.
>
> —Rita Mae Brown, from *A Note*

Use parallel structure to pair ideas

Parallel structure is also useful to pair ideas. The closer the similarity in structure, the more emphasis you will achieve.

> Being a grown-up means assuming responsibility for yourself, for your children, and—here's the big curve—for your parents. In other words, you do get to stay up later, but you want to go to sleep sooner.

—Wendy Wasserstein, from *Bachelor Girls*

■ Parallel structure in images also creates emphasis. Notice how the horse and the groom have a parallel stance—both tense, both with knees bent, both looking away—connected only by the hand on the rein.

33 | Find the Right Words

QUICKTAKE

- **How do you choose the right level of formality?** (see below)
  Informal: The reporter was all up in Senator Grimes's face about the scandal.
  Formal, college writing: The reporter confronted Senator Grimes about the scandal.
- **How do you choose the right words?** (see p. 507)
  Imprecise and incorrect: The senator said he had received bad council from someone.
  More precise and correct: Senator Grimes admitted accepting bad counsel from his financial advisor.
- **What is figurative language, and how can you use it in your writing?** (see p. 510)
  Literal: Senator Grimes was very nervous under the scrutiny of the press.
  Figurative: Senator Grimes melted under the scrutiny of the press.

Be Aware of Levels of Formality

Colloquialisms

Colloquialisms are words or expressions that are used informally, often in conversation but less often in writing.

> I'm not happy with my grades, but that's the way the cookie crumbles.

> I've had it up to here with all of Tom's complaining.

> Liz is always running off at the mouth about something.

Aside from carrying meanings that aren't always obvious to your reader, colloquialisms usually indicate a lack of seriousness that runs counter to what you'll be trying to accomplish in most academic and professional writing. Colloquialisms can suggest a flippant attitude, carelessness, or even thoughtlessness.

College writing does not mean, however, that you should try to use big words when small ones will do as well, or that you should use ten words instead of two.

Slang

The most conspicuous kind of language to be avoided in most college writing is slang. The next time a friend talks to you, listen closely to the words he or she uses. Chances are you will notice several words that you probably would not use in a college writing assignment. Slang words are created by and for a particular group—even if that group is just you and your friend.

> Joey's new ride is totally pimped out.

> The party was bumpin' with all my peeps.

Aside from being a fun way to play with language, slang asserts a sense of belonging to a group. But because slang excludes those who are not members of the group, it is best avoided in college writing.

STAYING ON TRACK

When to use *I*

You may have been taught to avoid the first person (*I, we*) in academic and professional writing. Some instructors feel that first-person references reflect a self-indulgence that is inappropriate outside of autobiography. Sentences beginning with *I* refer to the author and make him or her the subject. In a sentence such as *I think Florida's west coast beaches are better in every way than those on the east coast*, the reader's attention is divided between the beaches and the person evaluating the beaches.

Another reason some instructors prohibit use of the first person is the tendency of writers to overuse it. Some writers feel that nothing can be invalidated as long as each potentially arguable assertion starts with *I think* or *I feel*. I becomes a shield, which the writer uses to escape the work of building an argument.

Occasionally, the use of *I* is redundant. In the following sentence, the nature of the assertion clearly indicates that it's the writer's opinion:

Redundant *I*   I think the Panama Canal is the greatest engineering achievement of the United States.

Here you can safely drop *I think* without changing the sentence's meaning. Sometimes, however, you will want to indicate plainly that an assertion is tentative. *I* is critical to the meaning of this sentence:

Tentative *I*   I thought that the dim, distant light was a planet.

If you're unsure whether or not the first-person references are permissible, ask you instructor.

Exercise 33.1 Richard Chen wrote the following note to thank an acquaintance for meeting with him to talk about how she got started in her career. How would the language of the note change if Richard were writing a letter to a potential employer, thanking her for a similar meeting? Rewrite the note, making the potential employer the audience. Note how eliminating colloquialisms changes a letter's level of formality.

> Dear Rayna,
>
> It was really awesome of you to meet with me to chat about your editing gig. And, thanks for spotting me the coffee, girl; I owe you a solid.
>
> Anyway, I have to make a confession. I always had the impression that all editors were total wallflowers who got all fired up about boring stuff like comma placement. Yawn! But you blew my mind! For one, I had no idea that there were so many different types of editing. And, I didn't know that you could work on such interesting stuff. Finally (and this is really embarrassing...yipes!), I thought that you had to work your way up, like, you start out as a proofreader, then you get better and become an editor, and then when you get really good you become a writer. I'm sorry if I rubbed you the wrong way with that one—my bad!
>
> At any rate, I really learned a lot from our little talk, and let me know if any jobs open up at your place.
>
> See ya,
> RC

Exercise 33.2 The following paragraph was taken from a rough draft of a research paper for an environmental ecology class. The instructor asked the writer to eliminate any use of first person, colloquial language, unnecessarily big words, and wordiness. Use the advice from this section to revise the paragraph according to the instructor's comments.

Example Many geologists and conservationists in the United States have views that are diametrically opposed on whether to support or fight mining and commercialization in sacrosanct public acreage.

Rewrite Many U.S. geologists and conservationists disagree on whether to mine or commercialize public lands.

David Brower, who died in 2000, was a person who was the president of the American wilderness preservation club called the

Sierra Club. As this organization's preeminent leader he was the human personification of preservation. Brower took a no-holds-barred approach to fighting the infidels of mining and tourism in America's wilderness areas. I think his most perspicacious campaign against these factors that threaten the wilderness must have been when he published an ad to fight the commercialization of the Grand Canyon. His placement of newspaper advertisements telling people about plans to open businesses at the base of the canyon deterred this development. I think that most who believe in conservation would agree that these achievements make David Brower a hero for the American environment.

33b Be Aware of Denotation and Connotation

Words have both literal meanings, called **denotations**, and associated meanings, called **connotations**. The contrast is evident in words that mean roughly the same thing but have different connotations. For example, some people are set in their opinions, a quality that can be described positively as *persistent*, *firm*, and *steadfast* or negatively as *stubborn*, *bull-headed*, and *close-minded*.

In college and professional writing, writers are expected not to rely on the connotations of words to make important points. For example, the statement *It's only common sense to have good schools* carries high positive connotations but is not precise enough for college writing. Most people believe in common sense, and most people want good schools. What is common sense for one person, however, is not common sense for another; how a good school is defined varies greatly. You have the obligation in college writing to support any judgment with evidence.

Exercise 33.3 The following sets of words have negative connotations. Replace each set with (a) two words that each have a similar denotative meaning but a positive connotation, and (b) one word that has a similar denotative meaning but a neutral connotation. If you are unsure of the meaning of a word, use a dictionary.

1. skinny, gaunt, emaciated, bony, skeletal
2. cacophony, discord, racket, clamor
3. drudge, workaholic, plodder, drone
4. flakey, indecisive, wishy-washy, dithering
5. stubborn, pig-headed, inflexible, obstinate

Use Specific Language

Be precise

Effective writing conveys information clearly and precisely. Words such as *situation*, *sort*, *thing*, *aspect*, and *kind* often signal undeveloped or even lazy thinking.

Vague   The violence aspect determines how video games are rated.

Better   The level of violence determines how video games are rated.

When citing numbers or quantities, be as exact as possible. A precise number, if known, is always better than slippery words like *several* or *many*, which some writers use to cloak the fact that they don't know the quantity in question. If you know an approximate quantity, indicate the quantity but qualify it: *about twenty-five* tells readers much more than *many*.

Use a dictionary

There is no greater tool for writers than the dictionary. When you write always have a dictionary handy—either a book or an online version—and get into the habit of using it. In addition to checking spelling, you can find additional meanings of a word that perhaps you had not considered, and you can find the etymology—the origins of a word. In many cases knowing the etymology of a word can help you use it to better effect. For example, if you want to argue that universities as institutions have succeeded because they bring people together in contexts that prepare them for their lives after college, you might point out the etymology of *university*. *University* can be traced back to the late Latin word *universitas*, which means "society or guild," thus emphasizing the idea of a community of learning.

COMMON ERRORS

Words often confused

Words with different meanings that are pronounced in the same way are called **homonyms**. Be particularly careful that you select the correct one. These pairs can cause confusion.

bare—unadorned
bear—(1) an animal; (2) to carry

capital—(1) government seat; (2) material wealth; (3) uppercase letter
capitol—a building housing a government seat

(Continued on next page)

COMMON ERRORS *(Continued)*

cite—(1) to make mention of; (2) to quote as an example
sight—something seen
site—place, location

coarse—rough
course—plotted-out site or matter

counsel—(1) advice; (2) lawyer; (3) to advise
council—a deliberative body

complement—to go with, as in That tie complements that suit.
compliment—to flatter

fair—(1) just; (2) carnival
fare—(1) ticket price; (2) to get along

hear—to listen to
here—location

passed—went by
past—time before the present

patience—the state of calmly waiting
patients—people receiving medical care

peace—serenity
piece—a part of

plain—(1) simple; (2) level land
plane—(1) short for airplane; (2) level surface; (3) carpenter's tool

principal—(1) head of an organization; (2) a sum of money
principle—a basic law or guideline

wear—(1) to don clothes; (2) to erode
where—location

weather—climatic condition
whether—if

Other words do not sound exactly alike, only similar. The words in the following pairs are frequently confused:

accept—to receive
except (as preposition)—excluding

advice—a suggestion
advise—to suggest

affect—to act upon or to have an effect on something or somebody
effect—a change caused by an action

allude—to make reference to
elude—to evade

(Continued on next page)

COMMON ERRORS *(Continued)*

allusion—an indirect reference
illusion—a false impression

conscience—moral compass
conscious—aware

continually—(1) consistently; (2) regularly
continuously—without stopping

desert—(1) geographical feature; (2) to abandon
dessert—sweet snack

elicit—to bring out
illicit—unlawful

loose—not tight
lose—(1) to misplace; (2) to fail to win a game

personal—(1) individual; (2) private
personnel—staff

presence—opposite of absence
presents—(1) gifts; (2) introduces

respectfully—demonstrating respect
respectively—in the given order

Remember: Use a dictionary to check that you are using the right word.

 For step-by-step discussion, examples, and practice exercises, visit this page of the eText at **www.mycomplab.com**.

Exercise 33.4 This paragraph, from a research paper about space exploration, contains vague and incorrect language. Revise it to eliminate vague language, misused homonyms, and misused sound alike words. Information needed to eliminate vague language is included in parentheses.

Example   Astronauts have been exploiting space for quite a few years now.

Rewrite   Astronauts have been exploring space since at least the 1960s.

Space missions can adversely affect an astronaut's health. A more than minor culprit is the lack of gravity in space; one of the affects that weightlessness has on astronauts is that it causes bone loss, which might be really bad. A sort-of older (45) astronaut may have such serious bone deterioration that after a mission, her bones resemble those of an old lady (like an 80-year-old). Other continuous effects are the interruption of sleeping patterns and the deterioration of the immune system and mussels. But perhaps the scariest affect sited by experts is radiation exposure, especially during visits to Mars. None knows what the cancer risks from this exposure might be.

Exercise 33.5 Circle the correct word in parentheses in the following paragraph. Look up the words in a dictionary if you are not sure of their meaning.

Butchering a hog requires (patience, patients) and hard work. First, find a (cite, sight, site) outside (wear, where) you will have plenty of space. After killing the pig, dunk it in hot water to loosen the (coarse, course) hair. Scrape the hair with a knife (continually, continuously) until the skin is completely (bare, bear). Thread a gambling stick (threw, through) the hamstrings, and hang the pig head-down from a post. Remove the head, cut down the length of the underbelly, and remove the organs. Then cut down the length of the spine and remove the tenderloin, fatback, ribs, middlin' meat, shoulders, and hams (respectfully, respectively). While some people are squeamish about eating hogs' heads and organs, in (principal, principle) nearly every part of the animal is edible.

33d Use Effective Figurative Language

Figurative language—figures of speech that help readers get a more vivid sense of an object or idea—is what you use when literal descriptions seem insufficient.

Literal   The prosecutor presented a much stronger legal case than did the defense attorney.

Figurative   The prosecutor took the defense attorney apart like a dollar watch.

The two most common figures of speech are the simile and the metaphor. A **simile** usually begins with *as* or *like*, and makes an explicit comparison.

In the past talking about someone's children was like talking about the weather.

Metaphor is from a Greek term that means "carry over," which describes what happens when you encounter a metaphor: You carry over the meaning from one word to another. Metaphor makes a comparison without using *like* or *as*.

> She reached the pinnacle of her profession.

> [highest point ────────▶ best]

Two other forms of figurative language are **synecdoche**, in which the part is used to represent the whole (a hood ornament that represents a car) and **metonymy**, in which something related stands in for the thing itself (*White House* for the executive branch; *brass* for military officers).

If not used imaginatively, figurative language merely dresses up a literal description in fancy clothes without adding to the reader's understanding of the object or idea. The purpose of figurative language is to convey information vividly to help the reader grasp your meaning.

You'll want to avoid **clichés**, which are relics of figurative language, phrases used so often that they have become tired and stripped of meaning. Among countless others, the following expressions have hardened into clichés.

better late than never	out like a light
blind as a bat	playing with fire
easier said than done	pride and joy
hard as a rock	thin as a rail
ladder of success	water under the bridge
nutty as a fruitcake	wise as an owl

STAYING ON TRACK

Think fresh

You might find yourself resorting to clichés when you're low on inspiration or energy. Read your drafts aloud to yourself to identify clichés, listening for the phrases that you've used or heard before. Make a note of them and either change the clichés to literal description or, better still, create fresh new phrases to convey what you were trying to say with the cliché.

Cliché

> When we entered the old café with the screen door banging behind us, we knew we stood out like a sore thumb.

Specific

> When we entered the old café with the screen door banging behind us, we knew we stood out like our hybrid Prius in the parking lot full of pickup trucks.

Exercise 33.6 The following paragraph is filled with clichés. Underline each cliché and replace it with fresh language.

Example Cephalopods are a group of marine mollusks that many Americans would not touch with a ten-foot pole.

Rewrite Cephalopods are a group of marine mollusks that many Americans find distasteful.

However, in Japan and in the Mediterranean, squid, octopus, and cuttlefish are an important food source and sell like hot cakes. Unfortunately, myths about giant squid sinking boats and octopus drowning swimmers persist in the United States, and information that giant squid are weak as kittens and that an octopus has never drowned anyone falls on deaf ears. The Japanese attitude is a step in the right direction; they see the octopus as a cheerful, friendly creature and often use its image as a toy or mascot. Our culinary pleasures could grow by leaps and bounds if more of us opened our minds to the joys of fried calamari dipped in marinara sauce and squid sushi with plenty of wasabi. We need to wake up and smell the coffee in the United States that cephalopods are an underexploited marine resource.

34 | Write to Be Inclusive

QUICKTAKE

- **How do you avoid stereotypical assumptions?** (see below)
  Stereotype: Like all Southern men, the author was fiercely loyal to his mother.
  Stereotype avoided: The author was fiercely loyal to his mother.
- **How can you be inclusive about gender?** (see p. 514)
  Not inclusive: Who will be manning the information booth this year?
  More inclusive: Who will be staffing the information booth this year?
- **How can you be inclusive about race, ethnicity, and other differences?** (see p. 516)
  Not inclusive: He was raised in the usual large, Irish Catholic family.
  More inclusive: He was raised in a large family.

While the conventions of language change continually, three guidelines for inclusive language toward all groups remain constant.

- Do not point out people's differences unless those differences are relevant to your argument.
- Call people whatever they prefer to be called.
- When given a choice of terms, choose the more accurate one.

34a Be Aware of Stereotypes

Reject stereotypes

A **stereotype** makes an assumption about a group of people by applying a characteristic to all of them based on the knowledge of only a few of them. The idea that Asian women are submissive, for instance, is a stereotype; it tries to apply one personality trait to many individuals whose only shared characteristics are their gender and ethnicity. Such a stereotype is just as ridiculous as a belief that all Idahoans are potato farmers.

Of course you want to avoid obviously harmful (not to mention inaccurate) stereotypes such as *People on welfare are lazy, gays are effeminate,* or *NASCAR fans are rednecks.* More subtle stereotypes, however, may be harder to identify and eliminate from your writing. If you want to offer an engineer as an example, will you make the engineer a man? If you want your reader to envision a child living in subsidized housing, will you describe the child as an African American? Instead of using these examples that perpetuate stereotypes, try to choose cases that go against them.

Watch for assumptions about what's "normal"

Assumptions about what's "normal" or "regular" can create bias. Calling one person or group "normal" implies that others are abnormal.

Problematic norm

> Gloria Nuñez isn't like the regular sprinters at the Greater Detroit Meet; while other runners gingerly settle their feet into the blocks, Nuñez plants her prosthetic foot in the block and waits for the starting gun.

Better

> Gloria Nuñez is one sprinter at the Greater Detroit Meet who might surprise you; while other runners gingerly settle their feet into the blocks, Nuñez plants her prosthetic foot in the block and waits for the starting gun.

Exercise 34.1 Identify your pet peeves in writing. Do you have any words or phrases that you find unnecessary, annoying, or wrong? Write down as many of them as possible. Then, consider where and how you acquired the negative attitudes toward them.

Bring the list of your pet peeves and the sources of your attitudes. Then, discuss with your classmates when those words and phrases may be useful or appropriate.

34b Be Inclusive About Gender

Gender is a term that refers to the social designations of men, women, and their sexual orientations.

Avoid exclusive nouns and pronouns

Don't use masculine nouns and pronouns to refer to both men and women. *He, his, him, man,* and *mankind* are outmoded and inaccurate terms for both genders.

- Don't say *boy* when you mean *child.*
- Use *men and women* or *people* instead of *man.*
- Use *humanity* or *humankind* in place of *mankind.*

Eliminating *he, his,* and *him* when referring to both men and women is more complicated. Many readers consider *he/she* to be an awkward alternative. Try one of the following approaches instead.

- Make the noun and its corresponding pronoun plural. The pronoun will change from *he, him,* or *his* to *they, them,* or *theirs.*

  ### Biased masculine pronouns

  An undercover agent won't reveal his identity, even to other agents, if he thinks it will jeopardize the case.

  ### Better

  Undercover agents won't reveal their identities, even to other agents, if they think it will jeopardize the case.

- Replace the pronoun with another word.

  ### Biased masculine pronoun

  Anyone who wants to rent scuba gear must have his certification.

  ### Better

  Anyone who wants to rent scuba gear must have diver certification.

Use gender-neutral names for professions

Professional titles that indicate gender—*chairman, waitress*—falsely imply that the gender of the person doing the job changes the essence of the job being done. Terms like *woman doctor* and *male nurse* imply that a woman working as a doctor and a man working as a nurse are abnormal. Instead, write simply *doctor* and *nurse.*

Biased, gender-specific	Better, gender-neutral
chairman	chair, chairperson
clergyman	member of the clergy
congressman	representative or senator
fireman	firefighter
foreman	supervisor
hostess	host
mailman	mail carrier
manpower	personnel, staff
policeman	police officer
salesman	salesperson
stewardess	flight attendant
waitress	server
weatherman	meteorologist
workmen	workers

Eliminate bias when writing about sexual orientation

Sexual orientation refers to a person's identification as bisexual, heterosexual, homosexual, or transsexual. *Heterosexual* and *homosexual* carry a somewhat clinical connotation. Referring to people who are homosexual as *gays* can lead to confusion: It sometimes connotes men and women, sometimes just men. Instead, use *gay men* and *lesbians*. Again, the principle is to use terms that individuals in specific groups prefer.

34c Be Inclusive About Race and Ethnicity

Use the terms for racial and ethnic groups that the groups use for themselves. Use *black* to write about members of the Black Coaches' Association and *African American* to write about members of the Society for African American Brotherhood. Avoid outdated terms like *Negro*.

If you are still in doubt, err on the side of specificity. For instance, while *Latino(a)*, *Hispanic*, and *Chicano(a)* are all frequently accepted terms for many people, a term that identifies a specific country (*Mexican* or *Puerto Rican*) would be more accurate. *Asian* is currently preferred over *Oriental*; however, terms like *Vietnamese* and *Japanese* are even more specific. Also, *English* and *British* are different. The people who live in England are English, but people from elsewhere in Great Britain—Scotland, Wales, Northern Ireland—will be quick to tell you that they are not English. Call people from Wales *Welsh* and those from Scotland *Scots*.

When discussing an American's heritage, often the best term to use is the country of origin plus the word *American*, as in *Swedish American* or *Mexican American* (note that these terms are not hyphenated). Currently *black* and *African American* are acceptable. Some people prefer *Native American* over *American Indian*, but both terms are used. In Canada the preferred name for indigenous peoples is *First Peoples* (or Inuit for those who live in the far north). First Peoples is increasingly used by indigenous peoples in the United States in solidarity with their Canadian relatives. If you are writing about specific people, use the name of the specific American or Canadian Indian group (Cree, Hopi, Mi'kmaq, Ute).

34d Be Inclusive About Other Differences

Writing about people with disabilities

The *Publication Manual of the American Psychological Association* (6th ed.) offers good advice about putting people first, not their disability (76). Write *people who are deaf* instead of *the deaf* and *a student who is quadriple-*

gic instead of *a quadriplegic student.* Discuss *a woman who uses a wheelchair,* not *a wheelchair-bound woman.* Don't reduce people to their deficiencies.

Writing about people of different ages

Avoid bias by choosing accurate terms to describe age. If possible, use the person's age rather than an adjective, like *elderly* or *older,* which might offend. *Eighty-two-year-old Adele Schumacher* is better than *elderly Adele Schumacher* or *Adele Schumacher, an older resident.*

Writing about people of different religions

Avoid making assumptions about someone's beliefs or practices based on religious affiliation. Even though the Vatican opposes capital punishment, many Roman Catholics support it. Likewise, not all Jewish men wear yarmulkes. The tremendous variation within religions and among individual practitioners makes generalizations questionable.

Exercise 34.2 Read the descriptions of situations below and decide if inclusive language is or is not being used in each. If it is not, explain why. Then, explain how the language might be made more inclusive.

- A humor writer jokes about how nervous he is going to his lady doctor.
- A principal speaks to the school board about purchasing new materials to help teach the increasing number of Vietnamese children in her school.
- A writer for a liberal political blog calls Catholic beliefs about birth control "medieval."
- A comedian refers to some audience members as Afro-Americans.
- A reporter asks a runner who uses a specially designed prosthetic leg how it feels to race against normal runners.
- A talk show host jokes about bigoted white men.
- An interviewer asks an artist how her art reflects her Hispanic heritage.
- A caller to a radio show argues that a clergyman shouldn't advise married couples unless he is also married.

34e Recognize International Varieties of English

English today comes in various shapes and forms. Many applied linguists now speak of "World Englishes" in the plural, to highlight the diversity of the English language as it is used worldwide. English has long been established as the dominant language in Australia, Canada, New Zealand, the United Kingdom, and the United States, although many people in those countries also speak other languages at home and in their communities. Englishes used in these countries share many characteristics, but there also are differences in sentence structures, vocabulary, spelling, and punctuation. For example:

British English	Have you got your ticket?
U.S. English	Do you have your ticket?

British English	What's the price of petrol (petroleum) these days?
U.S. English	What's the price of gas (gasoline) these days?

Newer varieties of English have emerged outside of traditionally English-speaking countries. Many former British and U.S. colonies—Hong Kong, India, Malaysia, Nigeria, Papua New Guinea, the Philippines, Singapore, and others—continue to use a local variety of English for both public and private communication. Englishes used in many of these countries are based primarily on the British variety, but they also include many features that reflect the local context.

Indian English	Open the air conditioner.
U.S. English	Turn on the air conditioner.

Indian English	They're late always.
U.S. English	They're always late.

Philippine English	You don't only know.
U.S. English	You just don't realize.

Philippine English	I had seen her yesterday.
U.S. English	I saw her yesterday.

Singaporean English	I was arrowed to lead the discussion.
U.S. English	I was selected to lead the discussion.

Singaporean English	I am not sure what is it.
U.S. English	I am not sure what it is.

Remember that what is correct differs from one variation of English to another.

STAYING ON TRACK

Stereotypical images

Most Americans now realize that overtly racist images are offensive. The notable exception to this awareness is representations of American Indians. American Indian mascots used by college and professional sports teams have long been controversial. Most were adopted in the early decades of the twentieth century when European Americans enjoyed putting on paint and feathers and "playing Indian." Supporters of the mascots claim that they honor American Indians. Critics argue that the mascots perpetuate stereotypes of American Indians as primitive, wild, and bellicose. Furthermore, fans of schools that compete with those that have Indian mascots often create derogatory images of American Indians.

■ Sign over a service station in New Mexico

Subtle stereotyping comes through the media. Based on images in the news media, many Americans think that women in Islamic countries cover their faces in public, but this practice is typical only in Saudi Arabia and the most conservative sectors of Islamic society. While some people in Holland still wear wooden shoes, wooden shoes are hardly everyday Dutch footwear.

Exercise P7.1   The following passage contains several errors. These errors include errors in voice, agency, repetitive sentence structure, empty intensifiers, wordy phrases, tangled sentences, emphasis, parallelism, and easily confused words. Use the Common Errors guide inside the back cover of the book and information from Part 7 to help identify the errors and rewrite the passage.

In the activity known as competitive eating, participants compete against each other to consume large quantities of food in a short amount of time. Each eating competition is usually around 15 minutes, and the eater

who consumes the most food in that time, also known as a "gurgitator," wins. Up to $10,000 can be won in a professional competition.

Competitive eating arose from eating contests at county fares. These contests usually involve pie, hotdogs, and other fair foods. The annual Nathan's Hot Dog Eating Contest in Coney Island, another forerunner of competitive eating, has been held on July 4 almost every year since 1916. The televised coverage of the Nathan's competition is claimed to be responsible for the recent spike in popularity of competitive eating. Takeru Kobayashi and Joey Chesnut are a few superstars who have made their names at this competition. Kobayashi won the competition consistently from 2001 through 2006. He was beaten by Chesnut in 2007. Chestnut and Kobayashi tied at 59 hot dogs in 10 minutes in 2008. Chesnut one the subsequent overtime "eatoff."

A master of ceremonies presides over competitive eating contests to announce the competitors, and keeping the audience engaged with witty commentary. Judges also enforce the contest rules, the results of the contest are certified by them, and they announce the winner.

There are a few terms very unique to competitive eating. One term is "chipmunking," which is when an eater attempts to put as much food as possible in his or her mouth. This happens during the final countdown. Another term is "dunking," which is the practice of dunking food in water or other liquids to soften it, making it easier to chew and in swallowing. Dunking works most best with foods served in a bun. Dunking is an excepted practice in general, but chipmunking is not aloud always.

There is an expectation that eaters will keep their immediate space fairly clean during the contest. If an eater fails to do this, he or she may have points deducted from the final score. Also, if an eater vomits at any time during or immediately after the contest, he or she will be disqualified.

Understanding Grammar

You **can learn more and do more** with
MyCompLab and with the eText version of
The Penguin Handbook. To find resources in
MyCompLab that will help you use grammar
successfully, go to

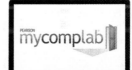

Resources

Grammar

> **Basic Grammar**

Adjectives and Adverbs | Articles | Conjunctions
Negatives and Double Negatives | Nouns |
Participles | Parts of Speech | Prepositions |
Pronouns | Quotations | Verb Form | Verb Tenses |
Verbs | Voice (active and passive)

> **Sentence Grammar**

Clauses and Phrases | Comma Splices |
Compound Sentences | Coordination and
Subordination | Fragments | Subjects and Verbs |
Misplaced and Dangling Modifiers | Objects |
Pronoun Reference and Pronoun Agreement |
Run-On Sentences | Avoiding Shifts | Transitional
Expressions

Review the Instruction and Multimedia resources within
each topic, then complete the Exercises and click on the
Gradebook to measure your progress.

In the **eText version** of *The Penguin Handbook*, you will also find extra
instruction, examples and practice exercises.

35 | Grammar Basics

QUICK*TAKE*

- **What are the parts of a sentence?** (see below)
  Subject: Hippopotamuses (noun)
  Predicate: kill (main verb) more humans (direct object) than any other African mammal (prepositional phrase).
- **What are phrases and clauses, and how can you tell the difference?** (see p. 533)
  Clause: Hippos will open their mouths wide
  Phrase: to warn other creatures to stay away.
- **What are the types of sentences?** (see p. 538)
  Simple: Hippos are vegetarian.
  Compound: Hippos are vegetarian, but they will attack other animals.
  Complex: Hippos attack other animals when they feel threatened.
  Compound-complex: Hippos may look fat and slow when they are on land, but a fully grown hippo can easily outrun a person

35a Sentence Basics

Sentences are the basic units in writing. Many people think of a sentence as a group of words that begins with a capital letter and ends with a period, but that definition includes grammatically incomplete sentences called **fragments** (see Section 36a).

Subjects and predicates

Regular sentences must have a subject and a predicate that includes a main verb. Typically the subject announces what the sentence is about, and the predicate says something about that subject or conveys the action of the subject.

Subject	Predicate
I	**want** a new iPhone.
By 1910, 26 million Americans	**were going** to the movies at nickelodeon theaters every week.

The exception to this rule is a class of sentences called **imperatives,** in which the subject is usually implied. In these sentences, we know that the subject is *you* without stating it.

> Quit bothering me.

> Help me carry in the groceries.

Sentence patterns

Sentences can be classified into four major patterns according to function.

- **Declaratives.** Declarative sentences make statements.

  The house on the corner was built in 2001.

- **Interrogatives.** Interrogatives are usually referred to as questions.

  Who will be the first to volunteer?

- **Imperatives.** Imperatives request or demand some action.

  Stop complaining.

- **Exclamations.** Exclamations are used to express strong emotion.

  What an incredible performance you gave!

Sentences can be classified as either **positive** or **negative.** A sentence can be made negative by inserting a negative word, usually *not* or a contracted form of *not* (*can't, isn't*).

Positive	Juanita has worked here for a year.
Negative	Juanita has **not** worked here for a year.

Sentences with transitive verbs (see Section 38c) can be considered as **active** or **passive** (see Section 30b). Sentences can be made passive by changing the word order.

Active	The House of Representatives selected Thomas Jefferson as president in 1800 when the electoral vote ended in a tie.
Passive	Thomas Jefferson **was selected** president by the House of Representatives in 1800 when the electoral vote ended in a tie.

Exercise 35.1 Identify whether or not each sentence is active or passive. If the sentence is passive, rewrite it to make it active.

Example There are so many places in the United States where supernatural creatures are reported to roam that it would take a lifetime to visit them all. (passive)

Rewrite You could spend a lifetime traveling across the United States and still not visit all of the places where supernatural creatures are rumored to roam. (active)

1. Do you know the phone number for the shrieking "Donkey Lady" in San Antonio, Texas?
2. Disagreements have arisen over whether the "Mothman" of Point Pleasant, West Virginia, simply warns about or actually causes disasters.
3. Stay away from the tall, green "Grinning Man" of Elizabeth, New Jersey, if you don't want to have nightmares.
4. "Wendigo psychosis," a craving for human flesh, was named after the malevolent Wendigo of the Algonquin people.
5. Victims of the goat-like Pope Lick Monster of Kentucky are attacked with a blood-stained axe!

35b Word Classes

Like players in a team sport who are assigned to different positions, words are classified into parts of speech. The different positions on a team have different functions. The parts of speech also serve different functions in sentences. And just as individuals can play more than one position on a team, so too can individual words belong to more than one part of speech. *Try* is a noun in *The third try was successful*, but a verb in *I would not try it*.

Nouns

A noun is the name of a person, place, thing, concept, or action. Names of particular persons, places, organizations, companies, titles, religions, languages, nationalities, ethnicities, months, and days are called **proper nouns** and are almost always capitalized. More general nouns are called **common nouns** and are seldom capitalized unless they begin a sentence (see Section 52a). Most common nouns can be made plural, and most are preceded by articles (*a, an, the*).

Nouns can be **possessive** (indicating ownership: *cat's, Ivan's*), **collective** (referring to a group: *family, jury*), **concrete** (referring to people, places, and things: *girl, truck*), and **abstract** (referring to qualities and states of mind: *humor, belief*). Multilingual writers should see Chapter 52 for more on count and noncount nouns.

Pronouns

Pronouns are a subclass of nouns and are generally used as substitutes for nouns. Pronouns themselves are divided into several subclasses.

- **Personal pronouns:** *I, you, he, she, it, we, they, me, him, her, us, them*

  I gave my old racquet to her. She gave me a CD in return.

- **Possessive pronouns:** *my, mine, his, hers, its, our, ours, your, yours, their, theirs*

  My old racquet is now hers.

- **Demonstrative pronouns:** *this, that, these, those*

  Those are the mittens I want.

- **Indefinite pronouns:** *all, any, anyone, anybody, anything, both, each, either, everyone, everything, many, neither, no one, none, nothing, one, some, someone, somebody, something*

  Everyone was relieved that the driver's injuries were minor.

- **Relative pronouns:** *that, which, what, who, whom, whose, whatever, whoever, whomever, whichever*

  The house, which hung off a steep ridge, had a stunning view of the bay.

- **Interrogative pronouns:** *who, which, what, where*

  What would you like with your sandwich?

- **Reflexive pronouns:** *myself, ourselves, yourself, yourselves, himself, herself, itself, themselves*

  The twins behaved themselves around their grandfather.

- **Reciprocal pronouns:** *each other, one another*

  The brothers didn't like each other.

See Chapter 39 for more on pronouns.

Exercise 35.2 The underlined words in the following paragraph are pronouns. Identify the function of each. Does it serve as a personal, possessive, demonstrative, indefinite, relative, interrogative, reflexive, or reciprocal pronoun?

> **Example** On November 20, 1820, a sperm whale rammed and sank the whaleship *Essex*, but all the sailors escaped with <u>their</u> lives.
> POSS

The ramming was no accident; after the whale hit the *Essex* once, <u>it</u> turned around to hit the ship a second time. The sailors found <u>themselves</u> adrift in three whaleboats, 1,200 miles from the nearest islands. However, the crew feared that <u>those</u> were populated by cannibals. After a month starving at sea, the sailors found a small island, <u>which</u> offered little to eat. Crushed by hunger, the crew convinced <u>each other</u> to eat a fellow sailor who had died of starvation. <u>Who</u> could say that <u>anybody</u> would act differently if placed in similar circumstances? <u>Their</u> chances of survival weakened with each passing day. Yet, first mate Owen Chase navigated <u>his</u> whaleship for eighty-eight days until the crew was rescued by a merchant ship.

Verbs

Verbs indicate actions, states of mind, occurrences, and states of being. Verbs are divided into two primary categories: **main verbs** and **auxiliaries**. A main verb must be present in the predicate. The main verb may be the only word in the predicate.

She slept.

When he heard the starting gun, Vijay sprinted.

Auxiliaries (often called *helping verbs*) include forms of *be, have,* and *do.* A subset of auxiliaries are **modals**: *can, could, may, might, must, shall, should, will, would.*

You will be satisfied when you see how well they painted your car.

She might have been selected for the lead role in the ballet if her strained muscle had healed.

See Chapters 37 and 38 for more on verbs.

Exercise 35.3 Underline the verbs in the following paragraph. Decide whether each verb is a main verb or an auxiliary verb. If it is an auxiliary verb, note whether or not it is a modal verb.

Example
     AUX NOT
     MODAL MAIN
   Frank Oz has created some of the best-known characters on *Sesame Street*, including Bert, Cookie Monster, and Grover.

  Frank Oz was born in Hereford, England, in 1944 and began staging puppet shows when he was 12. You may know him best as the voice of Yoda in the *Star Wars* series. Oz could have remained a puppeteer, but he has decided to embark on a second career as a movie director. You might have seen one of his movies such as *Indian in the Closet* or *In and Out*. The Muppet Fozzie Bear is named after Oz, using his first initial and his last name.

Verbals

Verbals are forms of verbs that function as nouns, adjectives, and adverbs. The three kinds of verbals are infinitives, participles, and gerunds.

- **Infinitives:** An infinitive is the base or *to* form of the verb. Infinitives can be used in place of nouns, adjectives, or adverbs.
  ⌐NOUN⌐
  To fly has been a centuries-old dream of people around the world.
             ⌐ ADJECTIVE ⌐
  Keeping your goals in mind is a good way to succeed.

- **Participles:** Participles are either present (*flying*) or past (*defeated*). They always function as adjectives.

  The flying insects are annoying.

  Napoleon's defeated army faced a long march back to France.

- **Gerunds:** Gerunds have the same form as present participles, but they always function as nouns.

  Flying was all that she wanted to do in life.

Exercise 35.4 Underline the verbals in the following paragraph and identify whether they are infinitives, participles, or gerunds. In addition, specify whether the participle is past or present.

Example
    GERUND
              PAST
              PARTICIPLE
   Casting the "evil eye" is a superstition recognized in cultures around the world.

> The evil eye is a focused gaze, supposedly causing death and destruction. Writings of the Assyrians, Babylonians, Greeks, and Romans all document an abiding belief in this supernatural concept. Old women and those thought to be witches are often accused of having the evil eye. To ward off the effects of the evil eye, people have resorted to praying, hand gestures, and purifying rituals.

Adjectives

Adjectives modify nouns and pronouns. Some adjectives are used frequently: *good, bad, small, tall, handsome, green, short.* Many others are recognizable by their suffixes: *-able* (*dependable*), *-al* (*cultural*), *-ful* (*hopeful*), *-ic* (*frenetic*), *-ive* (*decisive*), *-ish* (*foolish*), *-less* (*hopeless*), *-ous* (*erroneous*).

> The forgetful manager was always backed up by her dependable assistant.

Adjectives often follow linking verbs.

> That drumbeat is relentless.

Numbers are considered adjectives.

> Only ten team members showed up for practice.

See Chapter 40 for more about adjectives and adverbs.

Adverbs

Adverbs modify verbs, other adverbs, adjectives, and entire clauses. The usual suffix for adverbs is *-ly.* Many adverbs do not have suffixes (*then, here*) and others have the same form as adjectives (*fast, hard, long, well*).

> That drummer plays well. [modifies the verb *plays*]
>
> That drummer plays very well. [modifies the adverb *well*]
>
> That answer is partly correct. [modifies the adjective *correct*]
>
> Frankly, I could care less. [modifies the clause *I could care less*]

Conjunctive adverbs often modify entire clauses and sentences. Like coordinating conjunctions, they indicate the relationship between two clauses or two sentences. Commonly used conjunctive adverbs include *also, consequently, furthermore, hence, however, indeed, instead, likewise, moreover, nevertheless, otherwise, similarly, therefore, thus.*

> The Olympics brings together the best athletes in the world; however, the judging often represents the worst in sports.

Exercise 35.5 The underlined words in the following paragraph are modifiers. Label each modifier as adjective or adverb, and write which word it modifies.

Example

ADV
MOD LIVING

ADJ
MOD
WOMAN

ADJ MOD
WOMAN

After <u>initially</u> living the life of an <u>average</u> <u>middle-class</u>

ADV MOD BECAME

woman, Dorothy Parker <u>ultimately</u> became one

ADV MOD
INFAMOUS

ADJ MOD
WITS

ADJ MOD CENTURY

of the <u>most</u> <u>infamous</u> wits of the <u>twentieth</u> century.

Parker's father encouraged her to pursue "<u>feminine</u> arts" such as piano and poetry, but <u>just</u> following his death in 1913, she rushed into what turned out to be a <u>profitable</u> foray into the world of literature. <u>Almost</u> <u>immediately</u>, *Vanity Fair* purchased one of her poems, leading her into a <u>full-time</u> <u>writing</u> position with *Vogue*. It was <u>life-changing</u>, as Parker's flair for <u>clever</u> prose <u>swiftly</u> led her into the <u>inner</u> sanctum of New York <u>literary</u> society. Parker was fired from *Vanity Fair*'s editorial board in 1919 after <u>harshly</u> panning an advertiser's film. Despite her <u>early</u> departure from magazines, Parker gained <u>lasting</u> fame as a <u>prolific</u> writer and critic.

Prepositions

Prepositions indicate the relationship of nouns or pronouns to other parts of a sentence. Prepositions come before nouns and pronouns, and in this sense prepositions are "prepositioned." The noun(s) or pronoun(s) that follow are called the objects of prepositions.

PREP   OBJ   PREP   OBJ

She took the job **of speechwriter for the president.**

Here are some common prepositions.

about	behind	from	than
above	below	in	through
across	beside	inside	to
after	between	of	toward
against	but	off	under
among	by	on	until
around	despite	out	up
as	down	over	upon
at	during	past	with
before	for	since	without

Some prepositions are compounds.

according to	due to	in front of	next to
as well as	except for	in spite of	out of
because of	in addition to	instead of	with regard to

Exercise 35.6 Underline the prepositional phrases in the following paragraph and circle the prepositions.

Example (In) 2009, scientists exploring the extinct volcano Mount Bosavi (on) the Pacific island of Papua New Guinea found forty new animal species.

Until recently, the hard-to-reach land inside Mount Bosavi had been a 'lost world' because of the forbidding walls of the volcano. Among the species discovered by the science team are the giant Bosavi wooly rat and a fish that makes a grunting sound with its swim bladder. During their exploration of the volcano, the scientists also found over fifteen kinds of frog, including one with fangs! High above these other fascinating creatures lives the newly discovered silky cuscus, which dines upon fruits and leaves. Despite the disruption caused by their human visitors, both the giant rat and the cuscus seem to be friendly and without fear, following closely beside the teams as they made their way through the rainforest.

Conjunctions

Conjunctions indicate the relationship between words or groups of words. The two classes of conjunctions are **coordinate**, indicating units of equal status, and **subordinate**, indicating that one unit is more important than the other.

- **Coordinating conjunctions:** The seven coordinating conjunctions are *and, but, or, yet, for, so,* and *nor*.

  Do you want cake or ice cream?

  I graduated a semester early, but I had to go to work immediately to pay off loans.

- **Subordinating conjunctions:** Subordinating conjunctions introduce subordinate clauses. Common subordinating conjunctions are *after, although, as, because, before, if, since, that, unless, until, when, where, while*.

  Although the word *earwig* is Anglo-Saxon for "ear-creature," earwigs do not actually crawl into people's ears.

Exercise 35.7 Fill in the blanks in the following paragraph with an appropriate coordinating or subordinating conjunction. More than one conjunction may fit.

Example   Scientists used to believe that sharks attacked people intentionally, *but* they now assert that sharks attack humans only when mistaking them for natural prey.

Only four of the 400 species of shark attack humans: bull sharks, whitetips, tiger sharks, _____ great whites. _____ sharks committed 74 fatal attacks in the past 100 years, 75% of all shark-attack victims have survived. Peter Benchley, the author of *Jaws*, describes sharks as "fragile" _____ their numbers seem to be declining. _____ the populations of some shark species have declined by 80%, some nations have enacted laws to protect them. People are coming to see sharks as an important part of ocean environments, _____ they are acting accordingly.

Articles

There are two classes of articles:

- **Definite article:** *the*
- **Indefinite article:** *a, an*

Multilingual speakers should see Section 52d for more on articles.

Interjections

Interjections are words like *oops, ouch, ugh*, and *ah*. They are usually punctuated separately, and they do not relate grammatically to other words.

Exercise 35.8 Each underlined word in these paragraphs represents one of the word classes explained in this section. Identify nouns, pronouns, verbs, verbals, adjectives, adverbs, prepositions, conjunctions, articles, and interjections.

Example   In 1874, Colonel George Armstrong Custer

VERB   NOUN
announced the discovery of gold on French Creek

ADJ
near present-day Custer, South Dakota.

Gold! This discovery not only triggered the Black Hills gold rush but also gave rise to the lawless town of Deadwood, which reached a population of around 5,000 within the next two years. Many scheming business people flocked to Deadwood, hoping to strike it rich by offering supplies and entertainments, many of them illegal, to the gold miners. Deadwood also quickly gained a reputation as a place where murders, such as that of Wild Bill Hickok, were frequent and murderers went unpunished.

As the gold vein became the property of mining companies, Deadwood lost its rough and rowdy character and gradually settled down into a prosperous town. However, a fire on September 26, 1879, devastated the town, destroying over 300 buildings. Without the opportunities that characterized the town's early days, many of those who had lost their belongings in the fire left town to try their luck elsewhere.

 Clauses

Clauses are the grammatical structures that underlie sentences. Each clause has a subject and a predicate, but not all clauses are sentences. The variety of clauses is nearly infinite because phrases and other clauses can be embedded within them in a multitude of ways. Nevertheless, a few basic patterns are central to English clause structure.

Subject-verb-object

On the predicate side of a clause, you always find a main verb and often a direct object that is affected by the action of the verb.

  ⌐ S ¬ ⌐ V ¬⌐ DO ¬
Ahmad kicked the ball.

This basic pattern, called **subject-verb-object** or **S-V-O**, is one of the most common in English. Verbs that take objects (*kick, revise*) are called **transitive verbs**. Some transitive verbs can take two objects: a **direct object** that completes the sentence and an **indirect object**, usually a person, indirectly affected by the action.

  ⌐ S ¬ ⌐V ¬ ⌐ IO ¬⌐ DO ¬
Ahmed gave Sally the ball.

Clauses without objects

Not all clauses have objects.

  ⌐ S ¬ ⌐ V ¬
Maria slept.

  ⌐ S ¬ ⌐ V ¬
The engine runs rough. [*Rough* is an adverb, not an object.]

The staff cannot work on weekends. [*On weekends* is a prepositional phrase.]

This clause pattern is **subject-verb** or **S-V**. Verbs that do not require objects are called **intransitive verbs**. Many verbs can be both transitive and intransitive.

Intransitive   Ginny runs fast.

Transitive   Ginny runs the company.

For more on the verbs *lay/lie, set/sit,* and *raise/rise,* see Section 38c.

Linking-verb clauses

A third major pattern links the subject to a noun or an adjective that follows the verb and restates or describes the subject. The most commonly used verbs for this pattern are forms of *be.*

McKinley was president in 1900.

Rosalia Fernandez is the assistant manager.

The results of the MRI **were negative.**

What follows the verb is the subject complement, either a noun or noun phrase (*president, assistant manager*) or a predicate adjective describing the subject (*negative*).

Other linking verbs besides *be* are *appear, become, feel, look, remain,* and *seem.* These linking verbs often refer to people's perceptions or senses.

Jennifer **felt** nervous when she accepted the award.

Main versus subordinate clauses

All the examples of clauses we have looked at up to now can stand by themselves as sentences. These clauses are called **main** or **independent clauses**. Other clauses have the necessary ingredients to count as clauses—a subject and a main verb—yet they are incomplete as sentences.

Where you choose to go to college

Which was the first to be considered

As fast as my legs could pedal

These clauses are examples of **subordinate** or **dependent clauses**. They do not stand by themselves but must be attached to another clause:

I rode my bike as fast as my legs could pedal.

Subordinate clauses as modifiers

- **Adjective clauses:** Adjective clauses modify nouns and pronouns. They are also called **relative clauses** and usually begin with a relative pronoun.

  Steroids that are used to increase muscle density have many harmful side effects.

  The site where the fort once stood was washed away by a hurricane.

- **Adverb clauses:** Adverb clauses function as adverbs, modifying verbs, other adverbs, adjectives, and entire clauses. They begin with a subordinating conjunction such as *after, although, as, because, before, if, since, that, unless, until, when, where, while.*

Modifies verb	She **arrived** after we had carried all of our furniture into our new apartment.
Modifies adverb	Jeff laughed **nervously** whenever the boss came around.
Modifies adjective	The forward was not as **tall** as the media guide stated.
Modifies clause	When you see a person faint, **you should call 911.**

Exercise 35.9 Identify which of the three main clause patterns each of the following sentences exemplifies: subject-verb-object, subject-verb, or subject-linking verb.

> **Example** In 1954, the United States Supreme Court ordered school desegregation. **(Subject-verb-object)**

1. Arkansas Governor Orval Faubus refused to obey the order.
2. The Arkansas militia seemed impenetrable.
3. Nine African American students retreated from the school.
4. President Dwight Eisenhower ordered National Guard troops to escort the African American students.
5. The guardsmen were successful.

Exercise 35.10 The subordinate clauses in the following sentences are in italics. Identify whether they are adjective or adverb clauses.

ADVERB CLAUSE

Example *Although many cultures abhor the practice of cannibalism,* that it has taken place in many areas is indisputable.

1. Tribes in the West Indies *who sought dominance over neighboring peoples* often ate human flesh.
2. Some practitioners in New Guinea believed that consuming the flesh of enemies would give them strength, *which would transfer the special attributes of the conquered to themselves.*
3. It is important to note that not all tribes *who practiced human sacrifice* necessarily condoned consumption of the dead.
4. *Unless there were dire circumstances of famine* most tribes perceived cannibalism solely as a byproduct of military conquest.
5. *Because Mediterranean histories cite instances of cannibalism,* we must concede that it has had a long and diverse cultural existence.

35d Phrases

Phrases add to a sentence groups of words that modify or develop parts of the sentence. Some phrases can be confused with clauses, but phrases lack either a subject or a main verb.

Prepositional phrases

Prepositional phrases consist of a preposition and its object, including modifiers of the object. They can modify nouns, verbs, or adjectives.

┌NOUN┐ ┌ PREP PHRASE ┐
The **carton** of orange juice froze solid.

┌VERB┐ PREP / ┌ PHRASE ┐
They will **bring** the pizza on time.

┌ADJ┐┌ PREP PHRASE ┐
She was **rich** in spirit.

Verbal phrases

Each of the three kinds of verbals—infinitives, participles, and gerunds—can be used to create phrases.

- **Infinitive phrases:** Infinitive phrases can function as nouns, adverbs, and adjectives. As nouns they can be subjects, objects, or complements.

  ┌──────────── SUBJECT ────────────┐
  To succeed where others had failed was her goal.

- **Participial phrases:** Participial phrases are formed with either present participles (*flying*) or past participles (*defeated*); they function as adjectives.

  The freighter, listing noticeably to the port side, left the port without balancing the load.

- **Gerund phrases:** Gerund phrases formed from the present participle (*-ing*) function as nouns.

  ┌──── SUBJECT ────┐
  Feeding stray cats became my next-door neighbor's obsession.

Appositives

Appositive phrases modify nouns and are often set off by a pair of commas. They usually follow the noun they modify. They are quite useful as identifying tags for nouns.

Andy, my old linguistics teacher, became one of my best friends.

Absolutes

Absolute phrases are nearly clauses because they include a noun or pronoun and a verb; however, the verb is a participle ending in *-ing* or *-ed* and not a main verb. Absolute phrases can appear anywhere in a sentence and are set off by commas.

He struggled at the beginning of his speech, his voice trembling.

Exercise 35.11 Combine each set of sentences into one, using the type of phrase(s) listed in the parenthesis.

Example A chicken in Fruita, Colorado had his head chopped off and lived. This happened on September 10, 1945. (prepositional phrase).

Rewrite On September 10, 1945, a chicken in Colorado had his head chopped off and lived.

1. The headless chicken became a national celebrity. His name was Mike. (appositive)

2. Mike and his owner made about $4,500 a month. His owner was named Lloyd Olsen. They toured the country. (appositive, verbal)
3. Mike did not seem to know he had lost his head. His brain stem and jugular vein had been left intact. (absolute)
4. Mike was fed with an eyedropper. He gained six pounds. This happened in the two years after he lost his head. (verbal, prepositional)
5. The memory of Mike lives on. He is celebrated every May in Fruita, Colorado. This happens on "Mike, the Headless Chicken" Day. (absolute, prepositional)

35e Sentence Types

Simple sentences

A simple sentence consists of one main clause and no subordinate clauses. Simple sentences can be quite short.

┌ SUBJ ┐ ┌VERB┐
The two toy **figures spun** together.

Simple sentences can become quite long if phrases are added.

┌─────────── MAIN CLAUSE ───────────┐
The two toy figures spun together, standing on top of their round metal pedestal, teetering back and forth in a jerky, clockwise motion, slowing gradually.

Compound sentences

Compound sentences have two or more main clauses and no subordinate clauses. The main clauses are connected in one of three ways: (1) by a semicolon, (2) by a comma and a coordinating conjunction (*and, but, or, for, so, nor, yet*), or (3) by punctuation and a conjunctive adverb (*furthermore, however, indeed, nevertheless, therefore*).

┌──── MAIN CLAUSE ────┐ ┌──── MAIN CLAUSE ────┐
Mike walked to his car, **and** he opened the trunk.
┌──────────── MAIN CLAUSE ────────────┐ ┌────MAIN CLAUSE────┐
The theater enjoyed record attendance; **however,** rising costs took
all the profits.

Complex sentences

Complex sentences have one main clause and one or more subordinate clauses.

┌──── MAIN CLAUSE ────┐┌──── SUBORDINATE CLAUSE ────┐
Mike walked to his car **when** he got out of class.

Compound-complex sentences

Compound-complex sentences have at least two main clauses and at least one subordinate clause.

┌── MAIN CLAUSE ──┐┌── SUBORDINATE CLAUSE ──┐ ┌── MAIN CLAUSE ──┐
Mike walked to his car when he got out of class, but he had to go back for his briefcase.

> **Exercise 35.12** The following are simple sentences. Rewrite each as compound, complex, and compound-complex sentences.

Simple example	Baseball, America's national pastime, has endured decades of poor attendance, scandals, and players' strikes.
Compound	Baseball has endured decades of poor attendance, scandals, and players' strikes, yet it is still America's national pastime.
Complex	Baseball, which many consider America's national pastime, has endured decades of poor attendance, scandals, and players' strikes.
Compound-complex	While it has been called America's national pastime for over a century, baseball has endured many trials, yet the game has survived decades of poor attendance, scandals, and players' strikes.

1. Philip K. Wrigley, chewing gum entrepreneur, founded the All-American Girls Professional Baseball League in 1943, bolstering waning interest in baseball during World War II.
2. The league attracted women from all over the United States and Canada, providing them with a previously absent national venue to showcase their athletic talents.
3. The league peaked in 1948 with ten teams and over 900,000 paying fans.
4. Promoting an image of femininity among female athletes, the league insisted on strict regulations regarding dress and public behavior.
5. Lacking audience interest, the league folded in 1954.

36 | Fragments, Run-ons, and Comma Splices

QUICK*TAKE*

- **How do you find and fix fragments?** (see below)
  Error: Early traveling salesmen once literally drummed up business.
  Beating drums and ringing bells.
  Correct: Early traveling salesmen once literally drummed up business by beating drums and ringing bells.

- **What are run-on or "fused" sentences?** (see p. 544)
  Error: The first deadbeats were "debt beaters" they left their debts behind.
  Correct: The first deadbeats were "debt beaters." They left their debts behind.

- **What are comma splices, and how do you avoid them?** (see p. 547)
  Error: Dressed to the nines doesn't refer to the 1-10 scale, it's slang for "dressed to thine eyes."
  Correct: Dressed to the nines doesn't refer to the 1-10 scale. It's slang for "dressed to thine eyes."

Fragments

Fragments in speech and writing

Fragments are incomplete sentences. They are punctuated to look like sentences, but they lack a key element—often a subject or a verb—or else are a subordinate clause or phrase. In spoken language we usually pay little attention to fragments.

Missing subject; Missing verb	**Nothing like a hot shower when you're cold and wet.**
Missing subject	I was completely hooked on the game. **And played it constantly.**
Missing verb	**You too?**
Subordinate clause	**If you think so.**

In writing, however, fragments usually interrupt the reader. Consider another example of a full sentence followed by a fragment:

The university's enrollment rose unexpectedly during the fall semester. Because the percentage of students who accepted offers of admission was much higher than previous years and fewer students than usual dropped out or transferred.

Such fragments compel a reader to stop and reread. When a sentence starts with *because*, we expect to find a main clause later. But here, the *because* clause refers back to the previous sentence. The writer no doubt knew that the fragment gave reasons why enrollment rose, but a reader must stop to determine the connection.

In formal writing you should avoid fragments. Readers expect words punctuated as a sentence to be a complete sentence. They expect writers to complete their thoughts rather than force readers to guess the missing element.

Basic strategies for turning fragments into sentences

Incorporate the fragment into an adjoining sentence. In many cases you can incorporate the fragment into an adjoining sentence.

She saw him coming. ~~And~~ *a* looked away.

I was hooked on the ~~game. Playing~~ *game, playing* day and night.

Add the missing element. If you cannot incorporate a fragment into another sentence, add the missing element.

He *is* studying more this semester.

When aiming for the highest returns, ~~and also~~ *investors should think* ~~thinking~~ about the possible losses.

COMMON ERRORS

e Edit Help

Recognizing fragments

If you can spot fragments, you can fix them. Grammar checkers can find some of them, but they miss many fragments and identify other sentences wrongly as fragments. Ask these questions when you are checking for sentence fragments.

- **Does the sentence have a subject?** Except for commands, sentences need subjects:

  Jane spent every cent of credit she had available. And then applied for more cards.

- **Does the sentence have a complete verb?** Sentences require complete verbs. Verbs that end in *-ing* must have an auxiliary verb to be complete.

  Ralph keeps changing majors. He trying to figure out what he really wants to do after college.

(Continued on next page)

COMMON ERRORS *(Continued)*

- **If the sentence begins with a subordinate clause, is there a main clause in the same sentence?** A good test to determine if a subordinate clause is a fragment is to say "I think that" before a possible fragment.

  Even though Seattle is cloudy much of the year, no American city is more beautiful when the sun shines. ~~Which is one reason people continue to move there.~~

  Remember: 1. A sentence must have a subject and complete verb.
                    2. A subordinate clause cannot stand alone as a sentence.

For step-by-step discussion, examples, and practice exercises, visit this page of the eText at **www.mycomplab.com**.

Watch for these fragments

1. Pay close attention to sentences that begin with transitional words, coordinating conjunctions, and subordinating conjunctions. Among the most common fragments are those that begin with a transitional word (*also, therefore, however, consequently*), a coordinating conjunction (*and, but, or*), or a word indicating a subordinate clause (*although, because, if, since*). Prepositional or verbal phrase fragments are also common.

Transitional words and phrases such as *also, however,* and *therefore* mark movement from one idea to another, such as introducing another example, a change in direction, or a conclusion. Writers often produce fragments when trying to separate these shifts with a period.

Susan found ways to avoid working during her shift. ~~T,~~ ↑herefore making more work for the rest of the employees.

Compound predicates are linked by a coordinating conjunction such as *and, but,* or *or*. Because compound predicates share the same subject, the solution for a coordinating conjunction fragment is to incorporate it into the sentence with the subject.

Heroin use among urban professionals is on the rise in the United States. ~~A~~ ↑and also in Europe, after several decades during which cocaine was the preferred drug among this group.

2. Look for subordinate clause fragments. Subordinate clauses resemble sentences because they contain subjects and verbs. But subordinate clauses cannot stand alone as sentences because their meaning is dependent on another clause. Subordinate clauses begin with words such as *although, after, before, despite, if, though, unless, whether, while, when, who,* and *that.* Subordinate clause fragments often follow the sentence to which they actually belong. You can fix the subordinate clause fragment by incorporating it into the preceding sentence.

> A recent scientific study showed that wives of soldiers who were deployed to wars in Afghanistan and Iraq were more frequently diagnosed with sleep disorders, depression, and anxiety. ~~W,~~ while wives whose husbands were not deployed suffered fewer problems.

Or you can fix the subordinate clause fragment by turning it into a sentence.

> A recent scientific study showed that wives of soldiers who were deployed to wars in Afghanistan and Iraq were more frequently diagnosed with sleep disorders, depression, and anxiety. In comparison, the study also showed that wives whose husbands were not deployed suffered fewer problems.

3. Look for phrase fragments. Phrases also cannot stand alone as sentences because they lack either a subject, a verb, or both. There are many kinds of phrase fragments. Prepositional phrase fragments are easy to spot and fix.

> As Helen looked over the notes for her autobiography, she mused about how much her life had changed. ~~I,~~ in ways she could not have predicted.

> Andrew accepted the university's award for outstanding dissertation. ~~W,~~ with great dignity and humility.

Appositive phrases, which rename or describe a noun, are often fragments.

> For his advanced history course, Professor Levack assigned J. J. Scarisbrick's *Henry VIII.* ~~A,~~ an older text historians still regard as essential when studying sixteenth-century English history and politics.

Verbal phrase fragments are sometimes difficult to spot because verbals look like verbs. But remember: They function as adjectives, nouns, or adverbs.

> On their last trip to Chicago, Greta went to the Art Institute, but Roger didn't go. ~~Roger,~~ having visited that museum twice already.

4. Watch for list fragments. Do not isolate a list from the sentence that introduces it. Words or phrases such as *for example, for instance, namely,* and *such as* often introduce lists or examples. Make sure these lists are attached to a sentence with a subject and verb.

> Several Ben and Jerry's ice cream flavors are puns. ~~S,~~ such as Cherry Garcia, Phish Food, and The Full VerMonty.

Exercise 36.1 Revise each of the following to eliminate sentence fragments.

Example   Certain mammals, like flying squirrels and sugar gliders,

are varieties that actually ~~glide. Which~~ *glide, which* enables them to

survive when they are being hunted by nimble predators.

1. Flying squirrels, like typical squirrels except they have flaps of skin that allow them to glide.
2. Flying squirrels glide gracefully. From tree to tree with surprising ease.
3. To gain speed and momentum, flying squirrels often free-fall for several feet. Then to turn in midair, lower one arm.
4. One of the largest known varieties the Japanese giant flying squirrel. Two feet long from its head to its furry tail.
5. Gliding escapes predators and gathers food quickly.

Exercise 36.2 Find the fragments in the following paragraph and revise the paragraph to eliminate them.

Barton Springs still seems like a place not in Texas for those who come from elsewhere. Surrounding hills covered by live oaks and mountain juniper. And ground around the pool shaded by pecan trees whose trunks are a dozen feet in circumference. Banana trees and other tropical plants grow in the roofless dressing areas of the pool. With grackles whistling jungle-like sounds outside. The pool is in a natural limestone creek bed. Which is an eighth of a mile long. Fed by 27,000,000 gallons of 68° water bubbling out of the Edwards Aquifer each day.

36b Run-on Sentences

Run-on sentences (also called "fused sentences") are the opposite of sentence fragments. While fragments are incomplete sentences, run-ons jam together two or more sentences, failing to separate them with appropriate punctuation. And while fragments are sometimes acceptable, especially in informal writing, run-on sentences are never acceptable.

Fixing run-on sentences

Take three steps to fix run-on sentences: (1) identify the problem, (2) determine where the run-on sentence needs to be divided, and (3) choose the punctuation that best indicates the relationship between the main clauses.

1. Identify the problem. When you read your writing aloud, run-on sentences will often trip you up, just as they confuse readers. You can also search for subject and verb pairs to check for run-ons. If you find two main clauses with no punctuation separating them, you have a run-on sentence.

┌──── SUBJ ────┐ ┌── VERB ──┐
Internet businesses are not bound to specific locations or old
ways of running a business ˢ┌─┐ ᵛ┌─┐
they are more flexible in allowing
employees to telecommute and to determine the hours they work.

2. Determine where the run-on sentence needs to be divided.

Internet businesses are not bound to specific locations or old ways
of running a business | they are more flexible in allowing employees
to telecommute and to determine the hours they work.

COMMON ERRORS

Recognizing run-on sentences

When you read the following sentence, you realize something is wrong.

> I do not recall what kind of printer it was all I remember is
> that it could sort, staple, and print a packet at the same
> time.

The problem is that the two main clauses are not separated by punctuation. The reader must look carefully to determine where one main clause stops and the next one begins.

> I do not recall what kind of printer it was | all I remember is
> that it could sort, staple, and print a packet at the same time.

A period should be placed after *was*, and the next sentence should begin with a capital letter:

> I do not recall what kind of printer it was. All I remember is
> that it could sort, staple, and print a packet at the same time.

Run-on sentences are major errors.

Remember: Two main clauses must be separated by correct punctuation.

 For step-by-step discussion, examples, and practice exercises, visit this page of the eText at **www.mycomplab.com**.

3. Determine the relationship between the main clauses. You will revise a run-on more effectively if you determine the relationship between the main clauses and understand the effect or point you are trying to make. There are several punctuation strategies for fixing run-ons.

- **Insert a period.** This is the simplest way to fix a run-on sentence.

  Internet businesses are not bound to specific locations or old ways of running a business. They are more flexible in allowing employees to telecommute and to determine the hours they work.

  However, if you want to indicate the relationship between the two main clauses more clearly, you may want to choose one of these strategies.

- **Insert a semicolon (and possibly a transitional word indicating the relationship between the two main clauses):**

  Internet businesses are not bound to specific locations or old ways of running a business; therefore, they are more flexible in allowing employees to telecommute and to determine the hours they work.

- **Insert a comma and a coordinating conjunction** (*and, but, or, nor, for, so, yet*):

  Internet businesses are not bound to specific locations or old ways of running a business, so they are more flexible in allowing employees to telecommute and to determine the hours they work.

- **Make one of the clauses subordinate.**

  Because Internet businesses are not bound to specific locations or old ways of running a business, they are more flexible in allowing employees to telecommute and to determine the hours they work.

Exercise 36.3 Correct the following run-on sentences.

> Example   Japanese Kabuki theater surfaced in the early ~~1600s its~~ 1600s. Its origins are often linked to the public, improvised performances of Izumo Grand.

1. The original Kabuki troupes were mostly comprised of female dancers however male performers replaced them after the art became associated with prostitution.
2. Performances included several thematically linked elements such as dance, history, and domestic drama they lasted up to twelve hours.
3. In the 1700s, choreographers and special schools became commonplace Kabuki dance became more complex.
4. Kabuki costumes are often quite elaborate actors sometimes need assistance preparing for performances.

5. Since World War II, Western influences have altered the social position of Kabuki ticket prices have risen, making performances more accessible to tourists, but not the average Japanese citizen.

 Comma Splices

Comma splices are a kind of run-on sentence. They do include a punctuation mark—a comma—but it is not a strong enough punctuation mark to separate two main clauses. Comma splices often do not cause the same problems for readers as run-ons. The following sentence can be read aloud with no problem.

> Most of us were taking the same classes, if someone had a question, we would all help out.

On the page such sentences may cause confusion because commas are used to distinguish between elements within sentences, not to mark the boundary between sentences. Most readers see comma splices as errors, which is why you should avoid them.

Fixing comma splices

You have several options for fixing comma splices. Select the one that best fits where the sentence is located and the effect you are trying to achieve.

1. Change the comma to a period.   Most comma splices can be fixed by changing the comma to a period.

> It didn't matter that I worked in a windowless room for 40 hours a
> *week. On*
> ~~week, on~~ the Web I was exploring and learning more about distant
> people and places than I ever had before.

2. Change the comma to a semicolon.   A semicolon indicates a close connection between the two main clauses.

> It didn't matter that I worked in a windowless room for 40 hours a
> *week;*
> ~~week,~~ on the Web I was exploring and learning more about distant
> people and places than I ever had before.

3. Insert a coordinating conjunction.   Other comma splices can be repaired by inserting a coordinating conjunction (*and, but, or, nor, so, yet, for*) to indicate the relationship of the two main clauses. The coordinating conjunction must be preceded by a comma.

> Digital technologies have intensified a global culture that affects us daily in large and small ways, **yet** their impact remains poorly understood.

COMMON ERRORS

e Edit Help

Recognizing comma splices

When you edit your writing, look carefully at sentences that contain commas. Does the sentence contain two main clauses? If so, are the main clauses joined by a comma and a coordinating conjunction (*and, but, for, or, not, so, yet*)?

Incorrect The concept of "nature" depends on the concept of human "culture," the problem is that "culture" is itself shaped by "nature."

[Two main clauses joined by only a comma]

Correct Even though the concept of "nature" depends on the concept of human "culture," "culture" is itself shaped by "nature."

[Subordinate clause plus a main clause]

Correct The concept of "nature" depends on the concept of human "culture," but "culture" is itself shaped by "nature."

[Two main clauses joined by a comma and coordinating conjunction]

Treating the word *however* as a coordinating conjunction produces some of the most common comma splice errors. *However* does not function grammatically like the coordinating conjunctions *and, but, or, nor, yet, so,* and *for* (see page 624).

Incorrect The White House press secretary repeatedly avowed the Administration was not choosing a side between the two countries embroiled in conflict, however the developing foreign policy suggested otherwise.

Correct The White House press secretary repeatedly avowed the Administration was not choosing a side between the two countries embroiled in conflict; however, the developing foreign policy suggested otherwise.

[Two main clauses joined by a semicolon]

Remember: Do not use a comma as a period.

For step-by-step discussion, examples, and practice exercises, visit this page of the eText at **www.mycomplab.com**.

4. Make one of the main clauses a subordinate clause.   If a comma splice includes one main clause that is subordinate to the other, rewrite the sentence using a subordinating conjunction.

Because community
~~Community~~ is the vision of a great society trimmed down to the size of a small town, it is a powerful metaphor for real estate developers who sell a mini-utopia along with a house or condo.

5. Make one of the main clauses a phrase.   You can also rewrite one of the main clauses as a phrase.

Community—the vision of a great society trimmed down to the size of a small town—is a powerful metaphor for real estate developers who sell a mini-utopia along with a house or condo.

Exercise 36.4   The following sentences all contain comma splices. Eliminate the splices using the methods indicated in parentheses.

> **Example**   Accused Nazi propagandist Leni Riefenstahl was born in
> *1902. Her*
> Germany in ~~1902, her~~ films *Triumph of the Will* and *The*
> *Olympiad* are said to have captured the essence of the
> Nazi era. (Change comma to a period.)

1. Riefenstahl spent her early days performing in Germany as a dancer, a 1924 knee injury derailed her dance career, this accident led her to a successful, scandal-ridden life in film. (Insert a coordinating conjunction; change comma to a period.)
2. Early editing work prepared her to direct her first film, *The Blue Light*, however, national recognition was slow to come. (Change the comma to a semicolon.)
3. The year 1935 saw the release of Riefenstahl's film *Triumph of the Will*, which stunningly captured a Nazi Party rally, to be sure, this film forever cast a shadow over the director's career. (Change comma to a period.)
4. Her pioneering techniques such as the underwater camera in her documentary of the 1936 Berlin Olympics, *The Olympiad*, captured the spirit of athletics, her place in film history was solidified. (Make one of the main clauses a subordinate clause; insert a coordinating conjunction.)
5. The French imprisoned Riefenstahl because her films were considered Nazi propaganda, she was not an active member of the Nazi Party, her film career was forever damaged by such insinuations. (Make one of the main clauses a phrase; change comma to a period.)

37 | Subject-Verb Agreement

QUICKTAKE

- **How do you know if a subject is singular or plural?** (see p. 551)
  Singular: **Neither curling nor diving** is considered an extreme sport.
  Plural: Ernest Hemingway is believed to have said that **bullfighting, motor racing, and mountaineering** are the only real sports.
- **How do you choose the right verb for indefinite pronouns and collective nouns?** (see p. 553 and p. 555)
  Indefinite pronouns: **Some** say that this statement implies that a sport must involve peril. (plural)
  Collective nouns: This **generation** seems to like sports that involve peril. (singular)
- **What do you do with subjects that describe amounts, numbers, and pairs?** (see p. 556)
  Treat as singular: **Two decades** was all the time extreme sports needed to become mainstream.
  Treat as plural: **Baggy pants** are the choice of many extreme athletes.

Agreement in the Present Tense

When your verb is in the present tense, agreement in number is straightforward: The subject takes the base form of the verb in all but the third person singular. For example, the verb *walk* in the present tense agrees in number with most subjects in its base form:

First person singular	I walk
Second person singular	You walk
First person plural	We walk
Second person plural	You walk
Third person plural	They walk

Third person singular subjects are the exception to this rule. When your subject is in the third person singular (*he, it, Fido, Lucy, Mr. Jones*) you need to add an *s* or *es* to the base form of the verb.

Third person singular (add *s*)	He walks. It walks. Fido walks.
Third person singular (add *es*)	Lucy goes. Mr. Jones goes.

37b Singular and Plural Subjects

Sometimes it will be difficult to determine whether your subject is singular or plural, especially when subjects joined by *and* refer to the same thing or idea (*toast and jam, peace and quiet*) or when subjects are linked by *either . . . or* or *neither . . . nor.*

Subjects joined by *and*

When two subjects are joined by *and*, treat them as a compound (plural) subject.

> **Mary and Jane are** leaving for New York in the morning.

Some compound subjects are treated as singular. These kinds of compounds generally work together as a single noun. Although they appear to be compound and therefore plural, these subjects take the singular form of the verb.

> **Rock and roll remains** the devil's music, even in the twenty-first century.

Also, when two nouns linked by *and* are modified by *every* or *each*, these two nouns are likewise treated as one singular subject.

> **Each night and day brings** no new news of you.

An exception to this rule arises when the word *each* follows a compound subject. In these cases, usage varies depending on the number of the direct object.

> **The army and the navy each have** their own air forces.
>
> **The owl and the pussycat each has** a personal claim to fame.

Subjects joined by *or, either . . . or,* or *neither . . . nor*

When a subject is joined by *or, either . . . or,* or *neither . . . nor*, make sure the verb agrees with the subject closest to the verb.

> ┌─SING─┐ ┌─PLURAL─┐ ┌PL┐
> Is it **the sky or the mountains** that **are** blue?
>
> ┌─PLURAL─┐ ┌─SING─┐ ┌─SING─┐
> Is it **the mountains or the sky** that **surrounds** us?
>
> ┌─PLURAL─┐ ┌─SING─┐ ┌SING┐
> **Neither the animals nor the zookeeper knows** how to relock the gate.
>
> ┌─SING─┐ ┌─PLURAL─┐ ┌PL┐
> **Either a coyote or several dogs were** howling last night.

Subjects along with another noun

Verbs agree with the subject of a sentence, even when a subject is linked to another noun with a phrase like *as well as, along with,* or *alongside.* These modifying phrases are usually set off from the main subject with commas.

┌─────────── IGNORE THIS PHRASE ───────────┐
Chicken, alongside various steamed vegetables, is my favorite meal.

┌─ IGNORE THIS PHRASE ─┐
Besides David Bowie, **the Beatles are** my favorite band of all time.

Multilingual writers can find more on singular and plural subjects in Section 52c.

COMMON ERRORS
e Edit Help

Subjects separated from verbs

The most common agreement errors occur when words come between the subject and verb. These intervening words do not affect subject-verb agreement. To ensure that you use the correct verb form, identify the subject and the verb. Ignore any phrases that come between them.

┌─────────── IGNORE THIS PHRASE ───────────┐
Incorrect **Students** at inner-city Washington High reads more than suburban students.

Correct **Students** at inner-city Washington High read more than suburban students.

Students is plural and *read* is plural; subject and verb agree.

Incorrect **The Whale Shark,** the largest of all sharks, feed on plankton.

Correct **The Whale Shark,** the largest of all sharks, feeds on plankton.

The plural noun *sharks* that appears between the subject *the whale shark* and the verb *feeds* does not change the number of the subject. The subject is singular and the verb is singular. Subject and verb agree.

Remember: When you check for subject-verb agreement, identify the subject and verb. Ignore any words that come between them.

 For step-by-step discussion, examples, and practice exercises, visit this page of the eText at **www.mycomplab.com**.

Exercise 37.1 Underline the subject in the following sentences and decide whether it should be treated as singular or plural. Next, circle the verb. If the verb doesn't agree in number with the subject, revise so that it agrees.

Example   Various <u>regions</u> in Italy—including Tuscany,

possess

Lazio, and Umbria— (possesses) rich cultures that

revolve around food preparation and meals.

["Regions" is plural, so the verb needs to be changed to "possess."]

1. Some cite Rome's Marcus Gavius Apicius as the author of the first cookbook, written in the first century.
2. Each Italian city and town in Italy possess a historical rationale for the gastronomical traditions of today.
3. People in central Italy enjoy eating many types of meat, but neither beef nor liver outshine the popularity of the region's top meat, pork.
4. Cheese, as well as foods such as balsamic vinegar and olive oil, is sometimes named for the region where it is produced.
5. Almost every man and woman in America know spaghetti hails from Italy, but many fail to learn about the rich and varied Italian tradition of food.

37c Indefinite Pronouns as Subjects

The choice of a singular or plural pronoun is determined by the **antecedent**—the noun that a pronoun refers to. For instance, the sentence *My friend likes soup* might be followed by another sentence, *She makes a new kind daily.* The pronoun must be singular because *she* refers to the singular noun *friend.*

Indefinite pronouns, such as *some, few, all, someone, everyone,* and *each,* often do not refer to identifiable subjects; hence they have no antecedents. Most indefinite pronouns are singular and agree with the singular forms of verbs. Some, like *both* and *many,* are always plural and agree with the plural forms of verbs. Other indefinite pronouns are variable and can agree with either singular or plural verb forms, depending on the context of the sentence.

COMMON ERRORS

e Edit Help

Agreement errors using *each*

The indefinite pronoun *each* is a frequent source of subject-verb agreement errors. If a pronoun is singular, its verb must be singular. This rule holds true even when the subject is modified by a phrase that includes a plural noun.

A common stumbling block to this rule is the pronoun *each*. *Each* is always treated as a singular pronoun in college writing. When *each* stands alone, the choice is easy to make:

Incorrect   **Each** are an outstanding student.
Correct   **Each** is an outstanding student.

But when *each* is modified by a phrase that includes a plural noun, the choice of a singular verb form becomes less obvious:

Incorrect   **Each** of the girls are fit.
Correct   **Each** of the girls is fit.

Incorrect   **Each** of our dogs get a present.
Correct   **Each** of our dogs gets a present.

Remember: *Each* is always singular.

For step-by-step discussion, examples, and practice exercises, visit this page of the eText at **www.mycomplab.com.**

Exercise 37.2   Identify the underlined indefinite pronoun in each sentence as singular or plural. Then circle the verb and correct it if it does not agree in number with the pronoun.

>   *plural have*
> **Example**   Many (has) heard of the curse that strikes down those
>
>   who enter the tomb of Tutankhamen.

1. A newspaper article about the discovery of the tomb in 1922 by Howard Carter stated that an inscription cursed all who enters to a certain death.
2. Everyone believed in the curse, though, because writers such as Sir Arthur Conan Doyle and Marie Corelli had planted the seed of a "terrible curse" in the minds of the press.
3. Both was inspired by earlier writers, such as Louisa May Alcott and Jane Loudon Webb.

4. Each had published a mummy story prior to the discovery of the tomb.
5. No one have done more to perpetuate the myth than Webb, however, whose novel *The Mummy* (1828) invented the story of a mummy coming back to life to seek revenge.

37d Collective Nouns as Subjects

Collective nouns refer to groups (*administration, audience, class, committee, crew, crowd, faculty, family, fleet, gang, government, group, herd, jury, mob, public, team*). When members of a group are considered as a unit, use singular verbs and singular pronouns.

The **audience** was patient with the novice performer.

The **crowd** is unusually quiet at the moment, but it will get noisy soon.

When members of a group are considered as individuals, use plural verbs and plural pronouns.

The **faculty** have their differing opinions on how to address the problems caused by reduced state support.

Sometimes collective nouns can be singular in one context and plural in another. Writers must decide which verb form to use based on sentence context.

The **number** of people who live downtown is increasing.

A **number** of people are moving downtown from the suburbs.

Sports is one of the four main buttons on the newspaper's Web site.

Sports are dangerous for children under five.

Exercise 37.3 The following paragraph contains collective nouns that can be considered either singular or plural depending on the context. Select the form of the verb that agrees with the subject in the context given.

Example   The jury (is/are) ready to deliberate.

[*Jury* is considered singular.]

The jury (believe/believes) that they will resolve their differences in judgment.

[*Jury* is considered plural.]

The administration usually (try/tries) to avoid responsibility for issues concerning students living off campus but also (listen/listens) when the city government (complain/complains) about student behavior. The public (is/are) upset about large parties that last into the morning. The university formed a committee of students, faculty, and neighborhood residents to investigate the problem. Unfortunately, the committee (disagree/disagrees) about the causes of excessive noise.

37e Inverted Word Order

Writers use inverted word order most often in forming questions.

Cats are friendly.

Are **cats** friendly?

Writers also use inverted word order for added emphasis or for style considerations. Do not be confused by inverted word order. Locate the subject of your sentence, then make sure your verb agrees with that subject.

37f Amounts, Numbers, and Pairs

Subjects that describe amounts of money, time, distance, or measurement are singular and require singular verbs.

Three days is never long enough to unwind.

Some subjects, such as courses of study, academic specializations, illnesses, and even some nations, are treated as singular subjects even though their names end in -s or -es. For example, *economics, news, ethics, measles,* and *the United States* all end in -s but are all singular subjects.

Economics is a rich field of study.

News keeps getting more and more commercial.

Other subjects require a plural verb form even though they refer to single items such as *jeans, slacks, glasses, scissors,* and *tweezers*. These items are all pairs.

Your **jeans** look terrific.

My **glasses** are scratched.

Exercise 37.4 Identify whether the underlined subject is singular or plural. Circle the verb and correct it if it does not agree in number with the subject.

Example You might think that the United States ⟨is⟩ the ancestral home of the modern circus.

1. However, thanks is due to the Circus Maximus of Rome, where spectators enjoyed chariot races and other entertainments.

2. Politics was the catalyst for Julius Caesar's expansion of the Circus in 50 BC.

3. Eighteen centuries are how long it took for the circus as we know it to emerge in Europe and the Americas.

4. Acrobatics was a popular attraction of these early modern circuses as well as equestrian acts.

5. Forty-two feet were set as the circumference of the center ring, the distance for a team of horses to circle at full gallop.

6. With sideshow attractions including human oddities, pickled "specimens," and "hootchie-kootchie" girls, the ethics of the nineteenth-century circus was often questioned.

7. Today, animal rights stand as the largest controversy surrounding the large traveling circuses.

38 | Verbs

QUICKTAKE

- **How do you know which verbs are regular and which are irregular?** (see p. 561)
  Regular: We entered a film contest last year.
  Irregular: We made a short, low-budget version of a popular movie.
- **What are transitive and intransitive verbs?** (see p. 564)
  Transitive: In the movie, the Scottish warriors refuse to lay their **weapons** down.
  Intransitive: At the end, the hero lies in agony on the torturer's table.
- **How can you avoid shifts in tense?** (see p. 565)
  Incorrect: Just when the Na'vi were about to lose, the Pandoran wildlife comes to the rescue.
  Correct: Just when the Na'vi were about to lose, the Pandoran wildlife came to the rescue.

Multilingual writers can find more on verbs in Chapter 53.

38a Basic Verb Forms

Almost all verbs in English have five possible forms. The exception is the verb *be*. Regular verbs follow this basic pattern.

Base form	Third-person singular	Past tense	Past participle	Present participle
jump	jumps	jumped	jumped	jumping
like	likes	liked	liked	liking
talk	talks	talked	talked	talking
wish	wishes	wished	wished	wishing

Irregular verbs do not follow this basic pattern. See Section 38b for the forms of irregular verbs.

Base form

The base form of a verb is the one you find listed in the dictionary. This form indicates an action or condition in the present.

> I like New York in June.

> We talk often on weekends.

Third-person singular

The base form of the verb changes when used with third-person singular subjects. Third-person singular subjects include *he, she, it,* and the nouns they replace, as well as other pronouns, including *someone, anybody,* and *everything.* (See Section 37c.) Present tense verbs in the third-person singular end with an *s* or an *es.*

> Ms. Nessan speaks in riddles.

> He watches too much television.

Past tense

The past tense describes an action or condition that occurred in the past. For most verbs, the past tense is formed by adding *d* or *ed* to the base form of the verb.

> I called at nine, but no one answered.

> She inhaled the night air.

Many verbs, however, have irregular past tense forms. (See Section 38b.)

COMMON ERRORS

Missing verb endings

Verb endings are not always pronounced in speech, especially in some dialects of English. It's also easy to omit these endings when you are writing quickly. Spelling checkers will not mark these errors, so you have to find them while proofreading.

Incorrect	Jeremy feel as if he's catching a cold.
Correct	Jeremy feels as if he's catching a cold.
Incorrect	Sheila hope she would get the day off.
Correct	Sheila hoped she would get the day off.

Remember: Check verbs carefully for missing *s* or *es* endings in the present tense and missing *d* or *ed* endings in the past tense.

 For step-by-step discussion, examples, and practice exercises, visit this page of the eText at **www.mycomplab.com**.

Past participle

The past participle is used with *have* to form verbs in the perfect tense, with *be* to form verbs in the passive voice (see Section 30b), and to form adjectives derived from verbs.

Past perfect	They **had** gone to the grocery store prematurely.
Passive	The book **was** written thirty years before it **was published**.
Adjective	In the eighties, teased hair was all the rage.

Present participle

The present participle functions in one of three ways. Used with an auxiliary verb, it can describe a continuing action. The present participle can also function as a noun, known as a **gerund**, or as an adjective. The present participle is formed by adding *ing* to the base form of a verb.

Present participle	Wild elks **are** competing for limited food resources.
Gerund	Sailing around the Cape of Good Hope is rumored to bring good luck.
Adjective	We looked for shells in the ebbing tide.

Exercise 38.1   Write the correct form of each underlined verb using the clues given in parentheses.

Example   Although it sound^s (third person singular) simple, noodle^ing (present participle-gerund), or catch^ing (present participle-gerund) fish by using only your bare hands, is complicate^d (past participle-adjective).

Flathead catfish are the choose (past participle-adjective) prey for noodle (gerund) because they lives (base form) sedentary lifestyles in holes or under brush. A noodler begin (third person singular) by go (gerund) underwater to depths ranging from only a few feet to a daunt (present participle-adjective) twenty feet. Placing his or her hand inside a discover (past participle-adjective) catfish hole, a noodler use (third person singular) his or her arm as bait to luring (base form) the fish. If all go (third person singular) as plan (past participle-adjective), the catfish will swim forward and fastened (base form) itself onto the noodler's hand and arm. Because catfish often weigh up to 50 to 60 pounds, many a noodler has need (past participle) help lift (gerund) their catch out of the water.

38b Irregular Verbs

A verb is **regular** when its past and past participle forms are created by adding *ed* or *d* to the base form. If this rule does not apply, the verb is considered an **irregular** verb. Here are common irregular verbs and their basic conjugations.

Common irregular verbs

Base form	Past tense	Past participle
arise	arose	arisen
be (is, am, are)	was, were	been
bear	bore	borne or born
beat	beat	beaten
become	became	become
begin	began	begun
bend	bent	bent
break	broke	broken
bring	brought	brought
buy	bought	bought
choose	chose	chosen
cling	clung	clung
come	came	come
cost	cost	cost
creep	crept	crept
deal	dealt	dealt
dig	dug	dug
dive	dived or dove	dived
do	did	done
draw	drew	drawn
drink	drank	drunk
drive	drove	driven
eat	ate	eaten
fall	fell	fallen
feed	fed	fed
feel	felt	felt

(Continued on next page)

Common irregular verbs (Continued)

fight	fought	fought
fling	flung	flung
fly	flew	flown
forbid	forbade or forbad	forbidden
forget	forgot	forgotten or forgot
forgive	forgave	forgiven
freeze	froze	frozen
get	got	got or gotten
give	gave	given
go	went	gone
grow	grew	grown
hang	hung	hung
have	had	had
know	knew	known
lay	laid	laid
lend	lent	lent
lie	lay	lain
make	made	made
read	read	read
run	ran	run
say	said	said
see	saw	seen
send	sent	sent
shine	shone	shone
show	showed	shown or showed
sit	sat	sat
sleep	slept	slept
speak	spoke	spoken
spring	sprang or sprung	sprung
swim	swam	swum
take	took	taken
teach	taught	taught
tell	told	told
think	thought	thought
understand	understood	understood
wear	wore	worn
write	wrote	written

COMMON ERRORS

e *Edit* Help

Past tense forms of irregular verbs

The past tense and past participle forms of irregular verbs are often confused. The most frequent error is using a past tense form instead of the past participle with *had.*

	PAST TENSE
Incorrect	She had never rode a horse before.
	PAST PARTICIPLE
Correct	She had never ridden a horse before.
	PAST TENSE
Incorrect	He had saw many alligators in Louisiana.
	PAST PARTICIPLE
Correct	He had seen many alligators in Louisiana.

Remember: Change any past tense verbs preceded by *had* to past participles.

 For step-by-step discussion, examples, and practice exercises, visit this page of the eText at **www.mycomplab.com.**

Exercise 38.2 Underline the correct form of the irregular verbs in the following paragraph.

Example   Until recently, historians (see/<u>saw</u>) the Dark Ages as a period of cultural, social and economic stagnation, but new research (<u>shows</u>/shown) that a great deal of economic growth happened during that period.

The Dark Ages are (understand/understood) to have (took/taken) place between the Decline of the Roman Empire and the 1500s. Historians (think/thought) that little or no trade happened during the Dark Ages because spices, which (come/came) to Europe from the East, are not (written/wrote) about in documents from that time period. However, evidence that there (be/was) trade between Europe and the East has been found in the bones of rats. Bones (dug/dig) up in Italy and (knew/known) to be from the Dark Ages (is/are) from rats born in Egypt. Since rats (do/did) not travel by foot more than 100 feet from where they are born, the Egyptian rats probably (ride/rode) to Europe on ships. Thus, historians (felt/feel), we should (begin/begun) to rethink what we believe about this misunderstood period.

38c Transitive and Intransitive Verbs

Lay/lie, set/sit, and raise/rise

Do you know whether you raise or rise from bed in the morning? Do your house keys lay or lie on the kitchen table? Does a book set or sit on the shelf? *Raise/rise*, *lay/lie*, and *set/sit* are transitive and intransitive verbs that writers frequently confuse. Transitive verbs take direct objects, nouns that receive the action of the verb. Intransitive verbs act in sentences that lack direct objects.

The following charts list the trickiest pairs of transitive and intransitive verbs and the correct forms for each verb tense. Pay special attention to *lay* and *lie*, which are irregular.

	lay (put something down)	**lie (recline)**
Present	lay, lays	lie, lies
Present participle	laying	lying
Past	laid	lay
Past participle	laid	lain

Transitive Once you complete your test, please lay your pencil (direct object, the thing being laid down) on the desk.

Intransitive The *Titanic* lies upright in two pieces at a depth of 13,000 feet.

	raise (elevate something)	**rise (get up)**
Present	raise, raises	rise, rises
Present participle	raising	rising
Past	raised	rose
Past participle	raised	risen

Transitive We raise our glasses (direct object, the things being raised) to toast Uncle Han.

Intransitive The sun rises over the bay.

	set (place something)	sit (take a seat)
Present	set, sets	sit, sits
Present participle	setting	sitting
Past	set	sat
Past participle	set	sat

Transitive   Every morning Stanley **sets** two dollars (direct object, the amount being set) on the table to tip the waiter.

Intransitive   I **sit** in the front seat when it's available.

Exercise 38.3   Decide whether each of the sentences in the following paragraph calls for a transitive or intransitive verb and underline the correct choice.

Example   The eastern diamondback rattlesnake (will set/<u>will sit</u>) immobile for hours, sometimes coiled and sometimes stretched to its full length of seven feet.

A rattlesnake will often (lay/lie) in wait for its favorite meal: a rat. When you encounter one of these poisonous snakes, (set/sit) aside your assumptions about aggressive snakes; many are timid. You can tell a rattlesnake feels threatened if its tail (rises/raises) and you hear a sharp rattling sound. If you are hiking in the desert in the southwestern United States, do not (sit/set) down without carefully surveying the ground. To (rise/raise) your chances of avoiding a rattlesnake bite, make noise when you are hiking in wilderness areas.

 Shifts in Tense

Appropriate shifts in verb tense

Changes in verb tense are sometimes necessary to indicate a shift in time.

Present to past   I never **shop** [PRESENT TENSE] online anymore because I **heard** [PAST TENSE] that hackers **have stolen** [PRESENT PERFECT TENSE] thousands of credit card numbers used in Internet transactions.

Past to Future   Because Oda **won** [PAST TENSE] the lottery, she **will quit** [FUTURE TENSE] her job at the hospital as soon as her supervisor **finds** [PRESENT TENSE] a qualified replacement.

Inappropriate shifts in verb tense

Be careful to avoid confusing your reader with unnecessary shifts in verb tense. Once you reach the proofreading stage of your writing, dedicate one careful reading of your text to finding inappropriate tense changes.

Incorrect

PRESENT TENSE

While Brazil looks to ecotourism to fund rainforest

PAST TENSE

preservation, other South American nations relied on

foreign aid and conservation efforts.

The shift from present tense (*looks*) to past tense (*relied*) is confusing. The sentence attempts to compare Brazil with other South American countries, but the shift in tenses muddles the comparison. Correct the mistake by putting both verbs in the present tense.

Correct

PRESENT TENSE

While Brazil looks to ecotourism to fund rainforest

PRESENT TENSE

preservation, other South American nations rely on

foreign aid and conservation efforts.

Exercise 38.4 Read the entire paragraph and underline the correct verb tenses.

Example   The American Indian Movement (AIM) (originated/ originates) in Minneapolis in 1968.

Native American activists, including Dennis Banks and Russell Means, (created/create) AIM, a militant organization that fights for civil rights for American Indians. AIM members (participate/ participated) in a number of famous protests, including the occupation of Alcatraz Island (1969–1971) and the takeover of Wounded Knee (1973). The group (has helped/helps) Indians displaced by government programs, (will work/has worked) for economic independence for Native Americans, and (agitates/ has agitated) for the return of lands (seize/seized) by the U.S. government. In his book *Agents of Repression: The FBI's Secret War against the Black Panther Party and the American Indian Movement*, Ward Churchill (documented/documents) how the FBI (infiltrated/ infiltrates) AIM in an attempt to destroy it. While most local chapters of AIM (have disbanded/disband), Native American activists today still (fight/fought) for their autonomy and for compensation for centuries of oppression and economic injustice.

COMMON ERRORS

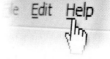

Unnecessary tense shift

Notice the tense shift in the following example.

Incorrect In May of 2000 the "I Love You" virus crippled [PAST TENSE] the computer systems of major American companies and irritated [PAST TENSE] millions of private computer users. As the virus generates [PRESENT TENSE] millions of e-mails and erases [PRESENT TENSE] millions of computer files, companies such as Ford and Time Warner are [PRESENT TENSE] forced to shut down their clogged e-mail systems.

The second sentence shifts unnecessarily to the present tense, confusing the reader. Did the "I Love You" virus have its heyday several years ago, or is it still wreaking havoc now? Changing the verbs in the second sentence to the past tense eliminates the confusion.

Correct In May of 2000 the "I Love You" virus crippled [PAST TENSE] the computer systems of major American companies and irritated [PAST TENSE] millions of private computer users. As the virus generated [PAST TENSE] millions of e-mails and erased [PAST TENSE] millions of computer files, companies such as Ford and Time Warner were [PAST TENSE] forced to shut down their clogged e-mail systems.

Remember: Shift verb tense only when you are referring to different time periods.

For step-by-step discussion, examples, and practice exercises, visit this page of the eText at **www.mycomplab.com**.

38e Shifts in Mood

Indicative, imperative, and subjunctive verbs

Verbs can be categorized into three moods—indicative, imperative, and subjunctive—defined by the functions they serve.

Indicative verbs state facts, opinions, and questions.

Fact Many same-sex couples in the United States are fighting for the right to marry.

| Opinion | Allowing same-sex couples to marry **will endanger** the institution of marriage. |
| Question | Why **do** some people **oppose** same-sex marriage? |

Imperative verbs make commands, give advice, and make requests.

Command	**Tell** me why you support same-sex marriage.
Advice	**Try** to think of same-sex marriage as a civil rights issue.
Request	**Could** you please **explain** how same-sex marriage is different from a civil union?

Subjunctive verbs express wishes, unlikely or untrue situations, hypothetical situations, requests with *that* clauses, and suggestions.

Wish	We **wish** that cultural prejudices **were** easier to overcome.
Unlikely or untrue situation	**If** heterosexual marriage **were** as sacred as some pundits would have us believe, there would be no divorce.
Hypothetical situation	**If** the right for heterosexual couples to marry **were** subject to a popular vote, the institution of marriage as we know it could be over.

The subjunctive in past and present tenses

Subjunctive verbs are usually the trickiest to handle. In the present tense subjunctive clauses call for the base form of the verb (*be, have, see, jump*).

It is essential that children **be** immunized before they enter kindergarten.

In the past tense they call for the standard past tense of the verb (*had, saw, jumped*), with one exception. In counterfactual sentences the *to be* verb always becomes *were*, even for subjects that take *was* under normal circumstances.

Indicative	I **was** surprised at some of the choices she made.
Subjunctive	If I **were** in her position, I'd do things differently.
Indicative	The young athletes found that gaining muscle **was** not easy.
Subjunctive	If being muscular **were** easy, everyone would look like Arnold Schwarzenegger.

Exercise 38.5 Replace the underlined verb with a verb in the correct mood using the clues in the brackets.

Example   Nitrogen Narcosis result[indicative] when nitrogen
                                    ^become
              levels in the bloodstream became [indicative] elevated
              because of pressure.

    This phenomenon is called "rapture of the deep" because the increase in nitrogen makes a diver feel as if she is [subjunctive] invincible. Being [imperative] very careful, however; this situation is dangerous. Often the combination of nitrogen and excessive oxygen overwhelm [indicative] the diver, causing her to wish that she could got [subjunctive] free of the breathing apparatus. A diver above the surface of the water experience [indicative] one atmosphere of pressure. How much do the pressure increase [indicative] if the diver is 100 feet below the surface? Imagining [imperative] having a 300 pound weight on your chest. That's right—the pressure triple [indicative]. It is crucial that a diver prepares [subjunctive] for the possibility of rapture occurring during a dive. Often divers would inhale [indicative] nitrous oxide to see how they would handle themselves if they was [subjunctive] in the throes of rapture of the deep.

39 | Pronouns

QUICK_TAKE_

- **How do you choose the correct pronoun case?** (see p. 571)
  Incorrect: She and me gave a better presentation than him.
  Correct: She and I gave a better presentation than he did.

- **How do you identify and correct errors in pronoun agreement?**
  (see p. 575)
  Incorrect: **Everybody** in the class had a chance to give their opinions.
  Correct: **All students** had a chance to give their opinions.

- **How do you identify and correct vague pronoun references?**
  (see p. 580)
  Vague: Tom thought he could run a marathon after he finished a 10K race.
  This was a mistake. [_This what?_]
  Better: Tom thought he could run a marathon after he finished a 10K race.
  This overconfidence was a mistake.

39a Pronoun Case

Subjective pronouns function as the subjects of sentences. **Objective pronouns** function as direct or indirect objects. **Possessive pronouns** indicate ownership.

Subjective pronouns	Objective pronouns	Possessive pronouns
I	me	my, mine
we	us	our, ours
you	you	your, yours
he	him	his
she	her	her, hers
it	it	its
they	them	their, theirs
who	whom	whose

People who use English regularly usually make these distinctions among pronouns without thinking about them.

> S   O   P   S   O   O   S   O
> I let him use my laptop, but he lent it to her, and I haven't seen it
> since.

Nonetheless, choosing the correct pronoun case sometimes can be difficult.

Pronouns in compound phrases

Picking the right pronoun sometimes can be confusing when the pronoun appears in a compound phrase.

> If we work together, you and **me** can get the job done quickly.

> If we work together, you and **I** can get the job done quickly.

Which is correct—*me* or *I*? Removing the other pronoun usually makes the choice clear.

Incorrect	Me can get the job done quickly.
Correct	I can get the job done quickly.

Similarly, when compound pronouns appear as objects of prepositions, sometimes the correct choice isn't obvious until you remove the other pronoun.

> When you finish your comments, give them to Isidora or **I**.

> When you finish your comments, give them to Isidora or **me**.

Again, the choice is easy when the pronoun stands alone.

Incorrect	Give them to I.
Correct	Give them to me.

We and *us* before nouns

Another pair of pronouns that can cause difficulty is *we* and *us* before nouns.

> **Us** friends must stick together.

> **We** friends must stick together.

Which is correct—*us* or *we*? Removing the noun indicates the correct choice.

Incorrect	Us must stick together.
Correct	We must stick together.

Exercise 39.1 Underline the pronoun in each sentence of the following paragraph and replace the pronoun if it is incorrect.

Example You and ~~me~~ /I should pay more attention to what we eat.

> If you and a friend go on a road trip, the ADA suggests that you and her limit your stops at fast-food restaurants. The association suggests us snack in the afternoon, provided we choose foods that are healthy for you and I. If your friend wants a cheeseburger for lunch, you should respond that you and her could split the meal. For your sake and me, it is not a good idea to snack after dark.

Who versus *whom*

Choosing between *who* and *whom* is often difficult, even for experienced writers. When you answer the phone, which do you say?

1. To **whom** do you wish to speak?

2. **Who** do you want to talk to?

Probably you chose 2. *To whom do you wish to speak?* may sound stuffy, but technically it is correct. The reason it sounds stuffy is that the distinction between *who* and *whom* is disappearing from spoken language. *Who* is more often used in spoken language, even when *whom* is correct.

COMMON ERRORS

_e Edit Help

Who or *whom*

In writing, the distinction between *who* and *whom* is still often observed. *Who* and *whom* follow the same rules as other pronouns: *Who* is the subject pronoun; *whom* is the object pronoun. If you are dealing with an object, *whom* is the correct choice.

Incorrect	Who did you send the letter to?
	Who did you give the present to?

Correct	To whom did you send the letter?
	Whom did you give the present to?

Who is always the right choice for a subject pronoun.

Correct	Who gave you the present?
	Who brought the cookies?

If you are uncertain of which one to use, try substituting *she* and *her* or *he* and *him*.

Incorrect	You sent the letter to she **[who]**?
Correct	You sent the letter to her **[whom]**?

Incorrect	Him **[Whom]** gave you the present?
Correct	He **[Who]** gave you the present?

Remember: *Who* = subject
Whom = object

For step-by-step discussion, examples, and practice exercises, visit this page of the eText at **www.mycomplab.com**.

Whoever versus *whomever*

With the same rule in mind, you can distinguish between *whoever* and *whomever*. Which is correct?

Her warmth touched **whoever** she met.

Her warmth touched **whomever** she met.

In this sentence the pronoun functions as a direct object: Her warmth touched everyone she met, not someone who touched her. Thus *whomever* is the correct choice.

Exercise 39.2 In the following sentences, fill in the blank with the correct pronoun: *who, whom, whoever,* or *whomever*.

Example   Kids _who_ have depression, attention deficit hyperactivity disorder, or social phobia are more likely than their peers to become addicted to the Internet.

1. Past research suggests that 1.4 percent to 17.9 percent of adolescents are addicted to the Internet, most of _____ live in Eastern nations rather than in Western nations.
2. Although there is no official diagnosis for Internet addiction, _____ uses the Internet so much that it interferes with everyday life and decision-making ability may be an addict.
3. Boys are more likely to become addicted to the Internet than girls, except for those for _____ depression and social phobias are a problem, but boys _____ use the Internet for more than 20 hours a week are at highest risk of all.
4. _____ suspects his or her child has an Internet addiction should monitor that child's Internet usage.
5. There is one residential treatment center for Internet addiction in the United States available for _____ has been diagnosed with this illness.

Pronouns in comparisons

When you write a sentence using a comparison that includes *than* or *as* followed by a pronoun, usually you will have to think about which pronoun is correct. Which of the following is correct?

Vimala is a faster swimmer than **him**.

Vimala is a faster swimmer than **he**.

The test that will give you the correct answer is to add the verb that finishes the sentence—in this case, *is*.

Incorrect	Vimala is a faster swimmer than him is.
Correct	Vimala is a faster swimmer than he is.

Adding the verb makes the correct choice evident.

In some cases the choice of pronoun changes the meaning. Consider the following examples.

She likes ice cream more than me. [A bowl of ice cream is better than hanging out with me.]

She likes ice cream more than I. [I would rather have frozen yogurt.]

In such cases it is better to complete the comparison.

She likes ice cream more than I do.

Possessive pronouns

Possessive pronouns are confusing at times because possessive nouns are formed with apostrophes, but possessive pronouns do not require apostrophes. Pronouns that use apostrophes are always **contractions**.

It's	=	It is
Who's	=	Who is
They're	=	They are

The test for whether to use an apostrophe is to determine whether the pronoun is possessive or a contraction. The most confusing pair is *its* and *it's*.

Incorrect	Its a sure thing she will be elected. [Contraction]
Correct	It's a sure thing she will be elected. [**It is** a sure thing.]

Incorrect	The dog lost it's collar. [Possessive]
Correct	The dog lost its collar.

Whose versus *who's* follows the same pattern.

Incorrect	Who's bicycle has the flat tire? [Possessive]
Correct	Whose bicycle has the flat tire?

Incorrect	Whose on first? [Contraction]
Correct	Who's on first? [**Who is** on first?]

Possessive pronouns before *-ing* verbs

Pronouns that modify an *-ing* verb (called a *gerund*) or an *-ing* verb phrase (*gerund phrase*) should appear in the possessive.

Incorrect	The odds of you making the team are excellent.
Correct	The odds of your making the team are excellent.

Exercise 39.3 The following sentences include all the pronoun uses explained in this section. Underline the correct pronoun in each sentence.

Example Phineas Gage was a railroad foreman (whom/<u>who</u>), in 1848, became a medical miracle.

1. (We/Us) students knew him as the man (who's/whose) head was pierced with a tamping iron and he survived.
2. (Him/His) surviving was due to one of the first neurosurgeries ever, which was nothing like surgeries you or (me/I) have ever heard about.
3. (Whomever/Whoever) knew Phineas before the accident, knew a different version of (his/him) after.
4. (Its/It's) shocking to see Phineas's skull and life mask in the Warren Anatomical Museum.
5. However, a recently discovered photo of Phineas showing (his/him) holding the iron is possibly more interesting than (them/they).

39b Pronoun Agreement

Because pronouns usually replace or refer to other nouns, they must match those nouns in number and gender. The noun that the pronoun replaces is called its **antecedent**. If pronoun and antecedent match, they are in **agreement**. When a pronoun is close to the antecedent, usually there is no problem.

Maria forgot **her** coat.

The band **members** collected **their** uniforms.

Pronoun and number shifts

When pronouns and the nouns they replace are separated by several words, sometimes the agreement in number is lost.

PLURAL
When the World Wrestling Federation (WWF) used **wrestlers** to represent nations, there was no problem identifying the **villains**.
SING   SING
He was the enemy if **he** came from Russia. But after the Cold War,
PLURAL
wrestlers can switch from **good guys** to **bad guys**. We don't
SING
immediately know how **he** has been scripted—good or bad.

Careful writers make sure that pronouns match their antecedents.

Collective nouns

Collective nouns (such as *audience, class, committee, crowd, family, herd, jury, team*) can be singular or plural depending on whether the emphasis is on the group or on the particular individuals.

Correct   The **committee** was unanimous in **its** decision.

Correct   The **committee** put **their** opinions ahead of the goals of the unit.

Often a plural antecedent is added if the sense of the collective noun is plural.

Correct   The individual committee **members** put **their** opinions ahead of the goals of the unit.

COMMON ERRORS

Indefinite pronouns

Indefinite pronouns (such as *anybody, anything, each, either, everybody, everything, neither, none, somebody, something*) refer to unspecified people or things. Most take singular pronouns.

Incorrect   **Everybody** can choose **their** roommates.
Correct   **Everybody** can choose **his or her** roommate.
Correct   **All students** can choose **their** roomates.
alternative

A few indefinite pronouns (*all, any, either, more, most, neither, none, some*) can take either singular or plural pronouns.

Correct   **Some** of the shipment was damaged when **it** became overheated.
Correct   **All** thought **they** should have a good seat at the concert.

A few are always plural (*few, many, several*).

Correct   **Several** want refunds.

Remember: Words that begin with *any*, *some*, and *every* are usually singular.

For step-by-step discussion, examples, and practice exercises, visit this page of the eText at **www.mycomplab.com**.

COMMON ERRORS

e Edit Help

Pronoun agreement with compound antecedents

Antecedents joined by *and* take plural pronouns.

Correct   **Moncef and Driss** practiced **their** music.

Exception: When compound antecedents are preceded by *each* or *every,* use a singular pronoun.

Correct   **Every male cardinal and warbler** arrives before the female to define **its** territory.

When compound antecedents are connected by *or* or *nor,* the pronoun agrees with the antecedent closer to it.

Incorrect   **Either the Ross twins or Angela** should bring **their** CDs.

Correct   **Either the Ross twins or Angela** should bring **her** CDs.

Better   **Either Angela or the Ross twins** should bring **their** CDs.

When you put the plural *twins* last, the correct choice becomes the plural pronoun *their.*

Remember:
1. Use plural pronouns for antecedents joined by *and.*
2. Use singular pronouns for antecedents preceded by *each* or *every.*
3. Use a pronoun that agrees with the nearest antecedent when compound antecedents are joined by *or* or *nor.*

 For step-by-step discussion, examples, and practice exercises, visit this page of the eText at **www.mycomplab.com**.

Exercise 39.4 In the following sentences, pronouns are separated from the nouns they replace. Underline the antecedent and fill in the pronoun that agrees with it in the blank provided.

> **Example** Ironically, <u>greyhounds</u> are rarely gray; *their* fur can be all shades of red, brown, gray, and brindle.

1. Canine experts disagree on the origin of the name "greyhound," but many believe _____ derives from "Greek hound."
2. For over 5,000 years, greyhounds have been prized for _____ regal bearing and grace.

3. Greyhounds were introduced into England by the Cretans around 500 BC, but _____ are best known as the mascot for America's number-one bus line.

4. King Cob was the first notable greyhound sire recorded after England began documenting canine pedigrees in 1858, and _____ fathered 111 greyhounds in three years.

5. Each greyhound King Cob fathered was of the purest pedigree, even though _____ great-grandfather was a bulldog.

Exercise 39.5 Underline the indefinite pronouns, collective nouns, and compound antecedents in the paragraph that follows. Circle the related pronouns, and, if necessary, revise them to agree with their antecedents. In some cases, you may have to decide whether the emphasis is on the group or individuals within the group.

Example   <u>Many stories</u> attempt to explain why the number 13 is considered unlucky, but (they) provide no evidence that Friday is a particularly unlucky day. In fact, if <u>everyone</u> *he or she* were to follow stories from Greek history, (they) might be avoiding ladders and sidewalk cracks on Tuesday the 13th.

Although few would admit it, he or she often take(s) extra precautions on Friday the 13th. Some are so paralyzed by fear that they are simply unable to get out of his or her bed when Friday the 13th comes around. The Stress Management Center and Phobia Institute estimate(s) that more than 17 million people admit to being extra careful as they drive and go about their business on this day. Perhaps they are right to be concerned! A team writing for a British medical journal has shown that there is a significant increase in traffic accidents on Friday the 13th. However, this fear seems to be directed toward cars. According to representatives from both airlines, neither Delta nor United Airlines suffer from any noticeable drop in travel on Friday the 13th.

39c Problems with Pronouns and Gender

English does not have a neutral singular pronoun for a group of mixed genders or a person of unknown gender. Referring to a group of mixed genders using male pronouns is unacceptable to many people. Unless the school in the following example is all male, many readers would object to the use of *his*.

| Sexist | **Each student** must select his courses using the online registration system. |

Some writers attempt to avoid sexist usage by substituting a plural pronoun. This strategy, however, produces a grammatically incorrect sentence that also risks putting off some readers.

| Incorrect | **Each student** must select their courses using the online registration system. |

One strategy is to use *his or her* instead of *his*.

| Correct | **Each student** must select his or her courses using the online registration system. |

Often you can avoid using *his or her* by changing the noun to the plural form.

| Better | **All students** must select their courses using the online registration system. |

In some cases, using *his or her* may be necessary. Use this construction sparingly.

COMMON ERRORS   e Edit Help

Problems created by the pronoun *one* used as a subject

Some writers use *one* as a subject in an attempt to sound more formal. At best this strategy produces writing that sounds stilted, and at worst it produces annoying errors.

| Sexist | **One** can use his brains instead of a calculator to do simple addition. |

| Incorrect | **One** can use their brains instead of a calculator to do simple addition. [Agreement error: *Their* does not agree with *one*.] |

(Continued on next page)

COMMON ERRORS *(Continued)*

Incorrect	When **one** runs a 10K race for the first time, you often start out too fast. [Pronoun shift error: *One* changes to *you*.]
Correct	**One** can use his or her brains instead of a calculator to do simple addition.
Correct	**One** can use one's brains instead of a calculator to do simple addition.

You're better off avoiding using *one* as the subject of sentences.

Better	Use your brain instead of a calculator for simple addition.

Remember: Avoid using the pronoun *one* as a subject.

For step-by-step discussion, examples, and practice exercises, visit this page of the eText at **www.mycomplab.com**.

Exercise 39.6 The following sentences contain examples of gender bias. Rewrite the sentences using subject and pronoun formations that are unbiased. Try to avoid using "his or her" constructions.

Example	When an American turns 18, he is bombarded with advertisements that market easy credit.
Revise	When Americans turn 18, they are bombarded with advertisements that market easy credit.

1. When someone is financially overextended, he often considers credit cards as a way of making ends meet.
2. One might begin to convince himself that credit is the only way out.
3. But each adult must weigh the advantages and disadvantages of her own credit card use.
4. Eventually, one may find himself deep in debt because of high credit rates and overspending.
5. Then, one option might be for the individual to find a debt consolidator to assist him.

 39d Vague Reference

Pronouns can sometimes refer to more than one noun, thus confusing readers.

The **coach** rushed past the injured **player** to yell at the **referee**. She was hit in the face by a stray elbow.

You have to guess which person *she* refers to—the coach, the player, or the referee. Sometimes you cannot even guess the antecedent of a pronoun.

> The new subdivision destroyed the last remaining habitat for wildlife within the city limits. They have ruined our city with their unchecked greed.

Whom does *they* refer to? the mayor and city council? the developers? the people who live in the subdivision? or all of the above?

Pronouns should never leave the reader guessing about antecedents. If different nouns can be confused as the antecedent, then the ambiguity should be clarified.

Vague   Mafalda's pet boa constrictor crawled across Tonya's foot. She was mortified.

Better   When Mafalda's pet boa constrictor crawled across Tonya's foot, Mafalda was mortified.

If the antecedent is missing, then it should be supplied.

Vague   Mafalda wasn't thinking when she brought her boa constrictor into the crowded writing center. They got up and left the room in the middle of consultations.

Better   Mafalda wasn't thinking when she brought her boa constrictor into the crowded writing center. A few students got up and left the room in the middle of consultations.

COMMON ERRORS   *e Edit Help*

Vague use of *this*

Always use a noun immediately after *this, that, these, those*, and *some*.

Vague   Enrique asked Meg to remove the viruses on his computer. This was a bad idea.

Was it a bad idea for Enrique to ask Meg because she was insulted? Because she didn't know how? Because removing viruses would destroy some of Enrique's files?

Better   Enrique asked Meg to remove the viruses on his computer. This imposition on Meg's time made her resentful.

Remember: Ask yourself "*this* what?" and add the noun that *this* refers to.

 For step-by-step discussion, examples, and practice exercises, visit this page of the eText at **www.mycomplab.com**.

Exercise 39.7 Revise the following to correct the underlined vague references.

Example   Tuberculosis (TB) is a disease caused by a bacterium called Mycobacterium tuberculosis. This was once the leading cause of death in the United States.

Rewrite   Tuberculosis (TB) is a disease caused by a bacterium called Mycobacterium tuberculosis. This disease was once the leading cause of death in the United States.

1. They used to call tuberculosis consumption because it seems to consume its sufferers.

2. Sanitariums were built to house and treat patients, since it was spread through the air when they coughed, sneezed, or spit.

3. One of these was Waverly Hills, in Kentucky, where patients were treated with bed rest, sunshine, fresh air and food, and surgery. This included a form of lung compression.

4. The patients at Waverly Hills were treated by some of the best nurses and doctors in the country. Because it was so contagious, they couldn't leave. They say some of them may still be there today.

5. Waverly Hills is said to be haunted. One is a nurse who hung herself in front of room 502. This was because she was pregnant and had also contracted tuberculosis.

40 | Modifiers

QUICK*TAKE*

- **How do you use comparatives and superlatives correctly?**
  (see below)
  Incorrect: The Great Seattle Fire of 1889 that destroyed 25 city blocks was the most large fire in the city's history.
  Correct: The Great Seattle Fire of 1889 that destroyed 25 city blocks was the largest fire in the city's history.
- **How do you identify and correct dangling modifiers?** (see p. 597)
  Incorrect: After decreeing that all new buildings had to be made of stone or brick, **the streets and sidewalks** were raised one or two stories higher than before, leaving a system of tunnels and rooms under the city.
  Correct: After decreeing that all new buildings had to be made of stone or brick, **Seattle's leaders** raised the streets and sidewalks one or two stories higher than before, leaving a system of tunnels and rooms under the city.

Choose the Correct Modifier

Modifiers come in two varieties: adjectives and adverbs. The same words can function as adjectives or adverbs, depending on what they modify.

Adjectives modify

nouns—*iced* tea, *power* forward
pronouns—He is *brash*.

Adverbs modify

verbs—*barely* reach, drive *carefully*
adjectives—*truly* brave activist, *shockingly* red lipstick
other adverbs—*not* soon forget, *very* well
clauses—*Honestly*, I find ballet boring.

Adjectives answer the questions *Which one? How many?* and *What kind?* Adverbs answer the questions *How often? To what extent? When? Where? How?* and *Why?*

Use the correct forms of comparatives and superlatives

As kids, we used comparative and superlative modifiers to argue that Superman was *stronger* than Batman and recess was the *coolest* part of the day. Comparatives and superlatives are formed differently; all you need to know to determine which to use is the number of items you are comparing.

Comparative modifiers weigh one thing against another. They either end in *er* or are preceded by *more*.

Road bikes are faster on pavement than mountain bikes.

The more courageous juggler tossed flaming torches.

Superlative modifiers compare three or more items. They either end in *est* or are preceded by *most*.

April is the hottest month in New Delhi.

Wounded animals are the most ferocious.

When should you add a suffix instead of *more* or *most*? The following guidelines work in most cases:

Adjectives

- For adjectives of one or two syllables, add *er* or *est*.

  redder, heaviest

- For adjectives of three or more syllables, use *more* or *most*.

  more viable, most powerful

Adverbs

- For adverbs of one syllable, use *er* or *est*.

  nearer, slowest

- For adverbs with two or more syllables, use *more* or *most*.

  more convincingly, most humbly

Some frequently used comparatives and superlatives are irregular. The following list can help you become familiar with them.

Adjective	Comparative	Superlative
good	better	best
bad	worse	worst
little (amount)	less	least
many, much	more	most
Adverb	**Comparative**	**Superlative**
well	better	best
badly	worse	worst

Do not use both a suffix (*er* or *est*) and *more* or *most*.

Incorrect	The service at Jane's Restaurant is more slower than the service at Alphonso's.
Correct	The service at Jane's Restaurant is slower than the service at Alphonso's.

Be sure to name the elements being compared if they are not clear from the context.

Unclear comparative	Mice are cuter.
Clear	Mice are cuter than rats.

Unclear superlative	Nutria are the creepiest.
Clear	Nutria are the creepiest rodents.

Absolute modifiers cannot be comparative or superlative

Absolute modifiers are words that represent an unvarying condition and thus aren't subject to the degrees that comparative and superlative constructions convey. How many times have you heard something called *very unique* or *totally unique*? *Unique* means "one of a kind." There's nothing else like it. Thus something cannot be *very unique* or *totally unique*. It either is unique or it isn't. The United States Constitution makes a classic absolute modifier blunder when it begins, "We the People of the United States, in Order to form a more perfect Union. . . ." What is a *more perfect Union*? What's more perfect than perfect itself? The construction is nonsensical.

Absolute modifiers should not be modified by comparatives (*more* + modifier or modifier + *er*) or superlatives (*most* + modifier or modifier + *est*). Note the following list of common absolute modifiers.

absolute	impossible	unanimous
adequate	infinite	unavoidable
complete	main	uniform
entire	minor	unique
false	perfect	universal
fatal	principal	whole
final	stationary	
ideal	sufficient	

Exercise 40.1 Decide whether each word in parentheses should be comparative or superlative. Rewrite the word, adding either the correct suffix (*-er* or *-est*) or *good, best, bad, worst, more, most, less,* or *least*. If you find an absolute modifier (a word that should not be modified), underline it.

> **Example**   Volkswagen's Beetle is the (good) *best* selling car in history even though it had the same body for 60 years and had undergone only <u>minor</u> mechanical changes.

1. The Model T is ranked second in sales, but it is perhaps (important) historically than the Beetle because it was the first car to be mass produced, paving the way for cars to be built (cheaply) and (quickly) than ever before.

2. Selling for about $300, the Model T wasn't the (expensive) car on the market in the 1920s, however; that unique honor belongs to the 1922 Briggs & Stratton Flyer, which sold for $125 to $150.

3. With a top speed of over 250 mph and a price well over $1,500,000, the Bugatti Veyron 16.4 is currently the (expensive) and (powerful) car in the world, but it is not the (fast). The SSC Ultimate Aero is (fast) than the Bugatti.

4. Although fast "muscle cars," such as the Camero, the Corvette, the Firebird, and the Mustang, are (fast) than the Aero, that they are also (expensive) makes them (attractive) to young drivers and therefore (dangerous), too.

5. The (safe) car in history, the 1957 Aurora, is also the (rare); the one Aurora that was ever built was considered a complete failure.

Double negatives

In English, as in mathematics, two negatives equal a positive. Avoid using two negative words in one sentence, or you'll end up saying the opposite of what you mean. The following are negative words that you should avoid doubling up:

barely	nobody	nothing
hardly	none	scarcely
neither	no one	

Incorrect, double negative	Barely no one noticed that the pop star lip-synced during the whole performance.
Correct, single negative	Barely anyone noticed that the pop star lip-synched during the whole performance.
Incorrect, double negative	When the pastor asked if anyone had objections to the marriage, nobody said nothing.
Correct, single negative	When the pastor asked if anyone had objections to the marriage, nobody said anything.

COMMON ERRORS

Irregular adjectives and adverbs

Switch on a baseball interview and you will likely hear numerous modifier mistakes.

> Manager: We didn't play bad tonight. Martinez hit the ball real good, and I was glad to see Adamski pitch farther into the game than he did in his last start. His fastball was on, and he walked less hitters.

While this manager has his sports clichés down pat, he makes errors with five of the trickiest modifier pairs. In three cases he uses an adjective where an adverb would be correct.

Adjectives	Adverbs
bad	badly
good	well
real	really

[*Bad*, an adjective modifying the noun *call.*] The umpire made a bad call at the plate.

[*Badly*, an adverb modifying the verb *play.*] We didn't play badly.

[*Good*, an adjective modifying the noun *catch.*] Starke made a good catch.

[*Well*, an adverb modifying the verb *hit.*] Martinez hit the ball well.

Exception: *Well* acts as an adjective when it describes someone's health: Injured players must stay on the disabled list until they feel **well** enough to play every day.

[*Real*, an adjective modifying the noun *wood.*] While college players hit with aluminum bats, the professionals still use real wood.

[*Really*, an adverb modifying the adverb *well.*] Martinez hit the ball really **well**.

The coach also confused the comparative adjectives *less* and *fewer,* and the comparative adverbs *farther* and *further.*

Adjectives

less—a smaller, uncountable amount
fewer—a smaller number of things

(Continued on next page)

COMMON ERRORS *(Continued)*

Less	Baseball stadiums with pricey luxury suites cater less to families and more to business people with expense accounts.
Fewer	He walked fewer hitters.

Adverbs

farther—a greater distance

further—to a greater extent, a longer time, or a greater number

Farther	Some players argue that today's baseballs go farther than baseballs made just a few years ago.
Further	The commissioner of baseball curtly denied that today's baseballs are juiced, refusing to discuss the matter further.

Remember: *Bad, good, real, less* (for uncountables), and *fewer* (for countables) are adjectives. *Badly, well, really, farther* (for distance), and *further* (for extent, time, or number) are adverbs. *Well* is an adjective when it describes health.

For step-by-step discussion, examples, and practice exercises, visit this page of the eText at **www.mycomplab.com**.

Exercise 40.2 Revise the following paragraph to eliminate double negatives. More than one answer may be correct in each case.

Example   One ~~can't~~ ^{can} hardly survey the history of the American film industry without encountering the story of the Hollywood Ten, a group of artists targeted as communists.

After the creation of the House Un-American Activities Committee (HUAC), Cold War paranoia could not barely hide itself in post–World War II America. HUAC followed on the coattails of the 1938 Special Committee on Un-American Activities. This earlier committee did not focus not solely on communists; extremists from both the far left and the far right were targeted. By the 1940s, however, HUAC focused not on neither white supremacist nor pro-Nazi groups, but instead on the supposed communist infiltration of Hollywood. Scarcely no one could escape the grasp of HUAC; actors, producers, and directors all came under scrutiny. By the end of the proceedings, not hardly nobody remained unscathed. Hundreds in the entertainment industry were either fired or appeared on the infamous HUAC blacklist.

Exercise 40.3 The following words in parentheses are tricky adjective-adverb pairs. Underline the word(s) being modified in the sentence, and circle the correct adjective or adverb from the pair.

Example   To ensure the success of their missions, NASA has tackled the challenge of enabling astronauts to eat (healthy/**healthily**) in space so that they can stay (good/**well**).

In the early days of manned space missions, NASA had (fewer/less) problems feeding astronauts. But the (further/farther) astronauts traveled, the (further/farther) NASA had to go to ensure healthy eating in space. For example, the Mercury missions of the early 1960s took (fewer/less) time than an actual meal, so NASA's (real/really) challenge didn't come until crews were in space for longer periods of time. However, these shorter trips worked (good/well) as tests for experimental astronaut foods. By the mid-1960s, the astronauts on the Gemini missions were offered better ways to prepare and enjoy food in space. Engineers eventually discovered that packaging food in an edible liquid or gelatin container would prevent it from crumbling and damaging the equipment (bad/badly). By the Space Shuttle expeditions of the 1980s and 1990s, (real/really) headway had been made in terms of (good/well) dining technology, and crew members could devise their own menus.

40b Place Adjectives Carefully

As a general rule, the closer you place a modifier to the word it modifies, the less the chance you will confuse your reader. This section and the next elaborate on this maxim, giving you the details you need to put it into practice. Most native speakers have an ear for many of the guidelines presented here, with the notable exception of the placement of limiting modifiers, which is explained in Section 40c.

Place adjective phrases and clauses carefully

Adjective clauses frequently begin with *when*, *where*, or a relative pronoun like *that*, *which*, *who*, *whom*, or *whose*. An adjective clause usually follows the noun or pronoun it modifies.

Adjective clause modifying *salon*: The **salon** where I get my hair styled is raising its prices.

Adjective clause modifying *stylist*: I need to find a **stylist** who charges less.

Adjective phrases and clauses can also come before the person or thing they modify.

Adjective phrase modifying *girl:* Proud of her accomplishment, the little **girl** showed her trophy to her grandmother.

Adjective phrases or clauses can be confusing if they are separated from the word they modify.

Confusing   Watching from the ground below, the kettle of broadwing hawks circled high above the observers.

Is the kettle of hawks watching from the ground below? You can fix the problem by putting the modified subject immediately after the modifier or placing the modifier next to the modified subject.

Better   The kettle of broadwing hawks circled high above the **observers** who were watching from the ground below.

Better   Watching from the ground below, the **observers** saw a kettle of broadwing hawks circle high above them.

See dangling modifiers in Section 40e.

Exercise 40.4   Underline the adjective phrases and clauses in the following sentences. If any phrase or clause could apply to more than one subject, revise the sentence to eliminate ambiguity.

Example   Arriving June 19, 1865, the Texas slaves were informed of their freedom by Union soldiers two years after the signing of the Emancipation Proclamation.

Rewrite   Arriving June 19, 1865, two years after the signing of the Emancipation Proclamation, Union soldiers informed Texas slaves of their freedom.

1. Now known as Juneteenth, Texas celebrates the day Texan slaves discovered their freedom.
2. A people's event that has become an official holiday, freed slaves celebrated annually their day of emancipation.
3. Celebrated vigorously in the 1950s and 1960s, the Civil Rights movement sparked a renewed interest in the Juneteenth holiday.
4. Still going strong, entertainment, education, and self-improvement are all activities included in the annual celebration.

Place one-word adjectives before the modified word(s)

One-word adjectives almost always precede the word or words they modify.

Pass the hot sauce, please.

When one-word adjectives are not next to the word or words being modified, they can create misunderstandings.

Unclear   Before his owner withdrew him from competition, the fiercest rodeo's bull injured three riders.

Readers may think *fiercest* modifies *rodeo's* instead of *bull*. Placing the adjective before *bull* will clarify the meaning.

Better   Before his owner withdrew him from competition, the rodeo's fiercest bull injured three riders.

Exception: predicate adjectives follow linking verbs

Predicate adjectives are the most common exception to the norm of single-word adjectives preceding words they modify. Predicate adjectives follow linking verbs such as *is, are, was, were, seem, feel, smell, taste,* and *look*. Don't be fooled into thinking they are adverbs. If the word following a linking verb modifies the subject, use a predicate adjective. If it modifies an action verb, use an adverb. Can you identify the word being modified in the following sentence?

I feel odd.

Odd modifies the subject *I*, not the verb *feel*. Thus, *odd* is a predicate adjective that implies the speaker feels ill. If it were an adverb, the sentence would read *I feel oddly*. The adverb *oddly* modifying *feel* would imply the speaker senses things in unconventional ways. Try the next one.

The bruise looked bad.

Since *bad* modifies *bruise, bad* is a predicate adjective implying a serious injury. *Looked* is the linking verb that connects the two. If we made the modifier an adverb, the sentence would read *The bruise looked badly*, conjuring the creepy notion that the bruise had eyes but couldn't see well. You can avoid such bizarre constructions if you know when to use predicate adjectives with linking verbs.

Put subjective adjectives before objective adjectives

When you have a series of adjectives expressing both opinion and more objective description, put the subjective adjectives before the objective ones. For example, in

the sultry cabaret singer

sultry is subjective and *cabaret* is objective.

Put determiners before other adjectives

Determiners are a group of adjectives that include possessive nouns (such as *woman's* prerogative and *Pedro's* violin), possessive pronouns (such as *my, your,* and *his*), demonstrative pronouns (*this, that, these, those*), and indefinite pronouns (such as *all, both, each, either, few,* and *many*). When you are using a series of adjectives, put the determiners first.

> our finest hour

> Tara's favorite old blue jeans

> those crazy kids

When you are using a numerical determiner with another determiner, put the numerical determiner first.

> both **those** tattoos

> all **these** people

Multilingual writers can consult Section 54c for more on the placement of modifiers.

Exercise 40.5 Underline the adjectives in the following paragraph. If any are placed ambiguously or incorrectly, revise them.

Example

influential American

Johnny Cash was an American influential country singer and songwriter.

Cash was known for his deep voice as well as his dark clothing and demeanor. These traits all earned him the nickname "The Man in Black." Keeping with his dark demeanor, much of Cash's music, especially that of his later career, echoed themes of sorrow, struggle moral, and redemption. One of his popular most songs, "Ring of Fire," was actually penned by his future wife, June Carter. The song may sound happy, but it is dark. It describes inner Carter's turmoil as she wrestled with her forbidden love for the wild, unpredictable Cash. Rocky Johnny Cash and June Carter's relationship was award-winning depicted in the 2005 film, *Walk the Line.*

Place Adverbs Carefully

For the most part, the guidelines for adverb placement are not as complex as the guidelines for adjective placement.

Place adverbs before or after the words they modify

Single-word adverbs and adverbial clauses and phrases can usually sit comfortably either before or after the words they modify.

Dimitri quietly **walked** down the hall.

Dimitri **walked** quietly down the hall.

Conjunctive adverbs—*also, however, instead, likewise, then, therefore, thus,* and others—are adverbs that show how ideas relate to one another. They prepare a reader for contrasts, exceptions, additions, conclusions, and other shifts in an argument. Conjunctive adverbs can usually fit well into more than one place in the sentence. In the following example, *however* could fit in three different places.

Between two main clauses

Professional football players earn exorbitant salaries; however, they pay for their wealth with lifetimes of chronic pain and debilitating injuries.

Within second main clause

Professional football players earn exorbitant salaries; they pay for their wealth, however, with lifetimes of chronic pain and debilitating injuries.

At end of second main clause

Professional football players earn exorbitant salaries; they pay for their wealth with lifetimes of chronic pain and debilitating injuries however.

Subordinating conjunctions—words such as *after, although, because, if, since, than, that, though, when,* and *where*—often begin **adverb clauses**. Notice that we can place adverb clauses with subordinating conjunctions either before or after the word(s) being modified:

After someone in the audience yelled, he **forgot** the lyrics.

He **forgot** the lyrics after someone in the audience yelled.

While you have some leeway with adverb placement, follow the advice in Section 40d: Avoid distracting interruptions between the subject and verb, the verb and the object, or within the verb phrase. A long adverbial clause is usually best placed at the beginning or end of a sentence.

COMMON ERRORS

 e <u>Edit</u> **Help**

Placement of limiting modifiers

Words such as *almost, even, hardly, just, merely, nearly, not, only,* and *simply* are called limiting modifiers. Although people often play fast and loose with their placement in everyday speech, limiting modifiers should always go immediately before the word or words they modify in your writing. Many writers have difficulty with the placement of *only.* Like other limiting modifiers, *only* should be placed immediately before the word it modifies.

Incorrect   The Gross Domestic Product only gives one indicator of economic growth.

Correct   The Gross Domestic Product gives only one indicator of economic growth.

Remember: Place limiting modifiers immediately before the word(s) they modify.

For step-by-step discussion, examples, and practice exercises, visit this page of the e Text at **www.mycomplab.com**.

Exercise 40.6   Rewrite each of the following sentences, moving the adverb to eliminate possible confusion. Place adverbs where they make the most logical sense within the context of the sentence. Underline the adverbs in your revised sentences.

Example   In the mid-1800s, Father Gregor Mendel developed experiments ingeniously examining the area of heredity.

Revise   In the mid-1800s, Father Gregor Mendel <u>ingeniously</u> developed experiments examining the area of heredity.

1. Mendel's work focused on initially hybridizing the Lathyrus, or sweet pea.
2. The Lathyrus possessed variations conveniently composed of differing sizes and colors.
3. Hybridizing the plants easily allowed Mendel to view the mathematical effects of dominant and recessive trait mixing.
4. By crossing white-flowered pea pods with red-flowered pea pods, Mendel proved successfully existing pairs of hereditary factors determined the color characteristics of offspring.
5. Though published in 1866, Mendel's theory of heredity remained unnoticed mostly by the biological community until the early 1900s.

Revise Disruptive Modifiers

The fundamental way readers make sense of sentences is to identify the subject, verb, and object. Modifiers can sink a sentence if they interfere with the reader's ability to connect the three. Usually, single-word modifiers do not significantly disrupt a sentence. However, avoid placing modifying clauses and phrases between a subject and a verb, between a verb and an object, and within a verb phrase.

Disruptive	The forest fire, no longer held in check by the exhausted firefighters, jumped the firebreak. [Separates the subject from the verb]
Better	No longer held in check by the exhausted firefighters, the forest fire jumped the firebreak. [Puts the modifier before the subject]
Disruptive	The fire's heat seemed to melt, at a temperature hot enough to liquefy metal, the saplings in its path. [Separates the verb from the object]
Better	At a temperature hot enough to liquefy metal, the fire's heat seemed to melt the saplings in its path. [Puts the modifier before the subject]

WRITING SMART

Split Infinitives

An infinitive is *to* plus the base form of a verb. A split infinitive occurs when an adverb separates *to* from the base verb form.

Infinitive = *To* + Base verb form

Examples: **to feel, to speak, to borrow**

Split infinitive = *To* + Modifier + Base verb form

Examples: **to strongly feel, to barely speak, to liberally borrow**

The most famous split infinitive in recent history occurs in the opening credits of *Star Trek* episodes: "to boldly go where no one has gone before." The alternative without the split infinitive is "to go boldly where no one has gone before." The writers in *Star Trek* no doubt were

(Continued on next page)

WRITING SMART *(Continued)*

aware they were splitting an infinitive, but they chose *to boldly go* because they wanted the emphasis on *boldly*, not *go*.

Nevertheless, many split infinitives are considered awkward for good reason.

Awkward	You have to get away from the city lights to better appreciate the stars in the night sky.
Better	You have to get away from the city lights to appreciate the stars in the night sky better.
Awkward	To, as planned, stay in Venice, we need to reserve a hotel room now.
Better	To stay in Venice as planned, we need to reserve a hotel room now.

When a sentence would sound strange without the adverb's splitting the infinitive, you can either retain the split or, better yet, revise the sentence to avoid the problem altogether.

Acceptable	When found by the search party, the survivors were able to barely whisper their names.
Alternative	When found by the search party, the survivors could barely whisper their names.

Exercise 40.7 Underline the disruptive modifiers in the following paragraph. You may find a modifying clause or phrase that separates major components of a sentence, or you may find a split infinitive. Rewrite the paragraph to eliminate the disruptions. More than one way of revising may be correct.

Example	The Catholic papacy, <u>because of conflict in the Papal States</u>, resided in France for more than seventy years.
Revise	Because of conflict in the Papal States, the Catholic papacy resided in France for more than seventy years.

In the thirteenth and fourteenth centuries, the Italian Papal States, because of militantly rivaling families, were consumed in chaos. In 1305 the cardinals elected, unable to agree on an Italian, a Frenchman as the new pope. He decided to temporarily remain in France. The papacy would, because of various religious and political reasons, remain in France until 1378. Rome, during the papacy's seventy-year absence, would lose both prestige and income.

40e Revise Dangling Modifiers

Some modifiers are ambiguous because they could apply to more than one word or clause. Dangling modifiers are ambiguous for the opposite reason; they don't have a word to modify. In such cases the modifier is usually an introductory clause or phrase. What is being modified should immediately follow the phrase, but in the following sentence it is absent.

> After bowling a perfect game, Surfside Lanes hung Marco's photo on the wall.

Neither the subject of the sentence, *Surfside Lanes*, nor the direct object, *Marco's photo*, is capable of bowling a perfect game. Since a missing noun or pronoun causes a dangling modifier, simply rearranging the sentence will not resolve the problem. You can eliminate a dangling modifier in two ways.

1. Insert the noun or pronoun being modified immediately after the introductory modifying phrase.

   > After bowling a perfect game, Marco was honored by having his photo hung on the wall at Surfside Lanes.

2. Rewrite the introductory phrase as an introductory clause to include the noun or pronoun.

   > After Marco bowled a perfect game, Surfside Lanes hung his photo on the wall.

Exercise 40.8 Each of the following sentences contains a dangling modifier. Revise the sentences to eliminate dangling modifiers according to the methods described in Section 40e. More than one way of revising may be correct.

Example	Though it preceded Woodstock, popular music history often obscures the Monterey Pop Festival.
Revise	Though the Monterey Pop Festival preceded Woodstock, it is often obscured by popular music history.

1. Lasting for three days in June of 1967, over thirty artists performed.
2. The largest American music festival of its time, attendance totaled over 200,000.
3. With artists such as Ravi Shankar, Otis Redding, and The Who, the fans encountered various musical genres.
4. Performing live for the first time in America, fans howled as Jimi Hendrix set his guitar on fire.
5. Establishing a standard for future festivals, Woodstock and Live Aid would eventually follow suit.

Exercise P8.1 The following passage contains several errors. These errors include fragments, comma splices, and run-on sentences as well as errors in subject-verb agreement, verb tense, verb endings, pronoun case, pronoun reference, and modifiers. Use the Common Errors guide on the back flap of the book and information from Part 8 to help identify the errors and rewrite the passage.

Although Charles Brockden Brown was not the first American novelist. He is the more frequently studied and republished practitioner of the "early American novel" between 1789 and 1820. His novels simply is often characterized as Gothic fiction, building plots around motifs such as ventriloquism, sleepwalking, and religious mania and drawing on medical Enlightenment-era writings.

Wieland or, The Transformation: An American Tale, also called *Wieland,* were Charles Brockden Brown's first work. It is set sometime between the French and Indian War and the American Revolutionary War, published in 1798. The plot details the horrible events that befall Clara Wieland, her brother Theodore, and Theodore's family. Clara and Theodore's father was a German immigrant who finded his own religion and came to America to spread it to the indigenous people. One night, while worshipped alone in his temple, he bursted into flames after a period of deteriorating health, he dies and they inherit his property. Theodore marries their childhood friend, Catharine Pleyel, they have four children.

Soon, Theodore and Catherine's brother, Henry, both begins to hear voices. At first doubtful about them, Clara eventually hears them, too. A mysterious stranger named Carwin appear and suggest that the voices might be caused by ventriloquism. The intrigue continues as she falls in love with Henry and Carwin tries to rape Clara, to tell her only that he believes her is under supernatural protection. Theodore then kills his family. Claims he was under the control of the voices. Clara thinks Carwin is to blame for Theodore's madness, and he admits to being a biloquist, or someone who can speak in two distinct voices, he did not tell Theodore to commit the murders. Theodore is going to prison, but escapes and went to Clara's house to kill her. Carwin stops him by using his very unique ability. Theodore comes to his senses, and then kills hisself. The novel ends as Clara's house burns down and she is forced to leave.

The novel is based on the true story of a multiple murder in 1781 that took place at Tomhannock, New York. James Yates killed his wife and four children and attempted to kill his sister under the influence of a religious delusion. Yates expressed no remorse for the murders in court.

Wieland, influential to later Gothic writers such Edgar Allan Poe and Mary Shelley.

PART 9

Understanding Punctuation and Mechanics

You **can learn more and do more** with MyCompLab and with the eText version of *The Penguin Handbook*. To find resources in MyCompLab that will help you use punctuation successfully, go to

Resources

Grammar

> **Punctuation and Mechanics**

Abbreviations, Capitalization, and Numbers | Apostrophes | Commas | Common Spelling Errors | End Punctuation | Italics and Quotation Marks | Other Punctuation | Semicolons and Colons

Review the tutorials (Read, Watch, Listen) within each topic, then complete the Exercises and click on the Gradebook to measure your progress.

In the eText version of *The Penguin Handbook*, you will also find extra instruction, examples and practice exercises.

41 | Commas

QUICK*TAKE*

- **What parts of a sentence should be set off with commas?** (see below)
  Incorrect: Although bears have a better sense of smell than bloodhounds there are reasons why the military cannot fly them into dangerous areas, and have them sniff out enemy combatants.
  Correct: Although bears have a better sense of smell than bloodhounds, there are reasons why the military cannot fly them into dangerous areas and have them sniff out enemy combatants.

- **When do you use commas with long modifiers?** (see p. 607)
  Restrictive: Anyone who thinks bears could be trained to carry out a military mission hasn't really thought the idea through.
  Nonrestrictive: The Pentagon, which recently added a virtual suggestion box to its Web site, has been receiving some unusual ideas.

- **How do you use commas with quotations?** (see p. 613)
  Incorrect: "Bears are the best sniffers", wrote someone.
  Correct: "Bears are the best sniffers," wrote someone.

41a Commas with Introductory Elements

Introductory elements usually need to be set off by commas. Introductory words or phrases signal a shift in ideas or a particular arrangement of ideas; they help direct the reader's attention to the writer's most important points.

Common introductory elements

Conjunctive adverbs	Introductory phrases
however	of course
therefore	above all
nonetheless	for example
also	in other words
otherwise	as a result
finally	on the other hand
instead	in conclusion
thus	in addition

When a conjunctive adverb or introductory phrase begins a sentence, the comma follows.

> Therefore, the suspect could not have been at the scene of the crime.

> Above all, remember to let water drip from the faucets if the temperature drops below freezing.

When a conjunctive adverb comes in the middle of a sentence, set it off with commas preceding and following.

> If you really want to prevent your pipes from freezing, however, you should insulate them before the winter comes.

Conjunctive adverbs and phrases that do not require commas

Occasionally the conjunctive adverb or phrase blends into a sentence so smoothly that a pause would sound awkward.

> Awkward　Of course, we'll come.
>
> Better　　Of course we'll come.

> Awkward　Even if you take every precaution, the pipes in your home may freeze, nevertheless.
>
> Better　　Even if you take every precaution, the pipes in your home may freeze nevertheless.

Exercise 41.1　Underline conjunctive adverbs, introductory phrases, and long introductory modifiers in the following sentences. Then set off those elements with commas when necessary.

> Example　Although king cobras have small fangs, one bite is poisonous enough to kill an elephant.

1. King cobras in fact have a poisonous bite from the moment they are born.
2. Even though king cobras carry lethal venom women in Thailand's King Cobra Club dance with the snakes' heads in their mouths.
3. Also many Southeast Asian countries worship the king cobra.
4. Above all avoid provoking king cobras; they are not aggressive animals if left undisturbed.
5. An antidote is available however if you are bitten by a cobra.

COMMON ERRORS

e <u>Edit</u> Help

Commas with long introductory modifiers

Long subordinate clauses or phrases that begin sentences should be followed by a comma. The following sentence lacks the needed comma.

Incorrect   Because teens and younger adults are so comfortable with and reliant on cell phone devices texting while driving does not immediately seem like an irresponsible and possibly deadly act

When you read this sentence, you likely had to go back to sort it out. The words *cell phone devices* and *texting* tend to run together. When the comma is added, the sentence is easier to understand because the reader knows where the subordinate clause ends and where the main clause begins:

Correct   Because teens and younger adults are so comfortable with and reliant on cell phone devices, texting while driving does not immediately seem like an irresponsible and possibly deadly act.

How long is a long introductory modifier? Short introductory adverbial phrases and clauses of five words or fewer can get by without the comma if the omission does not mislead the reader. Using the comma is still correct after short introductory adverbial phrases and clauses.

Correct   In the long run stocks have always done better than bonds.

Correct   In the long run, stocks have always done better than bonds.

Remember: Put commas after long introductory modifiers.

For step-by-step discussion, examples, and practice exercises, visit this page of the eText at **www.mycomplab.com**.

41b Commas with Compound Clauses

Two main clauses joined by a coordinating conjunction (*and, or, so, yet, but, nor, for*) form a compound sentence (see Section 35e). Writers sometimes get confused about when to insert a comma before a coordinating conjunction.

Use a comma to separate main clauses

Main clauses carry enough grammatical weight to be punctuated as sentences. When two main clauses are joined by a coordinating conjunction, place a comma before the coordinating conjunction in order to distinguish them.

> Sandy borrowed Martin's netbook on Tuesday, and she returned it on Friday.

Very short main clauses joined by a coordinating conjunction do not need commas.

> She called and she called, but no one answered.

Do not use a comma to separate two verbs with the same subject

| Incorrect | Sandy borrowed Martin's video camera on Tuesday, and returned it on Friday. |

Sandy is the subject of both *borrowed* and *returned*. This sentence has only one main clause; it should not be punctuated as a compound sentence.

| Correct | Sandy borrowed Martin's video camera on Tuesday and returned it on Friday. |

Exceptions to this rule occur when there is a lapse of time or after *said*.

> He did not study, and failed.

> "That's fine," he said, and went on reading.

COMMON ERRORS   e Edit Help

Commas in compound sentences

The easiest way to distinguish between compound sentences and sentences with phrases that follow the main clause is to isolate the part that comes after the conjunction. If the part that follows the conjunction can stand on its own as a complete sentence, insert a comma. If it cannot, omit the comma.

Main clause plus phrases

> Mario thinks he lost his passport while riding the bus or by absentmindedly leaving it on the counter when he checked into the hostel.

(Continued on next page)

COMMON ERRORS *(Continued)*

Look at what comes after the coordinating conjunction *or*:

> by absentmindedly leaving it on the counter when he checked into the hostel

This group of words is not a main clause and cannot stand on its own as a complete sentence. Do not set it off with a comma.

Main clauses joined with a conjunction

> On Saturday Mario went to the American consulate to get a new passport, but the officer told him that replacement passports could not be issued on weekends.

Read the clause after the coordinating conjunction *but*:

> the officer told him that replacement passports could not be issued on weekends

This group of words can stand on its own as a complete sentence. Thus, it is a main clause; place a comma before *but*.

Remember:

1. Place a comma before the coordinating conjunction (*and, but, for, or, nor, so, yet*) if there are two main clauses.

2. Do not use a comma before the coordinating conjunction if there is only one main clause.

 For step-by-step discussion, examples, and practice exercises, visit this page of the eText at **www.mycomplab.com**.

Do not use a comma to separate a main clause from a restrictive clause or phrase

When clauses and phrases that follow the main clause are essential to the meaning of a sentence, they should not be set off with a comma.

Incorrect	Sandy plans to borrow Felicia's CD collection, while Felicia is on vacation.
Correct	Sandy plans to borrow Felicia's CD collection while Felicia is on vacation.
Incorrect	Sandy plans to borrow Felicia's CDs while Felicia is on vacation, in order to put them on her iPod.
Correct	Sandy plans to borrow Felicia's CDs while Felicia is on vacation in order to put them on her iPod.

COMMON ERRORS

e Edit Help

Do not use a comma to set off a *because* clause that follows a main clause

Writers frequently place unnecessary commas before *because* and similar subordinate conjunctions that follow a main clause. *Because* is not a coordinating conjunction; thus it should not be set off by a comma unless the comma improves readability.

Incorrect   I struggled to complete my term papers last year, because I had a full-time job along with my course load.

Correct   I struggled to complete my term papers last year because I had a full-time job along with my course load.

But do use a comma after an introductory *because* clause.

Incorrect   Because Danny left his red jersey at home Coach Russell benched him.

Correct   Because Danny left his red jersey at home, Coach Russell benched him.

Remember: Use a comma after a *because* clause that begins a sentence. Do not use a comma to set off a *because* clause that follows a main clause.

 For step-by-step discussion, examples, and practice exercises, visit this page of the eText at **www.mycomplab.com.**

Exercise 41.2   Decide which of the coordinating conjunctions in the following sentences should be preceded by commas and add them.

> **Example**   Most people are familiar with the usual five senses, but there are four more accepted senses.

1. Thermoception is the sense of heat or its absence.
2. Because of the fluid-containing cavities of our inner ear we have a sense of balance, or equilibrioception.
3. Nociception is the perception of pain from the skin, joints, and body organs yet this does not include the brain.
4. Headaches do not originate from the brain because the brain has no pain receptors.
5. Proprioception is also known as "body awareness" and it refers to our unconscious knowledge of where our body parts are.

41c Commas with Nonrestrictive Modifiers

Imagine that you are sending a friend a group photo that includes your aunt. Which sentence is correct?

> In the back row the woman wearing the pink hat is my aunt.

> In the back row the woman, wearing the pink hat, is my aunt.

Both sentences can be correct depending on what is in the photo. If there are three women standing in the back row and only one is wearing a pink hat, this piece of information is necessary for identifying your aunt. In this case the sentence without commas is correct because it identifies your aunt as the woman wearing the pink hat. Such necessary modifiers are **restrictive** and do not require commas.

If only one woman is standing in the back row, *wearing the pink hat* is extra information and not necessary to identify your aunt. The modifier in this case is **nonrestrictive** and is set off by commas.

Distinguish restrictive and nonrestrictive modifiers

You can distinguish restrictive and nonrestrictive modifiers by deleting the modifier and then deciding whether the remaining sentence is changed. For example, delete the modifier *once synonymous with the Internet* from the following sentence:

> The proliferation of gadgets with downloadable apps including Twitter, Facebook, Skype, online games, and streaming movies have cannibalized the World Wide Web, **once synonymous with the Internet,** and have challenged the Web browser as the center of the Internet world.

The result leaves the meaning of the main clause unchanged.

> The proliferation of gadgets with downloadable apps including Twitter, Facebook, Skype, online games, and streaming movies have cannibalized the World Wide Web and have challenged the Web browser as the center of the Internet world.

The modifier is nonrestrictive and should be set off by commas.

In contrast, deleting *who left work early* does change the meaning of this sentence:

> The employees **who left work early** avoided driving home in the blizzard.

Without the modifier the sentence reads:

> The employees avoided driving home in the blizzard.

Now it sounds as if all the employees avoided driving home in the blizzard instead of just the ones who left early. The modifier is clearly restrictive and does not require commas.

Recognize types and placement of nonrestrictive modifiers

Nonrestrictive modifiers are used frequently to add details. You can add several kinds of nonrestrictive modifiers to a short, simple sentence (see Sections 35c and 35d).

> The student ran across campus,
>
> which left him panting when he got to class. [adjective clause]
> his backpack swaying back and forth. [absolute phrase]
> weaving his way down the crowded sidewalks. [participial phrase]

Nonrestrictive modifiers can be placed at the beginning of sentences.

> When he realized his watch had stopped, [adverb clause]
> With his thoughts on the intramural championship later that afternoon, [prepositional phrase]
> Rushing to get to class, [participial phrase]
>
> the student ran across campus.

They also can be placed in the middle of sentences.

> The student,
>
> who had woken up only fifteen minutes before class, [adjective clause]
> my old roommate, [appositive]
> wearing a ripped black trenchcoat, [participial phrase]
> with one arm in a cast and the other clutching a stack of books, [prepositional phrase]
>
> ran across campus.

Pay special attention to appositives

Clauses and phrases can be restrictive or nonrestrictive, depending on the context. Often the difference is obvious, but some modifiers require close consideration, especially appositives. An **appositive** is a noun or noun phrase that identifies or adds information to the noun preceding it.

Consider the following pair.

1   Apple's tablet computer the iPad introduced a class of devices between smartphones and laptops.

2   Apple's tablet computer, the iPad, introduced a class of devices between smartphones and laptops.

Which is correct? The appositive *the iPad* is not essential to the meaning of the sentence and offers additional information. Sentence 2 is correct.

Use commas around nonrestrictive clauses within a *that* clause

Restrictive clauses beginning with *that* sometimes have a nonrestrictive clause embedded within them.

Incorrect	I want you to know that despite all the arguments we have had over the past few months I still value your advice.
Correct	I want you to know that, despite all the arguments we have had over the past few months, I still value your advice.

Use commas to mark off parenthetical expressions

A **parenthetical expression** provides information or commentary that is usually not essential to the sentence's meaning.

Incorrect	My mother much to my surprise didn't say anything when she saw my pierced nose.
Correct	My mother, much to my surprise, didn't say anything when she saw my pierced nose.

Some parenthetical expressions are essential to the point of the sentence, especially ones that make contrasts, but they too are set off by commas.

Incorrect	The candidate's conversational skills not her résumé landed her the job.
Correct	The candidate's conversational skills, not her résumé, landed her the job.

However, do not use a comma when the parenthetical expression is one word and its function is not obviously parenthetical.

Incorrect	The Freshmen Studies course is, fundamentally, an introduction to writing arguments.
Correct	The Freshmen Studies course is fundamentally an introduction to writing arguments.

COMMON ERRORS

Commas with *that* and *which* clauses

Writers often confuse when to use commas to set off modifying phrases beginning with *that* and *which*. *That* clauses follow a hard and fast rule: They are used only as restrictive modifiers.

A *that* clause is a restrictive modifier: Omit commas

Two other women were wearing the same dress that Sherice bought specifically to wear to the awards banquet.

Which clauses are usually used as nonrestrictive modifiers. While *which* clauses can also function as restrictive modifiers, careful writers observe the difference and change *which* to *that* if the clause is restrictive.

A *which* clause is a nonrestrictive modifier: Use commas

A student government committee is recommending the allocation of an additional $10,000 for Black History Month festivities, which take place in February, in order to bring a nationally known speaker to campus.

When a *which* clause acts as a restrictive modifier, change *which* to that

Incorrect   The uncertainty which surrounded the selection of the new coach was created by the sudden and unexpected resignation of her predecessor.

Correct   The uncertainty that surrounded the selection of the new coach was created by the sudden and unexpected resignation of her predecessor.

Remember:

1.   *That* clauses are restrictive modifiers and do not take commas.

2.   *Which* clauses can be either restrictive or nonrestrictive, but careful writers use them as nonrestrictive modifiers and set them off with commas.

For step-by-step discussion, examples, and practice exercises, visit this page of the eText at **www.mycomplab.com**.

Use commas to mark off absolute phrases

An **absolute phrase** contains at least one noun or pronoun and at least one participle (see Section 35d). Absolutes can modify a noun or a whole sentence.

Incorrect	Her project completed Marianne decided to splurge on a beach vacation.
Correct	Her project completed, Marianne decided to splurge on a beach vacation.

Exercise 41.3 The underlined portions of the following paragraph are modifiers. Identify each modifier as either restrictive or nonrestrictive. Then set off the nonrestrictive modifiers with commas.

Example   Marcus Ulpius Traianus, a successful governor and soldier, became the Roman emperor in the year AD 98.
(Nonrestrictive modifier)

Trajan decided to use the Empire's coffers which were brimming with war booty to begin a massive building program. He commissioned the market Mercati Traianei and a lush new forum. In AD 113 he also built a column still on display in Rome today adorned with reliefs depicting his military victories. But the conditions that many Romans faced from day to day stood in stark contrast to the splendor Trajan created. Living in cramped apartment buildings people coped with dark, dirty, and sometimes cold homes.

41d Commas with Items in a Series

In a series of three or more items, place a comma after each item but the last one. The comma between the last two items goes before the coordinating conjunction (*and, or, nor, but, so, for, yet*).

Health officials in Trenton, Manhattan, and the Bronx have all reported new cases of meningitis.

Exercise 41.4 Insert commas to separate items in a series, following the academic convention. Some sentences may not require commas.

Example   Suburban residents unknowingly spread diseases among deer by feeding them salt, corn, and pellets.

1. White-tailed deer ground squirrels gray squirrels foxes raccoons coyotes opossums and armadillos often wander across my back yard.

2. White-tailed deer and coyotes are among the animals that have adapted best to urban habitats.
3. Deer find cover in urban green belts and thrive on young trees shrubs and flowers that homeowners plant.
4. White-tailed deer reproduce quickly because they have always been prey animals for wolves coyotes mountain lions bobcats and bears.
5. Elimination of predators curtailment of hunting and a high birth rate have led to deer overpopulation in many urban areas.

41e   Commas with Coordinate Adjectives

Coordinate adjectives are two or more adjectives that independently modify the same noun. Coordinate adjectives that are not linked by *and* must be separated by a comma.

> After the financial crisis of 2007–2010, the creators of credit-default swaps and other risky investments are no longer the **fresh-faced, giddy** kids of Wall Street.

Distinguish coordinate adjectives

You can recognize coordinate adjectives by reversing their order; if their meaning remains the same, the adjectives are coordinate and must be linked by *and* or separated by a comma. In the following example when the order of the adjectives changes, the description of *lifestyles* retains the same meaning:

> Because border collies are bred to herd sheep, their energetic temperaments may not suit city dwellers' more **sedentary, staid** lifestyles.

> Because border collies are bred to herd sheep, their energetic temperaments may not suit city dwellers' more **staid, sedentary** lifestyles.

Do not use commas to link cumulative adjectives

Commas are not used between cumulative adjectives. Cumulative adjectives are two or more adjectives that work together to modify a noun: *deep blue sea, inexpensive mountain bike*. If reversing their order changes the description of the noun (or violates the order of English, such as *mountain inexpensive bike*), the adjectives are cumulative and should not be separated by a comma.

The following example doesn't require a comma in the cumulative adjective series *massive Corinthian.*

Visitors to Rome's Pantheon pass between the massive Corinthian columns flanking the front door.

We know they are cumulative because reversing their order to read *Corinthian massive* would alter the way they modify *columns*—in this case, so much so that they no longer make sense.

Exercise 41.5 Identify each underlined adjective series as either coordinate or cumulative. Then insert commas to separate coordinate adjectives.

Example Krampus is a furry, demon-like creature that accompanies Santa Claus on his rounds during Christmastime.
(Coordinate)

In Austrian and Hungarian holiday folklore, Krampus punishes the naughty children, while Santa rewards the good. The naughtiest most unrepentant children are carted away by Krampus in a large basket or bag to be cast into the dark fiery pits of Hell. On nineteenth-century postcards, Krampus is often depicted with sharp curling horns, hooves, and a long red tongue. Menacing leering eyes flash as he threatens his charges with rough birch switches and rusty chains. More modern postcards show a well-dressed well-groomed devil. This dapper human-like Krampus is shown either flirting with or being bested by pretty young women. Krampus is still celebrated today around December 5 or 6 with raucous community festivals and parades. During these events, young men dressed as the dark forbidding figure accost adults, especially attractive single women.

Commas with Quotations

Properly punctuating quotations with commas can be tricky unless you know a few rules about when and where to use commas.

When to use commas with quotations

Commas set off phrases that attribute quotations to a speaker or writer, such as *he argues, they said,* and *she writes.*

"When you come to a fork in the road," said Yogi Berra, "take it!"

If the attribution follows a quotation that is a complete sentence, replace the period that normally would come at the end of the quotation with a comma.

Incorrect	"Simplicity of language is not only reputable but perhaps even sacred." writes Kurt Vonnegut.
Correct	"Simplicity of language is not only reputable but perhaps even sacred," writes Kurt Vonnegut.

When an attribution is placed in the middle of a quotation, put the comma preceding the attribution within the quotation mark just before the phrase.

Incorrect	"Nothing is at last sacred", wrote Emerson in his 1841 essay, "but the integrity of your own mind."
Correct	"Nothing is at last sacred," wrote Emerson in his 1841 essay, "but the integrity of your own mind."

When not to use commas with quotations

Do not replace a question mark or exclamation point with a comma.

Incorrect	"Who's on first," Costello asked Abbott.
Correct	"Who's on first?" Costello asked Abbott.

Not all phrases that mention the author's name are attributions. When quoting a term or using a quotation within a subordinate clause, do not set off the quotation with commas.

> "Stonewall" Jackson gained his nickname at the First Battle of Bull Run when General Barnard Bee shouted to his men that "Jackson is standing like a stone wall."

Even a quotation that is a complete sentence can be used in a subordinate clause. Such quotations should not be set off with commas. Pay special attention to quotations preceded by *that, which*, and *because*; these words are the most common indicators of a subordinate clause.

> It was Benjamin Franklin's conviction that "Those who would give up essential liberty to purchase a little temporary safety deserve neither liberty nor safety."

Exercise 41.6 Read the following paragraph for errors in comma usage with quotations. Some are used correctly. Cross out unnecessary commas, move misplaced commas, and add omitted commas.

Example When inspecting a painting for authenticity, try looking for an angle that catches the glare of lights. "You will not be able to see what the paintings show," asserts author James Elkins, "but you'll get a good look at the *craquelure.*"

Craquelure is, "the fine network of cracks that scores the surface of . . . paintings" (Elkins 20). Elkins explains that "few museum visitors realize how many paintings have been seriously damaged" and goes on to list possible hazards, such as damage by, "fire, water, vandalism, or just the wear and tear of the centuries" (20). Not all cracks are signs of legitimate age; indeed "Counterfeiters have faked cracks by putting paintings in ovens, and they have even rubbed ink in the cracks to make them look old" (Elkins 22). Though cracks often happen with mishandling, Elkins explains that, "most cracks in paintings that are not caused by accidents are due to the flexing of the canvas or the slow warping of the wood" (22). If you are serious about art history, you may want to learn how to read the cracks in art work. "*Craquelure* is not a hard-and-fast method of classifying paintings," admits Elkins "but it comes close" (24).

41g Commas with Dates, Numbers, Titles, and Addresses

Some of the easiest comma rules to remember are the ones we use every day in dates, numbers, personal titles, place names, direct address, and brief interjections.

Commas with dates

Use commas to separate the day of the week from the month and to set off a year from the rest of the sentence.

March 25, 1942

Monday, November 18, 2011

On July 27, 2012, the opening ceremony of the World Scout Jamboree will be televised.

Do not use a comma when the month immediately precedes the year.

12 June 1988

April 2013

Commas with numbers

Commas mark off thousands, millions, billions, and so on.

16,500,000

However, do not use commas in street addresses or page numbers.

page 1542

7602 Elm Street

Commas with personal titles

When a title follows a person's name, set the title off with commas.

Gregory House, MD

Jackie Hart, Vice President for Operations, reported that her company's earnings were far ahead of projections.

Commas with place names

Place a comma between street addresses, city names, state names, and countries.

Poughkeepsie, New York

Lima, Peru

Write to the president at 1600 Pennsylvania Avenue, Washington, DC 20500.

Commas in direct address

When addressing someone directly, set off that person's name in commas.

I was happy to get your letter yesterday, Jamie.

Yes, Virginia, there is a Santa Claus.

Commas with brief interjections

Use commas to set off brief interjections like *yes* and *no*, as well as short questions that fall at the ends of sentences.

The director said that, no, the understudy would not have to stand in for the lead tonight.

Have another piece of pie, won't you?

Exercise 41.7 The fictitious business letter that follows is missing commas with dates, numbers, personal titles, place names, direct addresses, and brief interjections. Insert commas where they are needed.

Mazaces' Headquarters
Cairo Egypt
December 13 332 BC

Parmenio
Commander of Syria
Damascus Syria

Dear Parmenio:

Thank you for your latest correspondence dated December 9 332 BC. I am pleased to hear the streets of Damascus remain quiet since our arrival in October 333 and that mighty Syria has adjusted herself to our presence.

To other matters. I write to request 4,000 of your most rested troops be sent to Egypt to arrive no later than January 1 331 BC. The fighting in Gaza was bitter and our enemy merciless; my soldiers are tired and need to recuperate before marching westward.

I busy myself with the construction of the city of Alexandria. Address future correspondence to 12 Conquest Avenue Alexandria where I will soon move in order to oversee the construction directly. Deinocrates head architect has seen to every detail, but of course detail requires time. I remain here until the spring when I intend for our armies to reunite and travel west to Thapsacus Mesopotamia where we will meet Darius King of Persia and secure his defeat for our mutual triumph and to the glory of Greece.

Sincerely,
Alexander the Great (Alex)

Exercise 41.8   The fictitious business letter that follows is missing commas with dates, numbers, personal titles, place names, direct addresses, and brief interjections. Insert commas where they are needed.

Jenkins Gallery Inc.
17 Resolution Boulevard
Boston MA 02116

June 28 2010

Samantha Rios
1818 Pleasant Lane
Peabody TX 01960

Dear Ms. Rios:

Thank you Samantha for your interest in exhibiting your work at The Jenkins Gallery during our September 15 2010 showcase. Unfortunately, we did not receive your materials until after our submission deadline of May 5 2010. This year, we received over 135000 submissions for our prestigious fall showcase; therefore, we hope you will understand that we cannot accept late entries. We would like to take this opportunity to encourage you to reapply next year. To answer your question about future opportunities at the Jenkins Gallery, yes we do see great potential in your work and hope to work with you in the future as well.

Sincerely,
Liam Jenkins Esquire

41h   Commas to Avoid Confusion

Certain sentences can confuse readers if you do not indicate where they should pause within the sentence. Use a comma to guide a reader through these usually compact constructions.

Unclear   With supplies low prices of gasoline and fuel oil will increase.

This sentence could be read as meaning *With supplies, low prices will increase.*

Clear   With supplies low, prices of gasoline and fuel oil will increase.

Exercise 41.9   Some of the sentences in the following paragraph are confusing because they lack clarifying commas. Add commas where readers need more clues about how to read the sentences.

Example   Using new ways of dating, scientists can now apply multiple techniques to determine an object's age.

Because geologists used both radiometric and fossil dating we now know that the Colorado River started carving the Grand Canyon only five or six million years ago. Scientists were able to accurately date the Shroud of Turin believed by many Catholics to be Christ's burial covering to between AD 1260 and 1390. This particular example of carbon dating challenged some believers to weigh faith against science. The mysterious Sphinx stands before the pyramid of Khafre dated using the "star method." Scientists determined that the Sphinx and its host pyramid are approximately seventy years younger than was originally believed.

41i Unnecessary Commas

Do not place a comma between a subject and a predicate

Incorrect   American children of immigrant parents, often do not speak their parents' native language.

Correct   American children of immigrant parents often do not speak their parents' native language.

However, you do use commas to set off modifying phrases that separate subjects from verbs.

Incorrect   Steven Pinker author of *The Language Instinct* argues that the ability to speak and understand language is an evolutionary adaptive trait.

Correct   Steven Pinker, author of *The Language Instinct,* argues that the ability to speak and understand language is an evolutionary adaptive trait.

Do not use a comma with a coordinating conjunction unless it joins two main clauses

Incorrect   Susana thought finishing her first novel was hard, but soon learned that getting a publisher to buy it was much harder.

Correct   Susana thought finishing her first novel was hard but soon learned that getting a publisher to buy it was much harder.

Correct   Susana thought finishing her first novel was hard, but she soon learned that getting a publisher to buy it was much harder.

Do not use a comma after a subordinating conjunction such as *although, despite,* or *while*

Incorrect   Although, soccer is gaining popularity in the States, it will never be as popular as football or baseball.

Correct   Although soccer is gaining popularity in the States, it will never be as popular as football or baseball.

Do not use a comma before *than*

Some writers mistakenly use a comma with *than* to try to heighten the contrast in a comparison.

Incorrect   Any teacher will tell you that acquiring critical thinking skills is more important, than simply memorizing information.

Correct   Any teacher will tell you that acquiring critical thinking skills is more important than simply memorizing information.

Do not use a comma before a list

A common mistake is to place a comma after *such as* or *like* before introducing a list.

Incorrect   Many hourly workers, such as, waiters, dishwashers, and cashiers, do not receive health benefits from their employers.

Correct   Many hourly workers, such as waiters, dishwashers, and cashiers, do not receive health benefits from their employers.

42 | Semicolons and Colons

QUICK*TAKE*

- **How do you use semicolons to link related ideas?** (see below)
  Incorrect: The first reports of an elephant arriving in the United States are from 1796; which may have been an elephant named Old Bet.
  Correct: The first reports of an elephant arriving in the United States are from 1796; they may have been referring to an elephant named Old Bet.
- **Where do you use colons?** (see p. 621 and p. 626)
  In a sentence: There is one elephant behavior that keepers look out for as a warning of possible aggression: rocking.
  With lists: Elephants need a few things to keep them healthy and happy: fresh food, plenty of water, room to roam, and the companionship of other elephants.

Semicolons with Closely Related Main Clauses

Why use semicolons? Sometimes we want to join two main clauses to form a complete sentence in order to indicate their close relationship. We can connect them with a comma and a coordinating conjunction like *or, but,* or *and.* However, using those constructions too often can make your writing cumbersome. Instead you can omit the comma and coordinating conjunction, and insert a semicolon between the two clauses.

Semicolons can join only clauses that are grammatically equal. In other words, they join main clauses only to other main clauses, not to phrases or subordinate clauses. Look at the following examples:

Incorrect   ⌐─────────MAIN CLAUSE─────────┐
Gloria's new weightlifting program will help her recover
           ┌──────────PARTICIPIAL PHRASE──────────
from knee surgery; doing a series of squats and presses
with a physical therapist.

Incorrect   ⌐─────────MAIN CLAUSE─────────┐
Gloria's new weightlifting program will help her regain
           ┌──────SUBORDINATE CLAUSE──────
strength in her knee; which required surgery after she
injured it skiing.

$$\overset{\text{\scriptsize————MAIN CLAUSE————}}{}$$

Correct   Gloria's new weightlifting program will help her recover
$$\overset{\text{\scriptsize————————MAIN CLAUSE————}}{}$$
from knee surgery; a physical therapist leads her through
a series of squats and presses.

COMMON ERRORS   Edit Help

Main clauses connected with transitional words and phrases

Closely related main clauses sometimes use a conjunctive adverb (such as *however, therefore, moreover, furthermore, thus, meanwhile, nonetheless, otherwise*; see the list in Section 41a) or a transition (*in fact, for example, that is, for instance, in addition, in other words, on the other hand, even so*) to indicate the relationship between them. When the second clause begins with a conjunctive adverb or a transition, a semicolon is needed to join the two clauses. This sentence pattern is frequently used; therefore, it pays to learn how to punctuate it correctly.

Incorrect (comma splice)	No one doubts that exercise burns calories, however, few people can lose weight by exercise alone.
Correct	No one doubts that exercise burns calories; however, few people can lose weight by exercise alone.

The semicolon separates the second main clause from the first. Note that a comma is also needed to separate *however* from the rest of the second clause.

Incorrect (comma splice)	The poster design left much to be desired, for example, the title was printed in garish red, orange, and green.
Correct	The poster design left much to be desired; for example, the title was printed in garish red, orange, and green.

Note that in addition to the semicolon, a comma separates *for example* from the rest of the second clause.

Remember: Main clauses that use a conjunctive adverb or a transitional phrase require a semicolon to join the clauses.

 For step-by-step discussion, examples, and practice exercises, visit this page of the eText at **www.mycomplab.com.**

Do not use a semicolon to introduce quotations

Use a comma or a colon instead.

Incorrect	Robert Frost's poem "Mending Wall" contains this line; "Good fences make good neighbors."
Correct	Robert Frost's poem "Mending Wall" contains this line: "Good fences make good neighbors."

Do not use a semicolon to introduce lists.

Incorrect	William Shakespeare wrote four romance plays at the end of his career; *The Tempest, The Winter's Tale, Cymbeline,* and *Pericles.*
Correct	William Shakespeare wrote four romance plays at the end of his career: *The Tempest, The Winter's Tale, Cymbeline,* and *Pericles.*

42b Semicolons Together with Commas

When an item in a series already includes a comma, adding more commas to separate it from the other items will only confuse the reader. Use semicolons instead of commas between items in a series that have internal punctuation.

Confusing	The church's design competition drew entries from as far away as Gothenberg, Sweden, Caracas, Venezuela, and Athens, Greece.
Clearer	The church's design competition drew entries from as far away as Gothenberg, Sweden; Caracas, Venezuela; and Athens, Greece.

Exercise 42.1 Decide where semicolons should go in the following paragraph. Add any semicolons that would repair run-on sentences, fix comma splices, or clarify a list. Also eliminate any incorrectly used semicolons and insert the correct punctuation.

Example	In the summer of 1947 a flying object crashed in eastern New Mexico; the incident feeds speculation that the government hides evidence of UFOs.

The media reported that the wreckage of a flying saucer had been discovered on a ranch near Roswell, military spokespeople came up with another explanation. They asserted that the flying saucer was actually a balloon, people stationed at the base, however, reported seeing unidentifiable bodies removed from the wreckage. Initially even UFO enthusiasts believed the government's reports; which seemed plausible at the time. The Air Force has declared the case closed they stated that the bodies at the crash sites were test dummies. Roswell, New Mexico, joins the list of rumored UFO hot spots that includes Delphos, Kansas, Marshall County, Minnesota, Westchester, New York, and Gulf Breeze, Florida.

42c Colons in Sentences

Like semicolons, colons can join two closely related main clauses (complete sentences). Colons indicate that what follows will explain or expand on what comes before the colon. Use a colon in cases where the second main clause interprets or sums up the first.

> Anthrozoology, the study of how animals and people relate to one another, sheds light on larger issues in human psychology: people's interactions with animals illustrate concepts of altruism, ethics, and taboo.

You may choose to capitalize the first word of the main clause following the colon or leave it lowercase. Either is correct as long as you are consistent throughout your text.

Colons linking main clauses with appositives

A colon calls attention to an appositive, a noun, or a noun phrase that renames the noun preceding it. If you're not certain whether a colon would be appropriate, put *namely* in its place. If *namely* makes sense when you read the main clause followed by the appositive, you probably need to insert a colon instead of a comma. Remember, the clause that precedes the colon must be a complete sentence.

> I know the perfect person for the job, namely me.

The sentence makes sense with *namely* placed before the appositive. Thus, a colon is appropriate.

> I know the perfect person for the job: me.

Never capitalize a word following a colon unless the word starts a complete sentence or is normally capitalized (see Chapter 49).

WRITING SMART

Punctuation following Quotations

Writing often requires quoting someone else's words. Use the correct sequence of punctuation marks when sharing a quotation with readers.

Place semicolons and colons outside quotation marks

Commas and periods that come after a quotation sit inside the quotation marks. The rule is different, however, for semicolons and colons: They sit outside the quotation marks. Because commas and periods always appear inside the quotation marks, semicolons and colons may seem incorrectly placed if you don't know that they follow a different rule.

> **Put commas and periods inside the quotation marks**
> "The length of a film," said Alfred Hitchcock, "should be directly related to the endurance of the human bladder."

> **Put semicolons outside quotation marks**
> Chicago mayor Richard Daley said, "The police are not here to create disorder. They're here to preserve disorder"; his misstatement hit at the truth underlying the violent treatment of protestors at the 1968 Democratic Convention.

> **Put colons outside quotation marks**
> "I believe, absolutely, that if you do not break out in that sweat of fear when you write, then you have not gone far enough": Dorothy Allison reassures would-be writers that they can begin on guts alone.

Remember: Little dogs (commas, periods) sleep in the house. Big dogs (semicolons, colons) sleep outside.

For more on using quotation marks correctly, see Chapter 46.

Colons joining main clauses with quotations

Use a colon to link a main clause and a quotation that interprets or sums up the clause. Be careful not to use a colon to link a phrase with a quotation.

> **Incorrect: noun phrase–colon–quotation**
> President Roosevelt's strategy to change the nation's panicky attitude during the Great Depression: "We have nothing to fear," he said, "but fear itself."

Correct: main clause–colon–quotation

President Roosevelt's strategy to end the Great Depression was to change the nation's panicky attitude: "We have nothing to fear," he said, "but fear itself."

Also, a colon is often used after a main clause to introduce an indented block quotation (see Section 24d).

42d Colons with Lists

Use a colon to join a main clause to a list. The main clauses in these cases sometimes include the phrases *the following* or *as follows*. Remember that a colon cannot join a phrase or an incomplete clause to a list.

Incorrect: noun phrase–colon–list

Three ingredients for soup: chicken stock, peeled shrimp, and chopped tomatoes.

Correct: main clause–colon–list

You can make a tasty soup with just three ingredients: chicken stock, peeled shrimp, and chopped tomatoes.

Incorrect: incomplete clause–colon–list

Volunteers aid biologists in: erosion control, trail maintenance, tree planting, and cleanup.

Correct: main clause without a colon

Volunteers aid biologists in erosion control, trail maintenance, tree planting, and cleanup.

COMMON ERRORS

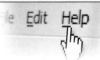

Colons misused with lists

Some writers think that anytime they introduce a list, they should insert a colon. Colons are used correctly only when a complete sentence precedes the colon.

Incorrect   Jessica's entire wardrobe for her trip to Cancun included: two swimsuits, one pair of shorts, two T-shirts, a party dress, and a pair of sandals.

(Continued on next page)

COMMON ERRORS *(Continued)*

Correct   Jessica's entire wardrobe for her trip to Cancun included two swimsuits, one pair of shorts, two T-shirts, a party dress, and a pair of sandals.

Correct   Jessica jotted down what she would need for her trip: two swimsuits, one pair of shorts, two T-shirts, a party dress, and a pair of sandals.

Remember: A colon should be placed only after a clause that can stand by itself as a sentence.

 For step-by-step discussion, examples, and practice exercises, visit this page of the eText at **www.mycomplab.com**.

Exercise 42.2   Decide where colons should go in the following sentences; add any that are necessary. Eliminate any incorrectly used colons and insert correct punctuation.

> **Example**   In the Philippines, you flirt with danger when you sing one song: "My Way," by Frank Sinatra.

1. Authorities do not know exactly how many people have been killed in the past few years in the Philippines for singing "My Way," but the number has been high enough to cause people to ask some questions, can the killings be blamed on violent culture? Or, is there something about the song that drives people to irrational anger?
2. One witness to many incidents of karaoke-related violence offers up an explanation for why Sinatra's song seems to make tempers flare, "Everyone knows it, and everyone has an opinion."
3. Karaoke-related assaults and killings have happened recently in countries other than the Philippines, however, including: Malaysia, Thailand, and the United States.
4. The prevalence of karaoke in the culture of the Philippines makes related violence statistically much more likely social gatherings almost always involve karaoke, and stand-alone karaoke machines can be found everywhere, including remote rural locations.
5. Karaoke singers everywhere can prevent violence by: showing respect to other singers, not hogging the microphone, and choosing songs that have not already been sung.

43 | Hyphens

QUICKTAKE

- **When do you hyphenate compound modifiers?** (see below)
  Incorrect: His apartment was on the second-story.
  Correct: He had a second-story apartment.
- **Which compound nouns are hyphenated?** (see p. 630)
  Incorrect: self awareness, city state
  Correct: self-awareness, city-state
- **How can hyphens help with clarity?** (see p. 631)
  Less clear: He tried to recreate the atmosphere Greenwich Village during the 1960s.
  Clearer: He tried to re-create the atmosphere Greenwich Village during the 1960s.

Hyphens (-) are frequently confused with dashes (—), which are similar but longer. Dashes are used to separate phrases. Hyphens are used to join words.

Hyphens with Compound Modifiers

When to hyphenate
Hyphenate a compound modifier that precedes a noun.
When a compound modifier precedes a noun, you should usually hyphenate the modifier. A compound modifier consists of words that join together as a unit to modify a noun. Since the first word modifies the second, compound modifiers will not make sense if the word order is reversed.

middle-class values	best-selling novel
self-fulfilling prophecy	well-known musician

Hyphenate a phrase when it is used as a modifier that precedes a noun.

step-by-step instructions	all-or-nothing payoff
all-you-can-eat buffet	over-the-counter drug

Hyphenate the prefixes *pro-, anti-, post-, pre-, neo-,* and *mid-* before proper nouns.

pro-Catholic sentiment   neo-Nazi racism

mid-Atlantic states   pre-Columbian art

Hyphenate a compound modifier with a number when it precedes a noun.

eighteenth-century drama   tenth-grade class

one-way street   47-minute swim

When not to hyphenate
Do not hyphenate a compound modifier that follows a noun.
Avoid using hyphens in compound modifiers when they come after the noun.

The instructor's approach is student centered.

Among serious video game players, *Mass Effect* and its sequels are well known.

Do not hyphenate compound modifiers when the first word is *very* or ends in *ly.*

newly recorded data   very cold day

Do not hyphenate chemical terms.

calcium chloride base   hydrochloric acid solution

Do not hyphenate foreign terms used as adjectives.

a priori decision   *post hoc* fallacy

Exercise 43.1 In the following sentences, decide where hyphens should be placed. Some sentences may require more than one hyphen and some sentences may need hyphens deleted.

    Example   Since there are few clear enemies of the state in the post‚Soviet era, political parties lack a galvanizing issue.

1. Some people consider the Electoral College to be un-democratic.
2. Independent candidates are often viewed as fly by night long shots with little or no hope of winning positions of power.
3. The tension surrounding the five week wait for the 2000 presidential election results was palpable.
4. Mostly-negative political ads are becoming more common.

5. Local candidates' political debates are rarely considered important enough to interrupt regularly-scheduled programming.
6. Candidates with free market economic policies are often popular with large corporations, which in turn make substantial donations to the candidates with favorable platforms.

43b Hyphens with Compound Nouns

A compound noun is made up of two or more words that work together to form one noun. You cannot change the order of words in a compound noun or remove a word without altering the noun's meaning. No universal rule guides the use of hyphens with compound nouns; the best way to determine whether a compound noun is hyphenated is to check the dictionary.

Some hyphenated compound nouns

T-shirt	heart-to-heart	play-by-play
sister-in-law	great-grandfather	speed-reading

Some compound nouns that are not hyphenated

oneself	heartland	speed of light
time zone	open house	playbook

While there's no set rule for all cases of compound nouns, some prefixes and suffixes that commonly require hyphens are *ex-*, *all-*, *self-*, and *-elect*.

All-American	president-elect
self-conscious	ex-employee

COMMON ERRORS

Hyphens with numbers
Whole numbers between twenty-one and ninety-nine are hyphenated when they are written as words.

Incorrect	twentysix
correct	twenty-six
Incorrect	sixteen-hundred
correct	sixteen hundred

(Continued on next page)

COMMON ERRORS *(Continued)*

Also, hyphens connect the numerators and denominators in most fractions.

> The glass is one-half full.

A few fractions used as nouns, especially fractions of time, distance, and area, do not take hyphens.

> A half century passed before the mistake was uncovered.

Remember: Numbers between twenty-one and ninety-nine and most fractions are hyphenated when written as words.

 For step-by-step discussion, examples, and practice exercises, visit this page of the eText at **www.mycomplab.com**.

43c Hyphens That Divide Words at the Ends of Lines

A hyphen can show that a word is completed on the next line. Hyphens divide words only between syllables.

> The Jackson family waited out the tor-
> nado in their storm cellar.

Unless you have a special reason for dividing words at the ends of lines, avoid doing it. One special situation might be the need to fit as much text as possible on each line of the narrow columns. Another might be the need to fit text inside the cells of a table.

43d Hyphens for Clarity

Certain words, often ones with the prefixes *anti-*, *re-*, and *pre-*, can be confusing without hyphens. Adding hyphens to such words will show the reader where to pause to pronounce them correctly.

> The courts are in much need of repair.

> The doubles final will re-pair the sister team of Venus and Serena Williams.

> Reform in court procedure is necessary to bring cases quickly to trial.

> The thunderclouds re-formed after the hard rain, threatening another deluge.

44 | Dashes and Parentheses

QUICK_TAKE_

- **When do you use dashes and parentheses rather than commas to set off information?** (see below)
  Regular emphasis: Marie set her pie, a lemon meringue, on the table.
  More emphasis: Mother scowled (after telling Marie in advance that she hated meringue).
  Greatest emphasis: Mother—who had planned this party for months—was about to lose her temper.

- **How do you type a dash?** (see p. 638)
  Incorrect: We can get home unless – heaven forbid! – I lost my credit card.
  Correct: We can get home unless—heaven forbid!—I lost my credit card.

Dashes and Parentheses vs. Commas

Like commas, parentheses and dashes enclose material that adds, explains, or digresses. However, the three punctuation marks are not interchangeable. The mark you choose depends on how much emphasis you want to place on the material. Dashes indicate the most emphasis. Parentheses offer somewhat less, and commas offer less still.

Commas indicate a moderate level of emphasis

Bill covered the new tattoo on his bicep, a pouncing tiger, because he thought it might upset our mother.

Parentheses lend a greater level of emphasis

I'm afraid to go bungee jumping (though my brother tells me it's less frightening than a roller coaster).

Dashes indicate the highest level of emphasis and, sometimes, surprise and drama

Christina felt as though she had been punched in the gut; she could hardly believe the stranger at her door was really who he claimed to be—the brother she hadn't seen in twenty years.

Exercise 44.1 Look at the modifying phrases that are underlined in the following paragraph. Use commas, parentheses, or dashes to set them off, based on the level of emphasis you want to create.

Example   Coffee‿ one of the most significant crops of all

time‿ has its origins in Africa‿like so many other

cornerstones of civilization‿.

Coffea arabica the official name for the bean was made popular in Yemen. The Shadhili Sufi used coffee to inspire visions and to stimulate ecstatic trances making coffee drinking a spiritual experience. The use of the beverage spread largely through other Muslims the Sufi had contact with, and by 1500 it was well known throughout the Arab world. Cafes originated in the Middle East. These early cafes one of the few secular public spaces Muslims could congregate were seen as subversive.

44b Dashes and Parentheses to Set Off Information

Dashes and parentheses call attention to groups of words. In effect, they tell the reader that a group of words is not part of the main clause and should be given extra attention. Compare the following sentences.

When Shanele's old college roommate, Traci, picked her up at the airport in a new car, a Porsche Boxster Spyder, she knew that Traci's finances had changed for the better.

When Shanele's old college roommate, Traci, picked her up at the airport in a new car (a Porsche Boxster Spyder), she knew that Traci's finances had changed for the better.

When Shanele's old college roommate, Traci, picked her up at the airport in a new car—a Porsche Boxster Spyder—she knew that Traci's finances had changed for the better.

The Porsche Boxster Spyder is weighted differently in these three sentences because of punctuation. In the first, it is the name of the car. But in the third, it's as if an exclamation point were added—a Porsche Boxster Spyder!

The lesson here is simple enough. If you want to make an element stand out, especially in the middle of a sentence, use parentheses or dashes instead of commas.

Dashes with final elements

A dash is often used to set off an element at the end of a sentence that offers significant comments about the main clause. This construction is a favorite of newscasters, who typically pause for a long moment where the dash would be inserted in writing.

> The *Titanic* sank just before midnight on April 14, 1912, at a cost of over 1,500 lives—a tragedy that could have been prevented easily by reducing speed in dangerous waters, providing adequate lifeboat space, and maintaining a full-time radio watch.

Dashes can also anticipate a shift in tone at the end of a sentence.

> A full-sized SUV can take you wherever you want to go in style—if your idea of style is a gas-guzzling tank.

Parentheses with additional information

Parentheses are more often used for identifying information, afterthoughts or asides, examples, and clarifications. You can place full sentences, fragments, or brief terms within parentheses.

> Some argue that ethanol (the pet solution of politicians for achieving energy independence) costs more energy to produce and ship than it produces.

Exercise 44.2 Insert dashes and parentheses in the following sentences to set off information.

> **Example**   Naples‸founded by the Greeks, enlarged by the Romans, and ruled later by the Normans, Hohenstaufen, French, and Spanish‸is one of the few European cities where the links to the ancient world remain evident.

1. Naples is a dirty and noisy metropolis in a spectacular setting a city that sprawls around the Bay of Naples with Mount Vesuvius at its back facing out to the islands of Procida, Ischia, and Capri.

2. The most famous eruption of Mt. Vesuvius the eruption that destroyed Pompeii and Herculaneum occurred in AD 79.

3. Some of the inhabitants of Pompeii decided to flee as the eruptions began, but they ran into several obstacles, such as darkness, unbreathable ash-filled air, and a continuous rain of pumice and *lapilli* small round droplets of molten lava.

4. The minor details in Pompeii graffiti scrawled on the walls give the city a living presence.

5. Herculaneum also known as Ercolano to the west of Pompeii was buried by a mudslide in the same eruption.

COMMON ERRORS

e **E**dit He**l**p

Do not use dashes as periods

Do not use dashes to separate two main clauses (clauses that can stand as complete sentences). Use dashes to separate main clauses from subordinate clauses and phrases when you want to emphasize the subordinate clause or phrase.

Incorrect: main clause–dash–main clause

I was one of the few women in my computer science classes— most of the students majoring in computer science at that time were men.

Correct: main clause–dash–phrase

I was one of the few women in computer science—a field then dominated by men.

Remember: Dashes are not periods and should not be used as periods.

For step-by-step discussion, examples, and practice exercises, visit this page of the eText at **www.mycomplab.com**.

44c Other Punctuation with Parentheses

Parentheses with numbers or letters that order items in a series

Parentheses around letters or numbers that order a series within a sentence make the list easier to read.

Angela Creider's recipe for becoming a great novelist is to (1) set aside an hour during the morning to write, (2) read what you've written out loud, (3) revise your prose, and (4) repeat every morning for the next thirty years.

Parentheses with abbreviations

Abbreviations made from the first letters of words are often used in place of the unwieldy names of institutions, departments, organizations, or terms. In order to show the reader what the abbreviation stands for, the first time it appears in a text the writer must state the complete name, followed by the abbreviation in parentheses.

The University of California, Santa Cruz (UCSC) supports its mascot, the banana slug, with pride and a sense of humor. And although it sounds strange to outsiders, UCSC students are even referred to as "the banana slugs."

Parentheses with in-text citations

The various documentation styles require that information quoted, paraphrased, or summarized from an outside source be indicated with a research citation. In several of the styles, including MLA (see Chapter 26) and APA (see Chapter 27), the citation is enclosed in parentheses.

E. B. White's advice on writing style is to use your natural voice (Strunk and White 70).

COMMON ERRORS   Edit   Help

Using periods, commas, colons, and semicolons with parentheses

When an entire sentence is enclosed in parentheses, place the period before the closing parenthesis.

Incorrect   Our fear of sharks, heightened by movies like *Jaws*, is vastly out of proportion with the minor threat sharks actually pose. (Dying from a dog attack, in fact, is much more likely than dying from a shark attack).

Correct   Our fear of sharks, heightened by movies like *Jaws*, is vastly out of proportion with the minor threat sharks actually pose. (Dying from a dog attack, in fact, is much more likely than dying from a shark attack.)

When the material in parentheses is part of the sentence and the parentheses fall at the end of the sentence, place the period outside the closing parenthesis.

Incorrect   Reports of sharks attacking people are rare (much rarer than dog attacks.)

Correct   Reports of sharks attacking people are rare (much rarer than dog attacks).

Place commas, colons, and semicolons after the closing parenthesis.

Incorrect   Although newspaper editors generally prize concise letters to the editor, (the shorter the better) they will occasionally print longer letters that are unusually eloquent.

(Continued on next page)

COMMON ERRORS *(Continued)*

Correct   Although newspaper editors generally prize concise
letters to the editor (the shorter the better), they will
occasionally print longer letters that are unusually
eloquent.

Remember: When an entire sentence is enclosed in parentheses,
place the period inside the closing parenthesis; otherwise, put the
punctuation outside the closing parenthesis.

 *For step-by-step discussion, examples, and practice exercises, visit
this page of the eText at* **www.mycomplab.com.**

Exercise 44.3 Decide where to add parentheses in the following sentences. Be careful to place them correctly in relation to other punctuation marks.

Example   *Saturday Night Live* (SNL) is a weekly late-night comedy-
variety show based in New York City.

1. *SNL* has been broadcast live by the National Broadcasting Company NBC
on Saturday nights since October 11, 1975.
2. The show was called *NBC's Saturday Night* until 1976 a short-lived variety
show hosted by Howard Cosell was also called *Saturday Night Live.*
3. On Saturdays that the show is broadcast live, the cast and crew have to
1 run through the show with props 2 do a full dress rehearsal 3 reorder
the script if any sketches are cut and 4 get ready to go live at 11:30 p.m.
EST.
4. The premature deaths of a few well-known cast members John Belushi,
Gilda Radner, Phil Hartman, Chris Farley, and Danitra Vance have given rise
to a superstition known as the "*Saturday Night Live* Curse."
5. Critics claim that talk of the show's being under a curse is ridiculous,
especially because a few untimely deaths are inevitable when a show
has had a cast of over 100 people "*SNL* is *Saturday Night Live* on NBC"
par. 14.

44d Other Punctuation with Dashes

Dashes with a series of items

Dashes can set off a series. They are especially appropriate when the series
comes in the middle of a sentence or when the series simply elaborates on
what comes before it without changing the essential meaning of the sentence.

Normally commas enclose nonessential clauses; however, placing commas around items separated by commas would confuse readers about where the list begins and ends.

> Rookie Luke Scott became the first player in Major League Baseball history to hit for the reverse cycle—a home run, a triple, a double, and a single in that order—in last night's game against the Diamondbacks.

Dashes with interrupted speech

Dashes also indicate that a speaker has broken off in the middle of a statement.

> "Why did everybody get so quiet all of a—"; Silvia stopped in her tracks when she noticed that the customer had a pistol pointed at the clerk.

COMMON ERRORS

e **Edit** **Help**

The art of typing a dash

Although dashes and hyphens look similar, they are actually different marks. The distinction is small but important because dashes and hyphens serve different purposes. A dash is a line twice as long as a hyphen. Most word processors will create a dash automatically when you type two hyphens together. Or you can type a special character to make a dash. Your manual will tell you which keys to press to make a dash.

Do not leave a space between a dash or a hyphen and the words that come before and after them. Likewise, if you are using two hyphens to indicate a dash, do not leave a space between the hyphens.

Incorrect　A well - timed effort at conserving water may prevent long - term damage to drought - stricken farms -- if it's not already too late.

correct　A well-timed effort at conserving water may prevent long-term damage to drought-stricken farms—if it's not already too late.

Remember: Do not put spaces before or after hyphens and dashes.

For step-by-step discussion, examples, and practice exercises, visit this page of the eText at **www.mycomplab.com.**

45 | Apostrophes

QUICK*TAKE*

- **How do you use apostrophes to show possession?** (see below)
  Jimmy's collar, alumni's donations, states' rights, passer-by's, Jim and
  Victoria's office, Sanjay's and Cho's performances *BUT* Aristophanes's plays,
  Moses's death

- **How do you use apostrophes to show omitted letters and
  numbers?** (see p. 641)
  No omissions: Do not tease me for liking 1970s rock and roll.
  Omissions: Don't tease me for liking '70s rock'n'roll.

- **Do you use apostrophes to make nouns plural?** (NO, see p. 642)
  Incorrect: Her three goal's registered her first hat trick.
  Correct: Her three goals registered her first hat trick.

45a Possessives

Nouns and indefinite pronouns (e.g., *everyone, anyone*) that indicate possession or ownership are in the **possessive case**. The possessive case is marked by attaching an apostrophe and an *-s* or an apostrophe only to the end of a word.

Singular nouns and indefinite pronouns

For singular nouns and indefinite pronouns, add an apostrophe plus *-s: -'s*.
Even singular nouns that end in *-s* usually follow this principle.

Iris**'s** coat

everyone**'s** favorite

a woman**'s** choice

**Official names of certain places, institutions, companies may or may
not add** *-'s* for singular nouns:

> *Governors Island, Teachers College of Columbia University, Mothers
> Café, Saks Fifth Avenue, Walgreens Pharmacy.* Note, however, that
> many companies do include the apostrophe: *Denny's Restaurant,
> Macy's, McDonald's, Wendy's Old Fashioned Hamburgers.*

Plural nouns

For plural nouns that do not end in -*s*, add an apostrophe plus -*s*: -'*s*.

> media**'s** responsibility

> children**'s** section

For plural nouns that end in -*s*, add only an apostrophe at the end.

> attorneys**'** briefs

> the Kennedys**'** legacy

Compound nouns

For compound nouns, add an apostrophe plus -*s* to the last word: -'*s*.

> my mother-in-law**'s** house

> mayor of Cleveland**'s** speech

Two or more nouns

For joint possession, add an apostrophe plus -*s* to the final noun: -'*s*.

> mother and dad**'s** yard

> Ben & Jerry**'s** Ice Cream

When people possess or own things separately, add an apostrophe plus -*s* to each noun: -'*s*.

> Roberto**'s** and Edward**'s** views are totally opposed.

> Dominique**'s**, Sally**'s**, and Vinatha**'s** cars all need new tires.

COMMON ERRORS

e Edit Help

Possessive forms of personal pronouns never take the apostrophe

Incorrect *her's, it's, our's, your's, their's*

> The bird sang in it's cage.

correct *hers, its, ours, yours, theirs*

> The bird sang in its cage.

Remember: It's = It is

For step-by-step discussion, examples, and practice exercises, visit this page of the eText at **www.mycomplab.com**.

Exercise 45.1   The apostrophes have been omitted from the following paragraph. Insert apostrophes in the appropriate places to indicate possession.

Example   Pompeii's ruins were excavated during the past two centuries.

    Its destruction was caused by an eruption of Mount Vesuvius in AD 79. Survivors stories contain accounts of tunneling through up to sixteen feet of debris after the disaster. The Naples Museums collection contains painted stuccos and other art objects from Pompeii that illustrate the delicate nature of the artisans techniques. More than five hundred residents bronze seals were found, and these helped identify the occupants of many destroyed homes. Pompeiis ruins provide the worlds most accurate snapshot of Hellenistic and Roman times.

Exercise 45.2   The apostrophes have been omitted from the following paragraph. Insert apostrophes in the appropriate places to indicate possession.

Example   James Cameron's *Avatar* won three Academy Awards.

    In 2009, James Camerons *Avatar*, starring Sam Worthington and Zoe Saldana, entranced audiences with the tale of an environmentally-themed, futuristic battle for the planet Pandora. The films commercial success was astounding. *Avatar* quickly became the highest grossing film of all time, wresting the title from Camerons *Titanic*. While Sam Worthingtons and Zoe Saldanas performances were strong, the films success rests largely on its innovative (and expensive) use of 3D technology. Development on the film began in 1994, and over its course involved groundbreaking work developing new cinematic technology and a new language for the films fictional Na'vi people. Officially, *Avatar*s budget was $237 million; however, other sources put its production costs as high as $310 million. Audiences adoration of the film continued into 2010 with a record-setting DVD release in April 2010. Plans are in the making for two sequels, indicating that the films success has justified the enormous budget in movie executives minds.

45b Contractions and Omitted Letters

In speech we often leave out sounds and syllables of familiar words. In writing these omissions are noted with apostrophes.

Contractions

Contractions combine two words into one, using the apostrophe to mark what is left out.

I am	⟶	I'm	we are	⟶	we're
I would	⟶	I'd	they are	⟶	they're
you are	⟶	you're	cannot	⟶	can't
you will	⟶	you'll	do not	⟶	don't
he is	⟶	he's	does not	⟶	doesn't
she is	⟶	she's	will not	⟶	won't
it is	⟶	it's			

Omissions

Using apostrophes to signal omitted letters is a way of approximating speech in writing. They can make your writing look informal and slangy, but overuse can become annoying in a hurry.

rock and roll	⟶	rock'n'roll
the 1960s	⟶	the '60s
neighborhood	⟶	'hood

45c Plurals of Letters, Symbols, and Words Referred to as Words

When to use apostrophes to make plurals

The trend is away from using apostrophes to form plurals of letters, symbols, and words referred to as words. In a few cases adding the apostrophe and *s* is still used, as in this old saying.

> Mind your p's and q's.

Words used as words are italicized and their plural is formed by adding an *s* not in italics, not an apostrophe and *s*.

> Take a few of the ***and**s* out of your writing.

Words in quotation marks, however, typically use apostrophe and *s*.

> She had too many "probably's" in her letter for me to be confident that the remodeling will be finished on schedule.

When not to use apostrophes to make plurals

Do not use an apostrophe to make family names plural.

Incorrect	You've heard of keeping up with the Jones's.
Correct	You've heard of keeping up with the Joneses.

Do not use apostrophes for indicating plurals of numbers and acronyms. They add only -*s*.

| 1890**s** | four CEO**s** | several DVD**s** |
| eight**s** | these URL**s** | the images are all JPEG**s** |

COMMON ERRORS

Do not use an apostrophe to make a noun plural

Incorrect	The two government'**s** agreed to meet.
correct	The two governments agreed to meet.
Incorrect	The video game console'**s** of the past were one-dimensional.
correct	The video game consoles of the past were one-dimensional.

Remember: Add only -*s* = plural
Add apostrophe plus -*s* = possessive

For step-by-step discussion, examples, and practice exercises, visit this page of the eText at **www.mycomplab.com**.

Exercise 45.3 In the following sentences some apostrophes were placed correctly, some were placed incorrectly, and others were omitted altogether. Cross out incorrectly used apostrophes and add apostrophes where necessary.

Example Americans have often loved their presidents´ nicknames
more than they loved the ~~president's~~ *presidents* themselves.

1. Texas VIP's and international diplomats alike affectionately referred to Lyndon B. Johnson as "Big Daddy."
2. There were no *ifs, ands,* or *buts* when the "Rough Rider," Theodore Roosevelt, rode into town.
3. Similarly, when old "Give, Em Hell," also known as Harry Truman, was on the Hill, congressmen could never catch up on their Z's.
4. Jimmy Carters staff learned quickly of his attention to small details, down to the dotting of is and crossing of ts.
5. The last twenty years has seen two George Bush's in the White House.
6. In the 1990's, George H. W. Bush was known as "No New Taxes."

46 | Quotation Marks

QUICK*TAKE*

- **How do you incorporate words from sources?** (see below)
  Direct quotation: Warren Zevon final piece of advice was to *"*enjoy every sandwich.*"*
  Paraphrase: Warren Zevon final piece of advice was to enjoy it all, even the small things.

- **How do you use periods and commas with quotation marks?** (see p. 649)
  Incorrect: Groucho Marx once said, "I was married by a judge; I should have had a jury"**.**
  Correct: Groucho Marx once said, "I was married by a judge; I should have had a jury**.**"
  Correct: Groucho Marx once said, "I was married by a judge; I should have had a jury" (Kanfer 45)**.**

- **How do you use colons and semicolons with quotation marks?** (see p. 650)
  Incorrect: As Flannery O'Connor wrote in 1955, "the truth does not change according to our ability to stomach it**;**" many today would do well to heed these words.
  Correct: As Flannery O'Connor wrote in 1955, "the truth does not change according to our ability to stomach it"**;** many today would do well to heed these words.

46a Direct Quotations

Use quotation marks to enclose direct quotations

Enclose direct quotations—someone else's words repeated verbatim—in quotation marks.

> Michael Pollan, the author of *Food Rules* and *The Omnivore's Dilemma*, argues that industrial agriculture uses too much fossil fuel to grow food: "We need to reduce the dependence of modern agriculture on oil, an eminently feasible goal—after all, agriculture is the original solar 'technology.'"

Even brief direct quotations, such as the repetition of someone else's original term or turn of phrase, require quotation marks.

> Michael Pollan, the author of *Food Rules* and *The Omnivore's Dilemma*, argues that reducing the amount of oil used to grow food is *"*an eminently feasible goal.*"*

Do not use quotation marks with indirect quotations

Do not enclose an indirect quotation—a paraphrase of someone else's words—in quotation marks. However, do remember that you need to cite your source not only when you quote directly but also when you paraphrase or borrow ideas.

> Michael Pollan, the author of *Food Rules* and *The Omnivore's Dilemma*, argues that reducing the amount of oil used to grow food would make food cheaper in hungry nations and lessen the impacts of global warming.

Do not use quotation marks with block quotations

When a quotation is long enough to be set off as a block quotation, do not use quotation marks. MLA style defines long quotations as more than four lines of prose or poetry. APA style defines a long quotation as one of more than forty words. In the following example, notice that the long quotation is indented (MLA style; in APA style it would be the same as a paragraph indent) and quotation marks are omitted. Also notice that the parenthetical citation for a long quotation comes after the period.

> Complaints about maintenance in the dorms have been on the rise ever since the physical plant reorganized its crews into teams in August. One student's experience is typical:
>> When our ceiling started dripping, my roommate and I went to our resident director right away to file an emergency maintenance request. Apparently the physical plant felt that "emergency" meant they could get around to it in a week or two. By the fourth day without any word from a maintenance person, the ceiling tiles began to fall and puddles began to pool on our carpet. (Trillo)
>
> The physical plant could have avoided expensive ceiling tile and carpet repairs if it had responded to the student's request promptly.

Set off quotations in dialogue

Dialogue is traditionally enclosed within quotation marks. Begin a new paragraph with each change of speaker.

> Before Jim and Lester walk fifty yards on a faint animal trail, they hear the brush rattle in front of them and the unmistakable snorting of a rhino. Jim crouches and looks through the brush. Lester watches Jim, wondering why he isn't retreating, then scrambles up a nearby tree. "Come on back," he yells to Jim, who is now out of sight.

After a few minutes Jim reappears. "I got right next to it but I never did get a good look. I was so close I could even smell it."

"The other one is still out there in the grass. And I heard a third one behind us toward the river."

"We better get out of here before it gets dark. Are you going to spend the night in the tree?"

"I'm thinking about it."

Exercise 46.1   The following sentences contain direct quotations (underlined) and paraphrases from Tony Horowitz's *Confederates in the Attic: Dispatches from the Unfinished Civil War* (New York: Pantheon, 1998). Add, delete, or move quotation marks as needed and correct the placement of citations and the setting of quotes if set incorrectly.

Example   After completing his wild and often contradictory ride through two full years, fifteen states, and the contemporary landscape of what he terms the South's Unfinished Civil War, award-winning journalist and cultural historian Tony Horowitz concluded: the pleasure the Civil War gave me was hard to put into words (387).

1. Horowitz's difficulty was finding words that might make sense, as he puts it, to anyone other than a fellow addict (387).

2. There are, Horowitz allows, clear and often-cited reasons why one might develop a passion for the Civil War, however. Everywhere, people spoke of family and fortunes lost in the war (384), Horowitz writes.

3. Horowitz notes that many Southerners, nostalgic for old-time war heroism, still revere men like Stonewall Jackson, Robert E. Lee, and Nathan Bedford Forrest—"figures that he refers to as the marble men of Southern myth (385)."

4. Civil War heroes were, after all, human. And these men, who for some command the status of gods, were also, in Horowitz's words, petty figures who often hurt their own cause by bickering, even challenging each other to duels. (385)

5. The Civil War was also unique because it marked the first war in which the rural landscape of the nineteenth-century United States met a new kind of war technology. Horowitz states: "It was new technology that made the War's romance and rusticity so palpable. Without photographs, rebs and Yanks would seem as remote to modern Americans as Minutemen and Hessians. Surviving daguerreotypes from the 1840s and 1850s were mostly stiff studio portraits. So the Civil War was as far back as we could delve in our own history and bring back naturalistic images attuned to our modern way of seeing (386)."

Titles of Short Works

While the titles of longer works such as books, magazines, and newspapers are italicized or underlined, titles of shorter works should be set off with quotation marks. Use quotation marks with the following kinds of titles.

Short stories	"Light Is Like Water," by Gabriel García Márquez
Magazine articles	"Race against Death," by Erin West
Newspaper articles	"Cincinnati Mayor Declares Emergency," by Liz Sidoti
Short poems	"We Real Cool," by Gwendolyn Brooks
Essays	"Self-Reliance," by Ralph Waldo Emerson
Songs	"Purple Haze," by Jimi Hendrix
Speeches, lectures, and sermons	"Zero to Web Page in Sixty Minutes," by Jean Lavre
Chapters	"Last, Best Hope of Earth," Chapter 8 of *The Civil War*, by Shelby Foote
Episodes of television and radio shows	"Treehouse of Horror," an episode of *The Simpsons*

The exception.   Don't put the title of your own paper in quotation marks. If the title of another short work appears within the title of your paper, retain the quotation marks around the short work. The title of a paper about Jimi Hendrix, for instance, might read:

The History of Hendrix: Riffs on "Purple Haze"

Other Uses of Quotation Marks

Quotation marks to indicate the novel use of a word

Quotation marks around a term can indicate that the writer is using the term in a novel way, often with skepticism, irony, or sarcasm. The quotation marks indicate that the writer is questioning the term's conventional definition. Notice the way quotation marks indicate skepticism about the conventional definition of *savages* in the following passage.

In the early days of England's empire building, it wasn't unusual to hear English anthropologists say that conquered native people were savages. Yet if we measure civilization by peacefulness and compassion for fellow humans, those "savages" were really much more civilized than the British.

Quotation marks to indicate that a word is being used as a word

Italics are usually used to indicate that a word is being used as a word, rather than standing for its conventional meaning. However, quotation marks are correct in these cases as well.

> Beginning writers sometimes confuse "their," "they're," and "there."

46d Misuses of Quotation Marks

Do not use quotation marks for emphasis

It's becoming more and more common to see quotation marks used to emphasize a word or phrase. Resist the temptation in your own writing; it's an incorrect usage. In fact, because quotation marks indicate that a writer is using a term with skepticism or irony, adding quotation marks for emphasis will highlight unintended connotations of the term.

> Incorrect   "fresh" seafood

By using quotation marks here, the writer seems to call into question whether the seafood is really fresh.

> Correct   fresh seafood

> Incorrect   Enjoy our "live" music every Saturday night.

Again, the quotation marks unintentionally indicate that the writer is skeptical that the music is live.

> Correct   Enjoy our live music every Saturday night.

You have better ways of creating emphasis using your word processing program: **boldfacing**, underlining, *italicizing*, and using color.

Do not use quotation marks around indirect quotations or paraphrases

> Incorrect   The airport security guard announced that "all bags will be searched and then apologized for the inconvenience to the passengers."

> Correct   The airport security guard announced, "All bags will be searched. I apologize for the inconvenience." [direct quotation]

> Correct   The airport security guard announced that all bags would be searched and then apologized for the inconvenience to the passengers. [indirect quotation]

Avoid using quotation marks to acknowledge the use of a cliché

You may have seen other writers enclose clichés in quotation marks. Avoid doing this; in fact, avoid using clichés at all. Clichés are worn-out phrases; fresh words engage readers more.

Incorrect	To avoid "letting the cat out of the bag" about forthcoming products, most large companies employ security experts trained in preventing commercial espionage.
Correct but stale	To avoid letting the cat out of the bag about forthcoming products, most large companies employ security experts trained in preventing commercial espionage.
Correct and Effective	To prevent their savvy competitors from peeking at forthcoming products, most large companies employ security experts trained in preventing commercial espionage.

46e   Other Punctuation with Quotation Marks

The rules for placing punctuation with quotation marks fall into three general categories.

Periods and commas with quotation marks

Place periods and commas inside closing quotation marks.

Incorrect	"The smartest people", Dr. Geisler pointed out, "tell themselves the most convincing rationalizations".
Correct	"The smartest people," Dr. Geisler pointed out, "tell themselves the most convincing rationalizations."

Exceptions occur when a parenthetical citation follows a short quotation. In MLA and APA documentation styles, the period follows the closing parenthesis.

Incorrect	"The smartest people," Dr. Geisler pointed out, "tell themselves the most convincing rationalizations." (52)
Correct	"The smartest people," Dr. Geisler pointed out, "tell themselves the most convincing rationalizations" (52).

Colons and semicolons with quotation marks

Place colons and semicolons outside closing quotation marks.

Incorrect	"From Stettin in the Baltic to Trieste in the Adriatic, an iron curtain has descended across the Continent;" Churchill's statement rang through Cold War politics for the next fifty years.
Correct	"From Stettin in the Baltic to Trieste in the Adriatic, an iron curtain has descended across the Continent"; Churchill's statement rang through Cold War politics for the next fifty years.

Exclamation points, question marks, and dashes with quotation marks

When an exclamation point, question mark, or dash belongs to the original quotation, place it inside the closing quotation mark. When it applies to the entire sentence, place it outside the closing quotation mark.

In the original quotation

"Are we there yet?" came the whine from the back seat.

Applied to the entire sentence

Did the driver in the front seat respond, "Not even close"?

Exercise 46.2 The following sentences use a variety of punctuation marks with quotations. Some are used correctly and some are not. Move the punctuation marks that are incorrectly placed in relation to the quotation marks.

Example	In her essay "Survival Is the Least of My Desires," the novelist Dorothy Allison describes herself as being "born poor, queer, and despised."

1. What does Allison mean when she tells gay and lesbian writers, "We must aim much higher than just staying alive if we are to begin to approach our true potential?"
2. She elaborates, "I want to write in such a way as to literally remake the world, to change people's thinking as they look out of the eyes of the characters I create" (212.)
3. "I believe in the truth"; this declaration forms the cornerstone of the philosophy Allison wants to pass on to gay and lesbian writers.

4. According to Allison, "I write what I think are "moral tales." That's what I intend, though I grow more and more to believe that telling the emotional truth of people's lives, not necessarily the historical truth, is the only moral use of fiction." (217)

5. "I believe the secret in writing is that fiction never exceeds the reach of the writer's courage", says Allison.

COMMON ERRORS

Quotations within quotations

Single quotation marks are used to indicate a quotation within a quotation. In the following example single quotation marks clarify who is speaking. The rules for placing punctuation with single quotation marks are the same as the rules for placing punctuation with double quotation marks.

Incorrect	When he showed the report to Paul Probius, Michener reported that Probius "took vigorous exception to the sentence "He wanted to close down the university," insisting that we add the clarifying phrase "as it then existed"" (Michener 145).
Correct	When he showed the report to Paul Probius, Michener reported that Probius "took vigorous exception to the sentence 'He wanted to close down the university,' insisting that we add the clarifying phrase 'as it then existed'" (Michener 145).

Remember: Single quotation marks are used for quotations within quotations.

For step-by-step discussion, examples, and practice exercises, visit this page of the eText at **www.mycomplab.com.**

47 | Other Punctuation Marks

QUICK*TAKE*

- **When do you use question marks?** (see p. 655)
  Incorrect: A group of artists and computer hackers wondered if there was a way to draw with the eyes? [a period should be used here]
  Correct: A group of artists and computer hackers wondered, "Is there a way to draw with the eyes?"

- **When do you use brackets?** (see p. 657)
  Incorrect: Describing the Battle of Tarawa, World War II photographer Norman Hatch said "they (the Japanese) were just mown down."
  Correct: Describing the Battle of Tarawa, World War II photographer Norman Hatch said "they [the Japanese] were just mown down."

- **When do you use ellipses?** (see p. 658)
  Full quotation: Author Seth Grahame-Smith explains how he equates slave-holders with vampires in *Abraham Lincoln: Vampire Hunter*: "Both creatures, basically slaveholders and vampires, steal lives—take the blood of others—to enrich themselves."
  Shortened quotation: Author Seth Grahame-Smith explains how he equates slaveholders with vampires in *Abraham Lincoln: Vampire Hunter*: "Both creatures . . . steal lives . . . to enrich themselves."

 **Periods**

Periods at the ends of sentences

Place a period at the end of a complete sentence if it is not a direct question or an exclamatory statement. As the term suggests, a direct question asks a question outright. Indirect questions, on the other hand, report the asking of a question.

Direct question	Mississippi opponents of the Confederate-themed state flag wonder, "Where does the state's pride in its heritage end and its respect for those offended begin?"
Indirect question	Mississippi opponents of the Confederate-themed state flag wonder where the state's pride in its heritage ends and its respect for those offended begins.

Periods with quotation marks and parentheses

When a quotation falls at the end of a sentence, place the period inside the closing quotation marks.

> Although he devoted decades to a wide range of artistic and political projects, Allen Ginsberg is best known as the author of the poem "Howl."

When a parenthetical phrase falls at the end of a sentence, place the period outside the closing parenthesis.

> Mrs. Chen, a grandmother in Seneca Falls, is training for her first 10K race (6.2 miles).

When parentheses enclose a whole sentence, place the period inside the closing parenthesis.

> Computer science researchers have been able to identify people in anonymous databases including Netflix's by collecting information on services such as Facebook, Flickr, and Twitter. (Even more unsettling to privacy advocates, researchers have been able to predict individual Social Security numbers by using publically available information.)

Periods with abbreviations

Many abbreviations require periods; however, there are few set rules. Use the dictionary to check how to punctuate abbreviations on a case-by-case basis.

> John F. Kennedy   Mr.   misc.   a.m.

The rules for punctuating two types of abbreviations do remain consistent: Postal abbreviations for states and most abbreviations for organizations do not require periods.

> OH for Ohio   ACLU for the American Civil Liberties Union
> CA for California   NRA for the National Rifle Association

When an abbreviation with a period falls at the end of a sentence, do not add a second period to conclude the sentence.

> **Incorrect**   Her flight arrives at 6:22 p.m..
>
> **Correct**   Her flight arrives at 6:22 p.m.

Periods in citations of poetry and plays

Use a period to separate the components of the following kinds of literary citations.

A poem divided into sections such as books or cantos

book.lines   *The Inferno* 27.79-84

A prose play

act.scene   *Beyond Therapy* 1.4

A verse play

act.scene.lines   *Twelfth Night* 3.4.194-98

Periods as decimal points

Decimal points are periods that separate integers from tenths, hundredths, and so on.

99.98% pure silver   98.6° Fahrenheit
on sale for $399.97   2.6 liter engine

Since large numbers with long strings of zeros can be difficult to read accurately, writers sometimes shorten them using decimal points. Notice how the decimal points make the second sentence easier to read than the first.

When the national debt rose over 13,000,000,000,000 dollars in 2010, the United States Congress passed legislation to limit the debt ceiling to 14,300,000,000,000 dollars.

When the national debt rose over $13 trillion in 2010 the United States Congress passed legislation to limit the debt ceiling to $14.3 trillion.

Exercise 47.1 Periods have been omitted from the paragraph that follows. You can see how confusing writing becomes without proper period placement. Add periods and capitalize the first words of sentences correctly to clear up the confusion.

Example   Mr.Clarence Saunders worked most of his life to develop the modern supermarket.

Mr Saunders started working as a grocer when he was 16 moving through various jobs in the field, including wholesale, he realized that grocers lost money by selling on credit at the age of 26 he formed Saunders-Blackburn Co, which dealt only in cash and urged its retail customers to do the same in 1916, on Jefferson St in Memphis, Tennessee, he opened the first self-service grocery store in the US, Piggly Wiggly by 1922, there were 1,200 stores in 29 states in 1923, however, Saunders went bankrupt and lost not only the enormous pink marble mansion he was building but also the rights to his own name trying to rebuild, he went on to create the Clarence Saunders Sole Owner of My Name Stores chain, which went into bankruptcy during the Great Depression in order to promote these stores Saunders founded a professional football team called the Clarence Saunders Sole Owner of My Name Tigers in 1930, the team, usually just called the Tigers, was invited by the NFL to join their organization, but Saunders refused

47b Question Marks

Question marks with direct questions

Place a question mark at the end of a direct question. A direct question is one that the questioner puts to someone outright. In contrast, an indirect question merely reports the asking of a question. Question marks give readers a cue to read the end of the sentence with rising inflection. Read the following sentences aloud. Hear how your inflection rises in the second sentence to convey the direct question.

Indirect question
Desirée asked whether Dan rode his motorcycle without a helmet.

Direct question
Desirée asked, "Does Dan ride his motorcycle without a helmet?"

Question marks with quotations

When a quotation falls at the end of a direct question, place the question mark outside the closing quotation mark.

Did Abraham Lincoln really call Harriet Beecher Stowe "the little lady who started this big war"?

Place the question mark inside the closing quotation mark when only the quoted material is a direct question.

Slowly scientists are beginning to answer the question, "Is cancer a genetic disease?"

When quoting a direct question in the middle of a sentence, place a question mark inside the closing quotation mark and place a period at the end of the sentence.

> Market researchers estimate that asking Burger World's customers "Do you want fries with that?" was responsible for a 15% boost in their french fries sales.

Question marks to indicate uncertainty about dates or numbers

Place a question mark in parentheses after a date or number whose accuracy is in question.

> After his escape from slavery, Frederick Douglass (1817?-95) went on to become a great orator and statesman.

Exercise 47.2 Periods and question marks have been omitted from the paragraph that follows. Add periods and question marks where needed and capitalize the beginnings of sentences.

> **Example**   What was so Earth-shattering about Friedan's naming of
>   the "problem with no name"?

>   Betty Friedan's *The Feminine Mystique* addressed the question, "Is this all" She examined why millions of women were sensing a gnawing feeling of discontent Friedan asked, "Can the problem that has no name somehow be related to the domestic routine of the housewife" and examined women's shifting place in postwar America What were women missing In asking these questions, Friedan legitimized the panic and uneasiness of many women who found the roles of mother and wife not wholly satisfying However, did this naming solve the "problem with no name"

47c Exclamation Points

Exclamation points to convey strong emotion

Exclamation points conclude sentences and, like question marks, tell the reader how a sentence should sound. They indicate strong emotion. Use exclamation points sparingly in formal writing; they are seldom appropriate in academic and professional prose.

Exclamation points with emphatic interjections

Exclamation points can convey a sense of urgency with brief interjections. Interjections can be incorporated into sentences or stand on their own.

> Run! They're about to close the doors to the jetway.

Exclamation points with quotation marks

In quotations, exclamation points follow the same rules as question marks. If a quotation falls at the end of an exclamatory statement, place the exclamation point outside the closing quotation mark.

> The singer forgot the words of "America the Beautiful"!

When quoting an exclamatory statement at the end of a sentence that is not itself exclamatory, place the exclamation point inside the closing quotation mark.

> Jerry thought his car would be washed away in the flood, but Anna jumped into action, declaring, "Not if I can help it!"

When the quotation of an exclamatory statement does not fall at the end of a sentence, place the exclamation point inside the closing quotation mark and place a period at the end of the sentence.

> Someone yelled "Loser!" when the candidate walked on stage.

47d Brackets

While brackets (sometimes called *square brackets*) look quite similar to parentheses, the two perform different functions. Brackets have a narrow set of uses.

Brackets to provide clarification within quotation marks

Quoted material sometimes requires clarification because it is removed from its context. Adding clarifying material in brackets can allow you to make the quotation clear while still accurately repeating the exact words of your source. In the following example the writer quotes a sentence with the pronoun *they*, which refers to a noun in a previous, unquoted sentence. The material in brackets clarifies to whom the pronoun refers.

> The Harris study found that "In the last three years, they [Gonzales Junior High students] averaged 15% higher on their mathematics assessment tests than their peers in Northridge County."

Brackets within parentheses

Since parentheses within parentheses might confuse readers, use brackets to enclose parenthetical information within a parenthetical phrase.

> Representative Patel's most controversial legislation (including a version of the hate crimes bill [HR 99-108] the house rejected two years ago) has a slim chance of being enacted this session.

Ellipses

Ellipses let a reader know that a portion of a passage is missing. You can use ellipses to keep quotations concise and direct readers' attention to what is important to the point you are making. An ellipsis is a string of three periods with spaces separating the periods.

Ellipses to indicate an omission from a prose quotation

When you quote only a phrase or short clause from a sentence, you usually do not need to use ellipses.

> Mao Tse-tung first used "let a hundred flowers blossom" in a Beijing speech in 1957.

Except at the beginning of a quotation, indicate omitted words with an ellipsis. Type a space between each ellipsis dot and between the ellipses and the words preceding and following them.

The original source

> "The female praying mantis, so named for the way it holds its front legs together as if in prayer, tears off her male partner's head during mating. Remarkably, the headless male will continue the act of mating. This brutal dance is a stark example of the innate evolutionary drive to pass genes onto offspring; the male praying mantis seems to live and die only for this moment."

An ellipsis indicates omitted words

> "The female praying mantis . . . tears off her male partner's head during mating."

Note: Retain any punctuation mark falling before the omitted passage if it clarifies the sentence. In this case the comma before the omitted passage would not make the sentence any clearer, so it was not retained.

Ellipses to indicate the omission of a whole line or lines of poetry

Using more than three periods is appropriate in just one instance: to signal the omission of a full line or lines of poetry in the middle of a poetry quotation. In such instances, use an entire line of spaced periods.

Original

My Shakespeare, rise; I will not lodge thee by
Chaucer or Spenser, or bid Beaumont lie
A little further, to make thee a room;
Thou art a monument, without a tomb,
And art alive still, while thy book doth live,
And we have wits to read, and praise to give.

—Ben Jonson, "To the Memory of My Beloved,
the Author, Mr. William Shakespeare" (1623)

Omitted lines of poetry

My Shakespeare, rise;

. . . .
Thou art a monument, without a tomb,
And art alive still, while thy book doth live,
And we have wits to read, and praise to give.

Ellipses to indicate a pause or an interrupted sentence

Ellipses can provide a visual cue that a speaker is taking a long pause or that a speaker has been interrupted.

"And the winner is . . . David Goldstein."

"That ball is going, going, . . . gone!"

"Be careful that you don't spill . . ."

Exercise 47.3 In the following quotations and A. E. Housman's poem "To an Athlete Dying Young," delete the underlined passages and punctuate the quotations with ellipses where necessary. Be sure to leave in clarifying punctuation.

Example   Robert Ward states, "The American culture positions its heroes such that they are destined to end in turmoil, problematizing the desire for eminent success. By elevating them to the position of gods, society gives heroes nowhere to go but down."

Rewrite Robert Ward states, "The American culture positions its heroes such that they are destined to end in turmoil. . . . By elevating them to the position of gods, society gives heroes nowhere to go but down."

Ward notes, "The phenomenon of the waning star is heavily represented in the last century of English and American culture, ranging from poetry to popular rock music." In 1896, chronicling the advantage of dying before the glory fades, A. E. Housman published the poem "To an Athlete Dying Young." The following is a passage from that poem:

> Now you will not swell the rout
> Of lads that wore their honors out,
> Runners whom renown outran
> And the name died before the man.
>
> So set, before the echoes fade,
> The fleet foot on the sill of shade,
> And hold to the low lintel up
> The still-defended challenge-cup.
>
> And round that early-laurelled head
> Will flock to gaze the strengthless dead,
> And find unwithered on its curls
> The garland briefer than a girl's.

Housman's verses extol the eternal glory of those who pass in their prime. Scholars such as Ona Click have noted the recent proliferation of Housman's theme, citing that "artists such as Neil Young have contemporized this notion with songs such as 'Hey Hey My My.' The song contrasts the fates of two rock stars who ultimately took two very different paths, Elvis Presley and Johnny Rotten of the Sex Pistols; while Presley died in a blaze of glory, Rotten's fleeting stardom waned and dulled the cultural memory of his initial rise to fame." In a related article, she notes this theme traveled into the 1980s as Bruce Springsteen's "Glory Days" recalled the tale of "those who outlive their primes and are forced to reduce their glory to nostalgic reminiscences and fleeting grasps at the past." Though we venerate our heroes, culture notes how their position is tenuous at best.

47f Slashes

Slashes to indicate alternative words

Slashes between two words indicate that a choice between them is to be made. When using slashes for this purpose, do not put a space between the slash and words.

Incorrect	Maya was such an energetic baby that her exhausted parents wished she had come with an on / off switch.
Correct	Maya was such an energetic baby that her exhausted parents wished she had come with an on/off switch.

The following are common instances of the slash used to indicate alternative words:

either/or	and/or	pass/fail
player/coach	win/lose	on/off

Slashes to indicate line breaks in short quotations of verse

Line breaks—where the lines of a poem end—are artistic choices that affect how we understand a poem. Thus it is important to reproduce them accurately when quoting poetry. The task is not difficult in MLA style when the quotation is four or more lines long: Simply indent the quoted lines 1 inch and mimic the line breaks of the original verse. When you quote three or fewer lines of poetry, however, and must integrate the quotation into the paragraph rather than setting it off in a block, use slashes to indicate line breaks. Type a space on either side of the slash.

> The concluding lines of T. S. Eliot's "Animula" offer a surprising revision of a common prayer. He writes, "Pray for Floret, by the boarhound slain between the yew trees / Pray for us now and at the hour of our birth." Replacing "death," the final word in the prayer, with "birth" at the end of this dark poem connotes an uneasy sense that we find ourselves adrift in a new and unfamiliar world.

Slashes with fractions

Place a slash between the numerator and the denominator in a fraction. Do not put spaces around the slash.

Incorrect	3 / 4
Correct	3/4

Slashes with dates

In informal writing, slashes divide the month, day, and year in a date. A longer format is appropriate for formal academic and professional writing. Omit the slashes, spell out the month, and place a comma after the day.

Informal   Javy, save 1/14/12 on your calendar; I reserved two tickets for the talent show.

Formal   It was a pleasure to meet you during my December 14 interview for Universal Oil's marketing internship. As we discussed, I will not be available for full-time employment until my graduation on May 12, 2012. However, I am hopeful that we can work out the part-time arrangement you suggested until that date.

Exercise 47.4 Take a look at the way the following paragraph uses all the punctuation marks discussed in this chapter: periods, question marks, exclamation points, brackets, ellipses, and slashes. Some are used correctly, and others are used incorrectly or omitted altogether. Correct any punctuation mistakes that you find, and add any necessary marks that have been omitted.

Example   Many ask, "Why have snakes become a symbol of religious devotion."?"

In 1996 alone, over sixty deaths occurred due to religious snake handling. Mark 16.18 in the King James version of the Bible states, "They shall take up serpents and if they drink any deadly thing it shall not hurt them . . ."! This passage instigated the formation of a religion which thrives among the Irish and English descendants living in Appalachia. (In the 1990s, over 2000 snake handlers lived in Appalachia alone.)

Snake handling has been investigated by both practitioners of the fine arts (Romulus Linney's *Holy Ghosts* (1971) examines snake handling in the South) and news media. One controversial case examined Rev Glenn Summerford who attempted to kill his wife by forcing her to handle rattlesnakes. The general public often sees snake handling as a frightening act of fundamentalism practiced by congregations [often assumed to be undereducated].

48 | Write with Accurate Spelling

QUICKTAKE

- **Do spelling checkers catch every spelling mistake?** (see below)
  Incorrect: Mini people believe their able two think four themselves, but a few experiments half shown that this is often knot the case.
  Correct: Many people believe they're able to think for themselves, but a few experiments have shown that this is often not the case.

48a Know the Limitations of Spelling Checkers

Spelling checkers do help you to become a better speller. But spelling checkers are quite limited and miss many errors. If you type *ferry tail* for *fairy tale,* your spelling checker will not catch the errors.

WRITING SMART

Electronic dictionaries

A number of reputable dictionaries are available on the Web. For a list check the Web site of your school's library. *The Merriam-Webster Dictionary* is available to everyone online at www.merriam-webster. com/dictionary/.

How do you look up a word if you have no idea about how it is spelled?

Use Google as a quick way to check if you have the right spelling. If your guess is incorrect, Google will suggest the correct spelling. Also, you can find definitions by using the "define:" operator in Google; for example, "define: crepuscular."

Exercise 48.1 The author of the following paragraph ran it through a spelling checker and took all of the checker's advice. The checker missed some errors and created a few new errors. Correct all the spelling mistakes in the paragraph.

Example	*It's* ~~Its~~ indicative of ~~Despond~~ *Desmond* Tutu's feelings of

solidarity with his parishioners that he opted to live in
~~Sowed,~~ *Soweto* a poor black neighborhood, rather than in

Houghton, a rich suburb.

Archbishop Despond Tutu's message to the peoples of South Africa is that all are "of infinite worth created in the image of god," and "to be treated . . . with reverence" (Wepman 13). Tutu maintains that this is true fore whites as well as blacks, a position that isn't popular wit some South African. It can be scene from the many awards tutu has received, not least among them the Nobel Peace Prize in 1984, that his commitment to morality and human freedom have had an effect the world over. Archbishop Despond Tutu is a ban who does not waist the potential of hiss powerful role as religious leader. On the contrary, the Archbishop seas many political problems as moral ones and speaks out frequently on human rights issues.

48b Distinguish Homonyms

Homonyms are pairs (*your, you're*) and trios (*their, there, they're*) of words that sound alike but have different spellings and meanings. They are tricky words to spell because we don't learn to distinguish them in spoken language, and spelling checkers don't flag them as errors because they correctly spell other words in their databases. It's easy to type *there* for *their* or *Web sight* for *Web site* and not catch the error when you proofread.

Exercise 48.2   Circle the correct homonyms in the paragraph that follows.

Example	The pitch drop experiment is a long-term experiment measuring the flow of a (peace/(piece)) of pitch, or bitumen, over many years.

This famous experiment was started in 1927 (by/buy) Professor Thomas Parnell of the University of Queensland to demonstrate that (sum/some) substances that (seem/seam) to be solid are actually (vary/very) (hi/high)-viscosity fluids. Parnell's first step was to (pour/poor) a heated sample of pitch into a sealed funnel. The pitch was then (aloud/allowed) to settle until 1930, at (which/witch) time the seal was cut. Over the (past/passed) seventy years, only (ate/eight) drops have fallen. To date, no (won/one) has ever (seen/scene) a drop fall. After Parnell (died/dyed) in 1948, John

Mainstone became the (hair/heir) to the experiment. Although scientists now (no/know) that pitch has a viscosity more that 230 billion times that of water (do/due) to (there/their) work, Parnell and Mainstone (one/won) the 2005 Ig Nobel Prize in Physics, a parody of the well-known Nobel Prize.

COMMON ERRORS

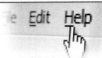

Commonly misspelled words

Is *accommodate* spelled with one *m* or two? Is *harass* spelled with one *r* or two? You'll find a list of words commonly misspelled at the URL below.

Remember: Always check a dictionary when you are unsure of how a word is spelled.

 For step-by-step discussion, examples, and practice exercises, visit this page of the eText at **www.mycomplab.com**.

48c Learn Spelling Rules

This section addresses four major categories of spelling rules: *i* before *e*; prefixes; suffixes; and plurals. While you'll see that each rule carries a number of exceptions, learning the rules is an important first step toward becoming a better speller.

I before *e*, except after *c* or when pronounced as *ay*

I before *e* is the classic spelling rule you probably learned in grade school. An *i* goes before an *e* except in two cases. The *i* follows the *e* when these letters follow *c* or when they are pronounced *ay*. Other exceptions follow on the next page.

> *i* before *e*: *brief, hierarchy, obedient*
> except after *c*: *receipt, perceive, ceiling*
> or when pronounced as *ay*: *eight, neighbor, heir*

Exceptions to the *i* before *e* rules

ancient	feisty	science
being	foreign	seismic
caffeine	forfeit	seize
conscience	height	species
counterfeit	heist	weird
efficient	leisure	
either	neither	

Prefixes

When adding a prefix to a word, retain the spelling of the root word. (See Sections 43a and 43b for help determining when a prefix–root word combination should be hyphenated.)

mis + spelling = misspelling
hemi + sphere = hemisphere
un + believable = unbelievable
un + nerve = unnerve

Suffixes

Double the root word's final consonant if

1. The root word ends in a consonant, and
2. A single vowel comes before the consonant, and
3. The root word is one syllable or the last syllable of the root is stressed.
   rappel + ed = rappelled
   control + ing = controlling
   recur + ence = recurrence
   hit + able = hittable

Do not double the root word's final consonant if

1. The root word ends in two consonants.
   lift + ing = lifting
   remind + ed = reminded
2. Two vowels come before the consonant.
   head + ing = heading
   repeat + ed = repeated
3. The last syllable of the root is not stressed.
   fó-cus + ed = focused
   tŕa-vel + ed = traveled
   lá-bel + ing = labeling

Drop the final *e* from a root word if the suffix begins with a vowel.

When adding a suffix that begins with a vowel to a root word that ends with an unpronounced *e*, drop the *e*.

fate + al = fatal
opportune + ity = opportunity
Greece + ian = Grecian

Exceptions.   Keep the *e* if it is preceded by a *c* (*enforceable, noticeable*) or a soft *g* (*advantageous, courageous*).

Keep the final e in a root word if the suffix begins with a consonant.

Keep the root word's final unpronounced *e* when the suffix begins with a consonant.

subtle + ty = subtlety
fortunate + ly = fortunately
appease + ment = appeasement

Exceptions

acknowledge + ment = acknowledgment
argue + ment = argument
awe + ful = awful
judge + ment = judgment
true + ly = truly
whole + ly = wholly

When adding a suffix to a root word ending with a consonant and y, change the y to an i.

beauty + ful = beautiful
crazy + ness = craziness
glory + fy = glorify
hungry + est = hungriest

Exceptions. When the suffix begins with an *i*, keep the *y* (as in *study, studying* and *dandy, dandyism*) in order to avoid a double *i*. Also keep the *y* when adding *'s* (*July's* heat, the *spy's* house). Other individual exceptions: *dryness, wryly, spryly*.

When adding a suffix to a root word ending with a vowel and y, retain the y.

pay + ment = payment
stay + ing = staying
boy + hood = boyhood
annoy + ance = annoyance

Exceptions

day + ly = daily   lay + ity = laity
gay + ty = gaiety   pay + ed = paid
lay + ed = laid   say + ed = said

Exercise 48.3 Each of the following root words ends in a consonant-vowel-consonant combination. Write the correct spelling of each word.

occur + ed = occurred
stop + ing = stopping

1. slap + ed
2. refer + ing
3. drop + ed
4. ship + ment
5. dim + er

6. run + ing
7. refer + ence
8. benefit + ed
9. commit + ment
10. forget + able

Exercise 48.4 Each of the following root words ends in a silent e. Write the correct spelling of each word. Pay attention to whether the first letter of the suffix is a consonant or a vowel.

continue + ous = continuous
state + ly = stately

1. definite + ly
2. pure + ist
3. spine + less
4. exercise + ing
5. imagine + ation

6. hate + ful
7. judge + ment
8. debate + able
9. like + able
10. nine + th

Plurals

You can make most words plural simply by adding *s*. Exceptions abound, however. The following rules will help you determine which words do not take just an *s* in the plural.

Compound nouns: Make the most important word plural.
To indicate more than one of a compound noun (several words combining to make a noun) make the most important word plural. Note that the last word isn't always the most important.

sisters-in-law
attorneys general
courts-martial

brigadier generals
passersby
power plays

Add *es* to words ending with *ch*, *s*, *sh*, *x*, *z*, or a consonant and an *o*.
Add *es* to words that end in *ch*, *s*, *sh*, *x*, or *z*, as well as to words that end with a consonant followed by an *o*.

ending with *ch*:
ending with *s*:

church, churches
dress, dresses

catch, catches
trellis, trellises

ending with *sh*:	wash, washes	radish, radishes
ending with *x*:	ax, axes	box, boxes
ending with *z*:	buzz, buzzes	quiz, quizzes
ending with consonant and an *o*:	hero, heroes	tomato, tomatoes

Exceptions

| memo, memos | photo, photos |
| piano, pianos | solo, solos |

With words ending in a consonant and *y*, change the *y* to an *i* and add *es*.

Words ending in a consonant followed by a *y* become plural by replacing the *y* with an *i* and adding *es*.

spy, spies
derby, derbies
philosophy, philosophies

With words ending in a vowel and *y*, add *s*.

If a vowel precedes the *y*, simply add an *s* to make the word plural.

day, days
buoy, buoys
lackey, lackeys

Irregular plurals

Some words are irregular in the plural; they don't follow any set rules in English. Some are Latin words that retain their Latin plural endings. The following is a partial list of irregular plurals.

Singular	Plural	Singular	Plural
alumnus	alumni	deer	deer
analysis	analyses	dice	die
axis	axes	fish	fish
bacterium	bacteria	focus	foci
basis	bases	half	halves
cactus	cacti	hypothesis	hypotheses
child	children	life	lives
crisis	crises	locus	loci
criterion	criteria	man	men
curriculum	curricula	medium	media
datum	data	memorandum	memoranda

Singular	Plural	Singular	Plural
mouse	mice	stimulus	stimuli
octopus	octopi	stratum	strata
ox	oxen	syllabus	syllabi
parenthesis	parentheses	thesis	theses
phenomenon	phenomena	thief	thieves
radius	radii	vertebra	vertebrae
self	selves	woman	women
species	species		

Exercise 48.5 In the following paragraph, singular words that should be plural are underlined. Make all the underlined words plural. Where necessary, change verbs so that they agree with the plural words.

Example Why Oscar Wilde, in 1885, brought Lord Queensbury to trial on charges of libel remains one of the great *mysteries* ~~mystery~~ of literary history.

Wilde, a successful author with two child and multiple follower in literary London, made a mistake when he pressed charge against the famous lord. By all account, Wilde was in jovial spirit when he arrived at the Old Bailey courthouse on April 3, 1895. Passerby may have seen the famous writer make one of his characteristically fantastic entrance: Wilde's carriage was outfitted with two horse, several servant, and all the pomp and circumstance his public character demanded. But the series of event that followed led up to one of the great crash of the Victorian era. Wilde lost the libel suit and was then himself tried, twice, based on the body of evidence amassed against him in the first trial. The medium were not sympathetic to Wilde, who had come to embody the multiple threat of moral indecency for conservative Victorian. In the day following his two trial and ultimate conviction for the newly illegal crime of gross indecency, both print article and caricature presenting story from the trial served as knife in the artist's back. Wilde was sentenced to two year of "hard labor," and upon his release from prison fled to France in exile. He died two year later. Wilde lived two life in his brief 47 years; he lived the first under the spotlight of fame, and the second under the glare of infamy. But his philosophy of art and beauty survive, as Wilde predicted they would.

49 Capitalization and Italics

QUICKTAKE

- **Which words do you capitalize?** (see below)
  Incorrect: Some americans are surprised to learn that most south africans are protestants, and while no sect has the majority, there are more pentacostals than any other denomination.
  Correct: Some Americans are surprised to learn that most South Africans are Protestants, and while no sect has the majority, there are more Pentacostals than any other denomination.

- **Which words do you italicize?** (see p. 675)
  Incorrect: An English major doesn't "have" to read Hermann Melville's novel "Moby Dick" or read any of his short stories, such as *Bartleby the Scrivener*, but it couldn't hurt.
  Correct: An English major doesn't have to read Hermann Melville's novel *Moby Dick* or read any of his short stories, such as "Bartleby the Scrivener," but it couldn't hurt.

 Capital Letters

Capitalize the initial letters of proper nouns and proper adjectives

Capitalize the initial letters of proper nouns (nouns that name particular people, places, and things), including the following:

Names	Sandra Day O'Connor	Bill Gates
Titles preceding names	Dr. Martin Luther King, Jr.	Mrs. Fields
Place names	Grand Canyon	Northwest Territories
Institution names	Department of Labor	Amherst College
Organization names	World Trade Organization	American Cancer Society
Company names	Motorola	JoJo's Café and Bakery
Religions	Protestantism	Islam

Languages	Chinese	Swahili
Months	November	March
Days of the week	Monday	Friday
Nationalities	Italian	Indonesian
Holidays	Passover	Thanksgiving
Departments	Chemistry Department	Department of the Interior
Historical eras	Enlightenment	Middle Ages
Regions	the South	the Midwest
Course names	Eastern Religions	Microbiology
Job title when used with a proper noun		President Nelson Mandela

Capitalize the initial letters of proper adjectives (adjectives based on the names of people, places, and things).

African American bookstore	Avogadro's number	Irish music

Avoid unnecessary capitalization

Do not capitalize the names of seasons, academic disciplines (unless they are languages), or job titles used without a proper noun.

Seasons	fall, winter, spring, summer
Academic disciplines (except languages)	chemistry, computer science, psychology, English, French, Japanese
Job titles used without a proper noun	The vice president is on maternity leave.

Capitalize titles of publications

In MLA and CMS styles, when capitalizing titles, capitalize the initial letters of all first and last words and all other words except articles, prepositions, and coordinating conjunctions. Even if it is one of those, capitalize the initial letter of the first word in the subtitle following a colon.

James and the Giant Peach

The Grapes of Wrath

The Writing on the Wall: An Anthology of Graffiti Art

COMMON ERRORS

e Edit Help

Capitalizing with colons, parentheses, and quotations

Capitalizing with colons

Except when a colon follows a heading, do not capitalize the first letter after a colon unless the colon links two main clauses (which can stand as complete sentences). If the material following the colon is a quotation, a formal statement, or consists of more than one sentence, capitalize the first letter. In other cases capitalization is optional.

Incorrect	We are all being integrated into a global economy that never sleeps: An economy determining our personal lives and our relationships with others.
Correct	We are all being integrated into a global economy that never sleeps: We can work, shop, bank, and be entertained twenty-four hours a day.

Capitalizing with parentheses

Capitalize the first word of material enclosed in parentheses if the words stand on their own as a complete sentence.

> Beginning with Rachel Carson's *Silent Spring* in 1962, we stopped worrying so much about what nature was doing to us and began to worry about what we were doing to nature. (Science and technology that had been viewed as the solution to problems suddenly became viewed as their cause.)

If the material enclosed in parentheses is part of a larger sentence, do not capitalize the first letter enclosed in the parentheses.

> Beginning with Rachel Carson's *Silent Spring* (first published in 1962), we stopped worrying so much about what nature was doing to us and began to worry about what we were doing to nature.

Capitalizing with quotations

If the quotation of part of a sentence is smoothly integrated into a sentence, do not capitalize the first word. Smoothly integrated quotations do not require a comma to separate the sentence from the rest of the quotation.

> It's no wonder the *Monitor* wrote that Armand's chili was "the best in Georgia, bar none"; he spends whole days in his kitchen experimenting over bubbling pots.

(Continued on next page)

COMMON ERRORS *(Continued)*

But if the sentence contains an attribution and the quotation can stand as a complete sentence, capitalize the first word. In such sentences a comma should separate the attribution from the quotation.

> According to Janet Morris of the *Monitor,* "The chili Armand fusses over for hours in his kitchen is the best in Georgia, bar none."

Remember: For elements following colons or within parentheses or quotation marks, capitalize the first letter only if the group of words can stand as a complete sentence.

 For step-by-step discussion, examples, and practice exercises, visit this page of the eText at **www.mycomplab.com.**

Exercise 49.1   Nothing in the paragraph that follows has been capitalized. Revise it as necessary.

Example   Sexting, the act of sending a text message containing a sexually explicit photograph, has brought attention to a legal gray area in the United States anti-child pornography laws.

Without a doubt, sexting has entered the popular culture of the english-speaking world. a 2008 survey in cosmogirl (sponsored by the national campaign to support teen and unplanned pregnancy) reported that 20% of american teens had sexted; similar results have been found in studies conducted in the uk. Recent episodes of teen dramas 90210 and degrassi have featured plot lines revolving around the dangers of sexting, as has an episode of law and order: svu. In february 2010, mtv aired a special, "sexting in america: when privates go public," that followed two very different teens and the devastating effects that sexting has had on their lives. while one teen suffers with the knowledge that a naked photo of herself will always follow her, another faces the legal ramifications of having forwarded a sext from his girlfriend to 70 people in a moment of anger. in most states, sexting can be considered a felony under child pornography laws, but many states are seeking to alter their laws in light of this new trend. in connecticut, for example, representative rosa rebimbas has introduced legislation to lessen the penalty for sexting between two consenting minors.

Exercise 49.2 Nothing in the paragraph that follows has been capitalized. Revise it as necessary.

Example   ^C ^A
courses in american history often disregard the founding
of the ^{FBI} fbi.

> the federal bureau of investigation (fbi) has long been considered an american institution that was fathered by president theodore roosevelt. during the early 1900s, the united states was going through what some referred to as the progressive era. (during this period, the american people believed government intervention was synonymous with a just society.) roosevelt, the president during part of this era, aided in the creation of an organization devoted to federal investigations. prior to 1907, federal investigations were carried out by agents-for-hire employed by the department of justice. on wednesday, may 27, 1908, the u.s. congress passed a law prohibiting the employment of agents-for-hire and enabling the establishment of an official secret service directly affiliated with the department. that spring, attorney general charles bonaparte appointed ten agents who would report to a chief examiner. this action is often considered to be the birth of the fbi.

 Italics

The titles of entire works (books, magazines, newspapers, films) are italicized in print. The titles of parts of entire works are placed within quotation marks.

Books	*The Brief Wondrous Life of Oscar Wao*
Magazines	*Make*
Journals	*Journal of Fish Biology*
Newspapers	*The Commercial Appeal*
Feature-length films	*Avatar*
Long poems	*Beowulf*
Plays, operas, and ballets	*Wicked*
Television shows	*The Office*
Radio shows and audio recordings	*The Fame Monster*
Paintings, sculptures, and other visual works of art	*Cloud Gate*
Pamphlets and bulletins	*Surrealist Manifesto*

Also italicize the names of ships and aircraft.

Spirit of St. Louis   *Challenger*
Titanic   *Pequod*

The exceptions.   Do not italicize the names of sacred texts.

The text for our Comparative Religions course, *Sacred Texts from around the World*, contains excerpts from the New English Bible, the Qur'an, the Talmud, the Upanishads, and the Bhagavad Gita.

Exercise 49.3 Underline any words in the following paragraph that should be italicized.

Example   Both controversial in their own right, the famed clothing designer Coco Chanel and the painter of <u>Guernica</u>, Pablo Picasso, are listed by <u>Time</u> magazine as two of the "Most Interesting People of the Twentieth Century."

Many think Coco Chanel is to fashion what the Bible is to religion. Consequently, various types of media have been used to try to capture the essence of this innovative designer. Films such as Tonight or Never preserve Chanel's designs for future generations, while the failed Broadway musical Coco attempts to embody her life's work. More recently, print and small screen have attempted to encapsulate the impact of the designer in specials like A&E Top 10: Fashion Designers and books such as Chanel: Her Style and Her Life. Chanel was as monumental and self-destructive as the Titanic. She almost single-handedly redefined women's clothing through the popularization of sportswear and the jersey suit. But she also sympathized with Hitler after the release of his book Mein Kampf and the relocation of the Jews, and her image was further tarnished by her wartime romance with a Nazi officer. However, after her initial success waned during World War II, magazines such as Vogue and Life welcomed her back. She reinvented herself and her clothing line in the 1950s, and today she stands as one of the most influential fashion designers in history.

50 | Abbreviations, Acronyms, and Numbers

QUICKTAKE

- **How do you use abbreviations?** (see below)
  Incorrect: Although he demands to be called "Dr. Hastings," Robert's
  Dr. of Phil. degree is strictly honorary.
  Correct: Although he demands to be called "Doctor Hastings," Robert's
  PhD is strictly honorary.
- **When do you spell out numbers?** (see p. 682)
  Incorrect: There are about 20,000,000,000 chickens in the world, which is
  about 3 chickens for every person.
  Correct: There are about 20 billion chickens in the world, which is about
  three chickens for every person.

Abbreviations

Abbreviations are shortened forms of words. Because abbreviations vary widely, you will need to look in the dictionary to determine how to abbreviate words on a case-by-case basis. Nonetheless, there are a few patterns that abbreviations follow.

Abbreviate titles before and degrees after full names

Ms. Ella Fitzgerald	**Dr.** Suzanne Smith	Driss Ouaouicha, **PhD**
Prof. Vijay Aggarwal	San-qi Li, **MD**	Marissa Límon, **LLD**

Write out the professional title when it is used with only a last name.

Professor Chin   **Doctor** Rodriguez   **Reverend** Ames

Conventions for using abbreviations with years and times

BCE (before the common era) and CE (common era) are now preferred for indicating years, replacing BC (before Christ) and AD (*anno Domini* ["the year of our Lord"]). Note that all are now used without periods.

479 **BCE** (or BC)

1610 **CE** (or AD, but AD is placed before the number)

The preferred written conventions for times are a.m. (*ante meridiem*) and p.m. (*post meridiem*).

> 9:03 a.m.
>
> 3:30 p.m.

An alternative is military time:

> The morning meal is served from 0600 to 0815; the evening meal is served from 1730 to 1945.

Latin abbreviations

Some writers sprinkle Latin abbreviations throughout their writing, apparently thinking that they are a mark of learning. Frequently these abbreviations are used inappropriately. If you use Latin abbreviations, make sure you know what they stand for.

cf.	(*confer*) compare
e.g.	(*exempli gratia*) for example
et al.	(*et alia*) and others
etc.	(*et cetera*) and so forth
i.e.	(*id est*) that is
N.B.	(*nota bene*) note well
viz.	(*videlicet*) namely

COMMON ERRORS   Edit Help

Making abbreviations and acronyms plural

Plurals of abbreviations and acronyms are formed by adding *s*, not *'s*.

> Technology is changing so rapidly these days that PCs become obsolete husks of circuits and plastic in only a few years.

Use *'s* only to show possession.

> The NRA's position on trigger locks is that the government should advocate, not legislate, their use.

Remember: When making abbreviations and acronyms plural, add *s*, not *'s*.

 For step-by-step discussion, examples, and practice exercises, visit this page of the eText at **www.mycomplab.com**.

In particular, avoid using *etc.* to fill out a list of items. Use of *etc.* announces that you haven't taken the time to finish a thought.

Lazy	The contents of his grocery cart described his eating habits: a big bag of chips, hot sauce, frozen pizza, etc.
Better	The contents of his grocery cart described his eating habits: a big bag of chips, a large jar of hot sauce, two frozen pizzas, a twelve-pack of cola, three Mars bars, and a package of Twinkies.

Conventions for using abbreviations in college writing

Most abbreviations are inappropriate in formal writing except when the reader would be more familiar with the abbreviation than with the words it represents. When your reader is unlikely to be familiar with an abbreviation, spell out the term, followed by the abbreviation in parentheses, the first time you use it in a paper. The reader will then understand what the abbreviation refers to, and you may use the abbreviation in subsequent sentences.

The Office of Civil Rights (OCR) is the agency that enforces Title IX regulations. In 1979, OCR set out three options for schools to comply with Title IX.

Exercise 50.1 The following is a paragraph from a research paper in which every word is spelled out. Decide which words would be more appropriate as abbreviations and write them correctly. Remember, this is formal academic writing; be sure to follow the conventions for using abbreviations in papers. When you have more than one abbreviation style to choose from, select the one recommended in this section. Note: The term "dense rock equivalent" is abbreviated DRE.

Example	Peter Francis, ~~Doctor of Philosophy~~ PhD, is among the scholars who have written introductory texts on volcanoes.

The unpredictable, destructive nature of volcanoes has attracted the interest of both scholarly and lay circles. Though it erupted in anno Domini 79, Mount Vesuvius is still famous because of its violent decimation of the city of Pompeii. Second to Vesuvius in destructive power is Mount Pelée, which in 1902 killed nearly thirty thousand people (id est, all but four of the citizens of Saint Pierre). Scholars like Professor George Walker have attempted to quantify and predict the effects of volcanoes. Professor Walker developed a system whereby volcanic eruptions are judged by magnitude, intensity, dispersive power, violence, and destructive potential. Walker began using a measurement called dense rock equivalent to measure unwitnessed eruptions. The actual volume of a volcano is converted into dense rock equivalent, which accounts for spaces in the rocks. Walker et alia have continued to perform research which will aid in the study of volcanoes.

 50b Acronyms

Acronyms are abbreviations formed by capitalizing the first letter in each word. Unlike other abbreviations, acronyms are pronounced as words.

AIDS for Acquired Immunodeficiency Syndrome
NASA for National Air and Space Administration
NATO for North Atlantic Treaty Organization
WAC for writing across the curriculum

A subset of acronyms is initial-letter abbreviations that have become so common that we know the organization or thing by its initials.

ATM for automated teller machine
HIV for human immunodeficiency virus
LCD for liquid crystal display
rpm for revolutions per minute
URL for Uniform Resource Locator

Familiar acronyms and initial-letter abbreviations such as CBS, CIA, FBI, IQ, and UN are rarely spelled out. In a few cases, such as *radar* (*ra*dio *de*tecting *a*nd *r*anging) and *laser* (*l*ight *a*mplification by *s*timulated *e*mission of *r*adiation), the terms used to create the acronym have been forgotten by almost all who use them.

Unfamiliar acronyms and abbreviations should always be spelled out. Acronyms and abbreviations frequent in particular fields should be spelled out on first use. For example, MMPI (Minnesota Multiphasic Personality Inventory) is a familiar abbreviation in psychology but is unfamiliar to those outside that discipline. Even when acronyms are generally familiar, few readers will object to your giving the terms from which an acronym derives on the first use.

The **National Association for the Advancement of Colored People (NAACP)** is the nation's largest and strongest civil rights organization. The **NAACP** was founded in 1909 by a group of prominent black and white citizens who were outraged by the numerous lynchings of African Americans.

COMMON ERRORS   e Edit Help

Punctuation of abbreviations and acronyms

The trend now is away from using periods with many abbreviations. In formal writing you can still use periods, with certain exceptions.

Do not use periods with

1. **Acronyms and initial-letter abbreviations:** AFL-CIO, AMA, HMO, NAFTA, NFL, OPEC
2. **Two-letter mailing abbreviations:** AZ (Arizona), FL (Florida), ME (Maine), UT (Utah)
3. **Compass points:** NE (northeast), SW (southwest)
4. **Technical abbreviations:** kph (kilometers per hour), SS (sum of squares), SD (standard deviation)

Remember: Do not use periods with postal abbreviations for states, compass points, technical abbreviations, and established organizations.

 For step-by-step discussion, examples, and practice exercises, visit this page of the eText at **www.mycomplab.com.**

Exercise 50.2 The following paragraphs from a research paper use some abbreviations correctly and some incorrectly. Revise the paragraphs, adding abbreviations where needed and spelling out the words where needed. You may also need to add or subtract punctuation marks such as parentheses and periods. Remember to make decisions based on whether or not the general population is familiar with the abbreviation.

> **Example**   Burning Man is an eight-day-long festival organized by
>   LLC
>   Black Rock City, ~~Limited Liability Company~~.
>   ^

The festival, which culminates in the burning of a giant man-shaped effigy, takes place on a playa in the Black Rock Desert in Nevada, 90 miles (150 kilometers) N-NE of Reno. Black Rock City, a temporary city which has its own DPW Department of Public Works, is an experiment in community and self-expression.

As the event has grown, one of the challenges faced by the organizers has been balancing the freedom of participants with the requirements of various land management groups, such as the Bureau of Land Management (BLM), and law enforcement groups, such as the DEA and the Reno PD. BMO (Burning Man Organization) is aware of the concerns about the festival's impact on the environment, so it encourages participants to Leave No Trace (L.N.T) of their visit to BRC. For example, participants are told to be very careful not to contaminate the playa with litter (commonly known as MOOP, or "matter out of place"). However, scientists are also concerned about how Burning Man contributes to global warming. Using several scales, including global warming potential (GWP), they are measuring how much greenhouse gases (chlorofluorocarbons, HFC's, PFCs) Burning Man participants will create. The scientists' CoolingMan website suggests ways to offset the damage caused by the festival, such as planting trees or investing in alternative energy solutions.

50c Numbers

In formal writing, spell out any number that can be expressed in one or two words, as well as any number, regardless of length, at the beginning of a sentence. Also, hyphenate two-word numbers from twenty-one to ninety-nine.

My office is twenty-three blocks from my apartment—too far to walk but a perfect bike riding distance.

When a sentence begins with a number that requires more than two words, revise it if possible.

Correct but awkward

Nineteen thousand six hundred runners left the Hopkinton starting line at noon in the Boston Marathon.

Better

At the start of the Boston Marathon, 19,600 runners left Hopkinton at noon.

The exceptions.   In scientific reports and some business writing that requires the frequent use of numbers, using numerals more often is appropriate. Most styles do not write out in words a year, a date, an address, a page number, the time of day, decimals, sums of money, phone numbers, rates of speed, or the scene and act of a play. Use numerals instead.

In **2011** only **33**% of respondents said they were satisfied with the City Council's proposals to help the homeless.

The **17** trials were conducted at temperatures **12–14**°C with results ranging from **2.43** to **2.89** mg/dl.

When one number modifies another number, write one out and express the other in numeral form.

In the last year all **four 8th** Street restaurants have begun to donate their leftovers to the soup kitchen.

Only after Meryl had run in **12 fifty**-mile ultramarathons did she finally win first place in her age group.

Exercise 50.3 All of the numbers in the following paragraph are spelled out. Decide where it would be more appropriate to use the numerals instead and revise. Remember to add hyphens where necessary.

Example   Caused by the dysfunction of two tiny joints near the
ears, a form of temporomandibular joint dysfunction
(TMJ) was identified in ~~nineteen hundred thirty-four~~
                                                    1934
by Doctor Costen.

Five hundred sixty is the number of times you heard a popping sound resonating from the jaw of the woman sitting next to you on the plane. She may be one of over nine point five million people suffering from TMJ, a condition that often causes symptoms such as popping, swelling, and aching in the jaw. At least one study has shown that women on hormone treatments are seventy seven percent more likely to develop TMJ symptoms. The disorder goes by at least six names, most of which include the initials TM, for temporomandibular: Costen's Syndrome, TMJ, TMD, TMJDD, CMD, and TMPD. Doctors currently prescribe at least forty nine different treatments for the disorder, ranging from one-dollar-and-fifty-cent mouth guards to prevent tooth grinding to a myriad of treatments which could cost thousands of dollars.

Exercise P9.1 The following passage contains several errors. These include errors in the use of commas, quotation marks, semicolons, colons, hyphenation, dashes, apostrophes, punctuation with quotations, question marks, brackets, ellipses, spelling, capitalization, italics, abbreviations, and numbers. Use the Common Errors guide inside the back cover of the book and information from Part 9 to help identify the errors and rewrite the passage.

The Marvel Family is a team of superheroes in the Fawcett Comics and DC Comics universes. DC refers to detective comics, one of the company's bestselling titles. The team which was created in 1942 by writer Otto Binder and Fawcett artists C C Beck; Mac Raboy; Ed Herron and Marc Swayze is an extension of Fawcetts Captain Marvel franchise. It includes Captain Marvel [Billy Batson] his sister Mary their friend Captain Marvel Junior and a rotating cast of other characters

One of the more whimsical characters in the marvel family is Mister Tawky Tawny a talking tiger who walks upright. In the Golden Age of comics nineteen thirties to nineteen fifties, Mister Tawky Tawny wanted to live among humans in civilization rather than in the wild or in the zoo. Thus in comics from this period he wears a Tweed business suit and carries himself in a formal dignified manner. Nonetheless he retains his fierce nature as he says dont let my cultured tones deceive you, sir, Tawny Bites"!

The modern day Tawky Tawny was a stuffed tiger doll which was animated by lord Satanus to help the Marvel Family fight Satanuss sister Blaze. Tawky Tawny calls himself a pooka that is a mythological celtic creature. Much like the animated Hobbes in the comic strip Calvin and Hobbes appears only to Calvin, Tawky Tawny is animated around only a few people Billy Mary and Uncle Dudley a Janitor at Billys school who helps out the Marvel's from time-to-time.

Tawky Tawny continues to change in Trials of Shazam! number ten—2008—Tawny revealed that the 10th Age of Magic has given him the ability to change into a giant sabre toothed tiger. And in the miniseries "Shazam!: The Monster Society of Evil" and its follow up series, "Billy Batson and the Magic of Shazam," Tawky Tawny is a shape-shifter who prefers his tiger form. Unfortunately in a battle with Mister Mind a highly-intelligent two inch worm Tawny was struck in mid-transition and became fixed in his humanoid form. He continues to live with Billy Batson causing much confusion for Billy's land-lady. What is next for Tawky Tawny!

PART 10

If English Is Not Your First Language

You **can learn more and do more** with MyCompLab and with the eText version of *The Penguin Handbook*. To find resources in MyCompLab that will help you complete your assignment successfully if English is not your first language, go to

Resources

Grammar

> **Basic Grammar**
>
> Articles | Nouns | Prepositions | Verb Form | Verb Tenses | Verbs

Review the tutorials (Read, Watch, Listen) within each topic, then complete the Exercises and click on the Gradebook to measure your progress.

In the **eText version** of *The Penguin Handbook*, you will also find extra explanation, examples and practice exercises.

51 | Write in a Second Language

QUICKTAKE

- How do you use English idioms? (see p. 690)
  Incorrect: Did he kick the calendar? [literal translation of Polish
  kopnąć w kalendarz with the same idiomatic meaning as "kick the
  bucket" in English]
  Correct: Did he kick the bucket?

51a Understand the Demands of Writing in a Second Language

If English is not your first language, you may have noticed some differences between writing in English and writing in your native language. Some of the differences are relatively easy to identify, such as the direction of writing (left to right instead of right to left or top to bottom), the uses of punctuation (€2,500.00 instead of €2.500,00), and conventions of capitalization and spelling. Other differences are more subtle and complex, such as the citation of sources, the uses of persuasive appeals, and the level of directness expected in a given situation.

Talk with other writers

When you write in an unfamiliar situation, it may be helpful to find a few examples of the type of writing you are trying to produce. If you are writing a letter of application to accompany a résumé, for example, ask your friends to share similar letters of application with you and look for the various ways they present themselves in writing in that situation. Ask them to read their letters out loud and to explain the decisions they made as they wrote and revised their letters.

Recognize the American style of writing

No simple generalizations can be made for every kind of writing in the United States, but writers who have been educated in other cultures often become aware of differences in style, especially in the workplace and in college. The fast pace of American life and the increasing use of fast digital technologies encourage a style of writing that values brevity.

The American style of writing is typically

- **more concise** than in cultures where the rich profusion of words is valued;
- **more direct** in announcing the topic at the beginning rather than leading up to the topic;
- **more topic focused**, keeping on the main idea rather than introducing digressions;
- **more explicit** in setting out reasons and evidence;
- **less conscious of politeness** in the desire to get to the main point;
- **more careful to distinguish the words of others** with the use of quotation marks;
- **more insistent that all writing is original** with serious consequences for plagiarism;
- **more conscious of giving the sources** of facts, figures, and the ideas of others.

Know what is expected in college writing

Understanding what is expected in college writing is as important as understanding English language conventions. College writers are expected to meet the expectations listed below. You will find detailed information on these expectations in other parts of this book.

WRITING SMART

A guide to expectations for writing in college

Address the specific demands of the assignment.	See Sections 2a and 2b for general assignment analysis. See Section 19a for analyzing research assignments.
Use the appropriate format and sources for particular disciplines.	See Chapters 11 to 15.
Pay close attention to document design.	See Chapters 16 to 18 for print, online, and presentation design.
Follow specific formatting rules.	See Sections 26l for MLA style. See Section 27g for APA style.

(Continued on next page)

WRITING SMART *(Continued)*

Understand and avoid plagiarism. The expectations are different in the United States from many other countries.	See Chapter 23, especially the Staying on Track box on Plagiarism in College Writing on p. 317.
Incorporate the words and ideas of others into your writing.	See Chapter 24.
Choose words carefully, and connect ideas clearly.	See Part 7.
Use accepted grammatical forms.	See Part 8. See Chapters 52, 53, and 54 for specific explanations of English grammar and mechanics for multilingual speakers.
Spell and punctuate correctly.	See Part 9.
Use your instructor's and peers' comments to revise and improve your writing.	See Chapter 4.

51b Use Your Native Language as a Resource

As you continue to develop your ability to write in English, you will find that many of the strategies you developed in your native language are useful in English as well. The ability to think critically, for example, is important in any language, although what it means to be "critical" may differ from one context to another. Imagery, metaphors, and expressions adapted from your native language may make your writing culturally richer and more interesting to read.

You can also use your native language to develop your texts. Many people, when they cannot find an appropriate word in English, write down a word, a phrase, or even a sentence in their native language and consult a dictionary or a handbook later; it helps to avoid interrupting the flow of thought in the process of writing. Incorporating key terms from your native language is also a possible strategy. For example, a term from Japanese can add flavor and perspective to a sentence: "Some political leaders need to have *wakimae*—a realistic idea of one's own place in the world."

51c Use Dictionaries

You can use regular English dictionaries for definitions, but most English dictionaries designed for native English speakers do not include all of the information that many multilingual English speakers find useful. For example, you may know the word *audience* but not whether and when *audience* can function as a count noun. Learner's dictionaries, such as the *Longman Dictionary of American English*, include information about count/noncount nouns and transitive/intransitive verbs (see Chapters 52 and 53). Many of them also provide sample sentences to help you understand how a word is used.

Some multilingual English speakers also find a bilingual dictionary useful. Bilingual dictionaries are especially useful when you want to check your understanding of an English word or when you want to find equivalent words for culture-specific concepts and technical terms. Some bilingual dictionaries also provide sample sentences. When sample sentences are not provided, check the usage in another dictionary or by searching for the word or phrase on the Web.

51d Understand English Idioms

Idioms are nonliteral expressions that gain a set meaning when they are used again and again. In the United States, for example, if someone has to "eat crow," he or she has been forced to admit being wrong about something. When people "walk a fine line," they are being careful not to irritate or anger people on different sides of an argument. Simpler examples of idiomatic usage—word order, word choice, and combinations that follow no obvious or set rules—are common even in the plainest English.

The way certain prepositions are paired with certain words is often idiomatic. It might be possible to use a preposition other than the one usually used, but the preferred combination is accepted as correct because it sounds "right" to longtime English speakers. Any other preposition sounds "wrong," even if it makes sense.

| "Incorrect" idiom | Here is the answer *of* your question. |
| Accepted idiom | Here is the answer *to* your question. |

Note that the second sentence is no more logical than the first. But to first-language English speakers, that first sentence sounds imprecise and strange. See Section 52e for more information on English preposition usage.

Placement order for modifiers is often idiomatic in English—or at least the rules are arbitrary enough that it may make more sense to memorize certain patterns than to try to place modifiers entirely by logic. Say you want to modify the noun *dogs* with three adjectives:

brown
three
small

In English, all these adjectives will be placed before the noun they are modifying. But in what order should they go? There are a number of possibilities:

Small three brown dogs
Three brown small dogs
Small brown three dogs
Three small brown dogs
Brown small three dogs
Brown three small dogs

Only two of these options may sound at all correct to first-language English speakers: "Three brown small dogs" and "Three small brown dogs." To put the adjective for number anywhere but first sounds wrong. The other two adjectives, describing size and color, also have a correct order to the ears of English speakers. Thus "three small brown dogs" sounds more natural than "three brown small dogs."

Though idioms may be frustrating, you can take comfort in the fact that many first-language English speakers struggle with them, especially when using prepositions. Because idioms are not governed by a single set of rules, you can only learn idioms one example at a time. Thus, the more you speak, read, and hear English, the better your grasp of idioms will become.

WRITING SMART

Use the Web to check English idioms

Many combinations of English words don't follow hard and fast rules but simply sound right to native speakers of English. If you are unsure whether you should write *disgusted with* or *disgusted for*, use Google or another search engine to find out how they are used.

Put the words inside quotation marks in the search box. You'll get many hits for both *disgusted with* and *disgusted for*, but you'll see about ten times more for *disgusted with*. You'll also notice that many of the hits for *disgusted for* will be examples of *disgusted*. For with *disgusted* at the end of one sentence and *For* at the beginning of the next sentence. You can use this method to determine that *disgusted with* is the better choice.

Exercise 51.1　Choose the idiom commonly used in English. If you are unsure, check a dictionary, Google, or another search engine to test the idiom.

1. The actor (suicided/committed suicide) after his wife's death.
2. He will be here (of/on) Sunday.
3. I have a question (for/of) you about your job.
4. Those (red, long/long, red) peppers are too hot (for/to) eat.
5. We were (drive/driving) as fast as we could.
6. (Knowing/To know) her is (to love/loving) her.
7. (A, The) last thing we want (do/to do) is (to make/making) trouble (on/for) you.
8. All he wants (do/to do) is (watching/to watch) television.
9. The cage held (five yellow fuzzy/five fuzzy yellow) chicks.
10. Her apartment is (on/at) the third floor.
11. The baby (borned/was born) healthy.
12. I am responsible (to/for) choosing a location (of/for) the party.

51e Understand and Avoid Plagiarism in English

The concepts of intellectual property and plagiarism differ across cultures. Some cultures, including the United States, Canada, the United Kingdom, and other English-speaking nations, place high value on individual expression. In the English-speaking world, people believe that words and ideas can be owned. Other cultures think that words and ideas belong to the culture, and students often copy word-for-word what authorities have written in the mistaken belief that there can be no improvement on those words.

Colleges and universities in the United States expect you to voice your own ideas and opinions, not string together sentences taken from printed books and articles and the Internet. Copying the words of others and submitting them as your own is considered plagiarism, which can have severe consequences for violaters. Students fail courses for comitting plagiarism and even are expelled from universities.

Does plagiarism mean you cannot use any words or ideas except your own? Not at all. Careful documentation of sources allows you to have it both ways. You can include the ideas and words of others if you acknowledge the sources of the ideas and words and carefully distinguish your words from the words of others. Indeed, in college you are expected to

- write about a topic that others have written about **but** make your own contribution to the discussion,
- discuss previous research and the opinions of experts **but** make clear your stance toward that research and where you agree and disagree with others,
- quote the words and include the ideas of others **but** document those sources accurately and use your words to advance the discussion.

You can avoid plagiarism by following a few basic rules.

If you want to	Then
Use a source in your project	You must cite your source in two places: where you use the source in your text and again at the end in a list. See Chapter 26 for MLA documentation and Chapter 27 for APA documentation
Use a sentence from a source	You must put the words inside quotation marks, include the page number, and introduce the quotation with a signal phrase. See Sections 23d and 24d.
Use a few words from a source	You must put the words inside quotation marks, include the page number, and introduce the quotation with a signal phrase. See Sections 23d and 24d.
Include a paraphrase or summary of an idea in a source using your own words	You must indicate the source with either a signal phrase or an in-text citation. See Section 24e.
Use the sentence structure of a source but switch out some of the words	You have committed plagiarism. You must use your own words in an original structure while accurately conveying the ideas of a source to have a true paraphrase. See Section 23e.
Include a visual (photograph, chart, graph, and so on) from a source	You should refer to the visual in your text, include a caption, and give complete citation information. See Section 24f.

(continued)

If you want to	Then
Include a fact that isn't common knowledge (e.g., biologists estimate the worldwide population of polar bears is between 20,000 and 25,000)	You must indicate the source with an in-text citation.
Include a fact that is common knowledge (e.g., the scientific name of the polar bear is *Ursus maritimus*)	You do not need to cite the source. When in doubt, cite the source.

52 | Nouns, Articles, and Prepositions

QUICKTAKE

- **How do you treat different kinds of nouns?** (see below)
  Incorrect: When we landed in the Memphis Airport, we asked for informations about transportation to Graceland, Elvis Presley's former Home.
  Correct: When we landed in the Memphis Airport, we asked for information about transportation to Graceland, Elvis Presley's former home.
- **How do you use articles correctly?** (see p. 699)
  Incorrect: A mother of a soldier held the picture of him up to a camera.
  Correct: The mother of the soldier held a picture of him up to the camera.
- **How do you use prepositions?** (see p. 702)
  Incorrect: Please leave the keys of the car to the hook.
  Correct: Please leave the keys for the car on the hook.

Kinds of Nouns

There are two basic kinds of nouns. A **proper noun** begins with a capital letter and names a unique person, place, or thing: *Theodore Roosevelt, Russia, Eiffel Tower.* In the following list, note that each word refers to someone or something so specific that it bears a name.

Proper nouns

Beethoven	Yao Ming	South Korea
Empire State Building	New York Yankees	Africa
Honda	Picasso	Stockholm
Thanksgiving	Queen Elizabeth	Lake Michigan

The other basic kind of noun is called a **common noun.** Common nouns do not name a unique person, place, or thing: *man, country, tower.* Note that the words in the following list are not names and so are not capitalized.

Common nouns

composer	athlete	country
building	baseball team	continent
company	painter	city
holiday	queen	lake

Common nouns can also refer to abstractions, such as *grace, love,* and *power.* In English, proper nouns are names and are always capitalized while common nouns are not names and are not capitalized.

Exercise 52.1 Underline the common nouns in the following paragraph once and underline the proper nouns twice. Correct any errors in capitalization.

Example In 1903, a fire in ₍C₎chicago led to the new safety ₍l₎Laws.

In 1903, Chicago opened the new iroquois theater on West Randolph street. Around christmas, the Theater held a performance of "Mr. blue beard" starring eddie Foy. Shortly after the play started, a light sparked causing a curtain to catch on fire. Elvira Pinedo said the crowd panicked after a giant Fireball appeared. This panic led to the deaths of more than six hundred people, many of whom died because bodies were pressed against doors that opened inward. Shortly after the Tragedy, mayor Carter h. Harrison was indicted and new laws demanded Theaters have doors that open outward, toward the lobby.

52b Count and Noncount Nouns

Common nouns can be classified as either *count* or *noncount.* **Count nouns** can be made plural, usually by adding -*s* (*finger, fingers*) or by using their plural forms (*person, people; datum, data*). **Noncount nouns** cannot be counted directly and cannot take the plural form (*information,* but not *informations; garbage,* but not *garbages*). Some nouns can be either count or noncount, depending on how they are used. *Hair* can refer to either a strand of hair, when it serves as a count noun, or a mass of hair, when it becomes a noncount noun.

Correct usage of *hair* as count noun

I carefully combed my few hairs across my mostly bald scalp.

Correct usage of *hair* as noncount noun

My roommate spent an hour this morning combing his hair.

In the same way, *space* can refer to a particular, quantifiable area (as in *two parking spaces*) or to unspecified open area (as in *there is some space left*).

If you are not sure whether a particular noun is count or noncount, consult a learner's dictionary. Count nouns are usually indicated as [C] (for "countable") and noncount nouns as [U] (for "uncountable").

Exercise 52.2 The following sentences include various types of plural nouns: count, noncount, and those that can be either, depending on how they are used. Underline the correct plural form from the choices provided.

> **Example** The first (animal/<u>animals</u>) in space were fruit flies.

1. In 1946, these tiny (astronaut/astronauts) were launched on an American rocket with some (corns/corn) to test the (effect of radiation/effect of radiations) at high (altitude/altitudes).
2. Fruit (fly/flies) match three-(quarter/quarters) of human disease (gene/genes), sleep every (night/nights), and reproduce very quickly, so replacing them does not cost a lot of (monies/money).
3. After fruit flies, scientists sent (moss/mosses), and then (monkeys/monkey).
4. The first (monkeys/monkey) to return from space safely was Albert IV, who was accompanied by eleven (mouses/mice) on his journey.
5. The Russian space program launched more than ten (dog/dogs) into space before launching (people/peoples).
6. Although (scientist/scientists) argue that the (information/informations) gathered from space missions using (animal/animals) has saved (life/lives), (activist/activists) argue that these (experiment/experiments) were cruel and unnecessary.

52c Singular and Plural Forms

Count nouns usually take both singular and plural forms, while non-count nouns usually do not take plural forms and are not counted directly. A count noun can have a number before it (as in *two books, three oranges*) and can be qualified with adjectives such as *many* (*many books*), *some* (*some schools*), *a lot of* (*a lot of people*), *a few* (meaning several, as in *I ate a few apples*), and *few* (meaning almost none, as in *few people volunteered*).

Noncount nouns can be counted or quantified in only two ways: either by general adjectives that treat the noun as a mass (*much* information, *little* garbage, *some* news) or by placing another noun between the quantifying word and the noncount noun (two *kinds* of information, three *piles* of garbage, a *piece* of news).

COMMON ERRORS

e Edit Help

Singular and plural forms of count nouns

Count nouns are simpler to quantify than noncount nouns. But remember that English requires you to state both singular and plural forms of nouns consistently and explicitly. Look at the following sentences.

Inorrect   The three bicyclist shaved their leg before the big race.

Correct   The three bicyclists shaved their legs before the big race.

In the first sentence, readers would understand that the plural form of *bicyclist* is implied by the quantifier *three* and that the plural form of *leg* is implied by the fact that bicyclists have two legs. (If they didn't, you would hope that the writer would have made that clear already!) Nevertheless, correct form in English is to indicate the singular or plural nature of a count noun explicitly, in every instance.

Remember: English requires you to use plural forms of count nouns even when a plural number is clearly stated.

 For more help using count and noncount nouns, try the exercises found on this page of the eText at **www.mycomplab.com**.

Exercise 52.3   The following paragraph includes many examples of singular/plural inconsistency. Correct any incorrect versions of nouns.

Example   In the history of fashion, many ~~word~~ *words* have lost their original ~~meaning~~ *meanings*.

Every year, thousands of bride and groom don traditional attire while attending their wedding. One garment associated with many of these traditional wedding is the groom's cummerbund or decorative waistband. This garment dates back many century to Persia where they were known as a "kamarband" or "loinband." The cummerbunds was first adopted by a few British military officer in colonial India and later by civilians. These cummerbund were traditionally worn with the pleats facing up to hold ticket stubs and other item. These day, however, cummerbunds are usually worn just for decoration.

52d Articles

Articles indicate that a noun is about to appear, and they clarify what the noun refers to. There are only two kinds of articles in English, definite and indefinite.

1. **the:** *The* is a **definite article**, meaning that it refers to (1) a specific object already known to the reader, (2) one about to be made known to the reader, or (3) a unique object.
2. **a, an:** The **indefinite articles** *a* and *an* refer to an object whose specific identity is not known to the reader. The only difference between *a* and *an* is that *a* is used before a consonant sound (*man, friend, yellow*), while *an* is used before a vowel sound (*animal, enemy, orange*).

Look at these sentences, identical except for their articles, and imagine that each is taken from a different newspaper story:

Rescue workers lifted the man to safety.

Rescue workers lifted a man to safety.

By use of the definite article *the*, the first sentence indicates that the reader already knows something about the identity of this man and his needing to be rescued. The news story has already referred to him. The sentence also suggests that this was the only man rescued, at least in this particular part of the story.

The indefinite article *a* in the second sentence indicates that the reader does not know anything about this man. Either this is the first time the news story has referred to him or there are other men in need of rescue. When deciding whether to use the definite or indefinite article, ask yourself whether the noun refers to something specific or unique, or whether it refers to something general. *The* is used for specific or unique nouns; *a* and *an* are used for nonspecific or general nouns.

A small number of conditions determine when and how count and noncount nouns are preceded by articles.

1. *A* or *an* is not used with noncount nouns.

Incorrect   The crowd hummed with an excitement.

Correct   The crowd hummed with excitement.

2. *A* or *an* is used with singular count nouns whose particular identity is unknown to the reader or writer.

Detective Johnson was reading a book.

3. ***The*** **is used with most count and noncount nouns whose particular identity is known to the reader.**
   The noun may be known for one of several reasons:

   ● The basic rule is that *a* or *an* is used on the first mention of a noun and *the* is used for every subsequent mention.

     I bought a book yesterday. The book is about Iraq.

   ● The noun is accompanied by a superlative such as *highest, lowest, best, worst, least interesting,* or *most beautiful* that makes its specific identity clear.

     This is the most interesting book about Iraq.

   ● The noun's identity is made clear by its context in the sentence.

     The book I bought yesterday is about Iraq.

   ● The noun has a unique identity, such as *the moon.*

     This book has as many pages as the Bible.

4. ***The*** **is not used with noncount nouns meaning "in general."**

   Incorrect   The war is hell.

   Correct   War is hell.

COMMON ERRORS

e Edit Help

Articles with count and noncount nouns
Knowing how to distinguish between count and noncount nouns can help you decide which article to use. Noncount nouns are never used with the indefinite articles *a* and *an*.

Incorrect   Maria jumped into a water.

Correct   Maria jumped into the water.

No articles are used with noncount and plural count nouns when you wish to state something that has a general application.

Incorrect   The water is a precious natural resource.

Correct   Water is a precious natural resource.

Incorrect   The soccer players tend to be quick and agile.

Correct   Soccer players tend to be quick and agile.

(Continued on next page)

COMMON ERRORS *(Continued)*

Remember:

1. Noncount nouns are never used with *a* and *an*.
2. Noncount and plural nouns used to make general statements do not take articles.

For more help using articles, see the exercises on this page of the eText at **www.mycomplab.com**.

Exercise 52.4 Underline the correct definite or indefinite articles for the nouns in the following paragraph.

Example   (A/An/The) First Earth Battalion was (a/an/the) secret
military unit established in 1979 by Lieutenant Colonel
Jim Channon, (a/an/the) U.S. soldier who had served in
(a/an/the) Vietnam War.

Channon wanted to establish (a/an/the) new military based on
New Age teachings. Members of the First Earth Battalion believed
that their first loyalty was to (a/an/the) planet, so they sought
nondestructive methods of conflict resolution. Channon referred
to members of (a/an/the) First Earth Battalion as "warrior monks"
because they would ideally have (a/an/the) dedication of (a/an/the)
monk and (a/an/the) skill of (a/an/the) warrior. (A/An/The) warrior
monk would learn different martial arts for self-defense, using
(a/an/the) attacker's strength against himself or herself. To
promote universal healing, (a/an/the) warrior monk would also use
(a/an/the) number of methods like yoga, qigong, and reiki. After
training, (a/an/the) warrior monk would also be able to become
invisible, bend metal with (a/an/the) mind, walk through walls,
calculate without (a/an/the) computer, and kill (a/an/the) goat just
by staring at it. In short, Channon imagined (a/an/the) army made
up of enlightened warriors who would promote peace and make
(a/an/the) Earth whole.

Exercise 52.5 The following paragraph includes properly and improperly used articles. Underline the articles, identify the types of nouns they modify (plural or singular, count or noncount), and correct any improperly chosen articles.

Example	Troy James Hurtubise <u>is</u> an inventor and
	Singular count
	conservationist from North Bay, Ontario, who is best
	Singular count
	known for attempting to develop the suit made for
	Noncount
	what he calls a "close-quarter bear research."

Rewritten	Troy James Hurtubise is an inventor and
	conservationist from North Bay, Ontario, who is
	best known for attempting to develop a suit made
	for what he calls "close-quarter bear research."

Hurtubise's obsession with the bears began in 1984 when he survived encounter with an adult grizzly bear. Inspired by a movie *Robocop*, Hurtubise decided to build a suit that would withstand the bear attacks. Strangely, he worked to make his suit fireproof as well. Seven years later, he introduced the suit, an *Ursus Mark IV*. Under consultation with a physicists, he tested the suit against the attacks by baseball bat wielding bikers, impact with a swinging 300-pound log, and a flamethrowers. These tests and their results can be seen in documentary *Project Grizzly*.

52e Prepositions

Prepositions are positional or directional words like *to, for, from, at, in, on,* and *with.* They are used before nouns and pronouns, and they also combine with adjectives and adverbs. Each preposition has a wide range of possible meanings depending on how it is used, and each must be learned over time in its many contexts.

Some of the most common prepositional phrases describe time and place, and many are idiomatic.

Incorrect	On midnight
Correct	At midnight
Incorrect	In the counter
Correct	On the counter

Incorrect	In Saturday
Correct	On Saturday
Incorrect	On February
Correct	In February

Over time, you may notice patterns that help you determine the appropriate preposition. For example, *at* precedes a particular time, *on* precedes a day of the week, and *in* precedes a month, year, or other period of time.

COMMON ERRORS   e Edit Help

Misused prepositions

The correct use of prepositions often seems unpredictable to multilingual speakers of English. When you are not sure which preposition to use, consult a dictionary.

Of for *about*	The report on flight delays raised criticism ~~of~~ about the scheduling of flights.
On for *into*	The tennis player went ~~on~~ into a slump after failing to qualify for the French Open.
To for *in*	Angry over her low seeding in the tournament, Amy resigned her membership ~~to~~ in the chess club.
To for *of*	The family was ignorant ~~to~~ of the controversial history of the house they purchased.

Remember: When you are uncertain about a preposition, consult a learner's dictionary intended for nonnative speakers of English. See Chapter 51 on the use of learner's dictionaries.

For a list of common verbs with prepositions that follow them, plus additional exercises, visit this page of the eText at **www.mycomplab.com**.

Exercise 52.6 Underline the proper preposition in parentheses in the following paragraph.

Example (<u>In</u>/On/At) the 1940s, several dozen pilots died trying to break Mach one, the speed of sound.

(In, On, At) that time, pilots were familiar (with/in/on) the "wall of air" that existed (in/on/at) the speed of sound. Many airplanes shattered (into/onto/from) a million pieces because of this "wall of air." Pilots were especially afraid (for/on/of) a condition called "compressibility," which would make them lose control (in/of/on) the plane. Air Force pilot Chuck Yeager tried to break the sound barrier (from/with/on) *Glamorous Glennis*, a plane named (from/for/to) his wife. (In/On/At) October 14, 1947, Yeager made an attempt to reach Mach one. The ground crew heard a boom (from/at/in) the distance and feared that *Glamorous Glennis* had crashed. They cheered (with/from/in) joy when they heard Yeager say (with/in/on) the radio a few moments later that he had broken the sound barrier.

Exercise 52.7 The following paragraph contains adjective-preposition phrases. Choose the correct preposition.

Example The Statue of Liberty was (full for/<u>full of</u>) significance for the millions of immigrants.

The United States remains (grateful to/grateful with) the people of France for the gift of the Statue of Liberty. France supported the colonists during the American Revolution and continues to be (proud for/proud of) its role in creating the United States. Although many Americans today are not (aware of/aware with) the importance of French support in the founding of their country, they are nonetheless (interested in/interested with) French culture and (fond of/fond with) its cuisine.

53 | Verbs

QUICKTAKE

- **How do you use different kinds of verbs correctly?** (see below)
  Incorrect: She intending to learn several skills that would help her becoming a superhero.
  Correct: She intends to learn several skills that will help her to become a superhero.

- **What are conditional sentences?** (see p. 711)
  Incorrect: If she **had talked** with me in private, I would not become so angry.
  Correct: If she **had talked** with me in private, I would not have become so angry.

- **What are phrasal verbs?** (see p. 713)
  Incorrect: She made out the story.
  Correct: She made up the story.

 Types of Verbs

The verb system in English can be divided between simple verbs like *run, speak,* and *look* and verb phrases like *may have run, have spoken,* and *will be looking.* In the verb phrases, the words that appear before the main verbs—*may, have, will,* and *be*—are called **auxiliary verbs** (also called **helping verbs**). Helping verbs, as their name suggests, exist to help express something about the action of main verbs: for example, when the action occurs (tense), whether the subject acted or was acted upon (voice), or whether or not an action occurred.

53b *Be* Verbs

Indicating tense and voice with *be* verbs

Like the other auxiliary verbs *have* and *do, be* changes form to signal tense. In addition to *be* itself, the **be verbs** are *is, am, are, was, were,* and *been.*

To show ongoing action, *be* verbs are followed by the present participle, which is a verb with an *-ing* ending:

Incorrect	I am think of all the things I'd rather be do.
Correct	I am thinking of all the things I'd rather be doing.

Incorrect	He was run as fast as he could.
Correct	He was running as fast as he could.

To show that an action is being done to, rather than by, the subject, follow *be* verbs with the past participle (a verb usually ending in *-ed, -en,* or *-t*):

Incorrect	The movie was direct by John Woo.
Correct	The movie was directed by John Woo.

Incorrect	The complaint will be file by the victim.
Correct	The complaint will be filed by the victim.

Verbs that express cognitive activity

English, unlike Chinese, Arabic, and several other languages, requires a form of *be* before the present or past participle. As you have probably discovered, however, English has many exceptions to its rules. Verbs that express some form of cognitive activity rather than a direct action are not used as present participles with *be* verbs. Examples of such words include *know, like, see,* and *believe.*

Incorrect	You were knowing that I would be late.
Correct	You knew that I would be late.

But here's an exception to an exception: A small number of these verbs, such as *considering, thinking,* and *pondering,* can be used as present participles with *be* verbs.

I am considering whether to finish my homework first.

Exercise 53.1 The following paragraph is filled with *be* verbs. In each case, underline the correct verb form from the choices provided in parentheses.

Example   Rosh Hashanah, one of the religious High Holy Days, (is celebrated/is celebrating) beginning on the second day of the seventh month of the Jewish calendar, Tishri.

Though many think it marks only the Jewish New Year, those who celebrate Rosh Hashanah (understand/are understanding) that it has many other meanings as well. Rosh Hashanah (is also called/are also called) the day of the blowing of the Shofar, the day of remembrance, and the day of judgment. It long (has been consider/has been considered) the only High Holy Day that warrants a two-day celebration; those who (observe/are observing) the holiday consider the two-day period one extended forty-eight-hour day. Families (feast/are feasting) on foods that (are sweetened/are sweetening) with honey, apples, and carrots, symbolizing the sweet year to come. Challah, the bread that (is eating/is eaten) on the Sabbath, is reshaped into a ring, symbolizing the hope that the upcoming year will roll smoothly.

53c Modal Auxiliary Verbs

Modal auxiliary verbs—*will, would, can, could, may, might, shall, must,* and *should*—are helping verbs that express conditions like possibility, permission, speculation, expectation, obligation, and necessity. Unlike the helping verbs *be, have,* and *do,* modal verbs do not change form based on the grammatical subject of the sentence (*I, you, she, he, it, we, they*).

Two basic rules apply to all uses of modal verbs. First, modal verbs are always followed by the simple form of the verb. The simple form is the verb by itself, in the present tense, such as *have,* but not *had, having,* or *to have.*

| Incorrect | She should studies harder to pass the exam. |
| Correct | She should study harder to pass the exam. |

The second rule is that you should not use modals consecutively.

| Incorrect | If you work harder at writing, you might could improve. |
| Correct | If you work harder at writing, you might improve. |

Ten conditions that modals express

- **Speculation:** If you had flown, you would have arrived yesterday.
- **Ability:** She can run faster than Jennifer.
- **Necessity:** You must know what you want to do.
- **Intention:** He will wash his own clothes.
- **Permission:** You may leave now.
- **Advice:** You should wash behind your ears.
- **Possibility:** It might be possible to go home early.
- **Assumption:** You must have stayed up late last night.
- **Expectation:** You should enjoy the movie.
- **Order:** You must leave the building.

Exercise 53.2 The following sentences contain modal auxiliary verbs. Some are used properly and some improperly. Identify the conditions they express (speculation, ability, necessity, and so on) and correct any incorrect modal usage.

Example Donnie is a Doberman Pinscher dog who can arranges his plush toys in geometric forms.

Revise Donnie is a Doberman Pinscher dog who **can arrange** his plush toys in geometric forms. (ability)

1. His owner rescued him from an animal shelter knowing that it might could take him a long time to bond with her, but it was a job she must be doing.
2. The producers of National Geographic Channel's *Dog Genius* show must have been impressed, or they would not have been featuring Donnie arranging his toys into circles, triangles, and parallel lines.
3. You should watch a video of the show so you can see Donnie arrange his toys to look like they are hugging and holding hands, as if he would be liking to communicate something.
4. Donnie also creates arrangements in which he matches toys that are like each other, as if he thinks monkeys might should always be with monkeys and frogs might should always be with frogs.
5. Scientists who study dogs like Donnie must to make sure that the dogs are not being coached, so they will often use remote video cameras and film the dogs when no humans are around.

53d Verbs and Infinitives

Several verbs are followed by particular verb forms. An **infinitive** is *to* plus the simple form of the verb. Here are common verbs that are followed by an infinitive.

afford	expect	promise
agree	fail	refuse
ask	hope	seem
attempt	intend	struggle
claim	learn	tend
consent	need	wait
decide	plan	want
demand	prepare	wish

Incorrect You learn playing the guitar by practicing.

Correct You learn to play the guitar by practicing.

Some verbs require that a noun or pronoun come after the verb and before the infinitive.

advise	instruct	require
cause	order	tell
command	persuade	warn

Incorrect I would advise to watch where you step.

Correct I would advise you to watch where you step.

A few verbs, when followed by a noun or pronoun, take an *unmarked infinitive*, which is an infinitive without *to*.

have	let	make

Incorrect I will let her to plan the vacation.

Correct I will let her plan the vacation.

Exercise 53.3 Complete the following sentences by choosing the proper verb, pronoun, and infinitive combinations from those provided in parentheses. Underline the correct answer.

Example Because reality television producers (to struggle/ struggle to) attract and keep a wide audience, they have developed many different formulas for their shows.

1. Shows in which a camera (follows/to follow) a person or a group of people around during their everyday life (refer to you/are referred to) as "documentary style."

2. The best known type of documentary style show (forces strangers living/forces strangers to live) together, (causing them to face/causing to face) a variety of conflicts.

3. Other documentary shows follow a professional or group of professionals as they (try completing/try to complete) a project, such as (opening/to open) a restaurant.

4. The extreme competition on some reality shows (causes to cheat participants/causes participants to cheat) against each other so that they will not be (chosen to leave/chosen leaving) the show.

5. A more positive type of show is the improvement or make-over show in which experts (advise to improve someone/advise someone to improve) his or her clothes, home, or overall life.

53e Verbs and *–ing* Verbals

Other verbs are followed by **gerunds**, which are verbs ending in *-ing* that are used as nouns. Here are common verbs that are followed by a gerund.

admit	discuss	quit
advise	enjoy	recommend
appreciate	finish	regret
avoid	imagine	risk
consider	practice	suggest

Incorrect   She will **finish to grade** papers by noon.

Correct   She will **finish grading** papers by noon.

A smaller number of verbs can be followed by either gerunds or infinitives (see Section 53d).

begin	hate	love
continue	like	start

With Gerund   She **likes working** in the music store.

With Infinitive   She **likes to work** in the music store.

 For more help using gerunds and infinitives, see the exercises on this page of the eText at **www.mycomplab.com.**

Exercise 53.4   The following sentences include verbs that should be followed by either gerunds or infinitives. Underline the correct gerund or infinitive from the options provided in parentheses. If both options are correct, underline both.

Example   Children enjoyed (to watch/<u>watching</u>) Pecos Bill in Disney's 1948 animated feature *Melody Time.*

1. Historians risk (misidentifying/to misidentify) actual origins when stories have been passed down simply by word of mouth.
2. Though some like (to believe/believing) that Edward O'Reilly found the story of Pecos Bill circulating among American cowboys, it is hard to prove.
3. The story of little Bill, who was raised by coyotes, fails (to go/going) away despite its ambiguous origins.
4. Despite the confusion, stories about Bill's bride Slue-Foot Sue and his horse Widow Maker continue (to spread/spreading) as part of Americana.
5. Because of the debate over authenticity, however, some consider (to call/calling) the story popular culture rather than folklore.

53f Conditional Sentences

Conditional sentences express *if-then* relationships: They consist of a **subordinate clause** beginning with *if*, *unless*, or *when* that expresses a condition, and a **main clause** that expresses a result. The tense and mood of the verb in the main clause and the type of conditional sentence determine the tense and mood of the verb in the subordinate clause.

```
┌─SUBORDINATE CLAUSE─┐ ┌──────MAIN CLAUSE──────┐
When the wind stops, the sea becomes calm.
```

Conditional sentences fall into three categories: **factual**, **predictive**, and **hypothetical**.

Factual conditionals

Factual conditional sentences express factual relationships: If this happens, that will follow. The tense of the verb in the conditional clause is the same as the tense of the verb in the result clause.

| Incorrect | When it rains, the ground would become wet. |
| Correct | When it rains, the ground becomes wet. |

Predictive conditionals

Predictive conditional sentences express predicted consequences from possible conditions. The verb in the conditional clause is present tense, and the verb in the result clause is formed with a modal (*will, would, can, could, may, might, shall, must,* and *should*) plus the base form of the verb.

| Incorrect | If you **take** the long way home, you enjoy the ride more. |
| Correct | If you **take** the long way home, you will enjoy the ride more. |

Hypothetical conditionals

Hypothetical conditional sentences express events that are either not factual or unlikely to happen. For hypothetical events in the past, the conditional clause verb takes the past perfect tense. The main clause verb is formed from *could have, would have,* or *might have* plus the past participle.

| Incorrect | If we **had fed** the dog last night, he would not run away. |
| Correct | If we **had fed** the dog last night, he would not have run away. |

For hypothetical events in the present or future, the conditional clause verb takes the past tense and the main clause verb is formed from *could, would,* or *might* and the base form.

Incorrect	If we **paid** off our credit cards, we can buy a house.
Correct	If we **paid** off our credit cards, we could buy a house.

For more help using conditionals, see the exercises on this page of the eText at **www.mycomplab.com.**

Exercise 53.5 Rewrite the following sentences to reflect the conditional category represented in the parentheses following the sentence.

Example	If you **were to show** irrational fear toward a common object or situation, you **would be diagnosed** with a phobia. (predictive)
Rewrite	If you show irrational fear toward a common object or situation, you will be diagnosed with a phobia.

1. If a child was terrified whenever he or she saw a clown, that child had coulrophobia. (factual)
2. If you were ever attacked by birds, you developed ornithophobia. (hypothetical)
3. If someone had claustrophobia, he would not be comfortable in a small cave. (factual)
4. If you develop heliophobia, you do not enjoy sunbathing. (predictive)
5. If a dentist has dentophobia, she has to find a new job. (hypothetical)

53g Participial Adjectives

The present participle always ends in *-ing* (*boring, exciting*), while most past participles end in *-ed* (*bored, excited*). Both participle forms can be used as adjectives.

When participles are used as adjectives, they can either precede the nouns they modify or they can come after a connecting verb.

> It was a thrilling book. [*Thrilling* modifies *book*.]

> Stephanie was thrilled. [*Thrilled* modifies *Stephanie*.]

Present participles like *thrilling* describe a thing or person causing an experience, while past participles like *thrilled* describe a thing or person receiving the experience.

Incorrect	Students were exciting by the lecture.
Correct	Students were excited by the lecture.

Exercise 53.6 The following paragraph includes participial adjectives. Underline each participial adjective once and the word being modified twice. Circle the phrasal verbs.

Example   The <u>whirling</u> <u>tornado</u> (lives up to) its reputation as one of the world's most <u>damaging</u> natural <u>disasters.</u>

Many tornadoes are made up of a special rotating thunderstorm called a supercell. A rising gust of warm wind combines with the raging storm; the warm air begins spinning as the rainfall causes a rushing downdraft. This interaction serves up a harrowing twister that is awful for those in its path. The United States faces up to the devastating distinction of hosting the world's most tornadoes per year; homeowners in the regions known as "Tornado Alley" and "Dixie Alley" are terrified when they see the funneling tornado heading for their houses.

53h Phrasal Verbs

The liveliest and most colorful feature of the English language, its numerous idiomatic verbal phrases, gives many multilingual speakers the greatest difficulty.

Phrasal verbs consist of a verb and one or two **particles**: either a preposition, an adverb, or both. The verb and particles combine to form a phrase with a particular meaning that is often quite distinct from the meaning of the verb itself. Consider the following sentence.

I need to **go over** the chapter once more before the test.

Here, the meaning of *go over*—a verb and a preposition that, taken together, suggest casual study—is only weakly related to the meaning of either *go* or *over* by itself. English has hundreds of such idiomatic constructions, and the best way to familiarize yourself with them is to listen to and read as much informal English as you can.

Like regular verbs, phrasal verbs can be either transitive (they take a direct object) or intransitive. In the preceding example, *go over* is transitive. *Quiet down*—as in *Please quiet down*—is intransitive. Some phrases, like *wake up*, can be both: *Wake up!* is intransitive, while *Jenny, wake up the children* is transitive.

In some transitive phrasal verbs, the particles can be separated from the verb without affecting the meaning: *I made up a song* is equivalent to *I made a song up*. In others, the particles cannot be separated from the verb.

Incorrect   You shouldn't **play** with love **around**.

Correct   You shouldn't **play around** with love.

Unfortunately, there are no shortcuts for learning which verbal phrases are separable and which are not. As you become increasingly familiar with English, you will grow more confident in your ability to use phrasal verbs.

54 | English Sentence Structure

QUICK*TAKE*

- **What is the subject of a sentence?** (see below)
  Incorrect: Is my favorite flavor of ice cream.
  Correct: Pistachio is my favorite flavor of ice cream.
- **What are the correct patterns for English sentences?** (see p. 716)
  Incorrect: The server brought her.
  Correct: The server brought her a whole salmon.
- **Where do you place modifiers?** (see p. 718)
  Unclear: After eating a few bites, the salmon was not fully cooked.
  Clear: After eating a few bites, she realized that the salmon was not fully cooked.

54a Subjects

With the exception of **imperatives** (commands such as *Be careful!* and *Jump!*) and informal expressions (such as *Got it?*), sentences in English usually contain a subject and a predicate. A **subject** names who or what the sentence is about; the **predicate** contains information about the subject.

⌐SUBJECT¬⌐PREDICATE¬
The lion is asleep.

Many languages allow the writer to omit the subject if it's implied, but formal written English requires that each sentence include a subject, even when the meaning of the sentence would be clear without it. In some cases, you must supply an **expletive** (also known as a *dummy subject*), such as *it* or *there*, to stand in for the subject.

| Incorrect | Is snowing in Alaska. |
| Correct | It is snowing in Alaska. |

| Incorrect | Won't be enough time to climb that mountain. |
| Correct | There won't be enough time to climb that mountain. |

Both main and subordinate clauses within sentences require a subject and a predicate. A main clause can stand alone as a sentence, while subordinate clauses can only be understood in the context of the sentence of which they're a part. Still, even subordinate clauses must contain a subject. Look at the underlined subordinate clauses in the following two correct sentences.

> We avoided the main highway <u>because it had two lanes blocked off.</u>

> We avoided the main highway, <u>which had two lanes blocked off.</u>

In the first example, the subject of the subordinate clause is *it,* a pronoun representing the highway. In the second sentence, the relative pronoun *which*—also representing the highway—becomes the subject. When you use a relative pronoun, do not repeat the subject within the same clause.

Incorrect   We avoided the highway, which it had two lanes blocked off.

In this sentence, *it* repeats the subject *which* unnecessarily.

Exercise 54.1   Underline all of the subjects in the following sentences. Some sentences may have more than one subject; some may appear to have none. If the sentence appears to have no subject, supply the needed expletive.

> **Example**   Though <u>you</u> may have heard of Lee Harvey Oswald and John Wilkes Booth, many lesser-known <u>individuals</u> have put presidents in harm's way.

1. Though some assassins are widely known, Charles Guiteau and Leon Czolgolsz are relatively obscure.
2. Guiteau shot President James Garfield in 1881, and was little doubt he would be hanged for the murder.
3. Twenty years later, Czolgolsz stood face to face with his victim, President William McKinley.
4. History books are littered with the names of would-be assassins such as Giuseppe Zangara, Samuel Byck, and Sarah Jane Moore.
5. You should protect your leaders because there is no way to tell what the future will bring.

Exercise 54.2   In the following sentences, underline main clauses once and subordinate clauses twice. Circle the subjects in each.

> **Example**   When (scientists) explain phenomena such as volcanoes and earthquakes, (they) often use the theory of plate tectonics.

1. Geologists based the theory on an earlier one that had observed that the continents fit together like pieces of a puzzle.
2. In the 1950s and 1960s, scientists found evidence to support the earlier theory, so they were able to confirm its hypothesis regarding continental drift.
3. Although water and earth appear to be distinctly separate, they share a similar underlayer called the asthenosphere.
4. This layer possesses high temperatures and high pressure, and these conditions allow for fluid rock movement.
5. As plates move around, they can create volcanoes or increase and decrease the size of oceans and mountains.

54b English Word Order

All languages have their own rules for sentence structure. In English, correct word order often determines whether or not you succeed in saying what you mean. The basic sentence pattern in English is subject + predicate. A **predicate** consists of at least one main verb (see Section 35a). Although it is possible to write single-verb sentences such as *Stop!* most English sentences consist of a combination of several words. A simple English sentence can be formed with a noun and a verb.

> Birds fly.

In the above sentence, the subject (birds) is taking the action *and* receiving the action. There is no other object after the verb. The type of verb that can form a sentence without being followed by an object is called an **intransitive verb**. If the verb is intransitive, like *exist,* it does not take a direct object.

Some verbs are **transitive**, which means they require a **direct object** to complete their meaning. The direct object receives the action described by the verb.

| Incorrect | The bird saw. |
| Correct | The bird saw a cat. |

In this sentence, the subject (the bird) is doing the action (saw) while the direct object (a cat) is receiving the action. A sentence with a transitive verb can be transformed into a passive sentence (*A cat was seen by the bird*). See Chapter 30 for active and passive sentences.

Some verbs (*write, learn, read,* and others) can be both transitive and intransitive, depending on how they are used.

Intransitive   Pilots fly.

Transitive   Pilots fly airplanes.

Most learner's dictionaries and bilingual dictionaries indicate whether a particular verb is transitive or intransitive. See Section 51c on the use of dictionaries.

In another simple pattern, the transitive verb is replaced by a linking verb that joins its subject to a following description.

The tallest player was the goalie.

Linking verbs like *was, become, sound, look,* and *seem* precede a *subject complement* (in this example, *the goalie*) that refers back to the subject.

At the next level of complexity, a sentence combines a subject with a verb, direct object, and indirect object.

INDIRECT   DIRECT
OBJ   OBJ
The goalie passed her the ball.

Passed is a transitive verb, *ball* is the direct object of the verb, and *her* is the indirect object, the person for whom the action was taken. The same idea can be expressed with a prepositional phrase instead of an indirect object.

DIRECT   PREP
OBJ   PHRASE
The goalie passed the ball to her.

Other sentence patterns are possible in English. (See Chapter 35.) However, it is important to remember that altering the basic subject + verb + object word order often changes the meaning of a sentence. If the meaning survives, the result may still be awkward. As a general rule, try to keep the verb close to its subject, and the direct or indirect object close to its verb.

Exercise 54.3 Label the parts of speech in the following sentences: subject (S), transitive or intransitive verb (TV or IV), linking verb (LV), direct object (DO), indirect object (IO), subject complement (SC), and prepositional phrase (PP). Not all sentences will contain all of these parts, but all will contain some.

Example
    S   *TV*   *DO*   *PP*
Hinduism includes several gods and heroes in its system
    PP
of beliefs.

1. Ganesh is the god of good luck.
2. Young Ganesh stood at the doorway to his mother's house.
3. He denied his father entry.
4. His father beheaded him.
5. His mother replaced his head with the head of an elephant.

54c Placement of Modifiers

The proximity of a modifier—an adjective or adverb—to the noun or verb it modifies provides an important clue to their relationship. Modifiers, even more than verbs, will be unclear if your reader can't connect them to their associated words. Both native and nonnative speakers of English often have difficulty with misplaced modifiers.

Clarity should be your first goal when using a modifier. Readers usually link modifiers with the nearest word. In the following examples, the highlighted words are adjective clauses that modify nouns.

Unclear	Many pedestrians are killed each year by motorists not using sidewalks.
Clear	Many pedestrians not using sidewalks are killed each year by motorists.
Unclear	He gave an apple to his girlfriend on a silver platter.
Clear	He gave an apple on a silver platter to his girlfriend.

An **adverb**—a word or group of words that modifies a verb, adjective, or another adverb—should not come between a verb and its direct object.

Awkward	The hurricane destroyed completely the city's tallest building.
Better	The hurricane completely destroyed the city's tallest building.

While single-word adverbs can come between a subject and its verb, you should avoid placing adverbial phrases in this position.

Awkward	Galveston, following the 1900 hurricane that killed thousands, built a seawall to prevent a future catastrophe.
Better	Following the 1900 hurricane that killed thousands, Galveston built a seawall to prevent a future catastrophe.

As a general rule, try to avoid placing an adverb between *to* and its verb. This is called a **split infinitive**.

Awkward	The water level was predicted to not rise.
Better	The water level was predicted not to rise.

Sometimes, though, a split infinitive will read more naturally than the alternative. Note also how the sentence with the split infinitive is more concise.

Without split infinitive	Automobile emissions in the city are expected **to increase by more than two times** over the next five years.
With split infinitive	Automobile emissions in the city are expected **to more than double** over the next five years.

Certain kinds of adverbs have special rules for placement. Adverbs that describe how something is done—called **adverbs of manner**—usually follow the verb.

The student listened **closely** to the lecture.

These adverbs may also be separated from the verb by a direct object:

She threw the ball **well**.

Adverbs of frequency are usually placed at the head of a sentence, before a single verb, or after an auxiliary verb in a verb phrase.

Often, politicians have underestimated the intelligence of voters.

Politicians have **often** underestimated the intelligence of voters.

It's common practice in English to combine two or more nouns to form a compound noun. Where two or more adjectives or nouns are strung together, the main noun is always positioned at the end of the string:

12-speed road **bike**, tall oak **tree**, computer **table**

Exercise 54.4 The following sentences include confusing modifiers. Underline the confusing modifiers, identify the broken rule (far away from modified word; adverb between verb and direct object; adverbial phrase between subject and verb; split infinitive), and rewrite the sentence clearly.

> **Example** Awareness of autism has increased through the life story of Temple Grandin <u>worldwide</u>. *(Far away from modified word)*
>
> **Revise** Awareness of autism has increased worldwide through the life story of Temple Grandin.

1. Doctors, seeing a bleak future for Grandin, told her parents that she should be institutionalized.
2. However, Grandin's mother was determined to not give up on her daughter.
3. Called often "weird" by her classmates, Grandin excelled in school and earned eventually a Ph.D. in animal science.
4. Grandin has used her ability unique to think visually to design facilities humane for livestock.
5. She has also to other people with autism become a hero.

Exercise 54.5 Underline all the adjectives and adverbs in the following sentences. Label adverbs of manner or adverbs of frequency, and correct improper word order where you find it.

> *adverb of frequency*
> **Example** Americans associate <u>often</u> cards and dice with <u>shady</u> gamblers <u>Las Vegas</u>.
>
> **Revise** Americans often associate cards and dice with shady Las Vegas gamblers.

1. By the fourteenth century, cards playing were used widely for gambling and predicting the future.
2. The invention of the printing press directly connects to the proliferation of card games standardized.
3. Ancient dice directly can be traced to Tutankhamen's tomb.
4. Gamblers hollowed frequently the center of an illegally rigged die.
5. These classic games have withstood well the test of time.

COMMON ERRORS

e Edit Help

Dangling modifiers

A dangling modifier does not seem to modify anything in a sentence; it dangles, unconnected to the word or words it presumably is intended to modify. Frequently, it produces funny results.

> **When still a girl**, my father joined the army.

It sounds like *father* was once a girl. The problem is that the subject, I, is missing:

> **When I was still a girl**, my father joined the army.

Dangling modifiers usually occur at the head of a sentence in the form of clauses, with a subject that is implied but never stated.

Incorrect After lifting the heavy piano up the stairs, the apartment door was too small to get it through.

Correct After lifting the heavy piano up the stairs, we discovered the apartment door was too small to get it through.

(Continued on next page)

COMMON ERRORS *(Continued)*

Whenever you use a modifier, ask yourself whether its relationship to the word it modifies will be clear to your reader. What is clear to you may not be clear to your audience. Writing, like speaking, is an exercise in making your own thoughts explicit. The solution for the dangling modifier is to recast it as a complete clause with its own explicit subject and verb.

Remember: Modifiers should be clearly connected to the words they modify, especially at the beginning of sentences.

 For more practice with modifiers, see the exercises on this page of the eText at **www.mycomplab.com.**

Exercise 54.6 The following sentences include dangling modifiers. Rewrite the sentences so that the relationship between subject, verb, and modifier is clear.

Example In his early thirties, France was dealt a hefty blow by Maximilien Robespierre.

Revise In his early thirties, Maximilien Robespierre dealt France a hefty blow.

1. His philosophical role model, Robespierre followed the writings of Jean Jacques Rousseau.
2. Elected on the eve of the French Revolution, the people were enthralled by his skillful oratory.
3. Gaining further power in the following years, his influence over domestic affairs was unmistakable.
4. A bloodbath known as the Reign of Terror, Robespierre ordered a rash of executions of members of the aristocracy and his political enemies.
5. After they tired of his aggressive tactics, he was overthrown by his own political party.

 For more explanation, examples, and practice exercises, visit the Common ESL Errors Workbook on this page of the eText at **www.mycomplab.com.**

Glossary of Grammatical Terms and Usage

The glossary gives the definitions of grammatical terms and items of usage. The grammatical terms are shown in blue. Some of the explanations of usage that follow are not rules, but guidelines to keep in mind for academic and professional writing. In these formal contexts, the safest course is to avoid words that are described as *nonstandard, informal,* or *colloquial.*

a/an   Use *a* before words that begin with a consonant sound (*a train, a house*). Use *an* before words that begin with a vowel sound (*an airplane, an hour*).

a lot/alot   *A lot* is generally regarded as informal; *alot* is nonstandard.

absolute   A phrase that has a subject and modifies an entire sentence (see Section 35d).

The soldiers marched in single file, their rifles slung over their shoulders.

accept/except   *Accept* is a verb meaning "receive" or "approve." *Except* is sometimes a verb meaning "leave out," but much more often, it's used as a conjunction or preposition meaning "other than."

She accepted her schedule except for Biology at 8 a.m.

active   A clause with a transitive verb in which the subject is the doer of the action (see Section 30b). See also passive.

adjective   A modifier that qualifies or describes the qualities of a noun or pronoun (see Sections 35b, 40a, and 40b).

adjective clause   A subordinate clause that modifies a noun or pronoun and is usually introduced by a relative pronoun (see Section 35c). Sometimes called a *relative clause.*

adverb   A word that modifies a verb, another modifier, or a clause (see Sections 35b, 40a, and 40c).

adverb clause   A subordinate clause that functions as an adverb by modifying a verb, another modifier, or a clause (see Section 35c).

advice/advise   The noun *advice* means a "suggestion"; the verb *advise* means to "recommend" or "give advice."

affect/effect   Usually, *affect* is a verb (to "influence") and *effect* is a noun (a "result"):

Too many pork chops affect one's health.

Too many pork chops have an effect on one's health.

Less commonly, *affect* is used as a noun and *effect* as a verb. In the following examples, *affect* means an "emotional state or expression," and *effect* means "to bring about."

The boy's affect changed when he saw his father.

The legislators will attempt to effect new insurance laws next year.

agreement   The number and person of a subject and verb must match—singular subjects with singular verbs, plural subjects with plural verbs (see Chapter 34). Likewise, the number and gender of a pronoun and its antecedent must match (see Section 39b).

all ready/already   The adjective phrase *all ready* means "completely prepared"; the adverb *already* means "previously."

The tour group was all ready to leave, but the train had already departed.

all right/alright   *All right*, meaning "acceptable," is the correct spelling. *Alright* is nonstandard.

allude/elude   *Allude* means "refer to indirectly." *Elude* means "evade."

He alluded to the fact that he'd eluded capture.

allusion/illusion   An *allusion* is an indirect reference; an *illusion* is a false impression.

The painting contains an allusion to the Mona Lisa.

The painting creates the illusion of depth.

among/between   *Between* refers to precisely two people or things; *among* refers to three or more.

The choice is between two good alternatives.

The costs were shared among the three participating companies.

amount/number   Use *amount* with things that cannot be counted; use *number* with things that can be counted.

A large amount of money changed hands.

They gave him a number of quarters.

an   See a/an.

antecedent   The noun (or pronoun) that a pronoun refers to (see Section 39b). *Jeff* is the antecedent of *his* in the following sentence.

Jeff stopped running when his knee began hurting.

anybody/any body; anyone/any one   *Anybody* and *anyone* are indefinite pronouns and have the same meaning; *any body* and *any one* are usually followed by a noun that they modify.

Anybody can learn English, just as anyone can learn to bicycle.

Any body of government should be held accountable for its actions.

anymore/any more   *Anymore* means "now," while *any more* means "no more."
Both are used in negative constructions.

No one goes downtown anymore.

The area doesn't have any more stores than it did in 1960.

anyway/anyways   *Anyway* is correct. *Anyways* is nonstandard.

appositive   A word or a phrase placed close to a noun that restates or modifies
the noun (see Section 35d).

Dr. Lim, my physics professor, is the best.

articles   The words *a*, *an*, and *the* (see Sections 35b and 52d).

as/as if/as though/like   Use *as* instead of *like* before dependent clauses
(which include a subject and verb). Use *like* before a noun or a pronoun.

Her voice sounds as if she had her head in a barrel.

She sings like her father.

assure/ensure/insure   *Assure* means "promise," *ensure* means "make certain," and
insure means to "make certain in either a legal or financial sense."

Ralph assured the new client that his company would insure the building at full
value, but the client wanted higher approval to ensure Ralph was correct.

auxiliary verb   Forms of *be*, *do*, and *have* combine with verbs to indicate tense
and mood (see Section 35b). The modal verbs *can, could, may, might, must,
shall, should, will,* and *would* are a subset of auxiliaries.

bad/badly   Use *bad* only as an adjective. *Badly* is the adverb.

He was a bad dancer.

Everyone agreed that he danced badly.

being as/being that   Both constructions are colloquial and awkward substitutes
for *because*. Don't use them in formal writing.

beside/besides   *Beside* means "next to." *Besides* means "in addition to" or "except."

Does anyone, besides your mother, want to sit beside you when you're coughing
like that?

between   See **among/between**.

bring/take   *Bring* describes movement from a more distant location to a nearer
one. *Take* describes movement away.

Bring me the most recent issue. You can take this one.

can/may   In formal writing, *can* indicates ability or capacity, while *may* indicates
permission.

If I may speak with you, we can probably solve this problem.

case   The form of a noun or pronoun that indicates its function. Nouns change case only to show possession: the **dog**, the **dog's** bowl (see Section 35b). See **pronoun case** (Section 39a).

censor/censure   To *censor* is to edit or ban on moral or political grounds. To *censure* is to reprimand publicly.

The Senate censored the details of the budget.

The Senate censured one of its members for misconduct.

cite/sight/site   To *cite* is to "mention specifically"; *sight* as a verb means to "observe" and as a noun refers to "vision"; *site* is most commonly used as a noun that means "location," but is also used as a verb to mean "situate."

He cited as evidence the magazine article he'd read yesterday.

Finally, he sighted the bald eagle. It was a remarkable sight.

The developers sited the houses on a heavily forested site.

clause   A group of words with a subject and a predicate. A main or independent clause can stand as a sentence. A subordinate or dependent clause must be attached to a main clause to form a sentence (see Section 35c).

collective noun   A noun that refers to a group or a plurality, such as *team, army,* or *committee* (see Section 37d).

comma splice   Two independent clauses joined incorrectly by a comma (see Section 36c).

common noun   A noun that names a general group, person, place, or thing (see Sections 35b and 52a). Common nouns are not capitalized unless they begin a sentence.

complement   A word or group of words that completes the predicate (see Section 35c). See also **linking verb**.

Juanita is my aunt.

complement/compliment   To *complement* something is to complete it or make it perfect; to *compliment* is to flatter.

The chef complemented their salad with a small bowl of soup.

The grateful diners complimented the chef.

complex sentence   A sentence that contains at least one subordinate clause attached to a main clause (see Section 35e).

compound sentence   A sentence that contains at least two main clauses (see Section 35e).

compound-complex sentence   A sentence that contains at least two main clauses and one subordinate clause (see Section 35e).

conjunction   See **coordinating conjunction**; **subordinating conjunction**.

conjunctive adverb   An adverb that often modifies entire clauses and sentences, such as *also, consequently, however, indeed, instead, moreover, nevertheless, otherwise, similarly,* and *therefore* (see Sections 35b and 40c).

continual/continuous   *Continual* refers to a repeated activity; *continuous* refers to an ongoing, unceasing activity.

Tennis elbow is usually caused by continual stress on the joint.

Archaeologists have debated whether Chaco Canyon was inhabited intermittently or continuously.

coordinate   A relationship of equal importance, in terms of either grammar or meaning (see Section 32c).

coordinating conjunction   A word that links two equivalent grammatical elements, such as *and, but, or, yet, nor, for,* and *so* (see Section 35b).

could of   Nonstandard. See **have/of.**

count noun   A noun that names things that can be counted, such as *block, cat,* and *toy* (see Section 52b).

dangling modifier   A modifier that is not clearly attached to what it modifies (see Section 40e).

data   The plural form of *datum*; it takes plural verb forms.

The data are overwhelming.

declarative   A sentence that makes a statement (see Section 35a).

Dover is the capital of Delaware.

dependent clause   See **subordinate clause.**

determiners   Words that initiate noun phrases, including possessive nouns (*Pedro's violin*); possessive pronouns (*my, your*); demonstrative pronouns (*this, that*); and indefinite pronouns (*all, both, many*).

differ from/differ with   To *differ from* means to "be unlike"; to *differ with* means to "disagree."

Rock music differs from jazz primarily in rhythm.

Miles Davis differed with critics who disliked his rock rhythms.

different from/different than   Use *different from* where possible.

Dark French roast is different from ordinary coffee.

direct object   A noun, pronoun, or noun clause that names who or what receives the action of a transitive verb (see Section 35c).

Antonio kicked the ball.

discreet/discrete   Both are adjectives. *Discreet* means "prudent" or "tactful"; *discrete* means "separate."

What's a discreet way of saying "Shut up"?

Over the noise, he could pick up several discrete conversations.

disinterested/uninterested   *Disinterested* is often misused to mean *uninterested.* Disinterested means "impartial." A judge can be interested in a case but disinterested in the outcome.

double negative   The incorrect use of two negatives to signal the same negative meaning.

We don't have no money.

due to the fact that   Avoid this wordy substitute for *because*.

each other/one another   Use *each other* for two; use *one another* for more than two.

effect   See **affect/effect**.

elicit/illicit   The verb *elicit* means to "draw out." The adjective *illicit* means "unlawful."

The teacher tried to elicit a discussion about illicit drugs.

emigrate from/immigrate to   *Emigrate* means to "leave one's country"; *immigrate* means to "settle in another country."

ensure   See **assure/ensure/insure**.

enthused   Nonstandard in academic and professional writing. Use *enthusiastic* instead.

etc.   Avoid this abbreviation for the Latin *et cetera* in formal writing. Either list all the items or use an English phrase such as *and so forth*.

every body/everybody; every one/everyone   *Everybody* and *everyone* are indefinite pronouns referring to all people under discussion. *Every one* and *every body* are adjective-noun combinations referring to all members of a group.

Everyone loves a genuine smile.

Every one of the files contained a virus.

except   See **accept/except**.

except for the fact that   Avoid this wordy substitute for *except that*.

expletive   The dummy subjects *it* and *there* used to fill a grammatical slot in a sentence.

It is raining outside.

There should be a law against it.

explicit/implicit   Both are adjectives; *explicit* means "stated outright," while *implicit* means just the opposite, "unstated."

Even though we lacked an explicit contract, I thought we had an implicit understanding.

farther/further   *Farther* refers to physical distance; *further* refers to time or other abstract concepts.

How much farther is your home?

I don't want to talk about this any further.

fewer/less   Use *fewer* with what can be counted and *less* with what cannot be counted.

There are fewer canoeists in the summer because there is less water in the river.

flunk   In formal writing, avoid this colloquial substitute for *fail*.

fragment   A group of words beginning with a capital letter and ending with a period that looks like a sentence but lacks a subject or a predicate or both (see Section 36a).

further   See **farther/further**.

gerund   An *-ing* form of a verb used as a noun, such as *running, skiing,* or *laughing* (see Section 35b).

good/well   *Good* is an adjective and is not interchangeable with the adverb *well*. The one exception is health. Both she feels *good* and she feels *well* are correct.

The Yankees are a good baseball team. They play the game well.

hanged/hung   Use *hanged* to refer only to executions; *hung* is used for all other instances.

have/of   *Have*, not *of*, follows *should, could, would, may, must,* and *might*.

I should have [not *of*] picked you up earlier.

he/she; s/he   Try to avoid language that appears to exclude either gender (unless this is intended, of course) and awkward compromises such as *he/she* or *s/he*. The best solution is to make pronouns plural (the gender-neutral *they*) wherever possible (see Section 39c).

helping verb   See **auxiliary verb**.

hopefully   This adverb is commonly used as a sentence modifier, but many readers object to it.

I am hopeful [not *Hopefully*] we'll have a winning season.

illusion   See **allusion/illusion**.

immigrate   See **emigrate from/immigrate to**.

imperative   A sentence that expresses a command (see Section 35a). Usually the subject is implied rather than stated.

Go away now.

implicit   See **explicit/implicit**.

imply/infer   *Imply* means to "suggest"; *infer* means to "draw a conclusion."

The ad implied that the candidate was dishonest; I inferred that the campaign would be one of name calling.

in regards to   Avoid this wordy substitute for *regarding*.

incredible/incredulous *Incredible* means "unbelievable"; *incredulous* means "not believing."

Their story about finding a stack of money in a discarded suitcase seemed incredible; I was incredulous.

independent clause See **main clause**.

indirect object A noun, pronoun, or noun clause that names who or what is affected by the action of a transitive verb (see Section 35c).

Antonio kicked the ball to Mario.

infinitive The word *to* plus the base verb form: *to believe, to feel, to act*. See also **split infinitive**.

infinitive phrase A phrase that uses the infinitive form of a verb (see Section 35d).

To get some sleep is my goal for the weekend.

interjection A word expressing feeling that is grammatically unconnected to a sentence, such as *cool, wow, ouch*, or *yikes*.

interrogative A sentence that asks a question (see Section 35a).

Where do you want to go?

intransitive verb A verb that does not take an object, such as *sleep, appear*, or *laugh* (see Sections 35c and 38c).

irregardless Nonstandard for *regardless*.

irregular verb A verb that does not use either *-d* or *-ed* to form the past tense and past participle (see Section 38b).

it is my opinion that Avoid this wordy substitute for *I believe that*.

its/it's *Its* is the possessive of *it* and does not take an apostrophe; *it's* is the contraction for *it is*.

Its tail is missing. It's an unusual animal.

-ize/-wise The suffix *-ize* changes a noun or adjective into a verb (*harmony, harmonize*). The suffix *-wise* changes a noun or adjective into an adverb (*clock, clockwise*). Some writers are tempted to use these suffixes to convert almost any word into an adverb or verb form. Unless the word appears in a dictionary, don't use it.

kind of/sort of/type of Avoid using these colloquial expressions if you mean *somewhat* or *rather*. *It's kind of hot* is nonstandard. Each is permissible, however, when it refers to a classification of an object. Be sure that it agrees in number with the object it is modifying.

This type of engine is very fuel-efficient.

These kinds of recordings are rare.

lay/lie   *Lay* means "place" or "put" and generally takes a direct object (see Section 38c). Its main forms are *lay, laid, laid. Lie* means "recline" or "be positioned" and does not take an object. Its main forms are *lie, lay, lain.*

He lays the papers down. He laid the papers down.

He lies down on the sofa. He lay down on the sofa.

less   See **fewer/less**.

lie   See **lay/lie**.

linking verb   A verb that connects the subject to the complement, such as *appear, be, feel, look, seem,* or *taste* (see Section 35c).

lots/lots of   Nonstandard in formal writing; use *many* or *much* instead.

main clause   A group of words with a subject and a predicate that can stand alone as a sentence (see Section 35c). Also called an *independent clause.*

mankind   This term offends some readers and is outdated. Use *humans, humanity,* or *people* instead.

may/can   See **can/may**.

may be/maybe   *May be* is a verb phrase; *maybe* is an adverb.

It may be time to go.

Maybe it's time to go.

media   This is the plural form of the noun *medium* and requires a plural verb.

The media in this city are biased.

might of   See **have/of**.

modal   A kind of auxiliary verb that indicates ability, permission, intention, obligation, or probability, such as *can, could, may, might, must, shall, should, will,* or *would* (see Section 35b).

modifier   A general term for adjectives, adverbs, phrases, and clauses that describe other words (see Chapter 40).

must of   See **have/of**.

noncount noun   A noun that names things that cannot be counted, such as *air, energy,* or *water* (see Section 52b).

nonrestrictive modifier   A modifier that is not essential to the meaning of the word, phrase, or clause it modifies and should be set off by commas or other punctuation (see Section 41c).

noun   The name of a person, place, thing, concept, or action (see Section 35a). See also **common noun** and **proper noun** (see Section 52a).

noun clause A subordinate clause that functions as a noun (see Section 35c).
That the city fails to pick up the garbage is ridiculous.

number See **amount/number**.

object Receiver of the action within the clause or phrase (see Sections 35c and 35d).

OK, O.K., okay Informal; avoid using in academic and professional writing. Each spelling is accepted in informal usage.

owing to the fact that Avoid this wordy, colloquial substitute for *because*.

parallelism The principle of putting similar elements or ideas in similar grammatical form (see Sections 32c, 32d, and 32e).

participle A form of a verb that uses *-ing* in the present (*laughing, playing*) and usually *-ed* or *-en* in the past (*laughed, played*). See Section 35a. Participles are either part of the verb phrase (*She had played the game before*) or used as adverbs and adjectives (*the laughing girl*).

participial phrase A phrase formed either by a present participle (for example, *racing*) or by a past participle (for example, *taken*). (See Section 35d).

parts of speech The eight classes of words according to their grammatical function: nouns, pronouns, verbs, adjectives, adverbs, prepositions, conjunctions, and interjections (see Section 35b).

passive A clause with a transitive verb in which the subject is being acted upon (see Section 30b). See also **active**.

per Try to use the English equivalent of this Latin word except in technical writing or familiar usages like *miles per gallon*.
The job paid $20 an hour.
As you requested [not *per your request*], I'll drive up immediately.

phenomena This is the plural form of *phenomenon* ("observable fact" or "unusual event") and takes plural verbs.
The astronomical phenomena were breathtaking.

phrase A group of words that does not contain both a subject and a predicate.

plenty In academic and professional writing, avoid this colloquial substitute for *very*.

plus Do not use *plus* to join clauses or sentences. Use *and, also, moreover, furthermore*, or another conjunctive adverb instead.
It rained heavily, and it was also [not *plus it was*] bitterly cold.

precede/proceed Both are verbs but they have different meanings: *precede* means "come before," and *proceed* means "go ahead" or "continue."

In the United States, the national anthem precedes every major league baseball game.

We proceeded to the train station.

predicate   The part of the clause that expresses the action or tells something about the subject. The predicate includes the verb and all its complements, objects, and modifiers (see Section 35a).

prejudice/prejudiced   *Prejudice* is a noun; *prejudiced* is an adjective.

The jury was prejudiced against the defendant.

She knew about the town's history of racial prejudice.

preposition   A class of words that indicate relationships and qualities (see Sections 35b and 52e).

prepositional phrase   A phrase formed by a preposition and its object, including the modifiers of its object (see Section 35d).

principal/principle   *Principal* means first in importance (*school principal, principal reason*). *Principle* applies to beliefs or understandings (*It goes against my principles*).

pronoun   A word that stands for other nouns or pronouns. Pronouns have several subclasses, including personal pronouns, possessive pronouns, demonstrative pronouns, indefinite pronouns, relative pronouns, interrogative pronouns, reflexive pronouns, and reciprocal pronouns (see Section 35b and Chapter 39).

pronoun case   Pronouns that function as the subjects of sentences are in the **subjective** case (*I, you, he, she, it, we, they*). Pronouns that function as direct or indirect objects are in the **objective** case (*me, you, him, her, it, us, them*). Pronouns that indicate ownership are in the **possessive** case (*my, your, his, her, its, our, their*) (see Section 39a).

proper noun   A noun that names a particular person, place, thing, or group (see Sections 35b and 52a). Proper nouns are capitalized.

raise/rise   The verb *raise* means "lift up" and takes a direct object. Its main forms are *raise, raised, raised*. The verb *rise* means "get up" and does not take a direct object. Its main forms are *rise, rose, risen*.

The workers carefully raised the piano onto the truck.

The piano slowly rose off the ground.

real/really   Avoid using *real* as if it were an adverb. *Really* is an adverb; *real* is an adjective.

The singer was really good.

What we thought was an illusion turned out to be real.

reason is because   Omit either *reason is* or *because* when explaining causality.

The reason he ran is that he thought he was late.

He ran because he thought he was late.

reason why   Avoid using this redundant combination.

The reason he's so often late is that he never wears a watch.

relative pronoun   A pronoun that initiates clauses, such as *that, which, what, who, whom,* or *whose* (see Section 35b).

restrictive modifier   A modifier that is essential to the meaning of the word, phrase, or clause it modifies (see Section 41c). Restrictive modifiers are usually not set off by punctuation.

rise/raise   See **raise/rise.**

run-on sentence   Two main clauses fused together without punctuation or a conjunction, appearing as one sentence (see Section 36b).

sentence   A grammatically independent group of words that contains at least one main clause (see Section 35a).

sentence fragment   See fragment.

set/sit   *Set* means "put" and takes a direct object (see Section 38c); its main forms are *set, set, set. Sit* means "be seated" and does not take a direct object; its main forms are *sit, sat, sat. Sit* should not be used as a synonym for *set.*

Set the bowl on the table.

Please sit down.

shall/will   *Shall* is used most often in first person questions, while *will* is a future tense helping verb for all persons. British English consistently uses *shall* with first person: *I shall, we shall.*

Shall I bring you some water?

Will they want drinks, too?

should of   See **have/of.**

sit/set   See **set/sit.**

some time/sometime/sometimes   *Some time* means "a span of time," *sometime* means "at some unspecified time," and *sometimes* means "occasionally."

Give me some time to get ready.

Let's meet again sometime soon.

Sometimes, the best-laid plans go wrong.

somebody/some body; someone/some one   *Somebody* and *someone* are indefinite pronouns and have the same meaning. In *some body, body* is a noun modified by *some,* and in *some one, one* is a pronoun or adjective modified by *some.*

Somebody should close that window.

"Some body was found on the beach today," the homicide detective said.

Someone should answer the phone.

It would be best if some one person could represent the group.

sort of See **kind of/sort of/type of**.

split infinitive An infinitive with a word or words between *to* and the base verb form, such as *to boldly go, to better appreciate* (see Section 40d).

stationary/stationery *Stationary* means "motionless"; *stationery* means "writing paper."

subject A noun, pronoun, or noun phrase that identifies what the clause is about and connects with the predicate (see Sections 35a and 35c).

subject-verb agreement See agreement.

subordinate A relationship of unequal importance, in terms of either grammar or meaning (see Section 32a).

subordinate clause A clause that cannot stand alone but must be attached to a main clause (see Section 35c). Also called a *dependent clause*.

subordinating conjunction A word that introduces a subordinate clause. Common subordinating conjunctions are *after, although, as, because, before, if, since, that, unless, until, when, where,* and *while* (see Section 35b).

such Avoid using *such* as a synonym for *very*. It should always be followed by *that* and a clause that contains a result.

It was a very [not *such a*] hot August.

sure A colloquial term used as an adverb to mean "certainly." Avoid using it this way in formal writing.

You were certainly [not *sure were*] correct when you said August would be hot.

sure and/sure to; try and/try to *Sure to* and *try to* are correct; do not use *and* after *sure* or *try*.

Be sure to [not *sure and*] take out the trash this morning.

Try to [not *try and*] finish first.

take See **bring/take**.

that/which *That* introduces a restrictive or essential clause. Restrictive clauses describe an object that must be that particular object and no other. Though some writers occasionally use *which* with restrictive clauses, it is most often used to introduce nonrestrictive clauses. These are clauses that contain additional nonessential information about the object.

Let's listen to the CD that Clarence bought.

Clarence's favorite music, which usually puts me to sleep, is too mellow for me.

transition A word or phrase that notes movement from one unit of writing to another.

transitive verb A verb that takes a direct object (see Sections 35c and 38c).

unique *Unique* means one of a kind. Things cannot be "very unique" or "more unique." They are either unique or not.

verb   A word that expresses action or characterizes the subject in some way. Verbs can show tense and mood (see Section 35b and Chapter 38).

verbal   A form of a verb used as an adjective, adverb, or noun (see Section 35b). See also **gerund, infinitive, participle.**

well/good   See **good/well**.

which/that   See **that/which**.

who/whom   *Who* and *whom* follow the same rules as other pronouns: *Who* is the subject pronoun; *whom* is the object pronoun (see Section 39a).

Sharon's father, who served in the Korean War, died last year.

Sharon's father, whom several of my father's friends knew, died last year.

will/shall   See **shall/will**.

-wise/-ize   See **-ize/-wise**.

would of   See **have/of**.

you   Avoid indefinite uses of *you*. It should only be used to mean "you, the reader."

The [not *your*] average life span in the United States has increased consistently over the past 100 years.

your/you're   The two are not interchangeable. *Your* is the possessive form of "you"; *you're* is the contraction of "you are."

Your car can be picked up after 5 p.m.

You're going to need money to live in Manhattan.

Answers to Selected Exercises

These pages provide answers to exercises from Parts 7–10 in *The Penguin Handbook*. For some exercises with multiple questions, only partial answers are given. For exercises with long paragraphs, many of the answers below are abbreviated versions of what the full answer would be. These are annotated as "shortened answers."

Chapter 30   Write with Power

Exercise 30.1 (p. 480)
Active and passive verbs are underlined. Possible revisions are in parenthesis (shortened answer):

It has been reported by researchers in neuroscience (Researchers in neuroscience have reported) that food advertising often succeeds because of the structure of our brains. Some people are surprised by this finding. (This finding surprises some people.)

Exercise 30.2 (p. 482)
The "be" verbs are in bold and the nouns are underlined in the sentences below. Possible revisions are in parenthesis (shortened answer):

Though few people celebrate the experience of pain, the human body **is** dependent (depends) on unpleasant impulses for survival. Without pain, an individual **is** at a disadvantage (The absence of pain disadvantages an individual) in terms of self-preservation.

Exercise 30.3 (p. 482)
The subject of each sentence is underlined below. Possible revisions are in parenthesis (shortened answer):

The observation of these old customs in parts of Europe where the inhabitants are Celtic proves their Druid origin. (Inhabitants of Celtic parts of Europe observed these old customs, proving their Druid origin.) To mark the beginning of winter, the burning of fires on November 1 was customary. (Druids burned fires on November 1 to mark the beginning of winter.)

Chapter 31   Write Concisely

Exercise 31.1 (p. 487)
Possible rewrite (shortened answer):

Because we cannot see a black hole up close, we must use our imaginations to consider its properties. For example, imagine jumping feet first into a black hole.

Exercise 31.2 (p. 488)

Possible replacements are in brackets (shortened answer):

In 1942, the American Office of Strategic Services (OSS) Chief William Donovan gathered six <u>incredibly respected</u> [prestigious] scientists to develop a truth serum. The American Psychiatric Association and the Federal Bureau of Narcotics, both <u>very respectable</u> [reputable] organizations, also participated in this <u>rather secretive</u> [covert] search for the truth drug.

Exercise 31.3 (p. 490)

Possible rewrite (shortened answer):

C. exigua is 3 to 4 centimeters in length, or 1.2 to 1.6 inches. This unique parasite makes its way into the spotted rose snapper through the gills and attaches itself at the base of the fish's tongue.

Exercise 31.4 (p. 492)

Possible rewrite (shortened answer):

Fossils can help paleontologists gain additional information about ancient eras in several ways. They aid in locating certain missing data regarding location, time, and traits of both past and future organisms.

Chapter 32   Write with Emphasis

Exercise 32.1 (p. 496)

Possible rewrite; main ideas are underlined twice and subordinate ideas are underlined once (shortened answer):

<u>Since popular representations of Jesus portrayed a thin, almost sickly man,</u> <u>men did not identify with Christianity as readily as women did.</u> <u>Those who wanted to change Jesus' image focused on his carpentry</u> because carpentry was associated with America's self-made man.

Exercise 32.2 (p. 500)

Replacement constructions are in brackets (shortened answer):

The first dark rides were built in the late 19th century and using [used] small l boats to carry riders through water-filled canals. These rides were called "scenic railways" or they were described as ["]pleasure railways.["] A dark ride does not have to be dark, but [the dark hides] ride mechanisms are hidden by dark, and [enhances the drama of the ride] the drama of the ride is enhanced by the dark.

Exercise 32.3 (p. 501)

1. Follow Route 22 N for 3 miles until you come to the Dewdrop Inn.
2. At the fourth traffic signal after the Dewdrop, make a sharp right turn onto Geoffrey Drive.

Chapter 33   Find the Right Words

Exercise 33.1 (p. 505)

Possible rewrite (shortened answer):

> Dear Rayna,
>   Thank you for meeting with me to discuss your work as an editor. I especially appreciate your generosity in providing the coffee.

Exercise 33.2 (p. 505)

Possible rewrite (shortened answer):

> The late David Brower was president of the Sierra Club, a group devoted to American wilderness preservation. As this organization's leader, Brower personified preservation.

Exercise 33.3 (p. 506)

Answers likely will vary. Possible responses below are marked (+) for positive connotation and (=) for neutral denotation.

  1. thin (+), slender (+), lean (=), trim (=)
  2. music (+), song (+), composition (=), tune (=)

Exercise 33.4 (p. 509)

Possible revision (shortened answer):

> Space missions can adversely affect an astronaut's health. A major culprit is the lack of gravity in space; one of the effects that weightlessness has on astronauts is bone loss, which can be severe.

Exercise 33.5 (p. 510)

Correct word choices are underlined (shortened answer):

> Butchering a hog requires <u>patience</u> and hard work. First, find a <u>site</u> outdoors <u>where</u> you will have plenty of space. After killing the pig, dunk it in hot water to loosen the <u>coarse</u> hair.

Exercise 33.6 (p. 512)

Clichés are underlined. Replacements will vary (shortened answer):

> However, in Japan and in the Mediterranean, squid, octopus, and cuttlefish are an important food source and <u>sell like hot cakes</u>. Unfortunately, myths about giant squid sinking boats and octopus drowning swimmers persist in the United States, and information that giant squid are <u>weak as kittens</u> and that an octopus has never drowned anyone <u>falls on deaf ears</u>.

Chapter 34   Write to be Inclusive

Exercise 34.1 (p. 514)
Answers will vary.

Exercise 34.2 (p. 517)
1. No; the writer could refer to his doctor without any gender specification, or make the doctor's gender secondary information.
2. Yes.

Exercise P7.1 (p. 519)
Possible rewrite (shortened answer):

In competitive eating, participants compete against each other to consume large quantities of food in a short amount of time. Each eating competition is usually around 15 minutes, and the eater, also known as a "gurgitator," who consumes the most food in that time period wins. The prize money for a professional competition can be up to $10,000.

Chapter 35   Grammar Basics

Exercise 35.1 (p. 525)
Rewrites will vary.
1. Active
2. Passive; People disagree about whether the "Mothman" of Point Pleasant, West Virginia, simply warns about or actually causes disasters.

Exercise 35.2 (p. 527)
Shortened answer:

The ramming was no accident; after the whale hit the *Essex* once, it [personal pronoun] turned around to hit the ship a second time. The sailors found themselves [reflexive pronoun] adrift in three whaleboats, 1,200 miles from the nearest islands.

Exercise 35.3 (p. 528)
Shortened answer:

Frank Oz was [aux modal] born [main] in Hereford, England, in 1944 and began [aux modal] staging [main] puppet shows when he was 12. You may [aux modal] know [main] him best as the voice of Yoda in the *Star Wars* series.

Exercise 35.4 (p. 528)
Shortened answer:

The evil eye is a focused [past participle] gaze, supposedly causing [present participle] death and destruction. Writings of the Assyrians, Babylonians, Greeks, and Romans all document an abiding [present participle] belief in this supernatural concept.

Exercise 35.5 (p. 530)

Shortened answer:

Parker's father encouraged her to pursue "feminine [adj mod. *arts*] arts" such as piano and poetry, but just [adv mod. *following*] following his death in 1913, she rushed into what turned out to be a profitable [adj mod. *foray*] foray into the world of literature. Almost [adv mod. *immediately*] immediately [adv mod. purchased], *Vanity Fair* purchased one of her poems, leading her into a full-time [adj mod. *position*] writing [adj mod. *position*] position with *Vogue*.

Exercise 35.6 (p. 531)

Items to be circled are in bold (shortened answer):

Until recently, the hard-to-reach land **inside** Mount Bosavi had been a 'lost world' **because of** the forbidding walls **of** the volcano. **Among** the species discovered **by** the science team are the giant Bosavi wooly rat and a fish that makes a grunting sound **with** its swim bladder.

Exercise 35.7 (p. 532)

Shortened answer:

Only four of the 400 species of shark attack humans: bull sharks, whitetips, tiger sharks, and great whites. While *or* Although sharks committed 74 fatal attacks in the past 100 years, 75% of all shark-attack victims have survived.

Exercise 35.8 (p. 532)

The word classes are in brackets (shortened answer):

Gold! [interjection] This [pronoun] discovery not only triggered the [article] Black Hills [adjective] gold rush [noun] but [conjunction] also gave rise to the lawless [adjective] town of Deadwood, which [pronoun] reached a [article] population of around 5,000 within [preposition] the next two years.

Exercise 35.9 (p. 535)

1. subject-verb-object
2. subject-linking verb

Exercise 35.10 (p. 536)

1. adjective clause
2. adjective clause

Exercise 35.11 (p. 537)

Rewrites may vary; some possible answers are given below.

1. Mike, the headless chicken, became a national celebrity.
2. Touring the country, Mike and his owner, Lloyd Olsen, made about $4,500 a month.

Exercise 35.12 (p. 539)

Possible solutions:

1. **Compound:** Philip K. Wrigley was a chewing gum entrepreneur, and he also began the All-American Girls Professional Baseball League in 1943. **Complex:** In 1943, when the onset of World War II threatened American interest in the sport of baseball, Philip K. Wrigley, chewing gum entrepreneur, began the All-American Girls Professional Baseball League. **Compound-Complex:** Philip K. Wrigley was primarily known as a chewing gum entrepreneur, but in 1943, when American involvement in World War II threatened interest in baseball, he pioneered the All-American Girls Professional Baseball League.

Chapter 36   Fragments, Run-ons, and Comma Splices

Exercise 36.1 (p. 544)

1. Flying squirrels are like typical squirrels except they have flaps of skin that allow them to glide.
2. Flying squirrels glide gracefully from tree to tree with surprising ease.

Exercise 36.2 (p. 544)

Possible rewrite (shortened answer):

Barton Springs still seems like a place not in Texas for those who come from elsewhere, with its surrounding hills covered by live oaks and mountain juniper, and the ground around the pool shaded by pecan trees whose trunks are a dozen feet in circumference.

Exercise 36.3 (p. 546)

Possible rewrites:

1. The original Kabuki troupes were mostly comprised of female dancers; <u>however,</u> male performers replaced them after the art became associated with prostitution.
2. Performances <u>that</u> included several thematically linked elements such as dance, history, and domestic drama lasted up to twelve hours.

Exercise 36.4 (p. 549)

Possible rewrites:

1. Riefenstahl spent her early days performing in Germany as a dancer. However, a 1924 knee injury derailed her dance career, detouring her into a successful, scandal-ridden life in film.
2. Early editing work prepared her to direct her first film, *The Blue Light*; however, national recognition was slow to come.

Chapter 37   Subject-Verb Agreement

Exercise 37.1 (p. 553)

Items to be circled are in bold; corrected verbs are in brackets.

1. <u>Some</u>, **cite**
2. <u>Each</u>, **possess** [possesses]

Exercise 37.2 (p. 554)

1. plural, enter
2. singular

Exercise 37.3 (p. 555)

The correct verb form is underlined (shortened answer):

The administration usually <u>tries</u> to avoid responsibility for issues concerning students living off campus but also <u>listens</u> when the city government <u>complains</u> about student behavior.

Exercise 37.4 (p. 557)

1. plural, are
2. singular, was

Chapter 38   Verbs

Exercise 38.1 (p. 560)

The correct form of the verb is underlined (shortened answer):

Flathead catfish are the <u>chosen</u> prey for <u>noodling</u> because they <u>live</u> sedentary lifestyles in holes or under brush. A noodler <u>begins</u> by <u>going</u> underwater to depths ranging from only a few feet to a <u>daunting</u> twenty feet.

Exercise 38.2 (p. 563)

Shortened answer:

The Dark Ages are (understand/<u>understood</u>) to have (took/<u>taken</u>) place between the Decline of the Roman Empire and the 1500s. Historians (<u>think</u>/thought) that little or no trade happened during the Dark Ages because spices, which (come/<u>came</u>) to Europe from the East, are not (<u>written</u>/wrote) about in documents from that time period.

Exercise 38.3 (p. 565)

The correct form of the verb is underlined (shortened answer):

A rattlesnake will often <u>lie</u> in wait for its favorite meal: a rat. When you encounter one of these poisonous snakes, <u>set</u> aside your assumptions about aggressive snakes; many are timid.

Exercise 38.4 (p. 566)

The correct form of the verb is underlined (shortened answer):

Native American activists, including Dennis Banks and Russell Means, <u>created</u> AIM, a militant organization that fights for civil rights for American Indians. AIM members <u>participated</u> in a number of famous protests, including the occupation of Alcatraz Island (1969–1971) and the takeover of Wounded Knee (1973).

Exercise 38.5 (p. 569)

The correct verb form is underlined (shortened answer):

This phenomenon is called "rapture of the deep" because the increase in nitrogen makes a diver feel as if she <u>were</u> invincible. <u>Be</u> very careful, however; this situation is dangerous.

Chapter 39   Pronouns

Exercise 39.1 (p. 571)

Corrections are in brackets (shortened answer):

If <u>you</u> and a friend go on a road trip, the ADA suggests that <u>you</u> and <u>her</u> [she] limit <u>your</u> stops at fast-food restaurants. The association suggests <u>us</u> [we] snack in the afternoon, provided <u>we</u> choose foods that are healthy for <u>you</u> and <u>I</u> [me].

Exercise 39.2 (p. 573)

1. whom
2. whoever

Exercise 39.3 (p. 575)

1. We, whose
2. His, I

Exercise 39.4 (p. 577)

Antecedents are underlined. Pronouns are in bold.

1. <u>name</u>, **it**
2. <u>greyhounds</u>, **their**

Exercise 39.5 (p. 578)

Items to be circled are in bold; replacement pronouns are in brackets (shortened answer):

Although <u>few</u> would admit it, **he or she** [they] often take extra precautions on <u>Friday</u> the 13th. <u>Some</u> are so paralyzed by fear that **they** are simply unable to get out of **his or her** [their] bed(s) when Friday the 13th comes around.

Exercise 39.6 (p. 580)

Possible rewrites:

1. When <u>some people become</u> financially overextended, <u>they</u> often consider credit cards as a way of making ends meet.
2. <u>Some</u> might begin to convince <u>themselves</u> that credit is the only way out.

Exercise 39.7 (p. 582)

Rewrites will vary.

1. Tuberculosis used to be called *consumption* because it seems to consume its sufferers.
2. Sanitariums were built to house and treat tuberculosis patients, since the bacterium was spread through the air when infected people coughed, sneezed, or spit.

Chapter 40   Modifiers

Exercise 40.1 (p. 586)

1. The Model T is ranked second in sales, but it is perhaps **more important** historically than the Beetle because it was the first car to be mass produced, paving the way for cars to be built **more cheaply** and **more quickly** than ever before.
2. Selling for about $300, the Model T wasn't the **least expensive** car on the market in the 1920s, however; that <u>unique</u> honor belongs to the 1922 Briggs & Stratton Flyer, which sold for $125 to $150.

Exercise 40.2 (p. 588)

Shortened answer:

After the creation of the House Un-American Activities Committee (HUAC), Cold War paranoia <u>could barely</u> hide itself in post–World War II America. HUAC followed on the coattails of the 1938 Special Committee on Un-American Activities.

Exercise 40.3 (p. 589)

Items to be circled are in bold (shortened answer):

In the early days of manned space missions, NASA had **fewer** <u>problems</u> feeding astronauts. But the **farther** astronauts <u>traveled</u>, the **further** <u>NASA had to go</u> to ensure healthy eating in space.

Exercise 40.4 (p. 590)

All sentences need revision. Possible rewrites:

1. <u>Now known as Juneteenth</u>, the day Texan slaves discovered their freedom, is celebrated in Texas.
2. Freed slaves celebrated annually their day of emancipation, <u>a people's event that has become an official holiday</u>.

Exercise 40.5 (p. 592)

Corrected modifier placement is in brackets (shortened answer):

> Cash was known for his <u>deep</u> voice as well as his <u>dark</u> clothing and demeanor. These traits all earned him the nickname "The Man in Black." Keeping with his <u>dark</u> demeanor, much of Cash's music, especially that of his <u>later</u> career, echoed themes of sorrow, struggle <u>moral</u> [moral struggle], and redemption.

Exercise 40.6 (p. 594)

1. Mendel's work <u>initially</u> focused on hybridizing the Lathyrus, or sweet pea.
2. The Lathyrus <u>conveniently</u> possessed variations composed of differing sizes and colors.

Exercise 40.7 (p. 596)

Possible rewrite with formerly disruptive modifiers underlined (shortened answer):

> In the thirteenth and fourteenth centuries, the Italian Papal states were consumed in chaos <u>because of militantly rivaling families</u>. In 1305, <u>unable to agree on an Italian</u>, the cardinals selected a Frenchman as the new Pope.

Exercise 40.8 (p. 597)

Possible revisions:

1. Lasting for three days in June of 1967, the festival presented over thirty artists.
2. The largest American music festival of its time, Monterey totaled over 200,000 in attendance.

Exercise P8.1 (p. 598)

Possible rewrite (shortened answer):

> Although Charles Brockden Brown was not the first American novelist, he is the most frequently studied and republished practitioner of the "early American novel" between 1789 and 1820, roughly. His novels are often characterized simply as Gothic fiction, building plots around motifs such as ventriloquism, sleepwalking, and religious mania. He also draws on Enlightenment-era medical writings.

Chapter 41   Commas

Exercise 41.1 (p. 602)

1. King cobras, <u>in fact</u>, have a poisonous bite from the moment they are born.
2. <u>Even though king cobras carry lethal venom</u>, women in Thailand's King Cobra Club dance with the snakes' heads in their mouths.

Exercise 41.2 (p. 606)

1. no comma
2. Because of the fluid-containing cavities of our inner ear, we have a sense of balance, or equilibrioception.

Exercise 41.3 (p. 611)

Modifiers are identified in parentheses (shortened answer):

Trajan decided to use the Empire's coffers, <u>which were brimming with war booty</u>, to begin a massive building program (nonrestrictive modifier). He commissioned the market <u>Mercati Traianei</u> and a lush new forum (restrictive modifier).

Exercise 41.4 (p. 611)

1. White-tailed deer[,] ground squirrels[,] gray squirrels[,] foxes[,] raccoons[,] coyotes[,] opossums[,] and armadillos are often in my back yard.
2. no commas necessary

Exercise 41.5 (p. 613)

Shortened answer:

In <u>Austrian and Hungarian holiday</u> (cumulative) folklore, Krampus punishes the naughty children, while Santa rewards the good. The <u>naughtiest, most unrepentant</u> (coordinate) children are carted away by Krampus in a large basket or bag to be cast into the <u>dark</u>, fiery (coordinate) pits of Hell.

Exercise 41.6 (p. 614)

Shortened answer:

Craquelure is "the fine network of cracks that scores the surface of . . . paintings" (Elkins 20). Elkins explains that "few museum visitors realize how many paintings have been seriously damaged," and goes on to list possible hazards, such as damage by "fire, water, vandalism, or just the wear and tear of the centuries" (20).

Exercise 41.7 (p. 617)

Shortened answer:

Mazaces' Headquarters
Cairo[,] Egypt
13 December 332 BC

Parmenio
Commander of Syria
Damascus[,] Syria

Dear Parmenio:

Thank you for your latest correspondence dated December 9[,] 332 BC. I am pleased to hear the streets of Damascus remain quiet since our arrival in October 333 BC and that mighty Syria has adjusted herself to our presence.

Exercise 41.8 (p. 618)

Shortened answer:

Jenkins Gallery[,] Inc.
17 Resolution Boulevard
Boston[,] MA 02116

June 28[,] 2010

Samantha Rios
1818 Pleasant Lane
Peabody[,] TX 01960
Dear Ms. Rios:

Thank you[,] Samantha[,] for your interest in exhibiting your work at The Jenkins Gallery during our September 15[,] 2010[,] showcase.

Exercise 41.9 (p. 619)

Shortened answer:

Because geologists used both radiometric and fossil dating[,] we now know that the Colorado River started carving the Grand Canyon only five or six million years ago. Scientists were able to accurately date the Shroud of Turin[,] believed by many Catholics to be Christ's burial covering[,] to between AD 1260–1390.

Chapter 42   Semicolons and Colons

Exercise 42.1 (p. 624)

Shortened answer:

The media reported that the wreckage of a flying saucer was discovered on a ranch near Roswell. Military spokespeople came up with another explanation; they asserted that the flying saucer was actually a balloon.

Exercise 42.2 (p. 627)

1. Authorities do not know exactly how many people have been killed in the past few years in the Philippines for singing "My Way," but the number has been high enough to cause people to ask some questions: Can the killings be blamed on violent culture? Or, is there something about the song that drives people to irrational anger?
2. One witness to many incidents of karaoke-related violence offers up an explanation for why Sinatra's song seems to make tempers flare: "Everyone knows it, and everyone has an opinion."

Chapter 43   Hyphens

Exercise 43.1 (p. 630)
1. Some people consider the Electoral College to be <u>undemocratic</u>.
2. Independent candidates are often viewed as <u>fly-by-night</u> long shots with little or no hope of winning positions of power.

Chapter 44   Dashes and Parentheses

Exercise 44.1 (p. 633)
Answers will vary.

Exercise 44.2 (p. 634)
1. Naples is a dirty and noisy metropolis in a spectacular setting—a city that sprawls around the Bay of Naples with Mount Vesuvius at its back, facing out to the islands of Procida, Ischia, and Capri.
2. The most famous eruption of Mount Vesuvius—the eruption that destroyed Pompeii and Herculaneum—occurred in 79 A.D.

Exercise 44.3 (p. 637)
1. *SNL* has been broadcast live by the National Broadcasting Company (NBC) on Saturday nights since October 11, 1975.
2. The show was called *NBC's Saturday Night* until 1976 (a short-lived variety show hosted by Howard Cosell was also called *Saturday Night Live*).

Chapter 45   Apostrophes

Exercise 45.1 (p. 641)
Shortened answer:

      <u>Its</u> destruction was caused by an eruption of Mount Vesuvius in AD 79. <u>Survivors'</u> stories contain accounts of tunneling through up to sixteen feet of debris after the disaster.

Exercise 45.2 (p. 641)
Shortened answer:

      In 2009, James Cameron['']s *Avatar*, starring Sam Worthington and Zoe Saldana, entranced audiences with the tale of an environmentally-themed, futuristic battle for the planet Pandora. The film['']s commercial success was astounding.

Exercise 45.3 (p. 643)
1. Texas <u>VIPs</u> and international diplomats alike affectionately referred to Lyndon B. Johnson as Big Daddy.
2. sentence is correct

Chapter 46   Quotation Marks

Exercise 46.1 (p. 646)

1. Horowitz's difficulty was finding words that might make sense, as he puts it, "to anyone other than a fellow addict" (387).
2. There are, Horowitz allows, clear and often-cited reasons why one might develop a passion for the Civil War, however. "Everywhere, people spoke of family and fortunes lost in the war," Horowitz writes (384).

Exercise 46.2 (p. 650)

1. What does Allison mean when she tells gay and lesbian writers, "We must aim much higher than just staying alive if we are to begin to approach our true <u>potential</u>"?
2. She elaborates, "I want to write in such a way as to literally remake the world, to change people's thinking as they look out of the eyes of the characters I create" (<u>212</u>).

Chapter 47   Other Punctuation Marks

Exercise 47.1 (p. 655)

Shortened answer:

Mr. Saunders started working as a grocer when he was 16. Moving through various jobs in the field, including wholesale, he realized that grocers lost money by selling on credit. At the age of 26, he formed Saunders-Blackburn Co., which dealt only in cash and urged its retail customers to do the same.

Exercise 47.2 (p. 657)

Shortened answer:

Betty Friedan's *The Feminine Mystique* addressed the question, "Is this all?" She examined why millions of women were sensing a gnawing feeling of discontent.

Exercise 47.3 (p. 660)

Shortened answer:

Ward notes, "The phenomenon of the waning star is heavily represented in the last century of English and American culture . . . ." In 1896, chronicling the perks of dying before the glory has time to fade, A.E. Houseman published the poem "To an Athlete Dying Young."

Exercise 47.4 (p. 662)

Shortened answer:

In 1996 alone, over sixty deaths occurred due to religious snake handling. Mark 16.18 in the King James version of the Bible states, "They shall take up serpents and if they drink any deadly thing it shall not hurt them . . .!"

Chapter 48   Write with Accurate Spelling

Exercise 48.1 (p. 664)
Shortened answer:

Archbishop <u>Desmond</u> Tutu's message to the <u>people</u> of South Africa is that all are "of infinite worth, created in the image of <u>God</u>," and "to be treated . . . with reverence" (Wepman 13). Tutu <u>maintains</u> that this is true <u>for</u> whites as well as blacks, a position that isn't popular <u>with</u> some South <u>Africans</u>.

Exercise 48.2 (p. 665)
Shortened answer:

This famous experiment was started in 1927 (by) Professor Thomas Parnell of the University of Queensland to demonstrate that (some) substances that (seem) to be solid are actually (very) (high)-viscosity fluids.

Exercise 48.3 (p. 668)
1. slapped
2. referring

Exercise 48.4 (p. 668)
1. definitely
2. purist

Exercise 48.5 (p. 670)
Shortened answer:

Wilde, a successful author with two <u>children</u> and multiple <u>followers</u> in literary London, made a mistake when he pressed <u>charges</u> against the famous lord. By all <u>accounts</u>, Wilde was in jovial <u>spirits</u> when he arrived at the Old Bailey courthouse on April 3, 1895.

Chapter 49   Capitalization and Italics

Exercise 49.1 (p. 675)
Shortened answer:

Without a doubt, sexting has entered the popular culture of the English-speaking world. A 2008 survey in *Cosmogirl* (sponsored by the National Campaign to Support Teen and Unplanned Pregnancy) reported that 20% of American teens had sexted; similar results have been found in studies conducted in the UK.

Exercise 49.2 (p. 675)

Shortened answer:

The Federal Bureau of Investigation (FBI) has long been considered an American institution that was fathered by President Theodore Roosevelt. During the early 1900s, the United States was going through what some referred to as the Progressive Era.

Exercise 49.3 (p. 676)

Shortened answer:

Many think Coco Chanel is to fashion what the Bible is to religion. Consequently, various types of media have sought to capture the essence of this innovative designer. Films such as *Tonight or Never* preserve Chanel's designs for future generations, while the failed Broadway musical, *Coco*, attempts to embody her life's work.

Chapter 50   Abbreviations, Acronyms, and Numbers

Exercise 50.1 (p. 680)

Shortened answer:

The unpredictable, destructive nature of volcanoes has attracted the interest of both scholarly and lay circles. Though it erupted in AD 79, Mt. Vesuvius is still famous because of its violent decimation of the city of Pompeii.

Exercise 50.2 (p. 681)

Shortened answer:

The festival, which culminates in the burning of a giant man-shaped effigy, takes place on a playa in the Black Rock Desert in Nevada, 90 miles (150 km) north to northeast of Reno. Black Rock City (BRC), a temporary city which has its own Department of Public Works (DPW), is an experiment in community and self-expression.

Exercise 50.3 (p. 683)

Shortened answer:

Five hundred sixty is the number of times you heard a popping sound resonating from the jaw of the woman sitting next to you on the plane. She may be one of over 9.5 million people suffering from TMJ, a condition that often causes symptoms such as popping, swelling, and aching in the jaw.

Exercise P9.1 (p. 684)

Suggested rewrite (shortened answer):

The Marvel Family is a team of superheroes in the Fawcett Comics and DC Comics universes. ("DC" refers to *Detective Comics*, one of the company's best-selling titles.) The team, which was created in 1942 by writer Otto Binder and Fawcett artists C. C. Beck, Mac Raboy, Ed Herron, and Marc Swayze, is an extension of Fawcett's Captain Marvel franchise. It includes Captain Marvel (Billy Batson), his sister Mary, their friend Captain Marvel, Jr., and a rotating cast of other characters.

Chapter 51   Writing in a Second Language

Exercise 51.1 (p. 692)

1. The actor committed suicide after his wife's death.
2. He will be here on Sunday.

Chapter 52   Nouns and Articles

Exercise 52.1 (p. 696)
Shortened answer:

In 1903, Chicago opened the new Iroquois Theater on West Randolph Street. Around Christmas, the theater held a performance of Mr. Blue Beard, starring Eddie Foy.

Exercise 52.2 (p. 697)

1. In 1946, these tiny astronauts were launched on an American rocket with some corn to test the effect of radiation at high altitudes.
2. Fruit flies match three-quarters of human disease genes, sleep every night, and reproduce very quickly, so replacing them does not cost a lot of money.

Exercise 52.3 (p. 698)
Shortened answer:

Every year, thousands of brides and grooms don traditional attire while attending their weddings. One garment associated with many of these traditional weddings is the groom's cummerbund or decorative waistband. This garment dates back many centuries to Persia, where they were known as a "kamarband" or "loin band."

Exercise 52.4 (p. 701)
Shortened answer:

Channon wanted to establish (a) new military based on New Age teachings. Members of the First Earth Battalion believed that their first loyalty was to (the) planet, so they sought nondestructive methods of conflict resolution. Channon referred to members of (the) First Earth Battalion as "warrior monks" because they would ideally have (the) dedication of (a) monk and (the) skill of (a) warrior.

Exercise 52.5 (p. 702)

Corrections are in brackets; types of nouns are in parentheses (shortened answer):

Hurtubise's obsession with [the] bears (plural, count) began in 1984 when he survived [an] encounter (singular, count) with an adult grizzly bear. Inspired by [the] movie (singular, count) *Robocop*, Hurtubise decided to build a suit (singular, count) that would withstand [the] bear attacks.

Exercise 52.6 (p. 704)

Shortened answer:

At that time, pilots were familiar with the "wall of air" that existed at the speed of sound. Many airplanes shattered into a million pieces because of this "wall of air."

Exercise 52.7 (p. 704)

Shortened answer:

The United States remains grateful to the people of France for the gift of the Statue of Liberty.

Chapter 53   Verbs

Exercise 53.1 (p. 706)

Shortened answer:

Though many think it marks only the Jewish New Year, those who celebrate Rosh Hashanah understand that it has many other meanings as well. Rosh Hashana is also called the day of the blowing of the Shofar, the day of remembrance, and the day of judgment.

Exercise 53.2 (p. 708)

1. His owner rescued him from an animal shelter knowing that it might take him a long time to bond with her, but it was a job she must do. (possibility, necessity)
2. The producers of National Geographic Channel's *Dog Genius* show must have been impressed, or they would not have featured Donnie arranging his toys into circles, triangles, and parallel lines. (assumption, speculation)

Exercise 53.3 (p. 709)

1. follows, are referred to
2. forces strangers to live, causing them to face

Exercise 53.4 (p. 710)

1. misidentifying
2. to believe

Exercise 53.5 (p. 712)

1. If a child <u>is</u> terrified whenever he or she <u>sees</u> a clown, that child <u>has</u> coulrophobia.
2. If you <u>had ever been</u> attacked by birds, <u>you could have developed</u> ornithophobia.

Exercise 53.6 (p. 713)

Items to be circled are in bold (shortened answer):

     Many tornadoes are **made up of** a special <u>rotating thunderstorm</u> called a supercell. A <u>rising gust</u> of warm wind **combines with** the <u>raging storm</u>; the warm air **begins spinning as** the rainfall **gives way to** a <u>rushing downdraft</u>.

Chapter 54   English Sentence Structure

Exercise 54.1 (p. 715)

1. Though some <u>assassins</u> are widely known, <u>Charles Guiteau</u> and <u>Leon Czolgolsz</u> are relatively obscure.
2. <u>Guiteau</u> shot President Garfield in 1881, and [there] was little doubt <u>he</u> would be hanged for the murder.

Exercise 54.2 (p. 715)

Items to be circled are in brackets.

1. [Geologists] based the theory on an earlier one <u>[that] had observed that the continents fit together like pieces of a puzzle</u>.
2. In the 1950s and 1960s, [scientists] found evidence to support the earlier theory, <u>so [they] were able to confirm its hypothesis regarding continental drift</u>.

Exercise 54.3 (p. 717)

1. Ganesh (S) is (LV) the god (SC) of good luck (PP).
2. Young Ganesh (S) stood (IV) at his mother's house (PP).

Exercise 54.4 (p. 719)

Replacement constructions are in brackets.

1. Doctors, <u>seeing a bleak future for Grandin</u>, told her parents that she should be institutionalized. (adverbial phrase between subject and verb) (Seeing a bleak future for Grandin, doctors told her parents that she should be institutionalized.)

2. However, Grandin's mother was determined to <u>not</u> give up on her daughter. (split infinitive) (However, Grandin's mother was determined not to give up on her daughter.)

Exercise 54.5 (p. 720)

1. By the <u>fourteenth</u> century, <u>playing</u> cards were used <u>widely</u> (adv. of frequency) for gambling and predicting the future.
2. The invention of the <u>printing</u> press connects <u>directly</u> (adv. of manner) to the proliferation of <u>standardized card</u> games.

Exercise 54.6 (p. 721)

1. Robespierre followed the writings of Jean Jacques Rousseau, his philosophical role model.
2. Elected on the eve of the French Revolution, he enthralled the people with his skillful oratory.

Index

Credits

Text Credits

Communication Education. Reprinted courtesy of Taylor & Francis via the Copyright Clearance Center.

EBSCO search for "Sustainable farm" on Academic Search Complete. Image courtest of EBSCO PUBLISHING.

Ecological Soceity of America. "A Cross-Regional Assessment of the Factors Affecting Ecoliteracy: Implications for Policy and Practice" by Sarah Pilgrim, David Smith, and Jules Pretty, ECO-LOGICAL APPLICATIONS, 17(6), 2007, pp. 1742-1751, a publication of the Ecological Society of America. Copyright 2007 by Ecological Society of America. Reproduced with permission via the Copyright Clearance Center.

LexisNexis archive search for "college organic farm". From the LexisNexis Academic website. Copyright 2010 LexisNexis, a division of Reed Elsevier Inc. All Rights Reserved. LexisNexis and the Knowledge Burst logo are registered trademarks of Reed Elsevier Properties Inc. and are used with permission of LexisNexis.

LexisNexis article search. From the LexisNexis Academic website. Copyright 2010 LexisNexis, a division of Reed Elsevier Inc. All Rights Reserved. LexisNexis and the Knowledge Burst logo are registered trademarks of Reed Elsevier Properties Inc. and are used with permission of LexisNexis.

Screen capture of Colby Magazine. Courtesy of Colby College.

Screen capture of Google Advanced Search. Reprinted courtesy of Google.

Screen capture of KU Libraries. Reprinted by permission of The University of Kansas Libraries.

Sustainable Endowments. Reprinted by permission of The Sustainable Endowments Institute.

USA TODAY, April 20, 2010. Reprinted with Permission.

Photo Credits

p. 64: Library of Congress
p. 69: Library of Congress
p. 260: NASA
p. 280: Cool Springs Press
p. 310: Greater Talent Network
p. 329: Library of Congress
p. 350: Penguin Press

Part 1 divider: Istockphoto
Part 3 divider: Shutterstock
Common Error Image: Istockphoto

Unless otherwise noted, all photos © Lester Faigley Photos.